REGULATING TRADE IN SERVICES IN THE EU AND THE WTO

This volume assesses the viability of various theories of economic integration that take into account the legal, economic, political and social challenges of incorporating free trade with the retention of a plurality of social welfare standards and consumer protection standards. Chapters cover the governance of trade in services at the European and global level; studies on the recent Services Directive and how this interacts with the principle of managed mutual recognition and harmonization in different sectors of the economy (social services, financial services); the recent case law of the European Courts on how the principle of free movement of services accommodates various national public interest concerns; and the interaction of the freedom to provide services with fundamental rights, including social rights. The operation of the principle of managed mutual recognition in other economic integration regimes, in particular in the context of the WTO, is also discussed.

IOANNIS LIANOS is a reader in European and Competition Law at the Faculty of Laws, University College London. He is also the Director of the Centre for Law, Economics and Society, the Institute of Global Law, and the Centre for Law and Governance in Europe at UCL.

OKEOGHENE ODUDU is Herchel Smith Lecturer in the Faculty of Law and Fellow in Law at Emmanuel College, University of Cambridge. He is the co-editor of the *Cambridge Yearbook of European Legal Studies* and was Deputy Director of the Centre for European Legal Studies between 2006 and 2011.

REGULATING TRADE IN SERVICES IN THE EU AND THE WTO

Trust, Distrust and Economic Integration

Edited by

IOANNIS LIANOS

and

OKEOGHENE ODUDU

CAMBRIDGE
UNIVERSITY PRESS

CAMBRIDGE UNIVERSITY PRESS
Cambridge, New York, Melbourne, Madrid, Cape Town,
Singapore, São Paulo, Delhi, Tokyo, Mexico City

Cambridge University Press
The Edinburgh Building, Cambridge CB2 8RU, UK

Published in the United States of America by Cambridge University Press, New York

www.cambridge.org
Information on this title: www.cambridge.org/9781107008649

First published 2012

Printed in the United Kingdom at the University Press, Cambridge

A catalogue record for this publication is available from the British Library

ISBN 978-1-107-00864-9 Hardback

CONTENTS

CONTRIBUTORS

ANTOINE BAILLEUX Professor at the Facultés Universitaires Saint-Louis (Brussels), *avocat* at the Brussels Bar

CHRISTOPHER BOVIS HK Bevan Chair, University of Hull

GARETH DAVIES Professor of European Law, VU University Amsterdam

PANAGIOTIS DELIMATSIS Associate Professor of Law and Co-director, Tilburg Law & Economics Center (TILEC), Tilburg University, The Netherlands

OLIVIER DE SCHUTTER Professor of Law, University of Louvain (UCL) and College of Europe (Natolin)

DAMIEN GERARD Research Fellow, Chair of European Law, Louvain University

VASSILIS HATZOPOULOS Associate Professor at the Democritus University of Thrace (Greece), Visiting Professor at the College of Europe, Bruges (Belgium), Honorary Lecturer at the University of Nottingham, Attorney-at-Law Member of the Athens Bar

ROBERT HOWSE Lloyd C. Nelson Professor of International Law at New York University School of Law

CHRISTIAN JOERGES Research Professor, University of Bremen (Centre of European Law and Politics and CRC Transformations of the State)

WOLFGANG KERBER Professor of Economics, Philipps University Marburg

JOHANNES LE BLANC Research Fellow, University of Zurich

IOANNIS LIANOS Reader in European Union Law and Competition Law, Faculty of Laws, University College London

JUAN A. MARCHETTI Counsellor, WTO

PETROS MAVROIDIS Edwin B. Parker Professor of Law at Columbia Law School, New York, Professor of Law at the University of Neuchâtel, and Research Fellow at CEPR

KALYPSO NICOLAÏDIS Professor of International Relations at Oxford University, and Director of the Centre of International Studies, Oxford University

OKEOGHENE ODUDU Herchel Smith Lecturer, Faculty of Law, University of Cambridge

FLORIAN RÖDL Head of Junior Research Group in the Cluster of Excellence 'Formation of Normative Orders', Goethe-University, Frankfurt

HARM SCHEPEL Professor of Economic Law, Kent Law School and Brussels School of International Studies, University of Kent

ROGER VAN DEN BERGH Professor of Law and Economics, Erasmus University Rotterdam

ACKNOWLEDGMENTS

The editors would like to thank the authors and Cambridge University Press for their patience during the long editorial process. In particular, we would like to thank Finola O'Sullivan and Richard Woodham from Cambridge University Press. The organization of the workshop in London and Cambridge would not have been possible without the generous support of the *Modern Law Review*, the Centre for Law and Governance in Europe, University College London, the Master and fellows of Emmanuel College, Cambridge and the Centre for European Legal Studies, Faculty of Law, University of Cambridge, to whom we also extend our thanks. Marta Maia and Julia Petrenko have provided excellent editorial assistance and also deserve praise.

ABBREVIATIONS

ASEAN	Association of South East Asian Nations
AVMS	Audio Visual Media Services Directive
BEREC	Body of European Regulators for Electronic Communications
CCBE	Council of Bars and Law Societies of Europe
CEN	European Committee for Standardization (Comité Européen de Normalisation)
CENELEC	European Committee for Electrotechnical Standardization (Comité Européen de Normalisation Électrotechnique)
CESR	Committee of European Supervisory Regulators
CMLR	Common Market Law Reports
DG	Directorate General
DPT	democratic peace theory
ECB	European Central Bank
ECHR	European Court of Human Rights
ECJ	European Court of Justice
ECMA	Electronic Communications Market Authority
ECR	Europeean Court Reports
EEA	Europeean Economic Area
EFTA	Europeean Free Trade Area
ERG	European Regulators Group
ERGEG	European Regulators Group for Electricity and Gas
ESC	European Securities Committee
ESRB	European Systemic Risk Board
ETSI	European Telecommunications Standards Institute
FSAP	Financial Services Action Plan
GATS	General Agreement on Trade in Services
GATT	General Agreement on Tariffs and Trade
ITU	International Telecommunications Union
JHA	Justice and Home Affairs
MBL	Swedish law on workers' participation in decisions
MFN	Most Favoured Nation
MiFID	Markets in Financial Instruments Directive
MRA	mutual recognition agreement
NRA	national regulatory authority
PTA	preferential trade agreement

RPT	regulatory peace theory
SHEC	safety and security, health and consumer protection
SPS	Sanitary and Phytosanitary Measures Agreement
TBT	Technical Barriers to Trade Agreement
TEU	Treaty on the European Union
TFEU	Treaty on the Functioning of the European Union
VCLT	Vienna Convention on the Law of Treaties

TABLE OF CASES

Introduction

IOANNIS LIANOS AND OKEOGHENE ODUDU

Trade in services is of significant importance for the global economy: in the European Union, 'services constitute the engine of economic growth and account for 70% of GDP and employment in most Member States'.[1] The liberalization of trade in services, at both the European level and more generally, has been and continues to be beset with difficulties. The difficulties arise not only from the specific characteristics of the different economic sectors in which services are provided, but also from the interaction of inter-State trade in services with diverse regulatory regimes that States have adopted either in order to promote the social welfare of their citizens or following pressure from specific domestic interests.

The tension between the logic of free trade and regulatory competition on the one hand and fair trade and harmonization on the other has long provided the conceptual framework within which several battles have taken place between the proponents of liberalization and market integration and the proponents of regulatory diversity and the defence of the 'social sphere'. At the international level, these tensions are often inherent in the debates between proponents of 'free trade' and proponents of 'fair' trade[2] – debates between those that highlight the benefits of 'trade' and those that focus on 'non-trade' elements such as the effects of trade liberalization on social and environmental development. Instances of deeper regional integration, as the European Union example illustrates,

[1] Directive 2006/123/EC of the European Parliament and of the Council on services in the Internal Market, OJ 2006 L376/76.

[2] J. Bhagwati and R. E. Hudec (eds.), *Fair Trade and Harmonization*, Vol. 1, *Economic Analysis* (Cambridge, MA: MIT Press, 1996); J. Bhagwati and R. E. Hudec, *Fair Trade and Harmonization*, Vol. 2, *Legal Analysis* (Cambridge, MA: MIT Press, 1996).

have resulted in calls for a more 'social Europe'[3] and, less abstractly, for the 'integration'[4] of various social clauses in the trade regime.

The conception of the 'economic' and the 'social' spheres as separate and antagonistic is the product of a specific view of the nature and aims of international or regional integration. Separation is thought of as a mechanism to promote greater convergence and similarity between the different units to be integrated: separation allows trade liberalization to be seen as a technical exercise, since social or distributive consequences are left outside the realm of economic integration. Social or political integration may follow separately, as the expected 'counter-movement' to the expansion of the market sphere.[5] The separation of the economic from the social has also been justified by a conceptualization of integration linked to expertise – authors of trading regimes have greater claims to expertise in efficiency than to that of equality, if one perceives these concepts as being in conflict.[6] At the international level, one might think of the functionalists' construction of different spheres and subsequently the substantive fragmentation of international law as an epiphenomenon of the transposition of the logical positivist's anxieties to the legal sphere. In the field of economic integration, the economist's rejection of distributive justice, perceived as a value external to economic expertise, can again be explained by the logical positivist connection, as it is illustrated by the two welfare theorems of economics,[7] following which the 'ethical foundations' of economics 'are now regarded to be a settled matter'.[8]

As contributors to this volume ably demonstrate, the separation thesis, and its positivistic and functionalist assumptions, underestimate the entanglement of the economic and the social. Tenants of the 'embedded liberalism'[9] thesis as well as their neo-liberal opponents would agree that

[3] A. Giddens, P. Diamond and R. Liddle, *Global Europe: Social Europe* (Cambridge: Polity Press, 2006).

[4] See Title 3 of the TEU, Articles 7, 9, 11 and 13.

[5] K. Polanyi, *The Great Transformation: The Political and Economic Origins of Our Time* (New York: Farrar and Rinehart, 1944).

[6] A. M. Okun, *Equality and Efficiency: The Big Trade Off* (Washington DC: Brookings Institution, 1975).

[7] M. Blaug, 'The Fundamental Theorems of Modern Welfare Economics, Historically Contemplated', *History of Political Economy* 39(2) (2007) 185–207.

[8] P. Dasgupta, 'What Do Economists Analyze and Why: Values or Facts?', *Economics and Philosophy* 21 (2005) 221–78, at 222. See also the criticism by H. Putnam and V. Walsh, 'A Response to Dasgupta', *Economics and Philosophy* 23 (2007) 359–64.

[9] J. G. Ruggie, 'International Regimes, Transactions, and Change: Embedded Liberalism in the Post-War Economic Order', *International Organization* 36(2) (1982) 379–415.

the process of European economic integration is re-embedding national considerations of the social sphere within the unified supranational institutional structures. At a time when the European Union declares the Charter of Fundamental Rights – containing a number of social rights – binding, progressively extends its aims and competence to cover areas of social regulation (i.e., social protection and environmental protection), and multiplies horizontal 'integration clauses', thus enabling the consideration of environmental concerns, sustainable development and social protection in all of the European Union's policies and activities,[10] it seems possible to abandon the decoupled/distinct spheres thesis in favour of one embracing 'holistic' theory of integration.[11]

Despite its certain political appeal, the concept of 'holistic integration' might nevertheless prove to be a slogan without content, if the dependent variable of integration is not reconceived to reflect the 'complex and multidimensional process of societal change' in the governance of the relationships between public and private actors at the national, international and supranational level that this concept of integration entails.[12] This volume suggests a new reading of the dependent variable of integration, relying on the concept of 'trust'.

The reference to the concept of 'trust' as consubstantial to that of integration may follow naturally from the emphasis recently put on managed mutual recognition as the cornerstone of economic integration.[13] Some scholars have noted the significance of 'mutual trust' in the process of harmonization, where, despite the efforts of establishing uniform rules, uncertainty remains as to the effective enforcement of these rules by the authorities of other Member States[14] (trust between Member States). Others emphasize the importance of trust in government, but also the need to institutionalize distrust at moments of major political

[10] See, e.g., Article 9 (social policy) and Article 11 (environment).

[11] I. Lianos, 'Shifting Narratives in the European Internal Market: Efficient Restrictions of Trade and the Nature of "Economic" Integration', *European Business Law Review* (2010) 705–60.

[12] P. de Lombaerde, E. Dorrucci, G. Genna and Fransesco P. Mongelli, 'Quantitative Monitoring and Comparison of Regional Integration Processes: Steps Toward Good Practice', in A. Kösler and M. Zimmek (eds.), *Elements of Regional Integration* (Baden-Baden: Nomos, 2008), 149–79, at 149.

[13] K. Nicolaïdis and G. Shaffer, 'Transnational Mutual Recognition Regimes: Governance without Global Government', *Law and Contemporary Problems* 68 (2005) 263–317.

[14] C. Barnard, *The Substantive Law of the EU* (Oxford: Oxford University Press: 2010), 189–90.

and legal change, as a way to reinforce the legitimacy of the political system[15] (trust of the citizens in the Union). The remit of this volume is broader, as it recognizes that the concept of trust is multidimensional and might refer to the existence of various trust relationships: between States, between States and the international/supranational level, between the private actors and the government (States or supranational level), and transborder relations between private actors. Trust can also take different forms: it can be inter-personal, as it relates to specific characteristics/similarities/familiarity between the different trust partners, or it can be 'system trust', when trust is provided to a third party and is based on factors other than similarity and familiarity. The hypothesis to be examined in this volume is the following: can the concept of integration be understood as related to that of increased levels of trust between different actors? Such an approach rejects the functionalist distinction between various spheres of integration – social, economic, political – but it also liberates the concept of integration from its usual analogy to centralism and uniformity. It thus breaks with the focus of integration studies on trade liberalization to the point that the removal of inter-State trade barriers is considered as one of the principal indicators of the success of the process of integration.

The questions arising from this new conceptualization of integration were examined by a number of scholars, lawyers, economists and political scientists, in a workshop at the Faculty of Laws, University College London, and at Emmanuel College, University of Cambridge, on 1 and 2 June 2009. This volume is the result of the participants' efforts to reflect on the topic of 'trust, distrust and economic integration'. Our aim was to test the 'trust theory of integration' in the most difficult area of trade in services, at both the European Union and the World Trade Organization (WTO) levels. Some of the contributions to this volume engage fully with the new conceptualization of economic integration and find that it provides a useful framework to analyze developments in the specific sector of services trade they examine. Others take a more sceptical position and refer to other theories explaining the evolution of trade regulation. In the end, any effort to theorize such complex phenomena as the regulation of trade in services and the emergence of multilateral or regional remedies relies on large cognitive structures, which are linked to the development of narratives ('embedded liberalism'), stories ('mutual

[15] I. Maher, 'Trust and EU Law and Governance', *Cambridge Yearbook of European Legal Studies* 12 (2010) 283–312.

recognition') and global accounts (functionalism, neo-functionalism). Choosing among competing explanations or global accounts depends on the relative plausibility of each narrative/story as measured by reference to a number of criteria: the portion of the facts that can be explained through that account; its consilience; and its internal coherence. This volume attempts to test the 'trust theory of integration' compared to other theoretical accounts and to develop a theoretical framework that could be later expanded to fit different processes of integration.

Part I of the volume introduces the 'trust theory of integration' and situates it with regard to competing accounts. In Chapter 1, Ioannis Lianos and Johannes Le Blanc examine the various theories of integration and discuss how the concept of integration, the dependent variable of this study, has received different interpretations by lawyers, political scientists and economists. Lianos and Le Blanc argue that the concept of economic integration owes a lot to functionalist theories. Based on this approach, neo-functionalism was able to construct a theory of regional integration employing the model of European integration as the archetypical paradigm of the concept. It follows that the functionalist approach and the concept of integration are profoundly linked: without the functionalist emphasis on the existence of separate functions, where national authority can be transferred to supranational institutions, there can be no integration. The chapter by Lianos and Le Blanc challenges the neo-functionalist view and seeks to show that the separate spheres approach – the distinctive characteristic of functionalism and of its neo-functionalist progeny – does not hold in the current state of the European integration process. Once the limits of the functionalist logic are displayed, the competing theories of international relations fail to conceptualize the dependent variable of 'integration'. Having recognized the need for a new approach to the concept of integration, Lianos and Le Blanc explore two alternatives. The first one – economic integration as efficient organizational creation – perfects the dependent variable suggested by functionalism. The second one – the 'trust theory of integration' – chooses instead to abandon the definition of the dependent variable suggested by functionalism and to focus on a different dimension that would represent the turn towards a holistic, as opposed to a functionalist, approach to integration, where the social, economic and political dimensions are embedded in each other. For Lianos and Le Blanc, the trust theory of integration provides a promising platform for reflection, not only for the European project of integration but also for all other projects of integration.

Part II of the volume aims to deconstruct the current narrative of economic integration, in particular in Europe, and to introduce a new approach that would engage with the concept of trust. Economic integration has long been associated with the concept of market access in order to bring within the scope of 'negative integration' important areas of economic and social activity and to subject them to the Procrustean logic of barriers to trade. Equivalence and mutual recognition (MR), in its judicial or regulatory variety, have also been thought of as complementary tools to negative integration and as an alternative to the paradigm of exhaustive or complete harmonization, the archetypical examples of 'positive integration'. The concept of trust having been long associated with mutual recognition, it is important to examine more closely this complex phenomenon, before extending the trust theory of integration to other dimensions of the integration process.

A comparison of the approach followed in the regulation of trade in services with that followed in other areas of free movement illustrates the operation of mutual recognition and its relation with the concept of trust. In Chapter 2, Vassilis Hatzopoulos examines why services present different challenges than the area of the free movement of goods for the principle of mutual recognition. He notes the decentralized and non-State origins of the measures; the important role of the recipient of services, which complicates any effort to regulate their content, services regulation being merely about process; the impossibility of a prior notification system for rules on services; the absence of extensive standardization; and, last but not least, the sensitive political stakes involved in the regulation of services. Hatzopoulos then proceeds to a detailed analysis of mutual recognition typology and of the practical implementation of the principle for a variety of State measures. He concludes that the 'proceduralization' of European governance and the experimentation with new modes of governance have transformed mutual recognition to the 'most far-reaching regulatory technique for the completion of the internal market', the concept being flexible and/or binding enough as each case requires. We are away from the sterile opposition between mutual recognition and harmonization or between mutual recognition and other new forms of soft law governance.

The Services Directive constitutes an excellent example of this mutation of the principle of mutual recognition, from a merely judicial instrument to a far-reaching regulatory tool. It is suggested that the concept of trust may serve as the common reference for the different forms of mutual recognition.

In Chapter 3, Gareth Davies explores the Services Directive as an example of market-making legislation, which works by indirect rather than direct means. Rather than adding significantly to the rules on free movement, Davies notes that the Services Directive develops communication and transparency mechanisms which will add to trust between Member States. Using ideas of oligopoly, regulatory competition and reflexive harmonization, he suggests that such transparency will lead to voluntary convergence of regulation, with a resulting increased tolerance for mutual recognition. This system is, however, likely to be unstable, given the fragmented and rapidly developing nature of services markets. The likely impact of the Directive on the services market demonstrates the dynamic interdependence between trust, mutual recognition and centralizing legislation.

The topic of mutual recognition is further explored in Chapter 4. Wolfgang Kerber and Roger van den Bergh critically assess the prevailing view that the principle of mutual recognition leads simultaneously to the removal of non-tariff barriers to trade and the implementation of an integrated market, the enabling of regulatory (institutional) competition, and the protection against a centralization of competences in a multi-level system of jurisdictions. They argue instead that the principle of mutual recognition leads to a number of serious (and so far not well-recognized) inconsistencies and problems, which are linked to a basic misunderstanding of its function with regard to the removal of trade barriers. According to them, the introduction of the rule of mutual recognition cannot be understood as an appropriate rule for the enabling of effective regulatory competition nor is it a suitable instrument for avoiding harmonization and centralization. Its introduction triggers a dynamic process of reallocation of regulatory powers between different regulatory levels in a multi-level system of regulation, and therefore has consequences for the vertical allocation of competences. In other words, it can be interpreted more as a test, whether the regulatory powers on the national level are still defendable or whether another solution for the allocation of regulatory powers seems to be superior, as, for example, centralization/full harmonization or the transition to a fully competitive system of regulations (with free choice of law). They conclude that mutual recognition seems to be more an alternative indirect path to harmonization and centralization, instead of offering a solution for the removal of barriers that simultaneously maintain the decentralized structure of competences. Since the introduction of mutual recognition also influences the vertical allocation of competences within a multi-level system of governance, they argue that the advantages of the removal of trade and mobility barriers also have to be balanced against the foregone manifold advantages of decentralization – leading to a much more ambivalent assessment of the long-term consequences of mutual recognition. On a theoretical level, this implies that the theory of international trade is relevant for the assessment not only of mutual recognition but also of the economic theory of federalism with its comprehensive analysis of all advantages and disadvantages of centralized and decentralized competences in a federal multi-level system of jurisdictions.

Chris Bovis' contribution in Chapter 5 examines the process of harmonization in the area of public procurement and public services and its interaction with the negative integration provisions of the Treaties. Bovis notes the wide margin of discretion the Member States enjoy in introducing public policy considerations with regard to public services, thus demonstrating that harmonization does not always lead to a lack of regulatory diversity.

The main components of the current paradigm of economic integration deconstructed, it is important to understand how the process of integration may accommodate regulatory pluralism. We start from the assumption that the main problem faced by economic integration regimes in services is not the existence of regulation – which is necessary either in order to address the risk of market failure in network industries or to promote efficient trade for credence goods, such as professional services and services where there is an important information asymmetry – but rather the distrust between national regulators and the risk of opportunistic behaviour. By providing for a process of administrative cooperation and exchange of information, the Services Directive facilitates trust-building between national actors (regulators or consumers). Harmonization and negative integration are not the only options on the table. This leaves enough room for diversity and regulatory pluralism that need to be managed, the topic of Part III, which considers the interaction between pluralism, trust and economic integration.

In Chapter 6, Ioannis Lianos and Damien Gerard examine how the trust theory of integration accommodates claims of regulatory pluralism. They start by describing the evolution of the case law of the Court of Justice of the European Union in assessing the existence of a State restriction of trade and the proportionality of the restriction(s) at stake in light of the alleged public interest to be safeguarded (the Internal Market test). They note that both the case law of the Court and the Internal Market policies of the European Commission increasingly take into account pluralistic concerns and regulatory diversity, each Member State embodying a specific political compact reflecting particular social choices and cultural traditions. This part of the volume builds on the dominant conception of economic integration as characterized by the absence of barriers and increased intra-area harmonization, which is, in essence, paradoxical to claims of pluralism. While the first section of the chapter highlights an evolution in the application of the Internal Market test revealing an emerging praxis of pluralism, the second reconceptualizes economic integration from the perspective of trust theory, in order to test if and how such an approach could accommodate regulatory pluralism. Lianos and Gerard consider that States put in place different mechanisms to govern the risk of cooperation with other States. Their focus on discrete governance mechanisms as risk management techniques displaces the unidimensional focus of integration theory on the erosion of barriers to exchange and regulatory sameness. Their analysis of the different governance mechanisms, put in place in various sectors of trade in services, illustrates the adjustments made in order to accommodate regulatory diversity and the porosity of the tripartite distinction between the market access/national treatment rule, the principle of equivalence and that of harmonization as discrete governance mechanisms. Building on the trust theory of integration, Lianos and Gerard note that, if the main problem faced by economic integration regimes is the distrust between national regulators, the different governance mechanisms cannot be thought of as constituting the different stages of a process of integration that leads ultimately to 'convergence' of regulatory systems, or any form of centralized control (EU regulation or the 'single' market's forces of supply and demand). The emphasis is on the establishment of institutions, formal and informal, with the aim to manage the risks of cooperation between diverse regulatory systems. Regulatory sameness is thus not the only desirable outcome but a possible outcome among others. What counts is the potential of these governance arrangements in generating inter-organizational system trust. The centrality of the mutual recognition principle in the process of European integration further illustrates the shift towards a trust-based conception of integration, focusing on regulatory interoperability. By disentangling the focus of integration from managing or suppressing conflicts from regulatory diversity establishing system trust between the different stakeholders, the trust theory of integration offers a real chance for regulatory pluralism.

The theme of regulatory pluralism is brilliantly explored by Kalypso Nicolaïdis in Chapter 7, in which she revisits the regulatory wars that marked the adoption of the Services Directive and the struggles surrounding mutual recognition in the EU. These conflicts struck a painful chord across European societies which had not yet come to terms with the tensions associated with enlargement and the gap between old and new Member States. They show that claims of regulatory pluralism are embedded in broader conflicts of identity. Nicolaïdis advocates the need for a regulatory peace theory, that is, a stable state of cooperation among regulators (broadly conceived) from different jurisdictions. A stable state of cooperation does not necessarily mean harmony, but rather the existence of mechanisms to manage the unavoidable mix of convergent and divergent interests and values between these actors, allowing them to pursue the public good in their own jurisdiction while minimizing negative externalities for outsiders. Building on 'democratic peace theory', she explores factors that make regulatory peace more likely both as characteristics of individual jurisdictions and as attributes of the interactions between them. Differences ought to be considered legitimate until proven otherwise. Managing differences does not necessarily require engineering convergence.

Establishing higher levels of trust between national regulators, between national regulators and international institutions and between citizens/consumers and national regulators or integration institutions thus becomes the principal aim of regimes of economic integration. However, in many instances, private parties intervene in the process of economic integration in various ways, such as delegation, self-regulation and standard-setting activity. The intervention of private parties in the economic integration process may render more complex the dynamics of the trust-building game. This is an additional challenge explored by two studies in Part IV of the volume.

In Chapter 8, Harm Schepel examines the (direct or indirect) horizontal application of the negative integration provisions to private parties, that is, the idea that private parties are directly bound by the free movement provisions of the EU Treaties. He notes that the full direct horizontal effect of the regimes of the free movement of workers, the freedom to provide services and the freedom of establishment – what he calls 'total market' – is the inescapable consequence of the Court's case law. He further notes that, if the Court persists in its case law on the horizontal scope of the prohibitions of the free movement provisions, it seems inevitable that it will have to expand the justification regime to the point of reducing the market disciplines imposed on private actors to very little. Based on this analysis, he criticizes the Court's elevation of freedoms of movement to fundamental rights (the 'total constitution'), as blurring the boundary between 'total market' and 'total constitution'. Schepel concludes that to impose norms onto private relationships that are conceptualized as both market freedoms and fundamental rights is 'in all likelihood a very bad idea that is bound to instil fear even in those who aren't afraid of either the total market or the total constitution'.

In Chapter 9, Panagiotis Delimatsis focuses on a trust-enhancing instrument identified in the proposed and the adopted Services Directive, namely, the creation of pan-European codes of conduct dealing with rules of professional ethics. While being soft-law instruments, codes of conduct enhance trust among Member States regarding the equivalence of services and service suppliers originating in other Member States. Exploring the application of the negative integration provisions of the Treaty and those of competition law, Delimatsis notes the Court of Justice, while well known as the most prominent trust-building institution, has adopted a lenient and deferential approach when examining arguments of ethics, professional secrecy, integrity and reputation of the profession and other qualitative elements that codes of conduct aim to preserve and enhance, thus deferring to local knowledge about the precise characteristics of the market and the nature of the profession. The deferential approach to rules of professional conduct is also present in the bottom-up approach followed by the Services Directive, which recognizes the role of national professional associations as essential at each and every stage of the constitution of European codes of conduct, from the decision on the content of pan-European codes of conduct to the surveillance of their implementation and the potential application of disciplinary sanctions. Harmonization through European non-binding regulation can go in tandem with greater involvement of national and, in this case, infra-national actors.

Part V of the volume turns to the much debated issue of regulatory competition and regulatory diversity as seeds of distrust in the social sphere. The public policy objectives States pursue may create additional costs to service providers that constitute barriers to trade. Competition among national regulatory systems may be preferable if it is a more efficient and equitable system. Regulatory diversity may increase economic efficiency, but it may also lead to a 'race to the bottom'. In this case, some form of coordination will satisfy various consumer preferences on the level of social services that need to be publicly provided. Defining the framework of cooperation or coordination is not, however, an easy task, in view of the distrust that exists between the different regulatory systems.

Olivier De Schutter's contribution in Chapter 10 turns to the debate between harmonization of social laws and regulatory competition in the EU. The recent case law of the Court of Justice allows companies to provide services across the EU from the Member State of their choice, with only limited possibilities for the host State to impose compliance with certain standards that go beyond the minimum provisions listed in the 1996 Posted Workers Directive. This, combined with the enlargement of the EU, has given rise to renewed fears about 'social dumping' in the EU, and casts doubt on the optimistic view that Member States would progressively converge towards higher social standards. The chapter discusses the plausibility of the 'race to the bottom' scenario in this context. It seeks to move beyond the usual dichotomy opposing de-regulation at domestic level and re-regulation at EU level. Instead, it shows that mechanisms allowing for an improved monitoring of the behaviour of Member States and for learning across jurisdictions could constitute a more promising avenue, provided certain institutional conditions are created.

The same topic, from a different angle, is explored in Chapter 11 by Christian Joerges and Florian Rödl. The authors argue that establishing trust may be understood as a way to manage the integration process, but it is not an adequate tool for the social sphere in its entirety. On the contrary, it reflects the commitment of the European project to the economic rationality of market integration and an attempt to keep the tensions between that commitment and the various welfarist traditions of the Member States latent. The authors question if it is economically sound and/or even a command of European solidarity to expose the labour markets of 'old Europe' to the cheap labour which the organizers of services can offer. They argue that it is much more likely that this type of competition will have disintegrative implications for the European project. The recent judgments of the Court where labour regulations were confronted with the logic of the Internal Market form the starting point of their analysis. The conceptualization of today's Europe as a 'federal union' tends to further a neo-liberal transformation of the social orders of the Member States. The authors propose a conflict-of-law approach – in which the validity of *all* legal norms of relevance in Europeanized constellations are of equal status – as the only way to grant and safeguard individual *and* social freedom.

Antoine Bailleux's contribution in Chapter 12 adopts a different standpoint, emphasizing how fundamental rights might enhance trust but also be a source of distrust. It appears from the Court of Justice's recent case law that fundamental rights are increasingly invoked in relation to free movement issues. In some instances, the 'rights talk' refers to a set of common values presented as the backbone of the European integration project and as the bedrock of trust relationships between the Member States. Such references to human rights strengthen the mutual recognition principle and – whether directly or indirectly – advance the cause of economic integration. In other cases, however, the fundamental rights discourse carries a divisive force, shielding the Member States' constitutional identities and regulatory diversity from the unifying dynamic of the Internal Market. Fundamental rights are used to express defiance *vis-à-vis* the regulatory standards of neighbouring States or to manifest distrust towards the ideology of market integration. Bailleux's chapter provides an analysis of this ambivalent relationship between trust, free movement and fundamental rights.

The conceptualization of economic integration in the area of EU services, as having the objective of establishing higher levels of trust between the actors in the process of economic integration should not conceal the relevance of the trust theory of economic integration in other contexts, such as the WTO and other attempts at regional economic integration. The establishment of trust is a constitutive element for all forms of economic integration, although it may take a different role in each of them. This is a topic examined in Part VI of the volume.

Chapter 13, by Juan Marchetti and Petros Mavroidis, delves into the anatomy of mutual recognition agreements (MRAs) in the WTO and argues that these are frequently concluded between States having a similar cultural background: Thus, they are based on an informal substratum of trust (a form of personalized trust), which is not supplemented by a formal institutional one, as is the case for deeper economic integration arrangements. Marchetti and Mavroidis argue that the multilateral regulatory framework encourages the signing of such agreements. It imposes, nonetheless, one important constraint: they have to be extended to all other interested WTO Members that are in a similar situation. The burden of persuasion associated with requests to extend MRA is quite heavy. It is, thus, rather easy for WTO Members to use recognition agreements and 'regionalize' trade across signatories only.

With all this in mind, Marchetti and Mavroidis explore who the WTO Members choose as MRA partners. Their important empirical study is confined to agreements that have been notified to the WTO. Their analysis shows that many MRAs come under a preferential trade agreement. Moreover, the majority have been signed across geographically proximate partners who usually share the same language as well. They conclude that cultural factors seem to be quite important in the selection of MRA partners, thus confirming theoretical analyses to this effect.

However, as Chapter 14, by Robert Howse, illustrates, the lack of institutional substratum may be problematic with regard to the importation of regulatory standards and principles from other, specialized international regimes into the WTO, the successful transplantation of regulatory standards being ultimately dependent on the domestic regulatory landscape, as well as on the institutions and norms of international regulatory cooperation. Howse argues that the WTO adjudicator – who has to *define*, in context, the appropriate relationship between the specialized regimes and the WTO and *adapt* the external standards and principles to the purposes of the WTO – cannot simply *apply* external norms in the WTO as if they were treaty norms to be interpreted in accordance with the Vienna Convention on the Law of Treaties. His study focuses on telecommunications, where the market access supposedly guaranteed by WTO free trade disciplines depends crucially on the shape of the domestic regulatory landscape, as well as on institutions and norms of international regulatory cooperation. This raises the question of where the dispute settlement organs of the WTO will go to find the regulatory standards and principles to interpret the scope and nature of Members' commitments under the General Agreement on Trade in Services (GATS) in specific contexts. Applying the regulatory and competition-related norms with respect to telecommunications therefore represents a delicate hermeneutic challenge for the dispute settlement organs that calls for a different approach. Howse suggests that a Global Administrative Law perspective should sensitize the WTO adjudicator to the complexity of the regulatory instruments used by the specialized regimes in question and the emergence of a regulatory culture necessary for the operation of these agreements.

PART I

The 'trust' theory of integration

1

Trust, distrust and economic integration: setting the stage

IOANNIS LIANOS AND JOHANNES LE BLANC

1. Introduction

The concept of integration, the dependent variable of this study, has received different interpretations by lawyers, political scientists and economists. Lawyers generally understand the concept as referring to 'legal integration', which is defined as 'the gradual penetration' of EU law 'into the domestic law of its member states'.[1] Economists prefer the concept of 'economic integration', defined as 'the elimination of economic frontiers between two or more economies'.[2] The removal of trade impediments between participating nations and 'the establishment of certain elements of cooperation and coordination between them' characterize the process of economic integration, as opposed to other forms of international cooperation.[3] Political scientists have been more reluctant to provide a ready-made definition of 'integration' and have focused their analysis on the 'political context in which integration occurs',[4] the dependent variable being generally

1 A.-M. Burley and W. Mattli, 'Europe Before the Court: A Political Theory of Legal Integration', *International Organization* 47(1) (1993) 41–76, at 43.

2 J. Pelkmans, 'The Institutional Economics of European Integration, in Integration Through Law: Europe and the American Federal Experience A General Introduction', in M. Cappelletti, M. Seccombe and J. H. H. Weiler (eds.), *Integration Through Law*, Vol. 1, *Methods, Tools and Institutions*, Book 1, *A Political, Legal and Economic Overview* (Berlin: de Gruyter, 1986), p. 318.

3 A. M. El-Agraa, *Regional Integration: Experience, Theory and Measurement*, 2nd edn (Macmillan, 1999), p. 1.

4 W. Mattli, *The Logic of Regional Integration – Europe and Beyond* (Cambridge University Press, 1999), p. 19.

conceived in broad and descriptive terms as the transfer of authority to a supranational level.[5]

The relatively recent emergence of the concept of 'integration'[6] owes a lot to functionalist theories, which were the first to break away from 'the traditional link between authority and a definite territory by ascribing authority to activities based in areas of agreement'.[7] States exercise several functions (activities), some of which require action at the international level. This transfer initiates the process of integration, which is driven by the continuous pursuit of these functions, in the context of an international institution created for that purpose. According to functionalism, '(e)very function is left to generate others gradually; in every case the appropriate authority is left to grow and develop out of actual performance.'[8] Based on this approach, neo-functionalism was able to construct a theory of regional integration employing the model of European integration as the archetypical paradigm of the concept. The functionalist approach and the concept of integration are profoundly interlinked: without the functionalist emphasis on the existence of separate functions, where authority can be transferred, there can be no integration, in the sense political scientists give to this term.

The aim of this chapter is to challenge this view. This can be done, first, by showing that the separate-spheres approach, the distinctive characteristic of functionalism and of its neo-functionalist progeny, does not hold in the current state of the European integration process.

[5] See, e.g., *ibid.*, p. 1, defining regional integration schemes as 'cases that involve the voluntary linking in the economic and political domains of two or more formerly independent states to the extent that authority over key areas of national policy is shifted towards the supranational level'.

[6] On the emergence of the theory of international economic integration, see Fritz Machlup, *A History of Thought on Economic Integration* (Macmillan Press, 1977), noting that economists in the inter-war era employed the negative noun of 'disintegration' of the world economy, probably as a consequence of the national protectionist legislation that followed the economic crisis of 1929. The positive noun of 'integration' was first employed after the Second World War in order to provide a conceptual vehicle for the efforts of 'integration of the Western European economy', the substance of which 'would be the formation of a single large market within which quantitative restrictions on the movements of goods, monetary barriers to the flow of payments and, eventually, all tariffs are permanently swept away': *ibid.*, p. 11, referring to Paul Hoffmann's official pronouncement to the Council of the Organization of European Economic Co-operation on 31 October 1949.

[7] W. Mattli, *The Logic of Regional Integration – Europe and Beyond* (Cambridge University Press, 1999), p. 21.

[8] *Ibid.*, pp. 21–2, referring to the work of David Mitrany, *A Working Peace System* (Chicago: Quadrangle Books, 1966).

As has been explained elsewhere, we are witnessing a gradual transformation from a process of 'economic integration' in the traditional sense of the word to a 'holistic approach', where economic, social and political dimensions are profoundly intertwined.[9] Secondly, the European competences have been expanding continuously to areas previously subjected to the exclusive competence of the Member States. It is thus extremely difficult to distinguish between the different dimensions and impact of the process of integration and the functional boundaries of EU and State competences.[10] Third, the 'legitimacy' or democratic deficit critique of the process of European integration has shown the limits of breaking the link between authority and territory, and the fact of ascribing authority to activities. However, each process has different implications as to the actors involved: while the functionalist logic can accommodate the participation of stakeholders in the process (industry, labour, consumers), it is doubtful whether it can extend to all of the affected constituencies, as would be required by the principle of democratic representation.[11]

The shortcomings of the current state of integration theory, including the dependent variable selected, will be examined in section 2 of this chapter. Our focus will be on the limits of the functionalist logic and on the alternatives suggested by competing theories of international relations. We will conclude that the main premises of functionalism have been seriously challenged. However, none of the competing theories has proposed a new conceptualization of 'economic integration' nor have they suggested a more precise definition of the dependent variable. This situation is unsatisfactory, as, without a clear definition of what is entailed by the concept of integration, the boundary between regional integration and international economic cooperation or other forms of international economic interaction is blurred.

Once the need for a new approach on the concept of integration is recognized, section 3 of the chapter proceeds to explore two alternatives.

[9] I. Lianos, 'Shifting Narratives in the European Internal Market: Efficient Restrictions of Trade and the Nature of "Economic" Integration', *European Business Law Review* 21(5) (2010) 705–60.

[10] R. Schütze, *From Dual to Cooperative Federalism – The Changing Structure of European Law* (Oxford University Press, 2010), pp. 190–213.

[11] G. Majone, 'Transaction-Cost Efficiency and the Democratic Deficit', *Journal of European Public Policy* 17(2) (2010) 150–75, noting that the democratic deficit of European integration can be explained by the EU leaders' propensity to avoid political transaction costs.

The first one – economic integration as efficient organizational creation – perfects the dependent variable suggested by functionalism, extending it this time to authority-legitimacy transfers and elaborates a sophisticated typology of different degrees of integration. The second one – the trust theory of integration – chooses instead to abandon the definition of the dependent variable suggested by functionalism and to focus on a different dimension that would represent the turn towards a holistic, as opposed to a functionalist, approach of integration, where the social, economic and political dimensions are embedded in each other. In our view, the trust theory of integration provides a promising platform of reflection, not only for the European project of integration but also for all other projects of regional integration. It can also clearly illustrate the important differences, as to the degree of integration, between the European integration project, for example, and the WTO Agreement framework, without, however, establishing a clear demarcation line between them.

2. 'Economic integration' beyond functionalism

The study of the concept of economic integration since the Second World War has been profoundly linked to the analysis of the phenomenon of regional integration.[12] Heavily inspired by neo-functionalist theory, the studies of regional integration in the 1950s and 1960s emphasized the different dimensions of the integration process and their interaction with each other.[13]

The concept of political integration was the main focus, with the economic and social dimensions of integration being 'causally connected with political integration'.[14] Political integration was defined as:

> the process whereby political actors in several distinct national settings are persuaded to shift their loyalties, expectations and political activities, towards a new centre, whose institutions possess or demand jurisdiction over the pre-existing national States. The end result of a process of political

[12] E. B. Haas, 'The Study of Regional Integration: Reflections on the Joy and Anguish of Pre-Theorizing', *International Organization* 24(4) (1970) 607–46.

[13] J. Nye, 'Comparative Regional Integration: Concept and Measurement', *International Organization* 22(4) (1968) 855–80, pp. 865 and 868, distinguishing between 'economic integration' (formation of transnational economy), 'social integration' (formation of a transnational society) and 'political integration' (formation of transnational political interdependence).

[14] Haas, 'The Study of Regional Integration', above, p. 632.

integration is a new political community superimposed over the pre-existing ones.[15]

This framework relied on the following conceptual core: a process of 'functional spill-over' and 'political spill-over', the two being interrelated.[16] Functional spill-over referred to a process of sector integration, starting with low-profile economic and technical sectors and progressively expanding to the whole economy.[17] Political spill-over described 'the incremental shifting of expectations, the changing of values and the coalescing at the supranational level of national interest groups and political parties in response to sectoral integration'.[18]

Regional integration could thus be distinguished from international trade liberalization, occurring almost during the same period, with the establishment of the General Agreement on Tariffs and Trade (GATT). Regional economic integration was perceived as an exception to the multilateralism of the GATT system, which did not include any preferential regime at the time of its conclusion.[19] Only Article XXIV GATT contained an exception to the most favoured nation (MFN) principle of Article I GATT, thus preventing multilateralism from operating in the specific setting of regional integration. The mechanism of spill-over, the constitution of supranational institutions where experts, rather than diplomats, played a central role, was largely absent from the GATT scheme, whose nature was purely intergovernmental.

The topic of this volume being the regulation of trade in services at the regional (EU) and international (WTO) level, it is important to examine the basic tenets of neo-functionalism, before moving to other approaches that have challenged its assumptions. Our aim is to uncover the theoretical underpinnings of 'economic integration', by looking to the actors involved, as these are defined by each theoretical framework, their motivations or their ways of operation.

[15] E. B. Haas, *The Uniting of Europe* (Stanford University Press, 1958), p. 16.

[16] A.-M. Burley and W. Mattli, 'Europe before the Court: A Political Theory of Legal Integration', *International Organization* 47(1) (1993) 41–76, p. 55.

[17] Haas, *The Uniting of Europe*, above, p. 297.

[18] Burley and Mattli, 'Europe before the Court', above, p. 55.

[19] Article XXIV GATT illustrates that regional integration was perceived as an exception to multilateralism. Preferential regimes were introduced in the GATT system with the Enabling Clause in 1979. See GATT BISD 26S 1980, pp. 203–5.

2.1 *The rise and fall of neo-functionalism*

Neo-functionalism's starting point is social differentiation: society is carved in various specialized and autonomous sectors, operating independently but gradually in more intensive cooperation with each other, as a consequence of the spill-over effect. Technocratic economic issues are perceived separately from contentious political or social ones. At the same time, they are profoundly interlinked within the same continuum. According to Haas, the initiator of the theory, 'the supranational style stresses the indirect penetration of the political by way of the economic because the 'purely' economic decisions always acquire political significance in the minds of the participants'.[20] At the same time, 'the measure of political success inherent in economic integration lies in the demands, expectations and loyalties of the political actors affected by the process, which do not logically and necessarily follow from statistical indices of economic success'.[21] It is clear in neo-functionalist theory that a 'purely' economic scheme 'does not by itself answer the basic political question whether the unified economy meets with the satisfaction of people active within it'.[22] The political and the economic dimension of integration are profoundly interlinked.

The main actors in the process of integration are experts operating independently of their national political constituents but who are at the same time checked by 'equally prescient national actors'.[23] They aim to promote, first, sectoral economic integration and, following 'spill-over', other forms of integration. The process of decision-making is incremental.[24]

The dependent variable of integration is the concept of 'authority-legitimacy transfer or sharing'.[25] Possible independent variables are institutionalization and the attitudes of actors.[26] Remarkably, neo-functionalism does not focus on the flow of goods, services and people across Member States as independent variables of integration.[27] The

[20] E. B. Haas, 'Technocracy, Pluralism and the New Europe', in Joseph S. Nye (ed.), *International Regionalism: A Reader* (Boston: Little, Brown, 1968), pp. 149–66, p. 152.

[21] Haas, *The Uniting of Europe*, above, p. 13. [22] *Ibid.*, p. 284.

[23] E. B. Haas, 'The Study of Regional Integration – Reflections on the Joy and Anguish of Pre-Theorizing', *International Organization* 24(4) (1970) 607–46, p. 627.

[24] *Ibid.* [25] *Ibid.*, p. 633. [26] *Ibid.*, p. 636.

[27] *Ibid.*, p. 610: 'The study of regional integration is concerned with explaining how and why states cease to be wholly sovereign, how and why they voluntarily mingle, merge, and mix with their neighbors so as to lose the factual attributes of sovereignty while acquiring new techniques for resolving conflict between themselves.' See also *ibid.*, p. 628.

dependent variable chosen is, of course, highly general and moving; hence, it does not relate to the existence of a holistic end-state or terminal condition: that of the 'amalgamated' variety, such as the federal union, or of the 'pluralistic' variety, such as a confederation. Domestic politics, the different dimensions of integration (economic, political and social) and the perception of States as multiple actors, active in the global as well as in the regional sphere, provide the matrix of the process of integration.

Although not necessarily limited to the study of European regional integration,[28] the process of European integration has profoundly influenced neo-functionalism. Eventually, the credibility of the theory was affected by its perceived inability to explain the difficulties faced by the European project in the 1970s,[29] following the '*chaire vide*' crisis and the opposition of General de Gaulle to British accession. The increasing role of 'national actors' challenged the neo-functionalist's belief that the integrated institutions were able to cope with the spill-over effect and consequently the possible 'collapse of legitimacy', caused by the absence of a clear central authority able to cope with 'complexly linked and highly controversial issues in the European agenda'.[30] Following this crisis, the process of integration seemed to arrive at a stalemate, thus questioning the predictions of neo-functionalist theory.

At this point, a new 'heroic actor', which until then had been ignored by neo-functionalist theory, made its entrance: the European Court of Justice (now the Court of Justice of the European Union).[31] The Court initiated a 'constitutional framework for a federal-type structure in Europe',[32] by developing the building blocks of European constitutionalism (direct effect, supremacy, general principles and protection of fundamental rights). Away from the conceptual fuzziness of neo-functionalism, where no clear indication was given on the

[28] For a study of Haas' influence on the study of Latin American integration, see W. Mattli, 'Ernst Haas's Evolving Thinking on Comparative Regional Integration of Virtues and Infelicities', *Journal of European Public Policy* 12(2) (2005) 327–48.

[29] E. B. Haas, *The Obsolescence of Regional Integration Theory* (Berkeley, CA: Institute of International Studies, University of California Berkeley, 1975).

[30] E. B, Haas, 'Turbulent Fields and the Theory of Regional Integration', *International Organization* 30(2) (1976) 173–212.

[31] J. H. H. Weiler, 'The Transformation of Europe', *Yale Law Journal* 100 (1991) 2403–2483, p. 2409.

[32] E. Stein, 'Lawyers, Judges, and the Making of a Transnational Constitution', *American Journal of International Law* 75 (1981) 1–27, p. 1.

dependent variable of integration,[33] the Court's rhetoric of legal coherence, '*effet utile*' as well as its federal understanding of the relation between the centre and the periphery provided a clear view of what the process of integration entailed. An additional advantage of the Court was that its legal-technical rhetoric was largely immunized by the risks of political spill-over and the reaction of national actors. Indeed, the Court had previously taken care to ally national judges to its cause, by empowering them to act independently of their domestic executive and, to a certain extent, legislative powers and to move away, in matters of European law, from their limited interpretative margin in civil law jurisdictions. Teleological interpretation became akin to 'functional spill-over', without its political inconvenience, so to speak.

The emergence of the Court as the principal actor in the integration process had profound implications on the type of dominant rationality that emerged. This was economically oriented towards the constitution of a 'single market' but relied heavily on a legalistic approach, the content of which was progressively defined by the jurisprudence of the Court. Legal integration, 'the gradual penetration of (EU) law into the domestic law of its member states',[34] was examined exclusively from a legal coherence perspective, with little emphasis given to external (to the legal system) sources of rationality.[35] Theoretical perspectives advocating an 'integration through law' approach adopted a more contextual perspective but still fell short of providing an overall conceptual framework that would explain the process of European integration.[36]

To cite an example, the broad definition of measures equivalent to quantitative restrictions adopted by the Court (in what is now Article 34 TFEU), the Member States incurring the burden to prove that the restriction of trade is justified by public interest objectives, can be explained by a specific conception of economic integration emphasizing regulatory uniformity across Member States or the absence of national trade barriers to the operation of the 'single market'. From this perspective, the position of the Court can be

[33] See E. B. Haas, 'The Study of Regional Integration – Reflections on the Joy and Anguish of Pre-Theorizing', *International Organization* 24(4) (1970) 607–46, p. 628, admitting that 'neo-functionalists do not agree on a dependent variable and therefore differ with each other on the point in time at which a judgment of how much successful integration is to be made'.

[34] Burley and Mattli, 'Europe before the Court', above, p. 43.

[35] K. Kaiser, 'L'Europe des Savants – European Integration and the Social Sciences', *Journal of Common Market Studies* 4(1) (1965) 36–46, pp. 39–40.

[36] Burley and Mattli, 'Europe before the Court', above, pp. 46–8.

compared to neo-functionalism, where spill-over leads inevitably to full economic unity.[37] Yet, it is important to note that neo-functionalists did not equate economic integration to regulatory sameness, but emphasized instead the progressive transfer of demands, expectations and loyalties of the political and economic actors to a new centre.[38] The Commission saw the opportunities offered by a broad definition of the concept of trade restriction and rushed to interpret the Court's jurisprudence as reinforcing its own powers.[39]

The legalistic approach followed by the Court led to a disconnection between the legal/narrow economic integration and its broader political and social dimensions. This is particularly apparent if one adopts a narrow definition of 'legal integration' or 'integration through law', accounting for a positivistic understanding, where law is hard and involves sanctions in case of non-compliance. In contrast to the purely economic dimension, the social dimension of integration has notoriously been left outside. Yet a broader understanding that would emphasize social practice and that would involve additional actors than courts,[40] may provide a slightly different account of the evolution of European integration and the emergence of social regulation at the EU level.[41] The Open Method of Coordination and other new methods of governance are the means through which the social dimension has been introduced in the economic integration project. The social dimension is now hardening with the development of a legislative programme that allegedly takes stock of the embeddedness of the economic and social dimensions.[42] This leads to a more holistic approach towards the Internal Market project,[43] which inevitably challenges the role of experts, the 'heroes' of integration for neo-functionalists, and re-emphasizes the role of national political actors in the process. The role of the latter has been the focus of realists/neo-realists approaches.

[37] Haas, *The Uniting of Europe*, above, p. 283. [38] *Ibid.*, p. 13.

[39] Communication from the Commission concerning the consequences of the judgment given by the Court of Justice on 20 February 1979 in Case 120/78 ('Cassis de Dijon'), OJ 1980 C256/2.

[40] G. de Búrca, 'Rethinking Law in Neofunctionalist Theory', *Journal of European Public Policy* 12(2) (2005) 310–26, p. 318.

[41] D. Ashiagbor, *The European Employment Strategy: Labour Market Regulation and New Governance* (Oxford University Press, 2005).

[42] M. Monti, 'A New Strategy for the Single Market at the Service of Europe's Economy and Society', Report to the President of the European Commission, 9 May 2010; Communication from the European Commission, 'A Single Market for the 21st Century', Brussels, 20 November 2007, COM(2007) 724 final.

[43] Lianos, 'Shifting Narratives in the European Internal Market', above.

2.2 *Realist and neo-realist approaches: the return to national actors*

The resurgence of realism, after the perceived failure of neo-functionalism to explain the role of national actors in the integration process, had important effects on the binary opposition between the European and the national levels that underpinned neo-functionalism. Moving away from this opposition, the realist view perceives the process of European integration as a 'rescue' of the nation State.[44] The theory insists on the complex bargaining between different States and the opportunity of side-payments as the driving forces of integration. In the realist's worldview, the European integration is a multi-level system of actors with different preferences aiming at the preservation of their sovereignty. The supranational institutions, such as the European Commission or the Court, are secondary actors that intervene to mobilize coalitions of governments for specific projects,[45] for instance the establishment of the Common Market.[46] While neo-functionalists stress the supranational authorities and the international experts' role in promoting integration, a realist perspective on European integration focuses on the role of States.

According to realists, the international system is characterized by anarchy and the relations between States are governed by the 'law of the jungle'.[47] Nation-States, not international organizations or transnational organizations, are the primary actors in this system.[48] Every State has to take care of its interests by itself. Vital interests for a State are the protection of its territory and the independence of its political decision-making from external powers, which might also relate to economic capabilities and its ability to deal effectively with poverty, diseases, natural disasters and other threats.[49]

[44] A. S. Milward, *The European Rescue of the Nation State*, 2nd edn (London and New York: Routledge, 2000), p. 4.

[45] D. Puchala, 'Domestic Politics and Regional Harmonization in the European Communities', *World Politics* 27(4) (1975) 496–520.

[46] W. Sandholtz and J. Zysman, '1992: Recasting the European Bargain', *World Politics* 42 (1989) 95–128.

[47] R. Aron, 'The Anarchical Order of Power', *Daedalus* 95(2) (1966) 479–502, p. 480.

[48] J. H. Herz. 'Political Realism Revisited', *International Studies Quarterly* 25(2) (1981) 182–97, p. 183.

[49] S. M. Walt, 'The Renaissance of Security Studies', *International Studies Quarterly* 35(2) (1991) 211–39, p. 213; R. Niebuhr, *Moral Man and Immoral Society* (New York: Charles Scribner's Sons, 1947), p. 15.

For realists, an increase in resources and capabilities by one State creates a dilemma for all members of the system and is easily perceived as a threat by its neighbours, which thereupon increase their own capabilities. The result is a never-ending struggle for power.[50] The most powerful States resulting from this rivalry for might are of course the most relevant ones in the international system. These dominant powers, the 'hegemons',[51] organize weaker States and enforce peace among them. This constellation lasts until the tide turns and formerly weak States may increase their might, finally challenging the hegemon. International organizations are only seen as a mere instrument by which powerful States attempt to defend and advance their national interests.[52]

International cooperation is possible as long as it leads to gains for the States involved. Realists agree that cooperation is more feasible when:

> large transactions can be divided up into a series of smaller ones, if transparency can be increased, if both the gains from cheating and the costs of being cheated on are relatively low, if mutual cooperation is or can be made much more advantageous than mutual defection, and if each side employs strategies of reciprocity and believes that the interactions will continue over a long period of time. '[53]

Diplomats play a key role in negotiations over cooperation. Their task is to mitigate the concerns of States and to increase the gains from cooperation. States will be more inclined to cooperate the better they understand the behaviour of their opponents. Open exchange of information and the creation of transparency in domestic processes are key factors for successful cooperation among States. An alternative strategy of a State fearing a potential turnaround of a current partner in the future is to integrate the opponent and itself into a cooperative structure in order to reduce the incentives of reneging in the future.[54]

[50] John H. Herz, 'Political Realism Revisited', *International Studies Quarterly* 25(2) (1981) 182–97.

[51] According to John H. Herz, 'Political Ideas and Political Reality', *Western Political Quarterly* 3(2) (1950) 161–78, p. 167, hegemony relations are a constellation in which 'one or a few of the members of sectional interests concerned "leads" the others'.

[52] H. J. Morgenthau, 'The Yardstick of National Interest', *Annals of the American Academy of Political and Social Science* 296 (1954) 77–84.

[53] R. Jervis, 'Realism, Neo-liberalism, and Cooperation: Understanding the Debate', *International Security* 24(1) (1999) 42–63, p. 52.

[54] R. Jervis, 'Realism in the Study of World Politics', *International Organization* 52(4) (1998) 971–91, pp. 986–7.

Neo-realists share the realist view of the unimportance of international organizations and other sub-national actors. They leave no doubt that it is the State and by no means other organizations that are capable of performing all crucial social, economic and security functions that nation States need in order to survive.[55] International organizations[56] are in neo-realist thought merely instruments by which powerful States realize their interests. These institutions have only limited independent effects since they are created, shaped and kept alive by States. The survival of international organizations therefore reflects more the power and influence of major States than the independent power of institutions themselves.[57]

The establishment of cooperation among States is seen in neo-realism as highly difficult and restricted by the States' struggle over the distribution of gains from cooperation.[58] Due to their preoccupation with their own relative position in the international system, the main objective of States is not the maximization of their gains from interaction but the prevention of other States from increasing their capabilities relative to their own. States will therefore defect from cooperation as soon as they perceive that the relative gains of partners are exceeding their own.[59]

Alliances are possible, but only under specific circumstances. They are feasible in a multi-polar system in which States interact closely in order to balance a major State or another alliance of States. In such a setting, each State is vitally dependent on the other and the defection of one member would jeopardize the security of all the other members of the alliance. The situation changes somewhat in a bipolar environment in which two major powers provide most of the security. Defections of minor partners in this case have only a minor impact upon the alliance as a whole. Since States find themselves in a self-help system in which each unit is required to look after itself, the most likely constellation that results is a balance of power. This is a direct consequence of the nature of

[55] K. N. Waltz, 'Globalization and Governance', *Political Science and Politics* 32(4) (1999) 693–700, p. 697; K. N. Waltz, 'Structural Realism after the Cold War', *International Security* 25(1) (2000) 5–41, p. 18.

[56] R. O. Keohane and J. S. Nye, *Power and Interdependence*, 2nd edn (New York: HarperCollins Publishers, 1989), p. 54.

[57] S. D. Krasner, 'Global Communications and National Power: Life on the Pareto Frontier', *World Politics* 43(3) (1991) 336–66; J. J. Mearsheimer, 'The False Promise of International Institutions', *International Security* 19(3) (1995) 5–49, p. 13; K. N. Waltz, 'Structural Realism after the Cold War', *International Security* 25(1) (2000) 5–41, p. 20.

[58] K. N. Waltz, *Theory of International Politics* (Boston: McGraw-Hill, 1979), p. 105.

[59] J. M. Grieco, 'Anarchy and the Limits of Cooperation: A Realist Critique of the Newest Liberal Institutionalism', *International Organization*, 42(3) (1998) 485–507, pp. 498–9.

the system itself and is most likely to perpetuate as long as at least some States try to preserve themselves.[60] But the international system is by no means static. It is a dynamic system in which 'structures shape and shove; they encourage States to do some things and to refrain from doing others.'[61] As a result, States permanently have to reconsider their own position relative to other States. This constant, dynamic change 'stimulates States to behave in ways that tend toward the creation of balances of power'.[62] The problem of a self-help system can be overcome in a situation of the hegemony of one powerful State which will prevent other States from defecting from negotiated conditions and, more generally, will regulate interaction among States.[63]

This theory of international relations has important implications for the theorizing of European integration.

First, the realist and neo-realist turn in international relations has shifted the focus of integration theory towards State interests and inter-State bargaining, that is, structural factors such as the position of the State in the international power distribution. The realist view questions the role of transnational elites or experts in the process of 'integration' and emphasizes instead the differences that exist between States and the subsequent regulatory pluralism that reflects their very different domestic political structures.[64] Integration is by no means an automatic process; it can be perceived instead as a form of unstable cooperation and intergovernmental bargaining between sovereign States, each following its own fixed preferences. To the integrationist logic of neo-functionalists, one could thus oppose the 'State-centred pluralistic and structured' approach of realists/neo-realists.[65]

Secondly, in the realist/neo-realist view, international organizations cannot solve the security dilemma that each State faces. For neo-realists,

[60] K. N. Waltz, *Theory of International Politics* (Boston: McGraw-Hill, 1979), p. 118.

[61] K. N. Waltz, 'Evaluating Theories', *American Political Science Review* 91(4) (1997) 913–17, p. 915.

[62] K. N. Waltz, *Theory of International Politics* (Boston: McGraw-Hill, 1979), p. 118.

[63] B. Buzan, 'Economic Structure and International Security: The Limits of the Liberal Case', *International Organization* 38(4) (1984) 597–624, p. 607; J. J. Mearsheimer, 'Back to the Future: Instability in Europe after the Cold War', *International Security* 15(1) (1990) 5–56, p. 47.

[64] S. Hoffmann, *Organisations Internationales et Pouvoirs Politiques des Etats* (Paris: Armand Colin, 1954).

[65] S. Hoffmann, 'Reflections on the Nation State in Western Europe Today', in S. Hoffmann (ed.), *The European Sisyphus. Essays on Europe, 1964–1995* (Boulder, CO: Westview Press, 1995), pp. 215–19.

States face two options in order to ensure their security: bandwagonning and balancing. Bandwagonning is the strategy of choice for weak States which are unable to balance against their stronger neighbours. Instead of increasing their own capabilities, they seek protection by strong States in exchange for important opportunities for a 'voice' within the organization.[66] Stronger State entities choose the balancing strategy.[67] The continuity between the technical/economic and the political dimensions of integration through the operation of the spill-over effect could thus be questioned.[68] In this tradition, the 'progress' of European integration is not due to a spill-over effect, but rather constitutes an epiphenomenon of the emergence of the hegemonic power of the United States, which pushed the medium and declining Western European powers to a strategy of 'balancing' by constituting the European Communities.[69]

Thirdly, these approaches can be opposed to the liberal position (see section 2.4), which presuppose a strong entanglement between domestic and international politics. One could employ the analogy of two-level games,[70] where processes occurring in the international level (high politics) influence considerably domestic politics and the formation of preferences at the national level (low politics).[71] The inverse syllogism is also true: domestic politics and economic interests largely explain national preferences represented at the international level.[72] For example, States delegate powers to international organizations with the aim to strengthen the authority of the executive branch, in particular as many

[66] A. Hirschman, *Exit, Voice, Loyalty: Responses to Decline in Firms, Organizations and States* (Cambridge, MA: Harvard University Press, 1970).

[67] K. N. Waltz, 'Evaluating Theories', *American Political Science Review* 91(4) (1997) 913–17, p. 915.

[68] S. Hoffmann, 'The European Community and 1992', in S. Hoffmann (eds.), *The European Sisyphus: Essays on Europe, 1964–1995* (Boulder, CO: Westview Press, 1995), p. 235.

[69] J. Grieco, 'Anarchy and the Limits of Cooperation: A Realist Critique of the Newest Liberal Intergovernmentalism', *International Organization* 42(3) (1988) 485–507.

[70] R. Putnam, 'Diplomacy and Domestic Politics: The Logic of Two-Level Games', *International Organization* 42(3) (1988) 427–60.

[71] P. Gourevitch, 'The Second Image Reversed: The International Sources of Domestic Politics', *International Organization* 23(4) (1978) 881–912.

[72] A. Moravcsik, 'Negotiating the Single European Act: National Interests and Conventional Statecraft in the European Community', *International Organization* 45(1) (1991) 19–56; A. Moravcsik, 'Preferences and Power in the European Community: A Liberal Intergovernmentalist Approach', *Journal of Common Market Studies* 31(4) (1993) 473–524.

of the domestic political constraints may not affect the international level.[73] For comparison, neo-functionalists would have emphasized the technical nature of decision-making in certain international cooperation settings, which would have required delegation to international experts and consequently the development of technocratic consensus.

The role of States being reaffirmed, it became difficult for neo-functionalists to argue that experts and/or the 'heroic' Court were running the show. However, the progress of economic integration post-Single European Act could not be adequately explained by the realist/neo-realist perspective as well, despite the best efforts made by some commentators.[74] The theory of federalism offers an alternative perspective.

2.3 Federalism

The federalist view highlights the transfer of authority and competences from the State level to the federal level as an important indication of integration.[75] Only significant transfers of sovereignty count. Federalism may take different forms: dual federalism is based on the idea that the federal level and the State have equal sovereignty (they are 'co-equals') and they exercise mutually exclusive competences in their own spheres; cooperative federalism supposes power-sharing between the federal and the State level in order to provide solutions to social problems.[76] This definition assumes that cooperative federalism lends itself to hierarchy, while dual federalism lends itself to heterarchy. Such dichotomy may, however, seem simplistic and does not exhaust the different meanings of the concept of federalism. Indeed, some authors have advocated a 'federal vision beyond the State', 'articulated around the concepts of mutual

[73] A. Moravcsik, 'Why the European Community Strengthens the State: International Co-operation and Domestic Politics', Center for European Studies Working Paper Series No. 52 (Cambridge, MA: Harvard University, 1994), also available at www.ces.fas.harvard.edu/publications/docs/pdfs/Moravcsik52.pdf.

[74] See G. Garrett, 'International Cooperation and Institutional Choice: The European Community's Internal Market', *International Organization* 46(2) (1992) 533–60.

[75] W. van Gerven, *The European Union: A Polity of States and Peoples* (Oxford: Stanford University Press and Hart Publishing, 2005); K. Lenaerts, 'Constitutionalism and the Many Faces of Federalism', *American Journal of Comparative Law* 38 (1990) 205–63; K. Nicolaïdis and R. Howse, *The Federal Vision: Legitimacy and Levels of Governance in the United States and the European Union* (Oxford University Press, 2001).

[76] R. Schütze, *From Dual to Cooperative Federalism – The Changing Structure of European Law* (Oxford University Press, 2009).

tolerance and empowerment'.[77] Kalypso Nicolaïdis notes that the distinguishing feature of 'federalism'

> lies precisely in *not* resolving the tensions which exist between the two poles: the One and the Many. In a federation, each part is itself a whole, not a part of a whole, and the whole itself is more than its parts. Neither is the One a simple expression of the Many – collaboration – nor are the Many simply components of the One – hierarchy. Instead, like fractals in our mental and material maps, each exhibits in its own scale its own version of a familiar pattern; each level operates as a whole albeit with multiple and subtle connections with other levels. Federalism in its essence does not mean bringing together different polities as one – however decentralized – polity. It means instead retaining what is separate *in spite of* all that is common.[78]

This 'federal vision' is characterized by a shift to 'open ended dynamics', 'shared competences' (including their exercise) arranged around principles of 'networked cooperation' and proportionality, the emergence of 'power checks' through 'mutual control' and 'federalism safeguards', the turn to 'multi-centred governance' achieved through 'non-hierarchical models of governance', the respect for principles of 'constitutional tolerance', mutual recognition and more broadly the existence of shared identities.[79] Nicolaïdis observes:

> This implies *inter alia* a shift in focus in the competence debate away from allocation of competences *per se* towards granting centre stage to the processes of change themselves and the mechanisms that make them sustainable, including governance structures and the many mechanisms of control among the actors involved at different levels, democratic input in the joint management of shared competences, and strategies of mutual empowerment between levels and actors involved in governance. In the end, it calls for a move 'beyond hierarchy' from vertical paradigms of multi-layered governance to more horizontal ones of multi-centred governance where the legitimacy of the system as a whole is grounded in mutual tolerance, mutual recognition, and mutual empowerment rather than in the design of common structures and the pursuit of homogenous practices.[80]

This conceptualization has important implications for the concept of integration:

[77] K. Nicolaïdis, 'Conclusion: The Federal Vision Beyond the Federal State', in K. Nicolaïdis and R. Howse, *The Federal Vision: Legitimacy and Levels of Governance in the United States and the European Union* (Oxford University Press, 2001).

[78] *Ibid.* [79] *Ibid.* [80] *Ibid.*

> *Integration* can be more about sustainable decentralization than centralization, horizontal mutual inclusiveness rather than vertical delegation of authority, and managing differences rather than engineering convergence.[81]

The 'federal vision' breaks with the unidimensional view of 'legal integration' and the latter's focus on regulatory sameness. Regulatory pluralism becomes essential in order to provide the necessary degree of flexibility, political inclusiveness and empowerment to the individual parts forming the 'federal' unit. Although this 'federal vision' may be relevant, if not applicable, to governance at the world level, the main thrust of the theory focuses, as was the case for neo-functionalism, on the European experiment of regional integration and looks unlikely to be applied as such at the WTO level.

2.4 Liberal regime theory: institutionalism and governance theory

The narrow conceptual focus of 'legal integration' is also at odds with the recent emphasis on the study of 'institutions' and 'governance'. The role of institutions, in particular in overcoming the problems arising from an anarchic international system, is the core subject of 'liberal institutionalism'. Liberal approaches differ from the realist school in that they reject the idea of States as the only important actors in international relations. Furthermore, the realist view of States as unitary or rational agents is questioned; power is pushed into the background by economic interests; and international institutions are believed to promote cooperation among States.[82] The liberal schools of thought, as the realist ones, do not represent a homogeneous theory but consist of several approaches, each one contributing to the understanding of the nature of inter-State relations.[83]

[81] *Ibid.*

[82] J. M. Grieco, 'Anarchy and the Limits of Cooperation: A Realist Critique of the Newest Liberal Institutionalism', *International Organization* 42(3) (1988) 485–507, pp. 489–90.

[83] According to Andrew Moravcsik, 'Taking Preferences Seriously: A Liberal Theory of International Politics', *International Organization* 51(4) (1997) 513–53, at least three variants can be differentiated: 'Ideational liberalism focuses on the compatibility of social preferences across fundamental collective goods like national unity, legitimate political institutions, and socio-economic regulation. Commercial liberalism focuses on incentives created by opportunities for transborder economic transactions. Republican liberalism focuses on the nature of domestic representation and the resulting possibilities for rent-seeking behavior.'

The study of international institutions and organizations becomes even more central in neo-liberal institutionalism (neo-liberals). Although in agreement with the core assumptions of neo-realism, which regards States as the most relevant actors pursuing their own interests, assumes rational behaviour by the actors and notes the anarchical character of the international system, neo-liberals believe that cooperation between States is possible.[84] Since cooperation does not arise automatically, as it always remains overshadowed by the fear of cheating, transaction costs may rise and the returns from the interaction are uncertain, institutions play a central role.[85] Institutions can 'reduce the uncertainty about the reliability of other States and, once in place, they lower the costs of securing specific agreement'.[86]

However, States are not perceived as unitary actors. Both the national and the international levels impact on decision-making in international relations.[87] It also follows that multiple channels link societies. Not only do official inter-State relations count but also trans-governmental and trans-national relations. These relations lead to strong transnational ties with high transaction rates, making States or sub-national actors in different countries economically dependent on one another. In contrast to interconnectedness, interdependence is always related to symmetric or asymmetric 'costly effects of transactions', since it restricts autonomy. The asymmetries in dependence allow an actor to influence the counterparts he is interacting with.[88] There are two dimensions of interdependence: sensitivity and vulnerability. In a stable framework, sensitivity refers to 'degrees of responsiveness within a policy framework – how quickly do changes in one country bring costly changes in another, and how great are the costly effects?'[89] Sensitivity of interdependence describes the costs that an actor has to bear if no action is taken in response. Vulnerability, however, 'rests on the relative availability and costliness of the alternatives that various actors face'.[90] The dimension of vulnerability stands for the costs that the actor faces by adapting to the changes.

[84] R. O. Keohane and J. S. Nye, *Power and Interdependence*, 2nd edn (New York: HarperCollins Publishers, 1989), p. xi, describe the two schools as 'complimentary'.

[85] J. Ikenberry, 'The Future of International Leadership', *Political Science Quarterly* 111(3) (1996) 385–402, p. 392.

[86] *Ibid.*, p. 392.

[87] R. O. Keohane and J. S. Nye, *Power and Interdependence*, 2nd edn (New York: HarperCollins Publishers, 1989), p. xi.

[88] *Ibid.*, pp. 9–11. [89] *Ibid.*, p. 12. [90] *Ibid.*, p. 13.

This complex interdependence has important implications for political processes. First, States are most likely to use asymmetrical interdependence, international organizations and transnational actors to attain their goals. Secondly, under complex interdependence there is no difference between high and low politics. This leads to a situation in which '[d]iscontented domestic groups will politicize issues and force more issues once considered domestic onto the interstate agenda'.[91] Thirdly, multiple channels of contacts among societies form and exercise a strong influence 'on the ability of statesmen to calculate the manipulation of interdependence or follow a consistent strategy of linkage'.[92] Numerous non-State actors, as well as State bureaucracies, interact permanently across borders. Fourthly, international organizations and institutions grow more important. Institutions can help 'set up the international agenda, and act as catalysts for coalition-formation and as arenas for political initiatives and linkage by weak states'.[93] By congregating representatives of different actors, international organizations can initiate coalitions of interest. In particular, weak States profit from their equal participation in organizations which provide these States with a forum for dialogue and cooperation.

The consequence of interdependence for political strategy is that the activities of all actors in the international system cause costs that other actors have to bear. Those actors, affected by the activities of others, will try to avoid having the burdens of adjustment forced upon them. The challenge is to 'generate and maintain a mutually beneficial pattern of cooperation in the face of competing efforts by governments (and non-governmental actors) to manipulate the system for their own benefit'.[94]

Closely intertwined with interdependence is the concept of 'regimes'. Regime theory is a reaction to and at the same time a correction of the theory of hegemonic stability of the realist school.[95] According to Keohane and Nye:

> [R]elationships of interdependence often occur within, and may be affected by, networks of rules, norms, and procedures that regularize behavior and control its effects. We refer to the sets of governing arrangements that affect relationships of interdependence as international regimes.[96]

[91] *Ibid.*, p. 33. [92] *Ibid.*, p. 34. [93] *Ibid.*, p. 35.

[94] R. O. Keohane and J. S. Nye, 'Power and Interdependence Revisited', *International Organization* 41(4) (1987) 725–53, p. 730.

[95] R. O. Keohane, *International Institutions and State Power* (Boulder, CO: Westview Press, 1989), p. 101.

[96] R. O. Keohane and J. S. Nye, *Power and Interdependence*, 2nd edn (New York: HarperCollins Publishers, 1989), p. 19.

The authors portray regimes as an important alternative tool to facilitate interaction among States. In the absence of authoritative institutions and therefore 'pervasive uncertainty' in the international system, regimes facilitate creating mutually advantageous agreements among several actors where *ad hoc* interaction would yield less efficient results.[97] Specific sets of regulations and procedures are developed to coordinate the interaction of States and transnational actors in multiple areas. Regimes order international behaviour and reduce conflict in the international system, they empower new groups to fight for their cause, they may increase the acknowledgment of common interests and they might initiate new policies.[98] While acknowledging the anarchical structure of the international system, neo-liberals claim that its negative effects can, at least partly, be overcome by this instrument.[99]

Regimes come in profoundly different shapes. They can be either formal or informal and can even be incorporated into inter-State agreements and treaties. Keohane and Nye differentiate between 'structure' and 'process': while structures focus on the distribution of capabilities among States, process refers to bargaining behaviour within a power structure. Regimes take an intermediate position between the international power structures and the bargaining processes among the players, that is, on the one hand, the regime is profoundly shaped by the distribution of power in the system, while, on the other hand, it has an impact on the bargaining process inside the system.[100]

Regimes are formed by States to diminish risks and conflicts of interest by coordinating the behaviour of actors.[101] They might also increase the efficiency of inter-State transactions by making agreement easier as they provide frameworks for establishing legal liability, 'they improve the quantity and quality of information available to actors' or they reduce other transaction costs, such as the costs of organization or of making side-payments.[102]

97 R. O. Keohane, *International Institutions and State Power* (Boulder, CO: Westview Press, 1989), pp. 106–8.

98 P. M. Haas, 'Do Regimes Matter? Epistemic Communities and Mediterranean Pollution Control', *International Organization* 43(3) (1989) 377–403, pp. 401–3.

99 J. M. Grieco, 'Anarchy and the Limits of Cooperation: A Realist Critique of the Newest Liberal Institutionalism', *International Organization* 42(3) (1988) 485–507, p. 486.

100 R. O. Keohane and J. S. Nye, *Power and Interdependence*, 2nd edn (New York: HarperCollins Publishers, 1989), pp. 20–1.

101 R. O. Keohane, *International Institutions and State Power* (Boulder, CO: Westview Press, 1989), p. 107.

102 *Ibid.*, p. 111.

Regimes are set up when organizational costs are lower than the expected return from the cooperation. The costs of setting up a regime need to be weighted to the costs of *ad hoc* decisions. If the latter are higher, the likelihood of the establishment of a regime is high. This is most likely to happen in environments where the 'issue density' is high, that is, in policy spaces where a high number of important issues arise.[103] Making agreements on certain issues in dense policy spaces tends to have a spill-over effect on neighbouring issues, because of the subsequent economies in organizational costs involved in reconciling distinct objectives. Regimes bringing together actors to discuss a wide range of issues also have a side effect in the form of side-payments. While side-payments usually raise transaction costs, these might be lowered by regimes because 'expectations that an integration arrangement can be expanded to new issue-areas permit the broadening of potential side-payments, thus facilitating agreements'.[104]

The central idea of regime functioning is that repeated interaction between States makes it possible to surmount the uncertainties arising from the prisoners' dilemma.[105] The 'shadow of the future' allows for a continuous interaction among players in an anarchical environment.[106] Assuming that players not only take short-term, but also long-term, benefits into account in an indefinitely repeated interaction, permanent cooperation without an enforcing power is possible even among egoistic actors.[107] However,

> [f]or cooperation to prove stable, the future must have a sufficiently large shadow. This means that the importance of the next encounter between

[103] R. O. Keohane, *After Hegemony* (Princeton University Press, 1984), p. 79; R. O. Keohane, *International Institutions and State Power* (Boulder, CO: Westview Press, 1989), p. 112.

[104] *Ibid.*, p. 113.

[105] States may behave in a tit-for-tat manner. States stick to rules they agreed upon as long as their counterparts do. See J. M. Grieco, 'Anarchy and the Limits of Cooperation: A Realist Critique of the Newest Liberal Institutionalism', *International Organization* 42 (3) (1988) 485–507, p. 493.

[106] R. Axelrod and R. O. Keohane, 'Achieving Cooperation under Anarchy: Strategies and Institutions', in D. A. Baldwin (ed.), *Neorealism and Neo-liberalism: The Contemporary Debate* (New York: Columbia University Press, 1993), p. 91: 'In Prisoner's Dilemma, concern about the future helps to promote cooperation. The more future payoffs are valued relative to current payoffs, the less the incentive to defect today – since the other side is likely to retaliate tomorrow.'

[107] A. Hasenclever, P. Mayer and V. Rittberger, *Theories of International Regimes* (Cambridge University Press, 1997), p. 34.

> the same two individuals must be great enough to make defection an unprofitable strategy.[108]

The prospect of future interaction is not, however, the only element determining cooperation. According to the 'sanctioning problem', the number of players in the game and their stance towards each other also matters. Three conditions decide whether an interaction is effective: '(1) players can identify defectors; (2) they are able to focus retaliation on defectors, and (3) they have sufficient long-run incentives to punish defectors.'[109] The higher the number of actors, the harder it gets to fulfil all three conditions; the incentive for free-riding increases. The stronger the sanctioning problem, the more likely it is that cooperation among the actors will break down. A possible scenario in which this problem may be overcome is when one powerful actor takes the initiative and rebuilds the system in such a way that sanctions become possible.[110]

In regime theory, neo-liberalism's stance towards the importance of the presence of a powerful hegemon to facilitate cooperation comes to light. Regimes, it is argued, can supplement a powerful player as a facilitator of cooperation among States. The positive effects of a regime hold even in the absence of a hegemon. It is therefore possible to create and maintain such institutions among comparably strong States.[111] To be sure, this does not mean that hegemony is antagonistic to regimes. The two models are often found in symbiotic relationship with one another. Hegemony in the context of regimes stands for a specific pattern of 'asymmetrical cooperation, which successful hegemons support and maintain'.[112] What appears to be a convergence of neo-realist and neo-liberalist theory is, in reality, a profoundly different perspective on hegemony and cooperation. The hegemon has to invest in the establishment and maintenance of institutions in order to make sure that those rules and norms are followed by other countries.[113]

108 R. Axelrod, *The Evolution of Cooperation* (New York: Basic Books, 1984), p. 174.

109 R. Axelrod and R. O. Keohane, 'Achieving Cooperation under Anarchy: Strategies and Institutions', in D. A. Baldwin (ed.), *Neorealism and Neo-liberalism: The Contemporary Debate* (New York: Columbia University Press, 1993), p. 94.

110 *Ibid.*, pp. 95–6.

111 R. O. Keohane, *After Hegemony* (Princeton University Press, 1984), p. 50; R. O. Keohane, *International Institutions and State Power* (Boulder, CO: Westview Press, 1989), p. 121; R. O. Keohane and J. S. Nye, *Power and Interdependence*, 2nd edn (New York: HarperCollins Publishers, 1989), pp. 42–6; see also A. Hasenclever, P. Mayer and V. Rittberger, *Theories of International Regimes* (Cambridge University Press, 1997), pp. 86–104.

112 R. O. Keohane, *After Hegemony* (Princeton University Press, 1984), pp. 46 and 49.

113 *Ibid.*, pp. 38–9 and 46.

2.5 Conclusions

Starting from similar assumptions about the nature of the international system, liberals and neo-liberals come to surprisingly different conclusions than their neo-realist counterparts. In contrast to realist thinking, liberals assume that actors, out of self-interest, interact closely and realize common interests. By interacting in regimes, they develop trust over time, although cheating is always a viable option.[114] By taking more actors, a wider time horizon, multiple channels of interaction and an increasing relationship of interdependence into account, (neo-) liberalism provides a highly complex and useful approach to the understanding of the relations among States and other actors. The theory assumes that, in order to realize their shared interest, States interact closely, form institutions to reduce transaction costs, and, by cooperating permanently under the 'shadow of the future', establish international regimes (of economic integration). The realist perspective in which power determines all interaction among States appears reductionist from this point of view since it ignores the complexity of inter- and transnational connections among them. Several aspects, however, remain disputed. In particular, neo-realists argue that institutions, regardless of how well they interconnect actors, do not solve the threat of cheating and the concerns over the higher relative gains of the other States involved.[115]

In conclusion, one could distinguish between approaches that recognize the specificity of the regional integration phenomenon, considered as *sui generis* to other forms of cooperation between States, from approaches that can easily be transposed to the global context. Neo-functionalism and federalism seem appropriate candidates for the first type, as they both presuppose the development of common understandings and shared meanings between elites of experts (neo-functionalism) or governments (federalism). On the contrary, realist/neo-realist approaches and liberal institutionalism or regime theories emphasize factors external to the individual motives of the actors involved, such as the nature and occurrence of the transactions, the development of interdependence or competition between the different States and the interests they represent.

[114] A. A. Stein, *Why Nations Cooperate* (Ithaca, NY: Cornell University Press, 1990), p. 53.

[115] J. M. Grieco, 'Anarchy and the Limits of Cooperation: A Realist Critique of the Newest Liberal Institutionalism', *International Organization* 42(3) (1988) 485–507, p. 487.

These intellectual perspectives set important challenges to the traditional concept of 'economic integration'. Integration cannot refer simply to an erosion of regulatory differences by the application of negative integration rules prohibiting national regulations or the European (federal) harmonization of national regulatory standards, as it was thought by the 'legal integration' approach. As previously explained, the 'legal integration' approach does not transpose the full complexity of the integration phenomenon. This is recognized by all the different approaches examined in the previous paragraphs, including the neo-functionalist one which, in opposition to the 'legal integration' approach that partially emanates from it, emphasizes the political as well as the social dimension of integration.

Once the 'legal integration' view is rejected, it is difficult, however, to find an answer to the question of what is entailed by the concept of economic integration. A possible way out is provided by the contextual framework of the 'integration through law' perspective: integration constitutes the transfer of legitimacy or authority across different political entities. The approach collapses the concepts of political and economic integration to 'a reciprocal relationship between the legal and political spheres' of European integration.[116] Yet, as Burley and Mattli observe, these approaches

> suffer generally from two problems: first, the nature of the relationship is often fuzzy and claims of cause and effect are qualified so as to be rendered almost empty. Second, the incentives for action are not spelled out.[117]

One could also add the relatively small importance granted by these theories to soft law, the bulk of the literature being on the role of the courts and legislative harmonization. In other words, the problem we suddenly face is the same as Haas identified as the main concern for 'pre-theories' of regional integration: what is the dependable variable that we are trying to explain? Is this always the one Haas once identified: the 'transfer of legitimacy-authority'? How could this be operationalized in the context of the different approaches examined in this study? What would be the measure of success of 'integration' if one adopts a more holistic perspective than that of 'legal integration', one that accepts regulatory pluralism and diversity?

[116] A.-M. Burley and W. Mattli, 'Europe before the Court', above, p. 46. [117] *Ibid.*

In the next section, we will provide two alternative accounts of the concept of integration that may accommodate the recent turn to a holistic view of economic integration and the increasing role of soft law norms in the integration process.

3. Two views of economic integration: efficient organizational creation and increasing levels of trust

Whatever theory of international relations one is adopting, it is clear that for all of them the dependent variable of integration is the same. This is because the theories attempt to explain why integration happens but are relatively silent, with the exception of neo-functionalists, on the dependent variable of integration as well as on the independent variables one should take into account in order to identify and measure the degree of integration. In his seminal contribution on *The Study of Regional Integration* Haas noted the existence of two competing 'pre-theories' of integration to neo-functionalism, each focusing on different variables: the federal approach assumed the transferability of the unitary framework of the State from the national to the regional level (the beyond-the-State version of federalism was not represented at the time); the communications approach focused on the relations between groups of people and the existence of important rates of transaction as measured by trade, mail and tourist flow indicators and by the rate of supranational group formations.[118] Each of the approaches proffered its own dependent variables: the federalist approach was the least ambiguous, the achievement of a federal union among the units studied being its 'terminal condition'.[119] Nonetheless, such an end-state is highly improbable in the context of international economic relations and, as we have explained, varies, according to the type of federalism adopted (dual federalism, cooperative federalism, the 'federal vision').

The question of the dependent variable of integration remaining unresolved, it is important to examine possible alternatives to the 'master concept' of 'authority-legitimacy transfer' leading to different types of 'terminal condition'.[120] For Haas, 'institutionalization' constituted an indicator for authority and legitimacy.[121] We will take this as the starting point of our quest for a dependent variable. A first option is to focus

[118] E. B. Haas, 'The Study of Regional Integration: Reflections on the Joy and Anguish of Pre-Theorizing', *International Organization* 24(4) (1970) 607–46, pp. 626–7.
[119] *Ibid.*, p. 630. [120] *Ibid.*, p. 633. [121] *Ibid.*

more precisely on the nature of the process of institution (organization) creation: integration could denote a process of efficient organizational creation. A second option is to surpass the concept of institution, which might appear formal and lead to a straitjacket effect, and instead adopt a broader concept, that of 'trust'. In our view, the latter option has a lot of potential to accommodate different forms of economic integration, while preserving the specificity of the concept, with regard to international cooperation.

3.1 Integration as a process of efficient organizational creation

According to the first approach, integration should be understood as a process of efficient organizational creation. Efficiency can be broadly defined as the satisfaction of the preferences of the constitutive units of an entity. The assumption is that any autonomous unit aims to satisfy its utility function and thus to promote efficiency. Autonomy refers to the decision-making capacity of the unit for the future. In international law, this autonomous unit refers essentially to the State. The preferences of these autonomous units are taken as a given. Preferences set the utility function of the actors and also affect their pay-off matrix.

The different autonomous units may interact with each other. Their interaction takes one of the following three forms: competition (when the unit attempts to maximize its utility at the expense of the utility of another unit); cooperation (when the unit maximizes its utility jointly with another unit); or co-opetition (where the unit develops a mixed strategy of competition in some areas and cooperation in other areas with other units).

The continuous interaction between autonomous entities requires the institution of some type of governance mechanisms in order to organize the transactions between them. The choice of a specific governance mechanism by these autonomous units is a function of the mechanism's comparative utility. We usually oppose markets to hierarchies, each forming the pole of a continuum that regroups different organizational forms, what Oliver Williamson calls 'hybrids'.[122] Starting with the assumption that the basic unit of our analysis is a unit capable of autonomy, the costs of transacting would refer to how much the autonomous unit is willing to trade its autonomy (decision-making capacity for the future) in order to obtain welfare benefits (higher satisfaction of

[122] O. Williamson, 'The Economics of Governance', *American Economic Review* 95 (2005) 1–18.

preferences). The transactions in which the autonomous units collect information on the amount of welfare benefits they might gain, in case they relinquish some degree of their autonomy, take place in the context of a market. The market is perceived as an institution facilitating the exchange of autonomy for welfare. In international society, 'the equivalent of the market is simply the place where states interact to cooperate on particular issues – to trade in power – in order to maximize their baskets of preferences'.[123] Joel Trachtman explains that 'the assets traded in this international market ... are peculiar to states: components of power, or jurisdiction', conceived as the 'institutionalized exercise of power'.[124]

The choice of the adequate institutional framework is a function of a comparison between the transaction costs of using the market mechanism versus the 'agency costs' involved in the governance of a more elaborate institution than the market,[125] such as a long-term bilateral agreement or an international regime, if we accept Robert Keohane's distinction between international regimes and international agreements.[126] The occurrence of significant transaction costs might lead the autonomous entity, after a comparative institutional analysis which would consider the transaction and agency costs, to opt for an international regime instead of an international agreement.[127] As Trachtman observes:

> [T]here appears to be little difference in theory between this question and the question of subsidiarity: once an international organization exists, and has plenary power ... what powers should it exercise at the center, and what powers should it devolve to decentralized units? All other things being equal, the question remains, where should responsibility be lodged? Thus, the transaction cost approach ... is applicable to the question of centralization or decentralization within an international organization.[128]

Transaction costs are significant if the complexity and the uncertainty of the subject matter make it difficult to write a complete treaty. Parties make agreements to apply and adapt broad 'rules of the game' (incomplete contracts). A dispute resolution mechanism and significant judicial

123 J. P. Trachtman, *The Economic Structure of International Law* (Cambridge, MA: Harvard University Press, 2008), p. 10.

124 *Ibid.*

125 *Ibid.*, p. 158: 'agency costs may be viewed as the costs of organization within an institution.'

126 R. O. Keohane, 'The Demand for International Regimes', in B. A. Simmons and R. H. Steinberg (eds.), *International Law and International Relations* (Cambridge University Press, 2007), pp. 18 and 29.

127 Trachtman, *The Economic Structure of International Law*, above, p. 159.

128 *Ibid.*, p. 176.

practice may reduce uncertainty and enhance the possibility of writing as comprehensive contracts as possible. The existence of a clear legal framework establishing liability for actions might facilitate that task. From this perspective, the choice of an international organization over an international agreement appears not to be motivated by some form of inability of States to satisfy their utility functions in the area covered by the agreement, for example for trade agreements the promotion of inter-State trade. The constitution of an international organization is instead the result of a comparative institutional analysis: 'international organizations are formed to establish a set of relationships more efficiently than the equivalent of the market (or agreement) in international society.'[129] The outcome of the comparative institutional analysis varies depending on the issues arising within a given policy space. Transactions characterized by a high degree of asset specificity are associated with higher degrees of transfer of authority to international organizations. Asset specificity refers, in our context, to the degree of reliance on other States 'to carry out their end of the bargain'.[130]

Joel Trachtman provides a 'matrix of institutional choice' that goes from the pole of regulatory competition involving externalization to majority voting within an international regime. Between them, he includes the intermediary categories of international agreements and dispute resolution (within the regime or outside it, i.e., arbitration).[131] Each of these forms of governance relates to a specific degree of integration. In most circumstances, the governance mechanism operates within a specific cluster of issues forming part of a distinct policy space. Of course, it is possible to link different issues clustered separately, but that would require side-payments (in order to modify the pay-off matrix of the other States, thus inducing cooperation) and eventually a revised comparative institutional analysis of the transaction and agency costs.

But what is the measure of efficiency if the focus is on the choice of the most optimal organizational structure for the accomplishment of States' preferences? For Trachtman, the success of an international regime depends on 'the (tautological) fact of political acceptance of a particular set of rules',[132] which becomes the ultimate test of efficiency. The success of the organizational structure of dispute resolution is, however, more difficult to measure. One could, of course, focus on compliance. But how would compliance be measured if one takes a broad conception of efficiency as it is entailed by the concept of holistic integration? Efficiency is not limited to

[129] *Ibid.*, p. 164. [130] *Ibid.*, p. 167. [131] *Ibid.*, p. 182. [132] *Ibid.*, p. 164.

the narrow promotion of intra-community trade. If the State pursues the satisfaction of its utility function, any constraint on the set of preferences of the State might theoretically lead to an inefficient outcome. For example, if a State is found liable for a restriction on intra-community trade, that would automatically frustrate the specific value from those included in the set of preferences the State was aiming to satisfy by adopting this measure. This would be unmistakably inefficient. Most often, the problem is accentuated by the relative fragmentation of policy areas, because of the distinction between the economic and the social dimensions of integration, and the impossibility of side-payments between areas included in the international regime and areas outside it.

The main flaw of this conception of integration is, however, that the main unit of analysis is the State: 'efficiency is defined in terms of maximization of state government preferences, without regard directly to the preferences of individual constituents.'[133] The citizens' preferences are aggregated at the level of the State. States serve as agents of the individuals in entering into international relations.[134] Furthermore, this approach does not take into account the transformative effect of integration on individual preferences. The approach neglects the formation of individual preferences, as it focuses only on the interaction between States. States attempt to maximize the aggregated exogenously given individual preferences of their constituents. Preferences are nevertheless constantly altered by individual internal responses to an external (social) environment in evolution. Preferences are relentlessly reconstructed during this interaction. Integration constantly shapes and transforms this external (social) environment of the constituents of the State. The purpose of integration should thus not only be confined to efficiency, perceived as the satisfaction of revealed/given preferences. Its aim is also to contribute to the process of preference-formation of the States and the constituents of the States.

It is well known that individual preferences may be influenced by legal norms. The 'market building' theory of the free movement rules of the Internal Market[135] illustrates this process of destruction of any

[133] *Ibid.*, p. 195. [134] *Ibid.*, p. 162.

[135] The European Internal Market is more a project of 'market building' than one of 'market maintenance'. Indeed, in contrast to the 'market maintenance' logic, 'market building' intervenes at the level of preference formation in an attempt to break up past path-dependencies and established national habits. Compare D. Regan, 'The Supreme Court and State Protectionism: Making Sense of the Dormant Commerce Clause', *Michigan Law Review* 84 (1986) 1091–1287, with M. P. Maduro, *We the Court* (Oxford: Hart Publishing, 1998), p. 98.

path-dependence on national rules, political processes, national economic markets and national products. Individual preferences cannot be an exception. Public choice theory also sheds light on how the internal political processes and the aggregation of individual preferences at the State level might be biased by interest group politics. States do not behave, in reality, like unitary actors responding to international circumstances in an effort to maximize the relative gains of their constituents (citizens).

3.2 *Integration as a higher intensity of institutional-based trust between actors interacting across national boundaries*

An alternative conceptualization of 'integration' should aim to open the black-box of the State, by taking into consideration its constitutive elements. This will add an additional layer in the consideration of preferences, this time inside the State. It would also recognize the endogenous character of individual preferences. Our suggestion is to define integration as the process of building increased levels of 'institutional-based' trust (or 'system trust') between actors interacting across national boundaries. This theory does not neglect the concept of the State, which is still present, as it sets the national boundaries defining the interactions between actors that are of interest to scholars of international/regional exchanges of jurisdiction. Interactions between these actors within the boundaries of a State are excluded from consideration. But the concept of the State is not as omnipresent as it was in the previous conceptualization of 'integration'.

Let us first define the term 'actor'. Actors are not only States, but also entities operating inside the black-box of the State: the national legislature, judiciary, national regulators and central administration, firms, consumers, citizens. In short, any entity that operates within the given policy space open to the type of interaction that is of interest counts. Each individual actor has a utility function based on a certain set of preferences that, in the case of 'public actors' (e.g., regulators) might be institutionalized and in some cases explicitly provided for in their constitutive charters (i.e., constitutions, regulatory statutes). These actors operate within a specific (social) environment, which can be characterized by principal–agency relations, relations of competition, cooperation and co-opetition. Actors do not behave or decide as atoms outside the social context: their action is instead embedded in concrete, ongoing systems of social relations. They dispose of the power to interact with other public or private actors across jurisdictions. Power relies on material and institutional (competence) capabilities and is subject to broad (social) environment constraints (interaction power).

We turn now to the concept of 'trust'. The term is employed in economics, organization theory and sociological literature in different ways.[136] One could define trust as 'an attitude involving a willingness to place the fate of one's interests under the control of others'.[137] Repeated interaction forms the primary basis for trust.

Andrew Kydd explains that

> trust is a belief that the other side prefers mutual cooperation to exploiting one's own cooperation, while mistrust is a belief that the other side prefers exploiting one's cooperation to returning it. In other words, to be trustworthy, with respect to a certain person in a certain context, is to prefer to return their cooperation rather than exploit them . . . Cooperation between two actors will be possible if the *level of trust* each has for the other exceeds some threshold specific to the situation and the actors.[138]

Increasing the intensity (level) of trust refers to 'the amount of discretion trustors grant trustees over their interests'.[139] Indeed, 'cooperation is possible when the level of trust for the other exceeds a minimum trust threshold for each party', which 'will depend on the party's own tolerance for the risk of exploitation by the other side'.[140] Consequently,

> to trust someone . . . is to believe it relatively likely that they would prefer to reciprocate cooperation. To mistrust someone is to think it is relatively likely that they prefer to defect even if they think one will cooperate.[141]

[136] See N. Luhmann, *Trust and Power* (New York: John Wiley, 1979), for a discussion of trust from the point of view of systems theory; J. Coleman, *Foundations of Social Theory* (Cambridge, MA: Harvard University Press, 1990), for a discussion of trust from a rational theory perspective; O. Williamson, 'Calculativeness, Trust, and Economic Organization' (1993) *Journal of Law and Economics* 453, for an economic perspective on trust. For sociological accounts of trust, see R. Hardin, *Trust* (New York: Russell Sage Foundation, 1998); R. M. Kramer and T. R. Tyler (eds.), *Trust in Organizations* (Thousand Oaks, CA: Sage, 1996); B. Barber, *The Logic and Limits of Trust* (Rutgers University Press, 1983); For the role of trust in international relations, see A. H. Kydd, *Trust and Mistrust in International Relations* (Princeton University Press, 2005).

[137] A. M. Hoffman, 'A Conceptualization of Trust in International Relations' 8(3) (2002) *European Journal of International Relations* 375, pp. 376–7.

[138] A. H. Kydd, *Trust and Mistrust in International Relations* (Princeton University Press, 2005), p. 6.

[139] *Ibid.*, p. 377. [140] *Ibid.* [141] *Ibid.*

The function of trust is to reduce uncertainty and complexity in social communication systems as 'it allows for specific (rather than arbitrary) assumptions about other social actors' future behaviour'.[142] It could thus be seen as a communicative medium reducing complexity.[143] Trust can take different forms: Luhmann distinguishes between 'personal trust', which is likely to develop when individual actors have frequent interactions and thus become familiar with each other's personal preferences and interests and thus indifferent to the institutional arrangements, and 'system trust', which relies on institutions to generate trust, rather than on personal interaction. Institutional-based trust constitutes a more 'advanced stage of trust production',[144] as its function is to generate trust on a massive scale. But trust also produces risk, in particular if there is limited information available about the future behaviour of the trustee. Risk is an unavoidable feature of trust because trust can be disappointed. For example, an offer of cooperation may be exploited by free riding, or not be reciprocated. There are thus two interrelated conditions for trust: risk and interdependence between the actors. In order to minimize the risk of defect, actors may develop various strategies.

An alternative way, other than trust, to reduce complexity and uncertainty is the exercise of interaction power. Power influences 'the selection of actions in the face of other possibilities'.[145] Power may not exclude risk but it may reduce it considerably: 'a social actor who considers using power usually can refer to "authoritative" and "allocative" resources, which can be deemed likely to find recognition by the subordinate actor'[146] and thus affect its incentives to act. Hegemonic power by one State, or the fight for hegemony, has been a feature of many historical periods in human history.[147] If powerful actors have few constraints on the exercise of their power, our capacity for trust in them is limited. Power is treated here as a relational construct, which connotes the degree of dependence of the actors on one another.

[142] R. Bachmann, 'Trust, Power and Control in Trans-Organizational Relations', 22 (2001) *Organization Studies* 337 (also available at www.sase.org/oldsite/conf1999/papers/reinhard_bachmann.pdf, p. 8).

[143] Luhmann, *Trust and Power*, above, pp. 42–3.

[144] Bachmann, 'Trust, Power and Control in Trans-Organizational Relations', above, p. 12.

[145] Luhmann, *Trust and Power*, above, p. 112.

[146] Bachmann, 'Trust, Power and Control in Trans-Organizational Relations', above, p. 16.

[147] See the analysis of different models of international relations and trust in A. H. Kydd, *Trust and Mistrust in International Relations* (Princeton University Press, 2005).

Actors are frequently found in situations where they have to decide whether to base their interaction/communication mostly on trust or on power, and the proportions of trust and power which should govern their relationship.

Trust and power should not, however, be viewed exclusively as alternatives. It is possible for power to appear in a 'de-personalized' form as 'system power'. System power can take the form of law, organization or a hierarchy which can develop shared meanings among the social actors and can thus 'mass-produce' trust. Standards of expertise are the main sources of 'system trust': they are integrated into organizational routines that may take the form of institutions (formal or informal). Institutions are thus the central precondition rather than an alternative to 'system trust'. The constitution of trust ultimately relies on the existence of strong institutions. As institutional-based or system trust is a condition for the efficient production of a high level of trust, the 'trans-organizational relations can be reconstructed as being controlled by the patterns of trust and/or power mechanisms'.[148]

It follows from this analysis that trust is a concept that takes significance in situations of uncertainty over the preferences or behaviour of interdependent actors in a specific social system. Its function is to reduce uncertainty and thus to induce welfare-enhancing cooperation between them. However, trust also produces risks when cooperation will be exploited or not returned. This will provoke mistrust, which could potentially deter welfare-enhancing activity from happening. Power or hegemonic control would be the other side of the coin: it is an alternative to trust and contributes to maintain control and avoid the slippery slope to a Hobbesian state of anarchy. The establishment of informal or formal institutions constitutes another available option in order to mitigate the risk of distrust by creating 'system trust'. Institutions will generate trust, as long as their constituents believe that they are effective in preventing situations of distrust. Institutions may also require the invention of a common grammar that will facilitate communication between the actors, the existence of a regime of sanctions for instances of mistrust or of a hierarchy that will exercise control over the action of the actors and will ensure that they are trustworthy ('system power').

In international trade regulation, trust can be considered as an objective concept describing a relationship between regulatory systems

[148] Bachmann, 'Trust, Power and Control in Trans-Organizational Relations', above, p. 24.

underpinned by a relationship between public and private actors.[149] The starting point is that, when States interact, they have incomplete information about the preferences and objectives of their counterparts, as well as their pay-offs and domestic pressures that are not evident to a counter-party.[150] As is also the case for individual relations, relations between States are shaped by social networks. Actions are embedded in concrete, ongoing systems of social relations. Consequently, the behaviour of the actors is driven not only by a pure interest calculation (calculative trust) but also by social norms and formal and informal institutions that support the specific relationship.

An important source of trust in this context would be the long history of interaction between these actors and their collective memory. Geographic proximity, common language, shared values and preferences facilitate interaction and thus build a certain level of 'personal trust' between the different actors.[151] The social network provides a source of information, but at the same time it also constitutes a mechanism that grants importance to 'reputational sanctions'.[152] Reputation helps to determine whether an actor would risk cooperating with another one.[153] To the extent that all actors are connected in a web of relations, even if there is no personal interaction, there is some assurance that the victim of a trust violation can take action to rectify the situation. The development of mutual dependence between exchange partners may, however, have ambivalent results as it may promote trust but also foster opportunistic behaviour (mistrust).

The network of social relations to which all actors belong provides not only a source of information about trustworthiness but also the opportunity for each actor to contribute to the reputation of another one, should other actors choose to provide information about a possible lack of trustworthiness. This reputational cost is particularly effective in closed social systems with membership, such as the European Union.

There is, however, a point where 'personal trust' is not sufficient to promote welfare-enhancing cooperation. The reason is that the more

[149] K. Nicolaïdis and G. Shaffer, 'Transnational Mutual Recognition Regimes: Governance without Global Government', *Law and Contemporary Problems* 68 (2005) 263–317, p. 298.

[150] A. T. Guzman, *How International Law Works – A Rational Choice Theory* (Oxford University Press, 2008), p. 92.

[151] See chapter 13 by Marchetti and Mavroidis in this volume.

[152] Guzman, *How International Law Works*, above, p. 33.

[153] On the value of reputation in international law, see *ibid.*, pp. 71–117.

complex the relationship and its environment becomes, the more uncertainty is generated over the future actions of the actors. As actors attempt to deal with uncertainty and the risk of mistrust, they may find it necessary either to exercise hegemonic power, if they have the capacity to do so (interaction power), or to elaborate institutions that will control occurrences of distrust. Institutions will have as their function to generate 'system trust'. They build on an existing level of trust, which is a necessary precondition of their existence. The reputation mechanism is one dimension of the story. Institutions will act as social networks implementing informal or formal sanctions to address mistrust. These could take the form of norms of exclusion in closed groups, of monitoring or of credible commitments that can also be a mechanism generating trust (trust-building tool).

There are different ways credible commitments may be established. First, there is a possibility of a rule which would cut off options. In our context, that could take the form of a prohibition of inefficient restrictions of inter-State trade (which comes to the same as a prohibition of measures having a protectionist intent) or the form of a broader prohibition of any obstacle to intra-EU trade.

Second, it is possible to arrange to suffer losses from a failure to act cooperatively (hostage taking). For example, the presumption of equivalence or mutual recognition shifts the burden of proof from the traders to the Member States in order to justify proportional restrictions of trade. This definitively increases the risk incurred by the regulation of the host State to be found illegal and thus sanctioned by the negative integration rules of the Treaty. Member States adopting regulations that are varying significantly from the regulations of the other Member States and thus fail to act cooperatively will suffer a higher likelihood of losing the case than States that are closer to the mean and which have taken proportional measures.

Third, an additional option would be to bring in a third party to oversee and even enforce the commitments an actor makes to others. In our context, that would require the intervention of a centralized EU institution, which will monitor the process and will enforce sanctions that would mitigate the risks of distrust, or a decentralized network that will ensure compliance through reciprocal monitoring and exclusion in case of non-compliance.

What is important here is to note that the definition of the concept of integration as an increased level of system trust is agnostic as to (i) the formal or informal character of the institutions generating trust (which could be either hard law or soft law or conventions); (ii) their public or private nature; (iii) the fact that institutions are centralized or decentralized; (iv) or even to the choice of personal over 'institutional-based'/ 'system trust'. We should recognize that there is a variety of trust-building tools which are very context-specific and do not necessarily form part of a continuum.

Turning to the example of the Internal Market, it seems that the existence of a high level of trust is a prerequisite for the application of the equivalence principle as regulators operate in a game of incomplete information. Kalypso Nicolaïdis observes that long-term contracts

> are obviously more sustainable when all parties are confident that the others abide by the letter and spirit of the contract . . . [S]uch confidence is based on the initial familiarisation and continued involvement with the foreign system, including through: obligations of transparency of regulatory systems, decision making process, and change in such system through the continued exchange of information between regulators; mutual monitoring that allows for the continued assessment of technical competence, capabilities, and efficiency as well as the foreign industries overall state of art in its capability to comply with the importing country's requirements; and finally, since there will always remain some information asymmetry, there needs to be trust that the foreign authorities will continue to have adequate regard for public health, safety and environmental concern.[154]

Host State regulators often lack information on the standards and practices of the home State regulators, but are asked to trust the standards and practices of the home State, according to the principle of equivalence. Extracting information on the regulatory regime of the home State constitutes an effective trust-building tool. Transparency, sustained exchange and monitoring will increase the level of trust between the home and the host States. The more important these costs of information are, the more attractive the harmonization of the standards would be, in particular as courts are ill-suited to perform this trust-building exercise at a lower cost. This explains why technically complex regimes, such as financial services, transports and communications, were harmonized before other areas in services trade. This is not to argue that the adoption of harmonized rules is a costless enterprise. However, an essential step of any negotiation process is the initially selective but

[154] Kalypso Nicolaïdis, 'Mutual Recognition of Regulatory Regimes: Some Lessons and Prospects', Jean Monnet Working Paper, 1997, available at http://centers.law.nyu.edu/ jeanmonnet/papers/97/97–07.html, at § 56.

gradually increasing exchange of information between the parties. This will avoid the costly quest for information on a case-by-case basis that is characteristic of the implementation of the principle of equivalence by courts. The process of negotiation will reduce uncertainty and therefore increase trust between actors.

Action at the Union level usually aims to facilitate the process of economic integration by providing a negotiated common set of rules/ standards. It usually intervenes, after it has been made clear in the implementation of the equivalence principle, that there are differences between the values protected by the regulatory regimes of the home and the host States. Action at the Union level may also intervene if the specific sector is subject to technically complex and detailed regulation that the courts are unable to cope with, in case they are required to apply the proportionality principle and therefore to compare the regulation of the host State with that of the home State. A regulatory regime may also be intrinsically complex if, for the accomplishment of its goals, it requires continuous supervision. The monitoring of technically detailed or intrinsically complex regulations involves important costs with respect to the acquisition of information and the implementation of the decision. The courts acquire this information on a case-by-case basis, without the benefit of prior knowledge or experience of the specific economic sector. Harmonization leads to a more manageable governance regime, as the focus will shift from courts to national regulators (be it the legislative power, a cabinet department or an independent regulatory authority) that will have the means to perform such a monitoring function more effectively. Monitoring by national regulators, under the supervision of the European Commission, could provide important economies of scale with regard to the acquisition of specialized knowledge (as this will not be done now on a case-by-case basis). Regulators have also an important prior experience of the economic sector. National regulatory regimes often include an independent authority which has the task to regulate the specific sector. These national regulatory authorities have contributed to the emergence of sector-specific harmonization standards. The involvement of independent administrative authorities operates as a credible commitment tool that the Member States will not adopt protectionist strategies. For example, the participation of independent regulatory national administrative authorities in the negotiation and enforcement of unified standards (as is the case with the Lamfalussy process in financial services or with the European regulators network in telecoms) ensures that concerns other than the very specific ones that are listed will be considered.[155] The harmonization process nonetheless requires an immense effort of negotiation and cautious drafting of an agreement between the various actors. The decision to proceed to harmonization or to rely on the operation of the equivalence principle will be a function of the comparison of these administrative costs, at least if we perceive harmonization as entirely motivated by utility.

Trust may, however, be an important concern, even after the adoption of a harmonized standard. As the Court noted in *Hedley Lomas*, 'member states must rely on trust in each other to carry out inspections on their respective territories'.[156] It is therefore important to impose on the parties additional obligations in order to render operational the harmonized standard. By imposing transparency (simplification) and an obligation of administrative cooperation between the regulatory authorities of the Member States, the Services Directive aimed precisely to address this concern.

One could identify three categories of trust relationships, on which the process of integration may operate. First, integration involves trust between national regulatory (norm-creation) actors, which would include national legislators, regulators, the judiciary, self-regulatory bodies and actors at the EU level of governance, EU institutions. Second, it will involve trust between different national regulatory bodies across Member States that interact directly in the negotiation process or indirectly through the resolution of conflicts from the extraterritorial application of their regulatory standards. Third, there should be trust between individual (non-normative) actors and the EU institutions ('trust in government'). The increased levels of trust between the different actors apply to all three relations ('total trust'). Total trust should be taken into account in order to examine the success of integration, not higher levels of trust in each relation. But how can we measure trust?

Measurement issues are certainly the most challenging aspect of this conception of integration. More research needs to be accomplished but there have already been some proposals for indicators measuring trust in international relations.[157] First, it is possible to identify policies that

[155] See the analysis by Lianos and Gerard in Chapter 6 of this volume.

[156] Case C-5/94, *The Queen* v. *Ministry of Agriculture, Fisheries and Food, ex parte Hedley Lomas (Ireland) Ltd* [1996] ECR I-2553, para. 19.

[157] On the measurement of trust, see A. M. Hoffman, 'A Conceptualization of Trust in International Relations', *European Journal of International Relations* 8(3) (2002) 375–401, pp. 385–93.

grant other States discretion over outcomes previously controlled by the first. For example, a majority voting system qualifies as an important discretion-granting policy. Second, the existence of mechanisms to oversee the exercise of discretion might also be a useful indicator. 'Methods of oversight that permit actors more leeway to make decisions are consistent with trusting relationships.'[158] For example, institutional-based trust may be promoted by the principle of mutual recognition as it increases the discretion of the home State to adopt regulatory standards that will differentiate from those of the host State without affecting the chances of its exports in the host State. The 'discriminatory market access test' or a national treatment rule in the law of the Internal Market also grants more discretion to the home State than the 'obstacles test', as only regulations that impose costs to foreign goods that have not been incurred by domestic goods are subject to judicial control under the second step of the assessment. Finally, issues of measurement also raise important difficulties within the traditional views of economic integration. A variety of indicators are often employed, such as, from the more simple ones, the extent of free trade of goods, services, free movement of capital and labour, the existence of supranational institutions and of monetary and fiscal coordination, to the more complex ones, such as the synchronization of business cycles, convergence of inflation rates and income and the degree of interpenetration of activities.[159] A common feature of all these methodologies is that they are all based on the theory and typology of economic integration of Balassa, with the corresponding emphasis on economic efficiency as measured by the removal of trade barriers.[160] These indicators assume the decoupling of the economic dimension from the political and social and are certainly inadequate if one adopts a holistic approach.

In contrast, if one adopts a 'cybernetic' approach, which would envision integration as having the aim to reach a 'security community',[161]

[158] *Ibid.*, p. 388.

[159] For a discussion, see Ph. De Lombaerde, 'Indicators of Economic Integration', *Statistika* 4 (2008) 340–5; Ph. De Lombaerde, *Assessment and Measurement of Regional Integration* (London: Routledge, 2008).

[160] B. Balassa, *The Theory of Economic Integration* (Homewood, IL: Richard Irwin, 1961).

[161] K. Deutsch, *Political Community and North Atlantic Area* (Princeton University Press, 1957), p. 5, defining integration as a process leading to the condition in which a group of people has 'attained within a territory a sense of community and of institutions and practice strong enough to assure for a long time, dependable expectations of peaceful change among its population'.

either of the amalgamated or of the pluralistic type,[162] the focus would be on communication channels in order to create interdependence between peoples.[163] This approach may accommodate pluralistic concerns, but its emphasis on the 'use of the same or equivalent patterns of living, and feeling among individuals, who are members of the various political units that make up the security community',[164] indicates that the principal focus is on patterns of communication between people rather than between institutions (formal or informal). Hence, the measurement indicators suggested by this approach do not take into account that the process of establishing institutional-based trust is of particular importance if one is to distinguish between the concept of integration and that of globalization, the latter also referring to the development of shared patterns of living.

[162] *Ibid.*, p. 6. An 'amalgamated' security community leads to the development of supreme institutions and the legal merger of, more than one, independent political units. A 'pluralistic' security community emphasizes cooperation of independent political units, rather than amalgamation.

[163] K. W. Deutsch, *Political Community at the International Level* (Sandy, UT: Global Publishing Co., 2006, first published 1954).

[164] K. W. Deutsch, 'Security Communities, International Politics and Foreign Policy', in J. N. Rosenau (ed.), *A Reader in Research and Theory* (New York: Free Press, 1961), pp. 98–9.

PART II

Unpacking the premises: mutual recognition, harmonization

2

Forms of mutual recognition in the field of services

VASSILIS HATZOPOULOS

1. Introduction

Mutual recognition is inscribed in Article 53 TFEU (formerly Article 47 EC) in respect of 'diplomas, certificates and other evidence of formal qualifications'. It has grounded the issuance of numerous 'transitory' measures of recognition of professional qualifications since 1964,[1] then the issuance of the sector-specific Directives for six health professions, architects and lawyers in the 1970s and 1980s and, finally, the General systems in the 1990s.[2] It is, however, with the Court of Justice's judgment in *Cassis de Dijon* and the corresponding Commission Communication that the principle of mutual recognition made its official entry into the EU legal order.[3] It is, finally, with the introduction of the 'new approach' in 1985 that mutual recognition gained its status as the central regulatory technique for the completion of the Internal Market.[4]

[1] See Directive 64/222/EEC, OJ 1964 L56/857; Directive 64/427/EEC, OJ 1964 L117/1863; Directive 68/364/EEC, OJ 1966 L260/6; and many other Directives, repealed by Directive 2005/36/EC, for the mutual recognition of professional qualifications, OJ 2005 L255/22.

[2] For these Directives, see below note 116 and the accompanying text.

[3] Case 120/78, *Rewe-Zentral (Cassis de Dijon)* [1979] ECR 648; Communication from the Commission concerning the consequences of the judgment given by the Court of Justice on 20 February 1979 in Case 120/78, OJ 1980 C256/2.

[4] Council Resolution of 7 May 1985 concerning a new approach on technical harmonization and standardization, 85/C 136/01, OJ 1985 C136/1; Council Resolution of 21 December 1989, concerning a global approach for conformity evaluation, 90/C 10/01, OJ C10/1. The system put into place has been reinvigorated recently by Regulation (EC) 764/2008 laying down procedures relating to the application of certain national technical rules to products lawfully marketed in another Member State and repealing Decision No. 3052/95/EC, OJ 2008 L218/21; Regulation (EC) No. 765/2008 setting out the requirements for accreditation and market surveillance relating to the marketing of products and repealing Regulation (EEC) No. 339/93, OJ 2008 L218/30, Decision No. 768/2008/EC on a common framework for the marketing of products, and repealing Council Decision 93/465/EEC, OJ 2008 L218/82.

Since mutual recognition has been around for half a century now, is it still worth wasting ink and paper on it, and is there anything special about mutual recognition in the field of services? The first part of this question may be answered easily, since a brief review of recent academic literature shows a revival of interest on this area of study.[5] The answer to the second part of the question will require more extensive developments and will, indeed, constitute the object of the present chapter. In order to give as complete an answer as possible, I am going to consider four issues: first, how services differ from goods in respect of mutual recognition; second, how mutual recognition 'combines' with other regulatory techniques, such as home country control, the country-of-origin principle etc., that are also used in the field of services; third, I am going to look into the main practical applications of mutual recognition in the area of services, before, fourth, putting forward some ideas on how such application could be enhanced.

2. Are services different from goods concerning mutual recognition?

The question is merely rhetorical, since the answer is clearly affirmative. The fact that mutual recognition is not extensively organized by the EU, nor 'imposed' by the Court of Justice (and national courts and authorities) in the field of services in such an extensive manner as in the field of goods, is not pure chance. Indeed, (a) the 'new approach' of legislation inaugurated in 1985 and based on mutual recognition,[6] (b) the issuance of Directives describing minimum safety and security standards and the EU marking enhancing mutual recognition, as well as (c) the obligation of transparency in respect of technical standards forcing 'pre-emptive'

[5] See, e.g., K. Armstrong, 'Mutual Recognition', in C. Barnard and J. Scott (eds.), *The Law of the Single European Market: Unpacking the Premises* (Oxford: Hart Publishing, 2002), pp. 225–67; M. Ortino, 'The Role and Functioning of Mutual Recognition in the European Market for Financial Services', *International and Comparative Law Quarterly* 56 (2007) 309–38; as well as the special issue of the *Journal of European Public Policy* 14(5) (2007) dedicated to this issue, including, among others, the following articles: A. Hé ritier, 'Mutual Recognition: Comparing Policy Areas' pp. 800–13; K. Nicolaïdis and S. Schmidt, 'Mutual Recognition "On Trial": The Long Road to Services Liberalisation', pp. 717–34; K. Nicolaïdis, 'Trusting the Poles? Constructing Europe through Mutual Recognition', pp. 682–98; J. Pelkmans, 'Mutual Recognition in Goods: On Promises and Disillusions', pp. 699–716; M. P. Maduro, 'So Close and Yet So Far: The Paradoxes of Mutual Recognition', pp. 814–25; and S. Schmitt, 'Mutual Recognition as a New Mode of Governance', pp. 667–81.

[6] See note 4 above.

mutual recognition, are all restricted to the area of goods. Academic literature follows suit. At least five reasons may account for such a discrepancy.

2.1 Decentralized and/or non-State origin of the measures

Goods are generally affected by regulations aimed at securing safety and security, health and consumer protection (SHEC).[7] These regulations are typically decided by the State – alone or in collaboration with the industry. Self-regulation and the use of voluntary standards is also an option, although rarely followed in matters endangering SHEC. At any rate, SHEC regulations tend to cover the entire territory for which they are decided; indeed, it is unlikely that the level of SHEC protection varies within a single Member State. Services regulations, on the other hand, tend to be much more diversified and their objectives much more complex than merely SHEC: cohesion and social policy, redistribution, protection of labour, a high level of 'public service', disciplinary organization of the professions, to name only a few. The content of such regulations very often varies within a single State. Moreover, depending on the constitutional settings of the State, such regulations may be adopted by sub-State units (federated States, municipalities etc.) or, indeed, by non-State entities such as trade unions, professional associations etc.

Therefore, it should come as no surprise that the 'stretching' of the Internal Market rules to cover 'private' measures started with Article 56 TFEU on services.[8] The Court is still today much readier to scrutinize non-State measures under the rules on services (and persons) than under the rules on goods.[9] It is now accepted that Article 56 TFEU may be violated by measures adopted by sports associations or federations,[10]

[7] The paternity of the acronym 'SHEC' and the term 'SHEC regulations' is attributed to Pelkmans, note 5 above, as well as in previous works of his.

[8] Case 36/74, *Walrave* [1974] ECR 1405.

[9] See V. Hatzopoulos, 'Trente ans après les arrêts fondamentaux de 1974, les quatre libertés: quatre?', in P. Demaret, I. Govaere and D. Hanf (eds.), *30 Years of European Legal Studies at the College of Europe – (30 ans d'études juridiques européennes au Collège d'Europe): Liber Professorum 1973/74–2003/04* (Brussels: PIE-Peter Lang, 2005), pp. 185–201; and, more extensively, see J. Snell, *Goods and Services in EC Law* (Oxford University Press, 2002), pp. 130–59.

[10] *Walrave*, above; Case 13/76, *Dona* v. *Mantero* [1976] ECR 1333; Case C-415/93, *Bosman* [1995] ECR I-4921; Case C-51/96 and 191/97, *Deliège* [2000] ECR I-2549; Case C-519/04 P, *Meca Medina* [2006] ECR I-6991.

professional associations,[11] insurance funds,[12] trade unions[13] and even automobile associations.[14]

At least three legal difficulties stem from the above state of affairs. For one thing, the extent to which the Internal Market rules are being stretched in order to cover private regulators may have reached its limits.[15] Second, to the extent that regional or local regulations are at stake, it is more difficult to establish their effect on intra-community trade and to subjugate them to the Treaty rules. Third, even if this hurdle is overcome, it is extremely complicated to apply mutual recognition to numerous regulations diverging at the sub-national level.

2.2 Services subject to non-incorporated rules

Services are, to a large extent, tailor-made to suit their recipients' needs. Moreover, it is difficult to define a service 'unit' as well as to identify the

[11] Case 292/86, *Gullung* [1988] ECR 111; Case C-309/99, *Wouters* [2002] ECR I-1577; Case C-506/04, *Wilson* [2006] ECR I-8613; Joined Cases C-94/04 and 202/04, *Cipolla* [2006] ECR I-11421.

[12] See, among several cases, Case C-158/96, *Kohll* [1998] ECR I-1931; Case C-157/99, *Smits and Peerbooms* [2001] ECR I-5437; and all the recent case law concerning the free movement of patients.

[13] Case C-438/05, *Viking* [2007] ECR I-10779; Case C-341/05, *Laval un Partneri* [2007] ECR I-11767.

[14] Case C-49/07, *MOTOE* v. *Greece* [2008] ECR I-4863.

[15] As the academic debate about the recent *Viking* and *Laval* judgments has shown; see, e.g., J. Cremers, J. E. Dolvik and G. Bosch, 'Posting of Workers in the Single Market: Attempts to Prevent Social Dumping and Regime Competition in the EU?', *Industrial Relations Journal* 38(6) (2007) 524–41; J. Malmberg and T. Sigeman, 'Industrial Actions and EU Economic Freedoms: The Autonomous Collective Bargaining Model Curtailed by the Court of Justice', *Common Market Law Review* 45 (2008) 1115–1146; M. Ronmar, 'Free Movement of Services vs National Labour Law and Industrial Relations Systems: Understanding the Laval Case from a Swedish and Nordic Perspective', *Cambridge Yearbook of European Legal Studies* 10 (2008) 493–521; D. Ashiagbor, 'Collective Labor Rights and the European Social Model', *Law and Ethics of Human Rights* 3 (2009) 222–66; C. Barnard, 'Viking and Laval: An Introduction', *Cambridge Yearbook of European Legal Studies* 10 (2008) 463–92; A. Dashwood, 'Viking and Laval: Issues of Horizontal Direct Effect', *Cambridge Yearbook of European Legal Studies* 10 (2008) 525–40; S. Deakin, 'Regulatory Competition after Laval', *Cambridge Yearbook of European Legal Studies* 10 (2008) 581–609; S. Sciarra, 'Viking and Laval: Collective Labour Rights and Market Freedoms in the Enlarged EU', *Cambridge Yearbook of European Legal Studies* 10 (2008) 563–80; C. Woolfson and J. Sommers, 'Labour Mobility in Construction: European Implications of the Laval un Partneri Dispute with Swedish Labour', *European Journal of Industrial Relations* 12 (2006) 49–68; see also R. Blanpain (ed.), 'The Laval and Viking Cases. Freedom of Services and Establishment v. Industrial Conflict in the European Economic Area and Russia', *Bulletin of Comparative Labour Relations* 69 (2009).

ingredients of a service. The active role played by recipients in the production of services leads some authors to talk about 'co-production'.[16] This explains why services regulations rarely concern the service itself; instead, they define the conditions that the service providers should themselves fulfil (qualifications, authorizations, entry into registers, deontology rules, provider's liability) or the circumstances under which the providers may offer their services (opening hours and days, location, price-fixing, access subject to a devolution system etc.). In other words, services regulations are essentially non-incorporated, in the sense that they concern the process and as such are not reflected in the actual 'content' of a service. Therefore, in principle, non-incorporated regulations exhaust their effects within the providers' 'home' country, while incorporated ones produce 'externalities' also felt in the 'host' State.[17] This, in turn, means that goods/services produced according to incorporated rules securing lower standards of (consumer, environment etc.) protection may be spontaneously resisted by consumers in the host State.[18] Non-incorporated regulations, on the other hand, will meet much lower resistance from consumers in the host State – and therefore local non-incorporated rules will be under greater pressure from regulatory competition.[19] If the host State is to safeguard its own standards of non-incorporated rules, it needs specifically to legislate acts of an essentially protective nature. Such rules are unlikely to yield to the effect of mutual recognition – or, if they do, the protective measures of the host State are given extraterritorial effect, since they are being complied with in the home State.

[16] L. Rubalcaba, 'Historical and Anthropological Origin of the Service Economy' in L. Rubalcaba, *The New Service Economy: Challenges and Policy Implications for Europe* (Cheltenham and Northampton: Edward Elgar, 2007), pp. 14–42.

[17] For the distinction between incorporated and non-incorporated regulations and the risk of the 'race to the bottom', see F. Scharpf, 'Introduction: The Problem-Solving Capacity of Multi-Level Governance', *Journal of European Public Policy* 4 (1997) 520–38; see also, more recently, G. Davies, 'Process and Production Method-Based Trade Restrictions in the EU', *Cambridge Yearbook of European Legal Studies* 10 (2008) 69–97; for a critical review of the distinction and of its legal consequence, see R. Howse and D. Regan, 'The Product/Process Distinction – An Illusory Basis for Disciplining Unilateralism', *European Journal of International Law* 11(2) (2000) 249–89.

[18] In the history of regulatory competition, next to stories of race to the bottom (also known as the 'Delaware effect'), there exist also stories of race to the top (also known as the 'California effect', after that state managed to impose its own higher standards of anti-pollution rules on the entire US).

[19] An imported vehicle having high CO_2 emissions or insufficient security devices is likely to raise more reactions than imported software programmed by an overtime worker.

2.3 No prior notification system of rules on services

The fact that most service-related measures are non-incorporated and that they are of a non-technical nature accounts for the lack of any system of prior notification of such measures. In the field of goods, Directive 98/34[20] requires that all 'technical specifications', 'technical rules' or 'other requirement' affecting the production, commercialization or, even, use of goods[21] be notified to the Commission prior to their entry into force. This notification is reinforced by a stand-still period, during which Member States may not enact the measure in question and which allows the Commission to initiate legislation, thus pre-empting national initiatives. Moreover, the Court has held that national measures that have not been duly notified are unenforceable.[22] The prior notification procedure is acknowledged as one of the great successes of the Internal Market strategy, as almost 900 measures are being notified every year to the Commission.[23] The commonest outcome of such notification is that an equivalence clause is inserted into the national measure: goods are admitted into the market which satisfy the prescribed 'or equivalent' rules. In this way, a system of 'pre-emptive recognition' is being introduced into national legislation by virtue of the notification Directive. This system only covers goods and – after the 1998 extension – information society services, which have a clearly pronounced technical aspect.

The 2006 Services Directive, for the first time, does foresee a prior notification obligation of national measures affecting services. This system, however, is much more limited in scope and intensity than the system for goods. First, it only concerns measures affecting the *establishment* of service providers, not the *service provision* itself. Second, the measures which need to be notified are enumerated in Article 15(7) of

[20] Directive 98/34/EC laying down a procedure for the provision of information in the field of technical standards and regulations, OJ 1998 L204/37; this Directive repealed Directive 83/189/EEC; its scope was extended by Directive 98/48/EC, OJ 1998 L217/18, to cover information society services.

[21] The Directive also covers measures concerning 'use' which affect the provision of services: see Case C-267/03, *Lindberg* [2005] ECR I-3245.

[22] Case C-194/94, *CIA Security* v. *Signalson* [1996] ECR I-2201; see, in this respect, the comment by P. J. Slot in *Common Market Law Review* 33 (1996) 1035–1050; and J. Coppel, 'Horizontal Effect of Directives, Case C-194/94, CIA Security International v. Signalson', *Industrial Law Journal* 26 (1997) 69–73; see also M. Dougan, 'The "Disguised" Vertical Effect of Directives?', *Cambridge Law Journal* 59 (2000) 586–612.

[23] J. Pelkmans, 'Mutual Recognition in Goods: On Promises and Disillusions', *Journal of European Public Policy* 14(5) (2007) 699–716, p. 707.

the Directive, presumably in an exhaustive way.[24] Third, Member States are not subject to any stand-still obligation, while the Commission's powers are limited to issuing individual decisions requiring the modification or repeal of the measures in question – but it has no general legislative powers. Last but not least, because of the more 'relaxed' nature of the notification obligation, it is contestable whether the *CIA Security* doctrine of non-enforceability of non-notified measures will be extended to the Services Directive.

2.4 *Absence of extensive standardization/certification*

The limited role played by technical rules in the field of services has a further consequence concerning the regulation thereof. In the field of goods, when technical standards or other requirements are too remote to subsume to mutual recognition, the regulator has an option: either to harmonize or to proceed by means of standardization. This second option has been used extensively since the introduction of the new approach in 1985.[25] The Commission gives a mandate to one of the EU standardization bodies (the CEN, the CENELEC or the ETSI), depending on the technological area, for the adoption of standards. These are non-binding, unless introduced into hard law, such as by Directive.[26] Therefore, standardization entails some degree of harmonization, *de facto* or *de jure* (depending on the binding/non-binding nature of the norms adopted), with the participation – in the standardization bodies – of industry representatives.

In the field of services, however, things are quite different. For the reasons already explained above, rules affecting services are not of a technical, but rather of a social, environmental, nature etc. Therefore, it is technically impossible and politically undesirable to have recourse to standardization in order to reduce disparities.

[24] These are (a) quantitative or territorial restrictions, (b) specific legal form requirements, (c) shareholding requirements, (d) restrictions on the mutual recognition of qualifications, (e) double cabinet restrictions, (f) minimum numbers of employees, (g) price-fixing, and (h) tying-in obligations.

[25] See note 4 above for a more detailed presentation of the new approach; and see V. Hatzopoulos, *Le principe communautaire d'équivalence et de reconnaissance mutuelle dans la libre prestation de services* (Athens and Brussels: Sakkoulas and Bruylant, 1999), pp. 419–35; the latter book is an improved version of the author's PhD presented in 1997 at the University of Strasbourg.

[26] On standards in the EU, see L. Boy, 'Normes', *Revue Internationale de droit économique* (1998) 115–46; J.-C. Graz, 'Quand les normes font loi: Topologie intégrée et processus différenciés de la normalisation internationale', *Etudes Internationales* 35 (2004), available at www.erudit.org/revue/ei/2004/v35/n2/009036ar.html (last visited 26 September 2010).

Moreover, the industry involved has less of an incentive to participate in non-technical standardization. Indeed, standards are in the interest of industry to the extent that they open up new markets. As explained above, spontaneous resistance to alien technical (incorporated) standards is much higher than resistance to non-incorporated standards; therefore, industry is keener on standardization of the former than on that of the latter. It is empirically proven that very often industry pushes forward the adoption of technical standards, while it holds back on non-technical (social, environmental etc.) ones.[27]

Therefore, the system of the adoption of standards and the certification of conformity of goods, carried out under the supervision of national accreditation authorities is not transposable as such in the area of services. It is interesting to note, in this respect, that the Commission has only issued two horizontal standardization mandates to the attention of CEN (M/340 of 8 October 2003 and M/371 of 16 July 2005) which have largely remained without effect: out of a total of 13,466 CEN publications only 36 standards (adopted or under adoption) concern primarily services, none of which is published in the *Official Journal* (therefore having binding effect)! The areas in which these standards have been adopted are: maintenance, transport, tourism, real estate, customer services, energy, installation management, translation and incineration.

The above lack of standards in the field of services has been highlighted by the Commission in its 'Europe 2020 Strategy' (COM(2010) 2020) and is likely to change to the extent that the Commission's recent Communication on 'a strategic vision for European standards' (COM(2011) 311 final) gets positively implemented. Therefore, alternative means – other than recourse to standards – should be used in order to facilitate mutual recognition.

2.5 Sensible political stakes

It has already been stated that service regulations are more often of a social, environmental nature etc., rather than of a purely technical/SHEC one. Except for the practical consequences presented above, this also bears its own intrinsic difficulty in respect of mutual recognition. Especially in the social field, there is no point in enquiring into the

[27] See J.-C. Graz, 'Quand les normes font loi: Topologie intégrée et processus différenciés de la normalisation internationale', above.

equivalence of different measures, without having regard to the more general policy into which they are integrated. Alas, it is much more complicated to judge the equivalence of *policies* rather than *measures*, for at least three reasons. First, it is often difficult to grasp the very content and objectives of various policies. Second, even if this first step has been completed successfully, it is difficult to judge the respective value of different policies: it is a political and highly ideological task. Third, there is the pressing issue of legitimacy: which supranational institution is in a position to second-guess policies decided by national representative bodies?[28]

This difficulty acquires extra weight if read against the distinction between incorporated and non-incorporated measures. Through the former kind of measures, the host State regulates the effects of goods/services in its own territory. Through the latter kind of measures, however, the host State pushes its own views onto other States, whose providers need to comply with the host State's regulations in order to have access to its market. There is, therefore, a strong element of extraterritoriality which runs counter to the very logic of mutual recognition.[29]

The difficulties of bridging divergent political traditions can best be illustrated by reference to services of general interest. It has proven impossible for '*service public*' countries, on the one hand, and common law countries, on the other,[30] to establish any common ground, or indeed any equivalence between their respective systems. This has led the Commission to intervene in various ways: by means of sector-specific Directives (in the field of telecommunications) or by dedicated Directive chapters (in other network industries, such as postal services or energy); by means of horizontal instruments of soft law (the 1996, 2000 and 2007 Communications); or by means of public consultations launched

[28] On the more general question of the mismatch between international trade, on the one hand, and social regulation at the national level, on the other, see M. P. Maduro, 'Is There Any Such Thing as Free or Fair Trade?' in G. de Búrca and J. Scott (eds.), *The EU and the WTO: Legal and Constitutional Issues*, 1st edn (Oxford and Portland, OR: Hart, 2001), pp. 259–82.

[29] *Ibid.*

[30] For these two concepts and their evolution under EC law, see C. Harlow, 'Public Service, Market Ideology and Citizenship' in M. Freedland and S. Sciarra (eds.), *Public Services and Citizenship in European Law: Public and Labour Law Perspectives* (Oxford: Clarendon Press, 1998), pp. 48–56; see also, in the same edited volume, G. Amato, 'Citizenship and Public Services – Some General Reflections', pp. 145–56.

through White and Green Papers.[31] And there is more to come.[32] In this sense, services of general interest constitute an illustration of the limitations of mutual recognition in the field of services.

3. Conceptual background

At this point, it is useful to enquire further into the nature and precise content of mutual recognition.

3.1 Equivalence: recognition

It has been observed by many writers that mutual recognition is a flexible means of regulation adapting to different regulatory needs.[33] A proof of flexibility and evolution is the fact that the very name of the principle has changed from 'equivalence and mutual recognition' to simply 'mutual recognition'. This change offers welcome clarifications concerning the content of the principle as, in the past, there was some confusion over whether recognition could take place without equivalence. Indeed, some

[31] See, in particular, Commission Communication, 'Services of general interest', OJ 1996 C281; Commission Communication, 'Services of general interest in Europe', OJ 2001 C17; Green Book on Services of General Interest, COM(2003) 270 final; White Book on Services of General Interest, COM(2004) 374 final; Commission Communication, 'Services of general interest including social services of general interest: a new European commitment', COM(2007) 725 final.

[32] For all these texts and for the ongoing Commission initiatives, see the dedicated Commission webpage at http://ec.europa.eu/services_general_interest/index_en.htm (last visited 27 September 2009); for a normative analysis, see the various contributions to J. V. Louis and S. Rodriguez (eds.), *Les services d'intérêt économique général et l'UE* (Brussels: Bruylant, 2006); see also H. Cox, J. Fournier and M. Girardot (eds.), *Les services d'intérêt économique général en Europe, régulation, financement, evaluation, bonnes pratiques* (Paris: CEEP/CIRIEC, 2000); P. Bauby, H. Coing and A. de Toledo (eds.), *Les services publics en Europe, Pour une régulation démocratique* (Paris: Publisud, 2007); and, more recently, U. Neergaard, R. Nielsen and L. Roseberry (eds.), *Integrating Welfare Functions into EU Law – From Rome to Lisbon* (Copenhagen: DJOF Publishing, 2009); and M. Krajewski, U. Neergaard and J. Van de Gronden (eds.), *The Changing Legal Framework for Services of General Interest in Europe – Between Competition and Solidarity* (The Hague: Asser Press, 2009).

[33] See, in chronological order, V. Hatzopoulos, note 25 above, pp. 59–72; K. Armstrong, 'Mutual Recognition' in C. Barnard and J. Scott (eds.), *The Law of the Single European Market: Unpacking the Premises* (Oxford: Hart Publishing, 2002), pp. 225–67; K. Nicolaïdis and S. Schmidt, 'Mutual Recognition "On Trial": The Long Road to Services Liberalisation', *Journal of European Public Policy* 14(5) (2007) 717–34; M. P. Maduro, 'So Close and Yet So Far: The Paradoxes of Mutual Recognition', *Journal of European Public Policy* 14(5) (2007) 814–25.

writers thought that the principle was about recognizing the equivalence of national regulations wherever such equivalence did exist,[34] while others thought that equivalence was a principle guiding the EU legislature while *recognition* bound the judiciary.[35] Others have always thought that *equivalence* was merely a factual situation entailing legal consequences, but that it is the principle of recognition which bears dynamism: recognition presupposes no equivalence, it is a dynamic process occasionally entailing 'activism', whereby situations which bear no actual equivalence are being recognized as equivalent.[36] In this respect, the various classifications set out below are highly instructive.

3.2 *Classifications*

3.2.1 Literature review

The fact that mutual recognition started as a judicial principle before being transformed into a regulatory technique is reflected in the classifications proposed by most authors. In chronological order, one may come across the following classifications. A first author distinguishes between mutual recognition as a 'general principle of EU law' underpinning all Internal Market situations, on the one hand, and mutual recognition as a 'legislative technique' on the other.[37] Along the same lines, Pelkmans distinguishes between 'judicial recognition' and 'regulatory recognition' without pushing as far as identifying any general principle.[38] Following an economic analysis, this author puts more weight on regulatory recognition, especially the kind of 'pre-emptive' recognition organized by the notification Directive.[39] Armstrong positions himself on the effects of recognition and distinguishes between 'active' recognition, when the host State authorities should actively seek to ascertain the degree of equivalence of their legislation with that of other Member States, on the one hand, and 'passive' recognition, when

[34] A. Mattera, 'Les principes de "proportionnalité" et de la "reconnaissance mutuelle" dans la jurisprudence de la Cour en matière de libre circulation des personnes et des services: de l'arrêt Thieffry aux arrêts Vlassopoulou, Mediawet et Dennemeyer', *Revue du Marché Unique Européen* 4 (1991) 191, p. 201.

[35] A. Bernel, *Le principe d'équivalence ou de 'reconnaissance mutuelle' en droit communautaire* (Zurich: Schulthess Polygraphischer Verlag, 1996), pp. 133 *et seq.*

[36] Hatzopoulos, note 25 above, pp. 63–4.

[37] Hatzopoulos, note 25 above; the very structure of the book follows this classification.

[38] Pelkmans, note 23 above.

[39] The difference of approach between the two may be explained by the fact that the former looks more into services while the latter looks into goods.

national authorities passively apply some system of recognition already agreed at EU level, on the other.[40] Trachtman thinks that one should distinguish between 'equivalence' which, whenever possible, should be acknowledged and given legal effects by national authorities and the Court of Justice, on the one hand, and 'mutual recognition' specifically established by common sector-specific rules, on the other. Lastly, Nicolaïdis and Schmidt distinguish, on the basis of the level of trust that underpins recognition, between 'pure' mutual recognition, when no instrument of harmonization/recognition exists, and 'managed' mutual recognition, whenever mutual recognition is aided by some secondary legislation.[41]

3.2.2 Yet another classification proposal

It is clear that the above classifications partly overlap. Moreover, they tend to leave out of the image another tentative source of mutual recognition obligations: the WTO. Therefore, it may be useful to propose yet another classification, based on four different criteria.

On the basis of the origin of mutual recognition obligations, one may distinguish between EU- and WTO-imposed mutual recognition. Within each legal order, we may further distinguish between legislative and judicial mutual recognition. While this distinction is familiar in the EU legal order, it is also valid within the GATS. Indeed, Article VII GATS foresees the institution of mechanisms of mutual recognition, 'which may be achieved through harmonization or otherwise'. Currently Article VII GATS is a dormant clause, and no mechanisms of mutual recognition have been instituted. This, however, may change and 'regulatory mutual recognition' may be organized at the WTO level. In the meantime, however, mutual recognition obligations may already be enforced by virtue of the GATS, through judicial means. Indeed, it would seem that 'market access' (Article XVI GATS), whenever scheduled by signatory States, bears in it, as part of the obligation of 'national treatment', an obligation of mutual recognition of services originating in other signatory States.[42]

[40] Armstrong, note 33 above. [41] Nicolaïdis and Schmidt, note 33 above.

[42] A. B. Zampetti, 'Market Access through Mutual Recognition: The Promise and Limits of GATS Article VII' in P. Sauvé and R. Stern (eds.), *GATS 2000: New Directions in Services Trade Liberalization* (Washington DC: Brookings Institution Press, 2000), pp. 283–306; see also J. Trachtman, 'Embedding Mutual Recognition at the WTO', *Journal of European Public Policy* 14(5) (2007) 780–99. These same authors explain that GATS Article II ('most favoured nation clause') grounds the duty to extend the scope of mutual recognition to services originating in any GATS signatory.

On the basis of the legal instrument organizing mutual recognition, several categories may be put forward, in the form of concentric circles. First, there are situations where no regulatory instrument helping mutual recognition exists (pure mutual recognition); in this case, mutual recognition stems from the general EU Treaty provisions on the Internal Market or the commitments scheduled by WTO States under Article XVI GATS. Second, there are situations where mutual recognition is underpinned by non-binding standards, common documents, mechanisms of exchange of information and/or coordination, or by administrative cooperation obligations. Third, mutual recognition may be organized by secondary legislation (or the equivalent under Article VII GATS), but in an imperfect, non-automatic way; the General System for the mutual recognition of diplomas, qualifications etc. would be a typical example. Fourth, mutual recognition may be organized in a quasi-automatic way through the text of secondary legislation (or the equivalent under Article VII GATS), based on some degree of prior harmonization.

On the basis of the degree of harmonization (or level of trust) on which mutual recognition is based, one may distinguish four situations:[43] (a) there has been some prior harmonization, in which case mutual recognition no longer operates on a 'mutual' basis between divergent regulations of different States, but rather in a 'centralized' way, by reference to commonly agreed standards/rules; (b) no harmonization is organized but there is some kind of 'pre-existing convergence' which facilitates mutual recognition; (c) no prior harmonization nor any apparent convergence, but administrative cooperation and/or judicial voluntarism do provide for some mutual recognition; (d) national rules are so different from one State to the next, that mutual recognition is impossible.

Last but not least, *on the basis of the way it is used by economic operators*, mutual recognition may fall into two broad categories. Either mutual recognition is organized by secondary legislation which, by the same token, provides for unfettered market access in other States; in this case, mutual recognition serves as a sword. Or the principle of mutual recognition is invoked before some administrative or judicial authority of the host State, in order to avoid some burden stemming from the host State regulatory framework; in this case, mutual recognition acts as a shield.

[43] See Hatzopoulos, note 25 above, p. 69.

3.2.3 Towards a theory of mutual recognition cycles?

The germs of the principle of mutual recognition are to be found, well before *Cassis de Dijon*, in *Van Binsbergen*. This case concerned a Dutch rule which required 'legal representatives' to be resident on the national territory. The Court held that, 'taking into account the particular nature of the services to be provided', such a requirement could be accepted 'where it is objectively justified'.[44] Where, on the contrary these two conditions (particular nature/objective justification) are not met, any restrictions on the activity would fall foul of Article 56 TFEU.[45] The same approach was confirmed in *Cassis de Dijon*, and then made explicit by the relevant Commission Communication.[46]

This first cycle of judicial mutual recognition was followed by regulatory mutual recognition, in the form of the 'passport' Directives in the field of insurance, banking and financial services. These are based on a clear distinction between, on the one hand, authorization requirements and, on the other, conditions of operation.[47] The former are put under 'home country control', and any authorization delivered by the home State is a valid 'passport' for entering the market in any other State. The conditions of operation, however, remain subject to shared control, in which the host State plays a predominant role; it is the host State's exclusive responsibility to make sure that the operators in question satisfy all professional and other rules applicable on its territory. Moreover, in order to foster mutual trust of the authorizations given, the Directives set out some substantive harmonization, at two levels. Not only are the minimum levels of liquidity and solvency of the undertakings harmonized, but so too are the rules concerning the keeping and publishing of accounts.[48] Therefore, this first generation of regulatory mutual recognition, based on home country control, was restricted in two ways: first, it concerned only the access to – not the exercise of – any given activity; second, it presupposed substantive harmonization.

[44] Case C-33/74, *Van Binsbergen* [1974] ECR 1299, paras. 12 and 14.

[45] *Ibid.*, para. 11.

[46] See note 3 above; for this Communication, see L. Gormley, 'Cassis de Dijon and Communication from the Commission', *European Law Review* (1981) 454.

[47] It is true that, in practice, such a distinction is not always easy to draw: see, e.g., Case C-347/02, *Commission* v. *France, Insurance* [2004] ECR I-7557.

[48] For a more detailed account of the early 'passport' system, see E. Lomnicka, 'The Home Country Control Principle in the Financial Services Directives and the Case Law', *European Business Law Review* (2000) 324–36; and Hatzopoulos, note 25 above, pp. 413–50.

The second generation of regulatory mutual recognition was clearly more ambitious. First and foremost, it was not restricted to the authorization but also concerned the operation of service providers in other Member States. What is more, it imposed only minimum harmonization. This second generation of regulatory mutual recognition was used for the first time in the 1997 modification of the 'TV Without Frontiers' Directive[49] (recently revisited in order to become the Audio Visual Media Services Directive).[50] The 'Electronic Signature'[51] and the 'E-Commerce'[52] Directives have followed suit. All of these Directives contain an 'internal market' clause whereby Member States must ensure freedom of reception and must not restrict the retransmission on their territory of television broadcasts from other Member States for reasons which fall within the fields coordinated by the Directive.[53] It has been observed that 'the purpose of the internal market clause is twofold: an extended application of the mutual recognition principle and the application of the law of the country of origin.'[54] The internal market clause,

49 Directive 97/36/EC modifying Directive 89/552/EEC on the coordination of certain provisions laid down by law, regulation or administrative action in Member States concerning the pursuit of television broadcasting activities, 'Television Without Frontiers Directive', OJ 1997 L202/60.

50 Directive 2007/65/EC, OJ 2007 L332/27; for this Directive, see, among many, F. Dehousse and K. Van Hecke, 'Towards an Audiovisual Media Directive: An Analysis of the Commission Proposal', Egmont European Affairs Publication (2006), available at http://aei.pitt.edu/9087/01/060606-AudioVis.directive.pdf (last visited 26 September 2010); P. Valcke and D. Stevens, 'Graduated Regulation of Regulable Content and the European AVMS Directive: One Small Step for the Industry and One Giant Leap for the Legislator?', *Telematics and Informatics* 24 (2007) 285–302, also available at http://law.kuleuven.be/icri/publications/948ti2007.pdf (last visited 26 September 2009); see also P. Valcke, D. Stevens, E. Lievens and E. Werkers, 'AVMS in the EU, Next Generation Approach or Old Wine in New Barrels?', *Communications and Strategies* 71 (2008) 103–18, also available at www.law.kuleuven.be/icri/publications/1149CS71_VALCKE_et_al.pdf?where= (last visited 26 September 2009); from a different perspective, see M. B. Nenova, 'The New AVMS Directive: Television Without Frontiers, Television Without Cultural Diversity', *Common Market Law Review* 44 (2007) 1689–1725.

51 Directive 1999/93/EC on a Community framework for electronic signatures, OJ 2000 L13/12.

52 Directive 2000/31/EC on certain legal aspects of information society services, in particular electronic commerce, in the Internal Market ('Directive on Electronic Commerce'), OJ 2000 L178/1.

53 'Television Without Frontiers Directive', Article 2a, para. 1.

54 M. Van Huffel, 'The Legal Framework for Financial Services and the Internet' in N. Nic Shuibhne (ed.), *Regulating the Internal Market* (Cheltenham and Northampton: Edward Elgar, 2006), pp. 144–80, p. 157.

however, is different from the passport system in at least three respects.[55] For one thing, home country control is a logical – almost undisputed – choice in the case of media and e-undertakings which never move away from home, while this choice is not as patently obvious in relation to financial institutions. Second, the European 'passport' corresponds to an authorization delivered by the competent home authorities, after making sure that the coordinated conditions are being met, and which is valid throughout the EU. The e-Directives, on the other hand, specifically rule that the relevant activities should be open, without a prior authorization being permitted.[56] This, in turn, raises the question of the responsibility borne by the home State: it may not authorize in advance but should, nevertheless, make sure that service providers established on its territory comply with the relevant provisions of the Directives.[57] Third, contrary to passports which are delivered following some or, lately, exhaustive[58] harmonization, the internal market clause is only based on minimal harmonization linked to the protection of the general interest. Therefore, the internal market relies to a greater extent on home State legislation and trust in home authorities. By the same token, it corresponds to a regulatory technique whereby 'competition [between legal orders] works as a substitute for harmonization'.[59]

Compared to the above 'passport' and 'internal market clause' systems, the 'country-of-origin principle' put forward by the draft Directive constituted a regulatory advance, in at least three respects. First and foremost, because it was deemed to govern not only the authorization and conditions of operation of the service activity but also to determine

[55] It has been observed, however, that the rights stemming from the E-Commerce Directive may serve as a 'second chance' passport and open the way for the provision of online financial services to providers who do not qualify for a 'real' passport under the relevant Directives; see Van Huffel, note 54 above.

[56] E-Commerce Directive, Article 4(1); E-Signature Directive, Article 3(1); the AVMS does not mention anything about the need of a prior authorization and leaves the choice to the Member States.

[57] On this issue, see Van Huffel, note 54 above, p. 151.

[58] Markets in Financial Instruments Directive 2004/39/EC ('MiFID'), OJ 2004 L145/1 (as modified by Directive 2006/31/EC, OJ 2006 L114/60, Directive 2007/44/EC, OJ 2007 L247/1, and Directive 2008/10/EC, OJ 2008 L76/33), replacing the Investment Services Directive 93/22/EC. The MiFID Directive is not a 'minimum' but rather a 'full' harmonization Directive, establishing 'a comprehensive regulatory regime governing the execution of transactions in financial instruments' (see its recital 5). The system has been further centralized after the 2008 financial crisis and the institution of the three central monitoring bodies of the European System of Financial Supervision (ESFS).

[59] Van Huffel, note 54 above, p. 176.

the applicable law, in case of a dispute. Hence the totality of the service provision (authorization, operation, conflict resolution) was to be covered by the country-of-origin principle. This difference also justifies the evolution of terminology from 'home country control' mainly used in the field of passport Directives to the more far-reaching 'country-of-origin principle'. Second, the draft Directive had an extremely wide scope, by no means restricted to services offered at a distance. Third, the level of harmonization put forward by the draft Directive was so elementary, that one could legitimately question whether the very term 'harmonization' is appropriate.[60] These three differences have stood in the way of the flourishing of the country-of-origin principle.

After the demise of the country-of-origin principle from the Services Directive, the likely way to proceed in the direction of services liberalization is either through more far-reaching judgments of the Court of Justice, or through sector-specific secondary legislation. In this sense, it is possible to identify some kind of cyclical movement in the implementation of the principle of mutual recognition into the EU legal order.

3.2.4 Mutual recognition as a general principle of EU law?

Irrespective of whether mutual recognition is put to work by the text of secondary law, it is submitted that it is a general principle of EU law, having general application. In order to acquire the status of a general principle of law, a principle needs either to be grounded on the text, the aims and the objectives of the Treaty, or to draw on international agreements to which the Member States or the EU are parties. Moreover, its content should be able to give rise to binding legal rules.[61] It has been explained above that: (a) the principle of mutual recognition is written

[60] For a critical evaluation of the content of the Services Directive, see C. Barnard, 'Unravelling the Services Directive', *Common Market Law Review* 45 (2008) 323–94; S. Griller, 'The New Services Directive of the EU, Hopes and Expectations from the Angle of (Further) Completion of the Internal Market' in H. F. Koeck and M. M. Karollus (eds.), *The New Services Directive of the EU* (FIDE XXIII Congress 2008, Congress Publications, Vol. 3, Vienna, 2008), pp. 379–423; V. Hatzopoulos, 'Legal Aspects in Establishing the Internal Market for Services' in J. Pelkmans, D. Hanf and M. Chang (eds.), *The EU Internal Market in Comparative Perspective: Economic, Political and Legal Analyses* (Brussels etc.: PIE-Peter Lang, 2008), pp. 139–89; V. Hatzopoulos, 'Assessing the Services Directive, 2006/123/EC', *Cambridge Yearbook of European Legal Studies* 10 (2008) 215–61; for more in detail, see V. Hatzopoulos, 'Que reste-t-il de la directive sur les services?', *Cahiers de Droit Européen* 3(4) (2008) 299–355.

[61] See T. Tridimas, *The General Principles of EU Law*, 2nd edn (Oxford University Press, 2006), pp. 25–6.

into the Treaty (Article 57 EC for diplomas etc.); (b) its scope has been generalized by the Court (*Van Binsbergen*, *Cassis de Dijon*), by the Commission practice and by the 'notification Directive' (pre-emptive mutual recognition)[62] and that it corresponds to one of the obligations that Member States have undertaken when signing the WTO Agreements.

It has also been explained, second, that the principle of mutual recognition constitutes the reverse of the principle of proportionality: the host State legislation will not be deemed necessary, and thus proportional, if its regulatory objectives are sufficiently secured by the rules of the home State. Therefore, the principle of proportionality starts (being operational) where mutual recognition stops (being operational).[63]

Third, the principle of mutual recognition is directly connected to the principle of mutual trust, itself stemming from Article 3 TEU (Member State solidarity), Article 4(3) TEU (Member State loyalty) and the principle of international law *pacta sunt servanda*.[64]

The fact that the principle of mutual recognition constitutes a general principle of EU law, already acknowledged by several Advocates General of the Court,[65] has been confirmed by the Court itself in its recent case law concerning the application of the procurement principles to tenders which fall outside the scope of the public procurement Directives. Starting with cases of *Commission* v. *France, Nord Pas de Calais* and *Telaustria*,[66] then in its judgments in *Coname*, *Parking Brixen* and *Contse*,[67] the Court has held the principle of mutual recognition to be of the same value as the principles of non-discrimination, equal treatment, transparency and proportionality.

[62] See the text accompanying note 23 above.

[63] Hatzopoulos, note 25 above, pp. 117–18. [64] *Ibid.*, pp. 119–20.

[65] Case C-5/94, *Hedley Lomas* [1996] ECR I-2553, as well as the Advocate General's Opinion delivered on 20 June 1995; Case C-87/94, *Commission* v. *Belgium, Walloon Buses* [1996] ECR I-2043, as well as the Opinion of Advocate General Lenz; Case C-11/95, *Commission* v. *Belgium, Cable TV* [1996] ECR I-4115; see also the Opinion of Advocate General Van Gerven in Case C-205/89, *Commission* v. *Greece, Pasteurised Butter* [1991] ECR I-1361, delivered on 10 January 1991; Advocate General Darmon's Opinion in Case C-154/93, *Tawil Albertini* [1994] ECR I-451, delivered on 17 November 1993; Advocate General Léger's Opinion in Case C-40/93, *Commission* v. *Italy, Dentists* [1995] ECR I-1319, delivered on 30 March 1995.

[66] Case C-225/98, *Commission* v. *France, Nord Pas de Calais* [2000] ECR I-7445; and Case C-324/98, *Telaustria* [2000] ECR I-10745.

[67] Case C-231/03, *Coname* [2005] ECR I-7287; Case C-458/03, *Parking Brixen* [2005] ECR I-8612; Case 234/03, *Contse* [2005] ECR I-9315.

The Commission's interpretative Communications are even more explicit in this respect.[68]

The immediate consequence of the principle of mutual recognition being a general principle of law is of a procedural order: even if the home and host State regulations are so different that no mutual recognition may take place between them, three elements should, nevertheless, be present. First, there should always be a procedure whereby the possibility of mutual recognition should be ascertained – no automatic rejection of the foreign good/service/professional is admissible.[69] Second, national authorities of the home and host States should do their best to cooperate with one another in order to achieve convergence points in their respective regulatory frameworks.[70] Third, foreign producers/professionals should have access to some means of judicial review of unfavourable decisions against them.

4. Practicalities

Having explored the conceptual background underlying the principle of mutual recognition, and before considering the ways in which mutual recognition may become more efficient, it is now time to turn to its basic applications. The two sections which follow correspond, to a large extent, to the distinction between pure mutual recognition (how it works) and managed mutual recognition (how it can be made to work better).

[68] The Commission interpretative Communication on the Community law applicable to contract awards not or not fully subject to the provisions of the Public Procurement Directives, OJ 2006 C179/2, foresees in its Article 1 that: 'Contracting entities from Member States have to comply with the rules and principles of the EC Treaty whenever they conclude public contracts falling into the scope of that Treaty. These principles include the free movement of goods (Article 34 TFEU), the right of establishment (Article 49 TFEU), the freedom to provide services (Article 56 TFEU), non-discrimination and equal treatment, transparency, proportionality and mutual recognition.' An equivalent formula is to be found in the Commission interpretative Communication on the application of Community law on public procurement and concessions to institutionalised PPP (IPPP), OJ 2008 C91/4, Article 2.1.

[69] See, in this respect, the case law concerning the mutual recognition of diplomas and professional qualifications under Articles 49 and 56 TFEU, notes 93–99 below and the corresponding text.

[70] See, in this respect, notes 74–82 below and the corresponding text.

4.1 General background

4.1.1 The four levels of mutual recognition

Mutual recognition applies at four levels, which may be presented in the form of concentric circles. First, and simply enough, documents are subject to mutual recognition. Whether they are issued purely by virtue of national law, or for the implementation of some common rule or standard, documents issued by the authorities of one Member State should be fully recognized in all the others.[71] Second, measures are subject to mutual recognition. Therefore, a measure requiring a guarantee deposit in one Member State should always be taken into account by the authorities of another Member State having a similar requirement. Third, to the extent that different measures (e.g., a prior authorization scheme and an obligation of registration) may serve the same policy (e.g., consumer protection), the evaluation of equivalence takes place at the policy level: provided the underlying policy is served at a comparable level (which is a question of fact), mutual recognition should apply.[72] Lastly, mutual recognition could also operate at a higher level of abstraction, that of the broader regulatory objective of a measure. An example of this application may be given by reference to the judgment in *Burbaud*:[73] the Portuguese system of acquiring professional qualifications should be taken into account by the French system for the recruitment of high-level civil servants, as both are aimed at securing that high skills are offered in the society.

4.1.2 Administrative cooperation

Irrespective of the level at which mutual recognition is to be put to work, it requires that administrative authorities of Member States work together – or, at least, familiarize themselves with one another and with their respective procedures and documents.[74]

71 See notes 86–92 below and the corresponding text for the practical implications of this first type of mutual recognition.

72 Hence, for example, in Case C-496/01, *Commission* v. *France, Medical Laboratories* [2004] ECR I-2351, France was condemned for refusing to refund medical analyses carried out by foreign laboratories on the ground of health protection, without looking at all into the authorization requirements that such laboratories had to comply with in their State of establishment.

73 Case C-285/01, *Burbaud* [2003] ECR I-8219.

74 According to my analysis above, administrative cooperation is one of the three 'procedural' attributes of the general principle of mutual recognition, the other two being (a) the existence of a procedure for the assessment of equivalence and (b) judicial control.

In a first series of cases, the Court built upon the specific cooperation obligations imposed by the texts of secondary legislation. In *IKA* v. *Ioannidis*,[75] the right of a Greek pensioner to claim a refund from his fund for treatment received in Germany under the terms of Regulation 1408/71[76] was at stake. The Court held that the authorities involved could not restrict themselves to a mechanical application of their obligations under Regulation 1408/71. Rather, they should '*in accordance with Article 10 EC* [now Article 4(3) TEU] . . . *cooperate* in order to ensure that those provisions are applied correctly . . . with a view to facilitating the freedom of movement of those insured persons are fully respected'.[77]

In *Kapper*,[78] a case where the German authorities were contesting the validity of a Dutch driving licence, the Court found a violation of Directive 92/439/EC[79] and of Articles 45, 49 and 56 TFEU. Not only did the Court completely rule out the possibility that a licence issued by the authorities of one Member State be invalidated by those of another Member State, but it also recognized the possibility of initiating infringement proceedings against States, the authorities of which fail to cooperate effectively.

A further step was taken in *Danner*,[80] where the Court rejected the Danish government's argument that the effectiveness of fiscal controls justified that pensions paid to residents by foreign funds did not qualify for a deduction from taxable income. The Court held that, even where

The latter is not a specific principle of mutual recognition and has been extensively examined elsewhere. The former – although connected to the duty of administrative cooperation – would require more analysis in its own right, if space were not a consideration.

75 Case C-326/00, *IKA* v. *Ioannidis* [2003] ECR I-1703; and, for a thorough presentation of this case, the comment by the present author in *Common Market Law Review* (2003) 1251–1268.

76 Council Regulation (EEC) No. 1408/71 on the application of social security schemes to employed persons, to self-employed persons and to members of their families moving within the Community, OJ 1971 L149/2, English Spec. Ed. Series I, Chapter 1971(II) 416. This Regulation has been modified at least thirty times, the last important modification extending its personal scope to cover nationals of non Member States legally residing within the EU: see Council Regulation (EC) No. 859/2003, OJ 2003 L124/1. It has recently been codified and repealed by Regulation (EC) No. 883/2004, OJ 2004 L166/1.

77 Case C-326/00, *IKA* v. *Ioannidis* [2003] ECR I-1703, para. 51 (emphasis added).

78 Case C-476/01, *Kapper* [2004] ECR I-5205.

79 Council Directive 91/439/EEC on driving licences, OJ 1991 L237/1, as amended by Council Directive 97/26/EC, OJ 1997 L150/41.

80 This case contains the bolder statement of the duty of cooperation between Member States' fiscal authorities, but almost all recent tax cases follow the same logic.

the secondary legislation in place (Directive 77/799)[81] does not effectively meet the legitimate objectives pursued by the host State's authorities, the latter are required to look into and to accept further evidence provided by the interested party, before imposing a restrictive measure.

Such an obligation may also be imposed upon Member States' authorities even in the absence of any specific text of secondary legislation. In *Oulane*, the Court held that the requirement that all Member States' nationals should possess a valid passport or identity card while in another Member State could not be imposed in an absolute way, if the person concerned was able to provide unequivocal proof of their nationality by other means.[82] This implies that the authorities in question may not rely only on the official documents they are familiar with, but may be required to take into account evidence, concerning the person's identity, by other means, probably in collaboration with the authorities of the Member State of origin of the person concerned.

4.1.3 Burden of proof: relation with country-of-origin principle

Through these cases it may be said that the Court, within the material limits of its capacity as an actor of negative integration, is, in some indirect and imperfect way, trying to foster positive cooperation obligations between Member States' authorities. This does not (and may not) go as far as a proper 'country-of-origin principle', since the home State authorities maintain the last word on the operation of foreign service providers in their territory. In this respect, the difference between the current situation and the one that would prevail under a fully fledged country-of-origin principle, like that of the Bolkestein draft, may be seen as associated with the onus of proof.[83] Under the country-of-origin principle, it would have been possible for service providers to be active in other Member States without having to look into or to comply with the requirements of the host State; it would be for the host State

[81] Council Directive 77/799/EEC concerning mutual assistance by the competent authorities of the Member States in the field of direct taxation, OJ 1977 L336/15.

[82] Case C-215/03, *Oulane* [2005] ECR I-1215.

[83] The idea that the difference between the case law on mutual recognition, on the one hand, and the (abandoned) country-of-origin principle, on the other, is merely a question of burden of proof is more fully developed by the present author in V. Hatzopoulos, 'Que reste-t-il de la directive sur les services?', *Cahiers de Droit Européen* 3(4) (2008) 299–355, p. 317; see also C. Barnard, 'Unravelling the Services Directive', *Common Market Law Review* 45 (2008) 323–94, p. 363.

authorities to prove that their requirements were necessary and proportionate to the legitimate policy objective pursued by them. As things stand right now, however, service providers still need to bear the enquiry and compliance costs in order for them to conform to the host State's requirements; they are helped, in this process, by mutual recognition and administrative cooperation. Seen from a slightly different perspective, the current situation may be seen as the 'worst of two worlds': Member States' administrative authorities are compelled to work with one another and to cope with documents unknown to them (as under the country-of-origin principle), while service providers still need to undergo the cost of compliance.[84]

4.2 *Specific applications*

According to the above, in most cases mutual recognition (at least in its pure, i.e., non managed, form) acts as a shield rather than a sword. It serves as part of the proportionality test of the host States' restrictive measures. In this context, mutual recognition may be seen to apply at different levels.

4.2.1 Documents, certificates, attestations

A distinction may be drawn depending on whether the document, certificate or attestation in question has Union origin. Many texts of secondary legislation provide for common documents to be put into place. This is true both in areas where EU law pushes forward a unification of the law, such as in the area of transport (where the use of common licences, conformity certificates, cabotage authorizations, transit documents, etc., is of the essence of the policy put into place), and in areas where the role of the EU is restricted to mere coordination, such as social security. Hence, for example, in *IKA* v. *Ioannidis*[85] and *Fitzwilliam*,[86] the Court held that documents E 111 (covering urgent medical care) and E 102 (certifying affiliation to a compulsory pension

[84] In this respect, two observations made by the House of Lords merit some attention, at least for being elegantly expressed: for one thing, 'there may be a gap between perceptions and legal rights, acting as a brake on service provision'; moreover, '[i]t may be that the appetite of small business for testing particular local restrictions on service activity through the courts is not strong'. House of Lords, 'Emerging Conclusions on the Revised Draft Services Directive', 25 Mai 2006, p. 3.

[85] Case C-326/00, *IKA* v. *Ioannidis* [2003] ECR I-1703.

[86] Case C-202/97, *Fitzwilliam* [2000] ECR I-883.

scheme) respectively, issued by the home States of the parties concerned, could not be put into doubt by the host authorities, but in exceptional circumstances. The Court took an additional step in *Kapper*, where at stake was the refusal of the German authorities to take into consideration a driving licence issued in the Netherlands, by virtue of Directive 91/439. Not only did the Court condemn such a refusal as being abusive, but it also held that the deficient application of mutual recognition could lead to Article 258 TFEU proceedings against the failing State. It is clear from the above that mutual recognition is not restricted merely to the formal validity of the document, but also covers the very content thereof.

Mutual recognition also covers 'purely national' documents unrelated to any Union document. Here again, a further distinction may be useful to draw, in order to appreciate the full breadth of mutual recognition. For one thing documents which are similar or serve a similar function should be mutually recognized. This expressly stems from the public procurement Directives, has been generalized by the Court's case law and subsequently articulated in Article 5(3) of the Services Directive, so that:

> Where Member States require a provider or recipient to supply a certificate, attestation or any other document proving that a requirement has been satisfied, they shall accept any document from another Member State which serves an equivalent purpose or from which it is clear that the requirement in question has been satisfied. They may not require a document from another Member State to be produced in its original form, or as a certified copy or as a certified translation.

More significantly still, Member States are obliged to recognize documents which are issued under clearly different conditions than those prevailing under their own legal order. Hence, in *Commission* v. *Greece, University Degrees*,[87] Greece was condemned, among other grounds, for failing to recognize degrees awarded by universities of other Member States by virtue of franchise agreements with local (private) educational establishments. The Greek government's argument, according to which higher education in Greece is reserved to State-owned establishments, was dismissed, since the Court held that the home State authorities were exclusively responsible for determining the conditions of delivery of the degrees in question. Therefore, Greece was made to give recognition to degrees awarded under conditions which, if present in a purely national setting, would fall foul of the Greek Constitution.

[87] Case C-274/05, *Commission* v. *Greece, University Degrees* [2008] ECR I-7969.

Mutual recognition also covers documents which perform different functions. In *Oulane*, discussed above,[88] the Dutch authorities were expected to adduce evidence concerning the identity/nationality of a person who had no identity card from other documents, such as social security cards, credit cards etc. Similarly, in *Commission* v. *The Netherlands, Security Services*,[89] the Dutch authorities were not allowed to require foreign security personnel to carry a special (professional) identity card, since their passports/identity cards issued by their home States would be enough to identify them.

4.2.2 Conformity certificates, standards etc.

What is true for certificates, attestations and other official documents is also true for conformity certificates, markings etc. By the same token, standards which fail to take into account those in force in other Member States are seldom accepted.

Many recent examples illustrate the point. In the parallel judgments in *Medipac* and *Commission* v. *Greece, EC Markings*,[90] the Court condemned the Greek public hospitals for excluding, from public tender procedures, pharmaceutical products bearing the EC mark. In *Commission* v. *Portugal, Plastic Pipes*,[91] the goods in question were altogether excluded from the Portuguese market. More significantly, in *Commission* v. *France, Nord Pas de Calais*,[92] the Court held that France was violating Article 56 TFEU (and Directive 93/37 on public works tenders) not because it excluded goods bearing non-national markings, but merely because the tender documents made reference only to national standards and measurements, thus making it more difficult for tenderers from other Member States to compete.

4.2.3 Professional qualifications

The field of professional qualifications is a test-bed for mutual recognition. Leaving aside the various texts of secondary legislation, now codified in Directive 2005/36 (managed mutual recognition), the ingenious application of mutual recognition by the Court needs to be highlighted. First, the Court, in its judgments in *Heylens*,

[88] See note 82 above and the accompanying text.

[89] Case C-189/03, *Commission* v. *The Netherlands, Security Services* [2004] ECR I-9289.

[90] Case C-6/05, *Medipac* [2007] ECR I-4557; Case C-489/06, *Commission* v. *Greece, EC Markings* [2009] ECR I-1797.

[91] Case C-432/03, *Commission* v. *Portugal, Plastic Pipes* [2005] ECR I-9665.

[92] Note 66 above.

Thieffry and *Vlassopoulou* established that the host State should, in all circumstances, take into account the qualifications and/or experience acquired in other Member States and may not rely on formal requirements. In the last ten years, and in parallel with the application of secondary legislation in this same field, the Court has, through the application of mutual recognition, launched the cornerstones of a common educational policy. According to the Court, the authorities of a Member State 'must take into consideration the professional qualification of the person concerned by making a comparison between the qualifications certified by his diplomas, certificates and other formal qualifications and by his relevant professional experience and the professional qualifications required by the national rules for the exercise of the profession in question'.[93] For one thing, the Court interprets extensively the concept of 'regulated profession' in order to cover not only professions the access to which is governed by legislative, regulatory or administrative measures, but also those who are governed by collective agreements, of a limited territorial validity.[94] Moreover, the obligation of mutual recognition extends to all public authorities, central and decentralized,[95] and to State-owned entities or companies towards their employees,[96] present and prospective: in the framework of a recruitment examination for civil servants, the mutual recognition of qualifications obtained in other Member States may require the organization of a different recruitment procedure.[97] More interestingly, the Court holds that the obligation of mutual recognition also covers degrees obtained in the host territory by virtue of franchise agreements with European universities, even though such degrees would run counter to the constitution of the host State, were they awarded in a purely national setting.[98] The Court has also held, where a Member State is late in transposing the General System Directive (Directive 89/48/EEC) into national law, it is nonetheless under a duty to recognize the relevant diplomas without, however, having the right to require compensatory measures (ascending but no descending direct effect).[99] This case law is always valuable, to the extent that transposition of Directive 2005/36 has

[93] Case C-313/01, *Morgenbesser* [2003] ECR I-13467, para. 57.
[94] Case C-234/97, *Bobadilla* [1999] ECR I-4773. [95] *Ibid.* [96] *Ibid.*
[97] Case C-285/01, *Burbaud* [2003] ECR I-8219.
[98] *Commission* v. Case C-274/05, *Commission* v. *Greece, University Degrees* [2008] ECR I-7969.
[99] Case C-102/02, *Beuttenmüller* [2004] ECR I-5405; see also Case C-141/04, *Peros* v. *TEE* [2005] ECR I-7163.

been a complicated task and the existence of strong guidelines from the Court plays an instrumental role in its proper implementation by Member States.[100]

In view of such extensive recognition obligations, it comes as no surprise that the Bologna process has been 'voluntarily' put into place, in order to secure some prior harmonization of the degrees which are, in any event, subject to mutual recognition. In this respect, the institution of the European Credit Transfer and Accumulation System (ECTS) for the implementation of the 2003 Berlin Declaration of the Ministers of Education is a decisive step towards more effective mutual recognition.

4.2.4 Guarantee deposits

Guarantee deposits with banks in other Member States should always, regardless of circumstance, be recognized. Any opposite solution would violate simultaneously (a) the free movement of service providers (being an indirect discrimination), (b) the free movement of banking services (being an absolute prohibition) and (c) the free movement of capital (being an absolute prohibition). Among several cases, two concerning Italy are representative.[101] In both cases, the principle of proportionality was breached, to the extent that the Italian authorities required a guarantee to be deposited with a credit institution established within national territory and ignored the amounts already deposited in the home State of the undertakings concerned.

4.2.5 Any other element of law or fact required for the issuance of authorization by the home State

Mutual recognition of guarantee deposits is just the beginning. Whenever the material requirements of the host State correspond – even if imperfectly – to the conditions for the delivery of an authorization or the inclusion in a register in the home State, the authorities of the host State should take into account the findings of those of the home State. In *Commission* v. *Italy, Sanitary Services*,[102] Italy was found in breach of Article 56 TFEU because the registration system in question did 'not exclude from its scope a provider of services who is established

[100] Several Member States have faced strong resistance in implementing the Directive, while others have communicated multiple combinations of texts (framework and/or sector-specific).

[101] Case C-263/99, *Commission* v. *Italy, Transport Consultants* [2001] ECR I-4195; Case C-279/00, *Commission* v. *Italy, Temporary Labour Agencies* [2002] ECR I-1425.

[102] Case C-358/98, *Commission* v. *Italy, Sanitary Services* [2000] ECR I-1255, para. 13.

in a Member State other than the Italian Republic and who, under the legislation of its Member State of establishment, already satisfies formal requirements equivalent to those under the Italian Law'. The Italian authorities should, before imposing any of the sanctions foreseen for breach of the registration procedure, examine whether the same or similar conditions as those required for registration were not already satisfied by the service providers in their home States. This recognition obligation may cover all the conditions pertaining to the authorization/registration of a service provider. It may not, however, cover the very authorization/registration as such, as this would be moving away from mutual recognition to the country-of-origin principle – a step not yet accomplished.

4.2.6 Other elements of law or fact testified by the home State

From the judgments of the Court in *Commission* v. *The Netherlands, Security Services* and *Oulane*, both discussed above, it becomes clear that the host State should also recognize and give effect to any document delivered by the home State authorities (identity cards and other means of identification, respectively), even if such document has not been specifically issued in relation to the provision of the services in question.

5. Enhanced (managed) mutual recognition

On the basis of the case law and in order to further accomplish the possibilities thus recognized, managed mutual recognition is progressively put into place. Depending on the substantial rules adopted, managed mutual recognition entails some degree of harmonization: while the 'passport' system was based on quite substantial harmonization of the very rules leading to the issuance of the passport by the home State, the 'general system' for the recognition of professional qualifications only harmonizes the type of and conditions for the imposition of compensatory measures by the host State. The Services Directive, for its part, falls short of any harmonization, but puts weight on administrative cooperation, the exchange of information, the use of electronic means and common documents, etc. If one looks briefly into the different systems of managed mutual recognition, without paying any attention to the substantial rules of each one of them, some basic 'horizontal' means of enhancing mutual recognition may be identified. These means may be distinguished in two broad categories: measures which tend to increase Member States' trust on mutual recognition and measures which tend to enhance the very effects of mutual recognition.

5.1 Measures to increase trust on mutual recognition

5.1.1 Strict rules on establishment

In the first section of this chapter, it was explained that mutual recognition is a source of regulatory competition: it allows undertakings the freedom to choose the regulatory framework (and hence the State) they deem better for their activity, and then to distribute their goods and services within the entire Common Market by virtue of the principle of mutual recognition. This freedom of choice, nevertheless, should not allow either continuous 'forum shopping' or arbitrary 'cherry picking'. In other words, the possibility of exit from a regulatory framework judged burdensome or otherwise inappropriate should not lead to an abuse of rights.

Against this background, the Court of Justice has developed its anti-fraud case law. Naturally, this case law has evolved in parallel with the very principle of mutual recognition it tends to correct. Therefore, in *Van Binsbergen*[103] and several subsequent cases, the Court has already held that:

> a Member State cannot be denied the right to take measures to prevent the exercise by a person providing services whose activity is entirely or principally directed towards its territory of the freedom guaranteed by Article 59 for the purpose of avoiding the professional rules which would be applicable to him if he were established within that State, such a situation may be subject to judicial control under the provisions of the chapter relating to the right of establishment and not of that on the provision of services.

In the same vein, in *Säger*, where the Court explicitly recognized, for the first time, that non-discriminatory measures may nevertheless violate Article 56 TFEU, the measures it viewed were liable 'to prohibit or otherwise impede the activities of a provider of services established in another Member State where he lawfully provides similar services':[104] the provider should be established in and compliant with the rules of one and the same State. This position was radically revisited in *VT4*,[105] where

[103] See Case 33/74, *Van Binsbergen* [1974] ECR 1299, para. 13; the same idea is also expressed in Case 246/80, *Broekmeulen* [1981] ECR 2311; Case C-148/91, *Veronica* [1993] ECR I-485; and Case C-23/93, *TV10* [1994] ECR I-4795.

[104] Case C-76/90, *Säger and Dennemeyer* [1991] ECR I-4221, para. 12.

[105] Case C-56/96, *VT4 Ltd* [1997] ECR I-3143, para. 22.

the Court held that '[t]he Treaty does not prohibit an undertaking from exercising the freedom to provide services if it does not offer services in the Member State in which it is established'. Thereafter, it was possible to be established in one Member State but only provide services to the attention of recipients in another Member State – and in compliance with the requirements of this State.[106]

This freedom opens up the way for abuse. This is the reason why most texts of secondary legislation organizing some kind of mutual recognition provide for strict nationality rules: in order to claim the benefits of managed mutual recognition, the undertakings should be compliant with the requirements of the Member State determined according to these nationality rules. The importance of nationality rules bears a negative correlation to the level of harmonization achieved by every single text of secondary legislation: it is when harmonization is unimportant that the prevention of the arbitrary choice of a legal order becomes important. In view of the fact that most recent EU texts are not harmonization-intensive, it may be that weight should be put on the determination of the appropriate nationality rules in order for them to reflect the specific nature of the activities covered by each text. Hence, for instance, the nationality rules included in the Television Without Frontiers Directive,[107] may no longer be appropriate since the 2007 amendment, whereby its scope was extended to cover also online (internet) services.[108]

5.1.2 Compulsory host State rules

In some circumstances it is not enough that the service provider complies with *some* rules but specifically with the host State rules. In these cases, the provider is left with no choice.

[106] See also the Court's judgments in Case C-212/97, *Centros* [1999] ECR I-1459; Case C-208/08, *Überseering* [2002] ECR I-9919; and Case C-321/05, *Hans Markus Kofoed* [2007] ECR I-5795. On the totality of the relevant case law, see A. Kjellgren, 'The Jurisprudence of the Court of Justice on Circumvention, Fraud and Abuses of Community Law' in M. Andenas and W.-H. Roth, *Services and Free Movement in EU Law*, 1st edn (Oxford University Press, 2001), pp. 245–78.

[107] Council Directive 89/552/EEC on the coordination of certain provisions laid down by law, regulation or administrative action in Member States concerning the pursuit of television broadcasting activities, OJ 1989 L298/23; modified by Directive 97/36/EC of the European Parliament and of the Council of 30 June 1997 amending Council Directive 89/552/EEC on the coordination of certain provisions laid down by law, regulation or administrative action in Member States concerning the pursuit of television broadcasting activities, OJ 1997 L202/60.

[108] See note 50 above.

The typical area where the application of the host State rules is important is the social field. Therefore, the Posted Workers Directive 96/71 foresees that the main characteristics of the employment relationship shall be governed by the host State regulation. This rule, however, has been progressively stripped of much of its content by the Court of Justice, in at least three respects. For one thing, it is henceforth clear that only legally binding rules and/or collective agreements,[109] having a general territorial scope,[110] may be forced upon foreign service providers posting workers. Second, it is also clear that all that is not expressly covered by the Directive is excluded from its scope and may not be imposed upon foreign service providers.[111] Third, the Court occasionally treats, under the rules on posted workers, situations which could qualify as 'establishment' – and therefore fully subject to the host State legislation: in *Laval*, despite the fact that the Latvian workers concerned were employed by Baltic, the Swedish subsidiary of Laval, the Court ignored an argument to this effect[112] and instead based its reasoning on the (legally imprecise) assumption that they were posted workers.

The application of compulsory host State rules is not restricted to the social field. Security is yet another area in which the host State may legitimately impose its own rules. For instance, Regulation 3118/93 opening up road haulage cabotage foresees that transport undertakings should observe host rules not only on tariffs, transport terms and working time (social preoccupations), but also concerning the weight and dimensions of the vehicle, the precautions for transporting dangerous products etc.

More generally, the application of compulsory host State *lois de police* in situations where the rules of some other State apply in principle – be it by virtue of some rule of private international law or by virtue of the EU mutual recognition principle – is not a legal novelty. In order to increase Member States' trust on mutual recognition, it could be useful to determine, on a case-specific basis, the sets of compulsory host State rules which should always be respected and could not yield to mutual recognition. The effort, currently under way, to define the contours of services of general interest at a level acceptable by all Member States may be a useful precedent in this respect.

[109] Case C-341/05, *Laval un Partneri* [2007] ECR I-11767; see also note 15 above for the rich commentary to this case.

[110] Case C-346/06, *Rüffert* [2008] ECR I-1989.

[111] Case C-319/06, *Commission* v. *Luxembourg, Posted Workers* [2008] ECR I-4323.

[112] See para. 43 of the judgment.

5.1.3 Provisional suspension of mutual recognition

Mutual recognition is based on trust. There are situations, however, in which trust is faltering. The home Member State may fail either at the regulatory level, by adopting measures which are deemed insufficient or inappropriate by the host State; or it may also fail at the implementation/individual level by failing to monitor and/or sanction specific providers. In both cases, it is crucial to allow the host State to suspend the effect of mutual recognition in order to secure interests judged vital.

The Service Directive is ambivalent in this respect. On the one hand, it allows for individual exceptions to the free movement of services (Article 18) in exceptional circumstances and subject to prior information of both the State making use of the exception and of the Commission. This procedure is apt to protect the host State's interests without allowing for protectionist excesses. It is likely, however, to be overshadowed by the possibility opened by Article 16(2) and (4), whereby Member States may freely (i.e., without following any specific procedure) introduce restrictions on the free movement of services, provided they are non-discriminatory, necessary and proportionate to some justified objective. Any attempt to conscribe the protectionist intent nurtured by such a general derogation clause will be curtailed by the lack of a prior notification system of restrictive measures.[113]

5.1.4 Consumer protection: service providers' liability

One of the main grounds invoked by Member States in order to restrict the free provision of services is consumer protection. In this respect, EU law is somewhat deficient. A Commission initiative to institute a common system of service providers' liability has not prospered,[114] although it stopped short of establishing a system of objective liability (as is the case for producer liability[115]) and provided only for a reversal of the onus of proof.

The Services Directive is not much more helpful. Compulsory information to be provided to service recipients (Article 22), mutual assistance between national authorities (Articles 28–31) and the alert mechanism (Article 32) do offer some assurance to consumers, but only

[113] For which see notes 20–24 above and the corresponding text.

[114] COM(1992) 482.

[115] Directive 85/374/EC on the approximation of the laws, regulations and administrative provisions of the Member States concerning liability for defective products, OJ 1985 L210/29.

in an indirect way. On the other hand, the only provision which explicitly deals with 'professional liability insurance and guarantees' relegates the issue to one for each individual Member State. Indicative of the impossibility to agree on common rules concerning providers' liability is the draft Directive on patients' rights.[116] Despite liability for medical malpractice being of paramount importance for patient mobility, and notwithstanding the fact that patients are particularly vulnerable 'consumers' (because of their medical condition and because of information asymmetries), the Directive foresees only that healthcare services are 'provided according to the legislation of the Member State of treatment': a compromise solution seriously compromising patient protection.

Therefore, breaking common ground concerning providers' liability could be a means to increase mutual trust between Member States (and their service recipients) and push further the application of mutual recognition.

5.2 *Measures to facilitate mutual recognition*

5.2.1 General Systems of mutual recognition

In the field of professional qualifications, the General Systems of mutual recognition have taken over the previous system of sector-specific rules.[117] Instead of harmonizing the conditions leading to each individual profession, the General Systems only harmonize the conditions for and the kinds of, compensatory measures available to the host State. The implementation of these General Systems has been a success story. The Court has consistently interpreted their terms broadly,[118] and has covered all cases which do not come within their scope by interpreting Articles 45, 49 and 56 TFEU in a way parallel to the Directives. In

[116] Directive 2011/42/EU, OJ 2011 L88/45.

[117] Council Directive 89/48/EEC of 21 December 1988 on a general system for the recognition of higher-education diplomas awarded on completion of professional education and training of at least three years' duration, OJ 1989 L19/16; Council Directive 92/51/EEC of 18 June 1992 on a second general system for the recognition of professional education and training to supplement Directive 89/48/EEC, OJ 1992 L209/25, modified several times; both these Directives have now been repealed and replaced by Directive 2005/36/EC of the European Parliament and of the Council of 7 September 2005 on the recognition of professional qualifications, OJ 2005 L255/22.

[118] See notes 93–99 above and the corresponding text.

Directive 2005/36, the EU legislature has thought appropriate to codify the General Systems and to expand their scope.

It may be that issues other than professional qualifications, such as for example, the issuance of authorizations or the entry into registers could also be the subject of some kind of a General System of mutual recognition.

5.2.2 Standardization: certification

Taking the previous point further, the role of standardization and certification in the field of services should be reviewed. The reasons which explain that this aspect of the service economy remains under-developed are fading. For one thing, it is only in these last twenty years that the service economy has been systematically studied and that the provision and trade in services has been scrutinized from an economic, legal, political and governance point of view.[119] Second, the development of new services, the massively increased demand and the possibility to provide many of them online increasingly allow for the 'banalization' and, therefore, the standardization of services. Such a standardization becomes all the more important for consumer protection since, today, it is on services that consumers spend most of their money. Moreover, the impact on services of the standards concerning the production, commercialization and use of goods should not be underestimated.[120]

Under these circumstances, the current lack of standards in the field of services should be seen as temporary. In the months and years to come it is to be expected that the EU standardization bodies will become more active in this field. Such a development is also underpinned by Article 26 (5) of the Services Directive, which foresees that 'Member States, in cooperation with the Commission, shall encourage the development of voluntary European standards'.

5.2.3 Administrative cooperation: networking

Mutual recognition depends largely on good faith and cooperation between national authorities.[121] The very term 'mutual' in a sense stresses the pro-active stance that national authorities should adopt.

[119] For an overview of the relevant literature, see Rubalcaba, note 16 above.

[120] See, e.g., Case C-267/03, *Lindberg* [2005] ECR I-3245: a 'technical rule' concerning the use of electronic betting machines had a direct impact on the provision of betting services.

[121] See notes 74–82 above and the corresponding text.

Administrative cooperation affects mutual recognition at, at least, three levels. (1) At a *psychological* level, administrative cooperation allows national authorities to get to know one another, both at the personal and at the operational levels, and to develop trust. (2) At a *practical* level, administrative cooperation allows agencies to get acquainted with each other's practices, techniques, documentation etc. (3) At an operational level, administrative cooperation makes it possible for national authorities to work closer together and resolve administrative deadlocks as they arise, and problems linked with the transborder nature of the legal situations with which they are faced.

To this end, the creation of points of contact and the establishment of networks are appropriate means. Hence, for example, the General Systems on the recognition of professional qualifications, as well as the e-signature Directive, foresee the establishment of national points of contact. Similarly, the network industries Directives provide for the networking of the different national regulatory authorities.[122]

It is, however, the Services Directive which is the most innovative text in this respect. It is, indeed, submitted that, after the abandonment of the country-of-origin principle, the Services Directive is not so much about direct services liberalization, but is rather a text – in fact the *first* EU text – aimed at regulatory reform at the Member State level.

Chapter VI of the Directive, on 'administrative cooperation', contains nine (out of a total of forty-five) provisions of the Directive. It is true that these provisions would have had more importance if the country-of-origin principle were still in place. Even after the abandonment of the country-of-origin principle, however, these provisions, together with the rules on administrative simplification (Chapter II of the Directive) do create their own dynamics.

Hence, the creation of one or more 'liaison points' in every Member State, responsible for the exchange of information between national authorities, will certainly help the application of the Directive (Article 28). In addition, a 'European network of Member States' authorities' will run an alert mechanism whenever it 'becomes aware of serious specific acts or circumstances relating to a service activity that could cause serious damage to the health or safety of persons or to the environment' (Article 32). An electronic system for the exchange of information

[122] See D. Geradin and N. Petit, 'The Development of Agencies at EU and National Levels: Conceptual Analysis and Proposals for Reform', *Yearbook of European Law* 23 (2004) 137–97.

(Article 34(1)) and some rules on the respective competences of the home and host States complete the rules on cooperation.

The creation of liaison points alongside the European network responsible for the alert mechanism will increase the flows of information exchange. This, in turn, will allow detailed comparisons to take place and will put national authorities under pressure to revise their unsatisfactory practices. This trend will be further reinforced by the obligation of self-evaluation of a long series of requirements and by periodic reporting and peer monitoring.

The detailed division of competences between national authorities (Articles 28–31), combined with the broad duty of cooperation stemming directly from Article 4(3) TEU,[123] will put national administrative authorities under strain: a mere effort to work together will not be enough: positive results in favour of the European citizen will be required. This, in turn, will prompt national administrations to find solutions which are commonly acceptable.

The use of unified documents (Article 5(2)) – if it materializes – will inevitably lead to a convergence of the conditions for their issuance and review, and more generally to a cross-fertilization between administrative cultures.

More importantly, the creation of points of single contact (Article 6) and the electronic filing of documents (Article 8) is set to change fundamentally the administrative structures – and possibly the very political configuration – of Member States. Public officials, being the mouth and hands of the State, exercise power over citizens: they can reject, seek further information, make observations, impose conditions and, occasionally, ask for bribes.[124] As soon as this 'vertical' relation gives way to a 'horizontal' one between officials of different administrations (i.e., between those serving in the points of single contact and those

[123] See, e.g., Case C-326/00, *IKA* v. *Ioannidis* [2003] ECR I-1703; and, for a thorough presentation of this case, the comment by the present author in *Common Market Law Review* (2003) 1251–1268; also Case C-476/01, *Kapper* [2004] ECR I-5205; Case C-215/03, *Oulane* [2005] ECR I-1215; for this general trend in the Court's case law, see V. Hatzopoulos, 'Assessing the Services Directive, 2006/123/EC', *Cambridge Yearbook of European Legal Studies* 10 (2008) 215–61, § 1.3.2.

[124] The 'visual' of a public official looking down, from behind his desk, with disdain over a sweaty citizen trying to get their case through, was presented in a very lively way by G. Davies, in the Conference on 'Services Liberalisation in the EU and the WTO', organized by the Europainstitut, Jean Monnet Center of Excellence, Economic University of Wien, Vienna, 5–6 March 2009.

competent for the delivery of the necessary authorizations and documents), the power relation is transformed into a mere bureaucratic one: what was the basis of power becomes the source of burden. By the same token, officials, faced with the difficulty and/or absurdity of administrative requirements and procedures, get a clear idea of how simplification may be achieved; in this way, simplification ceases to be an external and abstract requirement preached by 'good governance' officials and becomes an internal commodity having specific content. Therefore, there is a double incentive – both psychological and practical – for administrative simplification. Administrative simplification, in turn, reduces the need (or increases the scope) for mutual recognition.

5.2.4 Exchange of information and of best practices

In addition to the previous point, the system of periodic reporting and peer review offers a triple positive effect. First, national authorities are made to question their own practices in order to justify them to their peers. Second, the peers become familiar both with the measures and with the underlying organizational logic of other Member States' administrations. Therefore, when it comes to comparing their own system with those of their peers – in the process of applying mutual recognition – national authorities have all the necessary data. Third, in the absence of commonly agreed standards, the exchange of best practices which takes place in this framework may be highly beneficial.

5.2.5 Dispute resolution: SOLVIT and the Services Directive

A final point on how to make mutual recognition more efficient is related to dispute resolution. This problem has two interconnected aspects. The first aspect is that of disputes between the service provider and the authorities of the host (or, occasionally, home) State. In this respect, it has been observed, in relation to the case in *Bobadilla*, that a waiting time of twenty-five months for the preliminary ruling alone, plus the delay of the national judicial procedure, in order to achieve the recognition of her diploma in her own country, is not the benchmark of a properly working Internal Market.[125] It is not uncommon, in fact,

[125] I. V. Atanasiu, 'Some Reflections on the Role of the Court in Relation to "Social Europe"' in J. Baquero Cruz and C. Closa Montero (eds.), *European Integration from Rome to Berlin: 1957–2007, History, Law and Politics* (Brussels etc.: PIE-Peter Lang, 2009), pp. 173–84, p. 182.

for Member States, through protracted litigation, to attempt to delay implementation.

The second aspect of dispute resolution concerns disputes between service providers and their recipients. In this respect, four developments should be underlined. First, Regulation 44/2001 ('Brussels I') on jurisdiction[126] provides as the first criterion for special jurisdiction (i.e., other than the defendant's country of residence) 'the place of the performance of the obligation in question', which, in the case of services, is where 'the services were provided or should have been provided' (Article 5). This criterion, however, makes little sense for services provided at a distance (GATS mode 1), as well as for those where both the provider and the recipient move together to a third State (e.g., the tourist guide cases). It would, therefore, be useful to clarify (by means of soft law?) the way in which the Regulation should apply in the various situations of service provision falling under Article 56 TFEU.

Second, we are currently going through a phase of effervescence in the area of the rules applicable and of the execution of judgments in transborder situations. The adoption of the 'Rome I' Regulation on jurisdiction in contractual disputes,[127] on the one hand, and of the 'small claims' and 'European injunction',[128] on the other, should assist the resolution of transborder disputes.

Third, Article 27 of the Services Directive requires service providers to supply their contact details, to respond to complaints in the shortest possible time and 'to make their best efforts to find a satisfactory solution'.

Last but not least, the SOLVIT system, put into place by the Commission as a means of extra-judicial settlement of disputes relating to the Internal Market, occupies an increasingly important role.[129] This system consists of a network of online dispute resolution available both to undertakings and to consumers. The 'plaintiffs' contact the SOLVIT point of contact in their country. If the complaint is within the 'tasks' of the SOLVIT network, this contact point registers it within an electronic

[126] Council Regulation (EC) No. 44/2001 on jurisdiction and the recognition and enforcement of judgments in civil and commercial matters, OJ 2001 L16/1.

[127] Regulation (EC) No. 593/2008 on the law applicable to contractual obligations (Rome I), OJ 2008 L177/6.

[128] Regulation (EC) No. 861/2007 establishing a European Small Claims Procedure, OJ 2007 L199/1; Regulation (EC) No. 1896/2006 creating a European order for payment procedure, OJ 2006 L399/1.

[129] COM(2001) 702 final.

database and contacts the SOLVIT point in the Member State where the problem has occurred. The latter SOLVIT point, together with the authorities of the State concerned, tries to resolve the problem. This system, after a hesitant start, has gained increasingly in credibility, and the number of disputes settled increases year by year.[130] There are, however, two limitations to SOLVIT's potential. For one thing, it has limited competence *ratione materiae*.[131] Moreover, SOLVIT may mediate only between an individual and a State authority, not between two individuals.

6. Conclusion

Back in 1997, I identified five factors affecting the evolution of the principle of mutual recognition in services: (a) the 'proceduralization' of European governance and the increased recourse to soft law; (b) enlargement; (c) the impact of WTO law and the GATS; (d) technological evolution; and (e) globalization.[132] Of these, the last three are still as unpredictable as they were fifteen years ago. The major enlargements are over and their impact on EU institutions will be mastered, now that the Lisbon Treaty has entered into force. What has fundamentally changed in the last fifteen years is the very first factor, i.e., the regulatory culture of the EU and the experimentation with new modes of governance.[133] Hereafter, mutual recognition is no more situated on the 'soft' side of the various EU regulatory techniques. On the contrary, mutual recognition, especially in its managed form, stands out as the most far-reaching regulatory technique for the completion of the Internal Market. Its main advantage lies in the fact that, depending on (a) the level at which it operates (documents, measures, policies, regulatory objectives) and (b) the legal instruments chosen (Regulations,

[130] See the annual SOLVIT report at http://ec.europa.eu/solvit/site/docs/solvit2008_report_en.pdf.

[131] Recognition of professional qualifications and diplomas; access to education; residence permits; voting rights; social security; employment rights; driving licences; motor vehicle registration; border controls; market access for products; market access for services; establishment as self-employed; public procurement; taxation; and free movement of capital or payments.

[132] Hatzopoulos, note 25 above, pp. 476–7.

[133] See, among many, the excellent contributions in G. de Búrca and J. Scott, *Law and New Governance in the EU and the US* (Oxford and Portland, OR: Hart, 2006); see also the special issue of *Columbia Journal of European Law* 13(3) (2007).

Directives, standards, common documents etc.), it can be as binding and/or flexible as the case requires. Compared to the 'new modes of governance', such as the Open Method of Coordination (OMC), however, mutual recognition offers increased visibility and greater transparency.[134] Therefore, it would not be an exaggeration to say that mutual recognition is a *passage obligé* towards service liberalization.

[134] For a critique of the OMC, see V. Hatzopoulos, 'Why the Open Method of Coordination Is Bad for You: A Letter to the EU', *European Law Journal* 13 (2007) 259–92.

3

Trust and mutual recognition in the Services Directive

GARETH DAVIES

1. Introduction

To portray mutual recognition between States and central legislation only as alternatives is to give an overly static picture of their role and effects. In any realistic attempt at market-making they are intertwined and interdependent, and the concept of trust plays an important role in explaining the relation between them. In particular, whereas mutual recognition is usually said to require trust as a precondition, harmonizing legislation has trust as its effect, and sometimes its goal.[1] Yet this observation immediately shows how central legislation may in fact serve to create the conditions for decentralized mutual recognition, provided that post-legislative discretionary space remains.

Nicolaïdis suggests that an important way in which legislation creates trust and promotes mutual recognition is by creating mechanisms of 'mutual monitoring' and 'reciprocal spying' which prevent States from 'cheating'.[2] The core insight is that, where States have knowledge of each other's rules and practices, they are inhibited from adopting regulation that deviates too far from accepted norms or that fundamentally undermines the interests of their partners.[3] To do so would risk these partners calling into question the fundamentals of the mutual recognition system, and threatening precisely the trading profits that the State is

[1] This formulation is taken from the presentation by Professor R. Bachmann at the *Modern Law Review* workshop on The Regulation of Trade in Services: 'Trust, Distrust and Economic Integration', held in London and Cambridge in June 2009. I am grateful to the participants in this workshop for discussion and comments.

[2] K. Nicolaïdis, 'Trusting the Poles? Creating European through Mutual Recognition', *Journal of European Public Policy* 14(5) (2007) 682–98, p. 683.

[3] *Ibid.*

trying to win. Incomplete harmonization, focusing on coordination and transparency, may therefore serve to facilitate and stabilize mutual recognition.

Kerber and Van den Bergh, among others, have described the other side of the coin, how mutual recognition promotes harmonization.[4] They take the view that mutual recognition, which creates instability, is a dynamic principle one of whose major functions is to provoke the vertical reallocation of powers. They point out that mutual recognition confronts jurisdictions with each other's rules, revealing and contrasting the differences. Stable mutual recognition may emerge if the differences are unimportant. However, it is just as likely, perhaps more likely in the current state of European integration, that this confrontation will serve to highlight the need for future substantive harmonization. In other words, the extent to which States can tolerate each other's regulation is not always clear until they try, and trying may be exactly what persuades them that harmonization is a preferable alternative to tolerance.[5] The resulting harmonization may be substantive, but it may also have communicative elements, aimed at increasing knowledge of each other's rules, moving from what Nicolaïdis calls 'blind trust' to what she calls 'binding trust'.[6] The resulting mutual recognition may then be stretched by entrepreneurial States or economic actors until it reaches the limits of the newly established trust, leading to new calls for legislative intervention, so that, as she puts it, 'a new cycle then begins'.[7]

Into this context of an unstable and dynamic relationship between mutual recognition and harmonizing legislation, between the legislator and the courts, this chapter offers the Services Directive as an example of the above ideas at work. It suggests that the Directive is not of great substantive import, but is primarily a communicative measure, which in turn may make the substantive rules on free movement of services – which are greatly composed of mutual recognition – effective.

[4] W. Kerber and R. van den Bergh, 'Mutual Recognition Revisited: Misunderstandings, Inconsistencies and a Suggested Reinterpretation', *Kyklos* 61 (2008) 447–65; G. Davies, 'Is Mutual Recognition an Alternative to Harmonisation? Lessons in Tolerance and Trade from the European Union for the WTO and Other RTAs' in F. Ortino and L. Bartels (eds.), *Regional Trade Agreements and the WTO* (Oxford University Press, 2006), pp. 265–80.

[5] G. Davies, 'Is Mutual Recognition an Alternative to Harmonisation? Lessons in Tolerance and Trade from the European Union for the WTO and other RTAs', above.

[6] Nicolaïdis, above, p. 683. [7] *Ibid.*

2. The Services Directive

The Services Directive has been presented as an attempt to create a single market for services by laying down clear and far-reaching rules on free movement.[8] These are intended to create sufficient rights for providers, and to impose sufficient constraints on public authorities, so that free movement will become a reality. Given that the continued existence of diverse national standards and regulatory approaches within a single market can create problems of competition and consumer protection, the Directive also contains feedback mechanisms aiming to provide a basis for future harmonization to deal with these problems. The Directive thus appears to envisage a sequential process that can be briefly summarized as: (1) create the market; (2) analyze the problems created; and (3) take the necessary compensating measures.

It is argued here that this is not an adequate description of how the Directive will work. The primary problem of the Internal Market is not an absence of far-reaching free movement rules. These exist already as a result of the Treaties and the jurisprudence of the Court. Rather, the lack of free movement in practice results from a lack of motivation on the part of the States to implement these rules, a considerable room for discretion which allows States *de facto* to restrict such implementation, and an absence of any Union-level measures addressing these problems of enforcement and implementation. The rules already exist, but there is sufficient room for States to hinder their effective use, and this they do.

The Directive does not address these enforcement and implementation issues and does not take the substantive rules on free movement much further than the current position. The Directive will therefore not be sufficient to directly create a single market. Its contribution to the substantive right of free movement is relatively slight.

Instead, the Directive does something else. It provides for increased transparency in many ways, and for increased communication between national authorities in different States. This may help to create trust between national authorities, and can be more specifically analyzed using the theories of oligopoly and of regulatory competition. The limited number of States involved in the Internal Market suggests that the Directive may encourage regulatory collusion. States may voluntarily converge towards consensual standards and regulatory approaches that

[8] Directive 2006/123/EC of the European Parliament and of the Council on services in the Internal Market, OJ 2006 L376/76.

protect each State against regulatory pressure from migrant businesses, their customers in the market for regulation.

It remains to be seen whether this is beneficial or not. In general, collusion enabling providers to act independently of customers is not to be welcomed, but, where those providers are of laws and enjoy democratic legitimacy, whereas the customers – mobile businesses – do not, cooperation between national authorities may be a desirable counter-balance to the risks of migration-fuelled regulatory competition. Moreover, the resulting trust may lead to an increase in free movement, as States apply free movement rules more leniently and cooperatively to partner States with which they have reached a regulatory understanding.

In any case, oligopoly theory suggests that the Services Directive should be viewed in a slightly different light from the usual one in which it is presented. It appears to have a reflexive character, and to create a mechanism for convergence of rules which is unusual in being consensual, variable and dynamic, and entirely decentralized, and in which the Commission is potentially marginalized. The Services Directive may also turn out to be effective at creating an Internal Market, but via the creation of trust and understanding between States, rather than via the toughness of its rules on free movement.

The following sections of this chapter elaborate on this. In turn, they consider (i) the problems which a legal attempt to create a single market for services has to address (section 3); (ii) whether the Directive provides an effective free movement regime (section 4); and (iii) whether its communication and information provisions will contribute to voluntary convergence, and to inter-State trust and acceptance, and thereby indirectly lead to a working single market (section 5).

3. The problems of the Single Market for services

Insofar as the absence of a working Single Market for services can be attributed to legal failure, that failure can be most plausibly located in one or both of two places. On the one hand, it is arguable that the rights of free movement on which the market is based are insufficiently clear or far-reaching; they do not sufficiently constitute the market. On the other hand, whether or not those rules are in principle adequate, it is arguable that States do not implement or comply with them with enough enthusiasm or good faith, and the rules are not sufficiently enforceable to overcome the obstacles that this lack of national goodwill creates. The problems can thus be divided into those of substance, and those of enforcement and implementation.

Sustaining both of these problems is a deeper, non-legal one, which may be called the problem of trust. States are not motivated to fully apply free movement rules, because they do not have faith that this is in their own interests, for a number of reasons. They exploit the defects of the law because they can, and because they want to. This is something that requires attention in itself.

3.1 Inadequacies in the substantive rules

Under the current interpretation of the Treaty, the application of any national measure which might tend to make the cross-border provision of services or establishment less attractive, or which might hinder it in any way, is in principle prohibited unless the State in question can show that the application is necessary to achieve a justified goal, and is proportionate.[9] A body of case law makes clear that proportionality is to be interpreted in a free-movement-friendly way, and the Court subjects national measures to strict, even sceptical, scrutiny.[10] In the course of interpreting proportionality, the Court has laid down a number of rules to this effect. For example, national rules must not attempt to duplicate requirements contained in home State laws,[11] administrative requirements on service providers must be cheap and simple, and completion may not be a prerequisite for starting work,[12] and the consumer must be treated as reasonably self-sufficient, so that the imposition of paternalistic standards will not be permitted.[13]

In substance, these comprise a far-reaching market manifesto, and full compliance would result in a market in which movement between States was hardly more difficult than internal movement. In fact, this is a formulation that the Court has on occasion used; application of rules making cross-border movement more difficult than domestic movement is prohibited.[14]

9 Case C-55/94, *Gebhard* [1995] ECR I-4165; Case C-76/90, *Säger and Dennemeyer* [1991] ECR I-4221.

10 S. Weatherill, 'Protecting the Consumer Interest in an Integrated Services Market', Mitchell Working Paper 1/2007, available at www.law.ed.ac.uk/file_download/series/23_promotingtheconsumerinterestinanintegratedservicesmarket.pdf, p. 2 (last visited 26 September 2010).

11 Case 279/80, *Webb* [1981] ECR 3305.

12 Case C-58/98, *Corsten* [2000] ECR I-1919.

13 Case 120/78, *Cassis de Dijon* [1979] ECR 649; S. Weatherill, *EU Consumer Law and Policy* (Cheltenham: Edward Elgar, 2005).

14 E.g., Case C-422/01, *Skandia* [2003] ECR I-6817; Case C-281/06, *Jundt* [2007] ECR I-12231.

There is the market then; *voilà*! If compliance could be assumed, the market would exist already.

However, a practical problem with the substantive law is its high degree of abstraction. What is 'justified' and 'proportionate' is open to argument, and, while a distinct philosophy emerges from the case law of the Court, this is less accessible and forceful than explicit and specific rules would be.[15] Moreover, the Court links its decisions to the individual facts of the case before it, meaning that it is always open for a Member State to argue that the facts in a subsequent case justify drawing the line in a different place.[16] Necessity, justification and proportionality remain negotiated, ambiguous and open-textured concepts.

Moreover, the status of judicial interpretations as law is not self-evident in all Member States. The degree to which the Court's pronouncements should be abstracted and treated as generally binding interpretations of the Treaty – even if expressed as such – is not settled decisively as a matter of doctrine.[17] Nor, as a matter of practice, can judicial statements be expected to have the same general impact on regulatory authorities as a written law would have.

To the EU specialist, the substantive law is therefore remarkably complete and powerful. The 'right' interpretation – that the Court would give in a case – is not too difficult to predict, and it allocates free movers a high degree of protection against national regulatory hindrance. However, that law is not formulated in a way that will have maximum practical impact on the authorities required to apply it, and so does not fulfil its own potential.

3.2 The problems of implementation and enforcement

If States simply snub their noses at the law, then one might speak of legal delinquency, and the solution would not necessarily lie in better rules but in enforcement mechanisms. However, there are ways of resisting full application that fall short of such outright legal rebellion.[18] Primarily, in

[15] See Weatherill, 'Protecting the Consumer Interest in an Integrated Services Market', above, pp. 12–15.

[16] *Ibid.*

[17] G. Davies, 'Abstractness and Concreteness in the Preliminary Reference Procedure' in N. Nic Shuibhne (ed.), *Regulating the Internal Market* (Cheltenham: Edward Elgar, 2006), pp. 233–6 (also available as 'The Division of Powers between the European Court of Justice and National Courts' on ssrn.com).

[18] See generally F. Snyder, 'The Effectiveness of European Community Law: Institutions, Processes, Tools and Techniques', *Modern Law Review* 56(1) (1993) 19–54.

the context of the Internal Market, States may take a stance on the ambiguous concepts of necessity, justification and proportionality that is favourable to national interests or the regulatory *status quo*, and relatively unfavourable to free movement. By doing so, they can effectively block free movement by continuing to apply restrictive national rules, claiming that these are genuinely necessary and justified.

The State might lose if the matter is appealed all the way to the Court, but this is barely relevant in practice. First, commercial reality entails that service providers do not have years to spare for a protracted legal fight. Thus, in practice, the initial position of a State on the legitimacy of its national laws is the one that the service provider will generally have to live with. The theoretical possibility of legal challenge, particularly given the speed of most legal systems, not to mention cost, is not a viable basis for a working free movement regime. Second, even if legal challenge does result in a rejection of the State's regulatory provision and a vindication of free movement, the State is still able to treat the judgment as restricted to the facts, and to continue its restrictive behaviour in other spheres.

Member States are therefore able to exploit the lack of clarity of the law to claim that particular restrictive measures are in fact necessary and proportionate. Debunking such conservative readings of the law requires engagement with the nuances of EU law, which in reality entails an impractical level of litigation. The ambiguity of free movement law is therefore widely seen as a major reason for its limited effectiveness in practice.[19]

EU law does not address these enforcement problems. It does require that judicial protection of EU rights be 'effective', and the Court – and the Directive – have laid down some further requirements,[20] but the standards resulting do not require a legal process sufficiently speedy and accessible to meet the demands of commercial reality for small to

[19] Weatherill, 'Protecting the Consumer Interest in an Integrated Services Market', above, pp. 12–15; J. Pelkmans, 'Deepening Services Market Integration – A Critical Assessment', *Romanian Journal of European Affairs* 7(4) (2007) 5–32, section 4.2 (also available on ssrn.com); B. De Witte, 'Setting the Scene: How Did Services Get to Bolkestein and Why?', Mitchell Working Paper 3/2007, available at www.law.ed.ac.uk/file_download/series/28_settingthescenehowdidservicesgettobolkesteinandwhy.pdf, pp. 6–7 (last visited 26 September 2010).

[20] See S. Prechal, 'Free Movement and Procedural Requirements: Proportionality Reconsidered', *Legal Issues of Economic Integration* 35 (2008) 201–16; C. Barnard, 'Unravelling the Services Directive', *Common Market Law Review* 45 (2008) 323–94, pp. 354–6.

medium-sized service providers. Nor could this be so; it would amount to a revolution in domestic legal systems.

Most importantly, nothing in EU law makes it wrongful for a State to consistently take a conservative approach to the interpretative space that the law offers. The fact that time after time States take positions that EU law specialists consider highly unlikely to survive the scrutiny of the Court does not in itself amount to a violation of EU law, nor does it attract punishment or criticism from the Court or the Commission. Each case is decided on its merits, and the fact that a State has fought and lost analytically similar cases in the past is not relevant to the outcome, nor even to a claim for damages, unless those cases are so similar as to be identical – which, given the open texture of the law, is always arguably not the case.[21] The sanction for a wrongful standpoint is generally no more than being required to change that particular standpoint if the case is ultimately litigated and lost.

The fact that a State consistently takes losing legal positions on free movement is therefore merely part of the legal game. This is probably inevitable. The same applies to appeals within a domestic legal system; the fact that a judgment is overturned on appeal, or even that a court finds its judgments often overturned on appeal to the extent that it attracts a reputation as particularly conservative or radical or whatever, does not render that court or its judgments illegitimate or subject to sanctions. Respect for judicial independence is too high to permit this. A similar logic may be applied to national regulatory authorities. Moreover, the problem is not just with such authorities. National judges tend to defer to governmental assessments of necessity and proportionality,[22] and, once again, the mere fact of being consistently wrong does not attract sanctions.

Given the room which the open-textured nature of free movement law leaves for interpretation there is therefore nothing in EU law to prevent national authorities and courts from consistently taking conservative and free-movement-unfriendly positions with respect to the application of national rules. They are in principle obliged to follow the Court's interpretations, but are neither sanctioned nor prevented if they interpret autonomously and divergently. *De facto*, EU law does not guarantee free movement rights.

[21] Case C-224/01, *Köbler* [2003] ECR I-10239; Cases C-46 and 48/93, *Brasserie du Pecheur* [1996] ECR I-1029; Case C-129/00, *Commission* v. *Italy* [2003] ECR I-14637.

[22] M. Jarvis, *Application of EC Law by National Courts: Free Movement of Goods* (Oxford: Clarendon Press, 1998), pp. 220–1.

3.3 *The problem of trust*

Although the law leaves room for States to resist free movement, this does not necessarily mean that they will choose to do so. However, the fact that a Single Market for services is not considered to exist suggests that to a considerable extent such resistance does occur.

This situation may be described by saying that States and national authorities clearly exercise their interpretative discretion in a way that favours national interests more, and free movement less, than EU law would prefer. There is obviously a perception in Member States that maximizing free movement by seeking to minimize the obstacles caused by national regulation is not in fact in the national interest or in the interest of the regulatory authority in question and/or its direct clients.

The most obvious basis for this view is the perception that other States do not regulate adequately, or as well as the host State, so that admitting foreign service providers without subjecting them to the full range of national regulatory demands undermines quality on the local market to the detriment of local consumers. This perception is not likely to be based on a deep knowledge of foreign rules or inadequacies, but is the result of a precautionary approach which in turn is probably based partly on a presumption of local superiority, and partly on the natural inertia and suspicion of non-conformity that one may attribute to institutions generally.

However, it is suggested that this concern for consumers is not likely to be the major motivation for restricting market access. Consumer protection is often a repackaging of concerns about unfair competition, and in these cases the primary objection to exemption from local rules for foreign economic actors is the perception that this is unfair.[23] This is partly based on the substantive argument that through exemption they gain a market advantage over domestic competitors, by being subject to a lesser regulatory burden, and partly based on the formal view that all should be treated identically, a view which has strong European roots and has considerable legal and philosophical capital in the Member States.[24] There is a resistance to the argument that, because some actors

[23] E.g., Case C-384/93, *Alpine Investments* [1995] ECR I-1141; Case C-134/04, *Commission* v. *Italy* [2007] ECR I-6251; Cases C-94/04 and 202/04, *Cipolla and Others* [2006] ECR I-11421.

[24] See E. T. Beller, 'The Headscarf Affair: The Conseil d'Etat on the Role of Religion and Culture in French Society', *Texas International Law Journal* 39 (2004) 581–623; T. J. Gunn, 'Religious Freedom and Laïcité: A Comparison of the United States and France', *Brigham Young University Law Review* (2004) 419–506; M. Mahlmann, 'Religious Tolerance, Pluralist Society and the Neutrality of the State: The Federal

are different, they deserve to be treated differently. In this case, that argument would suggest that those subject to the regulation of their home State consequently deserve to have a different status under the regulation of the host State, but the concept of exemptions for difference is resisted on far more general and philosophical grounds, linked to matters such as the unity of the State and the blindness of public authority to categories of citizens.[25]

Less philosophically and more practically, national authorities may resist free movement out of concerns about where it will take them. The idea of special legal treatment for foreign-based providers entails a form of regulatory competition which is highly contested, and in fact probably rejected by most members of the European political class and the European public.[26] It raises the spectre of the race to the bottom, and States may resist free market access because they fear that if they are too open they will (a) encourage domestic firms to relocate abroad to low-regulation States, and (b) be participating in a game which will lead to a spiralling down of regulatory standards, not only harming national interests but also reducing national control over the quality of national markets.[27] Regulatory competition is a significant threat to the substantive regulatory autonomy of States, and it is hardly surprising therefore that they seek to resist forms of free movement which entail this.[28] Indeed, one of the issues which the law of the Internal Market has failed to address adequately is the fact that regulatory authorities often do not in fact appear to accept the fundamental principles upon which the Internal Market is based, namely, that economic actors should be able to operate throughout the EU while only being subject to a single regulatory jurisdiction. By contrast, both governments and the public are probably more sympathetic to a 'when in Rome, do as Romans do' rule: if you want to do business in X, comply with its rules.[29] The justice of this is certainly easier to explain and to grasp.

Constitutional Court's Decision in the Headscarf Case', *German Law Journal* 4(11) (2003) 1099–1116.

25 *Ibid.*

26 See De Witte, 'Setting the Scene: How Did Services Get to Bolkestein and Why?', above, pp. 9–10.

27 See J.-M. Sun and J. Pelkmans, 'Regulatory Competition in the Single Market', *Journal of Common Market Studies* 33 (1995) 67–89.

28 See F. Scharpf, 'Economic Integration, Democracy and the Welfare State', *Journal of European Public Policy* 4 (1997) 18–36.

29 K. Nicolaïdis and G. Schaffer, 'Transnational Mutual Recognition Schemes: Governance without Global Government', *Law and Contemporary Problems* 68 (2005) 263–317.

Finally, there is the issue of reciprocity. While economists may suggest that it is beneficial to open one's markets even if partner States do not do the same, this view does not attract much political support. Given the weaknesses of the law, open markets are not beyond question, and it may be assumed that States fear that if they are too obedient to EU law for their own good they will be in the position of having their domestic markets 'plundered' by foreign providers while their own providers will be unable to gain access to markets abroad. This is a situation which could be analyzed in game theoretical terms. Even if States believe in open markets generally, given that they also believe in reciprocity they are unlikely to make the first move unless they have some mechanism for protecting themselves against misuse of this generosity by their neighbours. This protection could lie in the possibility to re-close markets, but a sense of protection could also arise from a mechanism for creating trust between authorities in different States.

The problems may be summarized by saying that there is a lack of trust in foreign standards, and a lack of faith in the concepts underlying the EU market regime and in that regime as a whole.[30] States do not appear to feel confident that opening their markets to non-compliant service providers from other jurisdictions will not lead to serious local economic and social harm, largely because they fear that other jurisdictions do, or will, adopt low standards, and that they will be caught in the pincer between the need to prevent businesses leaving the country, and the desire to regulate in accordance with local preferences.

3.4 *Ways of addressing the legal problems*

Measures to increase the effectiveness of free movement law might take one of a number of forms. The most obvious would be to reduce the ambiguity which enables national resistance. This could be done by legislation spelling out the content of free movement law in a more precise and specific way. It could also be done by giving a procedural content to the assessment of necessity, justification and proportionality.[31] Providing lists of relevant factors and guidelines for their use would constrain national authorities and result in less deviation from the Court's preferred interpretative approach.

[30] See K. Nicolaïdis, 'Trusting the Poles? Constituting Europe through Mutual Recognition', *Journal of European Public Policy* 15(5) (2007) 682–98.

[31] See Davies, 'Abstractness and Concreteness in the Preliminary Reference Procedure', above, p. 232.

Another way of increasing effectiveness would be for EU law to directly address the procedural problems of enforcement – for example requiring extra-speedy judicial processes or appeals, or imposing a presumption of free movement rights while a case is pending. This approach is unlikely to be followed because of the degree to which it imposes on national legal systems and domestic procedure.

A third way is to address the issues of trust and motivation, to create a situation in which States perceive opening their markets to foreign service providers to be in their own interests, or to raise no or limited conflicts with other interests.

The following two sections of this chapter consider the extent to which the Services Directive offers any solutions such as these.

4. The Services Directive as a regime for free movement and regulatory competition

The Directive is presented as legislation promoting free movement by enacting free movement rights. This view is unsatisfying for three reasons. First, the Directive barely changes the existing law. Second, its limited scope means that, even if it is implemented in good faith, it does not address a sufficient range of issues to be properly market-opening. Third, there is little reason to think that its rights will be more concrete than those of the Treaty, since there is a continued avoidance of enforcement and implementation issues. It is true that the fact of setting rights out in legislation may encourage a fuller adoption of them than would be the case if they remained products of case law, but given the limitations of the substance of the Directive this is not enough to rebut the conclusion that the Directive does not provide sufficient or even particularly significant legal support for free movement.

4.1 Does the Directive take the law any further?

The chapter of the Directive on freedom of establishment is in substance an enactment of the Court's interpretation of Article 49 TFEU.[32] It

[32] There is a consensus on this. See, e.g., Weatherill, 'Protecting the Consumer Interest in an Integrated Services Market', above; Barnard, 'Unravelling the Services Directive', above; S. Griller 'The Services Directive: Two Steps Forward, How Many Back' in F. Breuss, G. Fink and S. Griller, *Services Liberalisation in the Internal Market* (Vienna: Springer, 2008), p. 225.

requires, as does the Treaty, in the view of the Court, that measures restricting access to the provision of a service as an established person must be justified by the pursuit of a legitimate interest, necessary for this, and proportionate. The chapter sets out lists of examples of measures which would be prohibited and which should be regarded with suspicion, but there is nothing in these lists which would surprise a lawyer.[33] The prohibited measures are ones that have long been prohibited as a result of judgments of the Court. The doubtful ones are to be assessed in light of the principles of justification and proportionality again.

Thus, while the codification of the case law may have a certain clarificatory value, this should not be overstated. The codification has been done in a relatively banal way, with the most obvious points being spelt out, but the more difficult points – what exactly is necessary and/or proportionate? – continue to be left open. The room for interpretation, dispute and *de facto* restriction of movement is therefore little changed from what it was before the Directive.[34]

The services chapter has attracted attention for its appearance of progress. While no longer referring to the country-of-origin principle, it essentially maintains it in substance. It restricts the application of host State service rules to foreign providers to such an extent that they are in principle, within the sphere of the Directive, almost as good as exclusively regulated by their home State. Host State rules can only be applied where justified by public policy, security, health or the environment, and the probability is – given the way these concepts have been interpreted in the past – that they will continue to be strictly enough interpreted that one may speak of exceptional derogations from the general rule of exclusive home State control.

Yet, alongside this far-reaching general idea, a number of provisos must be placed. Not least is the fact that the difference between the country-of-origin principle and the existing Treaty rules interpreted into Article 56 TFEU is not so great. Currently, Member States are entitled to apply national measures to foreign service providers wherever justified, necessary and proportionate, which seems open-ended, but in practice the Court has been restrictive, and the litigation success rate of States is

[33] Articles 9–15 of Directive 2006/123.

[34] Weatherill, 'Protecting the Consumer Interest in an Integrated Services Market', above, pp. 12–15; Pelkmans, 'Deepening Services Market Integration – A Critical Assessment', above, section 4.2; Griller, 'The Services Directive: Two Steps Forward, How Many Back', above.

low. While, for example, consumer protection is often cited as a reason for restricting market access which the Services Directive takes away, there are few cases in which it has actually been successfully relied upon.[35] Thus, the legal principle contained in the Directive is really very close in practice to the legal principle found in the existing case law – the more extensive derogations from free movement which are presently permitted tend to be unsuccessful anyway.[36]

Nevertheless, the fact that these cases on consumer protection were brought indicates that the open-ended justifications which the case law permits provided an opportunity for conservatism on the part of States. Given that, as it has been argued above that the commercial disadvantages of litigation often give States effective ownership of open-ended concepts, removing some of those concepts is likely to aid free movement. However, this is mitigated by the fact that, as a result of narrowing the category of exemptions to free movement, the ones that remain are likely to become more contested. If public policy remains the only justification for derogation, then we will probably see States straining to expand this concept and bringing ever more arguments within it.[37] Since the limits and definitions of public policy are as potentially open-textured as any others – 'sufficiently serious threat to a fundamental interest of society', 'interpreted strictly', 'proportionate'[38] – the challenge of preventing national authorities from misusing interpretative spaces for an over-restrictive approach to free movement has not been met.

A criticism of both the establishment and services chapters is that they appear to apply only to a limited class of public measures, namely, those restricting 'access to a service activity'.[39] This may be contrasted with the broader Treaty prohibition which, in the eyes of the Court, covers 'any measure which may hinder or make less attractive' the exercise of free

[35] Barnard, 'Unravelling the Services Directive', above, p. 367; Weatherill, 'Protecting the Consumer Interest in an Integrated Services Market', above, p. 2.

[36] Similarly, V. Hatzopoulos, 'Legal Aspects in Establishing the Internal Market for Services', College of Europe Research Paper in Law 6/2007.

[37] Barnard, 'Unravelling the Services Directive', above, p. 366. Cf. the plausible argument popular on the continent that the mandatory requirements will and should be interpreted into Article 16 just as they were interpreted into the almost identically worded Article 49 EC; Hatzopoulos, 'Legal Aspects in Establishing the Internal Market for Services', above; Pelkmans, 'Deepening Services Market Integration – A Critical Assessment', above; G. Davies, 'The Services Directive: Extending the Country of Origin Principle and Reforming Public Administration', *European Law Review* 32 (2007) 232–45, p. 235.

[38] Case C-36/02, *Omega Spielhallen* [2004] ECR I-9609.

[39] Article 9(1); Article 16(1).

movement.[40] The distinction lies in measures which do not directly concern access to a service activity as such, but do in fact make it harder to provide services abroad. These could be aspects of planning rules, the legal system, vehicle and property use, the integration of the family of the service providers, and tax issues, to which the Directive will not apply. Given that services are provided by people or organizations which must exist as people or organizations, as well as engaging in their service activity *pur sang*, the Directive is not wide enough in scope to function as a real market opener.[41] It does not even pretend to address the full range of legal factors which in fact make it difficult to supply services abroad. As a result, service providers will often have to fall back on the Treaty articles to establish the legal rights necessary for their activities, an undesirably messy legislative position.[42]

4.2 Enforcement and implementation again

Although the Directive does not substantially develop the substantive law, and is even narrower than the Treaty in some ways, it may stimulate national authorities to take account of free movement rights simply by virtue of being a Directive, explicitly addressed to them.[43] Commanding the attention of the national regulator is a useful, if insufficient, step in enforcing the law.

The administrative provisions of the Directive may also help with practical enforceability. These require States to make the administrative procedures associated with access to a service activity 'sufficiently simple', and accessible via a single point of contact, which must include an online contact point.[44] This should make it easier for service providers to establish what their legal position is, and encourage them to assert rights. An assertive approach is more probable where providers have a clear line of communication with the authorities, and do not feel lost in a sea of bureaucracy.

Nevertheless, these are rearguard arguments. Neither the mere fact of being written law, nor the simplification of the bureaucracy associated with cross-border movement addresses directly the continued weaknesses and ambiguities of the substantive law. It is difficult to believe that the delays and difficulties associated with dealing with local

[40] Case C-55/94, *Gebhard* [1995] ECR I-4165.
[41] Cf. Barnard, 'Unravelling the Services Directive', above, pp. 336–9.
[42] See also *ibid*., pp. 343–4. [43] *Ibid*., pp. 393–4. [44] Articles 5–8.

authorities are in themselves a significant enough obstacle to movement that addressing them in this procedural way will fundamentally change the level of market integration.

5. The Services Directive as a mechanism for inter-State cooperation

The Services Directive may not provide adequate free movement rights directly, but it does create mechanisms through which Member States can communicate with each other about issues and concerns relevant to service activities.[45] Looking at these mechanisms in light of theories about competition suggests they may be effective in helping to create inter-State consensus over levels and types of regulation and in helping States to accept each other's rules and service providers. The Directive may therefore contribute to free movement via an indirect – second order – mechanism. It can be seen as a type of reflexive law, encouraging States to react constructively to each other and converge voluntarily and flexibly.[46]

5.1 A regulatory oligopoly

The starting point for this perspective is a view of Member States as sellers on a market for regulation; each State offers its rules and hopes that this will attract and stimulate economic actors, who will use the State as a base for their service provision throughout the EU.[47] This is often described in terms of regulatory competition, and it is the fear of many that such competition between States may lead to a race to the bottom.[48] It is precisely the hard free movement rights to which the Directive is often presented as containing that raise this risk, because they make it possible for companies to choose their State of establishment independently of the location of their customers.

[45] See Articles 28–36. See also Articles 7 and 21.

[46] S. Deakin, 'Two Types of Regulatory Competition: Competitive Federalism versus Reflexive Harmonisation: A Law and Economics Perspective on Centros', *Cambridge Yearbook of European Legal Studies* 2 (1999) 231–60.

[47] See generally A. Ogus, 'Competition between National Legal Systems: A Contribution of Economic Analysis to Comparative Law', *International and Comparative Law Quarterly* 45 (1999) 405–18.

[48] For an overview in the EU context, see C. Barnard and S. Deakin, 'Market Access and Regulatory Competition', Jean Monnet Working Paper 09/01, available at http://centers.law.nyu.edu/jeanmonnet/papers/01/012701.html (last visited 26 September 2010).

However, not all markets function perfectly, and the market for regulation within the EU has some of the characteristics of an oligopoly – a relatively small number of providers dominate the market. In this case, the number of providers of regulation has a ceiling of the number of EU Member States.

In oligopolistic markets, the risk arises that the providers either collude – form a conscious cartel – or engage in non-collusive, parallel behaviour – they converge in products and prices even without explicit agreement to do so.[49] The result of either path may be that the providers collectively take on the characteristics of a dominant market actor, able to act to a significant extent independently of consumers – who are in this case the service providers subject to the regulation.[50] The risk of regulatory competition, by contrast, is that States become enslaved to migrating companies, who can dictate the terms of regulation.[51] The reply in terms of oligopoly is that by collusion or natural parallel behaviour States may once again assert their independence of those companies, and be able to act in their own interests – or those of their voters.

However, such oligopolistic parallelism does not happen in all markets. A number of factors make it more or less likely.[52] The first of these is the number of sellers in the market, and on the whole a smaller group is more likely to act as one than a larger group. The number of Member States in the EU, currently twenty-seven, is on the high side for either collusion or parallelism. However, for many kinds of service the EU may not be one market. For reasons of infrastructure, language, the availability of staff and physical location, among other issues, not every jurisdiction will be able to plausibly compete for the headquarters of all service providers. Thus, for any given service in any given part of the EU, there may be a smaller number of jurisdictions that are realistic options for establishment, and that are therefore in competition with each other. The EU may in fact consist of multiple smaller overlapping services markets.

A second factor which is considered to make collusion or parallel behaviour much more likely is the availability of information about what competitors are doing. It is sometimes possible for parallel behaviour to occur entirely without contact between firms if one makes clear pricing

[49] See, e.g., G. Monti, *EC Competition Law* (Cambridge University Press, 2007), pp. 308–11.

[50] See Ogus, 'Competition between National Legal Systems', above. The definition of dominance is from Case 85/76, *Hoffman La Roche* [1979] ECR 461. See also G. Monti, 'The Concept of Dominance', *European Competition Journal* 2 (2006) 31–52.

[51] See C. Barnard and S. Deakin, 'Market Access and Regulatory Competition', above.

[52] See A. Jones and B. Sufrin, *EC Competition Law* 3rd edn (Oxford University Press, 2008), pp. 871–3.

and policy announcements, and so behaves as leader for the others, who understand implicitly and independently that it is in their interests to follow the leader rather than undercut it. If there is contact between market actors, this further increases the chance of non-competition.

A large part of the Services Directive is devoted to increasing transparency and making information about regulatory demands available.[53] The administrative chapter is aimed at making requirements clear for service providers,[54] but if the information is 'out there' on clear websites, as is the intention, it will be equally available to the authorities of other States. It seems plausible that at the moment most national authorities have relatively little knowledge of the details of regulatory requirements of other States, and the publication of the details to providers will also significantly raise the level of information available to sister-authorities. Additionally, the Directive contains provisions requiring communications networks to be set up between national regulatory and supervisory authorities.[55] This is expressed to be primarily for the purpose of assisting each other with the supervision of specific providers, and exchanging information about reputability and so on. However, the fact that channels of communication are being created and kept open is likely to lead to an enhanced understanding of each other's regulatory content, methods and philosophy in general, as well as of plans for changes and developments. Almost inevitably, the creation of this network will be the beginning – or in some cases further development – of a conversation between regulatory authorities.

The third of the major factors determining the behaviour of oligopolists is the possibility to sanction members who depart from the terms of (implicit) agreements. The cartel that can sanction its members is much more stable than one which cannot, while if there is a potential price to be paid for non-parallel behaviour then market actors are more likely to continue along the parallel path.

Here the weakness of the Services Directive – that it does not actually guarantee free movement – becomes one of its key points. Under the regime that it introduces free movement continues to be conditional upon the good will of the host State, for all the reasons discussed above. However, the conversation about free movement is, as a result of the communication provisions of the Directive, no longer just between the service provider and the host State, but between national authorities. These speak to each other

[53] See Articles 7, 21 and 28–36. [54] Chapter II of the Services Directive.
[55] See Articles 28(2), 32(2) and 34.

directly about service regulation, and so implicitly, and probably explicitly, about access to each other's markets. Free movement was never guaranteed, and is still not guaranteed, but has changed from being conditional to being negotiated. As authorities speak to each other, they learn of each other's concerns – and these are probably largely shared – and of the reasons each may have to take a restrictive approach to service providers, and are capable of adapting to these reasons either by providing information to allay fears, or by adapting rules to meet concerns, or by offering deals – you take it easy on our management consultants and we'll not be too difficult about your architects. All of these strategies are likely to be used together, so that each State is effectively engaged in negotiating market access with its fellow Member States.

The sanction is then that a State which chooses to go its own regulatory way, without concern for the consensus of other States, may find that its providers have difficulty operating in other States. This need not be as a result of any conscious retribution. However, if there is a regulatory consensus about the proper level of protection or types of acceptable constraint, then a State will feel more confident and justified in, for example, interpreting public policy, justification or proportionality in a way that excludes providers departing notably from this consensus, or subject to a supervisory jurisdiction that does so. There is safety in numbers, and the possibility for consensus between many States makes it more likely and more defensible that non-conforming States will pay a price in market access. Added to this may be a price in political isolation. States playing the regulatory competition game at its hardest will not be pleased if other States are able to form a well-informed oppositional front. One may note, finally, that communicated consensus between States may strengthen their position even if service providers – or the Commission – do choose to litigate. The Court of Justice must itself then interpret the open norms, and a broad European consensus for a certain view is likely to carry more weight than an argument from a uniquely mono-national point of view.

5.2 *Collusion or democratic cooperation?*

The outcome of an oligopolistic market with high levels of communication and sanction is likely to be, in the absence of countervailing factors, coordinated behaviour.[56] In the context of a market for regulation, it

[56] See note 52 above.

seems likely that some degree of convergence of regulation will occur, as States realize that locating their regulation within a consensus band is in their own interests, as it prevents competition between them.

In a conventional market this would be seen as undesirable. However, in a conventional market the concern is usually to maximize the welfare of consumers, and to prevent sellers from organizing to hinder that goal. In a context of regulatory competition, matters change somewhat. The customers of laws are service providers, whose welfare is a concern, but by no means the exclusive or even major concern of policy in this area. By contrast, the end consumers of the services are democratically represented in the States – the sellers of law – giving these a legitimacy that they do not have in a normal market. The situation requires more careful analysis.

In the absence of international trade rules, States can make their own trade-offs between the costs and benefits associated with opening their markets, and different levels of regulation.[57] Low regulation may stimulate economic activity, but bring unwelcome consequences. High regulation may serve some consumer interests, but hinder economic activity. Opening the national market to foreign providers may create the risk of domestic producers locating abroad where regulation is lighter, but may also result in increased domestic competition and lower prices. All are legitimate factors to take into account.

However, if trade rules constrain a State to open its markets at least to some non-trivial extent – as both the Treaty and the Directive do – then that State loses the capacity to balance interests exclusively according to the preferences of its population.[58] One may hope that the joining of the trade area and the submission to the trade rules is a preference of the population, so that this is a non-issue, but in practice it is never quite so simple; populations would ideally like to be members of the trade area but not take all the consequences all of the time.

Giving States the capacity to cooperate and thereby gain a certain independence of migrating companies restores some balance to their

[57] See Sun and Pelkmans, 'Regulatory Competition in the Single Market', above; R. van den Bergh, 'Towards an Institutional Legal Framework for Regulatory Competition in Europe', *Kyklos* 53 (2000) 435–66; M. Trebilcock and R. Howse, 'Trade Liberalisation and Regulatory Diversity: Reconciling Competitive Markets with Competitive Politics', *European Journal of Law and Economics* 6 (1998) 5–37; J. Trachtman, 'International Regulatory Competition, Externalisation, and Jurisdiction', *Harvard International Law Journal* 34 (1993) 47–104.

[58] *Ibid.*

policy-making capacity. If the goal is that States are able to make policy reflecting the preferences of their populations, then it may be advantageous. Yet, while the resulting convergence to a consensus may reflect preferences better than an unfettered race to the bottom would, it may nevertheless not be optimal. The tendency of colluding sellers is to keep prices too high, and the tendency of cooperating States, freed from pressure from the consumers of their laws, may be to undervalue the advantages of limited regulation, and to overvalue their own institutional interests in a strong State-administered regulatory system.

5.3 *Variable and flexible cooperation*

An apparently attractive aspect of the situation created by the Directive is that it allows for variation and change within the overall framework of a movement towards consensus. A State that wishes to go its own regulatory path is still able to in any given area, while converging on others, provided it is prepared to accept the possible price in access and isolation. While the result of communication may be convergence, this is voluntary, and so reversible. Moreover, it need not be full convergence; the degree to which States are prepared to accept diversity is negotiable and dynamic, and may change and broaden as States come to understand each other better. Initial reactions to mutual learning may be an eagerness to agree terms, but as trust deepens States may be more and more able to accept divergent regulation. Collusion is an utterly flexible mechanism.

6. Conclusions

It is a difficult empirical question, beyond the scope of this chapter or the expertise of its author, whether communication and cooperation between States will in fact lead to optimal regulation or how far it will diverge from the optimum. However, whatever the outcomes, three *a priori* points may be made about the mechanisms involved, based on the preceding discussion.

(1) The relationship between the Directive and the market for services is not what it is commonly presented to be. The conventional presentation is that the Directive creates free movement; this leads to regulatory competition, which in turn may lead to agreement to Commission-led harmonization. In fact, it is suggested that a more important sequence will be as follows: authorities communicate and

learn about each other; this leads to convergence of regulation and acceptance of regulation; and as a result they open their markets to each other's providers. Limited voluntary harmonization therefore leads to free movement, rather than free movement leading to traditional EU harmonization.

(2) The absence of the EU or the Commission in the mechanism described is striking. While the Directive envisages that the States and the Commission will together form an information network with a view to harmonization where necessary, in fact the role of the Commission may be marginalized. If States are able to work together then they may see no need for true harmonization, and resist the loss of autonomy and flexibility that it entails.

(3) It is open to doubt whether an oligopolistic market for regulation is optimal, but it is worth noting that this market will be a dynamic and unstable one. The States collectively gain power as a result of cooperation, but that does not mean that actors such as firms and the Commission are entirely devoid of influence. For one thing, even where there is a functioning consensus, there is likely to be relative dissatisfaction in some States, who would rather locate the consensus elsewhere. Thus a role for traditional harmonization, or intervention from Brussels, is not completely absent. By strategic intervention, both the Commission and industry lobbies can do something to counteract a possible tendency among colluding States to overvalue selected interests and ignore others.

In summary, trust, legislation, mutual recognition and market-making are interdependent. Developments in one affect all of the others. Effective legislation or policy uses this fact to achieve indirect – second-order – as well as direct results. The Services Directive provides only a mildly reformed framework for substantive mutual recognition, but a greatly enhanced framework for trust and communication. It seems likely that this will contribute to the effectiveness of mutual recognition and market operation, and ultimately promote more selective, but more achievable and useful, and perhaps often voluntary, harmonization.

4

Mutual recognition in the global trade regime: lessons from the EU experience

WOLFGANG KERBER AND ROGER VAN DEN BERGH

1. Introduction

The introduction of the principle of mutual recognition is deemed as crucial for the important progress in completing the Internal Market in the EU. A large number of trade and mobility barriers between the EU Member States were eliminated through its application to national regulations by the European Court of Justice in its *Cassis de Dijon* jurisprudence. The transition from the country-of-destination to the country-of-origin principle helped the enforcement of the four fundamental freedoms of the EU (free mobility of goods and services as well as the production factors of labour and capital). This is the reason why, in the literature on international trade, the principle of mutual recognition is assessed as a crucial institutional innovation, which led to a far-reaching elimination of non-tariff barriers to trade and the achievement of economic regional integration within the EU.[1] Therefore, it is not surprising that also on the level of global trade the possibilities for the introduction of this principle are intensively discussed, in order to reduce the manifold barriers to a larger global economic integration. In this discussion, the EU is often seen as a model for the global efforts to reduce trade barriers.[2]

So far, the principle of mutual recognition does not really play a role within the framework of the WTO. All States, even if they are members

[1] J. Pelkmans, 'Mutual Recognition in Goods and Services: An Economic Perspective' in F. K. P. Schioppa (ed.), *The Principle of Mutual Recognition in the European Integration Process* (Basingstoke: Palgrave Macmillan, 2005), pp. 85–128.

[2] J. H. H. Weiler, 'Mutual Recognition, Functional Equivalence and Harmonization in the Evolution of the European Common Market and the WTO' in F. K. P. Schioppa (ed.), *The Principle of Mutual Recognition in the European Integration Process* (Basingstoke: Palgrave Macmillan, 2005), pp. 25–84.

of the WTO, still have the authority to enact regulations for products and services, which can lead to non-tariff trade barriers. Products that do not comply with these national regulations might be prevented from being imported, and only discrimination between domestic and foreign firms is prohibited according to the WTO rules (national treatment rule). From an economic perspective, it is entirely clear that, on the global trade level, the same problem of non-tariff barriers to trade exists as it did within the EU before the completion of the Internal Market. However, there is a decisive difference to the situation in the EU before the *Cassis de Dijon* judgment of the European Court of Justice: within the legal framework of the GATT and the WTO, there is no direct equivalent to the four fundamental freedoms of the EU and to the European Court of Justice, which, as a court, was able to make binding decisions with regard to the enforcement of the fundamental freedoms. However, also on the global level, there is a discussion over whether certain rules within the WTO framework (for example, with regard to 'like products') could not be interpreted in a way that would allow the application of the EU concept of 'equivalent regulations'. This might open up the prospect also of applying the principle of mutual recognition on the WTO level.[3] For example, Weiler is convinced that 'it will not be long before a WTO Panel and/or Appellate Body will pronounce a WTO version of the Doctrine of Parallel Functionalism (or mutual recognition)'.[4] Even if the principle of mutual recognition has so far not been applied within the WTO framework, there might be a possibility that on the global level non-tariff barriers to trade through national regulations might also be removed through the principle of mutual recognition.

This is closely linked to the discussion whether the application of the principle of mutual recognition within the EU might itself be a violation of the WTO rules. The decisive point is that the 'mutual recognition regime' of the EU implies that the national regulations of the EU have to be recognized mutually; however, this is not true for regulations of third countries, even if they seem to be equivalent to the regulations of the Member States. Therefore, the question has been raised whether this might be a discrimination which violates the most-favoured-nation

[3] For more detail, see J. P. Trachtman, 'Embedding Mutual Recognition at the WTO', *Journal of European Public Policy* 14 (2007) 780–99, pp. 787–93.

[4] J. H. H. Weiler, 'Mutual Recognition, Functional Equivalence and Harmonization in the Evolution of the European Common Market and the WTO' in F. K. P. Schioppa (ed.), *The Principle of Mutual Recognition in the European Integration Process* (Basingstoke: Palgrave Macmillan, 2005), pp. 25–84, p. 58.

principle of the WTO.[5] A sophisticated legal analysis leads Bartels to the surprisingly clear conclusion that the European system of mutual recognition of regulations is indeed not compatible with the WTO rules.[6] From our perspective, more important than this legal result are the reasons given: the decisive argument is that the European system of mutual recognition is a closed regime, because it encompasses only the EU Member States and excludes other countries. If it were an open system of mutual recognition, 'allowing all States to submit their regulatory regimes for review and possible acceptance for recognition',[7] it would presumably be compatible with the WTO rules. This also could be a hint to a possible path for an extension of mutual recognition regimes onto the global level. However, it is an open question whether such an 'open' system of mutual recognition would require a number of additional (institutional) preconditions in order to work satisfactorily.

Beyond this level of WTO rules, we already have an extensive application of mutual recognition in the realm of international trade, but at the level of bilateral trade agreements. In recent years, a large number of bilateral treaties concerning the mutual recognition of regulations between two (or more) States have been concluded, which were the result of direct negotiations between the participating States. These 'Mutual Recognition Agreements' determine under which conditions what kinds of specific regulations are recognized as equivalent by the parties to the treaties, i.e., that certain kinds of imports are allowed despite their non-compliance with the domestic regulations of the importing country.[8] There are three important differences between such treaties and the EU regime of mutual recognition: (1) mutual

[5] For arguments about why the EU system of mutual recognition leads to disadvantages for third countries and especially developing countries, see M. X. Chen and A. Mattoo, 'Regionalism of Standards: Good or Bad for Trade?', *Canadian Journal of Economics* 41 (2008) 838–63; J. P. Trachtman, 'Embedding Mutual Recognition at the WTO', *Journal of European Public Policy* 14 (2007) 780–99.

[6] L. Bartels, 'The Legality of the EC Mutual Recognition Clause under WTO Law', *Journal of International Economic Law* 8 (2005) 691–720. See, for a similar position, J. P. Trachtman, 'Embedding Mutual Recognition at the WTO', *Journal of European Public Policy* 14 (2007) 780–99.

[7] Trachtman, 'Embedding Mutual Recognition at the WTO', above, p. 795.

[8] For literature on Mutual Recognition Agreements, see G. Shaffer, 'Reconciling Trade and Regulatory Goals: The Prospects and Limits of New Approaches to Transatlantic Governance through Mutual Recognition and Safe Harbor Agreements', *Columbia Journal of European Law* 9 (2002) 29–77; K. Nicolaïdis and G. Shaffer, 'Transnational Mutual Recognition Regimes: Governance without Global Government', *Law and Contemporary Problems* 68 (2005) 263–317.

recognition is the specific result of bilaterally negotiated treaties and not the consequence of the application of a general principle within a court system as in the EU; (2) the application of mutual recognition does not follow general principles of equivalence (with general exceptions, such as health protection, etc.) but is negotiated specifically for particular regulations; both aspects open up many more possibilities for influencing the outcome of these negotiations through specific rent-seeking interests of domestic industries; (3) these mostly bilateral treaties on the application of mutual recognition lead more to a patchwork of different rules for mutual recognition instead of to an integrated economic area. It cannot be expected that the results of these bilateral negotiations lead to a consistent application of mutual recognition. We cannot discuss here the particular problems emerging through such a patchwork of bilaterally different applications of the principles of mutual recognition. The fundamental problems of bilateral trade agreements are well known in the literature on international trade and were one of the main arguments for establishing a multilateral system of global trade (such as the GATT–WTO system) in the first place. Within the context of the discussion about 'Mutual Recognition Agreements', a new and sophisticated literature emerged on the so-called 'Managed Mutual Recognition Regimes'.[9] In the final section of this chapter, we will see that this literature, which focuses on the 'management' of the principle of mutual recognition application, i.e., under what conditions this principle should or should not be applied, can be directly linked to our argument in this chapter, and therefore can help in our endeavour to understand how the principle of mutual recognition might be used productively on the level of global trade.

In this chapter, we do not wish to analyze the current problems of the (non-)application of the principle of mutual recognition in international trade and within the WTO framework. Our main focus is on the general assessment of this principle. We will demonstrate that in the academic discussion about mutual recognition there are serious misunderstandings about this principle and its long-term effects, which are also very relevant for the question of its application at the global level. Its current

[9] K. Nicolaïdis, 'Globalization with Human Faces: Managed Mutual Recognition and the Free Movement of Professionals' in F. K. P. Schioppa (ed.), *The Principle of Mutual Recognition in the European Integration Process* (Basingstoke: Palgrave Macmillan, 2005), pp. 129–89; K. Nicolaïdis and G. Shaffer, 'Transnational Mutual Recognition Regimes: Governance without Global Government', *Law and Contemporary Problems* 68 (2005) 263–317.

general assessment can be summarized as follows. There is a widespread consensus that the principle of mutual recognition is a very positive institutional innovation for removing non-tariff barriers to trade and implementing an integrated market.[10] The principle of mutual recognition has not only great advantages compared to the cumbersome (and often unsuccessful) strategy of harmonization of regulations through negotiations (with often painful political compromises). Mutual recognition is also deemed to be a strategy for removing trade and mobility barriers between countries without embarking on a path to harmonization and centralization. Therefore, the introduction of mutual recognition would defend decentralized competences. This is in line with the opinion in the literature about systems competition (institutional competition) as well as in the law and economics literature that the introduction of the principle of mutual recognition is a crucial institutional precondition for enabling positively assessed processes of regulatory competition.[11] From that perspective, the principle of mutual recognition is assessed as a quasi-ideal solution for simultaneously achieving: (1) the removal of non-tariff barriers to trade and the implementation of an integrated market; (2) the enabling of regulatory (institutional) competition; and (3) the protection against a centralization of competences in a multi-level system of jurisdictions as in the EU.

Our main thesis is that the principle of mutual recognition has to be assessed much more critically. We do not wish to deny that the introduction of mutual recognition in the EU has contributed greatly to the removal of trade and mobility barriers, and we would also agree that it

[10] J. H. H. Weiler, 'Mutual Recognition, Functional Equivalence and Harmonization in the Evolution of the European Common Market and the WTO' in F. K. P. Schioppa (ed.), *The Principle of Mutual Recognition in the European Integration Process* (Basingstoke: Palgrave Macmillan, 2005), pp. 25–84; J. Pelkmans, 'Mutual Recognition in Goods and Services: An Economic Perspective' in F. K. P. Schioppa (ed.), *The Principle of Mutual Recognition in the European Integration Process* (Basingstoke: Palgrave Macmillan, 2005), pp. 85–128; J. Pelkmans, 'Mutual Recognition in Goods: On Promises and Disillusions', *Journal of European Public Policy* 14 (2007) 699–716; K. Nicolaïdis and G. Shaffer, 'Transnational Mutual Recognition Regimes: Governance without Global Government', *Law and Contemporary Problems* 68 (2005) 263–317.

[11] H. Siebert and M. J. Koop, 'Institutional Competition: A Concept for Europe?', *Aussenwirtschaft* 45 (1990) 439–62; M. Streit and W. Mussler, 'Wettbewerb der Systeme und das Binnenmarktprogramm der Europäischen Union' in L. Gerken (ed.), *Europa zwischen Ordnungswettbewerb und Harmonisierung* (Berlin: Springer, 1995), pp. 75–107; F. Parisi and L. E. Ribstein, 'Choice of Law' in Peter Newman (ed.), *The New Palgrave Dictionary of Economics and the Law*, vol. I (London: Macmillan, 1998), pp. 236–41.

could have similar effects at the global level. According to our view, however, this principle leads to a number of serious (and so far not well-recognized) inconsistencies and problems, which are linked to a basic misunderstanding of its function with regard to the removal of trade barriers. We think that the introduction of the rule of mutual recognition can neither be understood as an appropriate rule for the enabling of effective regulatory competition nor is it a suitable instrument for avoiding harmonization and centralization. In our view, its introduction triggers a dynamic process of reallocation of regulatory powers between different regulatory levels in a multi-level system of regulations, and therefore has consequences for the vertical allocation of competences. Rather, the introduction of mutual recognition can be interpreted more as a test, whether the regulatory powers on the national level are still defensible or whether another solution to the allocation of regulatory powers seems to be superior, for example, centralization/full harmonization or the transition to a fully competitive system of regulations (with free choice of law). An empirical analysis of its effects within the EU would lead to the clear result that the introduction of this principle has not only led to a removal of trade and mobility barriers but has also *de facto* shifted competences from the Member States to the EU level. Therefore, we will argue that it seems to be more an alternative indirect path to harmonization and centralization, instead of offering a solution to the removal of barriers that simultaneously maintains the decentralized structure of competences. Since the introduction of mutual recognition also influences the vertical allocation of competences within a multi-level system of governance, we argue that the advantages of the removal of trade and mobility barriers have also to be balanced with the foregone manifold advantages of decentralization – leading to a much more ambivalent assessment of the long-term consequences of mutual recognition. So far, these effects have not been taken into account in the discussion about the principle of mutual recognition with regard to the EU Internal Market. On a theoretical level, this implies that not only the theory of international trade is relevant for the assessment of mutual recognition but also the economic theory of federalism with its comprehensive analysis of all advantages and disadvantages of centralized and decentralized competences in a federal multi-level system of jurisdictions.

In the next section, we will give a brief but comprehensive summary of our main general critique of the current view on the principle of mutual recognition, which draws on our previous work on mutual recognition, both on a theoretical level as well as with regard to the experiences within the EU.[12] This will encompass a short introduction to the application of the principle within the EU, a theoretical analysis of the rule of mutual recognition as a conflict-of-laws rule within a multi-level system of regulations, as well as an analysis of the inconsistencies and problems that have been caused by its introduction in the EU. Finally, it will be argued that this principle should be reinterpreted as a dynamic principle for triggering a process of reallocation of regulatory powers. On the basis of these insights, we will in the third section draw conclusions from these insights with regard to the discussion about the introduction of mutual recognition on the global trade level.

2. The principle of mutual recognition: theoretical analysis and the experiences within the EU

2.1 Mutual recognition within the EU: a short overview

Within the EU, the principle of mutual recognition was introduced through both the jurisprudence of the European Court of Justice and the Internal Market programme of the EU Commission for enforcing the fundamental freedoms through the removal of barriers to mobility between the Member States. With regard to the free movement of goods, Article 34 TFEU (ex Article 28 EC) was applied, which prohibits quantitative restrictions of imports and 'measures having equivalent effects' (with exemptions according to Article 36 TFEU (ex Article 30 EC)). In the *Dassonville* case (1974), the Court clarified that all rules enacted by Member States, which are capable of hindering, directly or indirectly, actually or potentially, intra-Community trade, can be seen as 'measures having equivalent effects' and therefore as infringing Article 34 TFEU (ex Article 28 EC).[13] This was the first clear decision that stipulated that the regulatory autonomy of the Member States could be restricted by the European rules for the enforcement of the free movement of goods. Article 36 TFEU (ex Article 30 EC) contains an exhaustive list of derogations, which, through the *Cassis de Dijon* decision[14] and

[12] See, in particular, W. Kerber and R. Van den Bergh, 'Mutual Recognition Revisited: Misunderstandings, Inconsistencies, and a Suggested Reinterpretation', *Kyklos* 61 (2008) 447–65.

[13] Case 8/74, *Procureur du Roi* v. *Dassonville* [1974] ECR 837.

[14] Case 120/78, *Rewe-Zentrale AG* v. *Bundesmonopolverwaltung für Branntwein* [1979] ECR 649.

later judgments of the Court, was developed into an open list of 'mandatory requirements'. They are capable of justifying the application of national regulations (for example, safety, health, environment and consumer protection), if four conditions are met: (1) equal treatment of foreign and domestic firms; (2) justification of the rules by reason of public interest; (3) necessity of the rules for attaining this public interest objective; and (4) proportionality of the rules to that objective.[15]

The principle of mutual recognition was introduced first by the European Court of Justice in the *Cassis de Dijon* decision, implying the transition from the traditional country-of-destination principle to the country-of-origin principle: goods, which were legally produced and sold in one Member State, should also be allowed to be sold in other Member States, if the objectives or effects of the national regulations are equivalent to those of the import State. It is important to note that the introduction of the principle of mutual recognition through the Court was a conditional one: it depended on the condition of the equivalence of the regulations. As a consequence, the criterion of 'equivalence of objectives or effects' of regulations became the central assessment criterion, i.e., whether the objectives of the regulations of the import country were sufficiently achieved by the regulations of the export country, or whether the import country could require compliance with stricter rules. The fulfilment of the 'equivalence' criterion implies that the application of the national regulations of the import country could be qualified as a trade barrier ('measure having equivalent effects') and an infringement of the free movement of goods, and therefore be declared inapplicable. In the meantime, this principle of mutual recognition has been extended to all other fundamental freedoms (for example, the freedom of establishment and the freedom to provide services, and even safety and security). With regard to the enforcement of mutual recognition, firms have to sue the Member States before the Court, if the application of certain national regulations leads to a prohibition of their imports. This judicial enforcement of the principle of mutual recognition for enforcing the fundamental freedoms can be cumbersome and risky, because there is a large grey area in the interpretation of the above-mentioned criteria for equivalence (for example, the necessity or the proportionality of national regulations). Therefore, Pelkmans is right in emphasizing the 'fairly high

[15] Case C-5/94, *Reinhard Gebhard* v. *Consiglio dell'Ordine degli Avvocati e Procuratori di Milano* [1995] ECR I-4165.

information, transaction, and compliance costs'[16] of this judicial way of enforcing the principle of mutual recognition.

Also, the EU Commission began to apply the principle of mutual recognition as a crucial strategy for implementing the Internal Market. In contrast to the judicial enforcement of mutual recognition ('judicial mutual recognition'),[17] the EU Commission applied this principle in a regulatory manner ('regulatory mutual recognition');[18] after the failure of the old approach to removing non-tariff barriers to trade through a full harmonization, the EU Commission stopped trying to prescribe in detail specific technical standards through regulations. Instead, it started to define only generally the objectives of Directives (as safety or health), and left the specific formulation of the technical standards to the Member States or standard-setting organizations. This 'new approach' of the Commission was endorsed by the Court in its *Foie Gras* decision[19] by requiring the Member States to include a mutual recognition clause in their technical regulations. This was supplemented by the Information Directive of the Commission,[20] which imposed a duty on the Member States to inform the EU about all new legislation that might have actual or potential effects on regulatory barriers to trade. Drafts of new national legislation with regard to safety, health and consumer protection have to be scrutinized by a special committee before being enacted by national parliaments. As a result of these rules, most of the drafts of such new legislation contain clauses providing for the equivalence of regulations. Pelkmans argues that the Commission thus succeeds in impeding the emergence of a large number of new regulatory trade barriers.[21] Therefore, a complex bundle of measures for a regulatory application of the principle of mutual recognition exists within the EU.

[16] J. Pelkmans, 'Mutual Recognition in Goods and Services: An Economic Perspective' in F. K. P. Schioppa (ed.), *The Principle of Mutual Recognition in the European Integration Process* (Basingstoke: Palgrave Macmillan, 2005), pp. 85–128, p. 103.

[17] J. H. H. Weiler, 'Mutual Recognition, Functional Equivalence and Harmonization in the Evolution of the European Common Market and the WTO' in F. Kostoris Padoa Schioppa (ed.), *The Principle of Mutual Recognition in the European Integration Process* (Basingstoke: Palgrave Macmillan, 2005), pp. 25–84.

[18] Pelkmans, 'Mutual Recognition in Goods and Services', above, p. 96.

[19] Case C-184/96, *Commission* v. *France (Foie Gras)* [1998] ECR I-6197.

[20] Directive 98/34/EC of the European Parliament and of the Council of 22 June 1998 laying down a procedure for the provision of information in the field of technical standards and regulations, OJ 1998 L204/37.

[21] J. Pelkmans, 'Mutual Recognition in Goods: On Promises and Disillusions', *Journal of European Public Policy* 14 (2007) 699–716.

2.2 *A theoretical framework: mutual recognition as a conflict-of-laws rule within a multi-level system of regulations*

Theoretically, the principle of mutual recognition can be interpreted as a conflict-of-laws rule that decides which legal rules have to be applied in cross-border contexts. For example, the country-of-origin principle (as a consequence of mutual recognition) stipulates that the relevant regulations for imported goods are those of the home country of the exporting firms. However, in the previous subsection, we have seen that the rule of mutual recognition, as it is applied by the Court, can only be applied as far as the objectives or effects of the regulations are equivalent (conditional mutual recognition). The country-of-destination principle, as it was applied before the *Cassis de Dijon* decision and still in use in most international trade contexts, requires that the imported goods have to comply with the regulations of the import country. Another possible rule is free choice of law, i.e., that firms are free to decide between the legal rules of different legal regimes, as is the case for contract law in international transactions. The introduction of the principle of mutual recognition can therefore be interpreted as a change of the conflict-of-laws rules with regard to regulations, implying a new delineation and therefore a redefinition of the regulatory powers between States.[22] However, it is crucial for the analysis of the development within Europe to take into account not only the changes with regard to the horizontal delineation of regulatory powers between Member States but also with regard to the vertical delineation of regulatory powers between the EU and the Member States. It is clear that the introduction of mutual recognition by the Court limited considerably the regulatory autonomy of the Member States and shifted some regulatory powers to the EU level.

An appropriate theoretical framework for the analysis of the effects of mutual recognition as an instrument for removing barriers to trade and mobility has to start theoretically with the notion of a multi-level system of jurisdictions (legal federalism).[23] On all of these levels (the global

[22] For an analysis of conflict-of-laws rules, see H. Muir Watt, 'Choice of Law in Integrated and Interconnected Markets: A Matter of Political Economy', *Columbia Journal of European Law* 9 (2003) 383–409; from an economic perspective, see F. Parisi and L. E. Ribstein, 'Choice of Law' in Peter Newman (ed.), *The New Palgrave Dictionary of Economics and the Law*, vol. I (London: Macmillan, 1998), pp. 236–41; and the conference volume of J. Basedow and T. Kono (eds.), *An Economic Analysis of Private International Law* (Tübingen: Mohr Siebeck, 2006).

[23] For multi-level legal systems (or multi-level governance), see G. Marks, L. Hooghe and K. Blank, 'European Integration from the 1980s: State-Centric v. Multi-Level

level, the EU level, the Member States level and, perhaps, even the regional level), there can be legal rules and regulations. The question then arises: what is the optimal vertical allocation of regulatory powers between the different levels of this multi-level system, i.e., what is the optimal degree of centralization/harmonization on the one hand or decentralization/regulatory competition on the other? Conflict-of-laws rules and rules for defining competences can be interpreted as any rule which defines and delineates the regulatory powers of the jurisdictions within such a multi-level system of legal regimes, both horizontally between the jurisdictions on the same level and vertically between the jurisdictions of different levels. Or, more precisely: to what extent should regulatory powers be centralized or decentralized? And, to the extent there is some degree of decentralized regulatory powers: what conflict-of-laws rule should be applied between the States horizontally, for example mutual recognition (conditional or unconditional), the country-of-destination principle or free choice of law? From that perspective arises the question of the optimal design of such a multi-level system of regulations. Our crucial point is that the question of the assessment of mutual recognition as a suitable conflict-of-laws rule can only be answered as part of this overall question for an optimal multi-level system of regulations.

For the question of how such a multi-level system of regulations should be structured, the economic theory of legal federalism can provide a large set of criteria which can be used for the analysis of the above-mentioned questions with regard to the optimal vertical allocation of regulatory powers and the proper conflict-of-laws rules. The economic theory of legal federalism can use the many theoretical and empirical insights from the general economic theory of federalism, the theory of inter-jurisdictional and regulatory competition, as well as law and economics and other approaches of institutional economics.[24] In the

Governance', *Journal of Common Market Studies* 34 (1996) 341–78; A. Héritier, M. Stolleis and F. W. Scharpf (eds.), *European and International Regulation after the Nation State: Different Scopes and Multiple Levels* (Baden-Baden: Nomos, 2004); W. Kerber, 'European System of Private Laws: An Economic Perspective' in F. Cataggi and H. Muir Watt (eds.), *The Making of European Private Law* (Cheltenham: Edward Elgar, 2008), pp. 64–97.

[24] See, e.g., C. M. Tiebout, 'A Pure Theory of Local Expenditures', *Journal of Political Economy* 64 (1956) 416–24; H. Siebert and M. J. Koop, 'Institutional Competition: A Concept for Europe?', *Aussenwirtschaft* 45 (1990) 439–62; F. H. Easterbrook, 'Federalism and European Business Law', *International Review of Law and Economics* 14 (1994) 125–32; V. Vanberg and W. Kerber, 'Institutional Competition among Jurisdictions: An Evolutionary Approach', *Constitutional Political Economy* 5 (1994)

following, only a very brief overview of the relevant criteria and the most important results of the research in legal federalism can be presented. Important criteria for the optimal vertical allocation of regulatory powers are costs (e.g., economies of scale, transaction and information costs, costs due to trade barriers, which often support centralization), heterogeneity of preferences and conditions (favouring more decentralized solutions), importance of local knowledge, innovation and adaptability of legal rules (which are usually better in the case of decentralization), political economy arguments as well as path dependencies (e.g., dynamic economies of scale). Regulatory competition can have important advantages with regard to innovation and efficiency of legal rules and can help solve political economy problems; however, regulatory competition can also lead to race-to-the-bottom problems and high information and transaction costs and suffer from incentive problems. It is also important to take into account that different conflict-of-laws rules can lead to different types of regulatory competition with different mechanisms and different advantages and problems.[25]

193–219; J.-M. Sun and J. Pelkmans, 'Regulatory Competition in the Single Market', *Journal of Common Market Studies* 33 (1995) 67–89; R. Van den Bergh, 'Economic Criteria for Applying the Subsidiarity Principle in the European Community: The Case of Competition Policy', *International Review of Law and Economics* 16 (1996) 363–83; R. Van den Bergh, 'Towards an Institutional Legal Framework for Regulatory Competition in Europe', *Kyklos* 53 (2000) 435–66; W. W. Bratton and J. A. McCahery, 'The New Economics of Jurisdictional Competition: Devolutionary Federalism in a Second-Best World', *Georgetown Law Journal* 86 (1997) 201–78; H. W. Sinn, 'The Selection Principle and Market Failure in Systems Competition', *Journal of Public Economics* 88 (1997) 247–74; W. E. Oates, 'An Essay on Fiscal Federalism', *Journal of Economic Literature* 37 (1999) 1120–1149; A. Ogus, 'Competition between National Legal Systems: A Contribution of Economic Analysis to Comparative Law', *International and Comparative Law Quarterly* 48 (1999) 405–18; J. P. Trachtman, 'Regulatory Competition and Regulatory Jurisdiction', *Journal of International Economic Law* 3 (2000) 331–48; D. C. Esty and D. Geradin (eds.), *Regulatory Competition and Economic Integration: Comparative Perspectives* (Oxford University Press, 2001); A. Marciano and J. M. Josselin (eds.), *The Economics of Harmonizing European Law* (Cheltenham: Edward Elgar, 2002); A. Marciano and J. M. Josselin (eds.), *From Economic to Legal Competition: New Perspectives on Law and Institutions in Europe* (Cheltenham: Edward Elgar, 2003); K. Heine and W. Kerber, 'European Corporate Laws, Regulatory Competition and Path Dependence', *European Journal of Law and Economics* 13 (2002) 43–71; W. Kerber, 'European System of Private Laws: An Economic Perspective' in F. Cafaggi and H. Muir Watt (eds.), *The Making of European Private Law* (Cheltenham: Edward Elgar, 2008), pp. 64–97.

25 For comprehensive catalogues of criteria for the optimal vertical allocation of competences, see R. Van den Bergh, 'Economic Criteria for Applying the Subsidiarity Principle in the European Community: The Case of Competition Policy', *International Review of*

In the meantime, a lot of theoretical and empirical research has been done regarding these issues. One clear result is that all initially discussed theses about the general positive or negative effects of centralization, decentralization or regulatory competition have been proved wrong. It very much depends on the type of regulation, on a number of specific conditions, and also on the applied conflict-of-laws rules, whether a more centralized or decentralized solution should be recommended, or whether regulatory competition can lead to more positive than negative effects (or *vice versa*). For solving the problem of the optimal allocation of a specific regulatory power, it is always necessary to make a specific analysis using the analytical tools offered by the theory of legal federalism. The result of a specific analysis usually is that there are both positive and negative welfare effects of centralized and decentralized solutions; often also both positive and negative effects can be expected in cases of regulatory competition. As a consequence, more or less complex trade-off problems emerge, leading to different optimal solutions for different regulations.[26] For some regulations, a more

Law and Economics 16 (1996) 363–83; R. Van den Bergh, 'Towards an Institutional Legal Framework for Regulatory Competition in Europe', *Kyklos* 53 (2000) 435–66; W. Kerber and S. Grundmann, 'An Optional European Contract Law Code: Advantages and Disadvantages', *European Journal of Law and Economics* 21 (2006) 215–36; W. Kerber, 'European System of Private Laws: An Economic Perspective' in F. Cafaggi and H. Muir Watt (eds.), *The Making of European Private Law* (Cheltenham: Edward Elgar, 2008), pp. 64–97. For different types of regulatory competition in dependence from different conflict-of-laws rules, see W. Kerber and O. Budzinski, 'Towards a Differentiated Analysis of Competition Laws', *ZWeR – Journal of Competition Law* 1 (2003) 411–48; H. Muir Watt, 'Choice of Law in Integrated and Interconnected Markets: A Matter of Political Economy', *Columbia Journal of European Law* 9 (2003) 383–409.

26 See, in general, D. C. Esty and D. Geradin (eds.), *Regulatory Competition and Economic Integration, Comparative Perspectives* (Oxford University Press, 2001); W. Kerber, 'European System of Private Laws: An Economic Perspective' in F. Cafaggi and H. Muir Watt (eds.), *The Making of European Private Law* (Cheltenham: Edward Elgar, 2008), pp. 64–97. For examples of such analyses in different fields of the law and regulations, see for corporate law K. Heine, *Regulierungswettbewerb im Gesellschaftsrecht. Zur Funktionsfähigkeit eines Wettbewerbs der Rechtsordnungen im europäischen Gesellschaftsrecht* (Berlin: Duncker and Humblot, 2003); for competition law, R. Van den Bergh, 'Economic Criteria for Applying the Subsidiarity Principle in the European Community: The Case of Competition Policy', *International Review of Law and Economics* 16 (1996) 363–83; W. Kerber, 'An International Multi-Level System of Competition Laws: Federalism in Antitrust' in J. Drexl (ed.), *The Future of Transnational Antitrust – From Comparative to Common Competition Law* (Bern: Kluwer, 2003), pp. 269-300; R. Van den Bergh and P. D. Camesasca, *European Competition Law and Economics: A Comparative Perspective* (London: Thomson, 2006), pp. 403–46; O. Budzinski, *The Governance of Global Competition: Competence*

centralized or harmonized solution can be recommended, whereas for other regulations decentralized regulatory powers are superior. As far as decentralized regulatory powers are more suitable, a further differentiation according to different conflict-of-laws rules is often necessary, because mutual recognition, country-of-destination principle or free choice of law can lead to different types of regulatory competition and therefore to different positive and negative welfare effects within the whole multi-level system of regulations. This implies that the question whether the principle of mutual recognition might be a superior conflict-of-laws rule in comparison to others, cannot be answered generally but depends on the type of regulation and a number of specific conditions. In the following subsection, however, we will show three crucial problems of the principle of mutual recognition which considerably question its general suitability as an appropriate conflict-of-laws rule within a multi-level system of regulations.

2.3 *Three crucial problems of the application of mutual recognition*

It has been seen as one of the important advantages of the principle of mutual recognition that mutual recognition helps to remove trade barriers without leading to centralization or harmonization. This thesis is fundamentally wrong and the result of a serious misunderstanding of mutual recognition. On the contrary, the introduction of mutual recognition (country-of-origin principle) implies the loss of the authority of a State to regulate its domestic markets. Although it is correct that the States still have the authority to enact regulations on products, these regulations do not address the domestic markets but only the domestic manufacturers of these products. If the preferences of citizens in different States differ on the regulation of markets with regard to consumer protection or health services, under an unconditional rule of mutual recognition these different objectives can no longer be fulfilled. This leads to a loss of welfare. Therefore, the advantages of the removal of trade barriers through mutual recognition should be balanced against

Allocation in International Competition Policy (Cheltenham: Edward Elgar, 2008); for (European) contract law, W. Kerber and S. Grundmann, 'An Optional European Contract Law Code: Advantages and Disadvantages', *European Journal of Law and Economics* 21 (2006) 215–36; R. Van den Bergh, 'The Uneasy Case for Harmonising Consumer Law' in K. Heine and W. Kerber (eds.), *Zentralität und Dezentralität von Regulierung in Europa* (Stuttgart: Lucius and Lucius, 2007), pp. 183–205.

the disadvantages of the non-fulfilment of the heterogeneous preferences of citizens for regulations in different States. If, however, the scope for satisfying different preferences should be maintained, then the introduction of mutual recognition would be a mistake and the traditional country-of-destination principle might be more appropriate. While these conclusions follow consistently from our theoretical framework in the previous subsection, these effects are entirely ignored in the discussion about mutual recognition (both on the theoretical level as well as in the discussion about the European Internal Market).[27] As a consequence, the thesis that the principle of mutual recognition protects decentralized competences for regulation is wrong. This is also confirmed by the experiences in the EU. Although the jurisprudence of the Court has protected the regulatory scope of the Member States for fulfilling heterogeneous preferences through its application of a conditional mutual recognition (equivalence of objectives or effects), it has done this through an explicit limitation of the application of mutual recognition. However, the manifold measures of regulatory mutual recognition through the EU Commission (subsection 2.1 above) lead to a large reduction in the remaining scope of the Member States for different regulations. Whereas the Internal Market literature sees this as a great success against old and new trade barriers,[28] the overall outcome is a far-reaching *de facto* harmonization that takes place under the explicit heading of mutual recognition. And, even if this regulatory method of mutual recognition does not lead to the desired degree of harmonization, then the direct path to harmonization according to Article 114 and 115 TFEU (ex Articles 95 and 94 EC) can be used. This direct path, which is also possible in the case of different regulatory objectives, has been facilitated through the introduction of a slightly modified qualified majority rule for the approximation of legal rules.

Another complex problem follows from another consequence of mutual recognition, namely, so-called 'reverse discrimination'. Whereas now firms from other Member States are allowed to offer their products with the regulations of their home States, domestic firms are still bound to the regulations of the import country. This potentially produces competitive

[27] One of the few exceptions is J. Pelkmans, 'Mutual Recognition in Goods and Services: An Economic Perspective' in F. K. P. Schioppa (ed.), *The Principle of Mutual Recognition in the European Integration Process* (Basingstoke: Palgrave Macmillan, 2005), pp. 85–128, p. 97.

[28] J. Pelkmans, 'Mutual Recognition in Goods. On Promises and Disillusions', *Journal of European Public Policy* 14 (2007) 699–716.

disadvantages for domestic firms if foreign regulations impose lower standards, and thus lower costs. Beyond the important problem of a potential race to the bottom in an ensuing regulatory competition process between States (treated separately in the next paragraph), two problems emerge. On the one hand, the question emerges of how these specific national regulations for domestic firms can be justified any longer, if on the same domestic markets other firms are allowed to sell their goods (produced according to other regulations), if all of these regulations are deemed as equivalent. For, in this case, the specific national regulations can no more be justified by the objective of consumer protection; rather they are only pure regulations for producers. It is interesting to see that the introduction of the principle of mutual recognition can transform the character of a regulation, here from a consumer regulation to a *de facto* producer regulation. It is hard to see how this kind of producer regulation can be defended from an economic policy perspective.[29] In addition, this kind of producer regulations leads to a well-known second problem: since these specific national producer regulations influence the international competitiveness of domestic firms, they are subject to manifold rent-seeking activities and industrial policy considerations with regard to domestic industry. Although this can also be seen as a mechanism for driving regulatory competition,[30] this can lead to very problematic effects. In sum, the overall implications of 'reverse discrimination' as a direct consequence of the principle of mutual recognition are complex and very problematic: it not only leads to an entirely inconsistent and economically indefensible structure of regulations within the integrated economic area, but also to a dangerous tendency towards regulatory policies driven by rent-seeking interests and industrial policy concerns. This undermines further the legitimacy of the remaining scope for national regulatory competences.

The most widespread and serious concerns about the application of the principle of mutual recognition refer to the already mentioned problem that its introduction might lead to a 'race to the bottom' with regard to regulatory standards. This potential problem of regulatory

[29] For a deeper discussion of some remaining economic reasoning, which are only convincing in very specific cases, see W. Kerber and R. Van den Bergh, 'Mutual Recognition Revisited: Misunderstandings, Inconsistencies, and a Suggested Reinterpretation', *Kyklos* 61 (2008) 447–65, p. 456.

[30] J.-M. Sun and J. Pelkmans, 'Regulatory Competition in the Single Market', *Journal of Common Market Studies* 33 (1995) 67–89.

competition has been studied extensively, both theoretically and empirically, and with regard to different kinds of regulations.[31] Similar to our conclusions with regard to the general working of regulatory competition in multi-level systems of regulations, also concerning the specific problem of the 'race to the bottom', no general conclusions are possible and therefore the answer has to be a differentiated one. It depends both on the specific regulations and on a number of conditions, whether we can expect positive 'race to the top' or problematic race-to-the-bottom processes of regulatory competition. Although empirical studies show that the dangers of race-to-the-bottom processes seem to be much exaggerated, such an outcome cannot be excluded. It is not surprising that this problem has been discussed intensively with regard to product regulations, which were first subjected to mutual recognition through the *Cassis de Dijon* jurisprudence of the Court and which at the same time are usually justified through consumer protection rationales. The question was whether consumers, who are considered to be less knowledgeable than producers about products, would be able to make meaningful choices between products that are produced according to regulations from different Member States. Our argument, however, focuses less on the probability of race-to-the-bottom processes that are caused by the introduction of mutual recognition. Instead, we ask which conflict-of-laws rule is better suited to deal with such a problem. We want to distinguish two cases:

(1) If consumers have serious problems assessing the regulations of different States, with the possible result of a race-to-the-bottom process, then there is a broad consensus that a (minimum) harmonization might be the superior solution in comparison with mutual recognition (country-of-origin principle).
(2) If, however, we do not have such a market failure, because consumers are capable of choosing meaningfully between products (manufactured according to different regulations), then the alternative rule of free choice of law would be superior to mutual recognition, because there are no good reasons why consumers but not producers should be able to choose freely between all regulations. The result would be a free Internal Market for regulations, which is controlled

[31] See the references in note 24 above; and, for an empirical study, see D. Vogel, *Trading Up: Consumer and Environmental Regulation in the Global Economy* (Cambridge, MA: Harvard University Press, 1995).

by a reputation mechanism for regulations (and perhaps linked with a duty for labelling with regard to the regulations used).[32]

Therefore, our argument can be summed up as follows: either there are serious race-to-the-bottom problems, then a (minimum) harmonization is superior to mutual recognition; or we do not have such problems, in which case a free choice of law should be recommended in preference to mutual recognition.

All of these serious problems demonstrate clearly that the principle of mutual recognition is not a good conflict-of-laws rule. Contrary to the overwhelming opinion in the literature, this principle does not protect decentralized competences; rather, it voids and delegitimizes the formally still existing decentralized regulatory competences. Under mutual recognition, they no longer refer to the regulation of domestic markets but only to the regulation of domestic producers (with multiple follow-on problems). In particular, the principle of mutual recognition no longer enables the satisfaction of heterogeneous preferences for the regulations of different Member States through different market regulations. As a consequence, these advantages of decentralization are lost and could only be defended through sticking to the old country-of-destination principle. Also, with regard to race-to-the-bottom situations, no stable situation ensues, because the transition to either a free market for regulations or harmonization is the superior solution compared to mutual recognition. This also implies that a free choice of law rather than the principle of mutual recognition is the proper conflict-of-laws rule for establishing regulatory competition.

2.4 Mutual recognition as a dynamic principle for the reallocation of regulatory powers in a multi-level system of regulations

These results indicate that the introduction of mutual recognition does not lead to a stable allocation of regulatory powers within a multi-level

[32] See, e.g., C. Koenig, J.-D. Braun and R. Capito, 'Europäischer Systemwettbewerb durch Wahl der Rechtsregeln in einem Binnenmarkt für mitgliedstaatliche Regulierungen', *Europäisches Wirtschafts- und Steuerrecht* (1999) 401–9; W. Kerber, 'Interjurisdictional Competition within the European Union', *Fordham International Law Journal* 23 (2000) 217–49; W. Kerber and R. Van den Bergh, 'Mutual Recognition Revisited: Misunderstandings, Inconsistencies, and a Suggested Reinterpretation', *Kyklos* 61 (2008) 447–65, p. 458.

system of regulations. Instead, they suggest that the introduction of this principle, with its considerable inconsistencies and consequent problems, leads to a dynamic process of changing the regulatory powers towards other and more stable solutions. Within a multi-level system of regulations, it is not the rule of mutual recognition that is a stable and suitable conflict-of-laws rule. In its place, stable conflict-of-laws rules are: (1) harmonization; (2) the country-of-destination principle (national treatment); and (3) free choice of law (leading to a free market for regulations). All of them might have their advantages and disadvantages, which we cannot discuss here, but all of them also lead to consistent solutions with regard to the allocation of regulatory powers within a multi-level system of regulations. However, the introduction of mutual recognition can lead to very positive effects, not as a new stable conflict-of-laws rule, as it has been interpreted widely in the literature, but as a dynamic principle that breaks up an old, traditional allocation of regulatory powers and helps to establish a new and better solution. A new interpretation of the principle of mutual recognition would interpret its introduction more as a kind of test: can the traditional allocation of regulatory powers (usually the national regulations with the country-of-destination principle) still be defended or should a new allocation of regulatory powers be chosen? This can be done either through harmonization (or centralization) or through free choice of law or a (not so rare) combination of (minimum) harmonization, free choice of law, and the country-of-destination principle.

Let us think about potential mechanisms for a change of the vertical allocation of regulatory powers within a multi-level system of regulations: both in the past within the EU and also currently on the global level: the basic idea is that, through a greater degree of market integration with less non-tariff barriers to trade, positive welfare effects arise. This implies the assumption that the old allocation of regulatory powers – with its national sovereignty that allows for non-tariff barriers to trade (and which is represented by the country-of-destination principle as conflict-of-laws rule) – is no longer the optimal solution for the allocation and delineation of regulatory powers within a multi-level system of regulations in the intended integrated economic area. How is it possible to change this allocation of regulatory powers? The most obvious solution is that the participating States agree on a new and better structure of regulatory powers. It is exactly this political bargaining solution which had failed in the past in the EU (the 'old approach' of full harmonization) and is also at least as hard to achieve on the global level. The fact that most of the existing mutual trade agreements are bilateral agreements shows the difficulties of agreeing a joint solution in such political bargaining processes. Therefore, the strategy of the Court in the 1970s to introduce the principle of mutual recognition of national regulations can be seen as a direct response to the failure of the political bargaining solution by the EU Member States to achieve progress with regard to the four fundamental freedoms, e.g., through direct measures of harmonization.[33] The decisive point is not that the principle of mutual recognition is the best solution for the removal of non-tariff barriers to trade; rather, its introduction (e.g., in the field of product regulations) triggered a dynamic process of testing the sustainability of the old solution and asking whether other kinds of allocation of regulatory powers within the European two-level system of regulations might be superior to the country-of-destination principle.

Therefore, both the judicial and the regulatory application of the principle of mutual recognition can be understood as a method for the reallocation of regulatory powers within the European two-level system of regulations. The approach of the Court is easy to interpret from an economic perspective: are there good reasons why a Member State insists on the compliance of its national regulations (e.g., because of different objectives due to different preferences in this State) or are the regulations of the export and import State with regard to their objectives or effects equivalent, which implies that the disadvantages of trade barriers are not balanced through comparably large advantages of the regulatory autonomy of the import State? In the first case, the maintaining of the country-of-destination principle can be defended. The additional criteria of a public interest objective, and the necessity and proportionality of the national regulation can be understood economically as an additional economic fine-tuning of the trade-off between the advantages of the national regulatory autonomy and the disadvantages of the non-removal of trade barriers. In the three decades since the *Cassis de Dijon* decision, a large number of national regulations with impact on all

[33] A similar process has taken place much later in the realm of the freedom of establishment. Here, the decisions of the Court of Justice in the *Daily Mail*, *Centros*, *Überseering* and *Inspire Art* cases have led to a *de facto* mutual recognition of national corporate laws within the EU – with the transition from the 'real seat theory' to the 'incorporation theory'. See K. Heine, *Regulierungswettbewerb im Gesellschaftsrecht. Zur Funktionsfähigkeit eines Wettbewerbs der Rechtsordnungen im europäischen Gesellschaftsrecht* (Berlin: Duncker and Humblot, 2003); K. Röpke and K. Heine, 'Vertikaler Regulierungswettbewerb und europäischer Binnenmarkt – die Europäische Aktiengesellschaft als supranationales Rechtsangebot', *ORDO* 56 (2005) 157–85.

four fundamental freedoms have been tested rigorously in a long step-by-step process with regard to their equivalence. This led to the necessity of a comprehensive justification of nearly all national regulations, which triggered a large number of reforms (albeit in very different ways). However, it also became clear early on that this method of using judicial mutual recognition as a means for changing the allocation of regulatory powers is limited to what it can achieve. Whereas judicial mutual recognition can replace the country-of-destination principle by the country-of-origin principle, it is not able to achieve (minimum) harmonization or a free market for regulations (through establishing free choice of law). Therefore, judicial mutual recognition is not a sufficient instrument for a comprehensive restructuring of regulatory powers within the European two-level system of regulations. As a consequence, rules might also be necessary which can be used for direct (minimum) harmonization (as Article 114 and 115 TFEU; ex Articles 95 and 94 EC) and indirect *de facto* harmonization (as the measures for regulatory mutual recognition).

However, we cannot conclude that within the EU we have sufficiently well-working mechanisms which ensure an appropriate adaptation of the vertical allocation of regulatory powers in this two-level system of regulations. This is confirmed by the broad and intense discussion of whether the factual reallocation of regulatory powers that has taken place in the last two decades in the EU might have led to too much harmonization and centralization of regulatory powers. An example is the manifold regulations in the realm of consumer protection and unfair business practices, which are to a large extent fully harmonized.[34] In this chapter, we cannot discuss this issue and the reasons for such a tendency for too much harmonization and centralization. However, we think that the misunderstandings about the long-term effects of the principle of mutual recognition that we have discussed in this section might be one important reason for this. The discussions about the Internal Market and the enforcement of the four fundamental freedoms have focused nearly exclusively on the problem of the removal of barriers to trade and mobility, and have not included costs in the form of the loss of the advantages of decentralized regulatory powers which have to be borne by

34 For a critique, see, e.g., R. Van den Bergh, 'The Uneasy Case for Harmonising Consumer Law' in K. Heine and W. Kerber (eds.), *Zentralität und Dezentralität von Regulierung in Europa* (Stuttgart: Lucius and Lucius, 2007), pp. 183–205; W. Kerber and S. Grundmann, 'An Optional European Contract Law Code: Advantages and Disadvantages', *European Journal of Law and Economics* 21 (2006) 215–36.

implementing either mutual recognition or harmonization for the removal of these barriers. The systematic use of the economic theory of legal federalism, which is capable of taking into account all the positive and negative effects of centralization and decentralization as well as of the advantages and disadvantages of regulatory competition under different conflict-of-laws rules, would prevent such a one-sided assessment of the effects of mutual recognition or harmonization. Also, the misunderstanding that mutual recognition would protect decentralized regulatory powers has prevented an earlier and more forceful resistance against too much centralization and harmonization. These lessons might be of considerable help, if we now turn to the question of the introduction of mutual recognition on the level of global trade.

3. Application of the principle of mutual recognition on the global level: some conclusions

To what extent can we recommend the introduction of mutual recognition on the global level considering the results of our theoretical analysis of this principle and the experiences of the EU? Can the EU be seen as a model for the global level? Or, to put the question differently, what considerations should be taken into account for attempts to apply the principle of mutual recognition to a larger extent on the global level?

A direct consequence of our analysis is that a pure introduction of the principle of mutual recognition as a conflict-of-laws rule would not be the real solution. Here, the same inconsistencies and problems would ensue. If national regulations were mutually recognized, national regulatory autonomy would be lost in the same way as it is in the EU, and the welfare losses caused by the non-fulfilment of the heterogeneous preferences of the citizens in different countries would be greater as such losses would occur on a global scale. The same kind of problems of 'reverse discrimination' would emerge, including the problematic incentives for industrial policy strategies with regard to national regulations, in order to boost the international competitiveness of domestic industries. Also here (minimum) harmonization in the case of race-to-the-bottom problems and a free market for regulations (free choice of laws) in the case of their absence would be superior conflict-of-laws rules than the principle of mutual recognition. We should understand also that, on the global level, the introduction of the principle of mutual recognition does not establish a solution, but constitutes the starting point for a dynamic process of critical scrutiny of the defensibility of the old solution of national regulatory autonomy and of searching for a better structure of regulatory powers within the global multi-level system of regulations. Similarly to the EU, such a process can lead to the maintaining of the old country-of-destination principle, to an explicit or implicit harmonization or centralization process, to a competitive system of regulations, or to a combination of these different stable solutions. We should also be aware that the introduction of mutual recognition does not in itself protect national regulatory powers or even ensure an effective process of regulatory competition; on the contrary, both our theoretical analysis as well as the experiences in the EU indicate that the introduction of this principle endangers both and therefore we also have to take these potentially negative effects of mutual recognition into account in a comprehensive analysis of all positive and negative effects of the introduction of mutual recognition on the global level.

However, as mentioned in the introduction, the institutional preconditions for the principle of mutual recognition are entirely different on the global level from those within the EU. It is true that a WTO panel or the Appellate Body might attempt to develop a criterion of equivalence of national regulations that might look similar to the criterion of 'equivalent objectives or effects' that was so powerful within the EU. But these institutions lack by far the legitimacy and the power of enforcement of the Court within the EU. Therefore, they will not be able to trigger a dynamic process of redefining national regulatory powers within the global trade regime as has been done through the process of judicial mutual recognition for the enforcement of the four fundamental freedoms within the EU. An important advantage in the EU is that the EU Treaties and therefore also (the jurisprudence with regard to) the four fundamental freedoms are directly applicable law in the Member States of the EU. This is not the case with the rules of the WTO. However, we would not deny that there might be a long-term perspective for establishing also a 'judicially' initiated dynamic process of restructuring regulatory powers in the global multi-level system of regulations using the mechanism of mutual recognition.[35] Nevertheless, we cannot expect that the process for the completion of the Internal Market can be a direct model for the global level. This is also true, because the possibilities for a regulatory application of mutual recognition (with its *de facto* harmonization effects) or for a direct harmonization of regulations through joint political decisions are much smaller within the weak institutional framework

[35] J. P. Trachtman, 'Embedding Mutual Recognition at the WTO', *Journal of European Public Policy* 14 (2007) 780–99.

of the WTO and the necessity of unanimous consent. Therefore, it is also less surprising that States try to lessen the disadvantages through non-tariff trade barriers – in a kind of bottom-up process – through 'Mutual Recognition Agreements' negotiated bilaterally between governments. In the introduction to this chapter, we briefly emphasized the inconsistencies and problems of such a patchwork approach. However, these institutional weaknesses of the political and judicial mechanisms for applying the principle of mutual recognition on the global level also very much limit the danger of too much harmonization and centralization on the global level. On the contrary, we can expect that the institutional preconditions on the global level do not lead to sufficient efforts for a proper restructuring of the regulatory powers from an economic perspective. This result of our analysis emphasizes again why all attempts to use a 'judicial' approach to mutual recognition within the WTO (perhaps along the lines of 'like products', as indicated in the introduction to this chapter) might be valuable shots for triggering a process of reallocation of regulatory powers within the global trade regime. Another important new group of institutional solutions for solving the problem of non-tariff barriers to trade and mobility on the global level are using entirely new forms of governance, for example the many forms of institutional solutions discussed under the heading of private regulations. In any case, it becomes clear that, on the global level, the institutional conditions for mutual recognition are very different, and that we might also have to look for entirely new institutional solutions using mutual recognition in order to trigger a dynamic process of reallocation of regulatory powers within the global multi-level system of regulations.

The previous paragraph referred to the problem of how to trigger a dynamic process of reallocation of regulatory powers with the principle of mutual recognition. However, the crucial question ultimately is what the optimal structure of regulatory powers is that should be achieved. What can be learnt from our theoretical analysis (briefly summarized in subsection 2.2 above) is that the problem of non-tariff barriers to trade cannot be solved in isolation from the much more complex and comprehensive problem of the overall design of the global multi-level system of regulations, because the solutions for the removal of non-tariff barriers to trade also influence the vertical allocation of regulatory powers. Thus, from the perspective of economic theory, we must not only use the theory of international trade and economic integration with its analysis of the welfare effects of barriers to trade and mobility. We also have to apply the economic theory of legal federalism, which can offer a lot of theoretical and empirical knowledge about the positive and negative welfare effects of a greater or lesser degree of centralization within a multi-level system of regulations. As we have seen in subsection 2.2, this theory also encompasses the theory of regulatory competition, which can demonstrate under what conditions and under what conflict-of-laws rules regulatory competition processes can emerge with either more positive or more negative welfare effects. Our point is that it is only through an overall analysis of all the advantages and disadvantages for welfare (or other normative objectives) that it is possible to derive the optimal structure of regulatory powers within such a global multi-level system of regulations. Since this optimal structure also requires the proper institutional framework as the set of jurisdictional rules for the optimal vertical and horizontal delineation of regulatory powers, it also encompasses the proper conflict-of-laws rules. Whether a pure or a conditional mutual recognition rule or – as we presume in most cases – other conflict-of-laws rules such as free choice of law or the country-of-destination principle or a (minimum) harmonization solution is superior is an endogenous result of such an overall analysis. Of course, we are aware that it is not possible to design an optimal multi-level system from scratch, using the large number of criteria developed in the theories of legal federalism and international trade and economic integration. It can only be done as a presumably slow step-by-step process starting from the *status quo*. From our perspective, it is important to understand that the welfare losses through non-tariff barriers to trade, which might be caused through decentralized regulatory powers, are only a part of the relevant welfare effects and have to be balanced with all other welfare effects that are caused by a different structure of regulatory powers in a multi-level system. For example, in the EU the potentially large positive welfare effects of decentralized regulatory powers, allowing for the fulfilment of different preferences but also maintaining an experimental process of innovative policy-making, often have not been sufficiently taken into account in the policies on the Internal Market and the four fundamental freedoms.

Another promising starting point for future research is the recent literature on so-called 'Managed Mutual Recognition Regimes'.[36] In this (primarily legal) literature, a complex analytical framework was

[36] See, in particular, K. Nicolaïdis, 'Globalization with Human Faces: Managed Mutual Recognition and the Free Movement of Professionals' in F. K. P. Schioppa (ed.), *The Principle of Mutual Recognition in the European Integration Process* (Basingstoke: Palgrave Macmillan, 2005), pp. 129–89; K. Nicolaïdis and G. Shaffer, 'Transnational Mutual Recognition Regimes: Governance without Global Government', *Law and Contemporary Problems* 68 (2005) 263–317; J. P. Trachtman, 'Embedding Mutual Recognition at the WTO', *Journal of European Public Policy* 14 (2007) 780–99.

developed, which is much more capable of describing and analyzing more clearly and realistically the many different forms of the application of the principle of mutual recognition than in the traditional European discussion on mutual recognition, which is very much focused on the European Internal Market. This new literature views itself much more as a contribution to global governance, which addresses a much broader problem than only non-tariff barriers to trade: 'the diffusion of mutual recognition regimes partakes in shaping a system of global subsidiarity that rejects (or at least does not unquestionably accept) the temptations of centralization and hierarchical constitutionalization of global economic relations.'[37] Therefore, its focus is relatively close to our perspective of an appropriate global multi-level system of governance. An important aspect of this notion of managed mutual recognition regimes is that the application of mutual recognition is seen as taking place under certain conditions; and the management dimension of this approach refers exactly to the determination of the conditions and the scope (including exceptions) for the application of mutual recognition: 'In this sense, mutual recognition regimes are always "managed", and thus differ from a pure "free trade" model by involving an (often highly) political process of assessment of mutual compatibility between national systems of governance.'[38] On the one hand, mutual recognition is here seen as one form of consensual extraterritorial application of law and analyzed as an alternative rule to the country-of-destination principle (national treatment) and to harmonization in existing mutual recognition regimes. This literature, on the other hand, has also clearly recognized that: (1) this also implies a balancing with the advantages of decentralized regulatory powers (and their specific political objectives); and (2) an 'essential harmonization' is the precondition for the application of mutual recognition.[39] For future research it would be very helpful to link the analytical framework that has been developed in the literature on 'Managed Mutual Recognition Regimes' to the economic theory of legal federalism and the dynamic interpretation of mutual recognition, as it was described here in this chapter.

[37] Nicolaïdis and Shaffer, 'Transnational Mutual Recognition Regimes', above, p. 263.

[38] *Ibid.*, pp. 264–5.

[39] J. P. Trachtman, 'Embedding Mutual Recognition at the WTO', *Journal of European Public Policy* 14 (2007) 780–99.

5

Public procurement and public services in the EU

CHRIS BOVIS

1. Introduction

The regulation of public procurement has been an instrumental component of the EU Common Market, as it has provided a platform for economic, legal and policy justifications in order to eliminate non-tariff barriers.[1]

Public procurement in the EU has been significantly influenced by the White Paper for the Completion of the Internal Market[2] and the Single European Act. Furthermore, law and policy[3] have been shaped by reference to the 1996 European Commission's Green Paper on Public Procurement[4] and the subsequent 1998 Commission Communication.[5] Public procurement regulation became an integral part of the Commission's 2000 Work Programme, which pledged to modernize the relevant legislation for the completion of the Internal Market and at the same time implement the Lisbon European Council's call for economic reform within the Internal Market.

The intellectual paternity of public procurement regulation can be traced in a neo-classical economic approach to market integration.[6] Public procurement has been identified as a serious non-tariff barrier and a hindrance

[1] See C. Bovis, *EC Public Procurement: Case Law and Regulation* (Oxford University Press, 2006).

[2] See European Commission, White Paper for the Completion of the Internal Market (COM) 85 310 final, 1985.

[3] See Directive 2004/18/EC on the coordination of procedures for the award of public works contracts, public supply contracts and public service contracts, OJ 2004 L134/114; and Directive 2004/17/EC coordinating the procurement procedures of entities operating in the water, energy, transport and postal services sectors, OJ 2004 L134/1.

[4] See the Green Paper on Public Procurement in the European Union: Exploring the Way Forward, European Commission, 1996.

[5] See European Commission, Communication on Public Procurement in the European Union, COM(1998) 143.

[6] See C. Bovis, 'Public Procurement and the Internal Market of the Twenty-First Century: Economic Exercise versus Policy Choice' in D. O'Keeffe and T. Tridimas (eds.), *EU Law*

to the functioning of a genuinely competitive Common Market. Its regulation, apart from seeking an endorsement of the *acquis communautaire* by Member States of the fundamental principles of the Common Market, aims primarily at introducing radical changes in the industrial base of the European Union. Integration of public markets, through the principles of transparency, non-discrimination and objectivity in the award of public contracts, will bring substantial savings to the public sector, rationalize and allocate more efficiently human and capital resources and increase the productivity and competitiveness of European firms.

Economic justifications for regulating public procurement aim at liberalizing and integrating the relevant markets of the Member States, by inserting competitiveness in the relevant product and geographical markets. This will, in turn, increase import penetration of products and services destined for the public sector and enhance the tradability of public contracts across the Common Market, resulting in significant savings and price convergence. Alongside the economic justifications, legal imperatives have emerged positioning the regulation of public procurement as a necessary ingredient of the fundamental principles of the Treaties, such as the free movement of goods and services, the right of establishment and the prohibition of discrimination on nationality grounds.[7] Finally, policy justifications of public procurement regulation have revealed a *sui generis* market place where the mere existence and functioning of antitrust and the influence of neo-classical economic theories[8] are insufficient to achieve the envisaged objectives of integration and liberalization. The European Court of Justice has referred to its presence and characteristics.[9] This *sui generis* market place is often

for the Twenty-First Century: Rethinking the New Legal Order (Oxford: Hart Publishing, 2005), Chapter 17.

[7] See C. Bovis, 'Recent Case Law Relating to Public Procurement: A Beacon for the Integration of Public Markets', *Common Market Law Review* 39 (2002) 1025–1056.

[8] See M. Bazex, 'Le droit public de la concurrence', *Revue Francaise de Droit Administratif* 14 (1998) 781–800; L. Arcelin, *L'Enterprise en droit interne et communautaire de la concurrence* (Paris: Litec, 2003); O. Guézou, 'Droit de la concurrence et droit des marchés publics: vers une notion transversale de mise en libre concurrence', *Contrats Publics* (March 2003) 43–7. See also A. Jacquemin and H. W. de Jong, *European Industrial Organization* (Macmillan, 1997); W. Möschel, 'Competition Law from an Ordo Point of View' in A. Peacock and H. Willgerodt, *German Neo-Liberals and the Social Market Economy* (Macmillan, 1989), p. 145.

[9] See Case C-223/99, *Agora Srl* v. *Ente Autonomo Fiera Internazionale di Milano*, and Case C-260/99, *Excelsior SNC di Pedrotti Runa and C* v. *Ente Autonomo Fiera Internazionale di Milano* [2001] ECR 3605; Case C-360/96, *Gemeente Arnhem Gemeente Rheden* v. *BFI Holding BV* [1998] ECR 6821; Case C-44/96, *Mannesmann Anlangenbau Austria AG et al.* v. *Strohal Rotationsdurck GesmbH* [1998] ECR 73.

referred to as *marchés publics* (public markets) and draws intellectual support from ordo-liberal theories.[10]

2. Public services under EU law

The application of public procurement rules, apart from serving to integrate intra-Community public sector trade, has served as a yardstick in order to determine the nature of an undertaking in its contractual interface when delivering public services. Public procurement regulation has prompted a distinctive category of markets within the Common Market, often described as public markets.[11] Public markets are such fora where the State and its organs would enter in pursuit of public interest.[12] Their respective activity does not resemble the commercial characteristics of private entrepreneurship, in as much as the aim of the public sector is not the maximization of profits, but the observance of public interest.[13] This fundamental factor provides the differential ground for the creation of *public markets* where public interest substitutes profit maximization.[14]

There are further variances that distinguish private from public markets. These focus on structural elements of the market place, such as competitiveness, demand conditions, supply conditions, the production process, and finally pricing and risk. These variances also indicate different methods and approaches employed in the regulation of public markets.[15] Public markets have monopsony structure tendencies (the

[10] See C. Bovis, 'Public Procurement and the Internal Market of the Twenty-First Century: Economic Exercise versus Policy Choice' in P. Nebia and T. Tridimas (eds.), *EU Law for the Twenty-First Century: Rethinking the New Legal Order* (Oxford: Hart Publishing, 2005), Chapter 17.

[11] See C. Bovis, 'Public Procurement within the Framework of European Economic Law', *European Law Journal* 4(2) (1998) 220–42.

[12] See P. Valadou, 'La notion de pouvoir adjudicateur en matière de marchés de travaux', *Semaine Juridique, Ed. Enterprise*, No. 3 (1991) 33–9.

[13] See M. A. Flamme and P. Flamme, 'Enfin l'Europe des Marchés Publics', *Actualité Juridique – Droit Administratif* 11 (1989) 651–78.

[14] On the issue of public interest and its relation with profit, see Case C-223/99, *Agora Srl* v. *Ente Autonomo Fiera Internazionale di Milano* [2001] ECR I-3605; and Case C-260/99, *Excelsior SNC di Pedrotti Runa and C* v. *Ente Autonomo Fiera Internazionale di Milano* [2001] ECR I-3605; Case C-360/96, *Gemeente Arnhem Gemeente Rheden* v. *BFI Holding BV* [1998] ECR I-6821; Case C-44/96, *Mannesmann Anlangenbau Austria AG et al.* v. *Strohal Rotationsdurck GesmbH* [1998] ECR I-73.

[15] See C. Bovis, *The Liberalisation of Public Procurement in the European Union and Its Effects on the Common Market* (Dartmouth: Ashgate, 1998), Chapter 1.

State and its organs often appear as the sole outlet for an industry's output) and function in a different way than private markets. In terms of its origins, demand in public markets is institutionalized and operates mainly under budgetary considerations rather than price mechanisms. It is also based on fulfilment of tasks (pursuit of public interest) and it is single for many products. Supply also has limited origins, in terms of the establishment of close ties between the public sector and industries supplying it and there is often a limited product range. Products are rarely innovative and technologically advanced, and pricing is determined through tendering and negotiations. The purchasing decision is primarily based upon the lifetime cycle, reliability, price and political considerations. Purchasing patterns follow tendering and negotiations, and purchases are often dictated by policy rather than price/quality considerations.

Within the remit of public markets, the funding of services of general interest by the State may emerge through different formats, such as the payment of a remuneration for services under a public contract, the payment of annual subsidies, preferential fiscal treatment or lower social contributions. However, the most common format is the existence of a contractual relation between the State and the undertaking charged to deliver public services. The above relation should, under normal circumstances, emerge through the public procurement framework, not only as an indication of market competitiveness but mainly as a demonstration of the nature of the deliverable services as services of 'general interest having non industrial or commercial character'. The latter description appears as a necessary condition for the applicability of the public procurement regime.

Article 106 TFEU (formerly Article 86 EC and Article 90 EEC) represents the legal cornerstone[16] of the competence of Member States to provide, organize and deliver public services. The term 'public service' (1) refers to a service which is offered to the general public, or (2) highlights that a service has been assigned a specific role in the public interest, or (3) refers to the ownership or status of the entity providing the service. In the latter situation, public service fuses with the concept of *public sector*, which covers the State and its organs, bodies governed by public law and finally undertakings controlled by public authorities. Two

[16] J. L. Buendia Sierra, *Exclusive Rights and State Monopolies under EC Law* (Oxford University Press, 1999), p. 330.

models for the treatment of public services have been developed, based on different theoretical and conceptual values. On the one hand, public services which capture general needs of the public are delivered through market-based mechanisms where the public sector interfaces or competes with private sector undertakings; this model is based on Article 106 TFEU, sectoral primary and secondary legislation, as well as State aid rules. On the other hand, public services which are described as essential facilities (for example, defence and policing purposes) should be sheltered from competition in order to ensure the integrity of their delivery.[17] The provision of these types of public services is the prerogative of the State and not affected by the thrust of EU law.[18]

2.1 Public service obligations, universal service obligations and services of general economic interest

Although the term 'public services' does not feature in the *acquis communautaire* relevant to Article 106 TFEU, surrogate concepts have contributed in constructing a notion where the State is expected or even obliged[19] to enter the market place in order to deliver directly or organize the delivery of public services. These surrogate concepts are reflected in the terms of *public service obligations* and *universal service obligations*, which have supported the liberalization process of sectoral policies of the European Union.[20] The term 'public service obligations' refers to specific quality and price requirements that are imposed by public authorities on the service provider in order to ensure that certain public interest objectives applicable at Community, national or regional level are met.[21] The term 'universal service obligations' denotes

[17] See T. Prosser, *The Limits of Competition Law* (Oxford University Press, 2005); also C. Graham, 'Essential Facilities and Services of General Interest', *Diretto e Politiche dell'Unione Europea* 1 (2007) 22–31, p. 29.

[18] See A. Moriceau, 'Services d'intérêt économique general et valeurs communes', *Revue du marché commun et de l'Union européenne* 519 (2008) 356–60, p. 358.

[19] See M. Ross, 'Article 16 EC and Services of General Interest: From Derogation to Obligation?', *European Law Review* 25 (2000) 22–38.

[20] See C. Bovis, 'Competition and Telecommunications' in *Encyclopaedia of Competition Law* (London: Sweet & Maxwell, 2007), Chapter 18; also C. Bovis, 'The Application of Competition Rules to the European Union Transport Sectors', *Columbia Journal of European Law* 11(5) (2005) 1–49.

[21] In the context of air transport, public service obligation is defined in Council Regulation 2408/92 as 'any obligation imposed upon an air carrier to take, in respect of any route which it is licensed to operate by a Member State, all necessary measures to ensure the provision of a service satisfying fixed standards of continuity, regularity, capacity and

contractual or regulatory requirements imposed by public authorities upon undertakings, with a view to maintaining regularity and affordability[22] in the provision of the relevant services.[23] Alongside public service obligations and universal service obligations, Article 106(2) TFEU has introduced the notion of 'services of general economic interest', a term whose significance has been augmented by virtue of Article 16 EC. The term 'services of general economic interest' is not defined further in the Treaty or in secondary legislation. The term refers to services of an economic nature which the Member States or the Community subject to specific public service obligations or universal service obligations by virtue of a general interest criterion. Thus, services of general economic interest cover services provided by utilities or network industries such as transport, water, postal services, energy and communications but are also extended to any other economic activities which may be subject to public service obligations.

2.2 *The characteristics of public services*

One of the fundamental characteristics of public services is their economic nature. The funding of public services, which may emerge through different formats such as remuneration under a contract, payment of annual subsidies, preferential fiscal treatment or lower social security contributions to an entrusted undertaking, reveals such a characteristic. This means that public services have a cost and a value attached to them. Cost reflects upon capital considerations, whereas value reflects upon revenue considerations. Even the provision of *social services of general interest*[24] which include health services, long-term care, social security, employment services and social housing is compatible with their economic character assessment.[25]

pricing, which standards the air carrier would not assume if it were solely considering its economic interest'.

22 See W. Sauter, 'Services of General Economic Interest and Universal Service in EU Law', *European Law Review* 2 (2008) 167–93, p. 172.

23 In the context of the Universal Services Directive 2002/22/EC, universal service obligations are services made available to the public at the quality specified to all end-users in their territory, independently of geographical location, and, in light of specific national conditions, at an affordable price.

24 European Commission, Green Paper on Services of General Interest, above.

25 European Commission, Communication from the Commission to the European Parliament, the Council, the European Economic and Social Committee and the Committee of the Regions, A Single Market for Twenty-First Century Europe Services

However, public services lack industrial or commercial character. The Court ruled[26] that the non-commercial or industrial character of a service is a necessary criterion, intended to clarify *needs in the general interest*. The Court recognized that there might be needs of general interest, which have an industrial and commercial character, and that it is also possible that private undertakings can meet needs of general interest which do not have an industrial or commercial character. Nevertheless, the test for needs of general interest which do not possess an industrial or commercial character is that the State or other public authorities choose themselves to meet these needs or to have a decisive influence over their provision. In parallel, the Court indicated[27] that, if an activity which meets general needs is pursued in a competitive environment, there is a strong indication that it possesses commercial characteristics.

The lack of commercial characteristics in a public service or the absence of competitive forces in markets within which a public service is delivered or organized represent a strong indication that the public service belongs to a *sui generis* market place. The first implication of such nature is the non-applicability of general competition law. In addition to the provisions of Article 106 TFEU, sector-specific regulation removed the treatment of financing public services from the general provisions of competition law and placed it within the State aid regime.[28] Furthermore, the *sui generis* nature of public service markets provides the conceptual bridge to engage the public procurement regime as a guardian of the principles of accountability and transparency in the delivery of services of 'general interest having non industrial or commercial character'.[29]

of General Interest, Including Social Services of General Interest: A New European Commitment, COM(2007) 725. See also C. Joerges and F. Rödl, '"Social Market Economy" as Europe's Social Model?', EUI Working Paper LAW No. 2004/8 (European University Institute, 2004).

[26] See Case C-360/96, *Gemeente Arnhem Gemeente Rheden* v. *BFI Holding BV* [1998] ECR 6821.

[27] See Case C-223/99, *Agora Srl* v. *Ente Autonomo Fiera Internazionale di Milano*; and Case C-260/99, *Excelsior SNC di Pedrotti Runa and C* v. *Ente Autonomo Fiera Internazionale di Milano* [2001] ECR 3605.

[28] See C. Bovis, 'Financing Services of General Interest, Public Procurement and State Aids: The Delineation between Market Forces and Protection', *European Law Journal* 11(1) (2005) 79–109.

[29] The term 'industrial and commercial character' features in the public procurement *acquis* and corresponds to the presence of market competitiveness supported through the factors of profitability and demand substitutability; see C. Bovis, 'Redefining Contracting Authorities under the EC Public Procurement Directives: An Analysis of

State aid *acquis* and jurisprudence have validated that services of general economic interest, which embrace the specific concept of public service obligations,[30] project certain characteristics such as the compensatory nature of their reimbursement and the need for market-oriented prerequisites for the selection of the entrusted undertaking of their delivery. These characteristics coincide conceptually with the repercussions of the *sui generis* market place of public services: their placement within State aid regulation and the need of the existence of public procurement as a competition benchmark.

This is reflected in the Commission's vision to utilize State aid regulation as a platform for the provision of essential public services through public service contracts.[31] The *Liikenne*[32] ruling confirms the above-mentioned approach, as the essential character of obligations for the provision of adequate services must be assessed by reference to elements that exceed the *stricto sensu* commerciality of the venture – and instead must demonstrate a combination of factors which include the

the Case C-44/96, Mannesmann Anlangenbau Austria AG et al. v. Strohal Rotationsdurck GesmbH', *Common Market Law Review* 39 (1999) 41–59.

30 Services of general economic interest and public service obligations conceptually merge through the medium of *public service contract*. See Regulation 1893/91, OJ 1991 L169. The concept of public service contracts, which covers contractual relations between competent authorities of Member State and undertakings and encapsulates contractualized obligations to provide adequate services to the public, introduces the need for principles of transparency and accountability in the selection process and methods of the entrusted undertaking to provide such services. A public service contract in the transport sector may cover: (i) transport services satisfying fixed standards of continuity, regularity, capacity and quality; (ii) additional transport services; (iii) transport services at specified rates and subject to specified conditions, in particular for certain categories of passenger or on certain routes; and (iv) adaptation of services to actual requirements.

31 See the European Commission's, 'XXIII Report on Competition Policy' (1993), point 534.

32 See Case C-412/96, *Kainuun Liikenne Oy* [1998] ECR 1515. The case elaborated on the ability of transport undertakings which are subject to a public service obligation to apply for the termination of such an obligation in whole or in part, under Article 4 of Regulation 1191/69. There is discretion on the part of Member States to grant such request, which entails that they can refuse even where the pursuit of public service obligations entails economic disadvantages for the relevant transport operator. However, such a refusal can only be based on the necessity of maintaining the provision of adequate transport services. The Court maintained that such necessity must be assessed having regard to: the public interest; the possibility of having recourse to other forms of transport and the ability of such forms of transport to meet the transport needs in question; and the transport rates and conditions which can be quoted to users. The Court implied that the competent authorities will choose the service that secures the lowest costs for the community if other services can be offered for equivalent conditions.

public interest, substitutability of services, price comparisons and the competitive environment in the relevant market.

The leap from the *stricto sensu* commercial assessment of a venture embracing public service obligations to the elaborate appraisal of substitutability assessment under a public service contract reveals that the competent authorities of Member States will choose the lowest cost service, if all available services can be offered under equivalent conditions. Such an observation brings into play the *compensatory* characteristics of services of general economic interest and public service obligations.

The compensatory element of public service contracts is clearly demonstrable in air transport services, where public service obligations[33] can only be conferred on operators by reference to a specific procedure, which links their compensation with a selection process based on a public tender.[34] The significance of this process is such as to allow Member States to determine the value of a public service by taking into account both the users' interests and costs incurred by the relevant operator. The criteria for calculating the compensation involve exclusively factors relevant to the operating deficit incurred on a specific route,[35] including a reasonable remuneration for the capital employed.[36] Thus, a contract to carry out public service obligations is awarded to the operator which requires the lowest financial compensation.[37] The compensation in the form of a public service contract

[33] The concept of public service obligation within the context of the air transport regime is defined in Regulation 2408/92 on access for air carriers to intra-Community air routes as 'any obligation imposed upon an air carrier to take, in respect of any route which it is licensed to operate by a Member State, all necessary measures to ensure the provision of a service satisfying fixed standards of continuity, regularity, capacity and pricing, standards which the air carrier would not assume if it were solely considering its economic interest'. OJ 1992 L240.

[34] Community rules on public procurement contracts do not apply to the awarding by law or contract of exclusive concessions, which are exclusively ruled by the procedure provided for pursuant to Article 4(1) of Regulation 2408/92.

[35] The implementation of a public service obligation must be transparent, and the selected transport operators are expected to account annually for the relevant costs, including fixed costs and revenues attributed to the relevant routes.

[36] Although Article 4(1)(f) of Regulation 2408/92, above, refers to the compensation required as just one of the criteria to be taken into consideration for the selection of submissions, the Commission considers that the level of compensation should be the main selection criterion, as other elements such as adequacy, fare prices and standards are constituent elements of the public service obligations themselves.

[37] See Case C-301/87, *France* v. *Commission* [1990] ECR I-307; Case C-142/87, *Belgium* v. *Commission* [1990] ECR I-959.

awarded through the tendering process reveals a neutral commercial operation between the relevant Member State and the selected air carrier. The neutrality of the transaction is based on reimbursement limited solely to sustained losses because of the operation of a specific route, and does not bring about any special benefit for the air carrier.[38] Compensation of costs incurred by a carrier which has not been selected according to the tendering process, or compensation which is not calculated on the basis of the lowest cost criterion, would be assessed under the general State aid rules.[39] Compensation will be considered as State aid if it diverts significant volumes of traffic or allows carriers to cross-subsidize routes on which they compete with other Community air carriers.[40]

2.3 The economic assessment of public services

The compensatory nature of the reimbursement for the provision of public services reflects two main elements: (1) the deficit-based calculation method for their value and, as a result, (2) the non-commercial nature of the markets within which such services are delivered. It is assumed that public services regarding public or universal obligations or services of general economic interest have minimal commercial value. Market forces cannot provide for the needs of the public, as a number of factors deter entry into the relevant market (profitability, set-up costs, risk, volume and levels of demand, intra-mode competition). Thus, the markets within which public service obligations are dispersed are *sui generis*. The most important repercussion of such finding is the true

[38] See Case 173/73, *Italy* v. *Commission* [1974] ECR 709.

[39] Reimbursement for public services to the Azores are excluded from the scope of Regulation 2408/92, but are subject to Articles 107 and 108 TFEU (formerly Article 87 and 88 EC). See Commission Decision of 6 July 1994, Case C-7/93 on reimbursement of the deficit sustained by TAP on the routes to the Atlantic islands, OJ 1993 C178.

[40] Article 4(1)(i) of Regulation 2408/92, above, obliges Member States to take the necessary measures to ensure that any decision to award public service obligations can be reviewed effectively. The Commission may carry out an investigation and make a decision where the development of a route is being unduly restricted under Article 4(3) of the Regulation. However, the Commission's powers under the Regulation are without prejudice to its exclusive powers under the State aid rules of the Treaty. Where there is clear evidence that the Member State has not selected the best offer, the Commission may request information from the State in order to examine whether the award of a public service obligation includes, in addition to compensation, elements of State aid. Such elements are likely to occur where a Member State has not selected the lowest offer in relation to the financial compensation to be paid to the air carrier.

relevance of the tools used to compare the value of a relevant service such as the private investor principle. The lack of a reliable comparator, the non-commercial nature of public service obligations and the calculation method for the reimbursement might pose problems in determining an objective and uniformly acceptable value for their delivery. It appears that there are difficult elements surrounding this, such as demand structure, infrastructure investment and costs, scale economies and revenue levels.

On the other hand, the market-oriented character of their award, as depicted in the tendering process, intends to establish a transparent and objective framework for their delivery. Interestingly, the competitive process for the award of public service obligations to the lowest offer reflecting the costs and revenue (i.e., the deficit) generated by the service runs in parallel with the application of public procurement rules for the delivery of services of a non-commercial nature.

The homogenous treatment of the relationship between Member States and public or private undertakings which are entrusted with the delivery of public services reflect upon a 'commissioning' role on the part of Member States. Such a commissioning role has the intention to remove the regulation of the relevant services from the remit of the general competition rules and place it within the framework of the State aid regime.[41]

3. The legal treatment of the financing of public services

3.1 Public services and State aid assessment

The European Commission and the European Courts (the Court of Justice and the General Court) have over the years developed a set of approaches to control the funding of public services and apply State aid *acquis* with a view to treating the funding of public services as compatible with the policies of the Treaties, and in particular with competition policy. The three approaches are: (1) the State aid approach; (2) the compensation approach; and (3) the *quid pro quo* approach.[42] Under the

[41] See C. Bovis, 'Public Procurement and Services of General Economic Interest' in M. Krajewski, U. Neergaard and J. van de Gronden (eds.), *The Changing Legal Framework of Services of General Interest – between Competition and Solidarity* (T. M. C. Asser Press, 2009).

[42] See A. Alexis, 'Services publics et aides d'état', *Revue du droit de l'Union Européenne* (2002) 63; D. Grespan, 'An Example of the Application of State Aid Rules in the Utilities

State aid approach,[43] all public service funding is treated as State aid within the meaning of Article 107(1) TFEU,[44] which may, however, be justified under Article 106(2) TFEU,[45] provided that the conditions of that derogation are fulfilled and, in particular, the funding complies with the principle of proportionality. On the other hand, under the compensation approach,[46] funding of public services is treated as State aid only if and to the extent that the remuneration paid to the entrusted undertaking provides an economic advantage, in as much as it exceeds an appropriate remuneration or the additional costs of providing those services. The test of appropriateness is determined by reference to the market price for the relevant services. The *quid pro quo* approach distinguishes between two categories of State funding of public services. On the one hand, in cases where there is a direct and manifest link between the State financing and clearly defined public service obligations imposed upon the entrusted undertaking, any sums paid by the State would not constitute State aid within the meaning of the Treaty. On the

Sector in Italy', *Competition Policy Newsletter*, No. 3 (October 2002), p. 17; Ph. Nicolaides, 'Distortive Effects of Compensatory Aid Measures: A Note on the Economics of the Ferring Judgment', *European Competition Law Review* 6(23) (2002) 313–19; Ph. Nicolaides, 'The New Frontier in State Aid Control: An Economic Assessment of Measures that Compensate Enterprises', *Intereconomics* 37(4) (2002) 190–7; C. Rizza, 'The Financial Assistance Granted by Member States to Undertakings Entrusted with the Operation of a Service of General Economic Interest: The Implications of the Forthcoming Altmark Judgment for Future State Aid Control Policy', *Columbia Journal of European Law* 9 (2003) 429–46; C. Bovis, 'Public Procurement, State Aids and the Financing of Public Services: Between Symbiotic Correlation and Asymmetric Geometry', *European State Aids Law Quarterly* (November 2003) 563–77.

[43] See Case C-387/92 [1994] ECR I-877; Case T-106/95, *FFSA and Others* v. *Commission* [1997] ECR II-229; Case C-174/97 P [1998] ECR I-1303; Case T-46/97 [2000] ECR II-2125.

[44] Article 107(1) EC defines State aid as 'any aid granted by a Member State or through State resources in any form whatsoever which distorts or threatens to distort competition by favouring certain undertakings or the production of certain goods . . . in so far as it affects trade between Member States'.

[45] Article 106(2) EC stipulates that: 'Undertakings entrusted with the operation of services of general economic interest . . . shall be subject to the rules contained in this Treaty, in particular to the rules on competition, insofar as the application of such rules does not obstruct the performance, in law or in fact, of the particular tasks assigned to them. The development of trade must not be affected to such an extent as would be contrary to the interests of the Community.'

[46] See Case 240/83, *Procureur de la République/ADBHU* [1985] ECR 531; Case C-53/00, *Ferring SA* v. *Agence centrale des organismes de sécurité sociale (ACOSS)* [2001] ECR I-9067; Case C-280/00, *Altmark Trans GmbH and Regierungspräsidium Magdeburg* [2003] ECR I-7747.

other hand, where there is no such link, or the public service obligations were not clearly defined, payments by public authorities would constitute State aid.

A hybrid assessment method between the compensation and the *quid pro quo* approaches has been introduced by the Court in *Altmark*,[47] in which subsidies are regarded as compensation for the services provided by the recipient undertakings in order to discharge public service obligations, and do not amount to State aid. Nevertheless, for the purpose of applying that criterion, four conditions must be satisfied: first, the recipient undertaking is actually required to discharge public service obligations and those obligations have been clearly defined; second, the basis on which the compensation is calculated has been established beforehand in an objective and transparent manner; third, the compensation does not exceed what is necessary to cover all or part of the costs incurred in discharging the public service obligations, taking into account the relevant receipts and a reasonable profit for discharging those obligations; fourth, where the undertaking which is to discharge public service obligations is not chosen in a public procurement procedure, the level of compensation needed has been determined on the basis of an analysis of the costs which a typical undertaking, well run and adequately provided with appropriate means so as to be able to meet the necessary public service requirements, would have incurred in discharging those obligations, taking into account the relevant receipts and a reasonable profit for discharging the obligations.

3.2 *Public procurement and public services*

The application of the State aid approach creates a gap in the treatment of funding of public services under State aid *acquis*, which is filled by the application of the public procurement regime or a specific tendering procedure, laid down for the award of public service contracts. The State aid approach presupposes that the delivery of services of general economic interest will emerge and take place in a different market, where the State and its emanations carry out a public function. Such markets are not susceptible to the private operator principle,[48] which has been relied

[47] See Case C-280/00, *Altmark Trans GmbH and Regierungspräsidium Magdeburg* [2003] ECR I-7747.

[48] See the Communication of the Commission to the Member States concerning public authorities' holdings in company capital (*Bulletin EC* 9–1984, point 3.5.1). The

upon by the Commission and the European Courts[49] to determine the borderline between market behaviour and State intervention. The State aid approach runs parallel with the assumption that services of general interest emerge and their delivery takes place within distinctive markets, which bear little resemblance with private markets in terms of competitiveness, demand and supply substitutability, and structure.

Settled case law of the European Courts differentiates between the economic nature of State intervention and the exercise of public powers.[50] The application of the private investor principle is confined to the economic nature of State intervention,[51] and is justified by the principle of equal treatment between public and private sectors,[52] which requires that intervention by the State should be subject to the same rules applicable to private undertakings. The non-economic character of State intervention[53] neutralizes the principle of private operator, for the

Commission considers that such an investment is not an aid where the public authorities sanction it under the same conditions as a private investor operating under normal market economy conditions. See also Commission Communication to the Member States on the application of Articles 92 and 93 of the EEC Treaty and of Article 5 of Commission Directive 80/723/EEC to public undertakings in the manufacturing sector, OJ 1993 C307/3, point 11.

49 See, in particular, Case 234/84, *Belgium* v. *Commission* [1986] ECR 2263, para. 14; Case C-142/87, *Belgium* v. *Commission (Tubemeuse)* [1990] ECR I-959, para. 26; and Case C-305/89, *Italy* v. *Commission (Alfa Romeo)* [1991] ECR I-1603, para. 19.

50 See Joined Cases C-278/92 to 280/92, *Spain* v. *Commission* [1994] ECR I-4103.

51 For example, where the public authorities contribute capital to an undertaking (Case 234/84, *Belgium* v. *Commission* [1986] ECR 2263; Case C-142/87, *Belgium* v. *Commission* [1990] ECR I-959; Case C-305/89, *Italy* v. *Commission* [1991] ECR I-1603), grant a loan to certain undertakings (Case C-301/87, *France* v. *Commission* [1990] ECR I-307; Case T-16/96, *Cityflyer Express* v. *Commission* [1998] ECR II-757), provide a State guarantee (Joined Cases T-204/97 and 270/97, *EPAC* v. *Commission* [2000] ECR II-2267), sell goods or services on the market (Joined Cases 67/85, 68/85 and 70/85, *Van der Kooy and Others* v. *Commission* [1988] ECR 219; Case C-56/93, *Belgium* v. *Commission* [1996] ECR I-723; Case C-39/94, *SFEI and Others* [1996] ECR I-3547) or grant facilities for the payment of social security contributions (Case C-256/97, *DM Transport* [1999] ECR I-3913) or the repayment of wages (Case C-342/96, *Spain* v. *Commission* [1999] ECR I-2459).

52 See Case C-303/88, *Italy* v. *Commission* [1991] ECR I-1433, para. 20; Case C-261/89, *Italy* v. *Commission* [1991] ECR I-4437, para. 15; and Case T-358/94, *Air France* v. *Commission* [1996] ECR II-2109, para. 70.

53 For example, where the public authorities pay a subsidy directly to an undertaking (Case 310/85, *Deufil* v. *Commission* [1987] ECR 901), grant an exemption from taxation (Case C-387/92, *Banco Exterior* [1994] ECR I-877; Case C-6/97, *Italy* v. *Commission* [1999] ECR I-2981; Case C-156/98, *Germany* v. *Commission* [2000] ECR I-6857) or agree to a reduction in social security contributions (Case C-75/97, *Belgium* v. *Commission* [1999] ECR I-3671; Case T-67/94, *Ladbroke Racing* v. *Commission* [1998] ECR II-1).

reason that profitability, and thus the *raison d'être* of private undertakings, is not present. It follows that services of general economic interest cannot be part of the same demand/supply equation, as other normal services the State and its organs procure by virtue of exercising public powers.[54]

Convergence emerges between public procurement and the State aid approach in light of the reasoning behind the *BFI*[55] and *Agora*[56] cases. Services of general economic interest are *sui generis*, having as their main characteristics the lack of industrial and commercial character, where the absence of profitability and competitiveness are indicative of the relevant market place. As a rule, the procurement of such services should be subject to the rigour and discipline of public procurement rules and classified as State aid, in the absence of competitive award procedures. In consequence, the application of the public procurement regime reinforces the general interest character of services of general interest as both non-commercial and industrial[57] and the existence of *marchés publics*.[58]

The compensation approach relies heavily upon the real advantage theory in determining the existence of any advantages conferred on undertakings through State financing.[59] Thus, under the real advantage theory, the advantages given by the State and threatening to distort competition are examined together with the obligations on the recipient of the aid. Thus, advantages constitute aid only if their amount exceeds the value of

[54] See the analysis in Joined Cases C-278/92 to 280/92, *Spain* v. *Commission* [1994] ECR I-4103.

[55] See Case C-360/96, *Gemeente Arnhem Gemeente Rheden* v. *BFI Holding BV* [1998] ECR I-6821.

[56] See Case C-223/99, *Agora Srl* v. *Ente Autonomo Fiera Internazionale di Milano*; and Case C-260/99, *Excelsior SNC di Pedrotti Runa and C* v. *Ente Autonomo Fiera Internazionale di Milano* [2001] ECR 3605.

[57] See Joined Cases C-83/01 P, 93/01 P and 94/01, *Chronopost and Others* [2003] ECR I-6993. The *Chronopost* ruling confirmed the private investor principle in State aid regulation, by indirectly accepting the State aid approach and therefore admitting the existence of *sui generis* markets within which services of general interest emerge and are delivered and that those markets cannot feasibly be compared with private ones. See also the earlier judgment of the General Court (the Court of First Instance at the time) in Case T-613/97, *Ufex and Others* v. *Commission* [2000] ECR II-4055.

[58] See C. Bovis, *EU Public Procurement: Case Law and Regulation* (Oxford University Press, 2006); M. Bazex, 'Le droit public de la concurrence', *Revue Francaise de Droit Administratif* 14 (1998) 781–800; L. Arcelin, *L'enterprise en droit interne et communautaire de la concurrence* (Paris: Litec, 2003); O. Guézou, 'Droit de la concurrence et droit des marchés publics: vers une notion transveraletransversale de mise en libre concurrence', *Contrats Publics* (March 2003) 43–7.

[59] See A. Evans, *European Community Law of State Aid* (Oxford: Clarendon Press, 1997).

the public service commitments which the recipient has been entrusted with or additional costs of providing those services. The compensation approach treats the costs offsetting the provision of public services as the baseline over which State aid should be considered. That baseline is determined by the market price, which corresponds to the given public/ private contractual interface and is demonstrable through the application of public procurement award procedures. The application of the compensation approach reveals a significant insight into the financing of services of general interest. A quantitative distinction emerges over and above which State aid exists. The compensation approach introduces an applicability threshold of State aid regulation, and that threshold is the perceived market price and terms and conditions for the delivery of the relevant services.

The application of the compensation approach is reflected in the *Stohal*[60] case, where an undertaking could provide commercial services and services of general interest, without engaging the public procurement rules. The rationale of the case runs parallel to the real advantage theory, up to the point of recognizing the different nature and characteristics of the markets under which normal (commercial) services and general interest services are provided. The distinction begins where, for legal certainty and legitimate expectations, the activities of undertakings of dual capacity are equally covered by the public procurement regime and the undertaking in question is considered as *contracting authority*, irrespective of the ratio of the delivery of commercial services to services of general interest. This finding might have a significant implication for the compensation approach in State aid jurisprudence: irrespective of any costs offsetting the costs related to the provision of general interest, the entire State financing could be viewed under the State aid approach. Nevertheless, the real advantage theory upon which the compensation approach seems to rely runs contrary to the apparent advantage theory, which underlies Treaty provisions[61] and

[60] Case C-44/96, *Mannesmann Anlangenbau Austria AG et al.* v. *Strohal Rotationsdurck GesmbH*, above. See also the analysis of the case by C. Bovis, *Common Market Law Review* 36 (1999) 205–25.

[61] According to Advocate General Léger in his Opinion on the *Altmark* case, the apparent advantage theory appears in several provisions of the Treaty, in particular in Article 102 (2) and (3) TFEU (formerly Article 92(2) and (3) EC) and in Article 97 TFEU (formerly Article 77 EC). Article 102(3) TFEU provides that aid may be regarded as compatible with the Common Market if it pursues certain objectives such as the strengthening of economic and social cohesion, the promotion of research and the protection of the environment.

the so-called effects approach[62] adopted by the Court in determining the existence of State aid.

The *quid pro quo* approach[63] introduces a distinction between two different categories of State funding for services of general interest: (i) the nature of the link between the financing granted and the general interest duties imposed; and (ii) the degree of clarity in defining those duties. The first category would comprise cases where the financing measures are clearly intended as a *quid pro quo* for clearly defined general interest obligations, or, in other words, where there is a direct and manifest link between the State funding granted and clearly defined general interest obligations imposed. The clearest example of such a link between State funding and clearly defined obligations are public service contracts awarded in accordance with public procurement rules. The contract in question should define the obligations of the undertakings entrusted with the services of general interest and the remuneration that they would receive in return. Examples falling into that category should be analyzed according to the compensation approach. The second category consists of cases where it is not clear from the outset that the State funding is intended as a *quid pro quo* for clearly defined general interest obligations. In those cases, the link between State funding and the general interest obligations imposed is either not direct or not manifest, or the general interest obligations are not clearly defined.

The *quid pro quo* approach appears *prima facie* consistent with the general case law on the interpretation of Article 107(1) TFEU. It also gives appropriate weight to the importance of services of general interest, within the remit of Article 14 TFEU and of Article 36 of the EU Charter of Fundamental Rights. On the other hand, the *quid pro quo* approach presents a major shortcoming: it introduces elements[64] of the nature of

[62] See Case C-173/73, *Italy* v. *Commission* [1974] ECR 709; Case 310/85, *Deufil* v. *Commission* [1987] ECR 901; Case C-56/93, *Belgium* v. *Commission* [1996] ECR I-723; Case C-241/94, *France* v. *Commission* [1996] ECR I-4551; Case C-5/01, *Belgium* v. *Commission* [2002] ECR I-3452.

[63] See the Opinion of Advocate General Jacobs in Case C-126/01, *Ministre de l'économie, des finances et de l'industrie* v. *GEMO SA* [2003] ECR I-13769.

[64] For example, the form in which the aid is granted (Case C-323/82, *Intermills* v. *Commission* [1984] ECR 3809, para. 31; Case C-142/87, *Belgium* v. *Commission* [1990] ECR I-959, para. 13; and Case 40/85, *Belgium* v. *Commission* [1986] ECR I-2321, para. 120), the legal status of the measure in national law (Commission Decision 93/349/EEC of 9 March 1993 concerning aid provided by the United Kingdom Government to British Aerospace for its purchase of Rover Group Holdings over and above those authorized in Commission Decision 89/58/EEC authorizing a maximum aid to this

public funding into the process of determining the legality of State aid. According to State aid jurisprudence, only the effects of the measure are to be taken into consideration,[65] and, as a result of the application of the *quid pro quo* approach, legal certainty could be undermined.

The *quid pro quo* approach appears to define State aid not only by reference to the effects of the measure, but also by reference to criteria of a purely formal or procedural nature. This means that the existence of a procedural or a substantive link between the State and the service in question lifts the threat of State aid regulation, irrespective of any effect the State measure has on competition. However, the Court considers that to determine whether a State measure constitutes aid, only the effects of the measure are to be taken into consideration, whereas other elements[66] typifying a measure are not relevant during the stage of determining the existence of aid, because they are not liable to affect competition. Moreover, the relevance of these elements may appear when an assessment of the compatibility of the aid[67] with the derogating provisions of the Treaty takes place. The application of the *quid pro quo* approach amounts to introducing such elements into the actual definition of aid. The presence of a direct and manifest link between the State funding and the public service obligations amounts to the existence of a public service contract awarded after a public procurement procedure. In addition, the clear definition of public service obligations amounts to the existence of laws, regulations or

operation subject to certain conditions, OJ 1993 L143/7, point IX), the fact that the measure is part of an aid scheme (Case T-16/96, *Cityflyer Express* v. *Commission* [1998] ECR II-757), the reasons for the measure and the objectives of the measure (Case C-173/73, *Italy* v. *Commission* [1974] ECR 709; Case 310/85, *Deufil* v. *Commission* [1987] ECR 901; Case C-56/93, *Belgium* v. *Commission* [1996] ECR I-723; Case C-241/94, *France* v. *Commission* [1996] ECR I-4551; Case C-5/01, *Belgium* v. *Commission* [2002] ECR I-3452) and the intentions of the public authorities and the recipient undertaking (Commission Decision 92/11/EEC of 31 July 1991 concerning aid provided by the Derbyshire County Council to Toyota Motor Corporation, an undertaking producing motor vehicles, OJ 1992 L6/36, point V).

65 See Case C-173/73, *Italy* v. *Commission* [1974] ECR 709, para. 27; Case 310/85, *Deufil* v. *Commission* [1987] ECR 901; Case C-56/93, *Belgium* v. *Commission* [1996] ECR I-723, para. 79; Case C-241/94, *France* v. *Commission* [1996] ECR I-4551, para. 20; and Case C-5/01, *Belgium* v. *Commission* [2002] ECR I-3452, paras. 45 and 46.

66 For example, the form in which the aid is granted, the legal status of the measure in national law, the fact that the measure is part of an aid scheme, the reasons for the measure, the objectives of the measure and the intentions of the public authorities and the recipient undertaking.

67 For example, certain categories of aid are compatible with the Common Market on condition that they are employed through a specific format. See Commission Guidelines on State Aid for Rescuing and Restructuring Firms in Difficulty, OJ 2004 C244/2.

contractual provisions which specify the nature and content of the undertaking's obligations. The borderline of the market price, which will form the conceptual base above which State aid would appear, is not always easy to determine, even with the presence of public procurement procedures. The State and its organs as contracting authorities (State emanations and bodies governed by public law) have wide discretion to award public contracts under the public procurement rules.[68] Often, price plays a secondary role within the award criteria. In cases when the public contract is awarded to the lowest bidder,[69] the element of *market price* under the compensation approach could be determined. However, when the public contract is to be awarded by reference to the most economically advantageous offer,[70] the market price might be totally different from the price the contracting authority is willing to pay for the procurement of the relevant services. The mere existence of a public procurement procedure cannot, therefore, reveal the necessary element of the compensation approach – the measure price that will determine the 'excessive' State intervention and introduce State aid regulation.

The *quid pro quo* approach relies on the existence of a direct and manifest link between State financing and services of general interest, indicated by the presence of a public contract concluded in accordance with the provisions of the public procurement Directives. Apart from the criticism it has received concerning the introduction of elements into the

[68] The Public Procurement Directives provide for two criteria under which contracting authorities award public contracts: the *lowest price* and the *most economically advantageous offer*. The first criterion indicates that, subject to the qualitative criteria and financial and economic standing, contracting authorities do not rely on any factor other than the price quoted to complete the contract. The Directives provide for the automatic disqualification of an 'obviously abnormally low offer'. See Case 76/81, *SA Transporoute et Travaux* v. *Minister of Public Works* [1982] ECR 457; Case 103/88, *Fratelli Costanzo SpA* v. *Comune di Milano* [1989] ECR 1839.

[69] An interesting view of the lowest price representing market value benchmarking is provided by Case C-94/99, *ARGE Gewässerschutzt* [200] ECR I-11037, where the Court ruled that directly or indirectly subsidized tenders by the State or other contracting authorities or even by the contracting authority itself can be legitimately part of the evaluation process, although it did not elaborate on the possibility of rejection of an offer, which is appreciably lower than those of unsubsidized tenderers by reference to the abnormally low disqualification ground.

[70] The meaning of the most economically advantageous offer includes a series of factors chosen by the contracting authority, including price, delivery or completion date, running costs, cost-effectiveness, profitability, technical merit, product or work quality, aesthetic and functional characteristics, after-sales service and technical assistance, commitments with regard to spare parts and components and maintenance costs, and security of supplies. The above list is not exhaustive.

assessment process of State aid, the interface of the *quid pro quo* approach with public procurement appears as the most problematic facet in its application. The procurement of public services does not always reveal a public contract between a contracting authority and an undertaking. It should be mentioned that the existence of dependency links, in terms of overall control of an entity by the State or another contracting authority, renders the public procurement regime inapplicable. Dependency presupposes a control similar to that which the State of another contracting authority exercises over its own departments. The 'similarity' of control denotes lack of independence with regard to decision-making. The Court in *Teckal*[71] concluded that a contract between a contracting authority and an entity over which the former exercises a control similar to that which it exercises over its own departments, and where that entity carries out the essential part of its activities with the contracting authority, is not a public contract, irrespective of whether that entity is itself a contracting authority.

On similar lines, public contracts which are awarded on the basis of exclusive rights granted to an undertaking by a law, regulation or administrative provision of a Member State,[72] as well as public contracts between the State and affiliated undertakings[73] are not subject to any competitive requirements.[74] In addition, the connection between the

[71] See Case C-107/98, *Teckal Srl* v. *Comune di Viano* [1999] ECR I-8121.

[72] See Article 6 of Directive 92/50/EEC relating to the coordination of procedures for the award of public service contracts, OJ 1992 L209/1.

[73] See Article 13 of the Utilities Directive 93/37/EEC concerning the coordination of procedures for the award of public works contracts, OJ 1993 L199/54.

[74] For the purposes of Article 1(3) of the Utilities Directive, an affiliated undertaking is one the annual accounts of which are consolidated with those of the contracting entity in accordance with the requirements of the Seventh Company Law Directive (Council Directive 83/349/EEC, OJ 1983 L193/1). These are service contracts which are awarded to a service provider affiliated either to the contracting entity or to a contracting entity participating in a joint venture formed for the purpose of carrying out an activity covered by the Directive. The explanatory memorandum accompanying the text amending the Utilities Directive (COM(1991) 347-SYN 36 1) states that this provision relates, in particular, to three types of service provision within groups. These categories, which may or may not be distinct, are: the provision of common services such as accounting, recruitment and management; the provision of specialized services embodying the knowhow of the group; and the provision of a specialized service to a joint venture. The exclusion from the provisions of the Directive is subject, however, to two conditions: the service provider must be an undertaking affiliated to the contracting authority and at least 80 per cent of its average turnover arising within the European Community for the preceding three years must derive from the provision of the same or similar services to undertakings with which it is affiliated.

State and entities that operate in the utilities sector and have been privatized is also too weak to sustain the presence of a public procurement contract for the delivery of services of general interest. Privatized utilities could be, in principle, excluded from the procurement rules when a genuinely competitive regime[75] within the relevant market structure would rule out purchasing patterns based on non-economic considerations. *Altmark* has created a number of problems.

The first condition, which requires the existence of a clear definition of the framework within which public service obligations and services of general interest have been entrusted to the beneficiary of compensatory payments, runs consistently with Article 106(2) TFEU jurisprudence, which requires an express act of the public authority to assign services of general economic interest.[76] However, the second condition, requiring the establishment of the parameters on the basis of which the compensation is calculated in an objective and transparent manner, departs from existing precedent,[77] as it establishes an *ex post* control mechanism by the Member States and the European Commission. The third condition, that the compensation must not exceed what is necessary to cover the costs incurred in discharging services of general interest or public service obligations, is compatible with the proportionality test applied in Article 106(2) TFEU. Nonetheless, there is an inconsistency problem, as the European judiciary is rather unclear as to the question of whether any

[75] The determination of a genuinely competitive regime is left to the utilities operators themselves. See Case C-392/93, *The Queen and HM Treasury, ex parte British Telecommunications plc*, OJ 1993 C287/6. The Utilities Procurement Directive 2004/17/EC, OJ 2004 L134, does not regard telecommunications utilities as contracting entities, since the sector has been subjected to competitive forces adequate to ensure the commercial character of its operation. See C. Bovis, 'The New Public Procurement Legal Framework', *European Public Law* 12(1) (2006) 73–109.

[76] See Case 127/73, *BRT* v. *SABAM* [1974] ECR 313, para. 20; Case 66/86, *Ahmed Saeed Flugreisen* v. *Commission* [1989] ECR 803, para. 55.

[77] The standard assessment criterion which applies under Article 106(2) TFEU only requires an examination of possible frustration of the performance of a particular public service task, thus allowing for an *ex post facto* application of Article 107(1) TFEU. See also the reasoning behind the so-called 'electricity judgments' of the Court of 23 October 1997: Case C-157/94, *Commission* v. *Netherlands* [1997] ECR I-5699; Case C-158/94, *Commission* v. *Italy* [1997] ECR I-5789; Case C-159/94, *Commission* v. *France* [1997] ECR I-5815; and Case C-160/94, *Commission* v. *Spain* [1997] ECR I-5851. A great deal of controversy exists as to whether the material standard of the frustration of a public service task under Article 106(2) TFEU had lost its strictness. See S. Magiera, 'Gefährdung der öffentlichen Daseinsvorsorge durch das EG-Beihilfenrecht?' in J. Ipsen and E. Schmidt-Jortzig (eds.), *Festschrift für Dietrich Rauschning* (Cologne: Carl Heymanns Verlag, 2001), pp. 269–89.

compensation for public service obligations may include a profit element.[78] Finally, the fourth condition establishes a comparison of the cost structures of both the recipient and a private undertaking which is well run and adequately provided to fulfil the public service tasks, in the absence of a public procurement procedure, inserts elements of subjectivity and uncertainty that will inevitably fuel controversy.

4. Conclusions

The relationship between public procurement and public services reveals a symbiotic flexibility embedded in the regime of regulating the award of public contracts, as well as a direct nexus with State aid regulation. That flexibility conferred on contracting authorities is augmented by a wide margin of discretion available to Member States to introduce public policy considerations in dispersing public services. State aid, as part of regional development or as part of a national or EU-wide industrial policy, is an inherent component of this symbiotic policy approach. This finding removes the often misunderstood justification of public procurement as an economic exercise and places it at the heart of an ordo-liberal interpretation of the European integration process.

Public services require State intervention for their provision, organization and delivery. This thesis has two implications: first, competition law has limited use in their regulation, mainly because of Article 106(2) TFEU; second, what can bring the provision, organization and delivery of public services into line with competition policy is State aid regulation. However, assessment instruments and methods under State aid policy, such as the private investor principle, show that public services which include public obligations, universal obligations and services of general economic interest, function in *sui generis* markets. They also reveal the non-commercial character of public services, in as much as the latter lack profitability, a character which points towards the *compensatory nature*

[78] See the Opinion of Advocate General Lenz, delivered on 22 November 1984, in Case 240/83, *Procureur de la République* v. *ADBHU* [1985] ECR 531 (p. 536). Advocate General Lenz in his Opinion held that the indemnities granted must not exceed the annual uncovered costs actually recorded by the undertaking, taking into account a reasonable profit. However, the Court, in the *ADBHU* case, did not allow for the permissibility of taking into account such a profit element. Interestingly, the approach of the Court of First Instance on Article 106(2) TFEU has never allowed any profit element to be taken into account, but instead focused on whether, without the compensation at issue being provided, the fulfilment of the specific public service tasks would have been jeopardized.

of the reimbursement of public service by the State and its organs. This finding exposes the deficit-based calculation method for their cost and value, which in turn renders their funding compatible with the EU Treaties, provided that the calculation method reflects market conditions and that the selection of the entrusted undertaking is transparent and based on objective criteria. Public procurement is the regime that can provide for transparency, objectivity and non-discrimination, as well as insert elements of competition in the provision, organization and delivery of public services.

PART III

The interaction between pluralism, trust and economic integration

6

Shifting narratives in European economic integration: trade in services, pluralism and trust

IOANNIS LIANOS AND DAMIEN M. B. GERARD

1. Introduction

At almost twenty-five years of distance, Cappelletti, Seccombe and Weiler, on the one hand, and Delmas-Marty, on the other, have associated the European integration process with the 'enigma of the "one and the many" that has haunted human civilisation throughout history',[1] that is 'the dilemma of reaching an equilibrium between, on the one hand, a respect for the autonomy of the individual unit, freedom of choice, pluralism and diversity of action, and, on the other hand, the societal need for cooperation, integration, harmony and, at times, unity'.[2] In 1986, Cappelletti, Seccombe and Weiler attempted to solve that dilemma, and thus the one of European integration, by resorting to the concept of federalism as embodying a 'societal philosophy and organizational principle which require a particular balancing of individual and communal interest – a balance between particular and general, peripheral and central, and between autonomy and heteronomy'.[3] In 2009, Delmas-Marty did so by resorting to the formula of 'multiple interactions – judicial and normative, spontaneous and imposed, direct and indirect, to link together legal ensembles – national and international',[4] as a way 'toward harmony'.[5]

[1] M. Delmas-Marty, *Ordering Pluralism – A Conceptual Framework for Understanding the Transnational Legal World* (Oxford and Portland, OR: Hart Publishing, 2009), p. 2.

[2] M. Cappelletti, M. Seccombe and J. H. H. Weiler, 'Integration Through Law: Europe and the American Federal Experience, A General Introduction' in M. Cappelletti, M. Seccombe and J. H. H. Weiler (eds.), *Integration Through Law*, vol. 1, *Methods, Tools and Institutions*, Book 1, *A Political, Legal and Economic Overview* (Berlin and New York: Walter de Gruyter, 1986), p. 4.

[3] *Ibid.*, p. 15. [4] Delmas-Marty, *Ordering Pluralism*, above, p. 14. [5] *Ibid.*, p. 16.

At the core of this tentative essay – a feeler, indeed – lies an attempt to uncover a relative shift in the narrative underlying the matrix of European integration – from one of unity and federalism to one of pluralism, harmony and multiple interactions, to trace and report on manifestations of that shift in the core praxis of the EU system – market integration – and to suggest an alternative conceptualization of its hidden ethos by means of the notions of mutual trust and distrust.[6] The area of services forms the empirical background illustrating that three-fold proposition, for in recent years it has presented an important source of tensions between market integration, regulatory diversity and social values, for example in the framework of the adoption of the Services Directive or of prominent cases decided by the Court of Justice. Those instances have further highlighted the historical complexity in promoting cross-border trade in a sector that is by essence 'uncommoditized', relies on interpersonal relations, involves local (and vocal) stakeholders and whose regulation reflects policy options anchored in deep identity-loaded social choices, while also accounting for by far the largest share of domestic and regional wealth.[7] In turn, those constraints have triggered a broad variety of policy interventions, including of a sectoral

[6] Cappelletti, Seccombe and Weiler relied on federalism as a method rather than in reference to an ideal or optimal state, in a way similar to Delmas-Marty when she emphasizes harmony as generation and multiple interactions as ongoing processes. Moreover, they rejected unity as an absolute value but presented it as only one dimension of federalism as a method and as one of the poles in the balancing process inherent to that method. Likewise, they viewed the failure of Europe to develop into a federal super-State as a virtue, and stressed the need to promote the emergence of transnational forms of law and government. Yet, beyond the epistemological weight of the 'F-word', they still viewed federalism as a frame, integration as the strength of the frame, the Union as the central authority and the US federal State as a comparative point of reference. Thus, if the approaches of Cappelletti, Seccombe and Weiler and Delmas-Marty may seem to converge from a methodological point of view, their starting point is different: the former explored ways to reach beyond the static model of the State and the international/national dichotomy, while the latter takes the pluralism of legal orders as a given and as the premise of an attempt to harness 'the Great Legal Complexity of the world'. Likewise, the former relied on federalism to capture the tension between autonomy and heterogeneity, while the latter views autonomy as the source of heterogeneity. Hence, the origins of their respective approach differ, and so do their respective ways to address the dilemma between the one and the many and, in turn, the narrative underlying their vision of the matrix of the EU system.

[7] The Internal Market in services has been continuously lagging behind in the EU economic integration process, with the result that only 20 per cent of services supplied in the EU have a cross-border dimension, whereas the sector accounts for 70 per cent of EU GDP, 68 per cent of employment and 96 per cent of new job creation, and constitutes the most important source of foreign direct investment (see European Commission, *The Internal Market – Ten Years Without Frontiers*, pp. 6 and 22; M. Monti, 'A New Strategy

nature, and form a particularly fertile ground for exploring complex market integration strategies and, generally, for observing a possible evolution in the management of regulatory diversity at EU level. This is the objective of section 2 below, which reviews successively legislative instruments and the case law of the Court in the area of services and beyond.

Eventually, then, the revelation of such an evolution will allow for the reformulation of the inner ethos of the European market integration process, moving away from the narrow imagery of the removal of national barriers to trade or regulatory sameness and towards a multi-dimensional paradigm based on the notion of 'system trust'. As a paradigm, it does not espouse a deterministic model, but embodies a stochastic process capable of evolving over time as a response to random political shocks that might alter the preferences and values of the actors and thus the probable systemic outcomes. In turn, that envisaged reformulation is a testament to and reveals a shift in the equilibrium between the one and the many in the EU system. Those preliminary propositions are developed in section 3 below, which is followed by concluding remarks.

2. The affirmation of pluralistic concerns in EU Internal Market law

The EU market integration programme, in both its negative and positive dimensions, has long been viewed as a process of re-regulation entailing the replacement of national economic regulations with EU rules,[8] in pursuance of a functional logic of unity whereby the unity of the market and the unity of law was to contribute to an overarching goal of political unity for Europe.[9] Thus, upon completion of the Customs Union in 1968, the Commission stated that the latter was to be followed by the achievement of an economic union, which required 'replac[ing] the old national policies with Community policies', notably through the

for the Single Market at the Service of Europe's Economy and Society', Report to the President of the European Commission, 9 May 2010, p. 53; Communication from the European Commission of 20 November 2007, 'A Single Market for the Twenty-First Century', Brussels, COM(2007) 724 final, p. 8).

8 See, e.g., A. R. Young, 'The Single Market – Deregulation, Reregulation and Integration' in Helen Wallace, Mark A. Pollack and Alasdair R. Young (eds.), *Policy-Making in the European Union*, 6th edn (Oxford University Press, 2010), pp. 107 *et seq.*

9 P. Pescatore, 'Les objectifs de la Communauté européenne comme principes d'interprétation dans la jurisprudence de la Cour de justice' in *Miscellanea W. J. Ganshof van der Meersch*, vol. 2 (Brussels: Bruylant, 1972), p. 351. On the classic notion of the unity of the European market, see, e.g., Case 14/68, *Walt Wilhelm and Others* v. *Bundeskartellamt* [1969] ECR 1, para. 5.

'harmonization or unification in the commercial, fiscal, social, transport, and other fields, as provided for in the Treaties'.[10]

In a context of economic crisis and political stagnation, the 1970s gave rise to the unfolding of a process of negative integration led by the Court. At the end of the transition period, the Court endowed successively the Treaty provisions guaranteeing the free movement of goods, persons and services, with direct effect,[11] thereby triggering a flurry of requests for preliminary rulings on the interpretation of those provisions. The most emblematical judgments of that period remain *Dassonville* and *Cassis de Dijon*, in relation to the free movement of goods, which established the sequence of analysis applied by the Court ever since, across all four freedoms: (i) a far-reaching definition of the notion of obstacle to trade, combined with (ii) the possibility to justify the said obstacle by means of mandatory (or imperative) requirements in the general interest applied in a proportionate manner, i.e., appropriate, necessary and reflecting the (lack of) equivalence of the regulatory framework in place in the country of origin.[12] Maduro has highlighted the institutional choice inherent to that sequence, 'namely that it leaves the ECJ to define the balance between free movement and regulatory aims and therefore to define the appropriate regulatory policy'.[13] In effect, the Court complemented the market-building approach advocated by the Commission with a view to breaking the path-dependence of actors from national systems and to promote the emergence of a new European majoritarian view reflecting 'Community-designed values and concepts'.[14] Even

[10] Declaration by the Commission on the occasion of the achievement of the customs union on 1 July 1968, OJ 1968 C7/5.

[11] With respect to the free movement of services, see Case 33/74, *Van Binsbergen* [1974] ECR 1299.

[12] Case 8/74, *Procureur du Roi* v. *Benoît and Gustave Dassonville* [1974] ECR 837, para. 5; and Case 120/78, *Rewe-Zentral AG* v. *Bundesmonopolverwaltung für Branntwein* (*Cassis de Dijon*) [1979] ECR 649, paras. 8–11 and 14–15.

[13] M. P. Maduro, *We the Court: The European Court of Justice and the European Economic Constitution: A Critical Reading of Article 30 of the EC Treaty* (Oxford: Hart Publishing, 1998), p. 59. On p. 62, the author illustrates his view as follows: 'After *Cassis de Dijon*, a stream of cases led the ECJ to adopt a policy of giving preference to labelling over mandatory requirements regarding the designation, composition or other characteristics of imported products, which led to a redefinition of many national regulatory policies on the characteristics and designation of goods.'

[14] *Ibid.*, p. 72. This is clearly apparent from *Cassis de Dijon*, where the Court, by deciding that the German rule on minimum alcohol content failed the necessity test, and replaced it with its own, namely, that the minimum alcohol content of beverages ought to be left to the arbitration of supply and demand, i.e., to the market.

though it also triggered legislative action, negative integration has therefore been viewed as a centralized mechanism of allocation of regulatory competence sheltered from the control of the EU political process.

With the endorsement by the European Council of the Commission White Paper on 'Completing the Internal Market' and the introduction by the Single European Act of qualified majority voting for the adoption of approximation measures,[15] the positive integration process was revitalized in the mid-1980s with a view to completing 'a fully unified internal market by 1992'.[16] To achieve that objective, mutual recognition and equivalence was to be favoured over the approximation of Member States' laws and regulations.[17] Yet, the Commission relied largely on the approximation provisions of the amended Treaty to achieve its ambitions. The vast majority of measures adopted in the framework of the Single Market legislative programme took the form of Directives.[18] In a decade, hundreds of them were adopted in a great variety of fields,[19] either based on product-specific performance requirements combined with fully harmonized provisions involving, for example, testing methods to guarantee consumer safety (pharmaceuticals, chemicals, automobiles, etc.) or covering large families of products and/or hazards and specifying minimum requirements to be met before being placed on the market, i.e., 'new approach Directives'.[20] Beyond its achievements in economic terms,[21] the Internal Market programme transformed radically the way many businesses are conducted in Europe and the success of the venture in 'breaking through the old structures inherited from the past',[22] did not come without traumatic consequences. Indeed, the

[15] See, respectively: (i) Conclusions of the Milan European Council of 28–29 June 1985, *Bulletin EC*, 1985, p. 6/13; and (ii) Single European Act, OJ 1987 L169/1.

[16] Communication of the Commission, 'Completing the Internal Market', 14 June 1985, COM(85) 310 final, p. 4.

[17] *Ibid.*, p. 6.

[18] A. Young, 'The Single Market – Deregulation, Reregulation and Integration', above, p. 119.

[19] The total body of Internal Market Directives amounted to 1,291 in 1995, and increased to 1,475 by 2002: European Commission, *The Internal Market – Ten Years Without Frontiers*, 2002, p. 10, available at http://ec.europa.eu/internal_market/10years/docs/workingdoc/workingdoc_en.pdf (last visited 15 July 2010).

[20] *Ibid.*, p. 20.

[21] For a review of the benefits associated with the Single Market, see European Commission, *The Internal Market – Ten Years Without Frontiers* (2002); and European Commission Staff Working Document, The Single Market: Review of Achievements, SEC(2007) 1521.

[22] Declaration by the Commission on the occasion of the achievement of the customs union on 1 July 1968, OJ 1968 C7/5.

enterprise was hardly politically neutral or value-free: it inevitably involved choices between conflicting values that profoundly affected business cultures and consumer preferences across the EU.[23] In turn, the magnitude of those choices led to deep and lasting criticisms of the centralized process whereby they were achieved.

In essence, the criticisms directed at the market integration process, in both its negative and positive dimensions, are rooted in a hiatus between the nature of the means and the magnitude of the ends pursued. Maduro, again, associates four shortcomings with the centralized model of integration, as follows: (i) lack of consideration for national diversity, including cultural and regulatory traditions; (ii) risk of reduction in legislative innovation and experimentation; (iii) risk of evasion in the absence of a developed sense of community or complex enforcement system; and (iv) questionable assumptions as to the EU's ability to bring added value to the process of economic regulation in terms of efficiency and democracy.[24] Those shortcomings have become encapsulated over time in one heavy-weighted and multi-faceted notion: that of (lack of) legitimacy of the Union as a regulatory and political body, under its two 'input' and 'output' aspects.[25]

Ironically, by aiming to achieve one of the main objectives set forth in the Treaty of Rome, the Internal Market programme also sowed the seeds of a profound transformation in policy-making at EU level. Indeed, the acknowledgment of the shortcomings pointed to above triggered a progressive evolution in the design of EU policies towards new modes of governance reflecting a willingness to improve the inclusiveness of decision-making and the effectiveness of policy outcomes, as clearly apparent from, for example, the White Paper on European

[23] Young, 'The Single Market – Deregulation, Reregulation and Integration', above, p. 112; and Maduro, *We the Court*, above, p. 147: '[M]any obstacles to trade come from different assessments of what is the right policy, in terms of choice between regulation and free trade or the types of appropriate regulation.'

[24] Maduro, *We the Court*, above, p. 114.

[25] See, e.g., K. Lenaerts and D. Gerard, 'The Structure of the Union According to the Constitution for Europe: The Emperor Is Getting Dressed', *European Law Review* 29 (2004) 321–2: '(i) input legitimacy relates to the direct legitimization of political power through the democratic participation of the citizens or their elected representatives in transparent decision-making and constitution-making procedures; and (ii) output legitimacy relates to the extent to which citizens see their preferences mirrored in the outcomes of political processes and therefore accept and support the political order as "valid".'

Governance.[26] The hypothesis underlying the present section associates that evolution, combined with increased diversity in EU membership and the quantitative and qualitative enlargement of the scope of EU competences,[27] with a move from unity to pluralism as the prevalent representation of the relation between the EU and the Member States, which is at the core of the Union's 'register of self-understanding'.[28] In other words, it endeavours to link the turn to governance with the emergence of a new narrative underlying the EU integration process – one of pluralism – from which insights can be derived to inform the design of its rules, the performance of its functions, the understanding of its ends and eventually the definition of its nature. In support of that view, it further postulates that the logic of pluralism has even permeated the Internal Market case law of the Court, in spite of the latter's long-standing stance as the ultimate guardian of the unity of the market and that of the law.

This is not the place for long developments on the notion of legal pluralism.[29] Yet, before turning to an examination of the manifestations thereof at EU level, some clarifications are required. Even though it took a different turn immediately after,[30] the very early case law of the Court enshrines the basic premise of a pluralistic account of the EU system, namely, the recognition that 'the municipal law of any Member State . . . and Community law constitute two separate and distinct legal orders'.[31] In effect, pluralism implies the coexistence of autonomous and valid sources of law, i.e., of different legal orders, within one and the same social field, that is, a territory or a population.[32] Pluralism therefore

[26] European Commission, European Governance – A White Paper, COM(2001) 428 final, available at http://ec.europa.eu/governance/white_paper/index_en.htm (last visited 5 February 2010).

[27] On the link between quantitative and qualitative increases in diversity and policy adaptations, see, e.g., E. Philippart and M. Sie Dhian Ho, 'From Uniformity to Flexibility: The Management of Diversity and Its Impact on the EU System of Governance' in G. de Búrca and J. Scott (eds.), *Constitutional Change in the EU: From Uniformity to Flexibility?* (Oxford: Hart Publishing, 2000), p. 300.

[28] N. Walker, 'Legal Theory and the European Union: A 25th Anniversary Essay', *Oxford Journal of Legal Studies* 25(4) (2005) 581–601, p. 600.

[29] For a recent thorough discussion, see, e.g., 'Le Pluralisme', *Archives de Philosophie du droit* 49 (2005) 499.

[30] Notably, by promoting the idea of the integration of EU law into the laws of each Member State (see, e.g., Case 6/64, *Costa* v. *ENEL* [1964] ECR 585, pp. 593, 594 and 596).

[31] See the first preliminary ruling issued by the Court in Case 13/61, *Van Rijn*, section A.

[32] See, e.g., R. Michaels, 'Global Legal Pluralism', Duke Public Law and Legal Theory Research Paper Series, No. 259 (July 2009), p. 3.

challenges the monopoly of the State as the unique and ultimate source of authority and enables the emergence of a transnational form of law resting on a disconnection between the concepts of State and constitution. In turn, the peace of such coexistence is guaranteed by cooperative mechanisms preventing conflicts between incompatible rules.[33] At EU level, by establishing 'institutions endowed with sovereign rights',[34] Member States not only created a binding system of shared powers and responsibilities backed by 'a complete system of legal remedies',[35] but also provided for a system of express and implied cooperation rules including, at primary level, the preliminary ruling procedure and the principles of precedence and direct effect and,[36] at secondary level, countless instruments determining the law applicable to a great variety of legal situations and organizing the meso-level of governance where the EU and the Member States interact through their respective institutional structure in the implementation of common policies.

Yet the EU transnational system is not one of 'pure' pluralism because it is fundamentally incomplete and emanates from the common volition of a diversity of nation States, each embodying a specific political compact reflecting particular social choices and cultural traditions. Consequently, the hybrid nature of the EU system carries particular constraints in terms of legitimation, which mandate the EU to live with, tolerate and indeed embed and experiment that diversity into its actual praxis. As explained hereinafter, the Union has precisely endeavoured in recent years to live by and deliver on that ontological requirement in the exercise of its competences, including of its historical commitment to market integration.[37] Before moving on, though, it is

[33] See, generally, Delmas-Marty, *Ordering Pluralism*, above.

[34] Case 26/62, *Van Gend &\ Loos*, above, p. 12.

[35] Case 294/83, *Parti écologiste 'Les Verts'* v. *European Parliament* [1986] ECR 1339.

[36] For a recent discussion of precedence as a conflicts rule, see H. G. Hofmann, 'Conflicts and Integration: Revisiting Costa v. ENEL and Simmenthal II' in M. P. Maduro and L. Azoulai (eds.), *The Past and Future of EU Law* (Oxford: Hart Publishing, 2010), pp. 62–6.

[37] Already in the early 1990s, in introducing his essay on *New Directions in European Community Law*, Snyder contended that, under a supranational umbrella, the Union 'increasingly recognises the validity of diverse national policies' so that, in effect, 'common market law, in a fragmented Europe, is thus mainly a co-ordinating device': F. Snyder, *New Directions in European Community Law* (London: Weidenfeld and Nicolson, 1990), p. 18. Likewise, Mattera has presented on various occasions in the past the principle of mutual recognition as a means allowing for the accommodation of national diversities: see, e.g., A. Mattera, 'L'article 30 du traité CEE, la jurisprudence "Cassis de Dijon" et le principe de la reconnaissance mutuelle – Instruments au service d'une Communauté plus respectueuses des diversités nationales', *Revue du Marché*

worth emphasizing anew the density of the cooperative interactions between the EU and national levels of government so that pluralism in the EU system is hardly one of closeness and separation. Moreover, it rests on a far-reaching institutional structure and elaborated constitutional principles, which condition and ensure the consistency of and compliance with its outcome.[38]

2.1 Affirmation of pluralistic concerns in EU Internal Market policies

A more 'holistic approach' integrating the pluralistic interests/preferences of the European polity is emerging in the European Commission's recent review of its positive integration programme.[39] In its Communication on the Citizen's Agenda, the Commission noted the importance of economic integration 'in making the EU stronger globally' but also emphasized the importance of the value of solidarity in achieving the objectives of the Union.[40] In accordance with the objectives set by the Constitutive Treaties,[41] the Union should aim to promote a higher quality of life, better social cohesion and greater environmental protection by

Unique Européen No. 4 (1992) 13; A. Mattera, 'L'Union européenne assure le respect des identités nationales, régionales et locales en particulier par l'application et la mise en œuvre du principe de reconnaissance mutuelle', *Revue du droit de l'Union européenne* No. 2 (2002) 217–39. Of course, Snyder was right to point to early instances of instruments relying heavily on the coordination of national rules (for a glaring example, see also Regulation 1408/71 on the application of social security schemes to employed persons and their families moving within the Community, OJ 1971 L149/2); yet the elaboration of those instruments remained centralized and coordination was arguably the result of regulatory constraints rather than the outcome of a conscious political choice. Likewise, mutual recognition, even though it carried the potential of giving transnational relevance to domestic requirements, was for a long time commanded centrally and poorly organized, with a consequent lack of certainty and effectiveness.

[38] To use the terminology of Delmas-Marty, cooperative interactions in the EU system are 'verticalized' (see Delmas-Marty, *Ordering Pluralism*, above. p. 17).

[39] On the 'holistic approach', see I. Lianos, 'Shifting Narratives in the European Internal Market: Efficient Restrictions of Trade and the Nature of "Economic" Integration', *European Business Law Review* 21(5) (2010) 705–60. On the importance of ensuring citizens' support for the project of the Internal Market and the need to reconcile the Single Market and the social and citizens' dimension in the context of the Treaty logic of the 'highly competitive social market economy', see M. Monti, 'A New Strategy for the Single Market at the Service of Europe's Economy and Society', Report to the President of the European Commission, 9 May 2010, Chapter 3.

[40] Communication from the Commission to the European Council, A Citizen's Agenda, COM(2006) 211 final.

[41] Article 3(3) TEU (after Lisbon) (formerly Article 2 TEU).

ensuring 'citizens' existing rights of access to employment, education, social services, health care and other forms of social protection across Europe'.[42] In order to achieve these aims, the Commission acknowledges the importance of working in partnership with national governments.

There are various manifestations of this shift of narrative on the objectives of economic integration in Europe. As is explained in the Commission's Communication on a 'Single Market for 21st century Europe', the Internal Market must be 'more responsive to the expectations and concerns of citizens'.[43] It follows that the Single Market policy goes 'hand in hand with social and environment policies to contribute to sustainable development goals' and needs to 'encompass a strong social and environmental dimension'.[44] The Commission's Staff Working Document accompanying the Communication also notes that the Single Market brought benefits to citizens 'in the form of more choice, higher quality and lower prices' but 'times have changed and Single Market policy should change accordingly, to ensure that it responds to the needs of today's citizens'.[45] Finally, in its recent Communication, 'Towards a Single Market Act', the Commission seems to have taken stock of the integration of the concept of 'social market economy' in the Treaty of Lisbon and proposed to conduct an 'in-depth analysis of the social impact of all proposed legislation concerning the single market'.[46]

The implications of this rhetorical shift are important. First, as the Commission acknowledges,

> [m]arket opening and economic integration have social and environmental impacts, which must be factored in – both in Europe and abroad. This requires a better assessment of the impact of decisions and a better collective capacity to anticipate, foster and manage changes implied by greater opening and technological developments. This also implies getting market prices to reflect their real costs on society and the environment,

[42] Communication from the Commission to the European Council, A Citizen's Agenda, COM(2006) 211 final, p. 5.

[43] Communication for the Commission to the European Parliament, the Council, the European Economic and Social Committee and the Committee of the Regions, A Single Market for the Twenty-First Century, COM(2007) 724 final, p. 3 (hereinafter Single Market for the Twenty-First Century Communication).

[44] *Ibid.*, pp. 3–4.

[45] Commission Staff Working Document, Instruments for a Modernized Single Market Policy (MSMP), SEC(2007) 1518, p. 5.

[46] According to the most recent Communication from the Commission to the European Parliament, the Council, the Economic and Social Committee and the Committee of the Regions, Towards a Single Market Act, COM(2010) 608 final, p. 23.

> as well as making *citizens* more aware of the social and environmental impacts of their *consumer* choices.[47]

It is further recognized that 'the ultimate objective of all economic activity is to provide the goods and services that citizens require in the most efficient manner'.[48] The conception of 'citizens as consumers' becomes 'clearly central to the Single Market', which should take 'more seriously' into account the distributional impact of the Internal Market policies, its social effects and the consumer/citizen side.[49] The new approach to positive market integration will be more evidence-based and 'impact-driven', relying on a number of tools, also employed in competition policy, such as sector inquiries, or specific to the Single Market policy, such as the 'consumer markets scoreboard', in order to provide information on how markets perform 'in terms of economic and social outcomes for consumers, and where intervention may be needed'.[50] The Commission will use an 'optimal mix of instruments' that would combine more flexible approaches to legislation (e.g., the Lamfalussy process) and non-binding tools (e.g., codes of conduct), as well as competition law and policy tools (e.g., competition advocacy) in a 'synergetic manner' to achieve greater welfare gains for European citizens/consumers.[51]

Second, there is a move from a 'more legalistic approach to a more economic approach' that focuses on both static (consumer choice, lower prices, better environmental standards) and dynamic (innovation) efficiency.[52] As the Commission explained in the Staff Working Document accompanying the Communication,

> [i]n the past, Single Market policy was mainly about 'integration through law'. The aim was to remove legal barriers to cross-border trade. This was achieved through 'negative' integration measures and 'positive integration measures'. In today's context, legal integration can no longer be the Single Market's sole or primary ambition.[53]

47 Single Market for the Twenty-First Century Communication, p. 10.

48 Commission Staff Working Document, above, p. 17.

49 *Ibid.*, p. 17.

50 *Ibid.*, p. 18.

51 *Ibid.*, pp. 8–15.

52 See F. Ilzkovitz, A. Dierx, V. Kovacs and N. Sousa, European Commission DG Economic and Financial Affairs, *European Economy, Steps towards a Deeper Economic Integration: The Internal Market in the Twenty-First Century, A Contribution to the Single Market Review*, No. 271 (January 2007), pp. 17–18.

53 Commission Staff Working Document, above, p. 5.

The emphasis put on regulatory differences as a sign of the success of the completion of the Single market is no longer the leitmotiv of the Internal Market project. For the Commission, 'policies need to be rethought so as to ensure that markets are not only integrated but can function well – thereby improving consumer welfare and raising productivity'.[54] The different social, economic and political context of various Member States may require different institutional choices for satisfying consumer welfare, for example, if this is the goal to achieve.

Third, the Commission recognizes the importance of developing an 'inclusive' perspective that will consider the interaction of the Internal Market project with other EU 'and national policies, among others to address adjustment costs'.[55] The interaction with other policies does not go one way only. Inge Govaere observes that 'social, environmental, and public health policy instruments are drafted with due regard to the internal market principles of non-discrimination and market access', so as to avoid 'an *ex post* interference of internal market law'; she cites the Commission's Communication on 'Opportunities, Access and Solidarity: Towards a New Social Vision for 21st Century Europe', drawing 'attention to issues of market access and non-discrimination in the social field'.[56] The Lisbon Treaty has also added a broad horizontal integration provision in Article 9 TFEU stating that '[i]n defining and implementing its policies and activities, the Union shall take into account requirements linked to the promotion of a high level of employment, the guarantee of adequate social protection, the fight against social exclusion, and a high level of education, training and protection of human health'.[57] Such broad policy integration provision did not exist in the previous Treaties, except in some specific areas such as environmental protection.[58] The inclusion of these provisions should prompt the Commission and arguably the Court to grant more importance to broader public interest concerns than the facilitation of intra-EU trade.

The success of the 'holistic approach' requires, however, important institutional changes in particular for the interaction between public authorities at the EU, the national and/or the local levels. Enhancing administrative cooperation between the different players is a key priority in the Commission's New Internal Market strategy. Following

[54] *Ibid.*, p. 7. [55] *Ibid.*, p. 20.

[56] I. Govaere, 'The Future Direction of the EU Internal Market on Vested Values and Fashionable Modernism', *Columbia Journal of European Law* 16 (2009) 67–80, p. 77.

[57] Article 9 TFEU. [58] Article 6 EC, now Article 11 TFEU.

a paradigm that has flourished in the enforcement of competition law, national administrations are included in a variety of networks[59] in the area of goods, services, consumer protection and social policy, where they exchange information with each other.[60] The Services Directive is a good example of this new approach that promotes cooperation, communication and exchange of information, by including an entire section (Chapter VI) on administrative cooperation between Member States, and by providing mechanisms for mutual assistance and joint monitoring.[61]

There is a perception that national action is a complement to EU action. The idea of a 'partnership' between Member States and the EU institutions, of a 'joint venture' in which Member States 'have a shared stake', is the new rhetoric advanced by the Commission,[62] in opposition to the prevalent perception that Member States and the Union have antagonistic interests, in particular with regard to the enforcement of the Internal Market rules. This partnership approach 'goes beyond the already established cooperation in a number of Single Market policy areas' and 'requires establishing and maintaining closer cooperation within and between the Member States, and with the Commission, in all areas that are relevant for the single market'. It also 'implies that Member States assume shared responsibility for and therefore a more proactive role in managing the single market'.[63] The Member States are encouraged to 'carry out regular evaluation and assessment of national legislation to ensure full compliance with single market rules and in so doing keep under review any use of exemptions or derogations provided for in existing single market rules'.[64]

[59] See, for an interesting survey, Commission Staff Working Document, Administrative Cooperation in the Single Market, SEC(2009) 881.

[60] See, e.g., the Internal Market Information System which facilitates cooperation between national administrations in the implementation of Internal Market legislation in the area of services or the European Public Administration Network (EUPAN) that aims to support the continuous development of national public administrations with the task of conceiving and implementing the Single Market. On the practical arrangements for the exchange of information between national authorities in the Internal Market, see Commission Decision 2009/739/EC setting out the practical arrangements for the exchange of information by electronic means, OJ 2009 L263/32.

[61] Chapter VI of Directive 2006/123/EC of the European Parliament and of the Council on services in the Internal Market, OJ 2006 L376/76. See our developments below.

[62] Commission Staff Working Document, above, p. 33.

[63] Commission Recommendation of 29 June 2009 on measures to improve the functioning of the Single Market, OJ 2009 L176/17, recital 5.

[64] *Ibid.*, para. 7.

The holistic approach also requires the broadening of the stakeholder's involvement in the management and monitoring of the Internal Market. The creation of European consumer centres, the 'points of single contact' introduced by the Services Directive,[65] the creation of consumer complaints networks or Single Market centres or the inclusion of users in advisory panels increase considerably the possibilities of participation by consumers in the management of the Internal Market and the integration of pluralistic concerns in the design of the Internal Market policies and their objectives.

2.2 Affirmation of pluralistic concerns in the EU Internal Market case law

As noted, it is postulated that the affirmation of pluralistic concerns has permeated up to the most sacred sanctuary of the logic of unity and of the one-dimensional imagery of market integration as entailing the removal of national barriers to trade, namely, the case law of the Court. To perceive a possible evolution in the Internal Market case law, while remaining mindful of the limits inherent to the casuistry, it is useful to go back in history to the early 1970s, following the completion of the transitional period.

In *van Binsbergen*, the Court endowed the equivalent of Article 56 TFEU, which prohibits 'restrictions on freedom to provide services within the Union', with direct effect so that it 'may therefore be relied on before national courts, at least in so far as they seek to abolish any discrimination against a person providing a service by reason of his nationality or of the fact that he resides in a Member State other than that in which the service is to be provided'.[66] At the time, the application of Article 56 TFEU was therefore premised on the existence of a direct discrimination, even though the Court hinted that an obstacle to trade could also derive from requirements 'which may prevent or otherwise obstruct the activities of the person providing the service'.[67] The Court then carved an exemption for those restrictions which 'have as their purpose the application of professional rules justified by the general good – in particular rules relating to organization, qualifications, professional ethics, supervision and liability – which are binding upon any person established in the state in which the service is provided'.[68] In turn,

[65] Article 6 of Directive 2006/123/EC.

[66] Case C33/74, *Van Binsbergen* [1974] ECR 1299, para. 27.

[67] *Ibid*., para. 10.

[68] *Ibid*., para. 12.

the assessment of such exemption was to be carried out 'taking into account the particular nature of the services to be provided'.[69] Like several of the early services cases, *van Binsbergen* involved a residence requirement, *in casu* for legal representatives other than attorneys, which was held contrary to Article 56 TFEU 'if the administration of justice can satisfactorily be ensured by measures which are less restrictive, such as the choosing of an address for service'.[70]

In the following years, in particular in the post-*Cassis de Dijon* era (i.e., the 1980s), the Court endeavoured to clarify the sequencing of its analysis and to broaden the scope of Article 56 TFEU, that is, of the range of restrictions capable of falling within its ambit. In a stream of insurance cases, for example, residence and licensing requirements were found to 'constitute restrictions on the freedom to provide services inasmuch as they increase the cost of such services in the State in which they are provided'.[71] Those restrictions may, however, be justified by 'imperative reasons relating to the public interest', if they are 'applied to all persons or undertakings operating within the territory of the state in which the service is provided' (i.e., in a non-discriminatory fashion), if they actually protect 'the interests which such rules are designed to safeguard' (i.e., appropriateness), if 'the public interest is not already protected by the rules of the state of establishment' (i.e., equivalence) and if 'the same result cannot be obtained by less restrictive rules' (i.e., necessity).[72] This presentation may appear somewhat misleading though, as the sequencing was not as clear at the time, but at least all elements that came to constitute the Internal Market test were present. The notion of mutual recognition acquired particular significance in the late 1980s, both at the level of the definition of the restriction and of its possible justification. Thus, in *Stichting Gouda*, for example, a restriction was found to arise out of the 'application of national rules which affect any person established in the national territory to persons providing services established in the territory of another Member State who already have to satisfy the requirements of that State's legislation', i.e., creating a so-called double burden.[73] In the same case, the Court came to exclude the possibility of justifying the national rules *a quo*, regulating advertising on cable television, 'if the requirements embodied in that legislation

[69] *Ibid.* [70] *Ibid.*, para. 16.

[71] See, e.g., Case C-205/84, *Commission* v. *Germany* [1986] ECR 3755, para. 28, and the references provided therein.

[72] *Ibid.*, paras. 27–9. [73] Case C-288/89, *Stichting Gouda* [1991] ECR I-4007, para. 12.

are already satisfied by the rules imposed on those persons in the Member State in which they are established'.[74] The reasoning, which may appear circular at first sight, was later clarified in *Säger*.

Indeed, in the early 1990s, *Säger* confirmed the expansion of Article 56 TFEU to non-discriminatory restrictions, thus moving towards a market access standard, and induced thereby a convergence of the test applicable to services with that applicable to goods at the time. Thus, the prohibition of barriers to trade in services was to cover not only direct discrimination 'but also the abolition of any restriction, even if it applies without distinction to national providers of services and to those of other Member States, when it is liable to prohibit or otherwise impede the activities of a provider of services established in another Member State where he lawfully provides similar services'.[75] The question from then on would rest with the substance of the term 'impede' or 'impediment to' the cross-border supply of services. Would the application of any domestic requirement to foreign-based services providers amount to a restriction? Or does it have to display certain plus-factors and, in the affirmative, which ones? An increase in the costs of the supply of services, but then, in what proportion? Eventually, *Säger* also clarified the stages of the proportionality assessment applicable to the justification phase of the Internal Market test: the domestic requirement(s) must be appropriate (i.e., 'objectively necessary') to ensure compliance with an imperative reason relating to the public interest that is not protected by the rules to which the service provider is subject in its Member State of establishment, and it must not exceed what is necessary to attain those objectives.[76] Over the same period, the Court further confirmed that Article 56 TFEU covers restrictions, including of a fiscal nature, affecting not only the suppliers but also the beneficiaries of services if they 'operate to deter' those seeking a particular service, such as pension, life, invalidity or sickness insurance coverage, 'from approaching insurers established in another Member State'.[77] Again, the actual contours of that deterrence requirement would remain a source of endless questioning from then on.

The convergence between the Internal Market test applicable to goods and services will last but with one important exception. In 1995, the

[74] *Ibid.*, para. 13.
[75] Case C-76/90, *Manfred Säger* v. *Dennemeyer & Co. Ltd* [1991] ECR I-4221, para. 12.
[76] *Ibid.*, para. 15.
[77] See, e.g., Case C-204/90, *Bachmann* [1992] ECR I-249, para. 31 (at stake, the deductibility of life insurance contributions).

Court declined indeed to extend to the area of services its *Keck and Mithouard* case law excluding non-discriminatory measures governing selling arrangements from the scope of the free movement of goods.[78] The relevant case, known as *Alpine Investments*, pertained to the prohibition of cold calling for the purpose of selling investment products; contrary to selling arrangements, the Court found, the prohibition at issue actually did 'directly affect access to the market in services in the other Member States [where customers are located] and is thus capable of hindering intra-Community trade in services'.[79] Indirectly, the Court refused therefore to distinguish between the service and the way it is supplied, while at the same time expressly relying on the notion of 'market access' that has come to qualify that of trade impediment. In passing, it also confirmed that restrictions on cross-border trade in services can emanate equally from the State of destination and from the State of origin of the supplier.[80] In the examination of the necessity of the prohibition on cold calling in light of the public interest in protecting investor confidence in the domestic financial markets, the Court upheld the measure and expressly allocated regulatory jurisdiction to the Member State from which the telephone calls were made by judging that it was 'best placed to regulate cold calling'.[81] In doing so, it insisted on the practical constraints relating to the control of calls emanating from another Member State and based its assessment on the effectiveness of such control.

This historical overview ends in the late 1990s/early 2000s with the *Smits & Peerbooms* case, where the Court confirmed that 'the special nature of certain services does not remove them from the ambit of the fundamental principle of freedom of movement' so that even social security rules – *in casu* a prior authorization scheme conditioning the benefit of the reimbursement of health treatments incurred abroad – are subject to the discipline of Article 56 TFEU.[82] The Court then examined the scheme both from the point of view of the beneficiary and from the point of view of one of the potential suppliers, and, while confirming the association between the notions of restriction and deterrence in relation to the former, volunteered a rather ill-defined standard for the determination of the scope of Article 56 as precluding 'the application of any

[78] Joined Cases C-267 and 268/91, *Keck and Mithouard* [1993] ECR I-6097, para. 16.
[79] Case C-384/93, *Alpine Investments* [1995] ECR I-1141, paras. 37–8.
[80] *Ibid.*, para. 30. [81] *Ibid.*, para. 48.
[82] Case C-157/99, *Smits and Peerbooms* [2001] ECR I-5473, para. 54.

national rules which have the effect of making the provision of services between Member States more difficult than the provision of services purely within one Member State'.[83] In retrospect, the question arises whether such statement does not represent the ultimate negation of regulatory diversity in so far as the cross-border supply of services would seem necessarily 'more difficult' and/or to 'involve additional costs' from a regulatory point of view, than doing so within a single Member State.

With the above background in mind, the following sections explore the latest case law of the Court in the area of services, with incursions beyond, with a view to highlighting an evolution in the application of the Internal Market test revealing an emerging praxis of pluralism. The two main stages of the test are reviewed successively: first, the interpretation of the notion of restriction to the freedom to provide services; and, second, the assessment of the proportionality of the restriction(s) at stake in light of the alleged public interest to safeguard.

2.2.1 Restriction criteria

A study of the most recent services case law of the Court reveals a lasting ambiguity as to the content of the notion of 'restriction' to trade. To be sure, those cases involving direct discrimination or poorly concealed protectionist measures are relatively straightforward, especially when they are reminiscent of past practices such as residence requirements or discriminatory taxation.[84] Situations where the supply of a particular service is prohibited or entrusted to a single operator are relatively unproblematic.[85] Cases pertaining to classic issues such as the posting of workers abroad have raised concerns related to the type of practice found to constitute a restriction, such as collective actions, but less as to the reasoning concerning the restrictive effects thereof.[86] Conversely, the

[83] *Ibid.*, para. 61 (and the references provided therein).

[84] See, e.g.: (i) Case C-546/07, *Commission/Germany*, 2010, not yet published, involving a residence requirement for those providers willing to conclude a works contract with Polish undertakings in order to provide services in Germany; and (ii) Case C-169/08, *Presidente del Consiglio dei Ministri*, 2009, not yet published, involving a local tax for stopovers made by aircraft or boats operated by persons having their tax domicile outside the territory of the region of Sardinia.

[85] See, e.g.: (i) Case C-36/02, *Omega* [2004] ECR I-9609, para. 25, where the operation of a laser game 'lawfully marketed in the United Kingdom' was prohibited in Germany; or (ii) the gaming cases, such as Case C-42/07, *Liga Portuguesa* [2009] ECR I-7633, para. 52; and Case C-258/08, *Ladbrokes/Lotto*, 2010, not yet published, para. 16.

[86] See, e.g., Case C-341/05, *Laval* [2007] ECR I-11767; and Case C-438/05, *Viking* [2007] ECR I-10779.

circumstances in which a measure applicable without distinction may be deemed to amount to a restriction – i.e., market access cases – continue to raise questions. Even if indicia of a possible 'turn to pluralism' are more apparent in the review of the proportionality of requirements aimed to safeguard public policy interests, two developments are worth mentioning at this stage.

2.2.1.1 A margin of diversity? The recent Italian auto insurance case, which involved the obligation for insurance providers to contract with any vehicle owner domiciled in Italy, offers a good starting point to illustrate the lasting ambiguity in the application of the market access criterion.[87] The Court starts with a now widespread formula according to which 'the term "restriction" within the meaning of Article [56 TFEU] covers all measures which prohibit, impede or render less attractive the freedom of establishment or the freedom to provide services'.[88] Interestingly, it then underlines that mere regulatory diversity, i.e., 'the fact that other Member States apply less strict, or more commercially favourable, rules to providers of similar services established in their territory', is not constitutive of a restriction.[89] That gesture towards the acceptance of a coexistence of different regulatory standards across the EU implies logically that a 'margin of diversity' ought to be left to Member States within which their domestic rules are not likely to be found restrictive of cross-border trade. Thus, only those measures found to 'affect access to the market for undertakings from other Member States' would be deemed to hinder intra-EU trade.[90] In turn, the Court of Justice considers that market access is affected in the case *a quo* because, by 'oblig[ing] insurance undertakings which enter the Italian market to accept every potential customer, that obligation to contract is likely to lead, in terms of organisation and investment, to significant additional costs for such undertakings'.[91] In particular, they 'will be required to re-think their business policy and strategy, *inter alia*, by considerably expanding the range of insurance services offered'.[92] The margin of diversity left to Member States appears therefore particularly thin and the notion of restriction on market access to be more a matter of

[87] Case C-518/06, *Commission* v. *Italy* [2009] ECR I-3491. See also, e.g., Case C-258/08, *Ladbrokes/Lotto*, 2010, not yet published, para. 15.

[88] *Ibid.*, para. 62.

[89] *Ibid.*, para. 63. A similar reference can already be found in Case C-384/93, *Alpine Investments* [1995] ECR I-1141, para. 27.

[90] *Ibid.*, para. 64. [91] *Ibid.*, para. 68. [92] *Ibid.*, para. 69.

degree – of 'scale' of 'changes and costs'[93] – than kind. In turn, that criterion continues to leave the scope of Article 56 TFEU wide open, quite unsettled and, in effect, a matter of case-by-case appreciation for the Court, which seeks to retain thereby the potential for allocating regulatory jurisdiction. This is equally apparent from, for example, a recent establishment case in which the Court found that a rule making the opening of new roadside service stations in Italy subject to minimum distances requirements between service stations affected access to the activity of fuel distribution.[94]

The notion of margin of diversity can be found in other recent cases relating, for example, to demographic limitations on the establishment of pharmacies in Spain.[95] In that case, the Court derived such margin from the 'power of Member States to organize their social security system' and to 'determine the level of protection which they wish to afford to public health and the way in which that level is to be achieved'.[96] Yet, the affirmation of that 'measure of discretion' did not seem to affect the actual assessment of the notion of restriction, which involved, it is true, a classic system of prior authorization.[97] Moreover, in another case involving 'the power of the Member States to organize their social security systems', the Court appeared to deny any margin of diversity by taking the view that Article 56 TFEU 'precludes the application of any national rules which have the effect of making the provision of services between Member States more difficult than the provision of services entirely within a single Member State'.[98] That case related, however, to a difference of treatment in the coverage of patients authorized to receive hospital care in another Member State. The same terminology was used in a case involving a different recovery period for taxes due on assets held inside or outside the territory of The Netherlands, which was deemed to 'make it less attractive for . . . taxpayers to transfer assets to another Member State in order to benefit from financial services offered there'.[99] Eventually, the 'more difficult' standard was merged

93 *Ibid.*, para. 70. 94 Case C-384/08, *Attanasio*, 2010, not yet published, para. 45.

95 Joined Cases C-570/07 and 571/07, *Blanco Pérez and Chao Gomez*, 2010, not yet published.

96 *Ibid.*, paras. 43–4. 97 *Ibid.*, para. 44.

98 Case C-211/08, *Commission* v. *Spain*, 2010, not yet published, para. 55. The reason for such a strict stance might lie with the similarities of the case with the earlier Case C-157/99, *Smits and Peerbooms* [2001] ECR I-5437.

99 Joined Cases C-155/08 and 157/08, *X and Passenheim-van Schoot* [2009] ECR I-5093, paras. 32 and 39.

with that of market access in a case involving the prohibition of advertising on national television networks for medical and surgical treatments carried out in private health care establishments in Italy.[100] Earlier on, in *Rüffert*, the Court held that a mere difference in the minimum rates of pay imposed in the country of supply of services and in that of establishment was such as to impose 'an additional economic burden that may prohibit, impede or render less attractive the provision of their services in the host Member State'.[101]

As noted, the Court appears more inclined overall to give operational significance to the notion of margin of diversity, i.e., tolerance for the coexistence of different regulatory systems across Member States, at the level of the proportionality review.[102] In contrast, at the prior level of the assessment of the existence of a restriction on trade, references to regulatory diversity, notably in relation to measures applicable indiscriminately, seem to have little impact on the interpretation of that concept, which continues to be associated with the loose notion of market access. The indeterminacy of that notion is further illustrated by the *Mobistar* case involving municipal taxes on mobile communications infrastructures (e.g., masts and antennae), which the Court interpreted as falling outside the scope of Article 56 TFEU.[103] Its reasoning started with a classic reminder of the fact that measures indiscriminately applicable may still amount to a restriction on cross-border trade if they are 'liable to prohibit or further impede the activities of a provider of services established in another Member State'.[104] It then resorted to a strict reading of Article 56 TFEU as precluding 'the application of any national rules which have the effect of making the provision of services between Member States more difficult than the provision of services purely within one Member State'.[105] It further added a third premise to its reasoning, namely, that 'measures, the only effect of which is to create additional costs in respect of the service in question and which affect in the same way the provision of services between Member States and that

[100] Case C-500/06, *Corporacion Dermoestetica* [2008] ECR I-5785, para. 33: 'Those rules are, therefore, liable to make it more difficult for such economic operators to gain access to the Italian market.'

[101] Case C-346/06, *Rüffert* [2008] ECR I-1989, para. 37.

[102] See, e.g., Case C-42/07, *Liga Portuguesa* [2009] ECR I-7633, paras. 58 *et seq.*

[103] Joined Cases C-544/03 and 545/03, *Mobistar/Commune de Fléron* [2005] ECR I-7723. Note, however, that the Court does not make express reference to the notion of 'access' in that case, even though it clearly involves a measure applicable 'without distinction to national providers of services and to those of other Member States' (para. 29).

[104] *Ibid.*, para. 29. [105] *Ibid.*, para. 30.

within one Member State, do not fall within the scope of Article [56 TFEU]'. That last statement appears difficult to reconcile with other cases, where the additional costs incurred by services providers due to domestic requirements in the host Member States were found constitutive of a restriction. Yet, the Court also held in *Mobistar* that there was 'nothing in the file to suggest that the cumulative effect of the local taxes compromises freedom to provide mobile telephony services', thereby hinting that, conversely, such cumulative effect could form the basis for a restriction. Then, again, the question arises of the magnitude of the cumulative costs necessary to form a restriction – i.e., when does a measure lose its neutrality to become restrictive – and of the unsatisfactoriness of a solution leaving that assessment in the hands of the Court on a case-by-case basis.

At this stage, the above findings suggest the following three considerations. First, the Court appears unwilling to limit the scope of Article 56 TFEU and of its own power to review the opportunity of national regulations affecting the supply of services, in a context of underdevelopment of the Internal Market in that important field of the economy. Second, the lack of established limitations on the scope of Article 56 TFEU shows the limits, paradoxically, of an Internal Market test based on the objective of removing national barriers to trade, for it does not reflect the variety of circumstances, demands and contexts involved in the enactment of domestic regulations. Third, it is often argued that the two parts of the Internal Market test are intertwined, or even interdependent, so that an allegedly 'light' restriction would be more prone to justification, and *vice versa*. Even if it may carry some truth from an empirical perspective, as apparent from some of the cases reviewed below, this truism remains problematic from a normative point of view and is of little help in identifying the narrative underlying the European economic integration process.

2.2.1.2 Taxing diversity? In tracing signs of a greater tolerance on the part of the Court for the coexistence of different regulatory standards, a second notable development in the recent Internal Market case law, with immediate consequences this time, relates to the Court's refusal to allocate regulatory jurisdiction in double taxation cases. Leaving the area of services to enter that of free movement of capital allows indeed for an interesting illustration of the pluralist hypothesis formulated above.

In essence, the Court was asked in various cases whether Article 63 TFEU prohibited the double taxation of dividends, i.e., the taxation of the same income in the country of origin of the income, by deduction at source, and then in the country of residence of the taxpayer as part of his revenues without providing for the possibility of setting off the former against the latter.[106] Even though the cases involved situations of double fiscal burden, susceptible of affecting investment decisions, the Court refused to find a restriction on the movement of capital between Member States in the absence of 'any distinction between dividends from companies established in [e.g., Belgium] and dividends from companies established in another Member State' as to the tax rate applicable in the taxpayer's country of residence.[107] Conversely, it considered that the situation resulted from the mere 'exercise in parallel by two Member States of their fiscal sovereignty' and that preventing double taxation in those cases would 'amount to granting a priority with respect to the taxation of that type of income to the Member State in which the dividends are paid',[108] which it was not prepared to do.

To justify its reluctance, the Court emphasized that direct taxation falls within the competence of the Member States, that it is for each Member State to organize its tax system and to define the tax base and the tax rate applicable to the taxation of dividends,[109] and, in particular, that 'no uniform or harmonization measure designed to eliminate double taxation has yet been adopted at Community law level',[110] with the consequence that 'Member States retain the power to define, by treaty or unilaterally, the criteria for allocating their powers of taxation, particularly with a view to eliminating double taxation'.[111] In other words, in the absence of 'any general criteria [provided for in EU law] for the attribution of areas of competence between the Member States in

[106] See, in particular, Case C-513/04, *Kerckhaert & Morres* [2006] ECR I-10967; and Case C-128/08, *Damseaux* [2009] ECR I-6823. See also Case C-194/06, *Orange European Smallcap Fund* [2008] ECR I-3747.

[107] Case C-513/04, *Kerckhaert & Morres*, above, para. 17. In contrast, the Court held that, in earlier cases in which it found a restriction, 'the laws of the Member States at issue did not treat in the same way dividend income from companies established in the Member State in which the taxpayer concerned was resident and dividend income from companies established in another Member State, thereby denying recipients of the latter dividends the tax benefits granted to others' (*ibid.*, para. 16, referring to Case C-35/98, *Verkooijen* [2000] ECR I-4071, Case C-315/02, *Lenz* [2004] ECR I-7063, and Case C-319/02, *Manninen* [2004] ECR I-7477).

[108] See, respectively, Case C-513/04, *Kerckhaert & Morres*, para. 20, and Case C-128/08, *Damseaux* [2009] ECR I-6823, para. 32.

[109] Case C-128/08, *Damseaux* [2009] ECR I-6823, paras. 24 and 25.

[110] Case C-513/04, *Kerckhaert & Morres*, above, para. 22.

[111] Case C-128/08, *Damseaux* [2009] ECR I-6823, para. 30.

relation to the elimination of double taxation', it is 'for the Member States to take the measures necessary'.[112]

The solution adopted by the Court in those cases is somewhat surprising in view of its past Internal Market case law, which included various attempts to compensate for a lack of legislative activity. Likewise, it is common ground that no 'nucleus of sovereignty' is beyond the reach of Union law.[113] Yet, the reasoning of the Court suffers little ambiguity: in the absence of any measure adopted at EU level with a view to preventing double taxation, generally, Article 63 TFEU does not require giving precedence to one regulatory solution, e.g., taxation at source, over another, e.g., taxation at the place of the taxpayer's residence. Is the Court suddenly stretching – i.e., taxing – the boundaries of regulatory diversity? A comparison with the *Laval* case reveals a possible willingness to defer to the legislature those cases involving policy choices in areas where no consensus at EU level has emerged.[114] Thus, in *Laval*,[115] the Danish and Swedish governments submitted that the right to take collective action in the context of negotiations with an employer fell outside the scope of Article 56 TFEU because, pursuant to Article 153(5) TFEU, the 'Community has no power to regulate that right'.[116] Yet, the Court held that the exercise of the right to collective action was to take place in compliance with EU law and therefore that it could not be excluded from the domain of freedom to provide services.[117] In effect, *Laval* involved alleged restrictions on the posting of workers abroad, a matter regulated by Directive 96/71/EC, thus reflecting a consensus reached previously at EU level,[118] the interpretation of which was precisely at stake.

The hypothesis of a greater deference for diversity in areas where no regulatory competence has been conferred upon or exercised by the Union is further explored below. Arguably, that deference is the sign of an evolution in the core praxis of the Union towards greater tolerance for the coexistence of varying regulatory standards. It is also consistent with

112 Case C-513/04, *Kerckhaert & Morres*, above, paras. 22–3.

113 See, e.g., K. Lenaerts, 'Constitutionalism and the Many Faces of Federalism', *American Journal of Comparative Law* 38(2) (1990) 205–62, p. 220.

114 As inspired by S. Francq, 'Note sous C-128/08, Damseaux', *Journal de droit international* (2010) 614–15.

115 Case C-341/05, *Laval* [2007] ECR I-11767.

116 *Ibid.*, para. 86.

117 *Ibid.*, paras. 87–8.

118 Directive 96/71/EC concerning the posting of workers in the framework of the provision of services, OJ 1997 L18/1.

a greater emphasis put on decentralized and/or participative/reflexive policy-making processes, and generally with a pluralist account of the narrative underlying European economic integration. Likewise, it is not excluded that it may be linked to a qualitative evolution in the nature of the questions put to the Court and a greater awareness of the possible implications of its rulings for Member States, including for their resources and, as a corollary, their redistributive powers. Furthermore, it might be construed as a propensity for taking competences (more) seriously in an echo of concerns voiced by various national actors over more than fifteen years, and thus as part of a response to challenges over the legitimacy of the Union as a regulatory and political body.

2.2.2 Proportionality review

As noted, indicia of a possible 'turn to pluralism' are more apparent from the proportionality branch of the Internal Market test, particularly at the level of the equivalence and necessity assessments, which have historically involved an inquiry as to whether the public policy interest pursued by the restriction on trade: (i) is not already satisfied by the rules imposed on the supplier in his country of establishment; and (ii) cannot be achieved by less restrictive means. This is not to say that no development has affected the application of the adequacy portion of the proportionality review. On the contrary, recent case law testifies to a stricter analysis of the 'consistent and systematic' character of the pursuit of the alleged justification ground(s). The application of that criterion appears to have been decisive in determining the outcome of various – including prominent – recent cases. For example, in *Rüffert*, the Court took issue with the fact that the higher rate of pay at issue was deemed necessary to protect construction workers when they are employed in the context of public works contracts but not in the context of private contracts.[119] In *Corporacion Dermoestetica*, it pointed to the inconsistency of rules prohibiting the advertisement of medical and surgical treatments on national but not on local television networks.[120] Likewise, in the area of establishment, the Court highlighted in *Blanco Pérez* the need to determine whether demographic limitations on the opening of pharmacies sought 'in a consistent and systematic manner to ensure that the provision of medicinal products to the public is reliable and of good

[119] Case C-346/06, *Rüffert* [2008] ECR I-1989, para. 40.
[120] Case C-500/06, *Corporacion Dermoestetica* [2008] ECR I-5785, para. 39.

quality'.[121] And, in the recent stream of gaming cases, emphasis was clearly put on whether restrictions were suitable for achieving objectives of, for example, consumer protection, 'inasmuch as they must serve to limit betting activities in a consistent and systematic manner'.[122] In effect, with a greater flexibility displayed in the equivalence and necessity inquiries as a result of a higher tolerance for regulatory diversity, the test of adequacy has acquired particular prominence in recent years and has risen to become a key aspect of the proportionality review, to the point of overshadowing the necessity requirement. The present section endeavours to substantiate that claim.

The starting point of the proportionality review in many recent services cases testifies to a willingness to depart from the fixed objective of the Europeanization of regulatory law, that is, of promoting at any rate the emergence of a new European majoritarian view aimed at breaking the path-dependence of actors from national systems.[123] Thus, in the Italian auto insurance case, for example, the Court made the following general proposition: 'it is not essential, with regard to the proportionality criterion, that a restrictive measure laid down by the authorities of a Member State should correspond to a view shared by all the Member States concerning the means of protecting the legitimate interest at issue.'[124] That language is clearly reminiscent of *Omega*, where the Court acknowledged that 'the specific circumstances which may justify recourse to the concept of public policy may vary from one country to another and from one era to another', and that 'it is not indispensable in that respect for the restrictive measure issued by the authorities of a Member State to correspond to a conception shared by all Member States as regards the precise way in which the fundamental right or legitimate interest in question is to be protected'.[125] In other cases, such as *Liga Portuguesa*, a similar finding to the effect that 'the mere fact that a Member State has opted for a system of protection which differs from that adopted by another Member State cannot affect the assessment of

[121] Joined Cases C-580/07 and 571/07, *Blanco Pérez and Chao Gomez*, 2010, not yet published, para. 95.

[122] Case C-258/08, *Ladbrokes/Lotto*, 2010, not yet published, para. 21. See also Case C-42/07, *Liga Portuguesa* [2009] ECR I-7633, para. 61; Joined Cases C-338/04, 359/04 and 360/04, *Placanica et al.* [2007] ECR I-1891, para. 53; and Case C-243/01, *Gamballi et al.* [2003] ECR I-13031, para. 67.

[123] See, generally, Maduro, *We the Court*, above, p. 72.

[124] Case C-518/06, *Commission* v. *Italy* [2009] ECR I-3491, para. 83.

[125] Case C-36/02, *Omega* [2004] ECR I-9609, paras. 31 and 37.

the need for, and proportionality of, the provisions enacted to that end' was rooted both in the absence of harmonization at EU level in the field of games of chance with, as a corollary, the freedom 'for each Member State to determine in those areas, in accordance with its own scale of values, what is required in order to ensure that the interests in question are protected', and in the 'significant moral, religious and cultural differences between the Member States'.[126]

Interestingly, those considerations displaying a principled tolerance for regulatory diversity are not limited to the area of services, but can also be found in establishment and free movement of goods cases. Thus, in *Blanco Pérez*, already discussed, the Court started its proportionality review with the observation that 'the fact that one Member State imposes more stringent rules than another in relation to the protection of public health does not mean that those rules are incompatible with the Treaty provisions on the fundamental freedoms' or at least 'is not decisive for the outcome of the cases before the referring court'.[127] Similarly, in the Italian *Trailers* case, the Court found that, 'in the absence of fully harmonizing provisions at Community level, it is for the Member States to decide upon the level at which they wish to ensure road safety in their territory' and 'the way in which that degree of protection is to be achieved', so that 'the fact that one Member State imposes less strict rules than another Member State does not mean that the latter's rules are disproportionate'.[128]

The immediate consequence of the above premise is, again, the recognition of a 'margin of diversity' to Member States in the exercise of their regulatory powers. As the Court stated in *Omega*, again: 'the need for, and proportionality of, the provisions adopted are not excluded merely because one Member State has chosen a system of protection different from that adopted by another State'.[129] At the stage of the proportionality review, however, that margin of diversity translates immediately in the recognition that 'the competent national authorities must . . . be allowed a margin of discretion within the limits imposed by the Treaty',[130] or, stated otherwise, that the diversity of national

[126] Case C-42/07, *Liga Portuguesa (Santa Casa)* [2009] ECR I-7633, paras. 57–8; Case C-258/08, *Ladbrokes/Lotto*, above, para. 19.

[127] Joined Cases C-580/07 and 571/07, *Blanco Pérez and Chao Gomez*, above, paras. 68–9.

[128] Case C-110/05, *Commission/Italy (Trailers)* [2009] ECR I-519, paras. 61 and 65.

[129] Case C-36/02, *Omega* [2004] ECR I-9609, para. 38.

[130] Case C-36/02, *Omega* [2004] ECR I-9609, para. 31. See also, e.g., Case C-518/06, *Commission* v. *Italy* [2009] ECR I-3491, para. 84; and Case C-258/08, *Ladbrokes/Lotto*, above, para. 19.

preferences entails 'a margin of appreciation' for Member States.[131] Even if the sequence of the Internal Market test embeds by essence a margin of discretion mechanism, providing for an additional national margin of appreciation in those cases characterized by the absence of regulatory consensus at EU level, as translated in EU-wide instruments, and/or in areas marked by profound moral, religious or cultural considerations, discloses the existence of a diversity of review standards and thus the emergence of a pluralist approach to the management of regulatory diversity. As Delmas-Marty observes, 'providing for a national margin of appreciation is the key to ordering pluralism' in so far as 'on the one hand, it expresses the centrifugal dynamic of national resistance to integration' and 'on the other, since the margin is not unlimited but bounded by shared principles, it sets a limit, a threshold of compatibility that leads back to the centre (centripetal dynamic)'.[132] In practice, the grant of an additional margin of appreciation is reflected directly in the operation of the equivalence and necessity inquiries embedded in the proportionality review of national restrictions to cross-border trade.

2.2.2.1 Equivalence in question The possible impact on the operation of the equivalence inquiry of the recognition of a broad margin of appreciation for national authorities is particularly apparent from the series of recent cases involving the gaming/gambling sector. Thus, in the *Placanica* and *Ladbrokes/Lotto* cases, the Court took as a premise that such margin ought to ensure Member States the freedom of designing 'their policy on betting and gambling according to their own scale of values and, where appropriate, to define in detail the level of protection sought'.[133] In *Liga Portuguesa*, the Court seems to have gone further by suggesting that the margin also ought to affect the implementation of the proportionality test in so far as the latter would then be carried out 'solely by reference to the objectives pursued by the competent authorities of the Member State concerned and the degree of protection which they seek to ensure', thus based on a self-centred perspective focusing on the

[131] Case C-110/05, *Commission/Italy (Trailers)* [2009] ECR I-519, para. 34.

[132] M. Delmas-Marty, *Ordering Pluralism*, above, p. 44. As Delmas-Marty further explains (*ibid.*, p. 51): 'Well understood, a national margin of appreciation is no doubt the best way to avoid simply juxtaposing differences and, instead, progressively rendering practices compatible. . . . its use must be rationalised by specifying the conditions that will enable it to order pluralism around shared guiding principles.'

[133] Joined Cases C-338/04, 359/04 and 360/04, *Placanica et al.* [2007] ECR I-1891, paras. 47–8; Case C-258/08, *Ladbrokes/Lotto*, above, paras. 19–20.

internal consistency of the domestic system.[134] In doing so, the Court appears to acknowledge that the public policy interests put forward in support of the restrictions at issue justify a particularly broad margin's width.

In that context, it is not difficult to anticipate the restrictive interpretation given to the principle of equivalence: 'A Member State is therefore entitled to take the view that the mere fact that an operator . . . lawfully offers services in that sector . . . in another Member State, in which it is established and where it is in principle already subject to statutory conditions and controls on the part of the competent authorities in that State, is not a sufficient assurance that national consumers will be protected against the risks of fraud and crime',[135] as determined by the host Member State in accordance with its 'own scale of values'.[136]

Some commentators contend that the above reasoning amounts to a 'blanket rejection of the application of the principle of mutual recognition in relation to online gambling services' and 'may potentially challenge the whole philosophy underlying [the application of Article 56 TFEU]'.[137] Others take the view that the condition of equivalence was simply not fulfilled, notably because of the extreme diversity of domestic legislations in the field of games of chance.[138] In a recent Opinion, Advocate General Mengozzi sheds some useful light on the tolerance shown by the Court for the lack of equivalence between the national regulatory frameworks at issue in the above cases.[139] In particular, while acknowledging a departure from the principle of equivalence as formulated in *Säger*,[140] he points to the exclusion of the gaming sector from the scope of the Services Directive and to the grant of offshore gaming licences by the authorities of Malta or Gibraltar as expressions of a lack of mutual trust between Member States in that field, whereas such mutual trust is the precondition for the mutual recognition of gaming

[134] Case C-42/07, *Liga Portuguesa (Santa Casa)*, above, para. 58.

[135] Case C-42/07, *Liga Portuguesa (Santa Casa)*, above, para. 69; and Case C-258/08, *Ladbrokes/Lotto*, above, para. 54.

[136] Case C-42/07, *Liga Portuguesa (Santa Casa)*, above, para. 57.

[137] A. Dawes and K. Struckmann, 'Rien ne va plus? Mutual recognition and the free movement of services in the gambling sector after the Santa Casa judgment', *European Law Review* 35(2) (2010) 236–62, pp. 259 and 262.

[138] Francq, 'Note sous C-128/08, Damseaux', p. 626.

[139] Opinion of Advocate General Mengozzi of 4 March 2010 in Joined Cases C-316/07, 358/07 to 360/07, 409/07 and 410/07, *Markus Stoß*, available at www.curia.eu (last visited 9 August 2010).

[140] *Ibid.*, paras. 95–6.

licences within the Union.[141] In other words, Advocate General Mengozzi implies that trust cannot be postulated but needs to be translated in operational and effective trust-building mechanisms of a cooperative nature in order to enable mutual recognition and the progressive convergence of national systems.[142] The link between the management of regulatory diversity and system trust is at the core of the attempt to reformulate the inner ethos of European market integration, as provided for in section 3 below.

2.2.2.2 Necessity, burden of proof and effectiveness Affirmations of a greater tolerance for regulatory diversity in cases involving policy areas characterized by the prevalence of domestic preferences over the expression of a consensus at EU level, aim particularly at the operation of the necessity inquiry: 'the fact that some Member States have chosen to establish a [regulatory] system different from that introduced by [another Member State] ... does not indicate that [the system] goes beyond what is necessary to attain the objectives pursued.'[143] Endowing Member States with an additional margin of appreciation while reviewing the proportionality of public policy justifications for domestic restrictions on trade impacts the necessity inquiry at two levels: (i) the definition of the burden of proof borne by Member States; and (ii) the assessment of the practical constraints faced by Member States in guaranteeing the effectiveness of the protection of the public interest(s) sought. Overall, those developments testify to a relaxation of the necessity inquiry, i.e., of a more lenient assessment compatible with the enhanced discretion left to Member States.

2.2.2.2.1 *The proof of the absence of less restrictive means* The performance of the necessity inquiry, as the last step in the Internal Market test, is often perceived as the most extreme form of counter-majoritarianism at EU level and is naturally prone to controversies – who is the Court to second-guess the opportunity of the means set forth by the Member States in pursuance of public policy objectives? In preliminary ruling cases, the Court of Justice leaves to the national court the actual assessment as to whether the domestic rule does not go beyond what is necessary to achieve the objective sought. Yet, it does often provide guidance, more or less subtly, to its national counterparts, at least as to

[141] *Ibid.*, paras. 97–8 and 103–4. [142] *Ibid.*, paras. 100–2.
[143] See, e.g., Case C-518/06, *Commission* v. *Italy* [2009] ECR I-3491, para. 85.

the level of scrutiny to be exercised and, conversely, the burden of proof incumbent upon the relevant Member State.[144]

Precisely, the Court adopted a particularly deferential position in some recent cases as to the intensity of the burden of proof carried by Member States. Thus, 'whilst it is true that it is for a Member State which relies on an imperative requirement to justify a restriction within the meaning of the [EU Treaties] to demonstrate that its rules are appropriate and necessary to attain the legitimate objective being pursued, that burden of proof cannot be so extensive as to require the Member State to prove, positively, that no other conceivable measure could enable that objective to be attained under the same conditions'.[145] While it is not exactly clear how that standard is supposed to translate in practice, it clearly indicates a willingness to refrain from questioning the means used to implement public policy objectives, to the extent that they appear 'adequate', and the effectiveness thereof.

2.2.2.2.2 *The effectiveness of the protection of the public interest(s) sought* The second notable evolution in the necessity inquiry associated with the recognition of a margin of appreciation consists in a greater sensitivity displayed toward the effectiveness of the means deployed to ensure the protection of the public interest(s) sought. In the online gaming cases, for example, the Court of Justice pointed to the 'substantial risks of fraud' caused by the 'lack of direct contact between consumer and operator' to substantiate the practical difficulties for the Member State of establishment to police effectively the practices of games suppliers on a host market and, as a result, to uphold the grant of exclusive rights to operate games of chance via the internet to a single operator, subject to the supervision of its domestic public authorities.[146] This approach is of course evocative of the reasoning adopted by the Court in the *Alpine Investment* case, discussed above, as to the effective means to police cold calling practices.[147] Similarly, in recent free movement of goods cases, the Court also underlined, in its review of the proportionality of the prohibition of or restrictions on the usage of certain goods,

[144] See, e.g., Case C-438/05, *Viking* [2007] ECR I-10779, paras. 87–9.

[145] See, e.g., Case C-518/06, *Commission* v. *Italy* [2009] ECR I-3491, para. 84; and, for a free movement of goods case, Case C-110/05, *Commission/Italy (Trailers)* [2009] ECR I-519, para. 66.

[146] Case C-42/07, *Liga Portuguesa (Santa Casa)*, above, paras. 69–70; and Case C-258/08, *Ladbrokes/Lotto*, above, paras. 54–5.

[147] Case C-384/93, *Alpine Investments*, above, paras. 47–9.

'that Member States cannot be denied the possibility of attaining an objective . . . by the introduction of general and simple rules which will be easily understood and applied . . . and easily managed and supervised by the competent authorities'.[148] Again, those considerations show a greater deference for Member States' discretion in devising the means adapted to the satisfaction of the level of protection set in accordance with domestic preferences.

The above section has attempted to identify signs of the emergence of a logic of pluralism in the core praxis of the EU system – economic integration, as driven by the ultimate guardian of the unity of the Union, namely, the Court of Justice. At this stage, the following conclusion surfaces: in those cases involving indiscriminately applicable measures pertaining to policy areas characterized by an absence of EU-wide consensus, as embodied in a legislative instrument adopted at EU level, the Court appears to display a principled tolerance of regulatory diversity,[149] which manifests itself in two interrelated phenomena: (i) a reluctance to proceed to a (re)allocation of regulatory jurisdiction and/or to define regulatory policy; and (ii) the recognition of a broad(er) margin of appreciation for Member States in the exercise of their regulatory powers. In doing so, though, the Court seems to exhibit a preference, at least in the area of services, for a more lenient proportionality review over a limitation of the scope of the notion of restriction on cross-border trade, which remains unsettled but also enables the Court to secure its prerogative of reviewing the opportunity of national regulations and/or to avoid creating safe harbours capable of evolving into loopholes in the EU economic integration system. The above findings call, however, for three remarks.

First, they are contingent on limitations inherent to the casuistry – i.e., on the nature, scope and timing of particular cases – and, at this stage, remain based on a review of a limited sample of about thirty cases. The ambition is therefore certainly not to express decisive conclusions but to highlight a tendency, which still carries meaning in view of the far-reaching positions held in the past by the Court, specifically in the field of market integration. The identification of the precise causes underlying that tendency is a subject for debate; overall, though, they appear to

[148] Case C-110/05, *Commission/Italy (Trailers)* [2009] ECR I-519, para. 67; Case C-142/05, *Mickelsson and Roos* [2009] ECR I-4273, para. 36.

[149] Interestingly, it denotes a growing influence of secondary law on the interpretation of primary EU law.

originate in an acknowledgment of existing limits to the interpretation of the market integration provisions of the EU Treaties, possibly informed by past experiences and a greater awareness as to their broad potential in affecting preference (re)formation and the design and implementation of redistributive policies.

Second, the above findings suggest a turn towards a more holistic approach in the application of the market freedom provisions revealing greater attention paid to values other than trade and, consequently, a willingness to depart from the one-dimensional paradigm of the erosion of national barriers to trade and its corollary, the isolation of the economic and social spheres. As a result, they trigger a fundamental question, that of the transformation of market-building into a 'market-deepening' project conditional on mutually agreed solutions, even if of a cooperative nature. Consequently, wouldn't that transformation both reveal and require a reformulation of the inner ethos of European economic integration, if not of the matrix of the whole EU system? Section 3 below explores one possible avenue to address that question.

Third, there is no doubt that protectionist measures remain inefficient and that their removal (will) remain a focus of the economic integration project, yet the above findings reveal the complexity of the notion of efficiency and the difficulty of devising principles capable of harnessing that complexity. The notion of margin of appreciation constitutes an important tool in that respect, in that it allows for a gradation in the intensity of the review of national regulations depending on the nature thereof and policy interests enshrined therein. In essence, the sequence of the Internal Market test itself embeds a margin of discretion mechanism; hence, by granting Member States an express 'margin of appreciation', the Court in fact adds width to that original or pre-existing margin of discretion. In turn, the Court reveals a practice of varying and adjusting the margin's width from case to case, i.e., the existence of a plurality of review standards, and discloses thereby a pluralist approach to the management of regulatory diversity. Such an approach carries great potential but is not immune from risks in terms of legal certainty and thus for the formal validity of the market integration rules. For Delmas-Marty, operating a pluralist approach is indeed dependent on two methodological conditions: 'transparency, which requires [international judges] to elaborate on the criteria serving as filters; and discipline, which implies that they respect these filters.' This is an exacting process, in particular on the part of a jurisdiction composed of judges with very different backgrounds.[150] Still, the stakes are high for, according to Delmas-Marty, 'judicial transparency and discipline, reasoning and self-limitation are the ingredients for realising the European Union's motto, "united in diversity".'[151] Moreover, 'committing to playing this game with determination and discipline' is nothing less than 'a way of showing that the union of peoples, including in other regions and at other levels, is not necessarily synonymous with uniformity, and that the universalism of values can adapt to the curves in space and time'.[152]

3. Pluralism, economic integration and the emergence of an ethos of mutual trust

The concept of 'economic integration' has been a marking element of post-war economic thinking over trade and international economic relations.[153] The concept suffered from an 'abundance of mutually contradictory definitions',[154] perhaps because of its dual essence: integration can be conceived of as a process, encompassing 'measures designed to abolish discrimination between economic units belonging to different national states', as well as a state of affairs, represented by 'the absence of various forms of discrimination between national economies'.[155] Its

[150] On the impact of the enlargement of the Court on the articulation of the legal reasoning supporting particular judicial decisions, see M. P. Maduro and L. Azoulai, 'Introduction' in M. P. Maduro and L. Azoulai (eds.), *The Past and Future of EU Law* (Oxford and Portland, OR: Hart Publishing, 2010), p. xix.

[151] Delmas-Marty, *Ordering Pluralism*, above, p. 58. [152] *Ibid.*

[153] On the emergence of the theory of international economic integration, see F. Machlup, *A History of Thought on Economic Integration* (Macmillan Press, 1977), noting that the term was first employed in business economics. Economists in the inter-war era employed the negative noun of 'disintegration' of the world economy, probably as a consequence of the national protectionist legislation that followed the economic crisis of 1929. The positive noun of 'integration' was first employed after the Second World War in order to provide a conceptual vehicle for the efforts of 'integration of the Western European economy' the substance of which 'would be the formation of a single large market within which quantitative restrictions on the movements of goods, monetary barriers to the flow of payments and, eventually, all tariffs are permanently swept away'. *Ibid.*, p. 11, referring to Paul Hoffmann's official pronouncement to the Council of the Organization of European Economic Co-operation on 31 October 1949.

[154] F. Machlup, *A History of Thought on Economic Integration* (Macmillan Press, 1977), p. 13.

[155] B.. Balassa, *The Theory of Economic Integration* (George Allen & Unwin Ltd, 1961), p. 1. For an extended analysis, see B. Balassa, 'Towards a Theory of Economic Integration', *Kyklos* 14 (1961) 1–17, p. 17. For a more 'outcome-oriented' definition, see J. Tinbergen, *International Economic Integration* (Elsevier, 1954), p. 95, defining integration as 'the creation of the most desirable structure of international economy,

meaning has been framed by the tensions between the 'liberalist' (market friendly) and the dirigist (State intervention friendly) ideals that characterized the political landscape of the post-war era.[156]

The development of the twin concepts of negative and positive integration, coined by Tinbergen in 1965,[157] and seen as complementary tools to remove discrimination and restrictions on movement in order to enable the market to function effectively, while promoting other broader policy objectives, was seen as a necessary compromise in order to make 'economic integration' acceptable to both camps. The different 'stages of integration', identified by Balassa,[158] as well as the distinction of the concept of 'integration' from that of 'cooperation',[159] were also inspired by the same narrative of removing barriers and achieving regulatory sameness to the point that they attracted the criticism that their final stage, the unitary State, was 'misconceived' for being inspired 'by a centralist rather than federal state model'.[160] Despite the absence of an authoritative definition of the term, Fritz Machlup noted in 1977 that a wide consensus existed as to the three essential conditions for economic integration: 'economic integration refers basically to division of labour', 'it involves mobility of goods or factors', and 'it is related to discrimination or non-discrimination in the treatment of goods and factors'.[161]

The main difficulty with this conceptualization of integration is that it does not accommodate the need for pluralism and diversity. By bringing in the economics of federalism as an additional analytical tool valuing diversity, economic integration theorists attempted a reconceptualization of the term that will make it more politically acceptable to the EU Member States and to the expected aspirations of the newly formed

removing artificial hindrances to the optimal operation and introducing deliberately all desirable elements of co-ordination or unification'.

156 *Ibid.*, pp. 7–10.

157 *Ibid.*, pp. 76–7. See also Pinder, 'Positive Integration and Negative Integration: Some Problems of Economic Union in the EEC', *World Today* 24 (1968) 88–110.

158 B. Balassa, *The Theory of Economic Integration*, 1st edn (George Allen & Unwin Ltd, 1961), p. 2.

159 B. Balassa, 'Towards a Theory of Economic Integration', *Kyklos* 14 (1961) 4–5, indicating that '[w]hereas cooperation includes various measures designed to harmonize economic policies and to lessen discrimination, the process of economic integration comprises those measures which entail the suppression of some forms of discrimination'. See also the transformation of the title of Jan Tinbergen's work to *International Economic Integration* (in 1954) from *International Economic Co-operation* (1945).

160 J. Pelkmans, *European Integration: Methods and Economic Analysis*, 3rd edn (Oxford University Press, 2006), pp. 8–9.

161 F. Machlup, *A History of Thought on Economic Integration* (Macmillan Press, 1977), p. 14.

European citizenry.[162] However, this was a risky analytical venture: once the need for diversity brings into the concept of economic integration a broader set of values than the more instrumental one of removing barriers to exchange, the concept loses its distinctive character and becomes confined to that of efficiency (broadly defined as the satisfaction of preferences of the different units of the entity). The question then boils down to identifying a measure of success for this kind of 'economic integration'. One could possibly imagine integration as a continuous and never-ending process of balancing the presence of different interests (integration as a process). But such a concept of integration will be devoid of purpose and thus semantically empty, not to mention unfit from a policy prescription perspective.

One could turn instead to studying institutions of governance, under the assumption that they may provide useful insights as to the interaction between the process of economic integration and the concept of pluralism. In that regard, the development of legal rules and informal arrangements in the EU can be viewed as part of a broad effort to mitigate the risks generated by the existence of interaction and interdependence between different regulatory systems. The more diverse the regulatory regimes are, the higher the risks involved. The process of managing these risks leads to the emergence of various governance mechanisms or tools, which present discrete characteristics.

Trade in services is probably the area where more differences lay across the regulatory regimes of EU Member States, as a result of the recent liberalization of the sector and the lack of expansive enforcement of the negative integration rules. It is also the area where the application of the principle of the freedom of movement led to the emergence of various governance mechanisms that defy the paradigm of positive (harmonization) versus negative integration (market access principle or national treatment). The hypothesis defended in this study is that the existence of a variety of governance mechanisms may be explained by the need to manage regulatory pluralism.

[162] J. Pelkmans, *European Integration: Methods and Economic Analysis*, 3rd edn (Oxford University Press, 2006), pp. 11–12. See also the analysis of optimal decision-making in W. Molle, *The Economics of European Integration – Theory, Practice, Policy*, 4th edn (Ashgate, 2001), pp. 23–5. The principle of subsidiarity enshrines this economic federalism view that a policy executed at the lowest level of government is thought more efficient because of higher participation, a greater ability to observe preferences, a higher degree of accountability and greater incentives for regulatory experimentation.

This analytical step becomes possible if we embrace a new paradigm of integration based on the concept of trust. To support this theory, one could note the revolution brought to the conceptual edifice of 'economic integration' by the principle of 'mutual recognition', a major innovation introduced by the European judiciary in *Cassis de Dijon*. Perceived initially as a tool of negative integration working alongside the broad 'obstacles to trade' approach in defining restrictions of trade, the principle of mutual recognition has evolved towards a mechanism of reallocation of jurisdictional authority, 'a hybrid at the intersection of both processes' (market access and harmonization).[163] Based on mutual trust, among regulators, mutual recognition has become the 'core paradigm' of 'economic integration', the 'starting assumption' before determining the need for 'a policed national treatment' or 'harmonization'.[164] This evolution displaces the unidimensional focus of integration theory on the erosion of barriers to exchange that underpinned the dilemma between negative and positive integration. Mutual recognition defies this paradigm and suggests a different perspective on economic integration, conceived of as a process of building increased levels of 'institutional-based' trust (or 'system trust') between actors interacting across national boundaries. The emphasis on the constitutive element of trust integrates some degree of marginalist thinking in integration theory that contrasts with the overall significance the classic economic integration theory accords to the erosion of barriers to exchange, to the point that the different stages of integration are conceived as a continuum going from the existence of barriers (and the resulting pluralism of regulatory cultures) to the absence of barriers to trade (and the resulting uniformity of the Single Market).

3.1 The emergence of discrete governance mechanisms

Governments regulate their economies for various reasons as explained by public interest, interest group or capture theory of regulation.[165] According to the principle of territoriality, these domestic policies apply to the territory controlled by the host Member State and affect

[163] K. Nicolaïdis, 'Mutual Recognition of Regulatory Regimes: Some Lessons and Prospects', Jean Monnet Working Paper (1997), available at http://centers.law.nyu.edu/jeanmonnet/papers/97/97-07.html, § 13 (last visited 20 September 2010).

[164] *Ibid.*, § 16.

[165] For an introductory analysis, see R. Baldwin and M. Cave, *Understanding Regulation* (Oxford University Press, 1999).

any economic operator that is economically active in its jurisdiction. The group of affected economic operators is not only limited to domestic service providers but also extends to foreign service providers that offer their services in the host Member State. Domestic policies will thus produce some form of extraterritorial effect, in particular as service providers established in other Member States (home State) may incur increased costs, as a result of the regulation imposed by the host State. First, the regulation of the host State may affect the objectives pursued by the home State to have access (for the benefit of economic operators established in its territory) to the host State's market. Second, the regulation of the service providers by the home State might affect the policy goals of the host State, as long as the foreign service providers established in the home State have access to the host State's market and the host State's regulation is rendered ineffective by the fact that some economic operators are established outside its jurisdiction. Indeed, it is theoretically possible for each State to adopt unilaterally measures in order to mitigate the negative externalities to its domestic policies generated by foreign service providers. However, in some circumstances this is not possible, for example because of the important costs of monitoring economic operators established outside its own jurisdiction or the ineffectiveness of controls, or even desirable, from a policy perspective. In these instances, cooperation with the foreign jurisdiction would be more effective in order to deal with these negative policy externalities.

It follows that the existence of negative domestic policy externalities that have cross-border effects constitutes the main reason for the emergence of a situation of cooperation between States. Moravcsik observes that:

> [n]ational governments have an incentive to co-operate where policy coordination increases their control over domestic policy outcomes, permitting them to achieve goals that would not otherwise be possible. This situation arises most often where co-ordination eliminates negative international policy externalities.[166]

In contrast, positive policy externalities, that is, policies that confer benefits on foreign groups in order to promote domestic policies, are often of little interest to international trade agreements or regimes. The 'purely internal situation' case law of the Court on restrictions of trade

[166] Moravcsik, 'Preferences and Power in the European Community', above, p. 485.

that disadvantage nationals[167] provides a good illustration of this lack of interest in positive cross-border externalities. The explanation is simple and relates to the absence of an incentive to cooperate in a situation of positive policy externality: 'Only where the policies of two or more governments create negative policy externalities for one another, and unilateral adjustment strategies are ineffective, inadequate or expensive, does economic interdependence create an unambiguous incentive to co-ordinate policy.'[168]

By entering into cooperation with other States, the host States incur risks. Cooperation is often initiated by conditional promises by which each State declares that it will act in a certain way on condition that the other State acts in accordance with its own commitments. This relation of reciprocity may take different forms. As Bilder explains:

> In general, a nation's decision to enter into an international [cooperation] ... can be said to involve considerations of risk when that nation believes that its commitment to the [cooperation] ... may, depending on the occurrence or non-occurrence of particular future events or outcomes as to which it is uncertain or in doubt, expose it to an eventual final outcome which is harmful in that its costs exceed its benefits. Typically, risk will be thought of in terms of probabilities.[169]

According to the same author, States may be concerned by one of the following broad types of risk:

> (1) The risk that the nation may later decide, for extraneous reasons, that it no longer wishes to participate in the agreement. For example, it may wish to get out of the agreement because some other nation has offered it a 'better deal'.
> (2) The risk that the intrinsic utility of the agreement to that nation may decline to the extent that the prospective benefits from the agreement no longer equal or exceed its costs. For example, the cost of performing its promise may increase or the value of what it has been promised may decline.

[167] See, e.g., Case C-212/06, *Government of the French Community and Walloon Government* v. *Flemish Government* [2008] ECR I-1683, para. 38. For an analysis, see A. Tryfonidou, 'The Outer Limits of Article 28 EC: Purely Internal Situations and the Development of the Court's Approach Through the Years' in C. Barnard and O. Odudu (eds.), *The Outer Limits of EU Law* (Oxford: Hart Publishing, 2009), pp. 197–243.

[168] Moravcsik, 'Preferences and Power in the European Community', above, p. 486.

[169] R. B. Bilder, *The Role of Trust in International Agreement* (1979), available at http://papers.ssrn.com/sol3/papers.cfm?abstract_id=912741, p. 7 (last visited 20 September 2010).

(3) The risk that the other nation concerned may not perform as promised. For example, a nation's treaty partner may completely withhold performance or may 'cheat'.[170]

The existence of risk will require recourse to various risk management techniques, such as 'provisions for easy withdrawal (from the mutual commitments), guarantees, timing of performance, verification and inspection, escrow, hostage, buffer zones, dispute settlement, [and] sanctions'.[171] One could envision these different risk management techniques as forms of regulation of risk. The term 'regulation' should not be perceived in its usual hierarchical dimension, in opposition to voluntary forms of governance such as networks, but as involving some form of action on the variables generating risk with the intention to manage uncertainty. The types of risks involved, the fact that the State will be risk-averse or risk-prone, the availability of information about the partner, the probability of occurrence of the risks or the existence of important opportunity costs in case of non-cooperation would impact on the choice of the institutional alternative to manage risk, and thus on the governance mechanism of the particular cooperative relationship.

In the context of cooperation aiming to mitigate negative domestic policy externalities with cross-border effects, different governance mechanisms will emerge. It has been argued that there are three main institutional alternatives or governance mechanisms to manage risk in international trade law.[172]

The first is the mutual commitment not to employ specific types of domestic regulation (a negative obligation). The conditional promises of the States may relate to the implementation of a national treatment rule. The latter prevents either State (home and host) from applying discriminatory standards to cross-border services; the State is otherwise free to set any standard that is not directly discriminatory to the foreign service providers.[173] In the field of services, the Court moved progressively to expand the conditional promise of non-discrimination (or the application of a national treatment rule) to include a market access rule,[174] where States commit not to adopt regulation that would affect the

[170] *Ibid.*, p. 8. [171] *Ibid.*, p. 11.

[172] S. Schmidt, 'Mutual Recognition as a New Mode of Governance', *Journal of European Public Policy* 14(5) (2007) 667–81, p. 671.

[173] K. Nicolaïdis and G. Shaffer, 'Transnational Mutual Recognition Regimes: Governance without Global Government', *Law and Contemporary Problems* 68 (2005) 263–317, p. 267.

[174] Case 76/90, *Säger* v. *Dennemeyer* [1991] ECR I-4221, para. 12.

market access of foreign service providers and establish barriers to trade, whatever that term means.[175] The starting point for both these rules is the existence of some form of negative cross-border domestic policy externalities. As noted, these arise 'where the policies of one nation impose costs on the domestic nationals of another,[176] thereby undermining the goals of the second government's policies'.[177] The main difference between the principles of national treatment and that of market access is the type of international negative domestic policy externalities that are of normative and practical interest, for the application of the prohibition principle. If, as it seems to be the case in the EU, the normative framework of the cooperation aims to achieve 'the elimination of all obstacles to intra-community trade in order to merge the national markets into a Single Market bringing about conditions as close as possible to those of a genuine internal market',[178] anything causing a potential disparity between legal orders and thus different economic conditions would be of interest to define the cross-border negative domestic policy externalities that will be the focus of the prohibition rule. In theory, the list of prohibited practices can include different domestic environmental pollution standards or other regulatory barriers imposing costs on cross-border service provision, competitive devaluation and different employment conditions leading to higher or lower labour costs, irrespective of the fact that the same rules apply to domestic firms.

Cooperation (in the form of a mutual commitment to a market access rule) can be particularly difficult to reach in situations where the governments have divergent policies, because of the different preferences to which they have to respond in the domestic arena. The variety of preferences translates into a different mix of societal interests, power struggles and bargaining positions between interest groups and the existence of a plurality of institutional structures across societies reflecting these interests. The objective of inter-State cooperation thus becomes to find a way to internalize negative policy externalities, that is, to restrain the

[175] On the different interpretations of this concept, see the analysis in I. Lianos, 'Shifting Narratives in the European Internal Market: Efficient Restrictions of Trade and the Nature of "Economic" Integration', *European Business Law Review* 21(5) (2010) 705.

[176] Here we will assume that the concept of non-nationals refers to foreign service providers or cross-border services providers.

[177] Moravcsik, 'Preferences and Power in the European Community', *Journal of Common Market Studies* 31(4) (1993) 473–524, p. 485.

[178] Case 15/81, *Schul* [1982] ECR 1409, para. 33.

domestic interests that affect foreign service providers and to devise an optimal division of the burden of adjustment. Cooperation emerges when the costs of coordination are outweighed by the common interest in reducing negative policy externalities (for example, when cooperation generates gains to powerful interest groups, if one adopts the capture or public choice theory of regulation, or more generally to the public interest, in conformity with the public interest theory of regulation).[179]

Second, the market access rule can be distinguished from the national treatment rule by focusing on the degree of internalization of cross-border negative domestic policy externalities. National treatment allows for the achievement of the goals of domestic policy, as long as this does not lead to a discrimination against cross-border service providers. Thus, a national treatment rule does not internalize all negative policy externalities, as cross-border service providers will still incur the costs of conforming to a different regulatory structure. In comparison, a broad market access rule has less potential to achieve the goals of domestic policies, but enables the internalization of negative externalities to a higher degree, as national rules are prohibited whenever they impose barriers to the market access of cross-border services. There are various interpretations of the concept of trade barriers, but, whichever is adopted, the scope of the prohibition rule is broader than under the national treatment rule.

Because of its potential breadth, with regard to the type of domestic regulations that it brings within its scope, the application of a pure market access rule is not politically achievable or even desirable in the EU. First, not all barriers to trade fall within the scope of the EU market access rule. For example, competitive devaluation is not prohibited for countries that do not participate in the Eurozone and the regulation of labour markets is largely outside the realm of the negative integration provisions of the Treaties. Second, EU Member States may restrict the freedom to provide cross-border services if this is justified by various recognized public interest objectives which are not protected by the home State's regulation to the same standard (efficient restrictions of trade).[180] Should this be the case, the host State's regulation will apply, subject to the proportionality principle. The latter will uncover situations of opportunistic behaviour, where the State would be arguing a

[179] Moravcsik, 'Preferences and Power in the European Community', above, p. 492.

[180] I. Lianos, 'Trust, Distrust and Economic Integration: Efficient Restrictions of Trade and the Evolution of the Law of the Internal Market', UCL Global Law Research Paper Series (forthcoming, 2011).

public interest justification with protectionist intent. Should this public interest justification prove successful, following judicial assessment, the host Member State may maintain measures that are restrictive of trade. The application of the market access rule is therefore conditioned by specific circumstances, in particular the absence of a legitimate justification for the restriction of trade. We will refer to this principle as 'conditional market access'.

The possibility of exceptions to the application of the market access rule, offered to the host State, is further qualified in the EU by an asymmetrical allocation of the burden of proof between the home and host State that disfavours the host State. This is achieved by the principle of equivalence, which creates a presumption that the home State's regulatory system internalizes all the cross-border negative policy externalities that it produces. It is for the host State to prove that this is not practically the case, for example because of some fundamental differences, which may relate to diverse regulatory cultures and policies determining mutual perceptions of regulatory effectiveness, different risk assessments, or more broadly the absence of 'regulatory compatibility' between the two regimes.[181] The principle of equivalence attenuates the possible neutralization of the market access principle by a frequent and inconsiderate use of exceptions. It constitutes a form of mutual recognition, as, by agreeing that their relations are governed by this principle, the home and the host State mutually recognize the compatibility of their regulatory systems.

The principle of equivalence thus constitutes a discrete governance mechanism compared to the market access and national treatment rules, as it involves a positive obligation imposed on the host State to 'recognize' the regulatory system of the home State. This involves a presumption of equivalence of the preferences maximized by the home State's regulation to those satisfied by its own regulation that is attached to it.

The practical assessment of the application of the equivalence principle is often left to a third independent party, the courts. As was rightly observed by Maduro, the courts do not assess whether the different national legislations are identical.[182] The principle of equivalence,

[181] K. Nicolaïdis and M. Egan, 'Transnational Market Governance and Regional Policy Externality: Why Recognize Foreign Standards?', *Journal of European Public Policy* 8(3) (2001) 454–73, p. 458.

[182] M. P. Maduro, 'So Close and Yet So Far: The Paradoxes of Mutual Recognition', *Journal of European Public Policy* 14(5) (2007) 814–25, p. 821.

operating as a presumption, dispenses with the need to integrate such an assessment into the judicial control. What the courts can do, however, is to define the negative policy externalities to foreign interests that need to be internalized for the principle of equivalence to operate fully.

Here, opinions diverge. Some authors argue that the role of the courts is to ensure the 'virtual representation' of all foreign interests that might be affected.[183] It follows that courts, such as the Court of Justice, will not simply look to the compatibility of the regulations of the home and host States, but will impose a solution which introduces the 'EU interests of market integration in the national decision-making process'.[184] This definition of the principle of equivalence requires the Court to intervene in order to ensure the virtual representation of *all* unrepresented foreign interests. This can take the form of either a proper balancing test that will *evaluate* the local benefits and the foreign costs and then assess their respective weight, or an 'institutional malfunctions' test.[185]

Other authors question the premises of the 'virtual representation' argument and instead advance a 'local/global equivalence' argument.[186] According to this view, foreign interests are often accounted for by local interests in decision-making. The interests of the local consumers might indeed be affected by a regulation that favours local producers and harms foreign producers/suppliers. But a strict environmental regulation that is indiscriminately applicable will also affect local suppliers of products whose production is not compatible with the stricter environmental standards and who might be obliged either to increase their costs considerably and thus lose market share or to exit the market. It might also

[183] M. P. Maduro, *We the Court – The European Court of Justice and the European Economic Constitution* (Oxford: Hart Publishing, 1998), p. 170. The assumption of the virtual representation argument is that, in the national political process, foreign interests are not usually taken into account, as they are not adequately represented. This might lead to a Kaldor–Hicks inefficiency, in particular when the foreign costs are greater than the local benefits of the regulation or when the foreign costs are disproportionate to the local benefits. For example, an environmental regulation might impose high costs on some foreign producers in order to satisfy the preferences of local consumers for a cleaner environment. The assumption is that the production of the foreign good has negative externalities on the host State's environment.

[184] Maduro, 'So Close and Yet So Far', above, p. 821.

[185] M. P. Maduro, 'Reforming the Market or the State? Article 30 and the European Constitution: Economic Freedom and Political Rights', *European Law Journal* 3(1) (1997) 55–82.

[186] D. H. Regan, 'Judicial Review of Member State Regulation within a Federal or Quasi-Federal System: Protectionism and Balancing "da Capo"', *Michigan Law Review* 99(8) (2001) 1853–1902, pp. 1859–1860.

affect local consumers that are unable to buy the more expensive environmentally friendly products. These local interests will oppose their home State's regulation, as its effect will decrease their welfare, and, by doing so, they will represent the foreign interests in the domestic political process. In other words, there is a vicarious consideration of the foreign producers' interests by the integration into the analysis of the interests of local consumers and/or some local suppliers.

The assumptions about the internalization of cross-border negative domestic policy externalities being exactly the opposite, each theory leads to a different degree of discretion for national regulatory systems and *in fine* to a different end point in their interaction. The virtual representation argument theory will be vindicated if, through the judge's intervention, the regulation under examination will internalize *all* the negative policy externalities of a domestic regulation to foreign interests: in other words, foreign interests will be integrated by judicial decision to the domestic weighing of interests, thus breaking the boundary between foreign and domestic interests: the 'foreign' and the 'domestic' spheres becoming one. In contrast, the local/global equivalence theory will internalize *some* negative policy externalities to foreign interests, presumably only those accounted for by local interests. The distinction between foreign and domestic will thus still be relevant, as it is possible that a different weighing of interests develops across jurisdictions, depending on the bargaining power of the various societal interests. As a result, there would be regulatory diversity, not sameness.

A third institutional arrangement/governance mechanism to deal with risks is for the parties to the cooperation to agree on *common* rules/standards of protection across jurisdictions, in other words to write a contract, implemented by a third party, which remains outside the control of the home or the host State. We thus move from regulatory compatibility to regulatory sameness or regulatory harmonization, at least as far as regulatory values are concerned. The same rules apply to all jurisdictions.

Harmonization is the preferred governance mechanism where the national treatment or market access principle cannot be enforced successfully. This may be caused by the fact that there are significant differences between the regulatory values of the home and the host States, which cannot be resolved on a case-by-case basis by the courts applying the market access rule or the principle of equivalence. There are various reasons for this. Courts may not have the legitimacy or the power to resolve the distributional conflicts between the winning and the losing societal interests in the home and host States, the task being delegated to the political process.

The application of the market access rule may be unsuited to sectors subject to technically complex regulation that requires an important amount of information and continuous supervision of the service provider. Furthermore, if there is economic interdependence between the jurisdictions, there is a high occurrence of cross-border negative policy externalities. In this case, harmonization may reduce transaction costs. Transaction costs include 'the cost of collecting information on the amount of welfare benefits'[187] the home or the host State might gain in order to determine their position as to the internalization of negative policy externalities in each case following the application of the market access rule. It also involves the costs of the *ad hoc* judicial examination of the justifications proffered by the State or the application of the principle of equivalence. The choice of harmonization as the adequate institutional framework will thus be a function of the comparison between these transaction costs and the costs entailed by harmonization.[188]

[187] J. P. Trachtman, *The Economic Structure of International Law* (Cambridge, MA: Harvard University Press, 2008), p. 10.

[188] These harmonization costs might be of different sorts: first, the costs related to the bargaining game over the terms of cooperation; second, 'agency costs'; and, third, the costs of 'mutual spying': see K. Nicolaïdis, 'Kir Forever? The Journey of a Political Scientist in the Landscape of Mutual Recognition' in M. Maduro (ed.), *The Past and Future of EU Law: The Classics of EU Law Revisited on the 50th Anniversary of the Rome Treaty* (Hart Publishing, 2010), p. 447, p. 453. It is obvious that the harmonization process requires an immense effort in identifying, negotiating and enforcing bargains, which might be achieved through side-payments and linkages. Costs may also rise due to the strategic behaviour of parties aiming to gain a better bargain (than the other) with regard to the distributional consequences of the arrangement. Communication between the States and the collection of information about the partners may also be costly. In the EU context, these costs are relatively minor, as the environment in which EU governments bargain is 'relatively information-rich', 'national negotiators are able to communicate at low cost and possess information about the preferences and opportunities facing their foreign counterparts, as well as the technical implications of policies that are of the greatest interest to them': see Moravcsik, 'Preferences and Power in the European Community', above, p. 498. Finally, agency costs arise usually after the negotiations have been concluded. They refer to the principal/agent relation between the States (principal) and the institution (agent) the States create to monitor and enforce their agreement. For example, the agreement may not be enforced at the desired (by the agents) level. In the presence of a decentralized enforcement of the common standards, the monitoring process involves 'mutual spying' by each of the parties to the agreement in order to identify instances of cheating and to put in place effective counter-strategies. This can take the form of networks involving personnel from all parties to the agreement ensuring a form of monitoring, regular meetings between the parties, the exchange of information, the development of appropriate sanctions in case of cheating, such as strategies to increase reputation costs – in other words, all conditions that favour the maintenance of the cartel between them.

However, the existence of discrete institutional alternatives cannot be limited to the principles of (pure) market access (national treatment), (conditional) market access (principle of equivalence) and harmonization. The terminology of 'mutual recognition' that now dominates the discourse about governance of economic integration projects indicates that those different institutional alternatives form part of a continuum,[189] which can be further creatively expanded with the emergence of new forms of governance, building on these foundational blocks.

There are various forms of 'mutual recognition'. Some authors, like Pelkmans, oppose 'judicial mutual recognition' to 'regulatory mutual recognition'.[190] Whilst 'judicial mutual recognition' proceeds to an *ad hoc* and *ex post* assessment of State measures, depending on the individual cases brought to the courts, 'regulatory mutual recognition' relies more on a systematic scrutiny of existing measures, by means of a screening mechanism, early warning systems (including the obligation to notify new measures), administrative cooperation among national authorities and mutual evaluation procedures, thus falling short of the rigidity of the 'harmonization' conceptual category. Mutual recognition can thus be perceived as a form of 'new governance' mechanism.[191] 'New governance' was an appropriate catch-all slogan to conceptualize the unlikeness of the 'new' 'regulatory mutual recognition' to the more established 'harmonization' category. By emphasizing the soft and somehow more collaborative and voluntary, rather than hierarchical and binding, character of the former,[192] its ambition was to describe a new phenomenon rather than to provide categorical and conceptual clarity. There was no attempt to advance and test explanations on the causes of this shift from old to 'new' governance methods that would have led to informed predictions on the evolution of EU governance in various fields.

[189] K. Nicolaïdis and G. Shaffer, 'Transnational Mutual Recognition Regime: Governance without Global Government', *Law and Contemporary Problems* 68 (2005) 263–317.

[190] J. Pelkmans, 'Mutual Recognition in Goods. On Promises and Disillusions', *Journal of European Public Policy* 14(5) (2007) 699–716.

[191] S. Schmidt, 'Mutual Recognition as a New Mode of Governance', *Journal of European Public Policy* 14(5) (2007) 667–81.

[192] G. de Búrca and J. Scott, *Law and New Approaches to Governance in the EU and US* (Oxford: Hart Publishing, 2006); J. Scott and D. M. Trubek, 'Mind the Gap: Law and New Approaches to Governance in the European Union', *European Law Journal* 8 (2002) 1–18; K. Armstrong and C. Kilpatrick, 'Law, Governance or New Governance? The Changing Open Method of Coordination', *Columbia Journal of European Law* 13 (2007) 649–77.

Possibly, this is due to the fuzziness of the 'mutual recognition' category. As Maduro once noted, the principle of mutual recognition conceals a dual nature.[193] First, it may constitute a governance mechanism, in the sense that it generates a process of regulatory competition and decentralization that can be distinguished from harmonization,[194] as previously explained. Second, it operates as a conflict-of-laws rule. Wolfgang Kerber and Roger van den Bergh have convincingly argued that mutual recognition aims to delineate the regulatory powers of jurisdictions and to test whether the traditional national regulatory autonomy is still defensible or if decentralization should be replaced by another allocation of regulatory powers that can take the form of either 'centralization (including measures of harmonization) or a free market for regulations (free choice of law)'.[195] As a conflict rule that determines which governance mechanism will prevail, it cannot be a form of governance in itself.[196]

Indeed, some formulations of the mutual recognition principle may lead to the extraterritorial application of the home State's law, thus providing economic operators with a limited right to choose among different national regulatory regimes. The application of a country-of-origin principle, where the host State accepts without any conditions the regulatory standards of the home State (pure mutual recognition) can lead initially to a system of intense regulatory competition between States, as economic operators are free to experiment with different regulatory systems. A country-of-origin principle may thus be compared to a uniform choice-of-law rule, where the applicable regulatory standards are always those of the home State, notwithstanding the fact that the practice affects the host State's domestic interests. The extraterritorial application of the home State's law that results from the country-of-origin rule increases the likelihood of a race to the bottom, where different regulatory systems enter into a spiral of scaling down their mandatory requirements in order to improve their position in the regulatory competition game. Ultimately, this might lead to a unification of law and to harmonization, where the most 'competitive' regulatory standard

[193] M. Maduro, 'So Close and Yet So Far: The Paradoxes of Mutual Recognition', *Journal of European Public Policy* 14(5) (2007) 814–25, p. 815.

[194] Schmidt, 'Mutual Recognition as a New Mode of Governance', above, p. 667.

[195] W. Kerber and R. Van den Bergh, 'Mutual Recognition Revisited: Misunderstandings, Inconsistencies, and a Suggested Reinterpretation', *Kyklos* 61 (2008) 447–65, p. 448.

[196] Maduro, 'So Close and Yet So Far', above, p. 815.

will prevail. Conflict-of-laws rules can easily become instruments of harmonization and integration.[197]

The decision to adopt choice of law as the optimal means of allocating regulatory competences between Member States is based on the assumption that a market for regulation will effectively satisfy the various regulatory preferences. However, a market for regulation may generate externalities, the race to the bottom being an obvious example. The provision of a free menu of regulatory options to economic operators would in this case not satisfy some domestic interests favouring high quality of services, safety, consumer protection or environmental standards. These values may not be taken into account by the market mechanism, because the total gains to be made by satisfying the marginal consumers of regulation (foreign entrepreneurs) and some infra-marginal consumers of regulation (domestic interests favouring low prices) will be more important than the costs to infra-marginal consumers of regulation (domestic interests – consumers and entrepreneurs – valuing environmental protection, consumer protection, social welfare) that put these values higher than lower prices in their scale of preferences. A mandatory allocation of regulatory competences would be an option in this case. The decision-making may be (i) exclusively delegated to a third party, (ii) shared between the affected jurisdictions, or (iii) permanently delegated to either the home or the host State. The country-of-origin principle may be perceived as an example of the third option, the regulatory competence being exclusively exercised by the home State. It does not thus constitute a free-menu choice-of-law system. One could certainly theoretically envision a country of the provision of services option, where regulatory competence will only be exercised by the host country and not by the home jurisdiction (for services that are cross-border). Such an option faces practical difficulties, because of the principle of territoriality in regulation and the difficulty of distinguishing *ex ante* between services that are provided cross-border, where the home State's regulatory regime will not apply, and services destined for the domestic market. There are also options (i) and (ii), which broadly correspond to the governance mechanism of harmonization and that of 'managed mutual recognition', where the parties to the cooperation

[197] P. Hay, O. Lando and R. D. Rotunda, 'Conflict of Laws as a Technique for Legal Integration' in M. Cappelletti, M. Seccombe and J. H. H. Weiler (eds.), *Integration Through Law*, Vol. 1, *Methods, Tools and Institutions*, Book 2 (Berlin: Walter de Gruyter, 1986), p. 161.

framework share the regulation of risks by effectively ensuring that negative cross-border policy externalities are internalized through mutual understandings concerning the required adjustments of the burden.

With this conceptual framework in mind, the next section explores the regulation of trade in services in the EU and the different governance tools chosen for various sectors, with a view to highlighting the emergence of hybrid governance tools that challenge the established conceptual categories of national treatment, market access and harmonization. The hypothesis is that this variety of governance tools exemplifies the efforts made in the EU to accommodate regulatory pluralism.

3.2 *A variety of governance tools in the area of services: adjustment to accommodate legal pluralism?*

The area of the free movement of services constitutes an interesting natural experiment for testing this proposition. Governments regulate trade in services for a number of reasons: they may be motivated by the need to promote the provision of some services in the marketplace that, absent regulation, would have never been provided; they may want to address externalities arising from the existence of natural monopolies or relational bargaining power because of an informational asymmetry; and they may have paternalistic concerns or pursue aims of distributive justice. The scope of negative policy externalities that are of concern for EU law is also broad, the market access rule operating under Article 56 TFEU covering all measures that have the potential to affect cross-EU trade. Consequently, the governance arrangements dealing with these negative externalities may cover various sectors of the economy and affect large societal interests.

3.2.1 The exclusion of the full operation of the principle of equivalence: the example of gambling

As noted, the Court of Justice recognized in *Liga Portuguesa* the need for Member States to develop their own scale of values with regard to the application of paternalistic regulation in order to preserve social objectives or to reduce criminal activity.[198] The fact that the Council has put in

[198] Case C-42/07, *Liga Portuguesa* [2009] ECR I-7633, para. 69: '[I]t should be noted that the sector involving games of chance offered via the internet has not been the subject of Community harmonization. A Member State is therefore entitled to take the view that the mere fact that an operator . . . lawfully offers services in that sector via the internet

place a Working Party on Establishment and Services on the legal framework for gambling and betting, which provided extensive information on the legal regime of the different Member States in this area might explain the cautious approach followed by the Court. After all, it was clearly explained in the progress report published by the Swedish presidency that Member States should be free 'to set the objectives of their policy on betting and gambling and, where appropriate, to define in detail the level of protection sought'.[199]

The Court could have applied the principle of equivalence as for all cases where EU harmonization has not been adopted. It chose instead a different starting point, that of the regulatory diversity of Member States. As explained in section 2.2 above, the result is that the burden of proof in proffering public policy justifications for measures restricting market access is now profoundly altered. Host States could dismiss an allegation of an Article 56 TFEU infringement by emphasizing the diversity of their regulatory regime: the once feared proportionality test is now to be carried out 'solely by reference to the objectives pursued by the competent authorities of the Member State concerned and the degree of protection which they seek to ensure'.[200]

This case exemplifies the emergence of a special category of judicial mutual recognition where the principle of equivalence does not operate, as it usually does under the framework established by the Court in *Cassis de Dijon*. This is not with the intention to promote gambling as an area of regulatory experimentation for Member States before making the choice of a more centralized or federal regulatory option. The objective is clearly to accommodate the variety of societal choices across the Member States in the Union.

in another Member State, in which it is established and where it is in principle already subject to statutory conditions and controls on the part of the competent authorities in that State, cannot be regarded as amounting to a sufficient assurance that national consumers will be protected against the risks of fraud and crime, in the light of the difficulties liable to be encountered in such a context by the authorities of the Member State of establishment in assessing the professional qualities and integrity of operators.'

199 See Council of the European Union, Swedish Presidency Progress Report, Legal Framework for Gambling and Betting in the Member States of the European Union, 25 November 2009, available at http://register.consilium.europa.eu/pdf/en/09/st16/st16571.en09.pdf at § 13; see also Council of the European Union, Conclusions on the Framework for Gambling and Betting in the EU Member States, 10 December 2010, available at www.consilium.europa.eu/uedocs/cms_data/docs/pressdata/en/intm/118398.pdf, noting the regulation of the gambling sector by national regulatory authorities and suggesting cooperation between them.

200 Case C-42/07, *Liga Portuguesa*, above, para. 58.

3.2.2 Delegation to the private sector and self-regulation (codes of conduct)

In other instances, regulation establishing barriers to trade is necessary to deal with market failure. Depending on which services sector comes into focus, the extent of regulation varies. Several factors such as increasing risks or the nature of the industry involved can determine the form of governmental action. In the sector of professional services, it might be necessary to maintain high professional standards and to ensure the quality of services for the benefit of the consumers. This regulation, pervasive in some economic sectors, is not always directly imposed by the State. It may emanate from a number of private professional associations/bodies to which the State has delegated the power to regulate professions. The definition of quality standards and other requirements for the exercise of professions is a highly information-intensive task, requiring an expert knowledge of the social and economic context of the profession, the expectations of consumers, the existing social (informal) norms that govern the exercise of professions (reputation effects). The reality of the regulatory space is complex enough, rendering improbable the choice of a simple command-and-control regulatory instrument. The self-regulation of professions also complicates any effort of harmonization at the EU level. The traditional harmonization tools would not have adequately addressed the plurality of actors and interests represented in the regulation of the professions in the various Member States. A different mechanism had thus to be chosen: Europe-wide codes of conduct.

According to Article 37 of the Services Directive,

> Member States shall, in cooperation with the Commission, take accompanying measures to encourage the drawing up at the Community level, particularly by professional bodies, organisations and associations, of codes of conduct aimed at facilitating the provision of services or the establishment of a provider in another Member State, in conformity with Community law.

This bottom-up approach emphasizes the involvement of the private sector and professional organizations/bodies across the Union, rather than interaction between national regulators. It was indeed felt that European codes of conduct, drafted by the professional bodies, would enable the pooling of expertise and specialized local knowledge on the minimum professional standards and would ensure quality across the Union. The pan-European codes of conduct could thus operate as a targeted trust-building tool accommodating the polyarchy of the regulation of the professions, where there is a multitude of national professional bodies involved. This approach has the dual effect of building more consumer trust on the quality of the services provided by professionals established elsewhere in the Union and of facilitating the interoperability of different regulatory environments.

One could contrast the regulation of the professions with another sector of the economy, where there is intensive quality regulation, but with less regulatory actors involved in this process. In public procurement markets, regulation aims to attain greater allocative efficiency, while ensuring greater quality of services and the performance of universal service obligations. Contrary to the delegated self-regulation of the professions, the regulation of procurement markets emanates directly from the State (it is not delegated to private bodies) and is horizontal in nature, as it applies to all sectors. It is also of relatively limited scope, as the standards imposed aim to preserve the transparency of the tender process and competition in the award of the contracts rather than specific and variable quality norms for each profession, as it is the case for the regulation of professions. The EU Directives that proceeded to the harmonization of the regulatory framework in this sector[201] thus offer an important discretion to Member States in regulating the award process and in ensuring the provision of services of general interest. The choice of the instrument of the Directive is justified by the relatively low degree of knowledge and sector-specific expertise requirements for the regulation of public procurement and the rather straightforward implementation process, compared to the difficulties that would have been incurred in the monitoring of the regulation of the professions at the European level, without the assistance of professional bodies and associations.

3.2.3 Balancing common standards and regulatory diversity by delegating to regulatory networks and agencies: the examples of energy and telecoms regulation

In other economic sectors, the pervasiveness and technicalities of the regulation, and consequently the greater degree of expert knowledge

[201] Directive 2004/17/EC of the European Parliament and of the Council of 31 March 2004 coordinating the procurement procedures of entities operating in the water, energy, transport and postal services sectors, OJ 2004 L134/1; Directive 2004/18/EC of the European Parliament and of the Council of 31 March 2004 on the coordination of procedures for the award of public works contracts, public supply contracts and public service contracts, OJ 2004 L134/114.

required, mandates the involvement in the EU harmonization process of national regulators. The process of developing interoperable standards across the Union requires their involvement. The aim is to share knowledge and to negotiate the development of common standards. The process is close to that of standard-setting organizations, with the difference that in this case the participants in the standard-setting are all stakeholders – Member States (national ministries and authorities, the Commission), business and industry representatives, consumer associations, not just the economic operators – and that their cooperation takes place or continues after the common standards have been established.

The development of EU harmonization in the regulation of utilities markets may provide a useful illustration of this cooperative partnership between Member States and between the Member States and the Union. For example, the Florence and the Madrid processes on the liberalization of the electricity and gas sectors in 1998 were thought of as completing the implementation of the first liberalization Directives of 1996, in view of the considerable opposition between the different Member States as to the degree of the opening up of the sectors to competition and the dismantling of national monopolies.[202] When the early EU steps towards liberalization were taken, utilities markets presented a heterogeneous configuration characterized by State ownership, vertical integration and monopoly. The Florence Electricity Regulatory Forum and the Madrid Gas Regulatory Forum provided the platforms for informal discussions and the exchange of ideas between the different stakeholders in order to ensure that the important differences that still separated the various domestic approaches could not curtail the achievement of the EU Internal Market in this sector.[203] This objective was largely achieved. The involvement of the stakeholders through this informal mechanism was an essential trust-building tool that eventually led to the development of more 'integrated' European standards, soon after the publication of the second liberalization package in 2003.

Cameron explains that the strategic considerations of security of energy supply or access to fossil fuels have traditionally weakened the

[202] P. D. Cameron, 'Creating an Internal Market in Energy: How Can the Tools Be More Effective?', Robert Schuman Centre, Policy Papers, 05/01, available at www.dundee.ac.uk/cepmlp/staff/pcameron_publications_RSCAS_policy_paper.pdf. One could also add the Citizen's Energy Forum, established in 2008 as a new regulatory platform based on the experience gained in the Florence and Madrid FORUMS. See http://ec.europa.eu/energy/gas_electricity/forum_citizen_energy_en.htm.

[203] *Ibid.*, p. 5.

force of arguments for energy market integration in the EU, in particular for Member States that rely on imports of energy and gas, and may explain the 'strong influence of public service considerations in the electricity and to a lesser extent the gas industry of the EU' that blocked the negotiations for a long time, in comparison to other regulated industries such as telecoms.[204] In telecoms, the Commission made use of the special powers given by Article 106(3) TFEU, which allow the issuance of Directives without requiring extensive negotiations with the Council and the European Parliament. However, in other sectors – especially energy and post – the use of a similar strategy would have clashed with the pronounced political resistance of some Member States. The Florence and Madrid fora can thus be explained by the need of the specific sector for an extensive and continuous trust-building process between the different stakeholders, something that was not considered that important in the development of the EU framework in the telecoms sector.

More importantly, the cooperation between Member States and between the Member States and the Commission continued even after the emergence of harmonized standards in these sectors. This is, in part, due to the specificities of the regulatory arrangements in the utilities sector. Electricity and telecoms have been traditionally regulated through public ownership or directly by government departments, less so by independent administrative authorities. Generally, with the main exception of the UK, there were initially no independent regulators in most of the EU Member States.[205] Central governments were the exclusive rule-setters and concentrated most of the regulatory powers. The choice of a government department to regulate often signalled that the objectives pursued by the State expanded beyond the usual focus of curbing the effects of market power and reducing negative externalities. A number of social or protectionist aims were also framing regulatory strategies.

The absence of a clear mandate with specific objectives and priorities for each national regulator, in conjunction with the strategic dimension

[204] *Ibid.*

[205] In contrast to the US, for most of the twentieth century there were very few NRAs in European countries. The situation was only altered when the UK began to create new agencies as part of the privatization process beginning in the 1980s. Note, however, that similar semi-independent bodies ('regulatory commissions') had already been developed in the UK during the nineteenth century: see C. D. Foster, *Privatization, Public Ownership and the Regulation of Natural Monopoly* (Oxford: Basil Blackwell, 1992), Chapter 2.

of these sectors made the development of regulatory interoperability and a level playing field between the different Member States an unachievable dream. Expanding the scope of the market and constraining national regulations with the implementation of EU competition rules would have been a possible option if the overall aim of the EU legislator was to dismantle the various national regulatory barriers to an internal market for electricity. The establishment of a European federal regulator could have been another option. In the event, none of these options was chosen. Instead, the European legislator imposed the establishment, in each Member State, of independent national regulatory authorities (NRAs),[206] which contribute to 'the development of the internal market and of a level playing field by cooperating with each other and with the Commission in a transparent manner'.[207] The NRAs were also integrated into a European network of regulators, called 'ERG' in telecoms and 'ERGEG' in energy,[208] both founded in order to promote cooperation between regulators, to draft guidelines and policy proposals and, more generally, to promote cognitive convergence at the EU level.[209]

[206] See, e.g., Article 23(1) of Directive 2003/54/EC of the European Parliament and of the Council of 26 June 2003 concerning common rules for the Internal Market in electricity and repealing Directive 96/92/EC, OJ 2003 L176/37, noting that 'Member States shall designate one or more competent bodies with the function of regulatory authorities. These authorities shall be wholly independent from the interests of the electricity industry. They shall, through the application of this Article, at least be responsible for ensuring non-discrimination, effective competition and the efficient functioning of the market.' Article 25 of Directive 2003/55/EC of the European Parliament and of the Council of 26 June 2003 concerning common rules for the Internal Market in natural gas and repealing Directive 98/30/EC, OJ 2003 L176/57.

[207] Article 23(12) of Directive 2003/54/EC, above.

[208] In the field of electronic communications, the Commission established the 'European Regulators Group' (ERG) in 2002. See Decision establishing the European Regulators Group for Electronic Communications Networks and Services, OJ 2002 L200/38 (as amended by Decision 2004/3445, OJ 2004 L293/20). In the energy sector, the European Regulators Group for Electricity and Gas (ERGEG) was established in 2003 as the Commission's formal advisory group of energy regulators. See Decision establishing the European Regulators Group for Electricity and Gas, OJ 2003L296/34. The Council of European Energy Regulators (CEER), a non-profit-making association of European electricity regulators, operates as a preparatory body for the ERGEG.

[209] For instance, see the Guidelines of Good Practice developed by the CEER and the ERGEG, at www.energy-regulators.eu. See also Common Position on the Approach to Appropriate Remedies in the New Regulatory Framework, ERG (03) 30 rev1.

It is possible to conceive the involvement of independent administrative regulators as a credible commitment[210] by the Member States that they will not adopt protectionist strategies in the future and that only regulatory measures that expert bodies such as national regulators judge as necessary for the normal operation of the industry (and justified by a market failure, externality or identifiable need to provide public services), will be adopted. Because of the nature of the European legislative process, however, Member States still enjoy a high degree of regulatory autonomy. The Directives merely set up a general framework that must be 'transposed' to the internal legislation of Member States. Whilst generally most – if not all – NRAs have broad duties and extensive powers to oversee their respective markets, their strategies and behaviour diverge widely.[211] Their degrees of discretion are different, their objectives and priorities vary,[212] the scope of their jurisdiction is dissimilar (e.g., some have concurrent jurisdiction with antitrust authorities) and their procedures to set tariffs are also very disparate.[213] Certainly, the European Commission, as the main governmental principal, casts a 'double shadow of hierarchy' over the sectoral governance agents (NRAs and the network of NRAs). This is achieved through the threat of further legislation and of enforcing EU competition law,[214] both options being employed effectively by the Commission.[215]

210 M. Thatcher, 'Delegation to Independent Regulatory Agencies: Pressures, Functions and Contextual Mediation', *West European Politics* 25 (2002) 125–47, p. 133; G. Majone, 'Two Logics of Delegation: Agency and Fiduciary Relations in EU Governance', *European Union Politics* 2 (2001) 103–22; G. Majone, 'The Regulatory State and Its Legitimacy Problems', *West European Politics* 22 (1999) 1–24, p. 4; G. Majone, 'The Politics of Regulation and European Regulatory Institutions' in J. Hayward and A. Menon (eds.), *Governing Europe* (Oxford University Press, 2003), Chapter 17.

211 See, e.g., M. Thatcher, 'Regulatory Agencies, the State and Markets: A Franco-British Comparison', *Journal of European Public Policy* 14(7) (2007) 1028–1047 (noting the similar formal structures but the different strategies of NRAs in France and the UK).

212 Objectives such as climate change and security of supply have been added to the long-standing aim of introducing competition for the benefit of consumers.

213 The most recent Directives significantly enhance the independence of NRAs in Member States. See Directive 2009/72/EC, OJ 2009 L211/55, concerning common rules for the Internal Market in electricity and repealing Directive 2003/54/EC, Chapter IX (Articles 35–40).

214 B. Eberlein, 'The Making of the European Energy Market: The Interplay of Governance and Government', *Journal of Public Policy* 28(1) (2008) 73–92.

215 See the energy sector enquiry in 2005, followed by a number of high-profile cases on competition law enforcement in the electricity and gas sector (in mergers, State aid and antitrust) and finally the recent third liberalization package adopted in 2009.

The recent third liberalization package in energy moved towards a more centralized governance structure.[216] This resulted in the creation of a formal agency in the energy sector, the 'Agency for the Cooperation of Energy Regulators' (ACER),[217] in charge of regulatory cross-border issues and the coordination of the work of NRAs. Likewise, the Commission launched a review of the current regulatory rules in the telecoms sector in November 2007.[218] The proposals for reform included the establishment of a European agency (the 'Electronic Communications Market Authority', ECMA) with powers to act centrally and to coordinate the actions of NRAs. The new package for electronic communications did not establish a strong central authority but introduced instead the Body of European Regulators for Electronic Communications (BEREC), which replaced the ERG as an exclusive forum for cooperation among NRAs and between NRAs and the Commission. The Office, an EU body with legal personality, would support BEREC and would have legal, administrative and financial autonomy. BEREC is more integrated into the EU legal framework than the ERG, but it is also a less centralized governance tool than the Commission's initial Proposal on the establishment of a European agency in the telecoms sector.[219]

While the European agency in the energy sector arose out of proposals made by the national regulatory authorities in the context of the ERG recognizing the value of voluntary cooperation between national regulatory authorities within an EU structure with clear competences and with the power to adopt individual regulatory decisions in a number of

[216] Regulation (EC) No. 714/2009 of the European Parliament and of the Council of 13 July 2009 on conditions for access to the network for cross-border exchanges in electricity and repealing Regulation (EC) No. 1228/2003, OJ 2009 L211/15; Regulation (EC) No. 715/2009 of the European Parliament and of the Council of 13 July 2009 on conditions for access to the natural gas transmission networks and repealing Regulation (EC) No. 1775/2005, OJ 2009 L211/36; Directive 2009/72/EC of the European Parliament and of the Council of 13 July 2009 concerning common rules for the Internal Market in electricity and repealing Directive 2003/54/EC, OJ 2009 L211/55; Directive 2009/73/EC of the European Parliament and of the Council of 13 July 2009 concerning common rules for the Internal Market in natural gas and repealing Directive 2003/55/EC, OJ 2009 L211/94.

[217] Regulation (EC) No. 713/2009 of the European Parliament and of the Council of 13 July 2009 establishing an Agency for the Cooperation of Energy Regulators, OJ 2009 L211/1.

[218] See Amended Proposal for a Regulation of the European Parliament and of the Council establishing the European Electronic Communications Market Authority (EECMA), COM(2008) 720, 2007/0249 (COD).

[219] Regulation (EC) No. 1211/2009 of the European Parliament and of the Council of 25 November 2009 establishing the Body of European Regulators for Electronic Communications (BEREC) and the Office, OJ 2009 L337/1.

specific cases,[220] in the area of electronic communications, the BEREC does not have any power to adopt individual regulatory decisions and is a much less integrated institution within the EU framework than ACER. Its aim is to contribute to a consistent regulatory practice by facilitating cooperation among NRAs, and between NRAs and the Commission. The BEREC does not duplicate the work of NRAs, but rather aims to develop greater policy consistency among NRAs by helping them to exchange information and knowledge on their practical experiences and by intensifying cooperation and coordination. As is clearly explained in Regulation 1211/2009, '[t]he EU regulatory framework sets out objectives to be achieved and provides a framework for action by national regulatory authorities (NRAs), whilst granting them flexibility in certain areas to apply the rules in the light of national conditions'.[221]

The different degree of integration into the EU structure of the European regulation of telecoms and energy may be explained by the varying levels of trust between national regulatory authorities in these two areas. The latter may be due to the variety of concerns addressed by energy regulation in comparison to the regulation of telecoms. Environmental concerns, security of supply and public service obligations are vague enough and provide more space for opportunistic behaviour by NRAs to promote protectionist interests than the comparatively fewer public interest objectives and principles that are integrated into the Union's legal framework for electronic communications. Because of the variety of objectives pursued and the possible occurrence of opportunistic behaviour, one could reasonably assume that there was a lower level of trust between NRAs in the energy sector, in comparison to the telecoms sector, which justifies the different patterns of evolution of institutional arrangements in these sectors, although, in both cases, the starting point was similar (loose networks of NRAs). It was felt that the need to limit the discretion of NRAs in the energy sector and that a regime more integrated into the EU institutional structure could have led to fewer instances of opportunistic behaviour. In the electronic communications sector, the regulatory framework did not promote pluralistic concerns but was mainly targeted at practices extending or reinforcing market power. This characteristic of the regulatory framework reduced the risk of opportunistic behaviour by NRAs and enabled cooperation between them, without the need to have recourse to a more centralized

220 Recital 3 of Regulation (EC) No. 713/2009, above.
221 Recital 3 of Regulation (EC) No. 1211/2009, above.

institutional framework. In conclusion, the higher level of institutional distrust between NRAs in the energy sector required the establishment of institutions different to those in the telecoms sector.

3.2.4 The evolution of regulatory networks to more solidified and centralized regulatory authorities: the example of financial services

In the financial services sector, the Lamfalussy process,[222] introduced in 2002 in securities regulation and in 2003 in banking and insurance, led to the development of a regulatory framework for the financial system in Europe, by integrating national regulatory authorities (NRAs) in the definition and operation of the newly adopted common standards. This approach, based on the cooperation of NRAs, followed the failure of the Single European Act to establish a European financial market, because of the difficulties faced in applying the principle of mutual recognition to banking, insurance and investment services.[223]

In the 1960s and 1970s, the financial systems of the Member States were largely incompatible with each other,[224] because of the different monetary systems, their loose cooperation in the monetary policy area, as well as the failure in integrating the freedom of cross-frontier provision of financial services in the EU *acquis*, notwithstanding the significant steps taken with regard to the right of establishment of foreign banks with the adoption of the first banking Directive in 1977.[225] These first attempts at EU harmonization contained a major innovation in so far as they institutionalized cooperation procedures through the creation of Committees composed of senior civil servants from the Member States as well as from the European Commission, thus associating both the Commission and the Member States in the initiation of legislation in

[222] Final Report of the Committee of Wise Men on the Regulation of European Securities Markets, February 2001, available at http://ec.europa.eu/internal_market/securities/docs/lamfalussy/wisemen/final-report-wise-men_en.pdf.

[223] E. Posner, 'The Lamfalussy Process: Polyarchic Origins of Networked Financial Rulemaking in the EU' in C. F. Sabel and J. Zeitlin (eds.), *Experimentalist Governance in the European Union: Towards a New Architecture* (Oxford University Press, 2010), p. 43, p. 46.

[224] J. Story and I. Walter, *Political Economy of Financial Integration in Europe: The Battle of the Systems* (Cambridge, MA: MIT Press, 1997).

[225] First Council Directive 77/780/EEC of 12 December 1977 on the coordination of the laws, regulations and administrative provisions relating to the taking up and pursuit of the business of credit institutions, OJ 1977 L322/30.

this area.[226] This cooperation expanded with the development of the European Monetary System in 1979.

The principle of equivalence with its deregulatory potential formed the cornerstone of the development of the European framework in this area. The Single European Act's strategy in the financial services sector was based on the belief that liberalization, in the sense of restricting regulatory barriers to trade, was a prerequisite to progress in the Internal Market.[227] This required a coordinated effort to achieve in view of the important proliferation of State and non-State actors in the political game: umbrella organizations representing banks, insurance companies and consumer associations, at both the EU and international levels, such as the International Federation of Stock Exchanges, the International Organization of Securities Commissions, the Basel Committee on Banking Supervision, international organizations involved in this area, such as the OECD, UNCTAD and the GATT, and major players in the global financial industry, such as the United States and Japan. The aim of market integration had also to accommodate concerns other than trade gains, such as financial stability, the need for prudential regulation, the preservation of the global competitiveness of the European financial services sector, the linkage of the financial services sector with monetary and more broadly economic policy.

As is illustrated by the choice of the instrument of harmonization by EU Directives, the simple operation of the equivalence principle through a case-by-case enforcement of the negative integration rules would have been inadequate, precisely because of the plurality of public interests to take into account and actors to involve. However, as Jonathan Story and Ingo Walter noted in their seminal study of financial integration in Europe,

> [f]inancial services proved the least amenable to legislative activism. Trust between Europe's financial centres was a scarce commodity. Competition prevailed over cooperation. Tax regimes differed. Ideas diverged about the role of capital markets.[228]

The result of the opposition between these divergent forces led to a stalemate for more than a decade, before the Council of the Union proposed the Financial Services Action Plan (FSAP), which was finally

226 J. Story and I. Walter, *Political Economy of Financial Integration in Europe: The Battle of the Systems*, above, p. 15.

227 *Ibid.*, p. 17. 228 *Ibid.*, p. 25.

adopted in March 2000. The FSAP included a number of legislative measures, defined across strategic objectives, with the objective of advancing convergence between the different financial systems of the Member States, in view, in particular, of the monetary union and the constitution of a single currency.[229] The bulk of the work for the FSAP was done by a Financial Services Policy Group, composed of representatives of the ECOFIN ministers and the European Central Bank, and put under the chairmanship of the Commission. The establishment of linkages between national bureaucracies and the European institutions active in the reform of the financial sector was an important part of this strategy. As was acknowledged in the FSAP,

> [a]t present, decisions on appropriate supervisory arrangements are determined at national level, and the supervision of the banking, insurance and securities sectors is predominantly conducted at that level. Member States have developed different models for performing these tasks. Mutual confidence in the effectiveness of partner country financial supervision and regulation – whether that be undertaken by a consolidated authority for the entire sector or by separate sectoral authorities that co-operate and co-ordinate effectively – is the key ingredient for successful cross-border supervision.[230]

An important ingredient of this new governance structure was the involvement of key stakeholders in order to promote 'a more inclusive and consensual approach in shaping policy from an early stage and in advance of drafting legislation', including not only the EU institutions or representatives of national regulators, but also market practitioners and consumers.[231] This constituted a major evolution from the framework existing at the time for cross-border cooperation, which consisted of bilateral memoranda of understanding between national supervisors. The collaboration with international private fora, such as the Basel Committee, or the constitution of new 'high level' European fora representing stakeholders and integrating them into the process of forging consensus, 'without prejudice to the Commission's legal right of initiative',[232] formed part of this new strategy. The creation by the Council of Economic and Finance Ministers in July 2000 of a Committee of Wise Men on the Regulation of European Securities Markets, under the chairmanship of Alexandre Lamfalussy, can also be explained by the need to

[229] COM(1999) 232, available at http://ec.europa.eu/internal_market/finances/docs/actionplan/index/action_en.pdf.

[230] *Ibid.*, p. 14 (emphasis added). [231] *Ibid.*, p. 16. [232] *Ibid.*

combine expertise in a rapidly evolving sector with the benefits of a 'committee of independent persons'[233] that would include in the process national regulators and the various groups and interests affected by the emerging regulatory framework.

Concretely, the Lamfalussy report initiated a new mechanism to promote convergence in the European financial supervisory practice, based on four levels.[234] At Level 1, the Commission can initiate a formal Proposal setting broad framework principles which can be adopted by the Council and the Parliament by means of Directive/Regulation, after a full consultation process under the normal EU legislative procedure. At the second level, new committees have been established: a European Securities Committee (ESC) in the area of securities and the European Banking Committee in the banking sector, with the mission to assist the European Commission in determining how to implement the details of the Level 1 framework. These Committees, composed of high-level Member State representatives, are chaired by the Commission. Their role in the process is central.

The Lamfalussy process thus recognized two layers in the legislation related to financial markets: basic political choices translated into broad but sufficiently precise framework norms (Level 1) and more detailed technical measures, in full conformity with this framework, which implement the objectives pursued by the legislation (Level 2). The ESC and other Level 2 committees have been vested with enough comitology powers to revise and update EU legislation, in addition to their advisory function. At Level 3 are committees composed of national regulators: the Committee of European Banking Supervisors (CEBS) and the Committee of European Securities Regulators (CESR), which work on joint interpretation, recommendations, consistent guidelines and common standards (in areas not covered by EU legislation) through a peer review process, and a comparison of regulatory practices across the Union to ensure consistent implementation and application. These Level 3 committees ensure a more effective cooperation between national supervisors and a convergence of regulatory and supervisory practices. At Level 4, the Commission can monitor the process by

233 Initial Report of the Committee of Wise Men on the Regulation of European Securities Markets, November 2000, available at http://ec.europa.eu/internal_market/securities/docs/lamfalussy/wisemen/initial-report-wise-men_en.pdf, p. 30.

234 Final Report of the Committee of Wise Men on the Regulation of European Securities Markets, 15 February 2001, available at http://ec.europa.eu/internal_market/securities/docs/lamfalussy/wisemen/final-report-wise-men_en.pdf, p. 19.

checking compliance in Member States and by taking legal action against Member States suspected of breach of the EU framework.

This process may be presented as a classic example of negotiation in the shadow of hierarchy,[235] where hierarchy is defined as any legislative and executive decisions 'that steer democratic governmental action at the national and European level'.[236] The process involves the Member States as long as they cooperate in the design and implementation of the common standards. In the absence of a cooperation strategy on their part, the Commission may still intervene. A 'double delegation of powers and functions' thus characterizes the governance arrangements in the financial services sector: this is exercised either 'upwards' from the national independent regulators to the Commission or 'downwards' from the European Commission to regulatory networks.[237] Coen and Thatcher conclude that European regulatory networks, such as the CESR, lack powers and resources, and exercise mainly an advisory (and secondary) role: for example, the CESR can shape policy 'in so far as it can influence the Commission'.[238]

Yet, other accounts of the operation of the Level 3 committees in the context of the Lamfalussy process report that the absence of a political consensus among the main principals (the European Parliament and the Council) in the creation of the Markets in Financial Instruments Directive (MiFID) at Level 1 left important political decisions to be taken by the CESR (acting as an agent) at Levels 2 and 3.[239] That led to an expansion of the CESR's role and its transformation into a 'central agenda setter' in the process.[240] The conceptualization of the CESR as operating in the shadow of hierarchy also does not consider that the European Commission's (the intermediary principal) initial proposals for introducing comitology in the financial sectors did not include the

[235] T. Börzel, 'European Governance: Negotiation and Competition in the Shadow of Hierarchy', *Journal of Common Market Studies* 48(2) (2010) 191–209, pp. 200–4.

[236] A. Héritier and D. Lehmkuhl, 'The Shadow of Hierarchy and New Modes of Governance', *Journal of Public Policy* 28(1) (2008) 1, p. 2.

[237] D. Coen and M. Thatcher, 'Network Governance and Multi-Level Delegation: European Networks of Regulatory Agencies', *Journal of Public Policy* 28(1) (2008) 49–71.

[238] *Ibid.*, p. 64.

[239] E. Posner, 'The Lamfalussy Process: Polyarchic Origins of Networked Financial Rulemaking in the EU' in C. F. Sabel and J. Zeitlin (eds.), *Experimentalist Governance in the European Union: Towards a New Architecture* (Oxford University Press, 2010), p. 43.

[240] *Ibid.*

establishment of Level 3 committees, such as the CESR, but only a Level 2 committee, the ESC. According to Posner, the development of an 'autonomous role' for the CESR, beyond its original mandate, was not expected by some of the principals in the process (the European Parliament and the Commission) and can be explained by a number of attributes: its members' expertise in a highly technical sector, the open consultation processes that enhanced its reputation as an expert technical body in touch with fast-changing market developments, the 'internal capacity-building processes' that included coordination through peer review or transparent benchmarking, the ongoing deliberation process and the existence of conflict-resolution mechanisms.[241] The conceptualization of regulatory networks as operating under the shadow of hierarchy provides thus a partial explanation of their operation and objectives. It is submitted that, besides the technical expertise, which could have been acquired through different means than the constitution of networks of NRAs, the Lamfalussy approach is intrinsically participatory, consensus-driven and based on open consultation with the aim of promoting convergence and building 'mutual trust to ensure better implementation' of the EU framework,[242] through mediation, delegation of tasks and information sharing. One could also note their contribution to the development of a 'common supervisory culture' through staff exchanges and training programmes.[243]

Furthermore, the theory of negotiation under the shadow of hierarchy does not provide an adequate theoretical framework to explain the replacement of the Level 3 committees with a more integrated and centralized institutional structure at the EU level, following the de Larosière report.[244] The theory fails to explain why the evolution towards a more centralized structure was required, in so far as the 'shadow of hierarchy' could already constrain the freedom of national supervisors to act. It is submitted that the high levels of distrust between national supervisors, because of a greater likelihood of opportunistic behaviour in a period of economic and financial crisis and the consequent development of a more intensive competition between Member

[241] *Ibid.*

[242] Communication from the Commission, Review of the Lamfalussy Process – Strengthening Supervisory Convergence, COM(2007) 727 final, p. 9.

[243] *Ibid.*, p. 7.

[244] The High-Level Group on Financial Supervision in the EU, Report, 25 February 2009, available at http://ec.europa.eu/internal_market/finances/docs/de_larosiere_report_en.pdf.

States increased the costs of cooperation between them under the current framework.[245]

We provide some context on the reform before moving to implications for our discussion on governance mechanisms. The Commission has recently made proposals for a reform of the institutional structure of the EU supervisory architecture and the constitution of a European System of Financial Supervisors. The proposals establish a new body, the European Systemic Risk Board (ESRB), with the aim of ensuring macro-prudential and macro-economic risks regulation and three European Supervisory Authorities (ESAs), the European Banking Authority (EBA), the European Insurance and Occupational Pensions Authority (EIOPA) and the European Securities and Markets Authority (ESMA), which will replace the existing Lamfalussy Level 3 committees.

The ESAs are EU bodies with legal personality; they have increased responsibilities to adopt technical standards by qualified majority voting, as well as a general power to ensure the consistent application of EU law. A more formal dispute settlement mechanism enables the ESAs to settle disagreements between national supervisory authorities, by adopting a binding decision. The new institutional arrangement is also justified by the development of a single rulebook in order to ensure a 'uniform application of rules in the EU', the main task of the ESAs being to monitor the implementation of the rules by the national supervisors.[246] In contrast to the Lamfalussy committees, the ESAs may take decisions requiring a national supervisory authority to take a specific action or to refrain from an action. In the event the national supervisory authority does not comply, the ESA may act as a last resort and adopt a decision directly applicable to the specific financial institutions.

These increased responsibilities for the ESAs, in comparison to Level 3 Lamfalussy committees, the 'comply or explain' approach followed with regard to national supervisors and better funding may lead to the emergence of a more centralized system at the EU level. However, they still confer an important role on national supervisors, because of their local knowledge and their close relation to the day-to-day operation of companies. The Commission does not exclude a further centralization of

[245] Communication for the Spring European Council, Driving European Recovery, COM (2009) 114 final, p. 6, noting 'the existing gaps in preventing, managing and resolving crises and the difficulties caused by a lack of cooperation, coordination, consistency and trust between national supervisors'.

[246] Proposal for a Regulation of the European Parliament and of the Council establishing a European Banking Authority, COM(2009) 501 final, p. 3.

the European system of financial supervision after the next review, to be completed in 2012, if this proves necessary.[247]

The internal organization of the ESAs and the ESRB illustrate also the evolution towards a more centralized model. The board of supervisors is certainly the main decision-making body of the ESAs. It includes as its voting members the heads of the relevant national supervisory authorities in each Member State. At the same time, the management board that prepares the ESA's work programme and adopts the rules of procedure includes a representative from the Commission and four elected members of the Board of Supervisors who 'shall act independently and objectively in the Community interest'.[248] A full-time independent chair of the ESA will be responsible for preparing the work and chairing the meetings of the Board of Supervisors and the Management Board, a noticeable change from the loose internal structure of the Level 3 Lamfalussy committees. The ESRB does not have a legal personality but is a new European body, whose strength lies in the composition of its General Board, comprising governors of national central banks, the President and Vice-President of the European Central Bank (ECB), a member of the European Commission and the chairs of the ESAs. The chair of the General Board is elected for a period of five years, and its activity is supported by the secretariat of the ECB. Although the ESRB cannot adopt binding decisions, it is anticipated that it will have an important moral authority because of its high-level composition.[249] It is apparent that these changes mark an evolution towards a more centralized governance mechanism.

3.2.5 Open Method of Coordination

The Open Method of Coordination (OMC) constitutes an additional route for coordination and constitution of a common regulatory culture. The method was first relied on for the coordination of employment policies at the Lisbon European socio-economic summit in 2000, and was later extended to a variety of policy areas, mainly in the fields of

[247] Communication for the Spring European Council, Driving European Recovery, above, p. 6.

[248] Proposal for a Regulation of the European Parliament and of the Council establishing a European Banking Authority, above, p. 9.

[249] Proposal for a Regulation of the European Parliament and of the Council on Community macro prudential oversight of the financial system and establishing a European Systemic Risk Board, COM(2009) 499 final.

economic policy and employment strategy,[250] where it was conceived of as a tool for the progressive Europeanization of domestic social policy.[251] The OMC has also expanded to a number of areas beyond social and economic governance (including fiscal policy), such as immigration and asylum, occupational health and safety, innovation policy and environmental protection. The exact content of this method varies considerably, depending on the characteristics of the policy field or the cross-sectoral, sectoral or sub-sectoral character of the reform, but the main ingredients of the OMC were defined by the Lisbon European Council's conclusions in 2000, according to which the OMC is a

> means of spreading best practice and achieving greater convergence towards the main EU goals. This method, which is designed to help Member States to progressively develop their own policies, involves:
>
> - fixing guidelines for the Union combined with specific timetables for achieving the goals which they set in the short, medium and long terms;
> - establishing, where appropriate, quantitative and qualitative indicators and benchmarks against the best in the world and tailored to the needs of different Member States and sectors as a means of comparing best practice;
> - translating these European guidelines into national and regional policies by setting specific targets and adopting measures, taking into account national and regional differences;
> - periodic monitoring, evaluation and peer review organised as mutual learning processes.
>
> ... A fully decentralised approach will be applied in line with the principle of subsidiarity in which the Union, the Member States, the regional and local levels, as well as the social partners and civil society, will be actively involved, using variable forms of partnership. A method

[250] L. Tholoniat, 'The Career of the Open Method of Coordination: Lessons from a "Soft" EU Instrument', *West European Politics* 33(1) (2010) 93–117; J. Zeitlin and M. Heidenreich (eds.), *Changing European Employment and Welfare Regimes: The Influence of the Open Method of Coordination on National Reforms* (Routledge, 2009); V. Hatzopoulos, 'Why the Open Method of Coordination Is Bad for You: A Letter to the EU', *European Law Journal* 13(3) (2007) 309–42; W. Kerber and M. Eckardt, 'Policy Learning in Europe: The Open Method of Co-ordination and Laboratory Federalism', *Journal of European Public Policy* 14 (2) (2007) 227–47; D. Ashiagbor, *The European Employment Strategy: Labour Market Regulation and New Governance* (Oxford University Press, 2005); C. Radaelli, 'The Open Method of Coordination: A New Governance Architecture for the European Union?', Report for the Swedish Institute for European Policy Studies, Stockholm (April 2003).

[251] See K. A. Armstrong, *Governing Social Inclusion: Europeanization through Policy Coordination* (Oxford University Press, 2010).

> of benchmarking best practices on managing change will be devised by the European Commission networking with different providers and users, namely the social partners, companies and NGOs.[252]

There are considerable differences in OMC modalities and procedures: the well-established and historic OMCs, such as the Broad Economic Policy Guidelines (BEPGs) and the European Employment Strategy (EES), involve EU institutions, the Parliament and the Council, which can issue joint recommendations to Member States for the implementation of the detailed BEPGs and the EES. In other cases, common European benchmarks and statistical indicators have been devised in order to facilitate cooperation and coordination between the different Member States. In the social sphere, the Member States are also required to prepare National Action Plans, National Strategy Reports or National Progress Reports, which are subjected to the peer review and mutual surveillance of the representatives of other Member States in sectoral committees, such as the Employment Committee, the Social Protection Committee and the Economic Policy Committee. A common characteristic of all OMC procedures is the non-reliance on binding legislation, but instead to 'voluntary' compliance and incentives, the coordination rather than harmonization of national policies, and the participation of a number of stakeholders and actors beyond Member States. The OMC thus fulfils a different aim than the traditional harmonization or market liberalization approach. According to Sabel and Zeitlin, 'the OMC was envisaged by its architects as a "third way" for EU governance between regulatory harmonization and fragmentation, capable of reconciling the pursuit of common European objectives with respect for national diversity while encouraging mutual emulation and experimental learning through comparison of different approaches to shared problems'.[253]

3.2.6 The 'new approach' to harmonization: taming regulatory diversity

Managing, rather than suppressing, diversity becomes an important concern in the regulation of intra-EU trade. Instead of adopting a detailed harmonization of national rules or excluding their application

[252] Presidency Conclusions – Lisbon European Council, 23 and 24 March 2000, available at www.consilium.europa.eu/uedocs/cms_data/docs/pressdata/en/ec/00100-r1.en0.htm.

[253] C. F. Sabel and J. Zeitlin, 'Learning from Difference: The New Architecture of Experimentalist Governance in the European Union', Eurogov, No. C-07–02.

through the joint operation of the principle of equivalence and the market access rule, the European Commission has since the late 1970s initiated a 'new approach' to harmonization, which proceeds by defining only the essential requirements that goods have to meet when they are marketed, and delegates the task of developing these standards to specific standard-setting bodies.[254] This approach is referred to below as 'managed harmonization' in order to illustrate its selective, partial and decentralized form in comparison with the classic exhaustive 'old' harmonization tool. The 'new approach' offers a considerable degree of flexibility to economic operators who are allowed to choose the way they conform to the requirements of the principle of mutual recognition. Member States are also more involved in the process as they can perform controls of the products for both the pre-market (conformity assessment modules) and post-market (market surveillance) stages. The new approach also establishes an early warning system requiring the notification of the adopted measures to the Commission and other Member States and the accreditation of the products by national conformity assessment bodies.

Market surveillance entails an effective cross-border administrative cooperation between Member States. Yet, originally, there was no systematic exchange of information between Member States concerning the criteria and procedures applied at national level for the assessment and surveillance of the bodies put in place, which has encouraged suspicion about uneven levels of implementation. The Commission quickly put in place mechanisms to increase the levels of confidence and trust between Member States, for the good operation of the system.[255] However, it also noted that 'Community harmonization legislation shall restrict itself to setting out the essential requirements determining the level of such

[254] Communication from the Commission of 7 May 2003 to the Council and the European Parliament enhancing the implementation of the New Approach Directives, COM (2003) 240 final.

[255] Regulation (EC) No. 764/2008 of the European Parliament and of the Council of 9 July 2008 laying down procedures relating to the application of certain national technical rules to products lawfully marketed in another Member State and repealing Decision No. 3052/95/EC, OJ 2008 L218/21; Regulation (EC) No. 765/2008 of the European Parliament and of the Council of 9 July 2008 setting out the requirements for accreditation and market surveillance relating to the marketing of products and repealing Regulation (EEC) No. 339/93, OJ 2008 L218/30; Decision No. 768/2008/EC of the European Parliament and of the Council of 9 July 2008 on a common framework for the marketing of products, and repealing Council Decision 93/465/EEC, OJ 2008 L218/82.

protection and shall express those requirements in terms of the results to be achieved'.[256]

3.2.7 Managed regulatory mutual recognition: the example of the Services Directive

The principle of regulatory mutual recognition offers an alternative governance mechanism to harmonization and judicial mutual recognition. It provides more flexibility than the 'new approach' as it 'obviates the need to set EU norms for a particular area or sector altogether – leaving it to Member States to set standards to protect public interest concerns, whilst avoiding that differential standards amount to barriers to trade'.[257] It also appeals to a different institution than courts, for dispute resolution, by providing mediation between conflicting interests at the regulatory level. Judicial mutual recognition may, however, evolve to regulatory mutual recognition. The free movement of goods offers an illustration of this evolution: following the *Cassis de Dijon* judgment of the Court,[258] the principle of mutual recognition was reframed and codified in legislative texts.[259]

The Services Directive provides an interesting illustration of regulatory mutual recognition.[260] It is well known that the initial draft of the Services Directive attempted to bring a substantial change from the *status quo*.[261] The country-of-origin principle, included in the initial version of the Proposal, subjected the provision of services (authorization, exercise, consumer protection) entirely to the rule and control of the home State, the host State not being able to impose additional

[256] Article 3(1) of Decision No. 768/2008/EC, above.

[257] Commission Staff Working Paper, Instruments for a Modernised Single Market Policy, COM(2007) 724 final, p. 10.

[258] Case 120/78, *Rewe-Zentral AG* v. *Bundesmonopolverwaltung für Branntwein* [1979] ECR 649.

[259] Regulation (EC) No. 764/2008 laying down procedures relating to the application of certain national technical rules to products lawfully marketed in another Member State and repealing Decision No. 3052/95/EC, OJ 2008 L218/21.

[260] Directive 2006/123/EC of the European Parliament and of the Council of 12 December 2006 on Services in the Internal Market, OJ 2006 L376/36.

[261] C. Barnard, 'Unravelling the Services Directive', *Common Market Law Review* 45 (2008) 323; G. Davies, 'Services, Citizenship and the Country of Origin Principle', Mitchell Working Paper Series No. 2/2007 (Europa Institute, Edinburgh University); B. de Witte, 'Setting the Scene: How Did Services Get to Bolkestein and Why?', Mitchell Working Paper Series No. 3/2007 (Europa Institute, Edinburgh University); M. Chang, D. Hanf and J. Pelkmans, 'The Services Directive: Trojan Horse or White Knight?', *Journal of European Integration* 32 (2010) 97–114.

requirements nor to monitor their enforcement. The country of origin would thus have led to a complete transfer of regulatory authority from the host State to the home State.

If one adopts the assumption that regulatory systems represent domestic preferences and institutional conditions at the domestic level determining the balance between divergent domestic interests,[262] such transfer of authority involves the acceptance that only foreign interests will be represented in the decision-making process. There should be a considerable level of trust between the different systems. A simple similarity of values and regulatory culture would not be sufficient. Nicolaïdis and Egan rightly remark that 'even high regulatory compatibility does not in itself produce absolute trust, and thus is not matched by full delegation of authority'.[263] One could, indeed, distinguish between the principle of 'pure' mutual recognition from that of 'managed mutual recognition', the latter enabling the host State to impose its own rules concerning the authorization, exercise and quality requirements on a cross-border service provider, of course as long as the principles of equivalence and proportionality are kept in sight. Kalypso Nicolaïdis explains:

> [a]s an outcome, managed mutual recognition can be contrasted with 'pure' mutual recognition in the same sense as managed trade can be contrasted with absolute free trade. Pure mutual recognition implies the granting of fully unconditional and open-ended rights (of action, access) to private market agents as a product of a free trade contract between states. In contrast, managed mutual recognition introduces conditionality in the contract. The four main dimensions along which mutual recognition can be managed or fine-tuned are: (a) prior conditions for equivalence, from convergence to inter-institutional agreements; (b) varying degrees of automaticity of access (for example, residual host country requirements); (c) scope of activities or features covered by recognition; and (d) *ex post* guarantees or safeguards, including mutual monitoring and ultimately provisions for reversibility.[264]

[262] If one follows the assumptions of liberal intergovernmentalism, see A. Moravcsik, 'Preferences and Power in the European community: A Liberal Intergovernmentalist Approach', *Journal of Common Market Studies* 31(4) (1993) 473–524, pp. 480–1.

[263] K. Nicolaïdis and M. Egan, 'Transnational Market Governance and Regional Policy Externality: Why Recognize Foreign Standards?', *Journal of European Public Policy* 8(3) (2001) 454–73, p. 470.

[264] K. Nicolaïdis, 'Kir Forever? The Journey of a Political Scientist in the Landscape of Mutual Recognition' in M. P. Maduro and L. Azoulai (eds.), *The Past and Future of EU Law* (Oxford: Hart Publishing, 2010), p. 451.

It is well known that the final version of the Directive did not include the principle of the country of origin, and replaced it with a 'freedom to provide services' clause. Article 16 of the Directive requires Member States to abstain from imposing their own requirements on cross-border service providers (but they can still impose them on their own national operators) except where justified by the four reasons enumerated in Article 16(1) and (3): public policy, public security, public health and protection of the environment. In comparison to the previous case law on imperative requirements of general interest, the latter offer only a limited opportunity to Member States to follow diverse public interest objectives. Furthermore, any such requirements have to comply with the principles of non-discrimination, necessity and proportionality. Article 16(2) lists a number of restrictions, for which there is a 'strong presumption' that they cannot be justified by the four public interest objectives referred to previously, 'since they will normally be disproportionate'.[265] However, this falls short of an obligation to refrain from all control.

It is possible to conclude that the scope of managed regulatory mutual recognition, introduced by the Directive, offers less room for regulatory diversity than judicial mutual recognition, as it curtails the discretion of the Member States to justify restrictive measures. Contrary to the Directive, the case law has always been open-ended on the list of reasons of public interest that can justify a restriction on the freedom to provide services. At the same time, the scope of application of the principle of managed regulatory mutual recognition is narrower than that of judicial mutual recognition.

First, a long list of sectors is excluded from the application of the Directive's principle of 'freedom to provide services'.[266] The Treaty provisions on the freedom to provide services (and the market access rule) may still apply in these sectors, and some of these services are already subject to sectoral regulation at the EU level (e.g., financial services, electronic communications and networks).

[265] European Commission, Handbook on the Implementation of the Services Directive, 2007, available at http://ec.europa.eu/internal_market/services/services-dir/index_en.htm, p. 39.

[266] *Ibid.*, pp. 10–13. The list is long: non-economic services of general interest, financial services, electronic communication services and networks, services in the field of transport, services of temporary work agencies and social services relating to social housing, childcare, support of families and persons in need, healthcare, audiovisual and radio broadcasting services, gambling activities, activities connected with the exercise of official authority and private security services.

Second, Article 1(6) of the Directive provides that it does not affect labour law or the social security legislation of the Member States, including all legal or contractual provisions concerning employment conditions, working conditions, health and safety at work and the relationship between employers and workers. The Directive has no impact on fundamental rights and supports the view that there is no inherent conflict between the exercise of fundamental rights and the fundamental freedoms of the Treaty; 'neither prevails over the other.'[267]

Third, Article 17 of the Directive contains a number of derogations from the principle of 'freedom to provide services': services of general economic interest and intellectual property rights are among the activities covered by these derogations, as well as a number of activities which have already been subjected to EU harmonization measures. Finally, Article 18 allows for derogations from the principle of 'freedom to provide services' on a case by case basis for safety reasons. This is done under strict conditions, in particular the requirement for the host Member State to assess whether the measures considered provide 'real added value' over measures adopted by the home State or to require the assistance of the home Member State prior to imposing these measures unilaterally. These numerous exceptions were placed in the Directive with the aim of attenuating the effect of the country-of-origin principle and in order to achieve consensus among Member States for its adoption.[268] The fact that they have been maintained, even after the abandonment of the country-of-origin principle, indicates that the Member States have gained some regulatory autonomy in these sectors, as it is improbable that the case law will head in an opposite direction and apply the market access rule in an expansive way.

It is significant that the Commission's Communication concerning the consequences of the *Cassis de Dijon* judgment in the area of the free movement of goods[269] emphasized only the Commission's role in implementing the principle of mutual recognition. The Services Directive goes much further and contains a number of provisions establishing administrative cooperation between Member States. The objective is to create an institutional mechanism in order to manage 'infrastructural heterogeneity' within Member States which can be a

[267] *Ibid.*, p. 15. [268] Chang, Hanf and Pelkmans, 'The Services Directive', above, p. 99.

[269] Communication from the Commission concerning the consequences of the judgment given by the Court of Justice on 20 February 1979 in Case 120/78, Cassis de Dijon, OJ 1980 C256/2.

barrier to cross-border cooperation.[270] The Directive first proceeds to an administrative simplification of the procedures and formalities applicable to service providers.[271] In particular, it requires Member States to set up 'points of single contact' as single interlocutors for service providers, thus enabling the collection and exchange of information between them. For example, Member States have to accept documents from other Member States which serve an equivalent purpose and which indicate that the requirement in question has been satisfied. Such measures of simplification as well as the provisions of the Directive on the quality of services increase the confidence of consumers in foreign providers of services. More importantly, the Directive promotes a deep level of administrative cooperation between the Member States, as a prerequisite to the operation of the principle of managed regulatory mutual recognition. The aim is 'to enhance both mutual trust between Member States and the confidence of providers and consumers in the Internal market'.[272]

Concretely, Chapter VI of the Directive sets out a system of cooperation based on the obligation of mutual assistance between the competent authorities of Member States.[273] This obligation is comprehensive, and encompasses also the possibility of finding and exchanging information between the different national authorities. The Internal Market Information System offers the technical means to promote communication between Member States.[274] This networked environment complements existing initiatives in other areas, such as the RAPEX (rapid alert system for non-food dangerous products), the RASFF (rapid alert system for food and feed) and the Consumer Protection Cooperation Network. Its aim consists in 'the building of mutual trust' and the establishment of a partnership where responsibility is 'shared' between the Member States

270 S. Weatherill, 'Promoting the Consumer Interest in an Integrated Services Market', Mitchell Working Paper Series No. 1/2007 (Europa Institute, Edinburgh University), available at www.law.ed.ac.uk/file_download/series/23_promotingtheconsumerinterestinanintegratedservicesmarket.pdf, p. 15 (last visited 26 August 2010).

271 Articles 5–8 of Directive 2006/123/EC.

272 European Commission, Handbook on the Implementation of the Services Directive, 2007, available at http://ec.europa.eu/internal_market/services/services-dir/index_en.htm, p. 7.

273 Articles 28–36 of Directive 2006/123/EC.

274 Commission Decision setting out the practical arrangements for the exchange of information by electronic means between Member States under Chapter VI of Directive 2006/123/EC of the European Parliament and of the Council in services in the Internal Market, OJ 2009 L262/32.

and the Commission.[275] Articles 30 and 31 of the Directive provide for a clear division of supervisory tasks between the different Member States in cross-border service provision, depending on the nature of the measures and rules envisioned: if these do not fall under the scope of the 'freedom to provide services', it is the host State which is responsible for supervising the activities of the provider; if the measures fall within the scope of Articles 16 and 17 and are thus prohibited, it is the home State that ensures compliance with its own national requirements and guarantees that the service provider has the required authorizations, the host State being only able to undertake factual checks on its own initiative under specific conditions.[276] Finally, if the host State benefits from a case-by-case derogation under Article 18, there is a specific procedure for managing these situations of breaking trust.[277]

One of the most innovative aspects of the Services Directive is the mutual evaluation process that enables Member States to comment on the reports submitted by other Member States after reviewing their legislation for conformity to the Directive.[278] The Commission will provide annually analyses and orientations on the application of these provisions in the context of the Directive. The recent Commission Communication, 'Towards a Single Market Act', reiterates the importance of the mutual evaluation mechanism and suggests its extension beyond the Services Directive.[279] This forms part of the broader strategy of the Commission to build a partnership with the Member States in the management of the Internal Market.[280] As was acknowledged by the Commission in its Recommendation on measures to improve the functioning of the Single Market,

> [t]he measures taken by the Member States and those taken by the Commission should complement each other. A coordinated and

[275] Commission Recommendation on measures to improve the functioning of the Single Market, OJ 2009 L176/17. According to the most recent Communication from the Commission, Towards a Single Market Act, COM(2010) 608 final, p. 31, the Commission will extend the application of the IMI to legislative areas other than that of the Services Directive.

[276] These conditions are set by Article 31(4) of Directive 2006/123/EC, above: the checks, inspections or investigations should not be discriminatory; they should not be motivated by the fact that the provider is established in another Member State; and they should be proportionate.

[277] Article 35 of Directive 2006/123/EC, above.

[278] Article 39 of Directive 2006/123/EC, above.

[279] Communication from the Commission, Towards a Single Market Act, above, p. 31.

[280] *Ibid.*, p. 32.

> cooperative approach – in partnership between the Commission and Member States – with a common objective of improved transposition, application and enforcement of single market rules, is vital to ensure the proper functioning of the single market. The partnership approach ... goes beyond the already established cooperation in a number of single market policy areas. It requires establishing and maintaining closer cooperation within and between the Member States, and with the Commission, in all areas that are relevant for the single market. It also implies that Member States assume shared responsibility for and therefore a more proactive role in managing the single market.[281]

In conclusion, these different case studies illustrate the porosity of the tripartite distinction between the market access/national treatment rule, the principle of equivalence and that of harmonization as discrete governance mechanisms. The emergence of different forms of cooperation in various sectors of trade in services, based on the development of the overarching principle of mutual recognition, as well as the failure of adopting a more horizontal and uniform approach for the regulation of trade in services, following the retreat of the country-of-origin principle from the final version of the Services Directive, illustrate the complex interaction between the centrifugal forces of pluralism and the centripetal tendencies of managing the risks of cooperation. These tensions eventually lead to the emergence of different cooperation equilibria in various sectors.

3.3 *Pluralism, trust and distrust*

The conclusion that one may draw from the survey of governance tools in the previous sections is that 'ideal' governance categories, such as national treatment, market access and harmonization, do not correspond to the much more complex reality of regulating inter-State trade in services. Managed market access, managed mutual recognition, managed harmonization, regulation through networks and agencies, governance by delegation to private parties, the Open Method of Coordination and other soft coordination mechanisms compose a much more complex picture of the various governance arrangements in the area of services trade. They also challenge common assumptions on the location of these different governance mechanisms in the continuum between the poles of regulatory diversity/regulatory pluralism and centralism/uniformity,

[281] European Commission, Recommendation on measures to improve the functioning of the Single Market, OJ 2009 L176/17, recital 5.

which can refer either to the adoption of common regulatory standards (harmonization) or to the free interplay of demand and supply in a 'single' market for regulations (pure mutual recognition with race to the bottom) or services (pure market access).

In this mapping exercise (see Figure 6.1), managed harmonization does not lead automatically to centralism and rests between the two poles. The active involvement of national independent regulatory authorities in the negotiation and evolving constitution of harmonized standards, as has been the case with the Lamfalussy process in the financial services sector and with the NRAs networks in the energy and telecom sectors, ensures that national diversities and regulatory cultures will be taken into account. The continuous involvement of these authorities in the process guarantees that this is not a one-off inclusion but a continuous interaction where experiences are shared and regulatory experimentation is valued. The Open Method of Coordination, with its emphasis on dialogue, partnership, peer review and benchmarking, seems also to influence the strategy followed by recent attempts of managed harmonization, such as the Services Directive, signalling the progressive abandonment of the strict format of detailed sectoral rules for more open-ended standards and relying on the continuous cooperation and interaction between national authorities to manage conflicts.

Yet, the market access-national treatment rule/mutual recognition/harmonization trilogy continues to be presented as the holy trinity of European Internal Market law. For example, in the recent *Ker-Optika* case on free movement of goods, the Court held that 'Article 34 TFEU [the equivalent to Article 56 TFEU for the free movement of goods] reflects the obligation to comply with the principles of *non-discrimination* and of

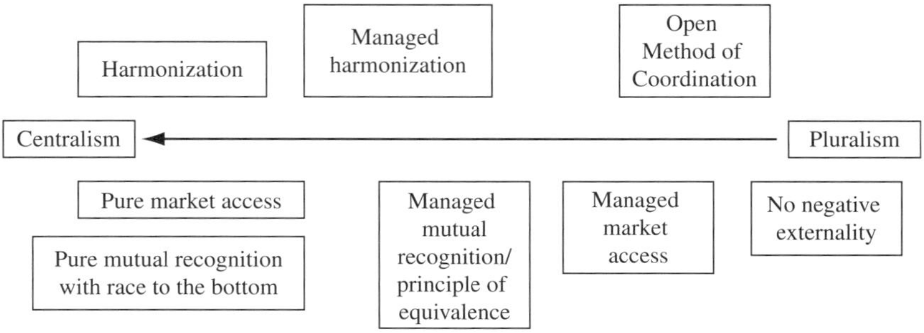

Figure 6.1 The poles of pluralism and centralism

mutual recognition of products lawfully manufactured and marketed in other Member States, as well as the *principle of ensuring free access of EU products to national markets*'.[282] There might be a reason explaining the stickiness of the trilogy in the imagery of the Internal Market project and the failure to fully capture the managed character of market access, recognition and harmonization.

A possible explanation is that the trilogy may perfectly explain the process of economic integration if the latter's aim is unidimensional: the erosion of barriers to trade with the removal of regulatory impediments and the convergence towards unified regulatory standards. However, in a legal order valuing regulatory pluralism, the outcomes of economic integration cannot be uniform. One should take into account the evolving objectives pursued by the different political and institutional entities that operate within the 'directly deliberative polyarchy' of the European regulatory area.[283]

In the polyarchic system of European governance, framework goals are jointly established by a multi-level institutional system comprising national ministries or national regulatory authorities, networks of national authorities, EU agencies and EU institutions, and private entities (through codes of conduct): this constructs an Internal Market framework within which the lower-level units (national administrations) can protect public health, social solidarity, consumers and the environment in ways that grow out of their own traditions. As Mario Monti noted in his report on 'A New Strategy for the Single Market',

> [t]he single market itself is today part of a context, which has dramatically changed. In turn, the actors to be involved in the initiative – Europe's policy makers and stakeholders – are more diverse and present a wider range of preferences and interests.[284]

The plurality of objectives and interests, 'economic' and 'social', embedded in the project of the Internal Market, cannot be brought to fruition within the simple framework of the market access/equivalence/

[282] Case 108/09, *Ker-Optika bt*, 2 December 2010, not yet published, para. 48 (emphasis added).

[283] C. F. Sabel and J. Zeitlin, 'Learning from Difference: The New Architecture of Experimentalist Governance in the European Union', Eurogov, No. C-07–02 (May 2007), p. 9.

[284] M. Monti, 'A New Strategy for the Single Market at the Service of Europe's Economy and Society', Report to the President of the European Commission, 9 May 2010.

harmonization trilogy that has long served as the mantra of the economic integration project. As we have previously shown, these principles are not the only conceivable conceptual categories of governance in the Internal Market: there is a multitude of other tools and possible combinations that can achieve stochastic equilibrium in a pluralistic setting. Some institutional arrangements may therefore work in some areas but not in others. The regulation of trade in services constitutes a telling example of this plurality of objectives and consequently institutional arrangements that break with the traditional categories and highlight a different, theoretically richer, conception of economic integration than the joint aims of regulatory sameness and the erosion of barriers to trade.

Nevertheless, this evolution contrasts with ambivalent rhetoric employed by the Commission. The completion of the Internal Market is seen as an economic modernization necessity and walks in tandem with deregulation (towards a 'single' market) or re-regulation at the EU level. Some have attempted to explain this apparent contradiction by the disembeddedness of the economic and the social dimensions in European integration, the economic being an EU competence and social policy being the exclusive choice of the Member States.[285] Others have more optimistically referred to the growing social regulation produced by the EU as an attempt to embed the Internal Market into a new social framework that is independent of the nation State.[286] Yet, despite the experimentation of the EU in social regulation (to be distinguished from the concept of social policy),[287] this remains a rather weak 'counter-movement' to the deregulatory paradigm shift brought by the Internal Market project.[288] The risk of a disembedded domineering market that will put an end to the 'embedded liberalism'[289] of the post-war consensus

[285] F. Scharpf, 'Economic Integration, Democracy, and the Welfare State', *Journal of European Public Policy* 4(1) (1997) 18–36.

[286] J. A. Caporaso and S. Tarrow, 'Polanyi in Brussels: Supranational Institutions and the Transnational Embedding of Markets', *International Organization* 63 (2009) 593–620.

[287] G. Majone, 'The European Community Between Social Policy and Social Regulation', *Journal of Common Market Studies* 31(2) (1993) 153–70.

[288] According to K. Polanyi, *The Great Transformation: The Political and Economic Origins of Our Time* (Beacon Press, 1944, reprint 2001), p. 132, a '"counter-movement" is a movement against market forces using "the principle of social protection aiming at the conservation of man and nature . . . using protective legislation, restrictive associations, and other instruments of intervention as its methods"'.

[289] J. G. Ruggie, 'International Regimes, Transactions, and Change: Embedded Liberalism in the Post-War Economic Order', *International Organization* 36(2) (1982) 379–415.

and the subsequent national versions of it,[290] constitutes the main source of fears and reactions to the 'completion' of the Internal Market project.

It is interesting to pause a little on the conceptualization by the European institutions of the problems faced by the project of economic integration and explain why it has not yet been 'completed'. In his report on the New Strategy for the Single Market, Mario Monti noted the emergence of an 'integration fatigue', eroding the appetite for a Single Market, as well as a 'market fatigue', leading to a reduced confidence in the role of the market. Both undermine the acceptance of the Internal Market project by the European citizens.[291] Monti clearly makes these comments in view of the dominant understanding of the aims of the Single Market as these were transcribed in the Commission's White Paper on Completing the Internal Market in 1985 where it was indicated that

> the objective of completing the internal market has three aspects . . . the welding together of the . . . markets of the Member States into one single market . . . ensuring that this single market is also an expanding market . . . [and] ensuring that the market is flexible.[292]

The Internal Market was thus conceived of as an exercise of unifying and expanding markets, where all sorts of barriers, physical, technical and fiscal, would shade away. This dominant rhetoric is still present in the way the European Commission envisions the project of the Internal Market and, more generally, economic integration. The rhetoric of 'barriers' and their ever expanding definition scarcely supports the idea that convergence of prices and costs of production across the Union is the aim of the Commission.[293] The Commission's report on the 'State of the Internal Market for Services', which served as the blueprint for the

[290] See the analysis of D. Bohle and B. Greskovits, 'Neo-liberalism, Embedded Neo-liberalism and Neocorporatism: Towards Transnational Capitalism in Central-Eastern Europe', *West European Politics* 30(3) (2007) 443–66.

[291] M. Monti, 'A New Strategy for the Single Market at the Service of Europe's Economy and Society', note 7 above.

[292] *Ibid.*, p. 14, citing European Commission, Completing the Internal Market, COM(85) 310 final.

[293] See, e.g., the assessment of financial integration by the European Commission, which employs two indicators, price and quantity. 'Price-based indicators include cross-country dispersions and measure discrepancies in prices that are related to the geographical origin of the services.' The Commission notes that, '[t]o the extent that financial products are comparable, an increase in integration should lead to higher convergence of prices and yields across countries'. The second category of indicators are quantity-based and 'follow the principle that integration should lead users of financial services to diversify geographically and to shop beyond national boundaries'. European Commission, Staff Working

reforms introduced by the Services Directive, is explicit on the identification not only of existing legal barriers to the development of services activities between Member States, but also of 'non-legal barriers' which create 'disincentives' for services trade, ranging from lack of information about the regulatory framework in other Member States to cultural/language differences and varied consumer habits across the Union.[294] Barriers are ubiquitous and changing: they are no longer to be found in the body of legal texts but rather in administrative practices, in particular in the discretionary power of appreciation left to national administrative authorities, and in the fact of regional or collective non-government rules and practices (in particular, in the regulated professions) or in the conduct of individual operators who still organize their economic activities around national boundaries.[295] One could imagine the extent of the Internal Market project, should the need to 'suppress' these 'barriers' be followed literally.

This approach is certainly negating any space for pluralism and regulatory diversity. If the objective is to become one, the different governance arrangements are provisional steps towards the ineluctable end-game of the emergence of the integrated market. Harmonization versus the pure market access principle becomes the only game in town. However, one can also find, in the Commission's rhetoric, germs of a different perspective on the aims of the project of the Internal Market.

Of particular interest is the analysis by the Commission in the 'State of the Internal Market for Services' report of the 'common origins of barriers'. These are essentially explained by three factors. The first is the lack of mutual trust between the authorities of the different Member States which leads to the 'simple evocation of general good objectives to justify obstacles, without verifying the equivalence of the protection offered in the country of origin or the proportionality of the restriction' and the 'automatic suspicion of services from other Member States'.[296] The main reason for this distrust is allegedly the 'ignorance' of the

Paper Document, European Financial Integration Report 2009, SEC(2009) 1702 final, p. 7. See also the various impact assessment measures developed for the evaluation of the Services Directive: H. Kox and A. Lejour, 'The Effect of the Services Directive on Intra-EU Trade and FDI', *Revue Economique* 57(4) (2006) 747–69. On issues of measurement of the progress of regional integration processes, see P. de Lombaerde, 'Indicators of Economic Integration', *Statistika* 4 (2008) 340–5.

[294] European Commission, Report from the Commission to the Council and the European Parliament on the State of the Internal Market for Services, COM(2002) 441 final, pp. 43–4.

[295] *Ibid.*, pp. 45–51. [296] *Ibid.*, p. 54.

implications of the principles of establishment and free provision of services, the lack of transparency and administrative cooperation between Member States and the 'lack of harmonization of the national rules, reflected in an excessive [*sic*] disparity between the levels of protection of the general good guaranteed by the national systems'.[297] Second, the Commission advances as an additional reason for the persistence of barriers the resistance to modernization of the national legal frameworks originating from the 'slightly outdated' regulation in some Member States, the weak monitoring of the judgments of the Court and the absence of a systematic approach against barriers to trade. Finally, the defence of purely national interests, which is 'firmly anchored in certain Member States' is advanced as a third explanatory factor for the pervasiveness of barriers to trade.[298]

Let us take stock of these reasons for the 'malaise' of the Internal Market project. It is noteworthy that economic protectionism does not constitute the principal worry, as one would have expected. On the contrary, economic 'modernization' in the sense of liberalization of trade and trust in the regulatory regime of other Member States are the focus of the Commission's attention. One could venture that the goal of economic modernization illustrates the mutation of the theoretical underpinnings of the Internal Market project from a legal-rule-based framework to a purely economic programme. But, at the same time, the reference to the necessary trust between national regulatory authorities offers a different conceptual background, where the problem is not so much the existence of domestic regulations, but rather the absence of interoperability between the different national regulatory systems. Regulatory compatibility and pluralism can thus be combined, under this view. What should be avoided is the absence of interconnection between the different national regulatory networks for reasons of distrust. The aim of the Internal Market project thus becomes transformed from an operation of forced regulatory convergence through harmonization or Single Market creation to an operation of establishing relations of trust between the different regulatory systems across the Union. Let the era of 'regulatory peace' begin![299]

This shift has profound consequences on the interaction between the concept of economic integration and pluralism. If the main problem

[297] *Ibid.* [298] *Ibid.*, p. 55.

[299] K. Nicolaïdis, 'Trusting the Poles, Mark 2: Towards a Regulatory Peace Theory', Chapter 7 in this volume.

faced by economic integration regimes is the distrust between national regulators, because of the risk of opportunistic behaviour (cheating, breaking of trust), the different governance mechanisms cannot be thought of as constituting the different stages of a process of integration that leads ultimately to 'convergence' of regulatory systems, or any form of centralized control (EU regulation or the 'single' market's forces of supply and demand). Regulatory sameness is not the only desirable outcome but a possible outcome among others. What counts is the potential of these governance arrangements in generating inter-organizational trust.[300] Regulatory sameness and centralism thus constitute irrelevant variables in evaluating the progress of the project of economic integration. Less regulatory pluralism or less diversity do not necessarily qualify as progress in economic integration.

One could thus envision an opposition between two poles, trust and power/control/authority, where it would be possible to map the different governance mechanisms as leaning towards one pole or the other, under the assumption that they constitute different organizing principles in managing risk. Authority or power will be an organizing principle of interdependence and uncertainty by reallocating decision-making rights.[301] Trust can be calculative and revolve around the idea of an advantageous cooperation where incentives for profit outweigh risk.[302]

Nevertheless, such a conceptualization overlooks that trust and power constitute functionally equivalent and not necessarily mutually exclusive means to reduce risk. Lane and Bachmann distinguish between 'interaction-based power', which derives from individually accumulated resources (size, economic power, political influence) and 'system power', which occurs in institutionalized form and 'rests in collectively binding arrangements' that constrain 'the options of opportunistic behaviour social actors might feel tempted to explore'.[303] The aim of 'system power' is to generate 'system trust', that is, 'to encourage social actors to trust each other on the grounds of collectively binding rules which

[300] On this concept, see I. Lianos and J. Le Blanc, 'Trust, Distrust and Economic Integration: Setting the Stage', Chapter 1 in this volume.

[301] B,. McEvily, V. Perrone and A. Zaheer, 'Trust as an Organizing Principle', *Organization Science* 14(1) (2003) 91–103, p. 92.

[302] O. E. Williamson, 'Calculativeness, Trust and Economic Organization', *Journal of Law and Economics* 36(1) and (2) (1993) 453–86. Williamson mentions that calculated trust is 'a subset of calculated risk'.

[303] C. Lane and R. Bachmann, 'Co-operation in Inter-Firm Relations in Britain and Germany: The Role of Social Institutions', *British Journal of Sociology* 48(2) (1997) 226–54, p. 232.

reduce the risk of trust'.[304] These can be enforced through an 'institutionalized threat of collective sanctions' or a more informal mechanism, such as the use of hostages, a balance of mutual dependence, and reputation costs. If the actors have a relationship of repeated interaction with a significant degree of interdependence, the latter can be equally effective in reducing the risks of cooperation. For example, as EU Member States have a relation of repeated interaction and a significant degree of interdependence, reputation costs in case of non-performance are extremely high. This may progressively lead to a weakening of the case for establishing formal institutions with the power to impose sanctions, through the means of hard law, and may favour the reliance on cooperation mechanisms, based on trust, such as networks or soft law, in sectors where the establishment of formal institutions, monitoring, safeguarding and formal controls may be costly (because of negotiation costs, monitoring and compliance costs).

It follows that trust and power/control cannot only be treated as substitutes but may also operate as complements in the context of the specific relationship of interdependence between organizations.[305] Yet this picture would be incomplete if one takes exclusively into account inter-organizational trust between Member States and does not include the other facets of 'total trust':[306] the trust between Member States as principals of the integrated EU institutions they put in place or trust in government, that is, the confidence of citizens/economic operators in their government and EU institutions. The trust game is thus more complex as each actor aims to increase its trustworthiness at different levels. For example, even if we conceive that the EU institutions, such as the European Commission and the European Court of Justice, are acting as agents of Member States, we are not in a system with one or few principals but rather twenty-seven diverse principals with different regulatory settings. In the absence of hegemonic control or veto power, each of the principals thus retains only a small fraction of control of the agent, and consequently it is more difficult and costly to hold agents to account.[307] In any case, each governance mechanism will dither between the following four poles: system power, system trust, personalized trust and 'interaction-based' power.

[304] *Ibid.* [305] B. Nooteboom, *Trust* (Cheltenham: Edward Elgar, 2002), pp. 11–12.

[306] On this concept, see I. Lianos and J. Le Blanc, 'Trust, Distrust and Economic Integration: Setting the Stage', Chapter 1 in this volume.

[307] N. Krisch, 'Global Administrative Law and the Constitutional Ambition', LSE Law, Society and Economy Working Papers 10/2009, p. 4.

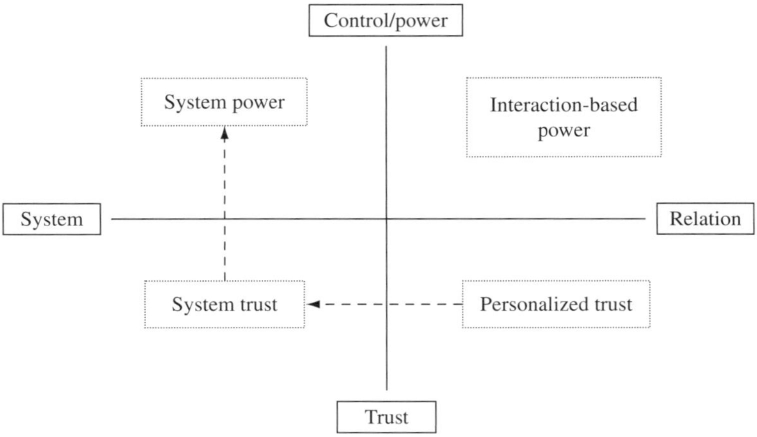

Figure 6.2 The trust/power relation

The focus on trust preserves the integrity of the governance system in as much as personalized trust facilitates system trust. It is easier to cooperate and move to a system of mutual recognition if there is some degree of familiarity or similarity with the partner's regulatory system. System trust also contributes to the emergence of system power when the risks of cooperation are substantial and justify the costs of establishing a heterarchical or hierarchical structure of monitoring and control, as is the case for regulatory harmonization (regulatory networks) or harmonization respectively.

This approach is not only the right one because it dissociates integration from centralism and thus preserves pluralism. It is also compatible with the evolution of EU integration and the emergence of hybrid governance mechanisms that challenge the existing conceptual categories of negative and positive integration or the market access/mutual recognition and harmonization trilogy. The centrality of the mutual recognition principle in the process of governance of the European Internal Market illustrates also a shift from the focus on centralism and uniformity towards managing diversity through regulatory interoperability, or, as Kalypso Nicolaïdis puts it in this volume, an era of 'regulatory peace'[308] that accommodates regulatory pluralism.

308 K. Nicolaïdis, 'Trusting the Poles? Mark 2' Chapter 7 in this volume.

4. Conclusion

The opposition of constitutionalists' and pluralists' accounts of post-national law has been an important trend in recent EU law and integration scholarship.[309] Transposing this debate to the economic integration realm one could establish an analogy with the tensions between the integrationist tendency of the proponents of an 'economic constitution' and the polyarchical conception of regulatory pluralism. These were initially accommodated by the decoupling of the economic and the social dimensions of integration and the institution of a functional pluralism where the decision-making power for social policy was allocated to the national level and that of economic and trade liberalization to the European level. Such dichotomy was of course transitive and operated as long as the economic effects of trade liberalization did not negatively affect the interests of powerful domestic groups. The assumption was that a 'counter-movement' will take place at the national level in order to compensate the affected domestic groups for the distributive consequences engendered by the process of trade liberalization.

However, the hierarchical structure of the EU legal order and its underlying monist constitutional dimension led to the emergence of intense normative conflicts between the logic of economic integration, perceived as trade liberalization, and that of national conceptions of social or distributive justice. Responding to this pressure, the realm of EU action was progressively extended to cover the field of social regulation,[310] thus slowly overthrowing the dichotomy between the economic and the social dimensions of European integration. As the social dimension was becoming part of the EU realm, the functional pluralism was replaced by a horizontal regulatory pluralism operating across different national regulatory systems, each of them attempting to influence the emerging social

309 N. MacCormick, *Questioning Sovereignty? Law, State and Nation in the European Commonwealth* (Oxford University Press, 1999); N. Walker, 'The Idea of Constitutional Pluralism', *Modern Law Review* 65 (2002) 317–59; N. W. Barber, 'Legal Pluralism and the European Union', *European Law Journal* 12 (2006) 306–29; M. P. Maduro, 'Contrapunctual Law: Europe's Constitutional Pluralism in Action' in N. Walker (ed.), *Sovereignty in Transition: Essays in European Law* (Oxford: Hart Publishing, 2003), 501; N. Krisch, 'The Case for Pluralism in Postnational Law', LSE Law, Society and Economy Working Papers 12/2009; P. Eleftheriadis, 'Pluralism and Integrity', Legal Research Paper Series, University of Oxford, Paper No. 43/2009, available at http://papers.ssrn.com/sol3/papers.cfm?abstract_id=1486151.

310 We use 'social regulation' in the broad sense, thus also including environmental regulation.

regulation system at the EU level, as a way to preserve the national arrangements and eventually to expand them in other jurisdictions.

Yet, the hard and fundamental character of legal norms protecting the principle of free movement in the EU legal framework, as well as the transformation of the political project of the Internal Market to a broader economic modernization venture, with the initiation of far-reaching reforms of national welfare systems, following the Lisbon agenda, signalled that the balance between trade and social protection to be achieved at the EU level would be politically unacceptable to a number of Member States and interest groups. The demands for social Europe that culminated with the reactions to the proposals for the Services Directive and the fear that eastward enlargement will spur a race to the bottom for social welfare systems led to a more vocal affirmation of the principle of regulatory pluralism.[311] As was examined in section 2 above, regulatory diversity and 'policy space' accommodating the Member States' various social and regulatory traditions made its entrance into the monolithic and market-integration-focused jurisprudence of the Court as well as into EU harmonization efforts.

The turn from market access and harmonization to the principle of mutual recognition encapsulates this recognition of regulatory pluralism as, at least a descriptive claim, for EU integration. Taking stock of regulatory pluralism thus carries an acceptance of the various structures of policy institutions and accordingly the diverse substantive regulatory outcomes across Member States in terms of policy production. Yet, the existence of cross-border negative domestic policy externalities requires some form of coordination among the plurality of regulatory systems that compose the EU. Here the analogy between regulatory pluralism and constitutional pluralism loses its appeal. Accounts of pluralism by constitutional/institutional law theorists emphasize the conflict of values between the whole and the parts as the main problem faced by a pluralistic legal order or the interaction between various heterarchical legal orders. Some offer overarching substantive principle or norms in order to resolve conflicts, such as subsidiarity, due process and democracy.[312] Others prefer a jurisdictional framework and the application

[311] N. Lindstrom, 'Service Liberalization in the Enlarged EU: A Race to the Bottom or the Emergence of Transnational Political Conflict?', *Journal of Common Market Studies* 48 (5) (2010) 1307–1327.

[312] M. Kumm, 'The Legitimacy of International Law: A Constitutionalist Framework of Analysis', *European Journal of International Law* 15(5) (2004) 907–31.

of conflict-of-laws rules[313] or some form of subject matter dualism and mutual respect between legal orders.[314] Others suggest a procedural framework, that of 'contrapunctual law' requesting from each system to integrate each other's concerns by communicating them and, more importantly, by integrating their different claims of validity within the context of a coherent and integrated European legal order.[315]

This study has defended a different perspective than that of managing values or regulatory conflicts. The emphasis has been on the establishment of institutions, formal and informal, with the aim to manage the risks of cooperation between diverse regulatory systems. Likewise, the hypothesis was that the emergence of different governance mechanisms in the regulation of trade in services entails that the risks of cooperation are variable. The latter depend on the degree of interaction between the Member States and the existence of regulatory pluralism. By disentangling the focus of integration from managing or suppressing conflicts and thus regulatory diversity to establishing system trust between the different components – Member States, European institutions, economic operators and citizens – the trust theory of integration, defended in this study, offers real chances to regulatory pluralism in the EU.

[313] See C. Joerges and F. Rödl, 'Reconceptualizing the Constitution of Europe's Post-National Constellation – By Dint of Conflict of Laws', Chapter 11 in this volume.

[314] P. Eleftheriadis, 'Pluralism and Integrity', Legal Research Paper Series, University of Oxford, Paper No. 43/2009, pp. 21–8, available at http://papers.ssrn.com/sol3/papers.cfm?abstract_id=1486151.

[315] M. P. Maduro, 'Contrapunctual Law: Europe's Constitutional Pluralism in Action' in N. Walker (ed.), *Sovereignty in Transition* (Oxford: Hart Publishing, 2003), p. 501, pp. 529–30.

7

Trusting the Poles? Mark 2: towards a regulatory peace theory in a world of mutual recognition

KALYPSO NICOLAÏDIS*

1. Introduction

There are all kinds of regulatory wars out there. Some wars pit 'regulatory cultures' against one another; others pit free traders against consumer protectors and all the variants of liberal, statist, technocratic or paternalistic approaches; others still confront low against high standards systems – in their race to the bottom (or the top) anything goes. And, in Europe of course, wars may pit Polish plumbers against local (imaginary) competitors. True, regulatory wars (or competition) may serve as useful selection mechanisms. But, as the 2008–11 financial crisis has amply demonstrated, there is little doubt that at least some lulls of regulatory peace would serve the greater good.

By 'regulatory peace' I mean a stable state of cooperation among regulators from different jurisdictions (usually countries), where 'regulators' stand for standards-setters in general, from legislators to agencies, standards organizations or accreditors. 'A stable state of cooperation' needs to be defined, as this does not of course mean harmony, but rather the existence of mechanisms to manage the unavoidable mix of convergent and divergent interests between these actors, mechanisms which allow them to pursue the public good in their own jurisdiction while minimizing negative externalities for outsiders, that is refraining from engaging in regulatory behaviour aimed at

* This chapter was first presented in Cambridge at the Modern Law Review conference, 1 July 2009. I thank the participants for greatly stimulating discussions and Ioannis Lianos for his further input. The paper includes and builds on an earlier publication, 'Trusting the Poles? Constructing Europe through Mutual Recognition', *Journal of European Public Policy* 15 (5) (2007) 682–98.

undermining the other side. For the purpose of this enquiry, the externalities in question stem from the movement of goods and services across borders. In a loose analogy to what is referred to in international relations (IR) as 'democratic peace theory' (DPT), we need to ask what are the factors that make regulatory peace more likely both as characteristics of individual jurisdictions and as attributes of the interactions between them. This is obviously a very ambitious endeavour, which would need to draw on the many strands of the burgeoning literature on domestic and transnational regulation as it relates to the free movement of goods and services across borders.[1]

Clearly, a 'regulatory peace theory' (RPT), if we choose to call it that, could only claim a loose analogy to its broader macro-political forebearer, DPT, as discussed briefly in the later part of this chapter. Nevertheless, I hope that this might prove a fruitful way to revisit some earlier analysis on the trade/regulation nexus.[2] I have argued in the past that a core component of regulatory cooperation is what I refer to as 'managed mutual recognition', which is itself predicated on producing and managing trust between parties, or indeed the lack thereof. Thus, a regulatory peace theory would need to explore the causes and implications of the resistance to mutual recognition for European and global governance – a vast research programme for which this volume is an important building block. My aim in this chapter is to lay out questions for future research rather than claim to provide the answers.[3]

In an article entitled 'Trusting the Poles?', I sought to encapsulate the essence of mutual recognition in the building of Europe. I used as my starting point the story of the mythical 'Polish plumber' attacked for stealing the job of non-existent French plumbers thanks to his lower

[1] Many of the relevant definitional and theoretical debates can be found in the leading journal in the field: see *Regulation and Governance*, published by Wiley-Blackwell. See also George A. Bermann, Matthias Herdegen and Peter L. Lindseth (eds.), *Transatlantic Regulatory Co-operation: Legal Problems and Political Prospects* (Oxford University Press, 2001).

[2] See, for instance, K. Nicolaïdis, *Regulatory Reform and International Market Openness* (Paris: OECD Publications, 1996), reprinted as part of the Jean Monnet Paper Series, Harvard Law School, 1997.

[3] This line of enquiry is part of a broader agenda spelled out in K. Nicolaïdis, 'Sustainable Integration: Towards EU 2.0?', Journal of Common Market Studies Annual Review Lecture, in *Journal of Common Market Studies* Annual Review 48 (2010) 21–54; and K. Nicolaïdis, 'EU 2.0: Towards Sustainable Integration', *Open Democracy*, 12 July 2010, available at www.opendemocracy.net.

home country standards. In spite of the witty response on the part of the Polish government with its poster modelling an attractive plumber 'staying at home', the story struck a painful chord across European societies which had not yet come to terms with the tensions associated with enlargement and the gap between old and new Member States. I argued that European integration has been and will continue to be flawed with conflicts, conflicts of interests embedded in broader conflicts of identity, and that these conflicts and the bargains they require exhibit similar patterns across a wide array of issues, as struggles around 'mutual' recognition. And, while the challenges and perils of recognition are universal, Europe can be seen as an experimental polity where, more formally than elsewhere, actors debate the contours of a norm which has migrated from regulatory praxis to mode of governance, and beyond, to political principle. If the 'Polish plumber' came to serve as the emblem for the denial of recognition in the EU, mutual recognition is no less conflictual when it comes to the status of refugees, Bosnians or cartoonists. Normatively, if 'managed mutual recognition' is to serve as a blueprint beyond International Political Economy, we need to analyze better the relationship between recognition and trust, blind and binding trust, deferential and interventionist recognition.

Section 2 of this chapter reproduces the original article published in 2007. In section 3, I build on this article to provide some *pistes* for a 'regulatory peace theory'.

2. Trusting the Poles? Constructing Europe through mutual recognition

This story could well start with the Dutch embassy in Berlin. From without, it advances like the bows of a ship between monuments symbolizing Germany's multi-faceted history. As you wander within, every space offers at least one vista from which to gaze at an adjacent space and from which one can be gazed at. There is no common grand entrance to awe the visitor with a sense of overarching commonality. Nevertheless, he who journeys through this maze of mutually open spaces cannot help but wonder whether the inspiration behind Koolhaas' design wasn't Europe itself. That is, the Union as it is becoming or as some of us wish it to become. A mosaic of intertwined mental and physical landscapes open to each other's soft influences and hard laws, and are bound together not by some overarching sense of common identity or people-hood but by the daily practice of mutual recognition of identities, histories and social contracts – what I have called elsewhere, our European 'demoi-cracy'.[4]

Such an idea of Europe is of course an idealization. Unlike Koolhaas' embassy, the European Union (EU) is built on the quicksands of archetypes, the construct of lawyers and political scientists fighting the twin perils of a post-modern Napoleonic vision of a harmonized continent and a Westphalian nostalgia for absolute sovereign autonomy. Nevertheless, like the embassy, it rests on solid foundations – in the law and politics of integration. And, like the embassy, it is predicated on some prevailing common notion of *appropriately intrusive trust*, the double movement of creating a claim on someone else and accepting the limits of such a claim ('I assume your space will be compatible with, since visible from, mine; but, in return, you trust that my gaze will not be overly intrusive and insistent, in the manner of Calvino's Palomar routine around the naked bosom on the beach').[5] It is this kind of trust, I believe, that is owed to all new members of the Union, including the Poles.

Perhaps to generalize, 'given the opaqueness of the other's intentions and calculations', trust needs to be predicated on identifying and strengthening the *ties that bind* in order to be sustainable.[6] The fabric of human intercourse is less often made of *blind trust* and more often the product of *binding trust* between individuals, groups, organizations or indeed countries. Trust of the first kind may only superficially be seen as deeper in that it is most often predicated on separateness at best, mutual ignorance at worst. But, if trusting the other is to seek to bind his to one's expectations, then such trust requires prior and continued knowledge about such other. International regimes and institutions can be seen as elaborate mechanisms for mutual monitoring, a consensual form of reciprocal spying predicated on residual amounts of trust, trust that we will each refrain from cheating in the blind spots of our commonly agreed standards. International regimes must strike a balance between acceptable *intervention* in each other's affairs and *deference* to each other's system. With time, the systems might come to be predicated on increasingly *blind* trust, where it is the mutual spying which becomes

4 See K. Nicolaïdis, 'We, the Peoples of Europe', *Foreign Affairs* (November 2004).

5 See I. Calvino, *Palomar* (Turin: Giulio Einaudi, 1983).

6 See A. B. Seligman, *The Problem of Trust*, 1st edn (Princeton University Press, 1997), p. 43; and A. Hoffman, 'A Conceptualization of Trust in International Relations', *European Journal of International Relations* 8(3) (2002) 375–401.

residual, only the amount necessary to reassure each other that continued trust is warranted. At some point, changes in the scale and purpose of the interaction and in background conditions – be they political, ideological social, economic or technological – may bring into question the whole design on which such a combination of binding and blind trust rests, requiring new additional amounts of binding trust. A new cycle then begins.

This article is a preliminary exploration into the sources and implications of the subtle balance between autonomy and connection, deference and intervention, *blind* and *binding* trust which underlies political and societal bargains around mutual recognition in the European Union. In order to do so, I start with the story of the Polish plumber explored in much greater detail in this volume.[7] I suggest a two-step approach to defining 'managed mutual recognition' which highlights the *preconditions* and the *limits* attached to it. I then seek to generalize this approach and explore the conflicts that lay behind the construction of Europe in other realms (justice and home affairs (JHA), diplomacy and freedom of expression) through the lenses of such managed mutual recognition as applied in the Single Market.

While the first two-fold comparison (with JHA) has been undertaken elsewhere,[8] the other two (recognition of State sovereignty and recognition of identities) can be considered as the two ends of the spectrum – from the broad macro to the micro level – and in this way emblematic of the function of recognition in international relations. Clearly, as the object of recognition changes – other countries' laws, other countries themselves, other 'others' – so do its preconditions, including the type of trust required. But I argue that the main patterns stay the same. Indeed, these areas illustrate the connection between recognition as a technical, legal or regulative norm to a more general form of transnational governance to a philosophical principle.[9] To be sure, recognition has become an increasingly fashionable concept in ethics and political theory as

[7] K. Nicolaïdis and S. Schmidt, 'Mutual Recognition on Trial: The Long Road to Services Liberalisation', *Journal of European Public Policy* 8(5) (2007) 717–34.

[8] S. Lavenex, 'Mutual Recognition and the Monopoly of Force: Limits of the Single Market Analogy', *Journal of European Public Policy* 8(5) (2007) 762–79.

[9] K. Nicolaïdis, 'Mutual Recognition among Nations' (PhD dissertation, Harvard University, 1993); K. Nicolaïdis, 'Mutual Recognition of Regulatory Regimes: Some Lessons and Prospects', Jean Monnet Paper Series, Harvard Law School, 1997; K. Nicolaïdis, 'We, the Peoples of Europe', *Foreign Affairs* (November 2004); F. K. P. Schioppa, *The Principle of Mutual Recognition in the European Integration Process* (Palgrave, 2005).

'liberation movements' around the world have learned to see themselves as objects of derecognition and subjects struggling for recognition.[10] In all social conflicts, in other words, 'resistance to an established social order is always driven by the moral experience of in some respect not receiving what is taken to be justified recognition'.[11] On such grounds, the recognition conception of Justice, translated in various kinds of non-discrimination laws and multicultural practices, has given rise to considerable debate, including on the virtues of restorative justice.

While this enquiry assumes that developments and ideas related to the economic, political and societal realms cannot but inform one another, I will not revisit these philosophical debates here, but instead focus on the actual and potential meaning of *mutual* recognition in the EU itself. In the EU context, it took a long time for observers and politicians alike to see that, in whatever guise, what I call 'pure mutual recognition' is far from a panacea. It necessarily constitutes a surrender of sovereignty, control, dominance, monopoly. In implementing it, States must constantly fine-tune the balance between the liberal imperative of recognition on the one hand and the republican constraints that need to be attached to it on the other. This chapter suggests that, as we explore different realms, we identify three variants of 'managed recognition' and the binding trust that ought to come along with it: recognition as embedded, constitutive and, indeed, mutual.

2.1 Trusting the Poles? The contested nature of mutual recognition

I have argued elsewhere that we may think of the current times as a Tocquevillian moment for the EU, an EU poised between its aristocratic past and an uncertain but irrevocable future where citizens enjoy the power of their collective *vetos*.[12] If so, we need to better understand the tensions that arise in the attempt to adapt the existing *ethos* of the EU to

[10] C. Taylor, 'The Politics of Recognition' in A. Gutman (ed.), *Multiculturalism: Examining the Politics of Recognition* (Princeton University Press, 1994); N. Fraser, 'From Redistribution to Recognition? Dilemmas of Justice in a "Post-Socialist" Age', *New Left Review* I/212 (July/August 1995) 68–93.

[11] A. Honneth, *The Struggle for Recognition: The Moral Grammar of Social Conflicts* (Polity Press, 1996).

[12] K. Nicolaïdis, 'UE: un moment Tocquevilien', *Politique Etrangère* 3 (September 2007) 497–509.

these changing circumstances. The story of the Polish plumber illustrates the great difficulty which comes along with such an adaptation.

It is striking that the 'no' to the draft Constitution started its inexorable rise in the French polls at the same time as discussions on the so-called 'Bolkestein Directive' reached their paroxysm. Ironically, the opponents of the Directive claimed with great vehemence that it was not liberalization of services in itself which they were targeting but only the principle of home country rule, which they claimed was a new principle for the EU, surreptitiously introduced by a neo-liberal Commission. In their view, this principle represented the soullessness of the market logic at its most extreme. It was symbolized by the infamous-to-be Polish plumber who, by gaining unfair competitive advantage through the application of his home country rule, threatens the integrity of the host State social contract.[13]

The conflictual nature of mutual recognition should come as no surprise.[14] This is a Janus-faced norm, usually branded as the 'easy option', and yet the hardest of all. As a horizontal transfer of sovereignty, it is both about respecting sovereignty and radically reconfiguring it – by delinking the exercise of sovereign power from its territorial anchor through a reciprocal allocation of jurisdictional authority to prescribe and enforce laws.

The real puzzle then is why the public trial of recognition in the EU and its unprecedented political visibility came so late. In fact, it has everything to do with our Tocquevillian moment for two reasons. First, because, in such a transitional moment, market regulation norms acquire a political resonance which they lacked until then, while the political class is unable to construct a public discourse that would prevent such migration to the public sphere from being captured by populists and demagogues. Second, this tension is made worse as the Union enlarges to encompass a degree of diversity of socio-historical systems now in competition beyond the 'mental absorption' capacity of its citizens. In short, at a turning point in our history, the issue of mutual recognition highlighted the instability of European bargains both between ideological families and between Member States, especially old and new ones, shifting from the former to the latter over time.

[13] K. Nicolaïdis and S. Schmidt, 'Mutual Recognition on Trial: The Long Road to Services Liberalisation', *Journal of European Public Policy* 14(5) (2007) 717–34.

[14] K. Nicolaïdis, 'Mutual Recognition among Nations' (PhD dissertation, Harvard University, 1993); *Ibid.*, 'Mutual Recognition of Regulatory Regimes: Some Lessons and Prospects', Jean Monnet Paper Series, Harvard Law School, 1997; K. Nicolaïdis and G. Shaffer, 'Managed Mutual Recognition Regimes: Governance without Global Government', *Law and Contemporary Problems* 68 (2005) 267–322, available at http://ssrn.com/abstract=728383 (last visited 15 September 2010).

2.1.1 Introducing managed mutual recognition

In this context, alternative regulative principles for the Single Market definitely bear different connotations with regard to diversity. The classic construct in the EU narrative on the Single Market is to contrast recognition with, on the one hand, national treatment (which if narrowly interpreted as a ban on discrimination does not solve the problem of regulatory fragmentation) and, on the other, harmonization (which is both impossible to attain and sustain, and irrelevant to problems of jurisdiction of control *per se*).[15] When we wish to generalize, the archetypical contrast of which this three-fold distinction is a category, is that between mutual recognition, that is, the engagement with differences, and (i) on the one hand, isolation, ghettoization or ignorance of these differences; and (ii) on the other hand, assimilation, or negation of these differences. In both cases, the other side must become like me, either upon entering my territory or through a process of harmonization. The move to mutual recognition comes with the acknowledgment that such sameness is usually neither feasible nor desirable. The denial of recognition comes in the form of the standard reply: your rules, or those governing the production of your products, the supervision of your firms or the training of your workers and professionals, do not have to be *the same as mine* but they need to be *compatible with mine*.

My first conceptual move in the international political economy (IPE) field has been to establish that in fact the deeper and more relevant contrast is one step removed from this one. It is between pure and managed mutual recognition, blind trust and binding trust, or between recognition as an alternative to versus an overarching concept encompassing elements of national treatment and harmonization. To a great extent, the distinction is parallel to that discussed by Joseph Weiler and others between the *Dassonville* jurisprudence – at least under one reading of its implications – of generalizing an *obstacles-based approach* to national regulation (all national rules are potentially subject to an assessment of illegality, and therefore to pure mutual recognition/home country rule by judicial *fiat*); and the more circumscribed *Cassis* doctrine of *functional equivalence*, especially as further constrained in *Keck*, which involves precisely the

[15] K. Nicolaïdis, *Mutual Recognition: The Next Frontier of Multilateralism?*, *Project Promethee Perspectives* (Paris, July 1989); See also K. Nicolaïdis, 'Mutual Recognition among Nations' (PhD dissertation, Harvard University, 1993); S. K. Schmidt, 'Mutual Recognition as a New Mode of Governance', *Journal of European Public Policy* 14(5) (2007) 667–81.

identification of the conditions and limits of recognition.[16] It must be noted here that only by migrating from the judicial to the legislative arena is it possible to spell out the full panoply of instruments for the management of recognition, which I have described elsewhere[17] as the attributes of recognition.[18] Therefore, while it is important to analyze the role of the rulings of the Court in the European story of mutual recognition, it is also true that all the Court could do when it came to designing this more sophisticated understanding of the principle was to provide a roadmap for politicians and technical experts later crafting the laws.[19]

Thus my second conceptual move is to ask what makes for sustainable recognition, in other words, how can institutions contribute in the entrenchment of *binding trust*. Binding trust is not only performative, based on what you do, but also *constitutive*, based on who you are – or who you should be – and involves therefore both an act of delineation of that other with whom I accept to interact, and a peeking inside his boundaries. Managed mutual recognition encapsulates the various ways in which this subtle balance can be struck through political bargains and the move from *ex ante* to *ex post* conditions (e.g., with less initial convergence we have

[16] J. Weiler, 'Mutual Recognition, Functional Equivalence and Harmonization in the Evolution of the European Common Market and the WTO' in F. K. P. Schioppa (ed.), *The Principle of Mutual Recognition in the European Integration Process* (Basingstoke: Palgrave Macmillan, 2005), pp. 25–84.

[17] K. Nicolaïdis, 'Mutual Recognition among Nations' (PhD dissertation, Harvard University, 1993); K. Nicolaïdis, 'Mutual Recognition of Regulatory Regimes: Some Lessons and Prospects', Jean Monnet Paper Series, Harvard Law School, 1997; and K. Nicolaïdis, 'Globalization with Human Faces: Managed Mutual Recognition and the Free Movement of Professionals' in F. K. P. Schioppa, *The Principle of Mutual Recognition in the European Integration Process* (Basingstoke: Palgrave Macmillan, 2005), pp. 129–89.

[18] As an outcome, managed mutual recognition can be contrasted with 'pure' mutual recognition in the same sense as managed trade can be contrasted with free trade. It involves complex sets of rules and procedures that may serve to reduce, if not eliminate, the open-endedness of access rights. The four main dimensions along which mutual recognition can be fine-tuned are: (1) prior conditions for equivalence, from convergence to inter-institutional agreements; (2) degree of automaticity of access; (3) scope of activities or features covered by recognition; and (4) *ex post* guarantees, including ultimately provisions for reversibility. Statically, variation along each of these dimensions can be seen to indicate how far parties have travelled down the road to full recognition. Dynamically, the management of mutual recognition can be viewed as a process involving evolving trade-offs between these dimensions.

[19] K. Nicolaïdis, 'Mutual Recognition among Nations' (PhD dissertation, Harvard University, 1993); K. Nicolaïdis and M. Egan, 'Regional Policy Externality and Market Governance: Why Recognize Foreign Standards?', *Journal of European Public Policy* 8(3) (2001) 454–73.

to accept more extensive mutual monitoring down the road) as well as between such conditions in general and the limits – in scope and effectiveness – that can be put around recognition. The key to these trade-offs consists in resolving conflicts that unfold over acceptable differences and acceptable deference.

2.1.2 The Services Directive in perspective

The idea that the working out of legitimate differences constitutes the most progressive challenge for Europe today remains relatively far from the left's ideological repertoire, especially parts of the French left, which shares with its Gaullist counterpart a lingering attachment to Europe as *Grande France*.[20] Whatever the actual flaws of the Bolkestein Directive, and there were many, to reject it wholesale, and to vilify the home country principle in doing so, is to fail to see the EU for what it has become, e.g., a 'mutual recognition space'. In fact, the rules adopted by the EU to 'complete' the Single Market in the last decade have created many kinds of firewalls against all-out competition *à l'americaine* through the kind of managed recognition discussed above.

This has long been the ambition of the European legislator, following on the Court's jurisprudence: to create a wide net for legislation on the Single Market and from this baseline only harmonize or retain host country control when differences are illegitimate. When should differences be considered so is the object of a vast literature – any pronouncement here is bound to be contested. Suffice to say that, to the extent that recognition ought to be conditional on some sort of convergence, we must first decide if it is for the sake of the 'Polish plumber' himself, in order to avoid *his* (unfair) exploitation, or for the sake of the 'French plumber', in order to avoid *her* (unfair) displacement. One way to reconcile both concerns is to ask whether a service provider on the move can live from his or her wages in the host country. And there is surely a link between legal transnational recognition and domestic social recognition, as workers struggling for wage increases tend to see the injustice of their situation in terms of misrecognition on the part of their own society too.

Indeed, the fate of the Polish plumber had been sealed a decade earlier by the so-called Posted Workers Directive which, in the wake of the *Rush Portuguesa* judgment, reinterpreted the 1980 Rome Convention which had instituted mutual recognition in the first place, precisely in order to

[20] Nicolaïdis, 'UE: un moment Tocquevilien', above.

avoid what can be called 'face-to-face social dumping'.[21] But national negotiators had fiercely disagreed on the scope of host/home country jurisdiction, agreeing for instance to include only 'universally applicable' collective agreements in the list of standards host countries were allowed to impose on foreign posted workers.

It may be argued that the Bolkestein Directive suffered from the ambiguities arising from this prior settlement, which it sought only to clarify (with a liberal bent) while removing remaining administrative obstacles to the operations of the employing firms themselves. Nevertheless, the draft Directive may have floundered precisely because it failed to 'manage' mutual recognition enough: its brand of recognition was too deferential to home State systems. Almost in mirror image, many of the opponents of the Directive failed to understand that mutual recognition could be more or less managed with home country principle at one end of the spectrum. Interestingly, as the debate reached an ideological stalemate, those seeking a compromise in the European Parliament and elsewhere tried to convey this idea by seizing on an exaggerated distinction between the (bad) country-of-origin principle and (good) mutual recognition.[22] There were certainly semantic reasons for this shift (mutual recognition 'sounds' progressive and desirable) but I would argue that the real distinction they were after was between the two forms of mutual recognition contrasted in this article, namely, 'pure' and 'managed'.

As the debate on services illustrates, a philosophy of recognition is based not only on reciprocal trust but also on the consensual delineating of the limits of such a trust. Can the Polish authorities be trusted to act in the interest of Polish workers? Can trade unions in the West be trusted to act in solidarity *with* not in protection *against* Polish plumbers? And what kind of externalities at the local level are created by such patterns of trust? Any interaction or interdependence, and thus all-the-more any formal integration process, is conditioned by the collective determining of where tolerable differences start and end between groups or nations.

[21] Nicolaïdis and Schmidt, 'Mutual Recognition on Trial: The Long Road to Services Liberalisation', above.

[22] For instance, E. Gebhardt, the (PES) rapporteur on the Services Directive, argued that the Socialist party was proposing to 'establish the principle of mutual recognition instead of that of country of origin in the directive, that is, that if one enterprise was established in one country legally it should be able to establish services in the whole of the EU not having to apply all the relevant country of origin principles [*sic*] but operating under a principle of minimum standards applicable in the host country. The "country of origin" principle is not a European answer to the problem – but mutual recognition and harmonization are.'

Obviously, the assumption that differences are legitimate until proven not so is conditioned by some kind of will to live together, some basic sense of commonality. It may well be the case that EU enlargement to eastern and central Europe has widened the perception of differences to such an extent, and thus so weakened the shared sense of belonging, that this underlying philosophy of 'legitimate differences' as the default option must be reinvented anew.

But enlargement was not the only culprit. Opposition to the Directive was based on two changing ideological frames: from the old vision of Europeanization as (good) 'non-discrimination' to Europeanization as (bad) globalization; and from associating the EU Single Market with *liberismo* to *liberalismo*, from free trade to economic liberalism. Under the first vision, the Single Market itself is an instrument against nationalism and a conveyor of solidarity; under the second, this solidarity function can only be fulfilled through convergence of rules. Under a progressive understanding of recognition, it is possible as a cosmopolitan and solidarist to defend liberty as free movement, or *liberismo*, without necessarily defending economic liberalism, or *liberalismo*, as an anti-State deregulatory ideology. Decisions by the Court may constrain the capacity of host States to police their territory but they do so by upholding *liberismo* not by promoting *liberalismo*. Ultimately, recognition, even in judicialized EU, has been a political decision. Indeed, as I will stress in the next sections, we are speaking here of recognition *of* acts of States *by* States and therefore a mechanism that highlights rather than denies State power.

2.2 From plumbers to refugees: recognition as embedded

It is worth noting that the 'No' campaigners in France – often lumping no to Bolkestein and to Giscard – hardly noticed a critical move contained in the draft Constitution, namely, the systematic extension of the principle of mutual recognition to the realm of Justice and Home Affairs, in other words the acceptance by judges and police forces throughout Europe of each other's procedures and judgments. While the move had been anticipated in practice, it testifies to the increased prevalence of the recognition paradigm beyond the strict realm of the Single Market.[23] Most spectacularly, September 11 accelerated the adoption of mutual recognition in the EU in the case of arrest warrants, e.g., final judicial decisions: 'wanted in one EU country, wanted everywhere in the EU'. In fact, recognition had been

[23] See Lavenex, 'Mutual Recognition and the Monopoly of Force', above.

adopted as the goal for the system of State responsibility for the examination of asylum claims since the 1990 Dublin Convention in order to ensure that applications would be constrained by a one-stop entry system: rejected in one country, rejected everywhere. No doubt such recognition was driven by division-of-labour considerations rather than by a sudden conversion to the business of trust. And therefore it is no surprise that the system has not been extended to this day to 'positive recognition', e.g., accepted once, accepted everywhere.

What can we learn from contrasting the fate of plumbers and refugees seeking to move *into* or *within* Europe? Lavenex argues that what serves as an instrument of liberalization in one sector, by expanding the societal *vis-à-vis* the governmental sphere, may work in the opposite direction in another.[24] In JHA, 'those benefiting from mutual recognition are not societal actors but State representatives'. In short, the field of justice and home affairs does not support the liberal credentials which characterize mutual recognition in the Single Market realm – neither *liberalismo* nor *liberismo*.

To be sure, there is a difference between recognizing who gets to be a criminal *across borders* and what gets to be a certified aircraft, or for that matter a certified lawyer, *across borders*, although both of the latter can kill too! Crucially, States have learned to delegate authority vertically to non-State bodies in areas pertaining to markets while parliaments are still in control in areas pertaining to justice; in that sense, recognition affects democratic accountability to different degrees in these different areas.[25]

Yet, Lavenex overstates the difference between the two realms for two reasons. First, we cannot say that recognition allows the free movement of products on one side and the free movement of (State) judgments on the other. In fact, recognition – at least as it relates to international relations (IR) – is always about granting extraterritorial jurisdiction to the acts of States (or bodies with delegated public authority), be they policies, regulations or laws and the ways in which States may help each other in enforcing these acts. The object of recognition is always embedded in a system of State practices.[26]

[24] *Ibid.*

[25] Nicolaïdis and Shaffer, 'Managed Mutual Recognition Regimes', above; Schmidt, 'Mutual Recognition as a New Mode of Governance', above.

[26] K. Nicolaïdis, 'Mutual Recognition of Regulatory Regimes: Some Lessons and Prospects', Jean Monnet Paper Series, Harvard Law School, 1997; Nicolaïdis and Egan, 'Regional Policy Externality and Market Governance', above.

Second, the insight that recognition is not *in and of itself* a liberal principle is fundamental but in fact not specific to JHA. When it comes to the movement of professionals, if a doctor has been struck off the register in France, he has also been struck off throughout the EU. True, we can contrast the initial core intent: to reduce regulatory duplication in order to expand EU-wide trade on the one hand, to reduce regulatory duplication in order to reduce EU-wide asylum application processing, and presumably successful ones, on the other. Whether the transnational enforcement of State acts curbs or on the contrary empowers individuals or society against the State depends on the context. The management of mutual recognition will generally involve a division of labour between host and home States – an area where again the difference between the two realms should not be overstated. In judicial matters for instance, the Member State issuing the warrant delegates the act of arresting a suspect to another – unwilling – host State who therefore lends out its monopoly of force. In trade or establishment, the host State may similarly conduct investigations of foreign firms or professionals in order to enforce their home State standards or codes of conducts. In both realms, the risks of 'collusion in State control' are real and need to be counter-balanced by enhanced individual rights – hence, the Commission Proposal on procedural rights in criminal matters, and the right of appeal devised for services providers in the Services Directive. But, then, such a need to embed mutual recognition in a system of rights may itself run counter to the queen of all objections: subsidiarity.

Indeed, the analogue between JHA and the Single Market is better served by using the Single Market in services rather than goods and considering the EU entry of third-country nationals. The asymmetry is clear. In principle, licensing of a non-EU lawyer by a public authority can be seen as analogous to granting a 'licence to stay' to an asylum-seeker. But the crucial difference here is that, in the case of asylum, EU States have not yet agreed on positive recognition, only negative recognition. Indeed, in both cases, State denial of the 'licence' will deny free movement – in the case of professionals, an inability to exercise their profession, either for lack of a diploma or for breach of a professional code of conduct.[27] The bias towards the banning rather than the permissive side in the case of JHA is not due to

[27] K. Nicolaïdis, 'Globalization with Human Faces: Managed Mutual Recognition and the Free Movement of Professionals' in F. K. P. Schioppa, *The Principle of Mutual Recognition in the European Integration Process*, above, pp. 129–89.

a structural difference in the 'object of recognition' – e.g., acts of States – but rather to the very nature of the acts that are being recognized (regulative versus coercive functions of the State) and the alternatives left on the table for the individuals concerned (consider where an 'unrecognized' lawyer versus a refugee will have to return to). In both cases, too, lack of trust (of the binding kind) may mean that recognition is so 'managed' that it becomes meaningless as Lavenex illustrates for JHA.

Thus, here again, recognition is predicated on binding trust. Both realms make clear that mutual recognition of State acts and harmonization or convergence of standards are not pure alternatives. In fact, recognition is predicated on convergence which may or may not require formal harmonization of the underlying standards, rules or criteria used by regulators, asylum law enforcers and diploma granters to grant entry. But, even the most adamant proponents of harmonization have to accept that recognition is a challenge that is posed above and beyond. The distinction between underlying laws and how such standards are interpreted applies across the board: given an existing level of convergence between asylum-granting or professional-training standards in different countries, should a host country recognize as valid the access granted by the home country authority? In JHA, recognition means that 'a Member State not only recognizes a law as being equivalent but recognizes the judicial act in its interpretation of all relevant provisions in a given case';[28] under Single Market rules, recognition means an ongoing acceptance of how a partner State interprets professional-training standards when accrediting licence-granting bodies. In both cases, ongoing recognition is predicated on trust that another State's enforcement of mutually compatible standards will result in mutually compatible decisions.

Recognition must remain embedded to remain sustainable. This was the message of the UK Court of Appeal which – after stating in 1998 that a discrepancy of approach between various Member States to the criteria of refugee protection did not matter unless deemed 'outside the range of tolerance' – refused recognition of French and German asylum jurisdiction because they did not acknowledge persecution by agents outside the State as grounds for granting refugee status. It is of little surprise that such a life-and-death difference in standards would fall outside the range of tolerance.

[28] Lavenex, 'Mutual Recognition and the Monopoly of Force', above, p. 765.

2.3 From acts of States to the constitution of States: recognition as constitutive

But recognition, of course, before concerning the 'acts of States' actually concerned the constitution of States themselves and their coming into existence as members of the international society. Since the Treaty of Westphalia (1648), a vast body of legal thinking and State practice has developed to regulate the emergence of new actors, e.g., States, in the international order. Here, the coveted price is *statehood*, defined as 'a claim of right, based on a certain legal and factual situation',[29] for example the requirements for statehood listed in the 1933 Montevideo Convention: a permanent population, a defined territory; government; and capacity to enter into relations with other States. To be sure, it seems that, at first sight, 'diplomatic recognition' is a far cry from the kind of regulatory and legal recognition as a mode of governance that occupies us in this volume, in that it is simply about bringing about sovereignty rather than the deeper horizontal sharing of sovereignty. And, yet more profoundly, it can also be seen as the foundational interventionist act on the part of the community of States. Indeed, we could argue that the circumstances of diplomatic recognition demonstrate, more vividly and tragically than with other realms, the import of appropriately 'managing' such recognition.

Europe's Tocquevillian moment started with a struggle for recognition of this kind, at the edges of the Union, namely, that of the republics emerging from the ashes of Yugoslavia. In this context, the conditional granting of recognition of constituent States as fully sovereign members of the international society was to be the foremost foreign policy instrument available to the EU. The story has been told often enough as to how an EU recognition strategy painstakingly designed in the course of 1991 to stall conflict actually contributed to increasing it.[30]

The basic assumptions made by European governments at the time were two-fold. First, recognition would lead to a change of unit of interaction and would therefore externalize the conflict, making it more legitimate for outside actors like the EU to intervene, which in turn was to deter Serbian aggression. Second, the EU could use the leverage of *conditional* recognition to enforce a change in the internal behaviour of its beneficiaries. Indeed, EU authorities, including the Badinter Commission of legal experts, went to a

[29] J. Crawford, *The Creation of States in International Law*, 1st edn (Oxford: Clarendon Press, 1979), pp. 31 and 119.

[30] R. Caplan, *Europe and the Recognition of New States in Yugoslavia*, 1st edn (Cambridge University Press, 2005).

considerable length in trying to devise such conditions, relying on and adapting traditional criteria for statehood.

And, here again, we see a balance between blind and binding trust, deferential and interventionist recognition. On the one hand, European States added to traditional Montevideo criteria for statehood – as with the requirement to hold a referendum on independence in Bosnia-Herzegovina, for instance. On the other hand, recognition itself is not supposed to introduce any *arbitrary* change in the subject which is recognized, namely, the boundaries of the new States which, according to the legal principle of *uti possidetis juris*, can only reflect the territorial *status quo* of the former Yugoslav republics (at the time, Montenegro could be recognized but not Kosovo).

Our original distinction between blind versus binding trust as underpinning two very different kinds of recognition is reflected in the long-standing debate between the *declaratory* and the *constitutive* schools of diplomatic recognition.[31] Advocates of the former argue that the role of recognition is simply to acknowledge that a territorial entity has satisfied the criteria of statehood but does not itself create States; those of the latter see a political or strategic role for recognition in that the very existence of a State depends on the political existence of other States and their acknowledgment of the attribute of sovereignty. Obviously, the reality is more subtle: Israel, Cyprus or Macedonia have existed as States short of universal recognition. But there is indeed what Caplan[32] calls a recognition paradox: recognition provides the very evidence of statehood – and acknowledgment of the rights associated with it – that may be needed to attract recognition in the first place. It is only after the fact that what is recognized as (pre-)existing, in fact comes to exist.

Clearly, the consequences of diplomatic recognition, if not totally unpredictable, must be considered as at least unintended. To the extent that recognition constitutes a bet with regard to a future state of affairs, it is generally *irreversible* and can best be understood through the analogy of tipping models with changing dynamics of the system before and after the fact of recognition. However much recognition may be predicated on future monitoring of the emerging States, it constitutes an abdication, an acknowledgment that we will continue to interact in spite of our differences. As with 'Single Market recognition', the conditional *ex ante* becomes conditional *ex post*. Binding trust implies that what you do is now my business, but, even if I am not happy with it, it is difficult to revert to the *status quo ante*.

[31] *Ibid.* [32] *Ibid.*

In the long run, of course, the recognition of the fledgling republics by the EU both enshrined (and, some would argue, precipitated) the disintegration of Yugoslavia, and constituted the prelude to the integration of these new States into the broader continent. It can also be argued that many EU conditions for recognition did bite and that it is more the EU's failure to take them seriously than their effectiveness *per se* which is to blame for the lack of progress in the area of minority rights.[33]

In a more detailed account, we would need to explore the historical cases of *mutual recognition* between two States which have hitherto coexisted in a State of war often by being each other's significant other: the two Germanies before 1974, the two Koreas, Israel and Palestine. Here more than anywhere else, we see that the decision to interact means acknowledging the other in spite of fundamental political differences and in order to narrow them. In the case of the two Germanies, the binding recognition eventually led to merger, in part because it kick-started a process which itself contributed to the end of the Cold War. As with international political economy (IPE), diplomatic mutual recognition can only be a stable equilibrium if truly constitutive of the other side rather than a means of accelerating convergence.

Generalizing from these regional and bilateral cases, mutual recognition is the very foundation of the international society of States as we know it and the subject of a whole body of international law. The most elementary expression as well as a facilitating factor for the web of diplomatic mutual recognition was the exchange of embassies which took place in the seventeenth century, creating islands of extraterritoriality. Of course, the exchange of rights and duties that ensued was not always symmetrical: witness, the treaties of capitulation between the Ottoman Empire and Western powers whereby European law was to be applied in Asia Minor for European citizens only. This was not of course recognition as we are discussing it here: the Ottomans were coerced into accepting the extraterritorial application of European law and such extraterritoriality was a one-way mechanism to protect the commercial interests and private property of traders. Which brings us to our third realm of recognition and the core feature of the kind of recognition which occupies us here.

[33] *Ibid.*, p. 183.

2.4 From sacred contracts to sacred symbols: recognition as mutual

To some extent, as Fukuyama reminds us with his *The End of History*, the Enlightenment project can be seen as an attempt at taming the lethal thriving for recognition that drove so many individuals to the fight to the death. If human intercourse could be organized around the politics of interest rather than the politics of identity, the violent struggle for honour would give way to the peaceful pursuit of mutually assured prosperity. We know what happened to the enlightenment project in the course of the twentieth century. But where are we today in Europe? From Sarajevo's no-man's land to Paris' suburbs, even our Kantian island Europe seems more than ever caught up in struggles about identity and their recognition rather than simple bargains over interests. Perhaps the story of the Polish plumber is also a mix between pure interest-based corporatism and the fear of loss of identity in an expanding Europe itself seen as serving as a 'Trojan horse for globalization'.

Indeed, we no longer understand 'European integration' to refer to what happens in and through Brussels but to refer to the integration of citizens within their respective national polities – or 'integration across Europe'. As Paris burnt in the fall of 2005, the flames licked the wounds of many beyond the *hexagon*. Social inclusion on the part of individuals and groups disenfranchised economically, ethnically or geographically is perhaps the foremost challenge of European politics today. Here, I argue, we need to understand the demands of these disparate actors – from *banlieusards* to strikers in the docks to illegal migrants – not only as struggles for recognition but as part of greater *mutual* recognition battles on the European scene.

The French philosopher, Paul Ricoeur,[34] may be seen as one of the most inspired exponents of this vision of conflictual consensus (*consensus conflictuel*) based on mutuality. While radical thinking about social recognition these days overlooks the importance of mutuality,[35] recognition, Ricoeur believed, speaks of the fundamental link uniting the members of a polity through Aristotle's 'political friendship', itself based on an even more fundamental relationship of an anthropological nature. Recognition takes us beyond the idea of politics as a simple game of redistribution between individuals well assured of their membership

[34] P. Ricoeur, *Parcours de la reconnaissance*, 1st edn (Trois Etudes, Paris: Stock, 2004).
[35] N. Fraser and A. Honneth, *Redistribution or Recognition? A Political–Philosophical Exchange* (London: Verso, 2003).

in society.[36] Instead, the idea of mutuality exceeds the kind of reciprocity which underpins the liberal contract and this 'plus' is 'constitutive' (again) of the political body.[37] Mutual recognition may acknowledge asymmetry (between, say, a victim and an accused) but it serves to tame otherness, to mediate the risk of violence by literally creating Arendt's *inter-esse*, this transitional space in-between individuals which makes for our politics. Recognizing the other cannot be solely a matter of positive law since it is based on 'an equivalence that can neither be measured nor calculated'. And mutuality is about assessing such equivalence beyond the emotional poverty of procedures and rights.

The cartoon controversy which blew up in Europe in the spring of 2006 can be used as a test case here.[38] We do not need to essentialize the relationship between Europe and Islam to acknowledge it as perhaps the most difficult *mutual* recognition challenge facing Europe today. If this is the case, there may be a common cause and common patterns to the denial of recognition with regard to the fate of our Polish plumbers and the fate of Mahomet cartoons on European soil. In both cases, passionate advocates saw grand principles pitted against one another. Freedom of movement against sacred social laws when it comes to plumbers; freedom of speech against sacred symbols when it comes to cartoons. Socialism versus neo-liberalism in one case. The West versus the rest in the other.

And yet in neither case can we accept the framing of the issue in such stark either–or terms. The real opposition is between self-righteousness on all sides and the difficult search for justice in a globalized world groping for ways to manage our increasingly conspicuous – if not actually greater – cultural and economic differences.

At the heart of both controversies lies the same paradox. If we want people from elsewhere to better integrate into our economies and our societies, we need to recognize the validity of at least *some* of their habits and rules from home. Only in the name of an old-fashioned defence of sovereignty and the absolute match between territorial, legal and administrative jurisdiction can we reject the multi-faceted demand for recognition.

[36] N. Fraser, 'From Redistribution to Recognition? Dilemmas of Justice in a "Post-Socialist" Age', *New Left Review* 212 (1995) 68–93.

[37] A. Garapon, 'Justice et reconnaissance', *Esprit* 323 (March–April 2006).

[38] K. Nicolaïdis, 'Europe and Beyond: Struggles for Recognition', *Open Democracy* (February 2006), available at www.opendemocracy.net/democracy-europefuture/recognition_3288.jsp (last visited 10 September 2010).

National treatment, or 'when in Rome, do as Romans do', will not do. If we want their countries to catch up, small businesses and people from eastern and central Europe cannot be asked to adapt all-over-again to each country's rule in a European space which is supposed to be borderless. Similarly, we cannot simply ignore the civic responsibilities – in Tariq Ramadan's words – that come with Europe's claim to primacy in the so-called dialogue of civilization with the Muslim world within and beyond our borders.[39] Most Muslims cannot be expected to buy our hard-earned fondness for blasphemy wholesale, here and now. Recognition, be it of home regulations or identities, means some degree of internalizing the interests and beliefs of others, as a precondition to freedom of movement on the one hand, and freedom of speech on the other.

This means, however, that recognition must not only be managed, as I have argued above, it must also be mutual.

Managed mutual recognition implies that acceptance of other people's norms can and must be reciprocal, conditional, progressive, partial, negotiated, dynamic and predicated on critical safeguards, which in turn makes it progressive and flexible over time. Thus, the Services Directive enables governments to enforce local rules pursuing social, environmental, health, security and consumer protection objectives, but only to the extent that these are 'necessary' and 'proportional' to the goals pursued. If countries of origin do their job, they will see their laws recognized to the extent that the Court, the Commission and other associated interests remain keen to enforce non-discrimination to the fullest. The sphere of mutual recognition should expand in tandem with the requisite level of convergence and tolerance between social systems.

Which brings us back to the cartoon clash. For Europeans to be truly reconciled with recognizing Muslim sensitivities, mutuality will certainly help. Muslim societies do not have to become like ours – although more freedom of speech in many of their countries would be welcome – but they must understand that many of us hold sacred the right to express disrespect for religion. Here, as with the Single Market, the spirit of proportionality would help. Moderates ought to argue on the fine points – should limits to free speech be legal or moral questions, should bans be considered in case of disrespect or only incitement to violence, etc. But surely, the hope is that, with time, and greater convergence, mutual knowledge and indeed healthy non-violent conflict, the scope for mutual recognition will expand here too.

[39] Tariq Ramadan, *Western Muslims and the Future of Islam* (Oxford University Press, 2005).

This is the (idealized) European vision, if there is one. Living with our differences and seeking to harmonize if and only if such differences are illegitimate in the eyes of either one of the parties involved. Recognition is a tough call on all sides of the political spectrum. The left fears 'social dumping' when recognition means importing market rules; libertarians fear 'political dumping' when recognition means importing curbs on free speech. Even if these fears can be exploited to demonize Polish plumbers or Muslim migrants, they must be assuaged. Ultimately, however, they must be transcended if we are to live in Europe and in the world as a community of others.

This article cannot do justice to the wide relevance of mutual recognition as a norm nor to the many different meanings of the idea itself. It only suggests some benchmarks for exporting recognition across seemingly disparate areas – Single Market, justice and home affairs, diplomacy, multicultural dilemmas. And, in doing so, it brings together a set of concepts that ought to accompany the quest for sustainable recognition: managed mutual recognition, binding trust and the accompanying features of recognition as embedded, constitutive and mutual.

The research agenda laid out here is to explore the commonalities between the various theatres where the struggle for recognition unfolds, from at least three disciplinary standpoints: trade law and international political economy; international relations; and political philosophy. In each of these realms, the resistance to mutual recognition and the preconditions for extending it are grounded in the same constraints of acceptable differences and necessary deference between the parties involved – in other words, the double anchor of the needs for sameness (harmonization) and separateness (national treatment). And these very patterns of resistance are the key to designing sustainable recognition regimes.

Many would argue that demands for recognition are so prone to conflict that societies are better off ignoring them, especially when it comes to transnational affairs. The Hegelian project of playing out and eventually resolving the struggle of recognition echoed by Kojeve's[40] universal State predicated on generalized mutual recognition continues to constitute a key political horizon in today's world. As a result, recognition holds an ever ambiguous ideological status. On the one hand, it can be seen as a second

[40] A. Kojéve, *Outline of a Phenomenology of Right* (Plymouth: Rowman & Littlefield Publishers Inc., 2000).

best, limiting the need for more harmonious strategies such as equality of chances and solidarity. On the other hand, struggles for recognition are at the heart of a progressive agenda for world politics. Obviously, the themes touched on above are relevant well beyond the confines of the EU. Increasingly, global institutions are designed to reflect our need to interact in spite of our differences and our capacity to agree on the limits of our mutual trust. With greater interdependence comes a greater awareness of differentiation and the need to work out patterns of recognition that are conditional, partial and managed and as such the only game in town.

3. Questions for a regulatory peace theory

Having laid out the normative landscape of mutual recognition as the concept expresses itself in Europe, can we draw on some of the chapters presented in this volume to start to move a step further? I suggested in the introduction to this chapter that it might be fruitful to develop collectively what may be called a 'regulatory peace theory' (RPT) drawing loose analogies with 'democratic peace theory' (DPT), a set of propositions in IR which together (1) argue that democracies do not go to war with each other (generally, that is); and (2) put forward a number of hypotheses as to why this is the case. In a nutshell, DPT argues that a majority of people in most contexts would never vote to go to war, unless in self-defence. Therefore, if all nations were democratic, there would be no wars for lack of aggressors.[41] Whatever the merits and limits of the original theories – which will not be discussed here – I will lay out some of the questions that may arise in using DPT as a heuristics for RPT.

3.1 From democratic peace theory to regulatory peace theory: conflict of sovereignties, conflict of laws

First, we obviously need to define what we mean by regulatory peace and what exactly is its converse. The proponents of DPT were able to agree that democratic peace between two countries consisted in the lack of significant armed conflict in the period at stake, that is, conflicts or wars

[41] For an early exposition of the theory, see M. Doyle, 'Kant, Liberal Legacies, and Foreign Affairs', *Philosophy and Public Affairs* 12(3) (1983) 205–35, pp. 207–8; see also M. W. Doyle, *Ways of War and Peace*, 2nd edn (New York: W. W. Norton, 1997); S. A. Bremer, 'Dangerous Dyads: Conditions Affecting the Likelihood of Interstate War, 1816–1965', *Journal of Conflict Resolution* 36(2) (1992) 309–41.

incurring more than a thousand deaths. Obviously, albeit elegant, such a definition has been criticized for its arbitrary character. But it does its job sufficiently well. RPT possibly offers a more complex challenge, as regulatory behaviour even while competitive cannot easily be identified as targeting a specific counterpart. A regulator might adopt 'war like' regulations without allowing us to determine whom they are meant to counter, or attack.

So, if regulatory peace is a state of relationship whereby regulators do not go to war with one another in order to manipulate the competitive environment between their countries, how do we define 'regulatory war'? Does it correspond to a kind of regulatory competition that is simply unmanaged, or would we prefer to define it as a question of degree, relating to the relationship between the normal ends of regulations and their manipulation so as to induce market advantage? Or should we probe more deeply the meaning of integration as explored by Cappelletti, Seccombe and Weiler (cited by Ioannis Lianos in this volume), that is, 'the dilemma of reaching an *equilibrium* between, on the one hand, a respect for the autonomy of the individual unit, freedom of choice, pluralism and diversity of action, and, on the other hand, the societal need for cooperation, integration, harmony and, at times, unity'.

At its broadest level of generality, RPT is about probing the conditions for sustaining such an equilibrium. At a more operational level, it is about the ways in which disagreements over applicable laws are resolved under a conflict-of-laws framework, as Christian Joerges and Florian Rödl as well as other authors have extensively discussed.[42] As they state in their chapter, '[courts] find themselves confronted with the collisions of the laws of ... functional regimes, which they take as merely legal conflicts and upon which they decide; however, at the heart of these conflicts lies the collision of the incommensurable rationalities of the differentiated functional subsystems.'

Second, therefore, we need to frame the specific question RPT is meant to address: when does this collision of incommensurable rationalities

[42] See Chapter 11 in this volume; as well as Christian Joerges, 'Informal Politics, Formalised Law and the "Social Deficit" of European Integration: Reflections after the Judgments of the ECJ in Viking and Laval', *European Law Journal* 15 (2009) 1–19; see also G. Teubner, 'Societal Constitutionalism: Alternatives to State-Centred Constitutional Theory?' in C. Joerges, I.-J. Sand and G. Teubner (eds.), *Constitutionalism and Transnational Governance* (Oxford: Hart Publishing, 2004), pp. 3–28; A. Fischer-Lescano, 'Regime Collisions: The Vain Search for Legal Unity in the Fragmentation of Global Law', *Michigan Journal of International Law* 25 (2004) 999–1045.

actually lead to explosions? In other words, 'under what conditions do (democratic) regulators refrain from going to war with each other?'; or 'can we design stable governance mechanisms for market integration (whereby the stability in question refers to the regulatory underpinnings of trade relations)?'; or 'what makes for stable relations in the transnational trade/regulatory nexus?' The way the core question is framed will of course affect how one goes about developing an RPT.

Third, we would need to distinguish between monadic and dyadic explanatory strategies. Where can we locate the greatest explanatory power? Is it, on one hand, in a monadic explanation which seeks to explain the propensity of individual democracies not to go to war regardless of their counterpart's type, that is, as a function of the characteristics of the units (in the DPT context, that democratic leaders must answer to war-averse voters, and therefore have incentives to seek alternatives; or that democracies tend to be wealthier than other countries, and the wealthy have more to lose with wars). So what can explain regulators' unilateral incentives to comply with the requirements of trade liberalization? The kind of variables highlighted by DPT would certainly be relevant, for example, transparency of decision-making, accountability, right of the opposition etc. But we would also need to turn to the regulatory culture of a given country, the degree of autonomy of its regulators *vis-à-vis* politics, the degree of fragmentation of its regulatory landscape, or, importantly, regulators' comfort with the trade culture and the kind of outcome that it seeks to pursue. Together, these factors will tell us the extent to which such-and-such regulatory body and its agents will likely be prone to collaborate with their counterparts across borders and avoid conflict.

On the other hand, dyadic explanatory strategies favour either conditional characteristics of decision-makers or relational features such as (in DPT) the fact that democratic statesmen have practice settling matters by discussion, not by arms, and do the same in foreign policy; or that democracies view non-democracies as threatening, and thus go to war with them over issues which would have been settled peacefully between democracies. Under RPT, such categories of explanation would focus on the commonalities and shared incentives of regulators across borders. In this vein, we would need to assess the different factors which may make regulatory cultures and decisions across borders more or less similar and compatible and connect this assessment with the 'tolerance for differences' characterizing regulators on both sides in conflict-of-laws situations. This would be an indicator of the compatibility between their different approaches even absent any coordination.

Fourth, still in the spirit of DPT, an RPT would need to tackle the distinction between institutional and normative factors and ask about their interrelationship. In other words, are the incentives facing regulators shaped by the institutions within which they are embedded (e.g., degree of centralization, hierarchy, accountability), or do they lie with norms, shared regulatory cultures and compatibility? What are the kinds of trade-offs that can be made between the two categories when assessing the ways in which regulators are likely to collaborate in order to facilitate trade relations?

3.2 Bringing mutual recognition back in: legal exegesis and regulatory peace theory

In the mid-1990s, the OECD conducted a broad exercise on regulatory reform around the world, where we assessed, *inter alia*, the extent to which the member countries were conducting their respective regulatory reform in a 'mutual-recognition-friendly' manner. Such an assessment could constitute a building block in the construction of an RPT to the extent that it characterizes both sides of the equation: the extent to which national regulators refrain from applying their own rules to incoming persons or products (unilateral recognition) as well as their capacity to exercise adequate regulatory control (as home State) over their economic agents operating abroad.

The next task in shaping an RPT would be to add to the characterization of the national regulators, their unilateral 'recognition-friendliness' and their mutual 'compatibility', an analysis of the kind of transnational or supranational trade-cum-regulatory frameworks within which such relations are embedded, and ask how they affect the incentives as well as the obligations of the various agents in the regulatory game.

Many of the chapters in this volume are clearly relevant to this exercise. In an integrated European (or globalized, for that matter) economy, regulatory war and peace, conflict and cooperation, are grounded in rules of the game adjudicated by courts and internalized (or not) by the various economic actors. Ioannis Lianos, in particular, provides an extensive and insightful overview of the jurisprudence on free movement as it relates to regulatory barriers to trade and how the Court of Justice has interpreted EU law injunctions over time, taking us down the different paths or impasses of regulatory conflict resolution.[43] For one, Lianos reminds us

[43] I. Lianos, 'Shifting Narratives in the European Internal Market: Efficient Restrictions of Trade and the Nature of "Economic" Integration', *European Business Law Review* 21(5) (2010) 705–60.

that the Court may have been tempted but has long refrained from interpreting any costs to trade and 'free movers' that arise from disparities in the laws and regulations of the Member States as restrictions on freedom of movement proscribed by the Treaties.[44] RPT is about how far not to go in overriding deeply seated social rationalities, as Joerges would put it. Instead, as emphasized by Advocate General (and scholar) Miguel Maduro in *Alpha Vita* and subsequent cases, 'to be considered as a restriction on trade, the supplementary cost imposed must stem from the fact that the national rules did not take into account the particular situation of the imported products and, in particular, the fact that those products already had to comply with the rules of their States of origin'. Consequently, 'the task of the Court is not to call into question as a matter of course Member States' economic policies', but to make sure that 'those States do not adopt measures which, in actual fact, lead to cross-border situations being treated less favourably than purely national situations'. Such a frame is clearly also contestable, as discussed by Lianos and other interpreters of EU jurisprudence. But it should be possible to say which factors of stability are privileged by which exegesis.

In short, the objective of the Internal Market has not been to reduce regulatory diversity as the means to reducing regulatory burdens to firms, but to obtain the same result – respect of a single rule – by changing the baseline in conflict of laws to the country-of-origin jurisdiction, and then, crucially, retreating from the extreme version of such a choice, on a case-by-case, sector-by-sector basis (see section 2.1.1 on managed mutual recognition).

Such a 'holistic approach' to integration, as Lianos calls it, does not amount to deregulation, a point long argued by many of us (against common wisdom) – a path which would be most prone to conflict. In short, 'taking into account' home State law clearly points to two regulatory (not deregulatory) roads: on the first, the home State satisfies the regulatory requisites of the host State; on the second, when this is not the case, the host State can justify obstacles to trade on various grounds broadly and ambiguously defined as 'mandatory requirements of general interest', even if these are directly discriminatory. As a result, given the second road, Member States as home States are unlikely to engage in aggressive forms of regulatory race to the bottom if they want to be in the trade game. Even if they do, the holistic approach allows for ultimate host State sovereignty.

[44] See also Ioannis Lianos and Damien Gerard, 'Shifting Narratives in European Economic Integration: Trade in Services, Pluralism and Trust', Chapter 6 in this volume.

This is where the sustainability of EU laws lies. An RPT would discuss the attributes of case law most prone to such sustainability.

But we need to take one more step. In a chapter in this volume, Gareth Davies brilliantly argues that the possibility and outcome of litigation is a sideshow and that, as a result, the obligations contained in a Directive like the Services Directive are not significant in and of themselves (indeed, they only serve to formalize existing jurisprudence grounded on the constructive ambiguity of words like 'legitimate' or 'proportional' regulations). What really matters is that the world in which regulators evolve is changing: networks are strengthened, contact points established, information shared and transparency increased not only for the operating agents but also for the regulators themselves. These are all part of what I call the *ex post* monitoring attribute of managed mutual recognition. In this vein, my argument has been that the latter has served to shift the transaction costs of cooperation from *ex ante* to *ex post*, from the political negotiations to the management of the contours of recognition once adopted. This 'trick' has successfully been used during the last two decades of EU rule-making to further the Single Market in light of political deadlocks. We have had (relative) regulatory peace thanks to such rule-making incrementalism.[45]

Of course, all is not well in the kingdom of integration. Regulatory peace is a process not an outcome, that needs to be nurtured over time. As I hope section 2 of this chapter amply demonstrates, and as argued in this volume by Wolfgang Kerber and Roger van den Bergh, mutual recognition is conflict-prone, which is precisely why it has (almost) always taken on a 'managed' form (but, contrary to what they say, it is still a form of decentralized regulation, albeit one with a non-territorial logic (the decentralization is centred around the individual or the firm as it were)).

There are many sources of conflict simply in interpreting when the assertion of host State control is legitimate. The conflict-of-laws logic is indeed conflictual when it involves first-order social choices. Should free movement be thought of as fundamental individual rights, thus elevating its status against public powers in the hierarchy of European norms? As the jurisprudence finesses the list of values that might justify limiting the reach of mutual recognition (the protection of the environment, paternalistic

[45] See K. Nicolaïdis, *Regulatory Reform and International Market Openness* (Paris: OECD Publications, 1996); and K. Nicolaïdis, 'EU 2.0: Towards Sustainable Integration', *Open Democracy*, 12 July 2010, available at www.opendemocracy.net (last visited 10 September 2010).

regulation that aims to mitigate the behavioural biases of consumers and information asymmetries, cultural diversity, a higher degree of public health and social protection, freedom of expression) should we not recast value-balancing not only as free trade against the almighty rest but elevate mutual recognition as a value in itself with all the requirements and caveats that it might involve? How do the obligations associated with free movement and the choice-of-regulation game affect European citizenship? Should States or a supranational body perform their own cost/benefit analyses on the basis of different values and different measurement mechanisms? If Maduro is right that 'different institutions may reach different and equally legitimate and efficient balances of the values concerned', how should these different 'balances' be adjudicated when they come into conflict through the mediation of those things and persons that move across borders? Is it enough to require that each State take the interest of others into account when doing so?[46] Is such internalization even necessary, if we can assume that there will always be national actors who share the interests of foreigners and therefore act and lobby unwittingly as proxies for outsiders?[47] And how can the Court decide on the under-representation (or not) of the interests of nationals of other Member States in the national political process without passing a judgment on this process as a whole, thus possibly disrupting the fragile balance involved in interest representation in domestic politics? Regulatory peace involves the kind of supranational assessment that cannot be in themselves 'right' or 'wrong' but that instead must correspond to an existing transnational equilibrium at a moment in time – an equilibrium that may vary with the prevailing 'mutual recognition threshold' – or acceptable differences prior to home rule.

The Services Directive (discussed in section 2 of this chapter as well as by other authors in this volume) amply demonstrate that this is a tricky business. For instance, the Court certainly does not want to grant an exception for the social field as a whole which would justify rejecting home country control

[46] For a discussion, see A. Menon and S. Weatherill, 'Transnational Legitimacy in a Globalising World: How the European Union Rescues Its States', *West European Politics* 31(3) (2008) 397–416; see also K. Nicolaïdis and G. Shaffer, 'Transnational Mutual Recognition Regimes: Governance without Global Government', *Michigan Review of International Law* 68 (2005) 267–322.

[47] See the discussion by I. Lianos, 'Shifting Narratives in the European Internal Market: Efficient Restrictions of Trade and the Nature of "Economic" Integration', *European Business Law Review* 21(5) (2010) 705–60. The original argument was developed by D. H. Regan, 'Judicial Review of Member State Regulation within a Federal or Quasi-Federal System: Protectionism and Balancing. da Capo', *Michigan Law Review* 99(8) (2001) 1853–1902.

wholesale as soon as it puts into question internal deals. So the said Court opens the black box of domestic politics and likes what it sees: collective agreements between management and labour where its exception-to-free-movement-imperative can be based not on the subject matter of the agreement but on the way such agreements affect the distribution of power between employers and employees, re-empowering the latter against the former. Outsiders cannot disregard such socially valuable deals simply because they are 'obstacles to trade'. If that was the case, trade union rights and traders' rights would simply be diametrically opposed. The deal has to be bad enough for outside workers, says the Court in *Viking* and subsequent cases – that is, simply wiping out any comparative advantage they might have – if we are to override it through country-of-origin jurisdiction. Is this a 'slippery slope' to more trade/regulatory wars over Polish plumbers? Not if Member States were to legislate over stuff they really care about, such as minimal wages, argue the likes of Pelkmans. Then host State law would clearly be applicable. So here regulatory peace comes at a price: the convergence among States of the realm of the law versus non-legal social accords.

3.3 *Blind versus binding trust and the transitivity of trust*

To be sure, it is not always so easy to open the black box of the State. The host State action in curbing a given freedom is usually blatant, but the home State action that might justify such a behaviour is not. As many chapters in this volume illustrate, the role of trust in economic integration needs to be theorized more systematically than has been done until now, including in my own 'Trusting the Poles?'. Trust has been defined as 'the willingness to take risk concerning the behavior of others' action in spite of non trivial probability of betrayal'. In this game, those doing the trusting are above all the regulators or law-makers who accept a withholding of their territorially defined authority over those working under their jurisdiction. But, of course, we need to ask where their own authority is coming from, if not entrusted by the public at large and the parts of society impacted by their action.

In this sense, the kind of relationships bound up with conflict-of-law and the trade-regulation nexus involve both direct and delegated trust. And the question we need to ask is whether trust is a transitive relationship (see Figures 7.1 and 7.2). If the French public trusts French authorities who in turn trust Polish authorities, has the original trust been delegated? And what if the Polish authorities have delegated part of their authority to regulatory bodies, certification agencies or universities

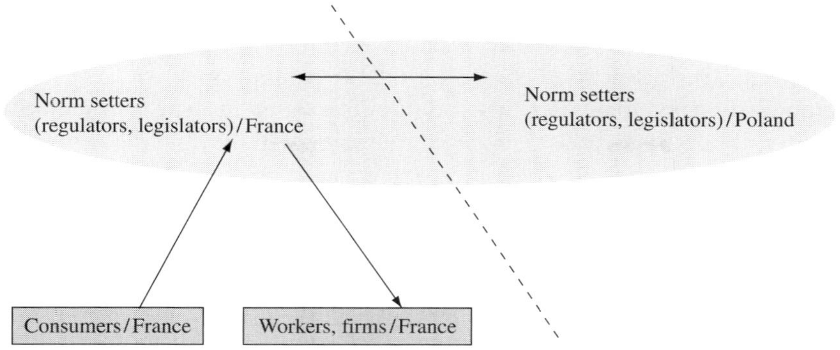

Figure 7.1 The transitivity of trust (1): delegated trust

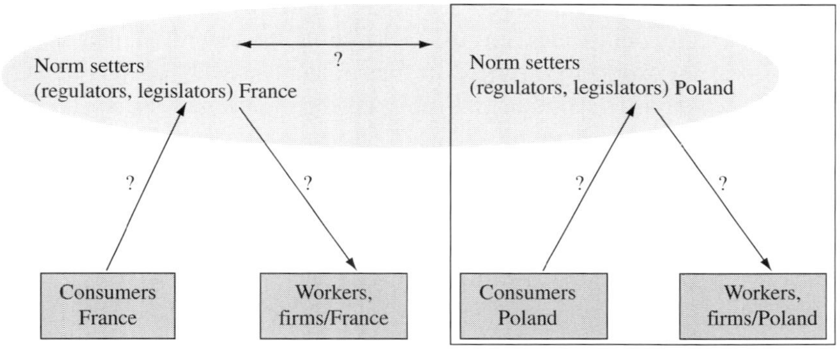

Figure 7.2 The transitivity of trust (2): opening the black box

whom they 'trust'? Should foreign authorities rely on the same trust, albeit mediated by their counterparts in the country at stake? And how is ongoing trust preserved over time in a situation when trust is delegated?

There are many dimensions to explore in assessing the role of trust in transnational trade-related regulatory politics. For instance, we can assess the pre-existing proclivity for trust (affective, reputational and identification-based) in a given relationship. We can ask whether trust in the first instance is primarily associated with such proclivity or is process-based, a result of an ongoing interaction.[48] We can also frame the issue in terms of principal–agent relations and information asymmetries.

[48] The former is more likely to be associated with what some authors call personalized trust (relations of confidence that come from familiarity), while the latter has more to do with systemic trust. We can also work with other distinctions, e.g., between

In section 2 of this chapter, I appealed to the idea of 'appropriately intrusive trust', which of course will vary with the parties and the situation involved. The distinction between blind and binding trust, with the latter grounded on the many ties that can bind regulators in their transnational cooperation, takes us back to managed mutual recognition and the argument developed by Davies. It is also meant to encapsulate in part the difference between trust as a prerequisite and trust as an objective of cooperation. To be sure, there needs to be a modicum of *a priori* trust to even contemplate regulatory delegation; but only by developing the 'ties that bind' can trust be built over time through the management of recognition – a binding to the other side's expectations of appropriate behaviour. This is not to say that time will necessarily bring convergence between regulatory systems – indeed part of the challenge associated with recognition is the need to build trust *in spite of* the lack of convergence. As the chapter by Juan Marchetti and Petros Mavroidis illustrates, mutual recognition agreements signed by the EU around the world have varied in their formats exactly on this basis.[49] Mutual recognition beyond a relatively convergent community like the EU must internalize the absence of familiarity through compensatory measures, not only the kind of *ex post* monitoring described by Davies but more broadly, careful delineation of the scope of (managed) mutual recognition, including, ultimately, reversibility. Paradoxically perhaps, it is only such a perspective of reversibility that will make recognition sustainable.

performative and constitutive trust, relational and calculative trust (e.g., intentions and identity versus rational risk calculation and predictability). A future research agenda on issues of trust in trade law and IPE would need to integrate more systematically the broad literature on trust in the fields of economics, sociology, psychology and philosophy. See, for instance, M. Saunders (eds.), *Organizational Trust: A Cultural Perspective* (Cambridge University Press, 2010); B. Misztal, *Trust in Modern Societies: The Search for the Bases of Social Order* (Cambridge: Polity Press, 1996); C. McLeod, 'Trust' in *The Stanford Encyclopedia of Philosophy*, available at http://plato.stanford.edu/entries/trust/ (last visited 10 September 2010); R. Bachmann and A. Zaheer (eds.), *Handbook of Trust Research*, 1st edn (Cheltenham: Edward Elgar, 2006); I. Marková and A. Gillespie (eds.), *Trust and Distrust: Socio-Cultural Perspectives* (Greenwich, CT: Information Age Publishing Inc., 2007).

49 For a discussion on the discriminatory nature of recognition regimes, see K. Nicolaïdis, 'Non-Discriminatory Mutual Recognition: An Oxymoron in the New WTO Lexicon?' in P. Mavroidis and P. Blatter (eds.), *Non Discrimination in the WTO: Past and Present, Journal of World Trade* (World Trade Forum Series, University of Michigan Press, 2000); see also M. Egan and K. Nicolaïdis, 'Regional Policy Externality and Market Governance: Why Recognize Foreign Standards?', *Journal of European Public Policy* 8(3) (2001) 454–73, reprinted in W. Mattli (ed.), *The Political Economy of Standardization* (Cambridge University Press, 2001).

There are of course limits to the recourse to network and 'mutual spying' as a way to create trust between regulators confronted with the need for mutual delineation. Sometimes, the game regulators play may simply consist in the consensual delineation of the limits of trust, a collective agreement that 'trust among us cannot extend to such and such area at least for the moment'. We would need to analyze how such delineation occurs and how it evolves over time. An analysis of the different forms of supranational organization to create and sustain such trust would discuss the difference between Commission prerogative, comitology and the creation of independent agencies on which governments bestow a degree of trust rather than trusting each other solely.

All these are only some of the issues bound up with assessing the role of trust in regulatory/trade relations. In sum, by moving from pure to managed mutual recognition, we move from recognition as one alternative among others to an overarching concept grounded on the assessment of equivalence between national regulations on the one hand, and the amount of trust between national authorities on the other. Once this conceptual move has been made, we can assess the factors that influence such trust in situations of incomplete contracting. The limits of recognition then correspond to the extent to which conditions for its application have not been met. This is the first-order trade-off. The second-order trade-off can be spelled out within these bounds: how exactly will it be managed? Through *ex ante* or *ex post* conditions, by reducing the scope activities covered or by increasing the degree of host country regulatory control? These are empirical questions.

3.4 *Bringing politics back in: the importance of cognitive frames*

Finally, recent developments in the EU have demonstrated that the analysis of the dynamics of the trade/regulation nexus must bring politics back in and take into account the influence of broader public opinion and sectoral interests – regulatory peace is a function also of transnational societal contracts. Indeed, as quickly sketched out in section 2 above, it is possible to argue that the EU has witnessed a fundamental change in societal involvement with issues of trade and regulatory sovereignty in the last two decades which can be depicted crudely as a change of cognitive frames.

Up to the 1980s, the EU's permissive consensus generally extended to these issues, leaving the management of transnational regulatory issues to experts. There were obviously tensions along the free movement–protection axis, but the issues at stake were mostly framed in technical terms related to the principles to be applied to trade (Figure 7.3).

During the 1990s and 2000s, the cognitive frame informing the public has progressively changed (Figure 7.4). A new dimension was added to people's apprehension of the issues at stake. The change was driven by socio-economics and the mobilizing of the fears and sense of vulnerabilities associated with structural changes in the global economy – in short, framing

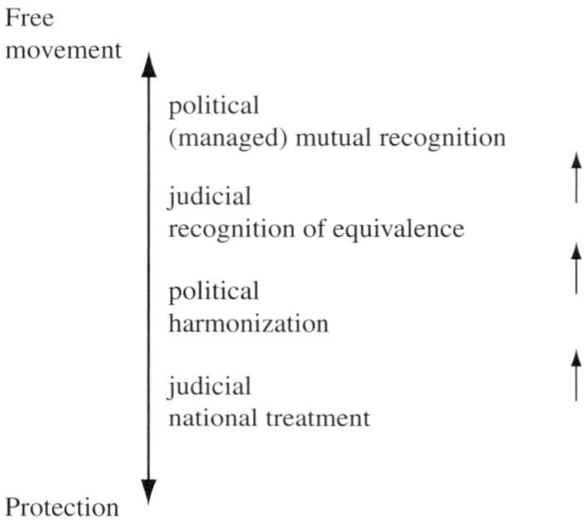

Figure 7.3 Basic frame in the perceptions of the trade–regulation nexus (1), 1960s–1980s: the trade axis

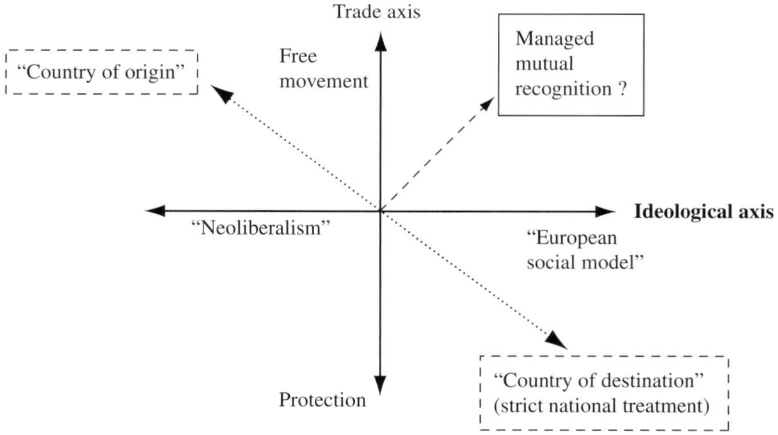

Figure 7.4 Changing frames in the perceptions of the trade–regulation nexus (2), 1990s–2000s: adding the ideological axis

Europeanization as globalization. This translated into calls to replace free trade by 'fair trade' benchmarks, making access to one's markets conditional on a convergence of underlying standards even in areas hitherto unscrutinized in the context of trade such as the environment and labour laws. In people's eyes, comparative advantage was increasingly becoming a byword for 'social dumping'. Worse, 'social dumping' at a distance was increasingly replaced by face-to-face 'social dumping' through the movement of workers (hence the 1996 Posted Workers Directive). All of this progressively amounted to a partial breakdown of trust in the compatibility of regulatory systems or the fairness of their confrontation.

Grounded on this socio-economic phenomenon, the change ultimately consisted in adding an ideological axis to people's perceptions of the issues at stake, an axis pitting 'neo-liberalism' against the 'European social model'. Increasingly, it would be along this dimension that hitherto technical principles having to do with conflict of law (rule of country of origin or destination) would come to be judged. In other words, a social resistance to the disembeddedness of global markets was progressively translated into a pointed resistance towards extraterritoriality. Under this new light, mutual recognition, a principle inscribed in the Treaties since 1957, was heralded and decried as a 'new principle', 'a political test for the left', while host country rule was equated with social solidarity.

With any change of cognitive frames of course comes a counter-frame. But, in this case, the counter-frame, which continued to hang on to the idea of Europeanization as 'non-discrimination' as well as 'globalization with a human face', was progressively losing its pregnance. The complementary argument, that most people prefer to stay put and would eventually return home, only gained credibility with the first wave of returns to central Europe after the financial crisis of 2008. In this context, 'legitimate differences' took on an increasingly narrow remit. Nevertheless, on the normative-ideological plane, the Single Market did continue to represent for many the anti-nationalist ideal embodied in the EU. In their eyes, a crucial difference had to be drawn between protectionist intent and solidarity rhetoric, or as stated earlier *liberismo* (the sanctity of freedom) and *liberalismo*; managing differences did not necessarily have to amount to engineering convergence; and differences ought to be considered legitimate until proven otherwise. In the end, if the challenge in Europe today is to re-embed liberalism by ensuring that horizontal delegation to other States does not amount to pure delegation to markets, it will need to better master the requisites of 'regulatory peace'.

PART IV

Private parties and the economic integration process

8

Who's afraid of the total market? On the horizontal application of the free movement provisions in EU law

HARM SCHEPEL

1. Introduction

To impose fundamental rights on constitutionally protected private economic relations is not a step to be taken lightly in liberal market democracies: it limits private autonomy, undermines the coherence of private law systems, and generally contradicts the tenets of liberty on which markets are supposed to be founded. The 'total constitution' is a fearsome thing. To impose market freedoms on constitutionally protected social relations is a step to be taken with great care in liberal market democracies: it implies, in the imagery of the great Karl Polanyi, 'no less than the running of society as an adjunct to the market. Instead of economy being embedded in social relations, social relations are embedded in the economic system.'[1] The 'total market' is a fearsome thing. To impose norms into private relationships that are conceptualized as both market freedoms and fundamental rights, then, is in all likelihood a very bad idea that is bound to instil fear even in those who aren't afraid of either the total market or the total constitution.

The thesis of this contribution is that this bad idea is unfolding rapidly in the context of the doctrine of the horizontal application of the free movement provisions of EU law.[2] My concern, however, is not so much

[1] K. Polanyi, *The Great Transformation* (Boston: Beacon Press, 2001), p. 60.

[2] Useful overviews in English include V. den Bogaert, 'Horizontality: The Court Attacks?' in C. Barnard and J. Scott (eds.), *The Law of the Single European Market – Unpacking the Premises* (Oxford: Hart Publishing, 2002), p. 123; J. Snell, 'Private Parties and the Free Movement of Goods and Services' in M. Andenas and W.-H. Roth (eds.), *Services and Free Movement in EU Law* (Oxford University Press, 2002), p. 211; E. J. Lohse, 'Fundamental Freedoms and Private Actors – Towards an "Indirect Horizontal Effect"', *European Public*

with the normative choice between a total constitution and a total market as it is to cut through the dead wood of marginal tinkering that obscures that choice in both the Court's case law and the literature. Both are marked by a striking ambivalence towards the idea of applying the free movement provisions to private actors. In the context of Article 34 TFEU, the Court at one point announced that 'it is impossible in any circumstances for agreements between individuals to derogate from the mandatory provisions of the Treaty on the free movement of goods',[3] only to hide that judgment away in a deep drawer ever since.[4] In the context of the free movement of workers and services, however, the Court held in *Walrave* that the prohibition of discrimination on the ground of nationality applies not just to acts of public authorities but also to 'rules of any other nature aimed at regulating in a collective manner gainful employment or the provision of services'.[5] Soon enough, on the basis of the particular constellation of facts in the case, the theory has developed that direct horizontal effect is limited by both a substantive condition and a personal one: it applies *only* to direct discrimination and *only* to those private bodies that have a regulatory function. To be sure, it is readily accepted that, in *Bosman*, the Court undermined the first condition, but, so the theory holds, not the second.[6] Similarly, in *Angonese*, the Court relaxed the second condition, but, so the theory hopefully posits, not the first.[7] It is still possible, then, to argue that the obligations enabling the freedom to provide services have no direct horizontal effect at all: one string of cases deals with a species of 'extended vertical direct effect' in that the obligations are applied to organizations that are functional equivalents to regulatory authorities; the other string of cases deals not with the horizontal effect of the free movement of services and

Law 13 (2007) 159–90; and A. Dashwood, 'Viking and Laval: Issues of Horizontal Direct Effect', *Cambridge Yearbook of European Legal Studies* 10 (2008) 525–40. In German, the choice is rather wider. Indeed, hardly a year goes by without another hefty monograph on the topic. See, e.g., M. Jaensch, *Die unmittelbare Drittwirkung der Grundfreiheiten* (Baden-Baden: Nomos, 1997); T. Körber, *Grundfreiheiten und Privatrecht* (Tübingen: Mohr Siebeck, 2004); K. Preedy, *Die Bindung Privater an die europäischen Grundfreiheiten- Zur sogenannten Drittwirkung im Europarecht* (Berlin: Dunckler & Humblot, 2005); and Ph. Förster, *Die unmittelbare Drittwirkung der Grundfreiheiten* (Peter Lang, 2007).

3 Case 58/80, *Dansk Supermarked* [1981] ECR 181, para. 17.

4 The most recent explicit rejection of horizontal direct effect of Article 34 is Case C-159/00, *Sapod Audic* [2002] ECR I-5031, para. 74.

5 Case 36/74, *Walrave and Koch* [1974] ECR 1405.

6 Case C-415/93, *Bosman* [1995] ECR I-4921.

7 Case 281/98, *Angonese* [2000] ECR I-4139.

workers *per se* but only with those provisions in as far as they implement the 'fundamental right' of non-discrimination.[8]

Sections 2 and 3 of this chapter are devoted to the deconstruction of this theory. Section 4 deals with a different theory of limitation that has dramatically turned into a theory of expansion: that of indirect effect. To some, the Court's decision in *Rioting Farmers*[9] to hold national authorities liable for failing to take adequate measures to remove physical obstructions to the free movement of goods seems like a promising idea which should be transported to the free movement of services *en lieu* of the doctrine of direct horizontal effect. In *Viking*,[10] however, both the Advocate General and the Court managed to suggest exactly the opposite: that the doctrine of indirect effect provides support for the idea that private parties are directly bound by the free movement provisions. The conclusion of the discussion so far will be that full direct horizontal direct effect of the regimes of the free movement of workers, the freedom to provide services and the freedom of establishment is the inescapable consequence of the Court's case law and that no effort to soften the blow survives scrutiny. Section 5 will deal briefly with the implications of this for the available public interest derogations from the free movement provisions. Section 6 concludes.

2. The institutional limitation: 'non-governmental regulatory bodies'

There can be little doubt that the Court's reasoning in *Walrave* was grounded in some notion of the functional equivalence to public authority of the International Cycling Union's power to issue 'rules aimed at regulating in a collective manner gainful employment and the provision of services'.[11] It held:

> The abolition as between Member States of obstacles to freedom of movement for persons and to freedom to provide services, which are fundamental objectives of the Community contained in Article 11 of the Treaty, would

[8] The theory is formulated in rudimentary form in P. Oliver and W. H. Roth, 'The Internal Market and the Four Freedoms', *Common Market Law Review* 41 (2004) 407–41, p. 426. Surprisingly, it seems to have *gained* currency after the trade union judgments in Case C-438/05, *Viking* [2007] ECR I-10779 and Case C-341/05, *Laval* [2007] ECR I-11767. See Dashwood, note 2 above; S. Prechal and S. A. de Vries, 'A Seamless Web of Judicial Protection in the Internal Market?', *European Law Review* 34 (2009) 5–25.

[9] Case C-265/95, *Commission* v. *France* [1997] ECR I-6959.

[10] Case C-438/05, *Viking* [2007] ECR I-10779.

[11] *Walrave and Koch*, note 5 above, para. 17.

> be compromised if the abolition of barriers of national origin could be neutralized by obstacles resulting from the exercise of their legal autonomy by associations or organizations which do not come under public law.
>
> Since, moreover, working conditions in the various Member States are governed sometimes by means of provisions laid down by law or regulation and sometimes by agreements and other acts concluded or adopted by private persons, to limit the prohibitions in question to acts of a public authority would risk creating inequality in their application.[12]

There is quite some support for the idea of fashioning this into some sort of generalized institutional test for direct effect. The personal scope of the Services Directive is limited to such bodies.[13] A respectable body of literature is committed to the general idea that horizontal effect is, or at least should be, limited to private entities that 'in a way take the place of public authorities',[14] to action that 'is not unlike State action',[15] or to instances where private parties are 'exercising regulatory tasks which would otherwise be exercised by public authorities in the state in question'.[16] And the Court seems stubbornly attracted to the idea, obsessively repeating the phraseology of *Walrave* in both apposite and inapposite places.

From the outset, however, there has been a tension between the explicit functionalism of *Walrave*'s mantra and the idea of a separate threshold test under the personal scope of the free movement provisions. The Court's reference to associations exercising their 'legal autonomy' points to a line of thinking that looks to establish some responsibility on the part of the State for the offending measures. Bluntly, the concern here is not to have the Member States 'get away' with something by mere formal classifications of organizations as 'private'. Even if the measure itself cannot be attributed to the State, it will still offend the free movement provisions if the power to take the measure stems from public action. The Dutch bar association in *Wouters* is probably the most obvious example of this, more obvious in any event than the UCI or UEFA, international organizations that cannot easily be said to derive their power from any particular grant of 'legal autonomy'. In *Viking*, the Court also considered that the organization of collective

[12] *Ibid.*, paras. 18 and 19.

[13] Article 4(9) of Directive 2006/123/EC on services in the Internal Market, OJ 2006 L376/36.

[14] Prechal and de Vries, note 8 above, p. 18.

[15] B. Cruz, 'Free Movement and Private Autonomy', *European Law Review* 24 (1999) 603, p. 618.

[16] P. A. J. Syrpis and T. A. Novitz, 'Economic and Social Rights in Conflict: Political and Judicial Approaches to Their Reconciliation', *European Law Review* 33 (2008) 411–27, p. 421.

action was 'covered' (*sic*) by the legal autonomy which trade unions enjoy pursuant to trade union rights accorded by national law.[17] It is perfectly obvious, however, that 'legal autonomy' cannot be a necessary condition under *Walrave*: that would directly contradict the functionalist logic underlying the references to the *effet utile* and uniformity of application of the Internal Market rules. 'Legal autonomy', then, is best understood not as an autonomous test but as an indication of something else.

The reference to 'collective regulation' represents a line of thinking that is more plausible under functionalist principles in as far as it sees to the activity engaged in by an organization and not to the source of its power. The idea here is clearly of functional equivalence to public regulatory authority, the realization that large chunks of modern economic life are regulated by private governance regimes of various descriptions such as, indeed, bar associations and sporting federations. What is far less obvious is whether the test seeks to identify inherently 'State-like' activity or just 'State-like' power to impede the freedom of movement. In many cases, these two categories will overlap: UEFA in *Bosman* and the bar association in *Wouters* can plausibly be seen to engage in the kind of regulatory activities that in both nature and effect are 'State-like' measures of the kind the free movement provisions seek to discipline. But only at a stretch could the same be argued for standard contract conditions of insurance companies,[18] or price-setting arrangements for medical services.[19]

One principled way to maintain *Walrave* as an autonomous test for the regulation of an inherently public nature would be to align it to the mirror image of the concept of an 'undertaking' under the competition rules.[20] There, the Court operates with a dichotomy not of public bodies and private entities, but of 'economic activities' on the one hand, and activities 'falling within the exercise of public powers' on the other,[21] a distinction it even uses to differentiate between the various activities of a

17 *Viking*, note 10 above, para. 35. In *Laval*, Advocate General Mengozzi relied heavily on the grant of 'considerable autonomy' and 'wide powers' to trade unions in the Swedish model of industrial relations in order to establish the analogy with the sports associations at issue in most of the relevant case law. Case C-341/05, *Laval* [2007] ECR I-11767, para. 160 of the Opinion. This may appear to leave some margin to argue that trade unions in less generous Member States could escape the free movement provisions. Dashwood's assessment here is apt: 'respectably arguable', but representing 'a forlorn hope'. Dashwood, note 2 above, p. 535.

18 See Case 251/83, *Haug-Adrion* [1984] ECR 4277.

19 See Case C-411/98, *Angelo Ferlini* [2000] ECR I-8081.

20 See, e.g., Snell, note 2 above.

21 The *locus classicus* here is Case C-41/90, *Höfner* [1991] ECR I-1979.

single entity.[22] It is clear, however, that the Court does not consider 'economic activities' immune from the free movement provisions: in *Wouters*, it was perfectly willing to apply the free movement provisions and the competition rules simultaneously.[23] The analogy with the competition rules is instructive. There, the Court is willing to exclude from the personal scope of Articles 101 and 102 TFEU 'public' activities and measures that most certainly offend the substantive prohibition of distorting competition.[24] Under the free movement provisions, however, it is precisely the ability to obstruct free movement that determines their personal scope whatever the nature or source of that ability: regulatory power, market power or even physical power. The point is made pointedly in *Ferlini* where the Court held it to follow from *Walrave* that Article 18 TFEU applies where a group or organization 'exercises a certain power over individuals and is in a position to impose on them conditions which adversely affect the exercise of the fundamental freedoms guaranteed under the Treaty'.[25] This collapse of the test under the personal scope was confirmed in *Laval*, where the ritualistic repetition of the *Walrave* rationale was followed by the mere observation that collective action is 'liable to make it less attractive, or more difficult' for the targeted foreign undertakings to carry out construction work in Sweden and therefore qualifies as a restriction of the freedom to provide services.[26] In *Viking*, finally, the Court seemed to let go completely of the *Walrave* test by explicitly denying any indication in the relevant case law 'that could validly support the view that it applies only to associations or to organizations exercising a regulatory task or having quasi-legislative powers'.[27] And yet, the implications of

[22] This development starts in Case C-82/01 P, *Aéroports de Paris* [2002] ECR I-9297, para. 74, and is taken to great complexity in Case C-39/07, *MOTOE* [2008] ECR I-4863, and Case 113/07 P, *SELEX* [2009] ECR I-2207.

[23] Case C-309/99, *Wouters* [2002] ECR I-1577.

[24] The Court's *effet utile* doctrine under the competition rules was, of course, devised to tackle precisely the problem of anti-competitive State measures. From the judgment in Case C-2/91, *Meng* [1993] ECR I-5751 onwards, however, that doctrine has been descending rapidly into farce. See W. Sauter and H. Schepel, *State and Market in EU Law* (Cambridge University Press, 2009), pp. 104 *et seq*.

[25] Case C-411/98, *Angelo Ferlini*, note 19 above, para. 50.

[26] *Laval*, note 17 above, para. 99. Advocate General Mengozzi, in para. 159 of his Opinion, makes the point more explicitly by arguing that the differences between private collective regulation on the one hand and industrial action on the other 'is important only in determining whether the collective action at issue constitutes an obstacle to the freedom to provide services', and has 'no bearing' on the question whether trade unions are in principle obliged to comply with the relevant provisions.

[27] *Viking*, note 10 above, para. 64.

this candour seem to have made the Court nervous enough to go to the extraordinary lengths of making the implausible argument that industrial action could still, after all, be classified as 'regulation' in that it should be regarded as 'inextricably linked' to the collective agreement the trade union was seeking to conclude.[28] No such escape route was available in *Angonese*, where the Court oddly rehearsed the *Walrave* rationale for the proposition that employment practices of a single undertaking were caught by the provisions on the free movement of workers.[29]

It is, then, it seems to me, impossible to maintain the view that there is an autonomous institutional test under the personal scope of the free movement provisions. Regulatory power and 'legal autonomy' are, rather, mere indications of what the Court is really looking for: the ability to obstruct free movement. Maduro unwittingly produced a fine summary of the case law in his view that 'the rules on free movement apply directly to any private action that is capable of effectively restricting others from exercising their right to freedom of movement'.[30]

3. The substantive limitation: 'direct discrimination'

In fairness, the Court obviously did not really, or at least not exclusively, rely on *Walrave* for the proposition that recruitment practices of single undertakings were subject to the discipline of Article 45 TFEU in *Angonese*. It supplemented the well-worn mantra with a brand new theory. With reference to its judgment in *Defrenne*,[31] the Court noted:

> The Court has ruled that the fact that certain provisions of the Treaty are formally addressed to the Member States does not prevent rights from being conferred at the same time to any individual who has an interest in compliance with the obligations thus laid down. The Court accordingly held, in relation to a provision of the Treaty which was mandatory in nature, that the prohibition of discrimination applied equally to all agreements

[28] *Ibid.*, para. 36. With Joerges and Rödl, 'Informal Politics, Formalised Law and the "Social Deficit" of European Integration: Reflections after the Judgments of the ECJ in Viking and Laval', *European Law Journal* 15(1) (2009) 1–19, p. 14, one would have thought that the right of collective action was intended to compensate precisely for the absence of regulatory power.

[29] *Angonese*, note 7 above, paras. 32 and 33.

[30] *Viking*, note 10 above, para. 43 of the Opinion. Maduro, of course, came to this conclusion without the slightest effort to work through the case law. Dashwood considers that Maduro's 'argument from first principles cannot be judged a success'. Dashwood, note 2 above, p. 534.

[31] Case 43/75, *Defrenne* [1976] ECR 455.

> intended to regulate paid work collectively, as well as to contracts between individuals.
>
> Such considerations must, *a fortiori*, be applicable to Article 45 of the Treaty, which lays down a fundamental freedom and which constitutes a specific application of the general prohibition of discrimination laid down in Article 18. In that respect, like Article 157, it is designed to ensure that there is no discrimination on the labour market.
>
> Consequently, the prohibition of discrimination on grounds of nationality laid down in Article 45 of the Treaty must be regarded as applying to private persons as well.[32]

The new rationale and the explicit exclusive reference to discrimination provide an alternative basis for the limitation of horizontal direct effect. In its modest form, the effort is just to limit the implications of *Angonese* on the personal scope of the free movement provisions.[33] In its more elevated manifestations, the theory would read *Angonese* with a 'fundamental rights twist' and hold that the prohibition of discrimination has undergone a 'crucial transformation' in that it is no longer primarily linked to market integration but to the protection of human dignity.[34]

This substantive theory is, of course, crucially dependent on the validity of some version of the institutional theory. The Court, after all, explicitly subjected UEFA to a 'market access' reading of Article 45 TFEU in *Bosman* that went far beyond mere discrimination.[35] More problematic still, the Court did the same for Article 49 TFEU in *Viking* and Article 56 TFEU in *Laval*.[36] Any attempt to limit horizontal direct effect to the prohibition of discrimination will thus have any chance of success only if it accepts the proposition that sporting federations and even trade unions are caught in a distinguishing, 'State-like' category of actors. The beauty of the substantive theory is, on the other hand, that its validity will in turn go a long way in keeping the institutional theory alive in that it disarms the import of *Angonese* itself in undermining it.

[32] *Angonese*, note 7 above, paras. 34 and 35. See also Case C-94/07, *Raccanelli* [2008] ECR I-5939, para. 45.

[33] See, e.g., Dashwood, note 2 above, p. 531 ('*Angonese* is not an authority for the application of the free movement provisions in horizontal situations in general, but only where direct discrimination practiced by a private sector employer impedes access to the labour market.').

[34] Prechal and de Vries, note 2 above, p. 17.

[35] *Bosman*, note 6 above, para. 96. See also Case C-176/96, *Lehtonen* [2000] ECR I-2681; and Case C-325/08, *Olympique Lyonnais* [2010] ECR I-2177.

[36] *Viking*, note 10 above, para. 72; and *Laval*, note 17 above, para. 99.

Let us, then, accept for the sake of argument that *Walrave* constitutes, if not a full-blown threshold test under the personal scope of the free movement provisions, then at least a valid basis for the differentiated application of their substance. The theory still remains weak at best. Some of the problems may seem like quibbles: for example, Dashwood's claim that *Angonese* only extends to direct discrimination is met not just by different understandings of the facts in *Angonese* itself,[37] but against the Court's repeated insistence that Article 18 TFEU covers indirect discrimination as well.[38] Even the claim that one can usefully distinguish between discrimination of any kind and other restrictions has been questioned, notably by Advocate General Mengozzi in *Laval* who even went so far as to caution against any attempt to impose such a limitation on the horizontal scope of Article 56 TFEU for the sake of 'the legal certainty of operators'.[39]

The deeper problem, however, lies in the relationship between the general prohibition of discrimination and the free movement provisions. If the theory is that Articles 45 and 56 TFEU insofar as they implement Article 18 TFEU create obligations for all private parties, while where they act as market freedoms they merely create obligations for Member States and 'State-like' organizations and associations, the implication must be that the scope of Article 18 is more limited than that of the free movement rules. Intuitive as that may seem, it is actually rather problematic. The Court has consistently held that the free movement provisions 'implement' the prohibition of discrimination in their respective domains and that, as a consequence, Article 18 only applies independently in areas not covered by those provisions.[40] With these mutually exclusive areas of application, the temptation is not just to have the free movement provisions 'implement' the prohibition of discrimination, but to have Article 18 'implement' Internal Market disciplines. And it can well be argued that the Court has not resisted. It has duly held that any rules that are compatible with Articles 45, 49 and 56 of the Treaty are also

[37] Advocate General Fennelly cautioned the Court against horizontal direct effect partly because 'the present case concerns an allegation of indirect discrimination on grounds of nationality, prohibition of which may present special problems and difficulties in the case of private economic actors'. *Angonese*, note 7 above, para. 41 of the Opinion.

[38] See, e.g., Case C-103/08, *A. Gottwald* [2009] ECR I-9117, para. 27.

[39] *Laval*, note 17 above, para. 228 of the Opinion. The statement seems a bit awkward in light of the fact that the Court itself is perfectly happy to make these distinctions in its choice of justification regimes. See below.

[40] Case 305/87, *Commission* v. *Greece* [1989] ECR 1461, para. 13.

compatible with Article 18,[41] but also that any rules that are incompatible with the free movement provisions are also incompatible with Article 18.[42] In *Ferlini*, it will be remembered, the Court claimed that it followed from *Walrave*, *Defrenne*, and *Bosman* that Article 18 applies to measures and actions that 'adversely affect the exercise of the fundamental freedoms guaranteed under the Treaty', language that seems clearly intended to convey an understanding of its scope that is closer to 'restriction' than it is to 'discrimination'.[43] It seems arguable, then, that, rather than Article 18 limiting the horizontal application of free movement provisions to discriminatory measures, the free movement provisions have stretched the horizontal application of Article 18 to capture any restriction of free movement.

4. The procedural alternative? Indirect effect

The relationship between market freedoms and fundamental rights also lies at the heart of the doctrine of the indirect effect of free movement, an issue that crops up in the discussion of horizontal direct effect in the most unexpected and contradictory ways. Faced with riots and protests physically obstructing transit routes at borders and tunnels, the Court decided to read the principle of Community loyalty into Article 34 TFEU in *Rioting Framers* and *Schmidberger* and devised a rule whereby Member States were held liable for not taking adequate measures to remove these 'barriers'.[44] On the face of it, these judgments were coping strategies for the absence of direct horizontal effect under the free movement of goods: to wit, *Rioting Farmers* was widely thought to be for the direct effect of Article 34 what *Marleasing* was for the direct effect of Directives.[45] Faced with the possibility of a strike by sailors unwilling to work under the rather worse conditions of a soon-to-be-reflagged ferry, however, both Advocate General Maduro and the Court in *Viking* relied on these judgments to hold trade unions *directly* liable under the freedom of establishment. True, the Court relied on them for the limited – and not very illuminating – observation that 'restrictions may be the result of actions by individuals or groups of such individuals rather than caused by the State', an observation it still held to 'support' the

41 Case 90/75, *Van Almeyde* [1977] ECR 1091, para. 27.
42 *Commission* v. *Greece*, note 40 above, para. 12.
43 *Angelo Ferlini*, note 19 above, para. 50.
44 *Commission* v. *France*, note 9 above; and Case C-112/00, *Schmidberger* [2003] ECR I-5659.
45 Case C-106/89, *Marleasing* [1990] ECR I-4135.

interpretation of Article 49 as being horizontally applicable.[46] Maduro, on the other hand, relied on them – and not on, say, *Walrave* or *Angonese* – to fashion his entire theory of direct horizontal effect. The thinking is deceptively simple and elegant: indirect effect and direct effect may differ in form, but 'there is no difference in substance': whether a case is brought against the public authorities for failure to rectify a problem or directly against the people causing the problem, the substantive issues and reconciliation of conflicting rights and freedoms are identical.[47] That being so, we can dispense with complex distinctions and categories under the personal scope of the free movement provisions and concentrate on complex distinctions and categories under their substance to come up with 'different levels of scrutiny' depending on the source and seriousness of the restrictions and the force and validity of competing claims.[48]

The novelty of Maduro's approach lies not in his reliance on indirect effect *per se*: it lies in the fact that most authors would draw exactly the opposite conclusion from the realization that indirect effect may well deal with identical substantive issues and lead to identical solutions to direct effect.[49] Most pointedly and authoritatively perhaps, Roth and Oliver rely on *Rioting Farmers* and *Schmidberger* for their suggestion that even *Defrenne*, in hindsight, 'went too far', and that the Court should abstain from applying the prohibition of discrimination directly to private persons altogether.[50]

There are at least two major problems with the theory. First, both Maduro and Roth and Oliver may be thought to read rather more into the obligations imposed on the public authorities in *Rioting Farmers* and *Schmidberger* than these judgments allow. In these cases, the remedy that the authorities were invited to provide consisted in wholly orthodox State tasks: to keep law and order, and to use the monopoly over the legitimate use of force to remove unruly citizens so that the transit of goods could be restored. Similarly, it is not unheard of that, in the last resort, collective action by trade unions is dealt with in like fashion. But it doesn't seem too fussy to point out that,

[46] *Viking*, note 10 above, para. 62. [47] *Ibid.*, para. 40 of the Opinion.

[48] *Ibid.*, para. 49 of the Opinion. Maduro has been charged with opening up a 'new can of worms' and introducing 'webs of complexity' by C. Barnard, 'Viking and Laval: An Introduction', *Cambridge Yearbook of European Legal Studies* 10 (2008) 463–92, pp. 469–72. Frankly, I have all sorts of problems with Maduro's approach, but I can't see how it produces more worms and complexity than the Court's current stance.

[49] See, e.g., Lohse, note 2 above.

[50] Oliver and Roth, note 8 above, pp. 428–9. These authors do, however, favour direct effect for 'collective regulation'.

surely, there is a difference between calling in the police to deal with physical obstruction of roads, tunnels and even construction sites on the one hand, and policing the market to the extent of interfering with insurance contracts, quality management standards, bylaws of professional associations and more to remove any 'restrictions' to free movement on the other. In the abstract, this extent of public intervention in the market is clearly at odds with the liberal tenets of the Internal Market. In the concrete, it may well be argued that the Court has refused to give *direct* horizontal effect to Article 34 TFEU precisely for fear of having to scrutinize private product standards, the procurement policies of supermarket chains, the labelling practices of small-scale 'home-grown' jam-makers and so on.

The main problem with Maduro's approach, however, lies in the fact that it presupposes the validity of the elevation of the free movement provisions to the status of 'fundamental' freedoms, or even rights. His observation that direct and indirect horizontal effect are identical 'in substance' was backed up with a copious footnote referencing works concerning the issue of the horizontal effect of fundamental rights in German and comparative constitutional theory, most notably Kumm's 'Who's Afraid of the Total Constitution?'.[51] The purpose and effect of that doctrine, however, are clearly to 'constitutionalize' private law in the sense of ensuring the primacy of the political constitution in economic and social life. To be sure, there are instances where the analogy fits: *Defrenne* may be the prime example, and at a stretch even *Angonese* and *Bosman* could be argued to be concerned with the injection of constitutional discipline into market relations. In the case of *Viking* and *Laval*, however, the analogy descends into a complete turn-around:[52] there, horizontal direct effect injects market discipline into the constitutionally protected rules of engagement of social partners. If we cannot distinguish between market freedoms and fundamental rights, we cannot distinguish between a constitutionalized market and a marketized constitution. We may manage to live without fear of the total constitution, but a total market is a much scarier proposition.

[51] M. Kumm, 'Who's Afraid of the Total Constitution? Constitutional Rights as Principles and the Constitutionalization of Private Law', *German Law Journal* 7 (2006) 341–69. Further references are to the magnificent R. Alexy, *A Theory of Constitutional Rights*, 1st edn (Oxford University Press, 2002); and M. Tushnet, 'The Issue of State Action/ Horizontal Effect in Comparative Constitutional Law', *International Journal of Constitutional Law* 1 (2003) 79–98.

[52] Joerges and Rödl, note 28 above, note 59.

5. The cushion: the justification regime

A more popular objection to direct horizontal effect finds its roots in the derogations available to private parties, the familiar list of public interest objectives that were obviously not identified with the interests and constraints of private parties in mind.[53] In *Bosman*, the Court seemed wholly unimpressed with the argument, and held:

> There is nothing to preclude individuals from relying on grounds of public policy, public security or public health. Neither the scope nor the content of those grounds is in any way affected by the public or private nature of the rules in question.[54]

The Court has shown itself quite liberal in some instances. In *Olympique Lyonnais*, it accepted the 'objective of encouraging the recruitment and training of young players' as an 'overriding reason in the public interest', albeit subject to scrutiny for proportionality.[55] More seriously, in *Laval* it accepted the protection of workers against 'social dumping' as such.[56] If horizontal direct effect is here to stay, however, there is little doubt that the Court will have to become more liberal still,[57] to the inevitable further detriment of the robustness and coherence of the justification regime. As it stands, the justification regime completely precludes the two main reasons why individuals would offend the rules of an Internal Market with undistorted competition: because it is in their best economic interest and because they feel like it. Whether one is ideologically inclined to accept the tenets of liberty and autonomy or not, it is difficult to argue that the freedom to define and pursue one's self interest is not at the very heart of the Internal Market.[58]

First, the shift from *Bosman* to *Olympique Lyonnais* is the familiar expansion of justifications expressly provided for in the Treaty to include

[53] See, e.g., H. Roth, 'Drittwirkung der Grundfreiheiten?' in O. Due, M. Lutter and J. Schwarze, (eds.), *Festschrift für Ulrich Everling* (Baden-Baden: Nomos, 1995), p. 1231, p. 1242; and Snell, note 2 above, p. 231.

[54] *Bosman*, note 6 above, para. 86. [55] *Olympique Lyonnais*, note 35 above, para. 39.

[56] *Laval*, note 17 above, para. 103.

[57] Advocate General Maduro proposes a balancing exercise which involves an assessment of 'the force and validity of competing claims of private autonomy'. *Viking*, note 10 above, para. 49 of the Opinion. In that light, it may be worth pointing out the obvious fact that the protection of private autonomy does not, and cannot, appear as a justification. See Oliver and Roth, note 8 above, p. 427.

[58] See, e.g., R. Streinz and S. Leible, 'Die unmittelbare Drittwirkung der Grundfreiheiten', *Europäische Zeitschrift für Wirtschaftsrecht* 15 (2000) 459.

the judicially created general category of 'overriding reasons in the public interest'.[59] For the category of 'State-like' associations engaged in 'collective regulation', this arrangement may be thought sufficient: one is entitled to expect 'State-like' measures to further 'public interest' objectives. The Court insists, however, that the open category of public interest objectives is open only to non-discriminatory measures: discriminatory action can only be justified under the headings of the objectives explicitly mentioned in Article 52.[60] And this presents a rather enormous problem for private individuals caught by the *Angonese* ruling: of all the reasons, good or bad, that employers and plumbers may have to choose their workers and clients, some of them may well be considered discriminatory, and none of them is very likely to make much sense under the headings of 'public policy, public security or public health'.

Even the general public interest justification has its limits, however: the Court insists that reasons of an 'economic nature' do not qualify.[61] The distinction between 'economic' reasons and other grounds is tenuous at best for measures taken by public authorities, and will likely be even less convincing for private action. The cultural and social benefits associated with the encouragement and training of young players in *Olympique Lyonnais*, for example, are to be produced by a fee paid to the clubs who encouraged and trained these players when they move to another club. It is hard to see a principled distinction that separates this policy of ensuring a return on investment and maintaining the financial viability of smaller clubs from 'economic' reasons. Similarly, the sinister connotations of 'social dumping' in *Laval* may well be thought to justify action to protect workers 'in the public interest'. But, again, it is difficult to see a bright line between protection against 'social dumping' and, say, protection against 'price competition'.[62]

If the Court persists in its case law on the horizontal scope of the prohibitions of the free movement provisions, it seems inevitable that it will have to expand the justification regime to the point of reducing the

[59] See Case C-55/94, *Gebhard* [1995] ECR I-4565, para. 37.

[60] See, e.g., Case C-153/08, *Commission* v. *Spain* [2009] ECR I-9735, paras. 36–7.

[61] See, e.g., Case C-260/04, *Commission* v. *Italy* [2007] ECR I-7083, para. 35.

[62] One could argue, of course, that, if the Court has been willing to fashion a non-economic public interest test under the competition rules, it may as well fashion an economic public interest test under the free movement rules. See Case C-519/04 P, *Meca-Medina* [2006] ECR I-6991, para. 45 (exempting the International Olympic Committee's anti-doping rules from the scope of Article 101 TFEU because they are 'justified by a legitimate objective' (*sic*)).

market disciplines imposed on private actors to very little. And that end result will be entirely in tune with the result of large chunks of the Court's case law in other areas which was supposed to ensure the 'effectiveness' of the Internal Market, from the *effet utile* doctrine to *Courage* v. *Crehan* to *CIA Security* and its progeny: very little useful effect at the cost of rather a lot of legal uncertainty and, preferably, fragmentation of national private law systems.[63]

6. Conclusion

Very few people, I suspect, would consider the Court's case law on the direct horizontal effect of the free movement provisions to be one of its proudest achievements. Maduro's Opinion from left field in *Viking* has had at least the merit of dispensing with the shaky premises and untenable distinctions that produce the cloudy incoherence of the Court's case law. By the same token, Maduro's cheerfulness should make us very wary: the total market may be a lot more fearsome than the total constitution, but the scariest position of all is to find ourselves unable to tell the difference.

[63] See Schepel, 'The Enforcement of EC Law in Contractual Relations: Case Studies in How Not To "Constitutionalize" Private Law', *European Review of Private Law* 5 (2004) 661–73, on the ramifications of Case C-453/99, *Courage* v. *Crehan* [2001] ECR I-6297 and Case C-194/94, *CIA Security* [1996] ECR I-2201.

9

The EU Services Directive and the mandate for the creation of professional codes of conduct

PANAGIOTIS DELIMATSIS*

1. Introduction

The European Commission's Proposal for a Services Directive (hereinafter 'the Proposal')[1] recognized the importance of the concept of trust in the achievement and the smooth functioning of a genuine internal market for services. The lack of trust reveals the absence of a 'thinking European' mentality[2] and is translated into protectionist interests that aim to foreclose foreign competition. Protectionism can be the result of the concern that foreign (intra- or extra-EU) suppliers deliver their services more efficiently or, on the contrary, that foreign suppliers are not as good as the domestic ones and therefore regulatory intervention is justified to internalize the ensuing externality. Following the first, rather self-interest approach or the second, more benevolent, public-interest approach, does not alter the result: domestic markets sometimes impose unduly burdensome restrictions which curtail the mobility of foreign professionals within the Union. Furthermore, the lack of trust negates the possibility of comparison and thus obliterates any motivation for domestic service suppliers to improve their services.[3]

* I am grateful to Petros Mavroidis, Aukje van Hoek, Vanessa Mak, Matteo Negrinotti, Linda Senden and the workshop participants for thoughtful insights. Remaining errors are the author's alone.

1 European Commission, Proposal for a Directive of the European Parliament and of the Council on Services in the Internal Market, COM(2004) 2, 13 January 2004.

2 European Commission, The State of the Internal Market for Services, COM(2002) 441 final, 30 July 2002, p. 45.

3 For the positive effects of mutual trust more generally, see the seminal work by F. Fukuyama, *Trust: The Social Virtues and the Creation of Prosperity*, 1st edn (New York: Free Press, 1995).

Hence, services and service suppliers from other Member States are viewed with suspicion and considered to threaten the allegedly 'exceptional' quality and safety of services produced domestically.[4] The abolition of the country-of-origin principle cynically demonstrates the absence of mutual trust at the current stage of European integration and how long and winding the road may be until mutual trust among the Member States is actually established. Building trust is a macro-process deeply rooted in the history of European integration and a continuous challenge for such a diverse region in terms of economic strength, regulatory approaches, or constitutional and cultural background.[5] In the end, this process forms an integral part of the *telos* of the European adventure.

Among the trust-enhancing instruments[6] identified in the proposed and the adopted Services Directive,[7] a prominent role is given to the creation of pan-European codes of conduct dealing with rules of professional ethics.[8] In the absence of the country-of-origin principle, the creation of codes of conduct at European level as a soft method of rule-making acquires new dynamics. Codes of conduct, while soft-law instruments, partake in the effort to guarantee a high level of quality and safety commensurate with the ever-increasing expectations of the EU citizens with a view to enhancing trust among Member States regarding the equivalence of services and service suppliers originating in other Member States.

This chapter aims to explore the impact of codes of conduct on the liberalization of professional services. Effective market access for service

[4] This suspicion typically takes the form of systematic application of the host country rules; the simple evocation of 'general good' objectives to justify obstacles, without verifying the equivalence of the protection in the country of origin or the proportionality of the restriction; the subjection of EU operators to the same system as that applied to third country undertakings; the presumption of circumvention of national rules by any cross-border service; or a particular zeal in regularly checking suppliers from other Member States. See European Commission, note 2 above, pp. 53–4.

[5] Also J. Delhey, 'A Trade-off between Enlargement and Integration? An Analysis of Trust between EU Nationalities', WZB Discussion Paper (July 2005), p. 13, available at http://bibliothek.wzb.eu/pdf/2005/i05–203.pdf (last visited 2 September 2010).

[6] Cf. European Commission Recommendation on measures to improve the functioning of the Single Market, OJ 2009 L176/17, Recital 9.

[7] Directive 2006/123/EC of the European Parliament and of the Council of 12 December 2006 on services in the internal market, OJ 2006 L376/36. For a detailed account of the Directive, see C. Barnard, 'Unravelling the Services Directive', *Common Market Law Review* 45 (2008) 323–94.

[8] Cf. recital 7 of the Services Directive.

suppliers can depend heavily on such codes, which are typically adopted by non-State, self-regulated bodies. While such (mostly voluntary) rules of conduct are aimed to improve the quality of the services supplied by the professionals subject to such rules, they can nevertheless hinder the intra-EU movement of professionals. Therefore, liberalization of factor mobility enshrined in primary and secondary EU law or agreed on during State-to-State negotiations at a multilateral level can be jeopardized by the adoption and application of such codes.

2. Setting the scene: the Services Directive

In 2002, the Commission, in its report on 'The State of the Internal Market for Services',[9] which formed part of the internal market strategy for services adopted by the Commission in December 2000,[10] was adamant about the never-ending tale of completing the internal market for services. Complex legal barriers have been substituted for physical and technical barriers, thereby reducing the possibility of a genuine, integrated, internal market for services. The fragmented approach of regulating service supply within the European Union is worrisome, as it negatively affects the competitiveness of European firms and leaves a high potential for growth untapped.[11] And yet, services account for two-thirds of total employment and for all new employment growth within the Union.[12]

That being said, services are more vulnerable to regulations impeding their supply. This chilling effect is due to the peculiar nature of services: services are typically non-tangible, non-storable and, above all, heterogeneous with limited possibilities of mass production. In addition, many of the most 'effective' barriers to free movement of services relate to pre- or post-establishment of juridical and natural persons.[13] In addition, quality, the 'holy grail' of every law or regulation governing services, is closely intertwined with the characteristics, qualifications, experience and so forth of

[9] European Commission, note 2 above. See also M. Monti, 'A New Strategy for the Single Market', 9 May 2010, p. 37.

[10] European Commission, Internal Market Strategy – Priorities 2003–2006, COM(2003) 238, 7 May 2003.

[11] European Commission, Towards a better functioning Single Market for services – building on the results of the mutual evaluation process of the Services Directive, COM(2011) 20, 27 January 2011.

[12] European Commission, New European Labour Markets, Open to All, with Access for All, COM(2001) 116 final, 28 February 2001.

[13] P. Delimatsis, *International Trade in Services and Domestic Regulations – Necessity, Transparency, and Regulatory Diversity* (Oxford University Press, 2007), p. 70.

each individual service provider. These characteristics of service regulations increase transaction costs and undermine the pursuit of efficiency when regulating this highly heterogeneous sector of the economy.

The Directive ambitiously aims to eliminate remaining legal barriers to the achievement of the Internal Market in services, while ensuring legal certainty for service suppliers and consumers. It adopts a horizontal approach based on the understanding that, while ubiquitous and diverse, several service sectors call for regulatory intervention to pursue a certain set of legitimate policy objectives which appears to be common to more than one sector such as consumer protection, the integrity of the profession, or ensuring the quality of the service.

The objective of the Directive is to enable both service suppliers and consumers to benefit from the fundamental freedoms guaranteed in Articles 49 and 56 TFEU, that is, the freedom of establishment and the freedom to provide services.[14] In this respect, the Directive consolidates previous Court of Justice case law on related issues.[15] While numerous sectors are excluded from its scope, the Directive applies to business services and covers, *inter alia*, most of the regulated professions within the EU. Additionally, *ratione materiae*, the Directive adopts a sweeping definition of the term 'requirements'.[16]

The Directive calls for the creation of single contact points for service providers, the establishment or maintenance of electronic procedures, the promotion of quality in services supplied and the establishment of effective administrative cooperation among the Member States. It also requires the review of national legislation and calls for mutual evaluation reports at the end of the transposition period.[17] Furthermore, it consolidates the legal framework for many services and has the potential to reduce the red tape and remaining barriers in the service sector, while promoting the modernization of practices and procedures, notably through the creation of one-stop shops.[18] The Directive also incorporates both mandatory and

[14] Cf. Article 16(2)(a).

[15] See, *inter alia*, Case C-55/94, *Gebhard* [1995] ECR I-4165, paras. 22–7.

[16] Article 4(7) of the Services Directive; also European Commission (DG Internal Market and Services), *Handbook on Implementation of the Services Directive* (2007), p. 16.

[17] European Commission Staff Working Paper on the process of mutual evaluation of the Services Directive, SEC(2011) 102 final, 27 January 2011.

[18] These points of single contact are not to be equated to the contact points envisaged in Directive 2005/36. Contrary to the latter, which essentially serve as information desks, the former should allow service suppliers to complete all procedures and formalities regarding access and exercise of service activities. This can also entail the recognition of professional qualifications.

voluntary best-endeavour provisions,[19] reflecting the intense bargaining that preceded its adoption. For the remaining obstacles to the free movement of services and the freedom of establishment, the Directive calls for respect of the principles of necessity, proportionality and non-discrimination.

Ratione personae, the Directive only applies to service suppliers that are nationals of an EU Member State (for natural persons) and to legal persons within the meaning of Article 54 TFEU[20] which are established in a Member State. On the other hand, services supplied by non-nationals of a Member State or by entities not established in any of the EU Member States fall outside the scope of the Directive.[21] Thus, services and service suppliers from non-EU Member States do not benefit directly from this new framework. Nevertheless, the endeavours to simplify procedures and 'screen' unnecessary obstacles to the supply of services across the EU as a result of the implementation of this Directive can reasonably be expected to generate indirect benefits for all non-EU services and service suppliers seeking to provide services within the EU.[22]

Thus, even in the absence of the country-of-origin principle, the effect of the Directive should not be underestimated. Rather, it is a major step towards further developing mutual trust. Fighting ignorance of EU law at the national level and lack of transparency regarding national measures affecting the delivery of services, as well as levelling the playing field with regard to the protection of public interest, is to a certain extent an appropriate way forward to further enhance trust among Member States. Mutual confidence cannot come 'out of the blue', and 'invisible hands' are simply a chimera when it comes to the cognitive part of trust, as exemplified by the unfortunate 'Polish plumber' narrative.

3. The mandate for the creation of pan-European codes of conduct

3.1 The legal obligation enshrined in the Services Directive

The Directive incorporates a convergence programme aiming at, *inter alia*, a targeted harmonization in specific areas such as access to the

19 Sometimes *within* a single provision. Cf. Article 26 of the Services Directive.

20 Article 54 TFEU makes reference to companies or other legal persons constituted according to the legislation of a Member State which have their registered office, central administration or principal place of business within the EU.

21 Also recital 37 of the Services Directive, above.

22 See, e.g., Article 15 of the Services Directive, above.

activity of judicial recovery of debts, private security services and the transport of cash and valuables. An important part of this chapter forms the mandate directed to the Member States and the Commission to encourage the establishment of pan-European codes of conduct. Article 37 of the Directive reads:

> Member States shall, in cooperation with the Commission, take accompanying measures to encourage the drawing up at Community level, particularly by professional bodies, organisations and associations, of codes of conduct aimed at facilitating the provision of services or the establishment of a provider in another Member State, in conformity with Community law.

In the absence of a top-down approach the country-of-origin principle would substantiate, the Directive puts an emphasis on the merits of a bottom-up approach in which the private sector is called upon to fulfil a decisive role and serve the objective of furthering European integration. While technically forming part of Chapter VII of the Directive, the mandate incorporated in Article 37 regarding the creation of pan-European codes of conduct is deemed an essential component of the Directive's most important objectives, as depicted notably in Chapter V of the Directive, to improve the quality of the services supplied within the Union and to enhance transparency as to the conditions regulating access to and exercise of a given profession in the various Member States.[23]

Codes of conduct appear to be particularly relevant for the so-called 'regulated professions'[24] within the EU legal order where compulsory registration with the corresponding professional associations also exists.[25] Regulated professions have two important characteristics: first, registration with the professional association is compulsory. Second, these professions are self-regulated for the most part. Compulsory registration allows for sanctions against those professionals who do not abide by the rules established by the professional body, including deontological rules usually contained in the sectoral codes of conduct. However, not all professions oblige the individuals concerned to register with the professional association. The mandate of Article 37 is equally – if not more – important for non-regulated professions, as the uniformity of

[23] Handbook, note 16 above, p. 62.

[24] Article 3(1)(a) of Directive 2005/36/EC of the European Parliament and of the Council of 7 September 2005 on the recognition of professional qualifications, OJ 2005 L255/22.

[25] The use of codes of conduct seems also to be appealing in respect of other areas of services such as information society services.

rules of ethics that apply to them across the Union can be even looser. A common set of rules for these professions will enhance quality and gain the trust of consumers, while allowing for the identification of those who may be 'cheating'.

3.2 *Why create pan-European codes of conduct?*

Codes of conduct exemplify the collapse of the traditional public/private divide and underscore the non-dichotomic reality that soft-law developments imply. Because of the manifest abundance of non-governmental collective rules in this area, including codes of conduct, Member States and the Commission recognize the beneficial effects of drawing up common sets of rules pertaining to issues such as independence, impartiality or professional secrecy, which would apply to a given profession exercised across the Union. As professional associations become the final 'masters' of the pursuit of the corresponding profession at a national level (setting both pre- and post-access-related rules), typically through a governmental act that delegates its regulatory powers to the associations, some alignment of the ethical or other rules regulating the profession may have positive effects for the integration of the EU services market. In addition, the risk of abuse may be particularly high in cases where domestic suppliers, in their function as members of the domestic professional association, may be called upon to decide on the aptitude of a service supplier originating in another Member State and intending to establish herself in that market or applying for an authorization to deliver her services in a cross-border manner.[26]

The *status quo* with diverse codes of conduct agreed exclusively at a national level hints at a national perception of the quality of services. Furthermore, the fact that some professions in a given Member State are not subject to a domestic code of conduct may create prejudice in other Member States with regard to the quality of the services supplied by the members of these professional associations and ultimately lead to a certain distrust (in particular, when the services are supplied cross-border) and to market fragmentation.[27] Therefore, the function of the codes of conduct is two-fold: they facilitate mobility of service suppliers (mobility-enabling function) and enhance trust in services and service

[26] Cf. Case C-169/07, *Hartlauer* [2009] ECR I-1721.

[27] European Commission (DG Internal Market and Services), *Enhancing the Quality of Services in the Internal Market: The Role of European Codes of Conduct* (2007), p. 6.

suppliers originating in other Member States (confidence-building function). Codes of conduct will lead to the identification of a minimum, acceptable level of quality when a given service is supplied and, more importantly, to the emergence of a European concept of 'quality of service' in given services sectors which would be an identifiable trait of these sectors throughout and beyond the Union.

The creation of pan-European codes of conduct would simplify the current conundrum with several national codes of conduct applying to situations which go beyond national borders. For instance, take the case of the Lawyers Establishment Directive,[28] which establishes a mechanism for the mutual recognition of professional titles of migrant lawyers desiring to practise under their home-country professional title. This Directive provides that a European lawyer must comply not only with the rules of professional conduct applicable in her home Member State but also with those of the host Member State, failing which she would incur disciplinary sanctions and exposure to professional liability.[29] Nevertheless, *quid iuris* when these rules are conflicting? Or with services for which it cannot be determined in which Member State they are actually supplied? Situations of this type call for coherent solutions. Finally, the nature of other rules such as limitations on the types of services that can be supplied or on the legal form under which such services are allowed to be supplied may have a dissuasive effect on professionals from other Member States otherwise capable of exercising the fundamental freedoms enshrined in Articles 49 and 56 TFEU.

3.3 *What content for the pan-European codes of conduct?*

The Directive does not contain any specific guidance with respect to the form of such codes of conduct nor to their content. For instance, it does not attempt to hint at what 'ensuring the quality' entails or what should be the level of protection pursued.[30] Rather, it bluntly spells out the *telos*

[28] Directive 98/5 of the European Parliament and the Council of 16 February 1998 to facilitate practice of the profession of lawyer on a permanent basis in a Member State other than that in which the qualification was obtained, OJ 1998 L77/36.

[29] *Ibid.*, Articles 6 and 7.

[30] The Court appears to be ready to accept the Commission deciding on the level of protection which may be acceptable at EU level, having regard to the public interest pursued by the various Member States: Case C-233/94, *Germany* v. *Parliament and Council* [1997] ECR I-2405, paras. 16 and 17; also C-168/98, *Luxembourg* v. *Parliament and Council* [2000] ECR I-9131, paras. 43–4.

of the mandate, that is, the facilitation of free movement pursuant to the Treaty.[31] Absent any further specifications under Article 37, the recitals preceding the main body of the Directive are highly informative. Thus, it is first made clear that pan-European codes of conduct should aim to ensure the quality of the service supplied and at the same time take into consideration the specificities of the profession at issue.

In Article 26(3), the link is made between quality assurance, consumer protection and cooperation between professional bodies and consumer associations at EU level. This provision requires that the Member States, together with the Commission, enact appropriate measures to instigate cooperation of private associations at the EU level to promote the quality of services, notably by facilitating the proper assessment of the competence of a given provider. Reducing the existing information asymmetries would lead to enhanced consumer protection and enable informed choices by consumers. Furthermore, the compatibility of codes of conduct with legally binding rules relating to professional conduct at national level and competition law at EU level should be ensured.[32]

In more general terms, codes of conduct typically codify traditional virtues that have demarcated a given profession for decades or even centuries,[33] usually going beyond what law prescribes.[34] They comprise rules relating to independence, impartiality, loyalty, professional competence and integrity, trustworthiness, confidentiality, conflict of interest, charging of fees and professional secrecy. Codes of conduct typically include rules about desirable behaviour (value orientation) and rules about prohibited behaviour (compliance orientation).[35] Such rules are related to professional conduct, but they may also call for a certain

[31] In this sense, codes of conduct have a *post*-law function in that they supplement and support the practical application of secondary law, *in casu*, the Services Directive. At the same time, they have a *para*-law function in that they are intended as an alternative to EU legislation. See L. Senden, *Soft Law in European Community Law* (Oxford: Hart Publishing, 2004), pp. 214–15.

[32] Recital 113 of the Services Directive. On the applicability of the EU competition rules to codes of conduct, see section 5 below.

[33] Cf. Article 2.2 of the Code of Professional Conduct, adopted by the Council of Bars and Law Societies of Europe (CCBE) in 1988 and most recently amended in 2006.

[34] The concept of codes of conduct also encompasses elements that, in practice, may be found in quality charters. The latter comprise exclusively rules describing the manner in which the service is to be provided.

[35] A. Nijhof, S. Cludts, O. Fisscher and A. Laan, 'Measuring the Implementation of Codes of Conduct – An Assessment Method Based on a Process Approach of the Responsible Organisation', *Journal of Business Ethics* 45 (2003) 65–78, p. 66.

private lifestyle.[36] Furthermore, depending on the specifics of the profession, they define the conflicting interests and ideally hierarchize them. For instance, Article 2.7 of the Code of Professional Conduct adopted by the Council of Bars and Law Societies of Europe (CCBE) stipulates that the primary allegiance of a lawyer should be to her client, sacrificing her own interest and that of her colleagues.[37]

In several professional services, such as legal services, codes of conduct may require that professionals be covered by professional liability insurance[38] for errors and omissions the level of which will depend on the nature and extent of the risk.[39] As compliance with this latter rule is typically reflected in the final price of the service delivered, agreement on common rules appears to be essential to avoid unfair price-based competition. For instance, competition can be distorted when domestic professionals are obliged to conclude such insurance, whereas cross-border suppliers or suppliers temporarily providing their services may not be bound by such a rule in their home State. The cross-border suppliers would not have to internalize any insurance cost in the final cost of their service and thus can offer the service at a lower price.

Finally, codes of conduct often include provisions on disciplinary sanctions in case the rules are not abided by, although often this deterrent is only used *in abstracto* and mentioned as a mere possibility.[40] However, civil or even penal sanctions cannot be excluded in the case of serious infringement.[41]

In addition to these basic, mostly fiduciary standards, of particular importance for our purposes are two areas where the Directive contains fairly detailed rules on the legality of restrictions: the first relates to commercial communications while the second refers to the establishment of multi-disciplinary practices.

Rules governing commercial communications typically form part of codes of conduct in several services sectors.[42] Restrictions ranging from outright prohibitions on advertising to strict control of content are particularly burdensome for professionals or legal persons who are not established in a given jurisdiction and thus they can become known in

[36] Cf. Article 2 of the International Code of Ethics adopted by the International Bar Association (IBA) in 1956, as amended in 1988.

[37] Note 33 above. [38] Cf. Article 23(5) of the Directive.

[39] The Services Directive hints at this possibility and the need for the conclusion of professional insurance cover. See recitals 98 and 99 and Article 23 of the Directive.

[40] Article 1.2.1 of the CCBE Code of Professional Conduct, note 33 above.

[41] European Commission, note 27 above, p. 9. [42] Article 4(12) of the Directive.

that market only through this type of promotional activity. Contrary to the case of goods, such rules impede the pursuit of a pan-European promotional campaign.

Article 24 of the Directive invites Member States (but also professional bodies and private associations regulating the pursuit of a given profession in a collective manner) to remove all outright bans on commercial communications by the regulated professions, such as bans on all advertising in one or more media of communication.[43] Manifestly, the Directive does not seek to question the utility of prohibitions on the *content*, but only those restrictions relating to the chosen *form* of commercial communication.[44] The link with codes of conduct is made in Article 24(2), which requires Member States to ensure that communications of this type are consistent with professional rules which are in conformity with EU law. These rules, usually enshrined in voluntary codes of conduct, set conditions and qualifications with respect to the independence, dignity and integrity of the profession or the appropriate conduct relating to professional secrecy. The Directive requires that such rules be non-discriminatory, justified by an overriding public interest requirement and compatible with the principle of proportionality. In addition, they have to be *specific* to the nature of the profession at issue. This specificity requirement calls for a case-by-case analysis of rules limiting commercial communications. The Directive acknowledges the need for a bottom-up approach whereby the professionals themselves should agree on pan-European rules governing the suitability of the content and methods of commercial communications in their own profession, which will form an integral part of the pan-European codes of conduct for this profession.[45]

Furthermore, Article 25 of the Directive seeks the removal of requirements limiting the exercise of different activities jointly or in partnership where such restrictions are not necessary to ensure the impartiality, independence and integrity of the regulated professions or to guarantee compliance with the rules governing professional ethics.[46] The Directive further specifies that several restrictions on such partnerships can be tolerated, such as certification, accreditation, technical monitoring and testing services, insofar as a close link with the objective of ensuring the independence and impartiality of the providers in question is established.[47]

[43] Also recital 100 of the Directive.
[44] In practice, the distinction between the two may not be made so straightforwardly.
[45] Recital 100 of the Directive. [46] Recital 101 of the Directive.
[47] Cf. Articles 25(3) and 39 of the Directive; also Handbook, note 16 above, p. 66.

However, in the case where Member States decide to allow the creation of multi-disciplinary partnerships, the Directive requires that Member States guarantee the prevention of conflicts of interest and the independence and impartiality of the providers. The Directive also alludes to the findings of the *Wouters* case by reiterating the importance of adopting rules of professional ethics, typically incorporated in professional codes of conduct, which are compatible with the activities that are represented in these partnerships, especially when professional secrecy may be put in jeopardy.[48] In addition, and again based on the Court's findings in *Wouters* and the Directive, a separate examination of the specific nature of the relevant professions is warranted to uphold or deny the legality of restrictions against multi-disciplinary practices.[49]

Harmonization with regard to rules of multi-disciplinary partnerships will also decrease the compliance costs for those service suppliers which have already adopted this business model in one Member State, but, due to restrictions in other Member States, they cannot exercise their fundamental freedoms guaranteed by the Treaty.[50] In fact, nowadays the clientele is increasingly sophisticated and hence the delivery of a complete range of services such as legal, accounting and tax advice within the same house renders the latter fairly attractive.[51] Moreover, restrictions on such partnerships may be more justifiable in certain services but not in others. Putting *Wouters* aside, it seems that there are feeble arguments justifying restrictions in partnerships between architects and engineers where the independence of professionals may not be as important as in other services such as legal services or accounting, the homogeneity of which is contentious at best.

It follows that, although the Directive adopts a rather liberal approach *vis-à-vis* the content of codes of conduct, allowing considerable room for manoeuvre to professional bodies to self-regulate their industry and establish deontological rules in coordination with their counterparts in other Member States, it adopts a more meddling stance towards the need for common rules relating to commercial communications and multi-disciplinary practices. The semantics are obvious: the chances that these categories of rules hinder the establishment of a genuine internal market

[48] Cf. Case C-309/99, *Wouters* [2002] ECR I-1577, para. 104.

[49] *Ibid.*, paras. 101–3; also European Commission, note 2 above, p. 19.

[50] European Commission, Extended Impact Assessment of Proposal for a Directive on Services in the Internal Market, Commission Staff Working Paper, SEC(2004) 21, 13 January 2004, p. 20.

[51] What the Court called the 'one stop shop advantage' in *Wouters*, above, para. 87.

and distort competition are high and therefore particular attention and action at EU level is warranted.

3.4 *Additional functions of codes of conduct*

Codes of conduct can be used by courts as supplementary means of interpretation.[52] This can be another reason for professional associations to use codes of conduct as a marketing tool,[53] i.e., to accentuate the importance and uniqueness of their profession for the entire society, which as a consequence may justify a different treatment from public regulatory authorities and courts at the national or, *in casu*, the supranational level.[54]

Thus, codes of conduct serve an imperative function for a given services (sub-)sector. They enunciate its professional norms and reassure external parties (consumers, colleagues, the government and society as a whole) of the integrity, competence and the high standards enforced and maintained in the sector.[55] Rules incorporated in codes of conduct thus aim to codify obligations that the professionals have to abide by to deserve the trust of their clients and of society overall. By adhering to such standards, professionals become trustworthy.

The CCBE Code of Conduct is again revealing in this respect when it emphasizes the role of legal professional privilege, noting that '[c]onfidentiality is . . . a primary and fundamental right and duty of the lawyer' and that '[w]ithout the certainty of confidentiality there cannot be trust'.[56] Indeed, confidentiality and professional secrecy protect the client from indiscreet disclosures which may harm his integrity and reputation.[57] Interestingly, the Code goes on to suggest that the respect for this principle serves not only the interest of the client, but also that of the administration of justice and therefore deserves to be protected by the State.[58] In *AM & S*,[59] the Court

52 Cf. Case C-506/04, *Wilson* [2006] ECR I-8613, para. 65; also Joined Cases C-94/04 and 202/04, *Cipolla* [2006] ECR I-11421, para. 63. In the WTO context, see Panel Report, *EC – Tariff Preferences*, para. 7.16.

53 European Commission, 'Instruments for a Modernised Single Market Policy', SEC (2007) 1518, 20 November 2007, p. 12.

54 Cf. Article 1.1 of the CCBE Code of Professional Conduct, note 33 above.

55 N. Higgs-Kleyn and D. Kapelianis, 'The Role of Professional Codes in Regulating Ethical Conduct', *Journal of Business Ethics* 19 (1999) 363–74, p. 364.

56 Article 2.3.1 of the CCBE Code of Professional Conduct, note 33 above.

57 Opinion of Advocate General Maduro in Case C-305/05, *Ordre des barreaux francophones and germanophones and Others* [2007] ECR I-5305, point 41.

58 Cf. ECHR, *Foxley* v. *United Kingdom*, Judgment of 20 June 2000, para. 50.

59 Case 155/79, *AM & S Europe Ltd* v. *Commission* [1982] ECR 1575.

of Justice concurred with this view and upheld the principle of confidentiality of written communications between lawyers and clients. More generally, confidentiality and professional secrecy is 'an obligation of discretion forming part of the ethics of a profession'.[60]

Viewed from this angle, codes of conduct also describe the conduct which the recipients of services are *entitled* to from professionals abiding by the codes of conduct and thus create expectations as to the quality standard for a given service. The role of the governing professional body is crucial on this score due to its autonomous, self-regulatory power and the control that it exerts over its members. Professional bodies are there to ensure that professional traditions are adhered to.

3.5 Materializing the mandate: a peculiar public–private partnership

Professional associations are called upon to set up pan-European codes of conduct for their own discipline, taking into account the peculiarities of their profession and ensuring that rules guaranteeing independence, impartiality, integrity and professional secrecy are agreed upon.[61] Moving away from command-and-control regulation, the Directive recognizes the reality of self-regulation in many business services and calls upon individuals concerned and their associations to participate in the shaping of rules and to decide on a common, pan-European set of rules on professional ethics and conduct of a non-coercive nature which would suit them best.[62] While the Directive remains silent as to the appropriate method for drawing up a code of conduct, the Commission underscored the significance of conforming to principles of good governance during that process.[63]

The procedures should be open, publicly accessible, fair, non-discriminatory and objective. They should be communicated in advance to all stakeholders involved (including consumers) to ensure transparency, inclusiveness and representativeness. Whereas allowing professional bodies to regulate their own matters boils down to a question of social coherence, this upgrading of the role of private associations also calls for reforms and restructuring to ensure compliance with current demands

[60] Opinion of Advocate General Maduro in Case C-305/05, *Ordre des barreaux francophones and germanophones and Others* [2007] ECR I-5305, point 37.

[61] Recital 114 of the Directive. [62] Proposal, note 1 above, 9.

[63] European Commission, note 27 above, p. 10.

for internal and external transparency, due process, legitimacy, accountability, fairness and inclusiveness.

While 50 per cent of European professional organizations have already drawn up a European code of conduct for their profession,[64] others are not that advanced or successful in their efforts to create such codes of conduct.[65] In addition, one can infer that the Commission is not always satisfied with existing codes of conduct, as it appears that several of them do not respect basic standards of transparency, participation, representativeness, integration or responsibility.[66] This would manifestly mean that, insofar as codes of conduct created at EU level are explicitly warranted and thus the role of codes of conduct should be viewed from a new perspective, existing codes of conduct would need to be revisited to ensure that they comply with fundamental principles of good governance.

It is for the Member States to take all the necessary measures to encourage professionals to implement the pan-European codes of conduct at the national level. Member States are allowed to take more stringent measures if they consider that the level of protection adopted at EU level is not commensurate with domestic preferences and peculiarities. By the same token, domestic professional bodies can seek higher levels of protection in their existing or future national codes of conduct.[67] Viewed from this angle, pan-European and national codes of conduct can coexist and complement each other. Nevertheless, in order not to deprive the Directive and the mandate relating to the creation of pan-European codes of conduct of its *effet utile*, Member States and professional bodies should be able to justify the particular situations that justify the stringency of the rules or conditions at the national level. The Commission, assisted by the Article 40 Committee, will be in charge of supervising the implementation of the Directive.

The creation of codes of conduct becomes a shared obligation of Member States and the Commission, which cannot be materialized without the active involvement of the private parties affected (or their associations) pursuant to Article 37. This tripartite approach aims to bring together the most important actors in the regulation of business services across the Union. Just as under Article 26 where Members are

[64] See, e.g., the codes of the Architects' Council of Europe and the European Tax Federation.
[65] European Commission, note 27 above, p. 10. [66] *Ibid.*
[67] Recital 115 of the Directive.

required to encourage action by private parties,[68] Article 37 requires that Member States, in cooperation with the Commission and (obviously) with associations representing service suppliers, such as professional bodies or chambers of commerce as well as consumer associations, take practical steps so that service suppliers and professional associations create codes of conduct at European level to enable full use of the freedom to provide services and the freedom of establishment.

This privileged role of the Commission is ordained not only by its function as *Hüterin der Verträge* (Guardian of the Treaties) according to Article 17(1) TEU,[69] but also in the aftermath of the Interinstitutional Agreement of 2003 on better law-making.[70] Abandoning the previous rigid top-down approach and in a clear shift away from hierarchical forms of governing,[71] the Union adopted a new legislative culture according to which consultations enhance the involvement of interested parties and improve the quality of the policy outcome,[72] whereas alternative modes of regulation of both a legislative and a non-legislative nature enacted at the periphery complement and sometimes replace legislative action at EU level to achieve more effectively the objectives pursued.[73] The binary objective of diversifying the Union's regulatory instruments and improving the regulatory environment is essentially driven by the concern to improve the effectiveness, legitimacy, transparency and legal certainty of regulation within the Union.[74] This has been in line with the paradigm shift in domestic administrative laws and practices across – mainly – developed countries in Europe and North

[68] Cf. Article 26(1)(b). In addition, under Article 26(5) of the Directive, the development of voluntary (obviously industry-driven) compatibility standards at EU level should be actively encouraged.

[69] Case C-531/06, *Commission* v. *Italy* [2009] ECR I-4103.

[70] European Parliament/Council/Commission, Interinstitutional Agreement on Better Law-Making, OJ 2003 C321/1.

[71] P. Craig and G. de Búrca, *EU Law – Text, Cases, and Materials*, 4th edn (Oxford University Press, 2008), p. 146.

[72] European Commission, Towards a reinforced culture of consultation and dialogue – General principles and minimum standards for consultation of interested parties by the Commission, COM(2002)704, 11 December 2002, p. 5; cf. Article 11 TEU.

[73] This is in accordance with the principle of subsidiarity. See Protocol No. 30 to the Treaty on the Application of the Principles of Subsidiarity and Proportionality. According to the Protocol, '[w]here appropriate and subject to the need for proper enforcement, EU measures should provide Member States with alternative ways to achieve the objectives of the measures'. *Ibid.*, para. 7.

[74] N. Walker and G. de Búrca, 'Reconceiving Law and New Governance', *Columbia Journal of European Law* 13 (2007) 519–37.

America towards less rigidity and more power-sharing with private parties.[75]

There are very good reasons for delegating the creation of such codes of conduct to the relevant bodies: First, it is the most cost-efficient solution due to the specialized knowledge of the professionals and their organized bodies, but also because of the professionals' ability to react more quickly and flexibly to new circumstances and adapt or revise their rules.[76] Second, the choice of this type of instrument leads to wider ownership of the policies at stake, which appears to be essential when it comes to enforcement and compliance with rules of a *non*-binding nature. Third, nowadays, legitimizing influential rules set out in the exercise of private authority which may by now be *de facto* binding and complied with by the individuals in their capacity as members of the professional associations becomes pressing, and hence an inclusive approach leading to the integration of these voices in rule-making and rule-shaping is required.[77] Fourth, the internationalization of the professions and the subsequent relativization of borders and jurisdictions also appear to advance this type of solution.[78] The desire inherent in this mandate is that, where EU institutions and politics have largely failed, private rule-making may provide solutions that will come from the fated expansion of business across borders and the increasing demands of customers for first-rate delivery of services regardless of geographical borders and competent fora.

Setting aside the concern that delegating regulatory power to professional bodies can constitute legitimizing a cartel with a wide ability to determine or influence the regulatory framework and access to the profession to the benefit of professionals/members of the 'club' but to the detriment of consumers,[79] the European Union moves towards a direction that aligns itself with the principle of subsidiarity[80] and the

[75] Cf. J. Scott and D. Trubek, 'Mind the Gap: Law and New Approaches to Governance in the European Union', *European Law Journal* 8 (2002) 1–18, p. 8.

[76] The Mandelkern Report used as the ultimate criterion the satisfaction of the user, and suggested that public intervention may be warranted only when the user is not satisfied. See Mandelkern Group on Better Regulation, Final Report (2001), pp. 14–15.

[77] After all, participation is one of the five principles of good governance identified in the Commission's White Paper on Governance.

[78] Cf., with respect to legal services, Case C-193/05, *Commission* v. *Luxembourg* [2006] ECR I-8673, para. 45.

[79] Cf. F. C. Zacharias, 'The Myth of Self-Regulation', *Minnesota Law Review* 93 (2009) 1147–1190, p. 1173.

[80] Also Lisbon European Council, Presidency Conclusions, 23–24 March 2000, para. 38.

2003 Interinstitutional Agreement.[81] The Agreement explicitly refers to codes of practice and sectoral agreements as examples of self-regulation.[82] It goes on to underscore that the choice of such a voluntary, decentralized instrument does not imply any preferred solutions by the EU institutions nor does it preclude any future action by them.

In this Agreement, a central role was entrusted to the Commission when recourse is made to alternative methods of regulation.[83] The involvement of the Commission is likely to become even more active when self-regulation substitutes EU action in an area that comes under EU competence, such as the creation and proper functioning of a genuine internal market for services. In addition, the Commission will report to the other EU legislating institutions on the successes or failures of this experimental transfer of regulatory power. In this regard, the Commission is bound to examine the extent of representativeness of the parties concerned, the sectoral and geographical coverage and the added value of the commitments at stake.[84] Even so, concerns remain regarding this peculiar intersection that may be occurring between the Commission and powerful professional associations, which can be neither transparent nor comprehensible to EU citizens, thereby creating a grey area of *de facto* legislating without democratic legitimacy.[85] Importantly, the Agreement stipulates that recourse to a legislative act based on a Proposal by the Commission may be necessary when the self-regulatory body fails to comply with the Treaty or when the competent legislative authority requests it. This is yet another piece of evidence that the classic 'Community method' is hale and hearty.

4. Applicability of Articles 49 and 56 TFEU to private action

In the universe of non-legislative, voluntary instruments adopted by private actors, the question of the possibility for the private parties affected to have recourse to legal remedies becomes pressing.[86] As with other soft-law instruments, codes of conduct can support a normative discourse similar to hard law. While violations of legal obligations are

[81] Interinstitutional Agreement, note 70 above. [82] *Ibid.*, para. 22.

[83] *Ibid.*, para. 17. [84] *Ibid.*, para. 23.

[85] Cf. the report by M. Ortega, 'On Institutional and Legal Implications of the Use of "Soft Law" Instruments', available at www.europarl.europa.eu (last visited 1 September 2010), p. 6.

[86] Cf. P. Delimatsis, 'The Enforcement of Transnational Private Regulation – The Case of Professional Services', TILEC Discussion Paper 2011-045, September 2011.

perhaps more striking, soft undertakings can stimulate 'accountability politics' provided that they entail manifest normative commitments.[87] Thus, a strategy of 'name and shame' can be very effective, notably in the area of professional services where individualism and personal reputation are still significant. As the boundaries between legally binding State action and essentially voluntary private action are increasingly blurred, and private authority sometimes emerges as a law-maker of similar effectiveness to public authority, the scope *ratione materiae* and the value of the fundamental freedoms is growing. It is commonplace now that the fragmentation of the internal market for services also results from the divergent standards adopted by non-public bodies in Member States, such as professional associations, sports federations, social partners drawing up collective agreements, or interested parties or groups adopting codes of conduct or collective rules in the exercise of their legal autonomy.

Settled case law of the Court makes clear that circumventing the abolition of State barriers to market integration through obstacles stemming from rules (or the application thereof) set out by associations or organizations not governed by public law that are entrusted with broad legal autonomy and regulatory power cannot be allowed.[88] Indeed, rules of *any* nature set out by private bodies aimed at regulating gainful (self-) employment and the supply of services in a collective manner can impede the functioning of the internal market and thus come within the purview of the free movement provisions of the Treaty.[89]

Recognizing that the activities of market participants can be significantly hampered by private action, the Court interpreted the fundamental freedoms in a broad manner with a view to enabling market participants to have adequate judicial protection and equal opportunities to gain access anywhere in the EU.[90] Consequently, the traditional approach, according to which horizontal effect was only applicable with regard to the rules of competition, whereas the rules on free movement only had vertical effect,

[87] K. W. Abbott and D. Snidal, 'Hard and Soft Law in International Governance', *International Organization* 54 (2000) 421–56, p. 452.

[88] Case 36/74, *Walrave* [1974] ECR 1405, paras. 17 and 23–4; Case 13/76, *Donà* [1976] ECR 1333, paras. 17 and 18; Case C-415/93, *Bosman* [1995] ECR I-4921, paras. 83–4; Case C-176/96, *Lehtonen* [2000] ECR I-2681, para. 35; Case C-309/99, *Wouters* [2002] ECR I-1577, para. 120.

[89] Case C-519/04, *Meca-Medina* v. *Commission* [2006] ECR I-6991, para. 24.

[90] Also D. Edward and N. Nic Shuibhne, 'Continuity and Change in the Law Relating to Services' in A. Arnull, P. Eeckhout and T. Tridimas (eds.), *Continuity and Change in EU Law – Essays in Honour of Sir Francis Snyder* (Oxford University Press, 2008), p. 243.

was abandoned.[91] Furthermore, the Court found that the provisions on the free movement of workers had not only vertical, but also horizontal, effect in *Clean Car*[92] and *Angonese*,[93] noting that the application of Article 45 TFEU only to public authority acts would disregard the fact that working conditions are typically governed by both public law and rules adopted by private persons. Thus, these rulings extended the *Defrenne* case law[94] into the area of free movement of workers.

The attempt of the Court to adopt a coherent approach towards the acceptance of the horizontal effect of the fundamental freedoms is more than obvious. In *Schmidberger*,[95] the Court found that private action should be subject to the provisions on the free movement of goods. In this case, it applied horizontally the fundamental freedom by balancing the fundamental right to freedom of expression of a group of individuals who were demonstrating against a transport company exercising its rights deriving from the Treaty relating to the free movement of goods.[96] Even if the action in *Schmidberger* was brought against the State, the facts in the record suggested that the State was a third party in a situation where the constitutional rights of one private party were being jeopardized by the actions of another.[97]

In *Viking*,[98] the Court had to decide, *inter alia*, on the horizontal effect of Article 49 TFEU on the freedom of establishment, that is, whether a private undertaking can derive rights from this provision on which it can rely against a trade union or an association of trade unions. The Court had no difficulty in confirming the application of its settled case law relating to horizontal effect also to Article 49 TFEU, *mutatis mutandis*.[99] The Court suggested that the collective action taken by the trade unions and the association thereof is liable to restrict the exercise of the freedom of establishment by another private party and thus violates Article 49 TFEU.[100] In previous cases, the Court applied the free movement provisions to private action, notably when its aim was to bear on working conditions and access to

[91] See, e.g., Case 41/74, *Van Duyn* [1974] ECR 1337, paras. 4–8.
[92] Case C-350/96, *Clean Car* [1998] ECR I-2521, paras. 19–21.
[93] Case C-281/98, *Angonese* [2000] ECR I-4139, paras. 33–4 and 36.
[94] Case 43/75, *Defrenne* [1976] ECR 455, paras. 31 and 39.
[95] Case C-112/00, *Schmidberger* [2003] ECR I-5659, paras. 57 and 62.
[96] Also Case C-265/95, *Commission* v. *France* [1997] ECR I-6959, para. 30.
[97] Advocate General Maduro's Opinion in *Viking*, Case C-438/05, *International Transport Workers' Federation and the Finnish Seamen's Union* [2007] ECR I-10779.
[98] *Ibid.* [99] *Ibid.*, para. 61. [100] *Ibid.*, paras. 72–3.

employment[101] or, in the case of sports associations, due to their powerful influence over the organization of professional sport.[102]

Accordingly, the Court, by rather focusing on the activity at stake, is determined to outlaw any provision of any nature which could be capable of preventing or deterring an EU citizen from leaving her home country to exercise her right to free movement. Any sign of disadvantaging the nationals of another Member State in the territory of a given Member State, which subsequently impedes or renders less attractive the use of the Treaty fundamental freedoms, can be sufficient to trigger the application of the free movement provisions.[103] In *Mobistar*, for instance, the Court submitted that rules which have the effect of making the provision of services between Member States more difficult than within one Member State are to be outlawed.[104]

In case the exercise of fundamental rights is in conflict with the exercise of the free movement, the Court will attempt to strike a balance between the facts of the case and the interests at stake. Nonetheless, neither fundamental rights nor fundamental freedoms are absolute.[105] The Court is willing to take up this daunting task, absent any serious attempt by the State to resolve the matter in a satisfactory manner. The Court's case law hints at the need for a more pro-active and reflexive reaction from the State when such issues are raised to avoid recourse to judicial means. Indeed, Member States can and should interfere with private rules by appropriate legislation or court decisions at any time. Given the risk of bias that may characterize private rules, State intervention may become essential in restoring the balance of rights and obligations or in complying with the obligations enshrined in the Treaty.

Nevertheless, this may not be the end of the story for our purposes of examining the consistency with EU law of restrictions based on codes of conduct. Even if non-discriminatory, a restriction on free movement cannot be sustained unless it pursues an EU-consistent legitimate objective, is justified by overriding reasons of public interest and complies with the proportionality principle. In *Gebhard*,[106] and more recently in

[101] Case C-281/98, *Angonese* [2000] ECR I-4139; and Case C-438/00, *Deutscher Handballbund* [2003] ECR I-4135.

[102] For the relevant case law, see note 88 above.

[103] Case C-442/02, *CaixaBank France* [2004] ECR I-8961, para. 11.

[104] Case C-545/03, *Mobistar* [2005] ECR I-7723, para. 30.

[105] Cf. Article 52(1) of the Charter of Fundamental Rights of the European Union. See also Advocate General Maduro's Opinion in *Viking*, note 97 above, point 23.

[106] Case C-55/94, *Gebhard* [1995] ECR I-4165.

Wouters, the Court found or implied that national measures liable to hinder or make less attractive the exercise of the right to free movement can be justified, based, *inter alia*, on professional ethics considerations. Hence, the protection of professional ethics can be considered as a legitimate, overriding reason of public interest.[107]

It follows that, when examining the compliance of codes of conduct rules with EU rules on fundamental freedoms, the rules of professional conduct and ethics will be examined as a justification for the violation of free movement rules. Therefore, what would seem to be of paramount importance under this constellation is the extent to which the measure that allegedly substantiates or is based on a rule of ethics and conduct complies with the principle of proportionality, that is, it is suitable for the attainment of the objective pursued and does not go beyond what is necessary in order to attain it.[108] Again, governmental rules may override compliance with such ethical rules. For instance, in the case of an organized campaign to combat illegal activities, such as money-laundering, limitations on the principles of confidentiality and professional secrecy can be considered as proportionate and justified.[109]

5. The relevance of EU competition rules

Rules of professional conduct come within the scope of EU competition law, as they organize and influence the exercise of a given profession.[110] The compatibility with EU law of rules contained in codes of conduct may be contentious when examined through the lens of competition law. Such an examination is, however, necessary to ensure that equally competitive conditions are offered to the economic operators active in the EU market.[111]

There are five principal categories of rules relating to professional services that may be inconsistent with EU competition rules. These relate to: price-fixing; recommended prices and minimum fees;[112] restrictions

[107] Or rules justified by the 'general good'. See also Cases 33/74, *Van Binsbergen* [1974] ECR 1299, para. 12; and Case 71/76, *Thieffry* [1977] ECR 765, para. 12. See, by analogy, with regard to the reputation of a given services sector, Case C-384/93, *Alpine Investments* [1995] ECR I-1141, paras. 42–4.

[108] See, *inter alia*, Case C-415/93, *Bosman*, above, para. 104; also Joined Cases C-171/07 and 172/07, *Apothekerkammer des Saarlandes* [2009] ECR I-4171.

[109] Case C-305/05, *Ordre des barreaux francophones and germanophones and Others* [2007] ECR I-5305, and the Opinion of Advocate General Maduro in this case.

[110] Case T-144/99, *Institut des mandataires agréés* [2001] ECR II-1087, para. 64.

[111] Case C-49/07, *MOTOE* [2008] ECR I-4863, para. 51.

[112] Also recital 73 of the Services Directive.

relating to commercial communications; entry requirements and reserved rights; and regulations relating to legal form, ownership and multi-disciplinary practices.[113] In several instances, professional bodies have included these types of restrictions in their codes of conduct and linked them to the proper conduct of the profession or the interests of the consumer.[114]

Empirical studies suggest that the theoretical perception alleging that a causal link exists between heavy regulation and better quality of professional services supplied does not hold.[115] Economic theory further demonstrates that delegating regulatory authority, i.e., granting to a professional body a monopoly right to self-regulate the pursuit of a professional service and thus allowing it to restrict entry to the profession, would generate important economic rents in the form of excess revenues for the incumbents.[116] Prices in this case would be higher without there being any indication of quality improvement. For instance, in *Cipolla*, the Commission argued that no causal link had been established between the setting of minimum levels of fees and a high qualitative standard of legal services.[117]

In *Meca-Medina*, the Court made explicit that, even in the absence of economic activity, the non-application of the provisions on free movement does not exclude the application of Articles 101 and 102 TFEU.[118] Rather, a separate analysis should be undertaken to examine (1) whether the rules governing the activity are created by an undertaking; (2) whether this undertaking restricts competition or abuses its dominant position; and (3) whether this restriction or abuse affects intra-EU trade.

The concept of 'undertaking' under EU law is relative. Case law gives a functional content to this concept by considering as an undertaking 'any entity engaged in an economic activity irrespective of its legal status and the way it is financed'.[119]

113 European Commission, Report on Competition in Professional Services, COM(2004) 83, 9 February 2004, p. 3.

114 See, more recently, the Commission Decision of 24 June 2004 on the recommended prices for Belgian architects, Case COMP/38.2549.

115 OECD, Competition in Professional Services, DAFFE/CLP(2000)2, 2000.

116 See J. Tirole, *The Theory of Industrial Organization* (Cambridge, MA: MIT Press, 1988).

117 Joined Cases C-94/04 and 202/04, *Cipolla* [2006] ECR I-11421, para. 63.

118 Case C-519/04, *Meca-Medina* v. *Commission* [2006] ECR I-6991, paras. 30–1.

119 Case C-41/90, *Höfner and Elser* [1991] ECR I-1979.

Liberal professions, *inter alia*, come under this definition. In *Wouters*, the Court ruled that lawyers are undertakings within the meaning of EU competition law, as they offer services against remuneration, and bear the financial risks that failures may entail.[120] By the same token, in *CNSD*,[121] customs agents were considered as undertakings, whereas, in *Pavlov*,[122] medical specialist doctors also came under this term. This would obviously apply to the overwhelming majority of the service suppliers delivering professional services. Furthermore, *à la Wouters*, the professional body should be considered as an association of undertakings that adopts a collusive behaviour pursuant to Article 101 TFEU in that it influences the conduct of its members on the market in the relevant services sector and directs them to act in a particular manner when they carry out their economic activity.[123] Thus, rules created in the exercise of the body's regulatory autonomy such as the adoption of codes of conduct (or of certain rules therein such as those relating to advertising or price-fixing) constitute a decision adopted by an association of undertakings within the meaning of Article 101(1) TFEU.[124] Like the concept of undertaking, the notion of an 'association of undertakings' is relative in that the activity under scrutiny becomes the decisive criterion.[125] Sufficient governmental involvement and mixed situations entailing public–private cooperation where the observance of predefined public interest criteria is warranted shields the body governing professional conduct from the purview of Article 101.[126] Nonetheless, the standard of review will be fairly strict in assessing the role of public authority in the measure under scrutiny. In *Van Eycke*, and later in *Arduino*, the Court clarified that a violation of Articles 4(3) TEU and 101 TFEU occurs when (1) a Member State divests its rules of legislative character through delegation to private economic actors of the responsibility to take decisions affecting the economic sphere, or (2) a Member State requires or even encourages collusive behaviour contrary to Article 101 or reinforces its effects.[127]

120 Case C-309/99, *Wouters*, above, para. 49.

121 Case C-35/96, *Commission* v. *Italy (CNSD)* [1998] ECR I-3851, para. 37.

122 Case C-180/98, *Pavlov* [2000] ECR I-6451.

123 Case C-309/99, *Wouters*, paras. 63–4.

124 *Ibid.*, para. 71. Also Case T-144/99, *Institut des mandataires agréés*, above, para. 62.

125 A. J. Vossestein's annotation of *Arduino* and *Wouters*, in *Common Market Law Review* 39 (2002) 841–63, p. 853.

126 Case C-35/99, *Arduino* [2002] ECR I-1529, paras. 37–9.

127 *Ibid.*, para. 35; and Case 267/86, *Van Eycke* [1988] ECR 4769, para. 16; also Case C-250/03, *Mauri* [2005] ECR I-1267, paras. 29–37.

Any activity, in turn, consisting of offering goods or services in a given market is deemed an economic activity.[128] Case law suggests that the concept of 'economic activity' is to be interpreted broadly to include any activity which is capable of being carried out by a profit-making organization and under market conditions.[129] An association of undertakings can itself be an undertaking if it performs such an economic activity. Non-profit entities are still to be considered as undertakings if they compete in the same market with entities which seek to make a profit.[130] The size of the entity or the extent of its economic success does not play a decisive role.[131] An entity can partially exercise public authority and not come under the purview of the competition rules, but still be subject to the competition rules if it undertakes additional activities within a competitive market on which a number of undertakings act in competition.[132] However, entities whose activities are exclusively social or of public interest and are not pursued in competition with other economic agents in the relevant market are excluded from the scope of competition rules.[133]

Decisions that affect trade between the Member States[134] and which *de facto* or *de jure* prevent, restrict or distort intra-EU competition are void by virtue of Article 101(2) TFEU. The so-called intra-Community clause is, again, interpreted broadly to cover any behaviour which may have an influence, direct or indirect, actual or potential, on intra-EU trade in a way that can hinder the attainment of the Single Market.[135] The relevant market can be the domestic market only or even certain regions thereof.[136] As the Commission puts it, in this type of case, 'the nature of the alleged infringement, and in particular its propensity to foreclose the national market, provides a good indication of the capacity of the agreement or practice to affect trade between Member States'.[137]

128 Case C-49/07, *MOTOE* [2008] ECR I-4863, para. 22.

129 Case C-264/01, *AOK Bundesverband* [2004] ECR I-2493, paras. 50 and 58.

130 Case C-222/04, *Cassa di Risparmio di Firenze* [2006] ECR I-289, paras. 122–3.

131 Opinion of Advocate General Lenz in C-415/93, *Bosman* [1995] ECR I-4921, point 255.

132 For instance, the city of Trier was deemed an undertaking: Case C-475/99, *Ambulanz Glöckner* [2001] ECR I-8089.

133 Case C-222/04, *Cassa di Risparmio di Firenze* [2006] ECR I-289, paras. 120–1.

134 Joined Cases 56/64 and 58/64, *Consten and Grundig* [1966] ECR 429. See also the Commission's Guidelines on the effect on trade concept contained in Articles 81 and 82 of the Treaty, OJ 2004 C101/81.

135 Case C-295/04, *Manfredi* [2006] ECR I-6619, para. 42.

136 Case C-475/99, *Ambulanz Glöckner* [2001] ECR I-8089, para. 38.

137 Commission's Guidelines, note 134 above, para. 77.

Regarding the effect, it should be appreciable (*de minimis* rule)[138] and is to be established based on both quantitative and qualitative elements.[139] Of particular importance is the attempt to identify those practices which are *capable* of hampering trade among Member States[140] in a manner which might harm the attainment of the objectives of the Single Market, notably by partitioning markets on a national basis or hindering the economic interpenetration in contrast to the objectives of the Treaty. In *CNSD*, the Court clarified that agreements extending over the whole of the territory of a Member State have, *by their very nature*, such an effect.[141]

Even so, these provisions do not aim to penalize every single agreement or decision that restricts the freedom of action of the parties or of one of them. Article 101 TFEU is to be interpreted in a manner that accommodates EU or national policies which are non-economic in nature.[142] Thus, courts should juxtapose the anti-competitive effects against the objectives of the agreements or decisions and the overall context in which the agreements or decisions are concluded or produce their effects. Furthermore, they have to examine whether the consequences which restrict competition are in fact inherent in the pursuit of those objectives and are limited to what is necessary to ensure the proper conduct of the profession, as it is organized in the Member State at stake.[143] In this analysis, then, the peculiarities of the domestic market and of the specific profession will have a central role.[144] In *Institut des mandataires agréés*, the Court of First Instance opined that the rule enshrined in the relevant codes of conduct had to be assessed against 'its impact on the freedom of action of the members of the profession and on its organization and also on the recipients of the services in question'.[145]

[138] Commission's Notice on agreements of minor importance which do not appreciably restrict competition under Article 81(1) of the Treaty establishing the European Community (*de minimis*), OJ 2001 C368/13.

[139] Joined Cases C-215/96 and 216/96, *Bagnasco and Others* [1999] ECR I-135, paras. 47 and 60.

[140] Case C-55/96, *Job Centre* [1997] ECR I-7119, para. 36.

[141] Case C-35/96, *Commission* v. *Italy (CNSD)* [1998] ECR I-3851, para. 48.

[142] R. Nazzini, 'Article 81 EC between Time Present and Time Past: A Normative Critique of "Restriction of Competition" in EU Law', *Common Market Law Review* 43 (2006) 497–536, p. 503. *Contra* O. Odudu, *The Boundaries of EC Competition Law – The Scope of Article 81* (Oxford University Press, 2006); also Case C-67/96, *Albany* [1999] ECR I-5751, paras. 52–60.

[143] Case C-519/04, *Meca-Medina* v. *Commission* [2006] ECR I-6991, paras. 42 and 47; and Case C-309/99, *Wouters* [2002] ECR I-1577, para. 97.

[144] Joined Cases C-94/04 and 202/04, *Cipolla* [2006] ECR I-11421, para. 68.

[145] Case T-144/99, *Institut des mandataires agréés* [2001] ECR II-1087, para. 65.

In *Wouters*, the Court found that outright prohibitions of multi-disciplinary practices in the legal profession are inconsistent with Article 101(1)(b) TFEU because they are liable to limit production and technical development,[146] as they do not allow the exploitation of the one-stop-shop advantage, the supply of 'full service' and the possible diminution of costs. However, the Court submitted that the rules at issue were designed to ensure the proper conduct of the profession and the sound administration of justice and therefore were justified and proportionate, thereby striking a balance between the anti-competitive behaviour and the pursuit of non-economic legitimate objectives which may, however, have pro-competitive effects. By the same thinking, anti-doping rules, while *prima facie* restrictive of competition, were justified because they were designed to ensure fair rivalry among athletes and complied with the principle of proportionality.[147] State compulsion can also function as a defence under Article 101. It cannot, however, be invoked when the national law merely allows, encourages or makes it easier for undertakings or associations to engage in autonomous anti-competitive conduct.[148]

It remains to be examined whether, when adopting rules enshrined in codes of conduct, the professional associations can act inconsistently with Article 102 TFEU relating to abuse of dominant position. Settled Court of Justice case law portrays this concept as 'a position of economic strength enjoyed by an undertaking which enables it to prevent effective competition being maintained on the relevant market by giving it the power to behave to an appreciable extent independently of its competitors, customers and ultimately of its consumers'.[149] Importantly, in *MOTOE*, the Court clarified that an undertaking can, *inter alia*, acquire a dominant position when it is granted special or exclusive rights enabling it to determine whether and under what conditions other undertakings can have access to the relevant market and supply their services. It further found that granting such special and exclusive rights to undertakings within the meaning of Article 106(1) TFEU would violate Articles 102 and 106(1) if it is liable to create a risk of an abuse of a dominant position.[150]

146 Case C-309/99, *Wouters* [2002] ECR I-1577, para. 90.
147 Case C-519/04 P, *Meca Medina* [2006] ECR I-6991.
148 Case C-198/01, *Consorzio Industrie Fiammiferi* [2003] ECR I-8055, paras. 52–6.
149 Case 27/76, *United Brands* v. *Commission* [1978] ECR 207, para. 65.
150 *Ibid.*, para. 50; also C-41/90, *Höfner and Elser* [1991] ECR I-1979, para. 29.

By analogy, a professional association which has been granted the power to self-regulate the conditions of a given professional activity, as well as the power to decide on the well-foundedness of applications for authorization to exercise a given professional activity, could be considered an undertaking to which a Member State has granted special rights within the meaning of Article 106(1). However, this would presuppose that a professional association that has previously been considered as an association of undertakings is also an undertaking itself for the purposes of Article 102. As noted earlier, economic activity is a precondition for the applicability of Article 102. A professional association, however, does not carry out an economic activity coming within this provision.[151]

Alternatively, Article 102 can apply if it can be proven that there is a collective dominant position where several undertakings which are legally independent of each other present themselves to act together on a particular market as a collective entity.[152] As all professionals can be regarded as undertakings within the meaning of EU competition rules, Article 102 TFEU could arguably apply in the case of a highly concentrated and homogenous profession such as accountancy if it can be ascertained that economic links exist between the undertakings or professional service suppliers which enable them to act together independently of their competitors, their customers and consumers.[153] In *Wouters*, the Court rejected the applicability of Article 102 to the legal profession arguing that lawyers 'are not sufficiently linked to each other to adopt the same conduct on the market with the result that competition between them is eliminated' and that the legal profession 'is highly heterogenous and is characterised by a high degree of internal competition' without sufficient structural links between lawyers.[154] Again, even if a collective dominant position is upheld, it needs to be demonstrated that abuse of such a position has occurred, as clarified in *Piau*.[155]

6. Conclusion

The implementation of the Directive should bring new dynamics to the creation of effective codes of conduct and the building of trust among the

[151] Case C-309/99, *Wouters* [2002] ECR I-1577, para. 112.
[152] Joined Cases C-395/96 and 396/96, *Compagnie Maritime Belge Transports SA* [2000] ECR I-1365, para. 36.
[153] *Ibid.*, paras. 42 and 111.
[154] Case C-309/99, *Wouters* [2002] ECR I-1577, paras. 113–14.
[155] Case T-193/02, *Piau* [2005] ECR II-209, para. 117.

peoples of the Union.[156] It is submitted that codes of conduct have been used as a vehicle for introducing several requirements and conditions applied to professionals to foreclose the relevant market and increase the rents for the incumbents over the years. Although it was correctly pointed out that codes of conduct create expectations on the part of third parties, the unpalatable truth is that, alone, they cannot result in consistently improved professional behaviour.[157]

Our analysis above demonstrated that the Court of Justice, while well known as the most prominent trust-building institution, has adopted a lenient and fairly deferential approach when examining arguments of ethics, professional secrecy, integrity and reputation of the profession and other qualitative elements that codes of conduct should aim to preserve and enhance. This approach is coupled with a country- and sector-specific proportionality test that is focused on the precise characteristics of the market and the nature of the profession and its inherent characteristics. More flexible solutions adopted in other countries will not automatically render disproportionate the solutions adopted in the Member State in question. However, the Court of Justice, as demonstrated in *Laval*,[158] is ready to condemn palpable cases of unjustified distrust.

Among the several provisions of the Directive, Article 15 provides that self-regulating professional bodies have to evaluate various restrictions enshrined in domestic codes of conduct regarding business structures and legal form, fixed pricing and territorial restrictions. The need for a revision of restrictions on commercial communications is also underscored. According to the Directive, some of these types of measures, including commercial communications, should form an integral part of any attempt to draw up codes of conduct at EU level for them to be meaningful. The task of creating such codes of conduct appears to be daunting, as will be their implementation once they are adopted at EU level. The Directive specifies that Member States will take accompanying measures encouraging professional associations to implement at national level the pan-European codes of conduct. As another piece of evidence of the bottom-up approach adopted, the role of national professional associations is essential at each and every stage of this process, from the decision on the content of the pan-European codes of conduct

156 European Commission, Single Market Act, COM(2011) 206 final, 13 April 2011, p. 11.

157 N. Higgs-Kleyn and D. Kapelianis, 'The Role of Professional Codes in Regulating Ethical Conduct', *Journal of Business Ethics* 19 (1999) 363–74, p. 365.

158 Case C-341/05, *Laval* [2007] ECR I-11767.

to the surveillance of their implementation and the potential application of disciplinary sanctions. While the Directive does not specify whether the codes of conduct drawn up at EU level will be binding, the long-term preferred constellation is obvious from the structure of the Directive: initially voluntary, the codes of conduct adopted at EU level will be transposed at the national level (replacing the current national codes of conduct, if needed) and gradually become binding, thereby ensuring a minimum level of homogeneity and acceptable professional conduct across the Union with regard to issues such as ethics, professional secrecy, integrity, impartiality, business structure, and advertising.

PART V

Seeds of distrust: regulatory competition and diversity in the social sphere

10

Transborder provision of services and 'social dumping': rights-based mutual trust in the establishment of the Internal Market

OLIVIER DE SCHUTTER

1. Introduction

European economic integration was perhaps the clearest expression of what J. G. Ruggie retrospectively referred to as the 'embedded liberalism' characteristic of the post-Second World War international economic order.[1] In this order, the reduction or elimination of trade barriers between modern Welfare States should serve to enhance the redistributive capabilities of each State *vis-à-vis* its own citizens, thus leading the regulatory State at domestic level to complement trade liberalization at international level: the gains from trade should benefit the Welfare State, just like the Welfare State should protect the losers from international trade, thus ensuring that international trade remains a politically desirable option.

This, however, presupposed that the Welfare State should not be obliged to renounce its regulatory functions under the pressure of trade liberalization. And it also assumed that, in their domestic policies, States are not primarily motivated by the need to improve their international competitiveness – that they are not mutating from Welfare States to 'national competitive States', to use the concept of J. Hirsch.[2] However, since the early stages of European integration, fears have been expressed that the lowering of barriers to trade and the free movement of capital within the EU, in addition to creating efficiency gains, also may create incentives for the EU

[1] J. G. Ruggie, 'International Regimes, Transactions, and Change: Embedded Liberalism and the Postwar Economic Order', *International Organization* 36(2) (1982) 379–415.

[2] J. Hirsch, *Der nationale Wettbewerbsstaat: Staat, Demokratie und Politik im globalen Kapitalismus* [*The Competitive National State: State, Democracy and Politics in Global Capitalism*] (Berlin and Amsterdam: ID-Archiv, 1995).

Member States to adopt legislation or policies that are considered desirable in order to benefit the most from the opportunities created by market integration or in order, at least, not to be put at a disadvantage as a result of such integration. This, it has been argued, may operate to the detriment of workers, particularly the least qualified, since these are much less mobile than capital. Indeed, calls for a more social Europe have been primarily motivated by this risk of 'social dumping', in the presence of the strong diversity of social protection legislation across the Member States and in the absence of a binding 'floor of rights'.[3]

This debate has been revived in recent years, particularly as the result of the enlargement of the EU in 2004. It has been particularly lively in the area of trade in services. Central to the debate has been the question whether the EU Member States can trust each other's legislation insofar as it relates to the protection of workers, or whether limits should be imposed on the principle of mutual recognition of domestic legislation in order to avoid the scenario of a 'race to the bottom' from materializing in the area of social standards. In revisiting the debate, this chapter argues in favour of a much more contextualized approach, taking into account the modalities of preference-formation at domestic level. Since the question of 'trust' between Member States depends, ultimately, on how trade unions and employers' organizations influence national policy-making, and on whether or not preference-setting at that level is hostage to the requirements of competitiveness in the Internal Market, it is only by focusing the attention on those decision-making processes that the question of trust may be addressed. In the context of the transborder provision of services, trust may travel in both directions: it may be seen as referring not only to trust in the regulation of the service provider by its home State, but also to trust in the fact that regulation in the receiving State is animated by the purpose of improving the situation of workers – including posted workers – rather than by protectionist motives. Which of these two competing understandings of trust should prevail in any particular case should depend, ultimately, on process-based considerations, related to the quality of democratic decision-making in the respective jurisdictions concerned.

This chapter recalls the stages of the debate on the protection of social rights in the transborder provision of services. It then examines whether the fears of 'regulatory competition' in this area are justified, and what

[3] See M. Rhodes, 'The Future of the "Social Dimension": Labour Market Regulation in Post-1992 Europe', *Journal of Common Market Studies* 30 (March 1992) 23–52.

the notion of trust may contribute to the discussion. It concludes by a call for moving beyond the de-regulation/re-regulation debate by refocusing our attention to the empowerment of actors at the national level. Our alternative is not between the 'race to the bottom' and a chimerical European Welfare State: it is between taking the institutions as they are or transforming them to ensure that they contribute to social progress.

2. The provision of services and labour rights: stages of progress towards regulatory competition

2.1 *Stage One: before the Posted Workers Directive*

Much of this story is well known, and it can be summarized briefly. In *Rush Portuguesa*, decided in 1990, the Court of Justice took the view that the provisions of the EEC Treaty relating to free provision of services precluded France from prohibiting a person providing services established in another Member State from moving freely on its territory with all his staff, or from making the movement of staff in question subject to restrictions such as a condition as to engagement *in situ* or an obligation to obtain a work permit. 'To impose such conditions on the person providing services established in another Member State', the Court noted, 'discriminates against that person in relation to his competitors established in the host country who are able to use their own staff without restrictions, and moreover affects his ability to provide the service.'[4] This meant that the local workforce could not be protected from foreign competition through the imposition of restrictive immigration rules. However, the Court added, 'in response to the concern expressed in this connection by the French Government', that 'Community law does not preclude Member States from extending their legislation, or collective labour agreements entered into by both sides of industry, to any person who is employed, even temporarily, within their territory, no matter in which country the employer is established; nor does Community law prohibit Member States from enforcing those rules by appropriate means.'[5]

The judgment was a source of considerable legal uncertainty at the time it was delivered, for it did not make clear which of the laws of the host Member State the service provider established in another Member State had to comply with, and which constituted disproportionate interference

[4] Case C-113/89, *Rush Portuguesa Lda* v. *Office national d'immigration* [1990] ECR I-1417, para. 12.
[5] *Ibid.*, para. 18.

with the freedom to provide services. Under one interpretation, all rules imposing burdens on service providers established in another Member State when they already comply with comparable rules in their country of origin should be considered as *de facto* discriminatory (since they impose a double burden on foreign service providers) and therefore prohibited under EU law. For example, where service providers already pay social security contributions for the same periods of employment and for the same workers in their home State, they should not have to pay social security contributions in the host State in which they post workers to perform a service, even where this would compensate for the fact that they do not comply with the legislation on minimum wages in the host State.[6]

Under another interpretation, certain rules applicable to employment relations in the host State are 'mandatory' in nature, and, due to their particular importance, they should be complied with even by a service provider established in another Member State. This latter interpretation would appear to be consistent with the 1980 Rome Convention on the Law Applicable to Contractual Obligations,[7] which, although it provides that a contract of employment in principle will be governed by the law of the country where the worker habitually carries out the work (i.e., the home State) (Article 6(2)), nevertheless provides that 'mandatory rules' should be complied with in the host State (Article 7). But the Rome Convention did not specify which rules could thus be considered mandatory, and neither *Rush Portuguesa*, nor the other judgments adopted by the Court in this area, seemed to provide for such specification.

2.2 Stage Two: the 1996 Posted Workers Directive

Following the *Rush Portuguesa* decision, negotiations began on what would become the Posted Workers Directive, finally adopted in 1996.[8] The Posted Workers Directive imposes an obligation on the host Member State to ensure at a minimum that service providers established in another Member State comply with the rules pertaining to: (a) maximum work periods and

[6] See, for instance, Joined Cases 62 and 63/81, *Seco SA and Another* v. *EVI* [1982] ECR 223; Case C-272/94, *Criminal Proceedings against Guiot* [1996] ECR I-1905; and Case C-164/99, *Portugaia Construções* [2002] ECR I-787, para. 16. These judgments prescribe the recognition by the receiving State of the sending State's legislation, but only when the latter may be considered to provide an equivalent protection for the worker.

[7] Convention on the Law Applicable to Contractual Obligations, OJ 1980 L266/1.

[8] Directive 96/71/EC of the European Parliament and of the Council of 16 December 1996 concerning the posting of workers in the framework of the provision of services, OJ 1997 L18/1.

minimum rest periods; (b) minimum paid annual holidays; (c) the minimum rates of pay, including overtime rates, but excluding supplementary occupational retirement pension schemes; (d) the conditions of hiring-out of workers, in particular the supply of workers by temporary employment undertakings; (e) health, safety and hygiene at work; (f) protective measures with regard to the terms and conditions of employment of pregnant women or women who have recently given birth, of children and of young people; and (g) equality of treatment between men and women and other provisions on non-discrimination (Article 3(1)). In principle, in order to be imposed on the service provider established abroad, the rules relating to these areas should be stipulated by law, regulation or administrative provision. But the Directive provides that, as regards the construction sector, they may also be contained in collective agreements or arbitration awards which have been 'declared universally applicable'.[9]

The difficulties of interpretation of the Posted Workers Directive stem from the fact that it seeks to pursue, simultaneously, three quite different objectives. On its surface, it aims at facilitating the transnational provision of services, by clarifying the labour legislation applicable to the employment relationship between the service provider and the workers he posts temporarily in another Member State for the duration of the service provided. It is in order to provide this clarity that the Directive specifies under which conditions the regulations applicable to employment relationships in the host Member State may be imposed on the service provider established in another State, defining strictly, for instance, which collective agreements may have to be complied with by that service provider.

But a second and no less important objective of the Directive was to protect workers' rights. The workers concerned fall into two categories. The local workforce, established in the host Member State, should be protected from the risks of 'unfair competition', by competitors operating under a regulatory framework less protective of workers' rights and therefore less costly to comply with.[10] In addition, the posted workers

[9] On this condition, see Article 3(8) of the Posted Workers Directive.

[10] As explained by the Court of Justice in Case C-341/05, *Laval un Partneri Ltd* [2007] ECR I-11767 (for a discussion of this case, see below), Article 3(1) of the Posted Workers Directive 'prevents a situation arising in which, by applying to their workers the terms and conditions of employment in force in the Member State of origin as regards those matters, undertakings established in other Member States would compete unfairly against undertakings of the host Member State in the framework of the transnational provision of services, if the level of social protection in the host Member State is higher' (para. 75).

themselves should be protected against the risks which would be entailed by an employment relationship being entirely regulated by the country of establishment, a regime which could be easily abused by unscrupulous employers tempted to resort to 'social dumping'. This explains why the Directive imposes an obligation on States to guarantee a core set of rules to posted workers: Article 3(1) of the Directive provides that the host Member State 'shall ensure' that these rules are effectively applied.

Finally – and this is a third objective, distinct from the two others – the Directive sought to protect the Member States themselves, in their regulatory capacity, allowing them to go beyond the minimum protection they are obliged to ensure. The Directive states in its preamble that 'the mandatory rules for minimum protection in force in the host country must not prevent the application of terms and conditions of employment which are more favourable to workers' (Recital 17), an authorization reiterated in Article 2(7). Since it would not be acceptable for a legislative instrument to derogate from the obligations of the Member States under the EU Treaties, this provision should not be seen as exempting the Member States from having to comply with the requirements of free provision of services (now under Article 56 TFEU). But it does imply that, provided it is not discriminatory and does not impose a disproportionate restriction on the provision of services (as would be the case if the posted workers were already protected under legislation 'equivalent in substance' in the Member State of establishment), the host State may impose compliance with its domestic legislation to the relationship between the posted workers and their employer.

In sum, it would seem consistent with these three objectives to interpret the Posted Workers Directive as clarifying the law applicable to posted workers in a transnational provision of services (a) by imposing on the host Member State to extend to posted workers a core set of rules applicable to the workers employed locally; and (b) by allowing the host Member State to extend its protection beyond that minimum, unless this represents a discriminatory or disproportionate interference with the freedom to provide services, as recognized now under Article 56 TFEU. In line with the case law of the Court based on that provision of the Treaty, the host Member State would be considered to impose a disproportionate restriction on the freedom to provide services if the protection it intends to grant to workers is already ensured by equivalent legislation in the Member State of establishment.

2.3 *Stage Three: the debate on the Directive on Services*

2.3.1 The 2004 Proposal for a Directive on Services in the Internal Market

It is precisely this balance which the initial Proposal of the European Commission for a Directive on Services in the Internal Market, in the form in which it was proposed in January 2004 as part of a package of measures to encourage growth and improve competitiveness in the EU,[11] created a risk of disrupting. The 'country-of-origin principle' was at the core of the Directive. This principle, which specific, sectoral Directives had already relied upon,[12] would have ensured that a service provider wishing to supply services to clients in another Member State would in general be subject only to the rules and regulations of the Member State where it is established. The country-of-origin principle was defined in the Commission's Proposal as implying that 'Member States shall ensure that providers are subject only to the national provisions of their Member State of origin which fall within the coordinated field [i.e., which concern any requirement applicable to access to service activities or to the exercise thereof]' (Article 16(1)(1)). This principle was to cover all national provisions relating to access to and the exercise of a service activity, 'in particular those requirements governing the behaviour of the provider, the quality or content of the service, advertising, contracts and the provider's liability' (Article 16(1)(2)). As stated in the extended impact assessment accompanying the Proposal:

> The barriers affecting the freedom to provide services require mainly that Member States refrain from applying their own rules and regulations to incoming services from other Member States and from supervising and controlling them. Instead they should rely on control by the authorities

[11] COM(2004) 2 final, p. 13.

[12] See, e.g., Article 2(1) of Council Directive 89/552/EEC of 3 October 1989 on the coordination of certain provisions laid down by law, regulation or administrative action in Member States concerning the pursuit of television broadcasting activities, OJ 1989 L298/23 (as amended by Directive 97/36/EC of the European Parliament and of the Council, OJ 1997 L202/60); or Article 3(1) of Directive 2000/31/EC of the European Parliament and of the Council of 8 June 2000 on certain legal aspects of information society services, in particular electronic commerce, in the Internal Market ('Directive on Electronic Commerce'), OJ 2000 L178/1. The lead author of the Proposal of the Commission on the Directive on Electronic Commerce, E. Crabit, was also closely involved within DG Internal Market in preparing the Proposal for a Directive on Services in the Internal Market (see E. Crabit, 'La directive sur le commerce électronique', *Revue du marché unique et de l'Union européenne* (2000) 749–834).

> in the country of origin of the service provider. This would remove the legal uncertainty and costs resulting from the application of a multitude of different rules and control measures to which cross-border service providers are currently subject.[13]

The impact assessment stated, rather candidly, that 'this means that Member States must have trust and confidence in each other's legal systems and control measures'.

Although the generalization of the country-of-origin principle went beyond the existing case law of the Court,[14] it was presented as fully preserving the Community *acquis* in the area of the posting of workers. Indeed, Article 17 of the proposed Directive stated that the country-of-origin principle did not apply to matters covered by Directive 96/71/EC. And, while Article 24 of the Proposal for a Directive on Services in the Internal Market contained 'specific provisions on the posting of workers', it did seem to preserve the full integrity of the system established by the Posted Workers Directive: it merely stated that the Member State of posting should in principle 'carry out in its territory the checks, inspections and investigations necessary to ensure compliance with the employment and working conditions applicable under Directive 96/71/EC', the imposition of certain types of obligations being excluded; and that the Member State of origin of the service provider should ensure that both its authorities and those of the Member State of posting receive the information necessary to ensure full compliance with the legal requirements imposed on the service provider.

There was a clear risk, however, that the country-of-origin principle would in fact entirely reverse the system of the Posted Workers Directive. In this Directive, the list of rules contained in Article 3(1) of the Directives constitutes a *minimum* protection the host State is obliged to provide. Once the Posted Workers Directive becomes a derogation to the principle of the country of origin, these rules come to define instead the *maximum* degree of protection a State may offer: while the matters 'covered' by the Posted Workers Directive, as listed in Article 3(1) of this instrument, were

[13] Extended impact assessment of the Proposal for a Directive on Services in the Internal Market, SEC(2004) 21, pp. 23–4.

[14] In a case concerning the legal basis of Directive 94/19 on deposit-guarantee schemes, the Court in fact explicitly denied that there existed a general principle of supervision by a home State: see Case C-233/94, *Germany* v. *European Parliament and Council of the EU* [1997] ECR I-2405, para. 64. The imposition of an across-the-board country-of-origin principle therefore constitutes an innovation.

'excluded' from the application of the country-of-origin principle (Article 17(5)), all the other aspects of the employment contract were to be regulated by the law of the State of establishment rather than by the law of the host State. Although the Proposal of the Commission did provide for the possibility of certain case-by-case derogations to the principle of country of origin (Article 19), none of them was really relevant to the protection of posted workers, and derogations seem to be premised, rather, on the need to ensure adequate protection of the recipient of services, rather than of those working for the service providers themselves. For some observers, this opened the way to 'social dumping', if we understand by this expression the choice of employers to work under a set of rules aimed at the protection of workers which allows them to be more cost-effective than potential competitors operating on the same market.[15] The timing was particularly ill-chosen. The Proposal was presented only weeks before the enlargement to ten new Member States. There were strong fears that the protection of workers was significantly weaker in those countries, giving the employers in those countries an unfair advantage in the Internal Market if they were authorized to provide services in accordance with the regulations imposed on them in the State of establishment only, with the exception of a minimum set of rules imposed by the State of posting in the areas listed in Article 3(1) of the Posted Workers Directive.[16]

Both the European Economic and Social Committee[17] and the European Parliament reacted with hostility to the Proposal. In a resolution of 16 February 2006,[18] the Parliament proposed to replace the country-of-origin principle by a reaffirmation of the freedom to provide services, implying that no restriction on that freedom shall be allowed which does not comply with the principles of non-discrimination, necessity and proportionality (Article 17(1)). It also proposed to state explicitly the primacy of Directive

[15] See, for a critique under this angle of the proposed Directive, O. De Schutter and S. Francq, 'La proposition de directive sur les services dans le marché intérieur: reconnaissance mutuelle, harmonization et conflits de lois dans l'Europe élargie', *Cahiers de droit européen* (2005) 603–60. See also R. Blanpain (ed.), *Freedom of Services in the European Union – Labour and Social Security Law: The Bolkestein Initiative* (The Hague: Kluwer Law International, 2006). For a longer discussion of social dumping and the ambiguity of its definition, see below.

[16] See, in particular, expressing this concern, D. C. Vaughan-Whitehead, *EU Enlargement versus Social Europe? The Uncertain Future of the European Social Model*, 1st edn (Cheltenham: Edward Elgar, 2003).

[17] See European Economic and Social Committee (EESC), Opinion of 9 February 2005, OJ 2005 C221/113.

[18] Doc. EP 369.610, P6_TA(2006)0061, 16 February 2006.

96/71/EC over the Directive on Services in the Internal Market (Article 3(1)), and the insertion of a provision recognizing that the provisions of this latter Directive on the freedom to provide services 'do not prevent the Member State to which the provider moves from imposing requirements with regard to the provision of a service activity, where they are justified for reasons of public policy, public security, environmental protection and public health. Nor do they prevent Member States from applying, in conformity with Community law, their rules on employment conditions, including those laid down in collective agreements' (Article 17(3)). In sum, rather than the revolution proposed by the European Commission through the country-of-origin principle, the Parliament proposed to reaffirm the case law of the Court, and to facilitate the exercise of the freedom to provide services by a series of measures which the initial Proposal of the Commission already contained (such as the establishment of single points of contact or administrative cooperation between the authorities of the State of establishment and those of the State where the service is provided).

2.3.2 The 2006 Directive on Services in the Internal Market

The new Proposal that the European Commission put forward in April 2006 took into account these concerns. Directive 2006/123/EC of 12 December 2006 on Services in the Internal Market,[19] adopted on the basis of this Proposal, explicitly states that it does not affect the Posted Workers Directive, and that therefore it 'should not prevent Member States from applying terms and conditions of employment on matters other than those listed in Article 3(1) of Directive 96/71/EC on grounds of public policy' (Recital 86). Indeed, the Directive should not affect labour law applied in accordance with national and Community law (Article 1(6)), and, as proposed by the Parliament, the primacy of Directive 96/71/EC is explicitly affirmed (Article 3(1)(a)). Although it contains a number of rules on administrative simplification, which aim to facilitate the exercise of freedom to provide services, the country-of-origin principle has disappeared: instead, as proposed by the Parliament, the principle of free provision of services is reaffirmed, which implies that any restrictions are allowable only insofar as they comply with the principles of non-discrimination, necessity and proportionality (Article 17).

[19] OJ 2006 L376/36.

2.4 *Stage Four: judicial imposition of regulatory competition*

The recent case law of the Court threatens to re-establish exactly the regime that the European legislator, after a fierce battle in 2004–5, had decided not to set up. In *Laval*,[20] the Court was asked by the Swedish Labour Court to deliver a preliminary ruling in a case opposing a Latvian contractor, Laval un Partneri Ltd, to a Swedish trade union. A subsidiary company of Laval intended to use Latvian posted workers on a construction site in the town of Vaxholm in Sweden, for the renovation and extension of school premises. It intended to pay these workers less than the minimum amount stipulated in a collective agreement concluded between, on the one hand, the Swedish building and public works trade union, in its capacity as the central organization representing construction workers, and, on the other, Sveriges Byggindustrier, the national organization for employers in the construction sector. This collective agreement imposed a number of pecuniary obligations on the employers, including on the hourly rate of pay and other matters referred to in Article 3(1), first subparagraph, (a) to (g), of Directive 96/71 (such as working time and annual leave), which went beyond those set out in the applicable Swedish legislation; some of them related to matters not referred to in that Article. Agreeing to the terms of this collective agreement would have extended the same obligations to Laval. However, Laval had signed, on 14 September and 20 October 2004, in Latvia, collective agreements with the Latvian building sector's trade union, of which 65 per cent of workers were members. None of the members of the Swedish trade unions parties to the collective agreement concluded with the Sveriges Byggindustrier were employed by Laval. Laval therefore considered that it should not conclude another, separate collective agreement for work to be performed in Sweden. A social conflict followed the refusal of Laval to agree to the terms of the collective agreement proposed by the Swedish unions. It led ultimately to other trade unions boycotting all Laval's sites in Sweden. In February 2005, the town of Vaxholm requested that the contract between it and Laval's Swedish subsidiary be terminated. A month later, Laval was declared bankrupt.

The main question submitted to the Court concerned the interpretation of both the Posted Workers Directive and of Article 56 TFEU. The Posted Workers Directive, it will be recalled, provided that, in the construction

[20] Case C-341/05, *Laval un Partneri Ltd* [2007] ECR I-11767. For useful commentaries, see A. R. Ganesh, 'Appointing Foxes to Guard Henhouses: The European Posted Workers' Directive', *Columbia Journal of European Law* 15 (2008) 123; S. Deakin, 'Regulatory Competition after Laval', *Cambridge Yearbook of European Legal Studies* 10 (2009) 581–609.

sector, the rules imposed on the service provider established abroad may be stipulated in collective agreements or arbitration awards which have been 'declared universally applicable'. Member States which have no system for declaring collective agreements or arbitration awards to be of universal application in the building sector may base themselves on collective agreements 'which are generally applicable to all similar undertakings in the geographical area and in the profession or industry concerned, and/or collective agreements which have been concluded by the most representative employers' and labour organizations at national level and which are applied throughout national territory', provided that their application to the service providers established abroad does not result in any discrimination between them and national undertakings in the same sector (Article 3(8)). In the decentralized Swedish system, however, management and labour set the wage rates through collective negotiations, 'on a case-by-case basis, at the place of work, having regard to the qualifications and tasks of the employees concerned':[21] the Court took the view that rates of pay set through such a decentralized procedure cannot be imposed on service providers established in other Member States, who cannot be obliged to negotiate with the local unions to that effect.

The Court acknowledged that the protection of the Posted Workers Directive was not to prevent application of terms and conditions of employment more favourable to workers. This, however, the Court said, 'cannot be interpreted as allowing the host Member State to make the provision of services in its territory conditional on the observance of terms and conditions of employment which go beyond the mandatory rules for minimum protection. As regards the matters referred to in Article 3(1), first subparagraph, (a) to (g), Directive 96/71 expressly lays down the degree of protection for workers of undertakings established in other Member States who are posted to the territory of the host Member State which the latter State is entitled to require those undertakings to observe. Moreover, such an interpretation would amount to depriving the directive of its effectiveness.'[22] The Court concluded that posted workers may not be protected through the legislation of the State of posting beyond the level of protection which must be guaranteed to these workers under Article 3(1), first subparagraph, (a) to (g), of Directive 96/71.[23]

Turning then to the requirements of Article 56 TFEU and to the question of whether the collective action resorted to by the Swedish unions was in violation of this provision, the Court took the view that 'the right of trade

[21] *Laval*, para. 69. [22] *Laval*, para. 80. [23] *Laval*, para. 81.

unions of a Member State to take collective action by which undertakings established in other Member States may be forced to sign the collective agreement for the building sector – certain terms of which depart from the legislative provisions and establish more favourable terms and conditions of employment as regards the matters referred to in Article 3(1), first subparagraph, (a) to (g), of Directive 96/71 and others relate to matters not referred to in that provision – is liable to make it less attractive, or more difficult, for such undertakings to carry out construction work in Sweden, and therefore constitutes a restriction on the freedom to provide services within the meaning of Article [56 TFEU]'.[24] While acknowledging that the right to take collective action is a fundamental right recognized under Community law (paras. 90–1), and thus may constitute an overriding reason of public interest justifying, in principle, a restriction of one of the fundamental freedoms guaranteed by the Treaties,[25] the Court notes that this right may be subject to certain restrictions, and must be exercised in accordance with national and EU law. The Court defines its role as having to balance the right to collective action against the freedom to provide services:

> Since the Community has ... not only an economic but also a social purpose, the rights under the provisions of the EC Treaty on the free movement of goods, persons, services and capital must be balanced against the objectives pursued by social policy, which include, as is clear from the first paragraph of Article 136 EC, *inter alia*, improved living and working conditions, so as to make possible their harmonization while improvement is being maintained, proper social protection and dialogue between management and labour.[26]

However, the Court considers that the obstacle to the freedom to provide services created by the collective action launched by the Swedish unions cannot be justified with regard to the objective of improving social protection, since, 'with regard to workers posted in the framework of a transnational provision of services, their employer is required, as a result of the coordination achieved by Directive 96/71, to observe a nucleus of mandatory rules for minimum protection in the host Member State' (para. 108). In other terms, collective action cannot seek to impose obligations on employers beyond the obligations the host State must impose in accordance with

[24] *Laval*, para. 99.

[25] *Laval*, para. 103. See, e.g., Joined Cases C-369/96 and 376/96, *Arblade and Others* [1999] ECR I-8453, para. 36; Case C-165/98, *Mazzoleni and ISA* [2001] ECR I-2189, para. 27; Joined Cases C-49/98, 50/98, 52/98 to C-54/98 and 68/98 to 71/98, *Finalarte and Others* [2001] ECR I-7831; Case C-36/02, *Omega* [2004] ECR I-9609, para. 35.

[26] *Laval*, para. 105.

Article 3(1) of the Posted Workers Directive. The Court concludes that the blockade imposed by the Swedish unions on the construction site of the company's subsidiary violates Community law and should not be allowed: Article 56 TFEU and the Posted Workers Directive preclude a trade union from resorting to collective action in order to force a provider of services established in another Member State to enter into negotiations with it on the rates of pay for posted workers and to sign a collective agreement the terms of which lay down, as regards some of the matters referred to in Article 3(1), first subparagraph, (a) to (g), of the Posted Workers Directive, more favourable conditions than those resulting from the relevant legislative provisions in the State concerned, while other terms relate to matters not referred to in Article 3 of the Directive.

A second question submitted to the Court in *Laval* concerned the Swedish law on workers' participation in decisions ('the MBL'). The Swedish courts interpreted Article 42 of the MBL as prohibiting taking collective action with the aim of obtaining the repeal of or amendment to a collective agreement between other parties. In 1989, it was held by the labour courts in a dispute concerning working conditions for the crew of a container ship named *Britannia*, flying a foreign flag, that that prohibition extended to collective action undertaken in Sweden in order to obtain the repeal or amendment of a collective agreement concluded between foreign parties, in a workplace abroad, if such collective action is prohibited by the foreign law applicable to the signatories to that collective agreement. In reaction, and with a clear intention to combat what they saw as a risk of 'social dumping' which workers would be prohibited from countering through collective action, the Swedish legislature adopted in 1991 the 'Lex Britannia'. This legislation restricted the scope of the principle expounded in the *Britannia* judgment, by providing that the prohibition to resort to collective action to undo an existing collective agreement shall apply only if an organization commences collective action by reason of employment relationships falling directly within the scope of the Swedish law. In practice, the 'Lex Britannia' thus authorized collective action against foreign service providers only temporarily active in Sweden, even in circumstances where such service providers had concluded a collective agreement in their home State.

When asked whether the 'Lex Britannia' violated EU law, the Court of Justice held that 'national rules, such as [the 'Lex Britannia'], which fail to take into account, irrespective of their content, collective agreements to which undertakings that post workers to Sweden are already bound in the Member State in which they are established, give rise to discrimination against such undertakings, in so far as under those national rules they are treated in the same way as national undertakings which have not concluded a collective agreement'.[27] Such discrimination, the Court reasoned, could not be justified under the EU Treaty. The Court noted that the 'Lex Britannia' 'is intended, first, to allow trade unions to take action to ensure that all employers active on the Swedish labour market pay wages and apply other terms and conditions of employment in line with those usual in Sweden, and secondly, to create a climate of fair competition, on an equal basis, between Swedish employers and entrepreneurs from other Member States'.[28] But this intention – to combat 'social dumping' – does not appear to the Court to correspond to the grounds of public policy, public security or public health, which may justify derogations from the freedom to provide services. The 'Lex Britannia' thus violates Community law.

Laval, which was decided on 18 December 2007, does not stand alone. It may be replaced in a broader context in which the Court increasingly appears to favour an interpretation of the requirements of Community law that seeks to encourage competition between the national regulatory systems, and that treats with suspicion any attempt by the Member States to limit the impacts of such competition on the protection of workers.[29] In *Viking*,[30] decided only a few days before *Laval*, the International Transport Workers' Federation and its local affiliate, the Finnish Seamen's Union, resorted to collective action in order to prevent Viking, a Finnish ferry operator, from reflagging a Finnish vessel as an Estonian vessel to escape the application of Finnish employment laws and the applicable collective agreement. The Court considered that such collective action, in the form of a strike and a boycott, should be treated as a restriction on the freedom of establishment recognized under Article 49 TFEU, since it has 'the effect of making less attractive, or even pointless . . . Viking's exercise of its right to freedom of establishment, inasmuch as such action prevents both Viking and its subsidiary, Viking Eesti, from enjoying the same treatment in the host Member State as other economic operators established in that State'.[31]

The Court acknowledged that the right to take collective action for the protection of workers is a legitimate interest which, in principle, justifies

[27] *Laval*, para. 116. [28] *Laval*, para. 118.

[29] See I. H. Eliasoph, 'A "Switch in Time" for the European Community? Lochner Discourse and the Recalibration of Economic and Social Rights in Europe', *Columbia Journal of European Law* 14 (2008) 467.

[30] Case C-438/05, *International Transport Workers' Federation and Finnish Seamen's Union* v. *Viking Line ABP and OÜ Viking Line Eesti* [2007] ECR I-10779.

[31] *Viking*, para. 72.

a restriction of the fundamental freedoms guaranteed by the Treaty, and that the protection of workers is one of the overriding reasons of public interest recognized in its case law.[32] However, even if they pursue a legitimate aim compatible with the Treaty and are justified by overriding reasons of public interest, restrictions on freedom of establishment are only acceptable insofar as they are suitable for securing the attainment of the objective pursued and do not go beyond what is necessary in order to attain it. While the Court recognized the legitimacy of unions seeking to safeguard the rights of *current* employees of the vessel, it expressed the view that any collective action going beyond that objective would be disproportionate: resorting to strikes or boycotts to avoid reflagging would be unacceptable, in the eyes of the Court, if it were established that the jobs or conditions of employment at issue were not jeopardized or under serious threat. Such would be the case, in particular, if the company concerned has agreed to a binding undertaking that the reflagging would not result in terminating the employment of any person employed by them at the time it is made, even if such undertaking does not include the renewal of short-term employment contracts or prevent the redeployment of any employee on equivalent terms and conditions.[33] In other words, collective action by unions may seek to protect the acquired rights of existing employees; it would be abusive if it were, instead, to discourage the exercise of freedom of establishment by companies seeking to relocate themselves to benefit from a more favourable regulatory environment.[34]

[32] Referring to the social provisions of the EC Treaty, the Court also noted that 'the Community has thus not only an economic but also a social purpose', which implied that 'the rights under the provisions of the Treaty on the free movement of goods, persons, services and capital must be balanced against the objectives pursued by social policy, which include, as is clear from the first paragraph of Article 136 EC, *inter alia*, improved living and working conditions, so as to make possible their harmonization while improvement is being maintained, proper social protection and dialogue between management and labour' (para. 79). The statement was reiterated in *Laval*, as we have seen.

[33] See para. 82 of the judgment and the tenth question referred to the Court of Justice by the Court of Appeal (England and Wales) (Civil Division).

[34] The distinction between these two purposes of resorting to collective action was put forward by Advocate General Maduro in the Opinion he delivered in the *Viking* case: 'collective action to persuade an undertaking to maintain its current jobs and working conditions must not be confused with collective action to prevent an undertaking from providing its services once it has relocated abroad. The first type of collective action represents a legitimate way for workers to preserve their rights and corresponds to what would usually happen if relocation were to take place within a Member State. Yet, that cannot be said of collective action that

3. Regulatory competition and fundamental social rights

3.1 Evaluating the impact of Laval (I): the static perspective

Any evaluation of the *Laval* case law should include both static and dynamic considerations. The most obvious question it raises concerns how conflicts between social rights and economic freedoms are resolved, in a static perspective. In line with the existing case law, the *Laval* judgment treats fundamental rights as primary law, and as having a hierarchical rank equivalent to, rather than superior to, the fundamental economic freedoms of EU law. The implication is that, when the exercise of a fundamental economic freedom appears in conflict with a fundamental right, the two rights must be balanced against one another.[35] The fundamental rights recognized as part of EU law include a number of social rights listed in the EU Charter of Fundamental Rights.[36] Therefore, the Member States may justify restrictions to fundamental economic freedoms by invoking the need to protect certain social rights recognized as fundamental, for instance the exercise of the right to resort to collective action. But they may do so only to the extent that such restrictions are not discriminatory *vis-à-vis* foreign service providers; and that such restrictions are both necessary for the protection of the social right concerned and proportionate to that objective.

A fundamental critique that has been levied against this approach is that it violates the decoupling between the economic and the social spheres in the European project. The project of European integration led to the attribution

merely seeks to prevent an undertaking that has moved elsewhere from lawfully providing its services in the Member State in which it was previously established' (para. 67). This latter form of collective action, in the view of the Advocate General, 'entirely negates the rationale of the common market' (para. 68).

35 See the Opinion of Advocate General Mengozzi, para. 84. Typical examples are Case C-67/96, *Albany International BV* [1999] ECR I-5751, paras. 59–62; Case C-112/00, *Schmidberger* [2003] ECR I-5659, para. 71.

36 Initially proclaimed as a political declaration in 2000, OJ 2000 C364/1, the Charter is not recognized as legally binding: see Article 6(2) of the Treaty on European Union as amended by the Treaty of Lisbon and the Treaty on European Union and the Treaty Establishing the European Community, signed at Lisbon, 13 December 2007, OJ 2007 C306/1 (referring to the EU Charter of Fundamental Rights in the revised form in which it was proclaimed on 12 December 2007, OJ 2007 C301/1). However, fundamental social rights not listed in the Charter of Fundamental Rights could nevertheless be recognized as part of the general principles of EU law as derived from international instruments for the protection of human rights binding upon the EU Member States, and from the common constitutional traditions of the Member States. For a discussion of the relationship between fundamental rights as part of the general principles of EU law and international human rights law, see I. de Jesus Butler and O. De Schutter, 'Binding the EU to International Human Rights Law', *Yearbook of European Law* 27 (2008) 277–320.

to the EU of the task of establishing an Internal Market, characterized by the protection of economic freedoms and the prohibition of distortions of competition (areas which were removed from politics to be made supranational), while the protection of social rights (the Welfare State) remained in the hands of the Member States (and thus subject to political contests at the national level): subordinating the latter to the economic freedoms of the Treaty would be in violation of this fundamental division of labour between the two levels. The main exponents of this critique summarize thus: 'Europe was conceived according to principles of a dual polity. Its "economic Constitution" was non-political in the sense that it was not subject to political interventions. This was its constitutional-supranational *raison d'être*. Social policy was treated as a categorically distinct subject. It belonged to the domain of political legislation, and, as such, had to remain national.'[37] Under this original scheme, 'trust' between the Member States takes on a very different meaning, almost at the opposite end to the interpretation given to the notion when it is used in the expression 'mutual trust': it is seen as referring to the notion that each State should trust that the social policies implemented in other Member States, since they are the outcome of democratic processes, seek to ensure a fair distribution of the gains from economic growth, and should not, presumptively at least, be treated as protectionist or as directed against the other Member States.

Even if we accept that the provision of social rights at the domestic level may be tested against the requirements of the economic freedoms constitutive of the Internal Market, another problem resides in the methodology of balancing social rights against these freedoms. Although the right to resort to collective action is not typical in this regard, social rights usually require from States that they take measures which ensure their progressive realization, to the maximum of the resources available to the State. Because both the level of achievement of these rights and the method by which they should be realized remain rather underspecified under the relevant international human rights instruments, States are granted a broad margin of appreciation at the level of implementation: the basic requirement is that they make progress towards the full realization of the rights concerned, and that they monitor progress. In this respect, what States need in order to discharge their obligations towards economic and social rights is not simply that no conflicting obligation is imposed on them, through other

[37] Ch. Joerges and F. Rödl, 'Informal Politics, Formalised Law and the "Social Deficit" of European Integration: Reflections after the Judgments of the ECJ in Viking and Laval', *European Law Journal* 15(1) (2009) 1–19, p. 5.

instruments: it is that they preserve the policy space they require to implement policies in areas such as health, education or social security, without being forced to limit themselves to what is 'strictly necessary' to comply with such obligations.

3.2 Evaluating the impact of Laval (II): the dynamic perspective

Adopting a static perspective is not enough. We must also ask which incentives are created, both for States and for economic operators, by the legal rule announced by the Court. It is here, in a dynamic perspective, that the notions of 'social dumping' or 'regulatory competition' intervene. The notion of 'social dumping' may of course be given various definitions, ranging from situations in which an employer deliberately violates existing legislation in order to achieve a competitive advantage to situations where practices as regards working conditions and wages comply with the applicable labour legislation and simply reflect different levels of productivity between workers, without entailing any distortion of competition.[38] The notion is used here to refer to the (perfectly legal) practice of companies locating their activities in the State, and thus under the regulatory regime, that will make compliance with social regulations least costly, in order to be the most competitive in the Internal Market. 'Regulatory competition' in turn refers to the choice of States to regulate wages and other working conditions in order to ensure that the companies established under their jurisdiction will not be placed at a competitive disadvantage as a result of higher labour costs being imposed on them than would be justified by the productivity of their workers, in comparison to companies established in other Member States who compete on the same markets.

It deserves notice that there are few restrictions to the potential 'abuse of the right to establishment' in EU law, when a company decides to reincorporate in a Member State other than its State of origin in order to benefit from a more favourable regulatory environment. In *Centros*, the Court expressed the view that 'the fact that a national of a Member State who wishes to set up a company chooses to form it in the Member State whose rules of company law seem to him the least restrictive and to set up branches in other Member States cannot, in itself, constitute an abuse of the right of

[38] For a discussion of these various definitions, see D. C. Vaughan-Whitehead, *EU Enlargement versus Social Europe? The Uncertain Future of the European Social Model* (Cheltenham: Edward Elgar, 2003), pp. 325–7.

establishment' as recognized in the Treaties.[39] Although the Court added that this should not be seen as an obstacle to the adoption by States of measures aimed at preventing fraud, for instance where it is established that the formation of the company intends to evade obligations towards private or public creditors,[40] the case was widely seen as promoting regulatory competition in corporate law in the EU.[41] *Centros* was reaffirmed in *Überseering*, a case in which a company incorporated in the Netherlands was denied by the German courts the capacity to be a party to legal proceedings in Germany without reincorporating in Germany, a restriction to freedom of establishment which the Court considered a violation of the rules of EU law on freedom of establishment.[42] Finally, in *Inspire Art*, decided in 2003, the Court considered that it was not an abuse of the right of establishment to seek to circumvent the more demanding conditions imposed under Dutch company law by incorporating in the United Kingdom, even if almost all the activities of the company do in fact take place in the Netherlands: 'the fact that a company does not conduct any business in the Member State in which it has its registered office and pursues its activities only or principally in the Member State where its branch is established is not sufficient to prove the existence of abuse or fraudulent conduct which would entitle the latter Member State to deny that company the benefit of the provisions of Community law relating to the right of establishment.'[43]

When it was presented with the Proposal for a Directive on Services in the Internal Market, the European Parliament insisted on a definition of

[39] Case C-212/97, *Centros Ltd* [1999] ECR I-1459, para. 27. [40] *Ibid.*, para. 38.

[41] See W. F. Ebke, 'Centros – Some Realities and Some Mysteries', *American Journal of Comparative Law* 48 (2000) 623–60; A. Looijestijn-Clearie, 'Centros Ltd – A Complete U-Turn in the Right of Establishment for Companies', *International and Comparative Law Quarterly* 49 (2000) 621–42; W. R. Roth, 'From Centros to Uberseering: Free Movement of Companies, Private International Law and Community Law', *International and Comparative Law Quarterly* 52 (2003) 177–208; M. Siems, 'Convergence, Competition, Centros and Conflicts of Law: European Company Law in the Twenty-First Century', *European Law Review* 27 (2002) 47–59; S. Deakin, 'Two Types of Regulatory Competition: Competitive Federalism versus Reflexive Harmonization: A Law and Economics Perspective on Centros', *Cambridge Yearbook of European Legal Studies* 1 (1999) 231–60.

[42] See Case C-208/00, *Überseering BV* v. *Nordic Construction Company Baumanagement GmbH* [2002] ECR I-9919.

[43] Case C-167/01, *Kamer van Koophandel en Fabrieken voor Amsterdam* v. *Inspire Art Ltd* [2003] ECR I-10155, para. 139. See E. Wymeersch, 'The Transfer of the Company's Seat in European Company Law', *Common Market Law Review* 40 (2003) 661–95; C. Kersting and C. P. Schindler, 'The ECJ's Inspire Art Decision of 30 September 2003 and Its Effects on Practice', *German Law Journal* 4 (2003) 1277–1299.

establishment requiring 'the actual pursuit of an economic activity at the place of establishment of the service provider', excluding therefore 'letter box' companies, established in one Member State with the sole purpose of working under its regulatory framework. The Court itself subsequently agreed that restrictions on the freedom of establishment could be justified in exceptional circumstances 'on the ground of prevention of abusive practices', for instance in order to 'prevent conduct involving the creation of wholly artificial arrangements which do not reflect economic reality, with a view to escaping the tax normally due on the profits generated by activities carried out on national territory'.[44]

However, the main safeguard against the risk of companies relocating in order to escape certain onerous regulatory requirements and hire workers under the terms of a domestic legislation less protective of the workers' rights stems from the fact that, for a number of EU Member States, the State of incorporation is not the decisive factor for the purposes of determining the State of establishment. These States rely instead on the 'real seat' doctrine, which presupposes that the company is considered to be established where it concentrates its activities or has its main place of business, thus creating a link between the 'nationality' of the company – the law under which it operates – and its 'residence' – its principal place of business.[45] A company will therefore not be authorized to rely on its freedom of establishment in order to develop activities in one Member State while remaining governed by the law of the Member State of origin (where it was initially incorporated), solely in order to benefit from the more favourable regulatory provisions of the latter. This is illustrated, for instance, by the *Cartesio* judgment of 16 December 2008.[46] The Hungarian law applicable did not allow a company incorporated in Hungary to transfer its seat abroad while continuing to be subject to Hungarian law as its personal law. This in practice obliged the company wishing to convert itself into a company governed by the law of another Member State, first to cease to exist as a Hungarian company. The Court refused to treat this as a disproportionate restriction on the freedom of establishment of companies; instead, it took the view that it is up to the national law of the Member State of

[44] Case C-196/04, *Cadbury Schweppes and Cadbury Schweppes Overseas* [2006] ECR I-7995 (para. 55).

[45] This constitutes a notable difference as compared to the US, where incorporation is decisive. See D. Charny, 'Competition among Jurisdictions in Formulating Corporate Rules: An American Perspective on the "Race to the Bottom" in the European Communities', *Harvard International Law Journal* 32 (1991) 423–56.

[46] Case C-210/06, *Cartesio Oktató és Szolgáltató bt* [2008] ECR I-9641.

incorporation to decide whether a company may transfer its registered office or its actual centre of administration to another Member State without losing its legal personality.

Thus, the freedom of establishment of companies is not unlimited. Certain restrictions are imposed on companies seeking to incorporate themselves under the laws of the Member State that impose the lightest burdens. These restrictions in turn diminish the pressure on States to relax their regulatory standards, since they are allowed to react to the clearest instances of abuse, such as the setting up of 'letter box' or 'front' subsidiaries.[47] Nevertheless, within these broad limitations summarized above, companies may choose where to establish themselves and, thus, under which rules to provide services across the EU. What are the consequences? Some have noted the disciplining virtue that could result from 'regulatory competition', in the meaning which has been referred to above: States will act more rationally, it has been suggested, if some degree of horizontal economic competition is organized, obliging them to offer the best 'fit' of regulation combined with a well-educated workforce and other advantages to the companies locating their activities within their jurisdiction.[48] However, there are also instances in which 'regulatory competition' may lead to sub-optimal outcomes: in what may be understood as one form of the 'prisoner's dilemma', States will legislate, not in accordance with the 'real' preferences of the domestic constituency (i.e., what that constituency would have chosen in the absence of competition from other jurisdictions), but taking into account the need to attract companies (or to stem their relocation abroad) as a source, primarily, of employment creation. The notions of 'social dumping' and of 'regulatory competition' both suggest the risk of a 'race to the bottom' in the presence of a variety of regulatory regimes coexisting in an area in which the factors of production are mobile and in which mutual recognition of these regulatory regimes is established.[49] A decisive question for the future direction of social rights in the

[47] Case C-196/04, *Cadbury Schweppes and Cadbury Schweppes Overseas* [2006] ECR I-7995, para. 68.

[48] See, e.g., J. P. Trachtman, 'International Regulatory Competition, Externalization, and Jurisdiction', *Harvard International Law Journal* 34(1) (1993) 48, pp. 51–3. For a comparison between the US and the EU debates on regulatory competition, see also C. Barnard, 'Social Dumping and the Race to the Bottom: Some Lessons for the European Union from Delaware?', *European Law Review* 25 (2000) 57–78.

[49] Cary has been credited with introducing the notion of the 'race to the bottom': see W. L. Cary, 'Federalism and Corporate Law: Reflections upon Delaware', *Yale Law Journal* 83 (1974) 663–705, p. 666. However, the idea had already been expressed with great clarity by Justice Brandeis, in *Liggett Co.* v. *Lee*, 288 US 517, 559 (1933) (Justice Brandeis,

EU is whether such a 'race to the bottom' is likely, and whether *Laval* encourages such an evolution.

But does it? In substance, the Court considers that the *minimum* (or 'mandatory') rules which the host Member State must impose compliance with on its territory in fact should be treated as the *maximum* level of protection that State may grant to workers posted on its territory: any further restriction to the freedom to provide services is likely to impose a disproportionate burden on the service provider, and collective actions seeking to coerce that service provider into agreeing to more favourable terms of employment are considered to constitute an abuse of the right to resort to collective action. This turns the Posted Workers Directive on its head. It also amounts to choosing, among the different objectives pursued by the Posted Workers Directive, the freedom to provide services above the other two objectives – the protection of the rights of workers and the preservation of the policy space of the host State. And it is premised on the idea that the application of any legislation at the place of posting which differs from the legislation imposed on the service provider in the State of establishment is *per se* a restriction on the freedom to provide services, *whether or not the legislation of the State of establishment provides an equivalent level of protection to workers.*

Thus, *Laval* reflects an understanding of mutual trust in the transnational provision of services in the EU which may be called 'blind': it is not conditional on the State of establishment of the service provider guaranteeing workers a level of protection of their rights equivalent to that ensured in the host Member State. In contrast, although it too suggests that the country-of-origin principle has its basis in the freedom to provide services,[50] the Opinion of Advocate General Mengozzi in the *Laval* case describes the first question submitted to the Court as being 'whether, in circumstances where a Member State has no system for declaring collective agreements to be of universal application, Directive 96/71 and Article [56 TFEU] must be interpreted as preventing trade unions of a Member State from taking, in accordance with the domestic law of that State, collective action designed to compel a service provider of another Member

dissenting), where he makes reference to the 'race of laxity' between states as businesses move to the state with the least demanding regulatory requirements.

50 See the Opinion of Advocate General Mengozzi, para. 132: '[T]he application of the "core" terms and conditions of employment that must be guaranteed by the host Member State to workers temporarily posted to its territory, under Article 3 of Directive 96/71, constitutes a derogation from the principle of application of the legislation of the Member State of origin to the situation of the service provider of that Member State that posts those workers to the territory of the first Member State.'

State to subscribe, by means of a tie-in agreement, to a collective agreement for the benefit of workers posted temporarily by that provider to the territory of the first Member State, *including cases* [*sic*] *where that provider is already bound by a collective agreement entered into in the Member State where it is established*' (para. 162). In his reading of Article 56 TFEU, 'host Member States, and in particular their courts, [should] assess the equivalence or essential similarity of the protection already available to posted workers under legislation and/or collective agreements in the Member State where the service provider is established, in particular as regards the pay such workers receive' (para. 264), and only if there exists such an equivalent protection of workers should restrictions on the freedom to provide services resulting, *inter alia*, from collective action by unions, be considered disproportionate. It is significant that these qualifications are absent from the reformulation by the Court of the question of interpretation it was submitted.[51] The remainder of the judgment confirms that, in the view of the Court, it does not matter whether or not the foreign service provider is bound, in the Member State of establishment, by rules ensuring a protection of workers equivalent to that they would be guaranteed by the extension to such workers of collective agreements concluded in the State of posting by the local unions for the benefit of the local workforce. It is in that sense that *Laval* may be said to organize regulatory competition between the EU Member States.

Similar considerations apply if we examine the second part of the judgment, which concerns the allegedly discriminatory character of the 'Lex Britannia' adopted in 1991 by the Swedish legislature in order to combat 'social dumping'. The Court takes the view that it is discriminatory not to apply a rule prohibiting collective action aimed at setting aside collective agreements already concluded between labour and management to collective action against service providers established in another Member State. Again in contrast to the position of Advocate General Mengozzi,[52] the

[51] *Laval*, note 10 above, paras. 51–3.

[52] The view of Advocate General Mengozzi was that, taking into account 'the extent of the coverage of collective agreements in the Swedish building sector and the possibility, deriving from the regime established by the MBL, of compelling domestic employers not affiliated to an employers' organisation to conclude an agreement of that kind by means of the right granted to trade unions to take collective action, the Swedish system appears, by subjecting a foreign service provider to the latter regime, to ensure the equal treatment provided for by Article 3 of Directive 96/71 as between that provider and the domestic undertakings carrying on business in the Swedish building sector which are in a similar situation' (para. 193 of the Opinion). That Opinion accepts the premise of the 'Lex Britannia', that employers operating in Sweden and having concluded collective

judgment of the Court thus seems to rely on the assumption that collective agreements concluded abroad must be trusted in principle to offer a sufficiently high level of protection of workers. Whether such trust should be blind or should instead be seen as a rebuttable presumption that the protection of workers is sufficiently robust is not clear. The Court does note at one point that the 'Lex Britannia' 'fails to take into account, *irrespective of their content*, collective agreements to which undertakings that post workers to Sweden are already bound in the Member State in which they are established'.[53] This suggests that collective agreements which are insufficiently protective of workers may not shield the foreign service providers who concluded them from having to face collective action by Swedish unions. But the remainder of the judgment of the Court does not refer back to this proviso, and suggests instead that the EU Member States should trust collective agreements concluded in another Member State as ensuring a level of protection equivalent to collective agreements concluded under their own jurisdiction.

4. Mutual trust in social Europe

In defence of the *Laval* and *Viking* cases, it may perhaps be said that they rely, albeit implicitly, on the notion of mutual trust: each Member State should agree to treat the protection of workers that any other Member State achieves at domestic level as equivalent in principle to its own, and this should suffice to justify a presumption that the service provider established in another Member State, and operating under the laws of that State, should be allowed to provide services throughout the Union, without being required to comply with the regulations of the host State, with the exception of the set of mandatory rules defined in the Posted Workers Directive. Such a presentation would be misleading, however. As noted above, the notion of mutual trust, with all the positive connotations it conveys, could be used in almost the exactly opposite way, to refer instead to the need to trust the receiving Member State that seeks to impose its rules on the service provider posting workers on its territory, without presuming that any rule going beyond the bare *minimum* is discriminatory in intent, or imposes burdens in fact that should be treated, presumptively, as violating the European

agreements under a foreign legislation may be treated as having concluded no collective agreement at all. Implicit is that such foreign collective agreements may not be trusted, and are no substitute for the conclusion, in Sweden, of collective agreements with the Swedish unions.

53 *Laval*, note 10 above, para. 116 (emphasis added).

compact. But the presentation of *Laval* and *Viking* as based on a notion of mutual trust also fails for two other reasons that go beyond the semantics.

First, this presentation tends to underestimate the imbalance that results from a situation in which companies are free to move, within certain limits, from one jurisdiction to another, without the free movement of workers constituting a credible counterweight to this mobility of capital.[54] As Lord Wedderburn already stated forcefully in 1973, 'the true correlative to an international agreement securing the right to capital the right to move and, therefore, organize across the boundaries of national states would be an agreement securing to collective organizations of workpeople the right to take common action in negotiating, bargaining with and, if need be, striking against the multinational enterprises . . . It is not true free movement of labour but free international trade union action which is the true counterpart to free movement of capital.'[55] It is particularly disquieting therefore that, in *Viking*, the transnational organization of labour is seen as potentially 'abusive',[56] since it could discourage companies from exercising their freedom of establishment. Indeed, the absence of robust social competences at the European level is an argument in favour of, not against, the exercise of transnational collective action, since no regulation can be expected to intervene at European level to counter the impact of companies relocating in order to benefit from the most favourable regulatory environment.

Second, the judgments in *Laval* and *Viking* appear very deferential to the result of domestic processes through which norms ensuring the protection of workers are set. However, there can be a wide gap between the regulatory framework applicable in any Member State and its effective implementation. For instance, in a review conducted by Vaughan-Whitehead on the impact of enlargement of social Europe, it has been noted that in a number of central and eastern European countries, complaints mechanisms were hardly ever made use of by the concerned workers, because of a fear of reprisals in fast-changing and fragile economic contexts.[57] The same study

[54] See, for instance, on the very limited flows of cross-border migration within the EU, L. Tsoukalis, *The New European Economy Revisited*, 3rd edn (Oxford University Press, 1997), pp. 117–21.

[55] K. Wedderburn, 'Industrial Relations' in H. R. Hahlo, J. G. Smith and R. W. Wright (eds.), *Nationalism and the Multinational Enterprise: Legal, Economic and Managerial Aspects* (Leiden: A. W. Sijthoff, and Dobbs Ferry, NY: Oceana Publications, 1973), p. 249.

[56] See, in particular, the Opinion of Advocate General Maduro, paras. 70–1.

[57] D. Vaughan-Whitehead, 'The World of Work in the New EU Member States: Diversity and Convergence' in D. Vaughan-Whitehead (ed.), *Working and Employment Conditions in New*

documents practices, such as certain employers systematically outsourcing the hiring of workers to employment agencies in order to avoid the payment of certain contributions and having a direct legal relationship with workers, or the practice of under-declaring wages, that may undermine certain social protection schemes. Such problems – sometimes resulting in the outright violation of the social legislation applicable – seem to a certain extent unavoidable so long as the standards of living remain relatively low: as Vaughan-Whitehead noted, referring to the situation prevailing at the time of enlargement of the EU in 2004, 'living standards [in the new Member States of central and eastern Europe] have so far not developed enough to induce employees to choose their working patterns on the basis of other criteria – for instance, the need to take care of children or the wish to have more leisure time, and so on – than the basic necessity to escape from poverty'.[58] The implication, however, is that trust between jurisdictions in principle should be based not only on substantive considerations – i.e., what regulatory framework is in place in the State of establishment, and which protection it grants to workers –but also on process-based considerations, such as the effectiveness of social dialogue at domestic level and the existence of monitoring mechanisms, whether at domestic or at international level, ensuring that the interests of workers are adequately taken into account.

Yet, pointing at the weaknesses of the *Viking–Laval* line of cases does not necessarily imply that the converse attitude – blindly trusting the domestic political processes in the receiving State – would necessarily be correct. The question of which level of mutual trust is desirable or acceptable between the EU Member States cannot be separated from certain hypotheses about the formation of preferences at domestic level. But how such preferences are formed cannot be merely assumed: it must be tested empirically, and, if necessary, it must be transformed.

The process of national policy-making is in fact far more complex than is generally assumed in the usual 'regulatory competition' scenarios. The idea of 'regulatory competition' is premised on the view that States will seek to create a regulatory environment as favourable as possible to the undertakings established under their jurisdiction, in order to attract them, as a source of capital mobilization and employment creation, transfers of technologies, and fiscal revenues, for the State concerned. But this is in fact a highly reductionist view. It impoverishes our understanding of States'

EU Member States: Convergence or Diversity? (Geneva: International Labour Office, 2005), pp. 1–43, p. 16.

[58] *Ibid.*, p. 16.

behaviour just like the idea of the *homo economicus*, in classical economics, impoverishes our understanding of the behaviour of the individual. It underestimates the complexity of decision-making processes at the domestic level – and in particular the weight of workers' unions in our advanced Welfare States.[59] It is precisely the reality of the contest of the definition of the 'public interest' in each State that is ignored when the national preferences of each State are predefined, or depoliticized, based on a view of governments as systematically seeking to attract foreign capital by creating a regulatory environment favourable to the undertakings established on their territory.[60] Instead, while it is acknowledged that 'social policy regulations that have (or are perceived as having) the effect of reducing profits and hence capital incomes are . . . vulnerable to increased capital mobility', the 'race to the bottom' in this area 'will at least be impeded by the political commitment of national governments to social policy purposes and by the resistance of unions and other groups that would suffer from deregulation and setbacks'.[61] The literature adopting a 'varieties of capitalism' approach also warns that the respective national response strategies within the EU may vary critically depending on the organizational power of trade unions and employers' organizations in each State, with widely diverging outcomes across States.[62]

[59] This is not to say that States cannot be treated as 'rational actors', for instance to describe their position in international negotiations. For instance, the 'liberal intergovernmentalist' model of international negotiations adopted by A. Moravcsik takes as its departure point 'the assumption that states act rationally or instrumentally in pursuit of relatively stable and well-ordered interests at any given point in time'. A. Moravcsik, *The Choice for Europe. Social Purpose and State Power from Messina to Maastricht*, 1st edn (London and New York: Routledge, 1998), p. 18. But Moravcsik rightly distinguishes the formation of national preferences as a separate and contested moment, noting that his 'rationalist framework of international cooperation' does not assume that States are 'unitary in their internal politics'. Quite the contrary in fact: 'National preferences – the underlying "states of the world" that states seek to realize through world politics – are shaped through contention among domestic political groups. The unitary-actor assumption maintains only that once particular objectives arise out of this domestic competition, states strategize as unitary actors *vis-à-vis* other states in an effort to realize them'. *Ibid.*, p. 22.

[60] See, in contrast to the classical 'regulatory competition' approach that obliterates this dimension, D. C. Esty and D. Geradin, 'Regulatory Co-opetition', *Journal of International Economic Law* (2000) 23555, p. 238.

[61] F. Scharpf, 'Introduction: The Problem Solving Capacity of Multi-Level Governance', *Journal of European Public Policy* 4 (1997) 520, p. 524.

[62] G. Menz, *Varieties of Capitalism and Europeanization: National Response Strategies to the Single European Market*, 2nd edn (Oxford University Press, 2008); and see, for an earlier contribution, G. Menz, 'Re-regulating the Single Market: National Varieties of Capitalism and Their Responses to Europeanization', *Journal of European Public Policy* 10(4) (2003) 532–55.

The reductionist view of the formation of the political preferences of each State not only seems to assume, without justification, that the interests of the business community will be systematically prioritized above those of workers or of the public as a whole. It also underestimates the potential role of what Scharpf refers to as 'political imitation', i.e., of the process through which each State seeks inspiration from the others, in making decisions of its own.[63] Communication between jurisdictions matters, not only because it may lead to a 'race to the bottom' in certain areas, as States observe each other and do not wish to have their competitiveness undercut by the regulatory choices made in other States, but also because 'best practices' can be shared, and relied upon by various groups within the State, to force a 'race to the top'.

Indeed, at the core of the idea of democratic experimentalism, as pioneered in particular in the work of Ch. Sabel and J. Zeitlin,[64] is the intuition that governance in multi-level (or federal) entities should be conceived in order to encourage local experiments (the search, in each sub-unit, for innovative solutions to the problems with which all units are confronted), combined with a pooling of the results following such experiments (on the basis of the evaluation made of those experiments). In this view, the combination of decentralized experimentation with the pooling of information and evaluations performed jointly should allow all sub-units of the system to benefit from the progress in understanding made in local settings. Such collective learning may potentially result in the empowerment of groups at the domestic level, whose inability to propose credible alternatives may otherwise lead to their marginalization within the political process. It is precisely the potential of such collective learning that is underestimated in the scenarios of 'regulatory competition' that assume that States act with the

[63] F. Scharpf mentions 'political imitation' as a possible factor weighing against the pressure exercised on national regulators by 'regulatory competition', in areas such as process regulations or taxation of mobile factors or households where such competition may exist (F. Scharpf, *Governing in Europe: Effective and Democratic?*, 1st edn (Oxford University Press, 1999)), pp. 90–1. He then states, however, that such 'political imitation' will not be considered further in his examination of the regulatory competition debate.

[64] See, in particular, C. F. Sabel and J. Zeitlin, 'Learning from Difference: The New Architecture of Experimentalist Governance in the European Union', *European Law Journal* 14 (2008) 271; and C. F. Sabel and J. Zeitlin (eds.), *Experimentalist Governance in the European Union: Towards a New Architecture*, 1st edn (Oxford University Press, 2010). See also O. Gerstenberg and C. F. Sabel, 'Directly Deliberative Polyarchy: An Institutional Ideal for Europe?' in Ch. Joerges and R. Dehousse (eds.), *Good Governance in Europe's Integrated Market*, vol. 11, Book 2, 1st edn (Oxford University Press, 2002), pp. 289–342.

main or even the sole purpose of enabling undertakings established on their territory to increase their competitiveness: such scenarios simply ignore the reality of democratic self-determination.

It is clear, of course, that 'democratic experimentalism', and the collective learning that it seeks to encourage, only have chances of succeeding if certain institutional conditions are fulfilled, both at EU and at national levels. Prominent among them are: (1) at national level, a strong involvement of national actors, including parliaments and civil society organizations, and the establishment of an institution specifically tasked with identifying good practices from foreign experiences and with examining whether they should inspire developments in the domestic setting; (2) at EU level, the development of a set of outcome indicators which may allow for different national experiences to be compared against one another, and the creation of a forum in which those experiences can be examined in the light of the specific national context from which they have emerged. Institutions matter, in that sense. But the important message here, in the context of the discussion of mutual trust in the provision of services across borders, is that neither full harmonization nor full decentralization, combined or not with mutual recognition, are desirable (or objectionable) in the abstract: the allocation of competences across different levels of governance and the rules regarding mutual recognition in the regime of trade in services can only be evaluated in combination with specific modes of political organization, at each level, and of the capacity of the different actors involved to bring about certain results.

5. Conclusion

This paper has examined the debate on the impact of the transborder provision of services on the protection of the fundamental rights of workers. In this context, the question of the role of trust in the mutual recognition of services regulation in the EU is essentially whether a presumption may be established in favour of recognizing the regulation of the State of establishment of the service provider as equivalent, in the degree of protection it provides to the worker, to that of the State of posting. We now see why this question is one that cannot be appropriately addressed without asking a series of other, interrelated questions. One is whether the State of establishment of the service provider, beyond having in place a regulatory framework that complies with the requirements of the fundamental social rights of workers, also has a well-functioning institutional framework – including labour inspectorates, social dialogue at company and sector levels, and courts – ensuring that these rights are effectively protected.[65] Another is whether the decision-making process within the State is sufficiently inclusive and organized in order to ensure that the policy choices of the State – its 'public interest' – will not be captured by particular factions, but will instead be the outcome of deliberative procedures, informed by the choices made in other States.[66] Even when both these conditions are fulfilled, however, the risk of 'regulatory competition' remains present, albeit in a limited sense: the risk is that, as the result of the non-cooperative behaviour of one or more EU Member States, all States will be hesitant to raise the levels of protection of workers' rights, in order not to impose excessive regulatory costs on companies established under their jurisdiction. In 1996, the Posted Workers Directive sought to respond to this risk, by requiring from the State of posting that it ensure compliance, at the very least, with a core set of rules ensuring a *minimum* protection of workers.[67] The recent case law of the Court of Justice redefines this *minimum* as a *maximum*: it now appears that States shall not be allowed to move beyond the imposition of this core set of rules, as any attempts to do so would be treated, presumptively, as a disproportionate restriction to the freedom to provide services across borders.[68]

In recent years, the debate on 'regulatory competition' has moved beyond the simplistic view that States were always motivated primarily, in their regulatory choices, by considerations linked to the need to attract foreign capital, even at the price of the protection of the rights of workers. A more complex picture has emerged both within the economics of federalism and public choice theory and outside that research programme, for instance in the writings of proponents of democratic experimentalism. These authors have reminded us that decision-making in democratic polities is the result both of the competition of various groups seeking to influence outcomes and of deliberative processes: the alternative to harmonization and the imposition of top-down regulations that could freeze the search for alternatives, then, may be to empower those among these groups that have a progressive agenda, and to strengthen such processes. They also put forward that decentralized decision-making (and the resulting 'competition' between sub-units of a multi-layered system of governance) can in fact have benevolent effects: by encouraging local experimentation and collective

[65] See the text corresponding to notes 57–8 above.
[66] See the text corresponding to notes 59–62 above.
[67] See the text corresponding to notes 8–9 above.
[68] See the text corresponding to notes 73–4 above.

learning, it can broaden our political imagination and increase the voice of groups that would otherwise be marginalized, because they would have no alternative to oppose the discourse prioritizing competitiveness that would have been tested elsewhere. Whether these benefits can outweigh the risks of regulatory competition, in an area such as the transnational provision of services, cannot be decided in the abstract: it will depend, primarily, on whether unions and civil society actors at domestic level manage to mobilize effectively, and can push for the adoption of the best practices identified in other jurisdictions, or whether instead they will be overpowered by the pressure exercised by the business community, in favour of the kind of 'laxity' that Justice Brandeis feared.[69] Let us not forget: it was on the 'strength of the trade union movement in European countries' and on the 'sympathy of European governments for social aspirations' that the experts who worked with Bertil Ohlin to prepare the 1955 report on the 'Social Aspects of European Economic Co-operation' were basing their optimism[70] – and their ghosts are still haunting the European house.

69 See note 52 above.

70 B. Ohlin *et al.*, 'Social Aspects of European Economic Co-operation', Report by the Group of Experts on Social Aspects of Problems of European Economic Co-operation, International Labour Office, Geneva, 1956 (reproduced in *International Labour Review* 74 (1956) 99).

11

Reconceptualizing the constitution of Europe's post-national constellation – by dint of conflict of laws

CHRISTIAN JOERGES AND FLORIAN RÖDL*

1. Introduction

'Trust' can be understood and operationalized as a response to the great variety of policy objectives pursued in the regulation of services and the need to 'manage' the integration process. It is a response, however, which is not adequate for the social sphere in its entirety. It reflects instead the commitment of the European project to the economic rationality of market integration. Tensions between that commitment and the various welfarist traditions of the Member States could be kept latent in the 'golden age' of 'embedded liberalism'. With the expansion and deepening of the integration process they are coming increasingly to the fore. The December 2007 judgments of the European Court of Justice in *Viking* and *Laval* and the later *Rüffert* case on the compatibility of national collective labour law with European prerogatives have prioritized European economic freedoms over the social objectives of national labour law. That jurisprudence has met with fierce criticism. In the conflicts law perspective of this chapter, the claim to supremacy of economic freedoms over national labour law seems indeed unwarranted. Is it at least economically sound and/or even a command of European solidarity to expose the labour markets of 'old Europe' to the cheap labour which the organizers of services can offer? It seems much more likely that this type of competition will have disintegrative implications.

Why introduce labour law cases in a volume dedicated to free trade in services? Why refer to conflicts law in a project exploring the importance of trust for the accomplishment of a European market for services? To

* Translated by Harry Bauer, London.

state just two quite obvious bundles of reasons: the ever growing importance of the service economy and of its legal notions is perceived, on the one hand, as a threat to the accomplishments of labour law, and, on the other, where services are privatized, as a threat to the provision of public services through the welfare State. These developments have not come to a rest, however: they are instead the background to constant tensions both in national societies and at the European level. Neither did the appeal of labour law to social justice and its critique of market rationality lose its social and political importance, nor did the politics of privatization and Europeanization destroy the realm of public services. 'Conflicts', the second notion we are going to employ, reflects these tensions, the presence of movements and counter-movements within and between the Member States and the European Union. Suffice it here to recall the unfortunate French referendum on the Constitutional Treaty of 18 July 2003[1] on which the Bolkestein draft Directive[2] has had a quite significant effect.[3] The later parliamentary discussion and intergovernmental negotiations were anything but harmonious. The compromise which was finally adopted[4] will require complex implementation processes. The Services Directive did not institutionalize the Bolkestein principle of home State control. Its *modus operandi* can instead be characterized as a 'managed mutual recognition',[5] which has much in common with the comitology procedures employed in particular in the fields of social regulation.[6]

The complex state of European services law mirrors the state of the Union as a whole. We refrain here from any systematic account, but simply underline our view that the current constitutional situation should not be equated with that of a federal State, not even a federal

[1] OJ 2004 C310/1.

[2] See COM(2004) 2 final of 25 February 2004 and the explanatory Commission Staff Working Paper, Extended Impact Assessment of Proposal for a Directive in Services in the Internal Market, SEC(2004) 21 of 13 January 2004.

[3] See D. della Porta and M. Caiani, *Quale Europa? Europeizzazione, identità e conflitti* (Bologna: Molino, 2005); J. Schild, 'Ein Sieg der Angst – das gescheiterte französische Verfassungsreferendum', *Integration* 28 (2006) 187–200.

[4] Directive 2006/123/EC of the European Parliament and of the Council of 12 December 2006 on services in the internal market, OJ 2006 L376/36.

[5] K. Nicolaïdis and S. K. Schmidt, 'Mutual Recognition on Trial: The Long Road to Services Liberalisation', *Journal of European Public Policy* 14 (2007) 717–34.

[6] See J. Falke, 'Umsetzung der Dienstleistungsrichtlinie – statt befürchteten Sozialdumpings erhoffte Verwaltungsreform' in A. Fischer-Lescano, F. Rödl and C. Schmid (eds.), *Europäische Gesellschaftsverfassung. Zur Konstitutionalisierung sozialer Demokratie in Europa* (Baden-Baden: Nomos, 2009), pp. 203–29.

State *in statu nascendi*.[7] We should underline, however, what we have explained elsewhere in much detail,[8] namely, that our reservations against the federalization of Europe is not just indebted to political realism but also rests on normative grounds. The conceptualization of today's Europe as a 'federal union' tends to further a neo-liberal transformation of the social orders ('*Sozialverfassungen*') of the Member States. The alternative of a constitution under conflicts law, which we defend, suggests that, with the establishment of the Common Market, characterized by the opening of national borders for goods and services, and far-reaching supranational regulation of the resulting cross-border competition, the Union has become the arena for a number of horizontal legal collisions between Member States as well as vertical legal collisions between the Community and the Member State level. Instead of ascribing – quasi-federally – supremacy at a grand scale to the European level, the European '*Verfassungsverbund*'[9] represents in our understanding a third way between the federal State and pure confederation. In that '*Bund*',[10] the validity of *all* legal norms of relevance in Europeanized

7 Even after the ratification of the Treaty of Lisbon, the Member States remain the 'masters of the Treaty' (see the Maastricht judgment of the German Bundesverfassungsgericht, *Brunner* v. *The European Union Treaty* [1994] 1 CMLR 57) (para. 112), confirmed by the judgment of 30 June 2009 on the Treaty of Lisbon. The English translation of the German Constitutional Court's judgment of 30 June 2008 on the Treaty is available at https://www.bundesverfassungsgericht.de/entscheidungen/es20090630_2bve000208.en.html.

8 Ch. Joerges, 'What Is Left of the European Economic Constitution? A Melancholic Eulogy', *European Law Review* 30 (2005) 461–89; F. Rödl, 'Labour Constitution' in A. von Bogdandy and J. Bast (eds.), *Principles of European Constitutional Law*, 2nd edn (Oxford: Hart Publishing, 2010), pp. 623–58; Ch. Joerges and F. Rödl, 'Informal Politics, Formalised Law and the "Social Deficit" of European Integration: Reflections after the Judgments of the ECJ in Viking and Laval', *European Law Journal* 15 (2009) 1–19; see, also, F. W. Scharpf, *Governing in Europe: Effective and Democratic* (Oxford University Press, 1999); M. Höpner and A. Schäfer, 'A New Phase of European Integration: Organized Capitalisms in Post-Ricardian Europe', *West European Politics* 33 (2010) 344–68.

9 On this notion, see I. Pernice, 'Die dritte Gewalt im europäischen Verfassungsverbund', *Europarecht* (1996) 27–43.

10 For a reconstruction of that concept, see Ch. Schönberger, 'Die Europäische Union als Bund', *Archiv des öffentlichen Rechts* 129 (2004) 81–119, thereby not avoiding the work of the dark lord of German constitutional law, Carl Schmitt, *Verfassungslehre*, 9th edn (Berlin: Duncker and Humblot, 1993), p. 363. According to Schmitt, the *Bund* is an entity established by a free agreement between the constituent Member States. It establishes a lasting order, charged with the realization of the objectives common to the Member States among which the achievement of the lasting peace is paramount. As such, the *Bund* requires a significant change in the legal and political status of the Member States; for a detailed analysis, cf. M. Avbelj, 'Theory of European Bund' (PhD thesis, European University Institute, Florence, 2009), Chapter 3, pp. 109 *et seq*.

constellations is of equal status. It should then – as a modern and universal conflict of laws has always demanded in its original area of international private law – try to establish a careful settlement between the competing substantial legal concerns of the involved politico-democratic units.[11]

2. The conflicts-law approach to the European constellation

We are by no means the only ones to plead for a turn to conflict of laws at all levels of governance.[12] It may, therefore, be useful to start with a note explaining the specifics of our approach by contrasting it with our most prominent neighbour, namely, Gunther Teubner, who resorts to conflict of laws as a means of operationalizing (juridifying) systems theory at all levels of governance,[13] and the suggestion developed in collaboration with Andreas Fischer-Lescano to reconstruct transnational law as a law of regime collisions.[14]

To restate their core argument briefly: the societal division of labour, so fundamental for societal modernity, can no longer be framed by the nation State. Instead, the highly differentiated societal spheres, which are domestically already only reflexively governable, push their respective law beyond the boundaries of the nation State. These processes trigger functional transnational legal regimes – some of public, some of private, some of hybrid character – to emerge, which manifest themselves as

[11] See F. Rödl, 'Weltbürgerliches Kollisionsrecht. Über die Form des Kollisionsrechts und seine Gestalt im Recht der Europäischen Union' (PhD thesis, European University Institute, Florence, 2008). As an American position with quite interesting affinities, albeit without particular interest in the defence of political democracy, see P. Schiff Berman, 'Choice of Law and Jurisdiction of the Internet: Towards a Cosmopolitan Vision of Conflict of Laws Redefining Governmental Interests in a Global Era', *University of Pennsylvania Law Review* 153 (2005) 1819–1892.

[12] We draw in the following in parts on Ch. Joerges and F. Rödl, 'Zum Funktionswandel des Kollisionsrechts II. Die kollisionsrechtliche Form einer legitimen Verfassung der post-nationalen Konstellation' in A. Fischer-Lescano *et al.* (eds.), *Soziologische Jurisprudenz. Festschrift für Gunther Teubner* (Berlin: Walter de Gruyter, 2009), pp. 599–612.

[13] See, e.g., G. Teubner, 'Societal Constitutionalism: Alternatives to State-Centred Constitutional Theory?' in Ch. Joerges, I.-J. Sand and G. Teubner (eds.), *Constitutionalism and Transnational Governance* (Oxford: Hart Publishing, 2004), pp. 3–28.

[14] G. Teubner and A. Fischer-Lescano, 'Regime-Collisions: The Vain Search for Legal Unity in the Fragmentation of Global Law', *Michigan Journal of International Law* 25 (4) (2004) 999–1045.

autonomous legal constitutions. After the erosion of the State's ability to govern and due to the solipsism of the highly differentiated subsystems, courts come into play both as fora and as actors alike in this situation. They find themselves confronted with the collisions of the laws of these functional regimes, which they take as merely legal conflicts and upon which they decide; however, at the heart of these conflicts lies the collision of the incommensurable rationalities of the differentiated functional subsystems. The judicial mediation of conflicts – and here their form under the conflict of laws becomes significant – should not give precedence to one societal rationality over the other, in order to reconstitute societal hierarchies; instead, it is important that none of the competing rationalities gains absolute primacy; all rationalities should be given as far-reaching a validity as possible, even in the case of conflict.

Our resort to conflict-of-laws methodologies is equally comprehensive. In our understanding, however, conflict of laws is a response to the complexity of conflict constellations in our societies, a response which requires the coordination or balancing of conflicting concerns. The 'proceduralization of the category of law'[15] is a response to this *problématique* within constitutional democracies.[16] This is a notion which we retain in our reinterpretation of European law as a 'new type of conflict of laws'. The challenges of the European constellation are, however, distinct in two ways. We start from a failure of democracy of nation

[15] The notion of proceduralization was first developed by Rudolf Wiethölter in his analysis of the litigation on the constitutionality of Germany's co-determination law: R. Wiethölter, 'Entwicklung des Rechtsbegriffs am Beispiel des BVG-Urteils zum Mitbestimmungsgesetz und – allgemeiner – an Beispielen des sog. Sonderprivatrechts' in V. Gessner and G. Winter (eds.), *Rechtsformen der Verflechtung von Staat und Wirtschaft* (Opladen: Westdeutscher Verlag, 1982), pp. 38–59; Jürgen Habermas took the notion up systematically in his *Between Facts and Norms*, 2nd edn (Cambridge, MA: MIT Press, 1998), pp. 427–46. For a more recent philosophical account, see C. Lafont, 'Procedural Justice? Implications of the Rawls–Habermas Debate for Discourse Ethics', *Philosophy and Social Criticism* 29 (2003) 167–85; and for the transposition into European law as a 'law of law production' (*Rechtfertigungsrecht*), see M. Everson and J. Eisner, *The Making of a European Constitution: Judges and Law Beyond Constitutive Power* (Abingdon: Routledge-Cavendish, 2007), pp. 22 and 28; and M.-S. Kuo, 'From Myth to Fiction: Why a Legalist-Constructivist Rescue of European Constitutional Ordering Fails', *Oxford Journal of Legal Studies* 29 (2009) 1–24.

[16] On this interdependence, see also F. Rödl, 'Regime-Collisions, Proceduralised Conflict of Laws and the Unity of the Law: On the Form of Constitutionalism beyond the State' in R. Nickel (ed.), *Conflict of Laws and Laws of Conflict in Europe and Beyond – Patterns of Supranational and Transnational Juridification* (Antwerp: Jutersentia, 2011), pp. 263–78.

States, which European law is to cure.[17] As Christian Joerges and Jürgen Neyer framed it back in 1997:

> The legitimacy of governance within constitutional states is flawed in so far as it remains inevitably one-sided and parochial or selfish. The taming of the nation-state through democratic constitutions has its limits. [If and, indeed, because] democracies presuppose and represent collective identities, they have very few mechanisms to ensure that 'foreign' identities and their interests are taken into account within their decision-making processes.[18]

If the legitimacy of supranational institutions can be designed to cure these deficiencies – as a correction of 'nation-State failures', as it were – they may then derive their legitimacy from this compensatory function.

The responses that European law can provide are, however, limited. The European Union is not a comprehensive polity; it lacks a *Kompetenz-Kompetenz* and its legislative activities remain restricted to 'limited fields'. The most important limitation, which has begun to come to the fore quite dramatically in the recent jurisprudence of the Court, stems from the 'social deficit' of the integration project. Fritz Scharpf's

[17] It is worth noting that Jürgen Habermas has already pointed to the 'ever greater gap between being passively affected and actively participating' in his very first essay on European integration: J. Habermas, *Staatsbürgerschaft und nationale Identität* (Zurich: Erker, 1990), reprinted as Annex II to Jürgen Habermas, *Between Facts and Norms*, 2nd edn (Cambridge, MA: MIT Press, 1999), pp. 491–516, p. 503. The Luhmannian parlance should not distract from Habermas' democratic concerns. They coincide with our argument that the supranational European conflicts law has to counter the democratic deficits of nation States: its inability to include those concerned in national decision-making.

[18] Ch. Joerges and J. Neyer, 'From Intergovernmental Bargaining to Deliberative Political Processes: The Constitutionalisation of Comitology', *European Law Journal* 3 (1997) 273–99, p. 293; for an update, see Ch. Joerges, '"Deliberative Political Processes" Revisited: What Have we Learnt about the Legitimacy of Supranational Decision-Making', *Journal of Common Market Studies* 44 (2006) 779–802. A very similar argument has been developed by Robert Howse and Kalypso Nicolaïdis. They write: '[Our] horizontal reading of subsidiarity and supremacy follows directly from the limits of the notion of sovereignty in a world where laws and actions within a polity increasingly have external effects. Supremacy and subsidiarity therefore can be defined in a dialectic way as complementary principles to deal with the fundamental conundrum of transnational democracy. Supremacy serves as a meta-norm of conflict of law between Member States such as to enhance the representation of foreigners inside the jurisdiction of every Member State and to ask when and to what extent these interests should trump the domestic social contract.' See R. Howse and K. Nicolaïdis, 'Democracy without Sovereignty: The Global Vocation of Political Ethics' in T. Broude and Y. Shany (eds.), *The Shifting Allocation of Authority in International Law: Considering Sovereignty, Supremacy and Subsidiarity* (Oxford: Hart Publishing, 2008), pp. 163–91, p. 167.

notion of the 'decoupling' of the (largely European) economic constitution from the (primarily national) social constitution captures this *problématique* well. What we praise as Europe's chance to cure its democracy deficits turns into a threat here. Europe simply does not have the means to develop an equivalent to the welfare traditions of the democracies of Western Europe. Undoubtedly, a destruction of Europe's '*Sozialstaatlichkeit*' is a democratic problem only if one assumes that democratic governance presupposes that the European citizens *should* be in a position to influence the economic and social organization of their societies.[19]

These remarks should suffice as a basis for the following elaboration of our three-dimensional conflict-of-laws approach. In each of the three dimensions, we will take up a *problématique* of exemplary importance. We will first comment upon the tensions resulting from the disjuncture of the economic and social spheres, which seemed to be in equilibrium during the 'golden age' of 'embedded liberalism'[20] (section 2.1 below). We will then illustrate the second dimension of our approach by referring to the European handling of problems of the risk society, herein defending the notions of transnational problem-solving which take law – not exclusively – as a product of judicial legal practice, but provide for the participation of both experts and societal actors, and for procedures which ensure the democratic legitimacy of the outcome that this generates (section 2.2 below). Our third point concerns the normative relationship between civil and public constitutions. The empirical emergence of para-legal 'civil constitutions' (*Zivilverfassungen*),[21] especially in the transnational context, can hardly be doubted. However, we argue that the coexistence of civil and public constitutions should not be seen as a factual pluralism of autonomous and equivalent normative orders. At this point, we would, instead, like to introduce an asymmetry, which has to exist in the relationship between civil and public constitutions. This argument is grounded in the fact that every civil constitution and its

[19] On this premise, see Ch. Joerges, 'What Is Left of the European Economic Constitution? above, note 8.

[20] The term has been coined by G. Ruggie, 'International Regimes, Transactions and Change: Embedded Liberalism in the Postwar Economic Order', *International Organization* 36 (1982) 379–415.

[21] G. Teubner, 'Societal Constitutionalism: Alternatives to State-Centred Constitutional Theory?' above, note 13.

law are made subject to examination under the public constitution.[22] We illustrate this point with the process of European norm-generation (section 2.3 below).

2.1 *The first dimension: the recent responses of the Court to the social disembedding of the European economy*

The recent jurisprudence of the Court on the impact of European primary and secondary law on national labour law has attracted unprecedented Europe-wide critical attention. We were among the first to articulate such critique,[23] which we do not need to reiterate here. Suffice it to underline the conflict-of-laws dimension of the, by now, (in)famous decisions in *Viking*[24] and *Laval*.[25] In both cases, the Court has attributed an extremely far-reaching and rigid meaning to the supremacy doctrine. European economic liberties were applied to Finnish trade unions in order to restrict their exercise of the right to strike in *Viking*; the Posted Workers Directive was interpreted as a comprehensive regulation which restricted the right to strike as guaranteed under the Swedish constitutional law in *Laval*. As Loïc Azoulai has pointed out,[26] this jurisprudence represents a move away from the original construction of the Common Market, from 'partial integration' to a regime of 'total integration'.[27] The revolutionary character of this move becomes apparent in the most basic exercise that students of conflict of laws have to undertake in the search for the applicable law, namely, that of 'characterization'. Economic liberties and collective labour law are very distinct species; to assign supremacy to the former ignores this difference. Similarly, a Directive with very limited objectives and the

[22] See Ch. Möllers, 'Transnational Governance without a Public Law?' in Ch. Joerges, I.-J. Sand and G. Teubner (eds.), *Constitutionalism and Transnational Governance* (Oxford: Hart Publishing, 2004), pp. 329–37.

[23] Ch. Joerges and F. Rödl, 'Informal Politics, Formalised Law and the "Social Deficit" of European Integration: Reflections after the Judgments of the ECJ in Viking and Laval', *European Law Journal* 15 (2009) 1–19.

[24] Case C-438/05, *International Transport Workers' Federation, Finnish Seamen's Union* v. *Viking Line ABP, OÜ Viking Line Eesti* [2007] ECR I-10779.

[25] Case C-341/05, *Laval un Partneri Ltd* v. *Svenska Byggnadsarbetareförbundet, Svenska Byggnadsarbetareförbundets, avdelning 1, Svenska Elektrikerförbundet* [2007] ECR I-11767.

[26] L. Azoulai, 'The Court of Justice and the Social Market Economy: The Emergence of an Ideal and the Conditions for Its Realization', *Common Market Law Review* 45 (2008) 1335–1356.

[27] *Ibid.*, p. 1346.

unspecified 'social dimension' of the Union cannot trump the labour and social constitution (*Arbeits-* and *Sozialverfassung*) of a Member State.

Let us briefly restate the institutional background to these objections:[28] the primarily economic orientation of the integration project and its detachment from statal welfare functions has never been substantially changed. During the formative era of the European Economic Community, this configuration did not cause serious concerns. It seemed safe to assume that both spheres could peacefully coexist: while the Common Market would provide all those involved with increases in prosperity, the Member States would remain responsible for the (re)distribution of these gains. Implicit to this was the assumption that the freedom of trade and services in the Common Market would not lead to direct Europe-wide wage competition among workers from different Member States; given that the price of human labour, if measured on the basis of its productivity, was at a comparable level throughout the Community, distortions of this initial equilibrium – this was the third assumption – could be counter-balanced by readjustments in the then still flexible exchange rates.[29]

These assumptions are of a constitutive importance for the defence of statal welfare functions because all welfare States restrict wage competition among employees through minimum legal working conditions and/or the legal sanctioning of collective bargaining. It is the very objective of labour law to exempt labour, the fictitious commodity, from the regular competitive market mechanisms. To be sure, the opening of national economies for free trade in goods and services threatens these historically grown, but also hard won, limitations. This threat is felt whenever a new State whose limiting mechanisms are less effective or geared towards lower standards becomes a member of the Union. This is why enlargement has caused foreseeable social tensions that could not be sufficiently cushioned by transfer payments.[30]

However, the competition in goods exerts pressure on the welfare States of 'old Europe' only indirectly, and is much softer than an imposition of

[28] See, more comprehensively, Ch. Joerges and F. Rödl, '"Social Market Economy" as Europe's Social Model?' in L. Magnusson and B. Stråth (eds.), *A European Social Citizenship* (Brussels: Lang, 2005), pp. 125–58, also available as EUI Working Paper Law No. 2004/8; also F. Rödl, 'Labour Constitution' in A. von Bogdandy and J. Bast (eds.), *Principles of European Constitutional Law*, 2nd edn (Oxford: Hart Publishing, 2010), pp. 623–58.

[29] Ch. Joerges and F. Rödl, '"Social Market Economy" as Europe's Social Model?', above.

[30] See G. Ross, 'Assessing the Delors Era and Social Policy' in St. Leibfried and P. Pierson (eds.), *European Social Policy: Between Fragmentation and Integration* (Washington, DC: Brookings Institution, 1995), pp. 357–88.

direct wage competition through legal *fiat*, which is precisely what happened in the *Rüffert* case.[31] At issue was the compatibility with European law of legislation on social clauses in public procurement tenders, in Germany's so-called *Tariftreuegesetz*. This type of legislation is a weak *ersatz* for an industry-wide collectively binding wage agreement. It has been enacted in a number of *Länder*, not only with social democratic governments, and requires 'loyalty' (*Treue*, compliance) with local collective agreements.[32] Firms which make contracts with a public authority are therefore bound to pay their employees according to the locally relevant wage agreements. By dint of this instrument, which is also correctly termed a 'small extension of a collective agreement', the binding force of industry-wide wage agreements can, at least in the area of public work, be enhanced. This is of particular importance in the construction industry. This legislative technique (*Tariftreuegesetzgebung*) was contested on legal grounds in Germany, but, in the end, its constitutional validity was clearly confirmed by Germany's constitutional court.[33]

The Court, however, declared Lower Saxony's *Tariftreuegesetze* to be incompatible with the freedom of services as guaranteed by Article 56 TFEU and the Posted Workers Directive.[34] This Directive stipulates that a number of core labour provisions, which are prescribed by law or by a legally binding collective agreement in the building industry, also apply to employees who are posted into the host State only temporarily. The Court interpreted this Directive in a surprisingly extensive way. The Court declared that any conceivable means other than those explicitly named in the Directive for extending domestic working conditions to posted workers were prohibited by the Directive.[35] The German mode of extending collective agreements limited to the public sector seemed so implausible to the Court that it did not pass the first step of the justification test for the limitations of fundamental freedoms: it seemed incomprehensible that the law was indeed meant to protect employees.[36]

[31] Case C-346/06, *Rüffert* v. *Land Niedersachsen* [2008] ECR I-1989.

[32] For an overview, see Th. Schulten and M. Pawicki, 'Tariftreueregelungen in Deutschland', *WSI-Mitteilungen* 61 (2008) 184–90.

[33] Bundesverfassungsgericht, judgment of 11 July 2006, available at www.bundesverfassungsgericht.de/entscheidungen/ls20060711_1bvl000400.html.

[34] Directive 96/71/EC, OJ 1997 L18/1.

[35] The Court again did not mention, let alone discuss, the Opinion of Advocate General Bot (Advocates General Mengozzi and Maduro were treated likewise in the *Laval* and *Viking* judgments).

[36] Case C-346/06, *Rüffert* v. *Land Niedersachsen* [2008] ECR I-1989, para. 40.

Once again, the Court assigned supremacy to the economic 'laws' (to the economic rationality) of the European market over the social objectives of national legislation. It thereby touched upon a condition which is of central symbolic and practical importance for the survival of the modern welfare State under conditions of open borders and transnational markets. To be sure, legislation such as that at issue in *Rüffert* has always been, and is bound to remain, politically contested.[37] However, it is for precisely this reason that the legitimacy of European intervention into such a contested field is extremely problematical. The Court has taken a clear position against a classical concern of the labour law of all Western European democracies.

The *Rüffert* ruling illustrates rather drastically that societal conflicts can underlie collisions of different – in this case, economic and social – 'rationalities', which nation States had managed to pacify by the recognition of both the 'laws' of the market *and* the exemption of labour relations from ordinary market governance. The seemingly neutral appeal to a legal rule, which subjects these orders to the general discipline of a federal order or to the European principle of primacy, seems simply misplaced. Similar reasons militate against a general precept of proportionality or mutual considerateness. In constellations such as that of the *Rüffert* case, an application of such principles would foster the 'invasion of the market' into spheres which have been exempted from its rules after decades of social and constitutional contestation. European law and its institutional actors should understand and respect the societal backdrop of the shape of Union competencies, according to which the articulation of social rights largely remains with the Member States.

2.2 *The second dimension: substantive conflicts law against technocratic rule*

While Europe has failed to develop transnational labour and social constitutions, Europeanization exerted remarkably progressive and modernizing effects in the field of so-called social regulation, in particular, the regulation of health and safety at work, and environmental and consumer protection. As, in the 1980s, all institutional actors agreed that

[37] See, with many references, M. Kittner, *Arbeitskampf. Geschichte, Recht, Gegenwart* (Munich: C. H. Beck, 2005).

integration should be pushed ahead by the 'completion' of the Internal Market, it became quickly apparent that this project required extensive regulatory and institutional reforms. Advocates of a neo-liberal market-Europe found this irritating, but the development did not really come as a surprise as Europe's striving for market building encountered a number of nationally established regulatory practices which it could not easily abolish: thus, extensive regulatory reforms seemed to be a more attractive alternative.

In view of its problem-solving ambition, modern regulatory politics requires that expertise be taken into account, for example, when it deals with the uncertainties of the risk *problématique*, complex economic issues or the social implication of a particular policy choice. Furthermore, expert advice may, thanks to its inherent 'objective' authority, help to ensure the cooperation of societal actors. With regard to all these aspects, the European level of governance was badly equipped for the tasks that the promotion of the integration project required. Thanks to some cunning of reason, this weakness translated into innovative experimentation. For the architects of the Internal Market, it was not really an option to establish a hierarchically structured bureaucracy or European agencies modelled on American patterns. Instead, it seemed obvious to return to those practices with which Europe had already established a level-transcending, continuously active, 'political administration', i.e., the committee system as first developed in agricultural policy.

In official parlance, this institutional arrangement is termed 'comitology'.[38] The obscurity of the term rivals the complexity of its task to reduce the functional and structural tensions of the Internal Market project. Often enough, the implementation of pertinent regulatory policies touches upon politically sensitive topics. The comitology system has then to mediate between functional requirements and normative concerns. The composition of committees will therefore mirror the task of taking different strands of expertise into account before coming to a

[38] For details, see J. Falke, 'Komitologie – Entwicklung, Rechtsgrundlagen und erste empirische Annäherung' in Ch. Joerges and J. Falke (eds.), *Das Ausschußwesen der Europäischen Union: Praxis der Risikoregulierung im Binnenmarkt und ihre rechtliche Verfassung* (Baden-Baden: Nomos, 2000), pp. 43–159; E. Vos, 'EU Committees: The Evolution of Unforeseen Institutional Actors in European Product Regulation' in Ch. Joerges and E. Vos (eds.), *EU Committees: Social Regulation, Law and Politics* (Oxford: Hart Publishing, 1999), pp. 19–47; and, most recently, E. Vos, 'Fifty Years of European Integration, Forty-Five Years of Comitology' in A. Ott and E. Vos (eds.), *Fifty Years of European Integration: Foundations and Perspectives* (The Hague: T. M. C. Asser Press, 2009), pp. 31–56.

practical synthesis. Thus, comitology more or less succeeds in adequately mirroring the given plurality of interests and political diversity which have to be balanced in the implementation process.

In our opening remarks on the conflicts approach, we introduced comitology as a mode of conflict mediation that cannot be understood as merely an 'application' of law to the problem at hand. The irrefutable need to include scientific and practical expertise in the search for the proper regulatory measure also affects its transnational operation. An exclusively judicial treatment of these collisions would be confronted with an irresolvable dilemma, as only two equally inadequate possibilities would be available: courts could either stress the territorial scope of a Member State's regulation, according to the tradition of public conflict of laws,[39] and would thereby fail to build up the Internal Market; or they could, instead, establish a pure country-of-origin principle, which would realize a liberalist conception of conflict of laws[40] – and would thus risk the discontent of the citizens of the Union with such deregulatory perspectives. The 'third way' we are advocating is transnational substantive provisions which are neither identical with the provisions of one of the concerned jurisdictions nor represent prerogatives from a superordinate federal level; these norms retain instead the function of conflicts rules, they are 'substantive norms in the conflict of laws' (*kollisionsrechtliche Sachnormen*).[41] In contrast to the norms of public and liberalistic conflict of laws, such substantive solutions cannot emerge in strictly and exclusively legal operations. Instead, these substantive responses have to be generated in procedures which mirror their political implications and mediating functions. It is precisely for this reason that comitology is an appealing institution. Its 'regulatory committees' resemble 'mini-councils', whose legitimation is derived from the delegation by democratically legitimated Member State governments. With the inclusion of

[39] For this tradition, see exemplarily G. Kegel and I. Seidl-Hohenveldern, 'Zum Territorialitätsprinzip im internationalen öffentlichen Recht' in A. Heldrich, D. Henrich and H. J. Sonnenberger (eds.), *Konflikt und Ordnung. Festschrift für Murad Ferid* (Munich: C. H. Beck, 1978), pp. 233–77.

[40] St. Grundmann, 'Das Internationale Privatrecht der E-Commerce-Richtlinie', *Rabels Zeitschrift* 67 (2003) 246–97.

[41] This notion was first coined by E. Steindorff, *Sachnormen im Internationalen Privatrecht* (Frankfurt: Klostermann, 1958); for a modernized version, see P. Schiff Berman, 'Choice of Law and Jurisdiction of the Internet: Towards a Cosmopolitan Vision of Conflict of Laws Redefining Governmental Interests in a Global Era', *University of Pennsylvania Law Review* 153 (2005) 1819–1892.

competing concerns and the introduction of scientific and practical expertise, a 'praxis as discovery procedure'[42] has been established, which is based upon the productivity of the cooperative handling of complex conflict situations; some significant pieces of evidence indicate that the considerations of problems are usually conducted in an objective-deliberative manner, which is – unfortunately until today overly – insulated from the broader public.

These failures are by no means a particularity of the European constellation. At all levels of governance, the edge of bureaucracy with regard to knowledge and power threatens to undermine the constitutionally foreseen relationship of legislation, government and bureaucracy.[43] Everywhere, and hence also in supranational contexts, it is important to prepare for the risks posed by increasingly detached European and international functional bureaucracies and expert circles.[44] Some appropriate safeguards can be discerned in the comitology system, for example, the transparency of comitology committees towards the European Parliament and the recognition of the rights of the individual citizen to information,[45] as well as the safeguard clauses in all pertinent secondary legislation, which do not allow permanent opt-outs, but ensure political rights to renewed consultation and

[42] The term was coined as a contrast to F. A. von Hayek's 'competition as a discovery procedure': it alludes to the social and political embeddedness of markets and to deliberative potentials of the 'economy as polity'; see Ch. Joerges, *Verbraucherschutz als Rechtsproblem* (Heidelberg: Recht und Wirtschaft, 1981), pp. 111 *et seq.*; Ch. Joerges, 'Quality Regulation in Consumer Goods Markets: Theoretical Concepts and Practical Examples' in T. Daintith and G. Teubner (eds.), *Contract and Organization* (Berlin: de Gruyter, 1986), pp. 142–63; Ch. Joerges, 'A New Type of Conflicts Law as the Legal Paradigm of the Postnational Constellation' in Ch. Joerges and J. Falke (eds.), *Karl Polanyi, Globalisation and the Potential of Law in Transnational Markets* (Oxford: Hart Publishing, 2011), pp. 465–501.

[43] See the seminal study of W. Schluchter, *Aspekte bürokratischer Herrschaft. Studien zur Interpretation der fortschreitenden Industriegesellschaft* (Frankfurt: Suhrkamp, 1972, reprint 1985), pp. 145–76.

[44] We are in agreement with R. Schmalz-Bruns' apposite phrase that this is the 'normative knell point of constitutionalisation of supranational-administrative legislation': R. Schmalz-Bruns, 'An den Grenzen der Entstaatlichung' in P. Niesen and B. Herborth (eds.), *Anarchie der kommunikativen Freiheit* (Frankfurt: Suhrkamp, 2007), pp. 269–94, p. 290.

[45] See Article 5, para. 5, of the Council Decision laying down the procedures for the exercise of implementing powers conferred on the Commission, OJ 1999 L184/23, on the one hand, and Case T-188/97, *Rothmans International* v. *Commission* [1999] ECR II-2463, on the other.

decision-making.[46] However, more advanced proposals regarding a deeper and primarily procedural constitutionalization of the comitology system have to consider two difficulties. The first concerns the barriers of incomprehension between experts and the general public. The second results from the socio-economic and cultural dependencies of risk politics. Constitutionalization has to take into account the fact that a plurality of expertise in the decision-making process has to be guaranteed, and that the social and political plurality of Europe is respected in order to allow European publics to observe each other mutually and to raise awareness of the concerns of others.[47] If all these considerations complicate unitary decisions, then this is, at least normatively, no disadvantage; on the contrary, it corresponds to the plurality of the EU. The practical prospects of these suggestions being implemented are, however, slim. Regulatory politics reacts in its dominant strands with a centralizing 'scientification' to the increase of regulatory tasks and the growth of socio-economic diversity, the latter being mainly a result of the Eastern enlargement; this strategy only accepts the objections to environmental and health risks, which can be backed by scientific proof, as relevant. In this way, the normative potential of comitology is being eroded.[48] It is increasingly replaced by European agencies, which work on cognitively understood risk analyses, while the risk management itself remains with the politically responsible actors – as if the cognitive-scientific and

[46] See Article 95, paras. 4–8 and 10 EC (now Article 114 TFEU), and, as a recent quite spectacular example, the Decision of the European Council of 2 March 2009 upholding Austria's import prohibition on genetically modified maize; see www.gmo-compass.org/eng/news/422.cultivation_ban_gm_maize_austria_hungary_remains.html and the analysis of M. Weimer, 'Applying Precaution in Community Authorisation of Genetically Modified Products – Challenges and Suggestions for Reform', RECON Online Working Paper 2009/14, Oslo, 2009.

[47] For the concept of a European public, we refer to the work of Klaus Eder, in particular, his 'Zur Transformation nationalstaatlicher Öffentlichkeit in Europa', *Berliner Journal für Soziologie* 10 (2000) 167–84.

[48] But, for a more positive account, see E. Vos, 'EU Committees: The Evolution of Unforeseen Institutional Actors in European Product Regulation' in Ch. Joerges and E. Vos (eds.), *EU Committees: Social Regulation, Law and Politics* (Oxford: Hart Publishing, 1999), pp. 19–47, pp. 49 *et seq*. In her account, she could not yet include the more recent moves initiated by the Commission on the basis of Articles 290 and 291 TFEU. Both the Communication of 9 December 2009 (COM(2009) 673 final) on delegated acts and the Proposal for the exercise of implementing powers of 9 March 2010 (COM(2010) 83 final) seek to strengthen the Commission's role significantly and one-sidedly.

practical-political dimensions of risk regulation could be clearly kept apart. The factual strengthening of scientific consultation in European risk politics accommodates the interest into common European and unitary decisions, and facilitates the integration of European policy into global efforts; in the end, this fact also tends to accommodate the marketing strategies of global corporations, which do not want to be concerned with the impact of legal regulations on the well-being of domestic pigs or of innovation in genetic engineering on Polish agriculture. It is in this tendency to detach European regulatory policies from their distributive implications that the disjunction of market integration and social integration is reproduced.

2.3 The third dimension: conflicts of public constitutionalism and private transnationalism

Even if these governance arrangements by which Europe organizes the economic and social regulation of the Internal Market often include non-governmental actors, in the above-outlined 'old' comitology an administrative component still dominates. For the practically enormously influential area of standardization, which affects all aspects of production and consumption, the opposite relationship exists. Here, national bureaucracies and the European Commission are in no way absent, but they have taken a role on the sidelines – as observers and facilitators.

In Europe, this change in position took place in 1985 by dint of the 'new approach to technical harmonization and standards'. Its (success) story is fantastic:[49] after the cumbersome efforts, which had occupied the EEC from 1969, to eliminate the so-called non-tariff barriers to trade had turned out to be in vain, Lord Cockfield designed a bundle of shrewdly tuned measures on behalf of the European Commission. By these means, European legislation unburdened itself significantly by focusing on essential safety requirements. The concretization of the latter was delegated to the European standardization organizations, CEN, CENELEC and ETSI. The inclusion of non-State actors signified *de facto* a delegation of legislative competencies. At a first glance, this might seem downright paradoxical: the regulation of this 'private transnationalism' (Harm Schepel) has turned out to be far more intense than in previously public

[49] See the reconstruction by H. Schepel, *The Constitution of Private Governance* (Oxford: Hart Publishing, 2005), especially at pp. 35 *et seq*.

policy fields, which are now covered by new governance arrangements. Widely accepted and stable procedures have emerged, which synthesize legal principles, professional standards and participation opportunities, and lead repeatedly to consensual problem-solving.

Significantly, European standardization shares many characteristics with – by now threatened – comitology features.[50] In particular, it has refrained from centralization, and, with its non-unitary network structure, guarantees that national delegations can make their perspectives/viewpoints heard. Not only the bureaucracies, but also courts, are always latently and, at times, actually present. Standardization happens in their shadow. It has detached itself from State law, but remains transparent and in contact with governmental actors. For Schepel, the recipe for successful standardization is that its procedures follow political, and not economic or scientific, standards: fair procedures, transparency, openness and balanced interest representation are the yardsticks according to which consultations within the respective institutions are geared. They foster neither scientific knowledge nor economic efficiency, but aim at the recognition of their results by State law.[51]

Thus, we are confronted with a constellation in which coercive State law and the norm-generation of non-State actors complement each other productively. The assertion that the process of standardization develops and maintains such sensitivity at all levels of governance seems, at least, plausible to us, as Schepel's observations coincide with historical studies reconstructing the transformation of the one-dimensionally construed consumer into a politically active market citizen,[52] with sociological analyses diagnosing the moralization of markets[53] and with a plethora of economic sociological studies conceptualizing markets as social institutions.[54] To generalize this point, law can, and should, be based on the fact that the modern economy and its markets do not function like automatons following the money-mediated steering mode of supply and

[50] It seems worth noting that the 2007 reform of the new approach seems to preserve the qualities we are praising; see the thorough analysis by J. Falke, 'Produkt- und Lebensmittelsicherheit in der Europäischen Union und in der WTO' in J. Falke and Ch. Joerges (eds.), *Handelsliberalisierung und Sozialregulierung in transnationalen Konstellationen* (Baden-Baden: Nomos, forthcoming, 2012).

[51] H. Schepel, *The Constitution of Private Governance*, above note 49, p. 223.

[52] K. Soper and F. Trentmann (eds.), *Citizenship and Consumption* (New York: Palgrave Macmillan, 2007).

[53] N. Stehr, *Die Moralisierung der Märkte* (Frankfurt: Suhrkamp, 2007).

[54] J. Beckert, *Beyond the Market: The Social Foundations of Economic Efficiency* (Princeton University Press, 2002).

demand. Instead, they have to determine politically important regulations. Law can assume that the producers of these norms are, in principle, interested in their recognition, especially by constitutional law. Therefore, law can, and should, influence the very generation of these regulations.

As in the case of comitology, we have to ask ourselves to what extent such interactions can be understood under the conflict-of-laws approach. In contrast to questions of recognition, with which the conventional law of conflicts is confronted in relation to foreign law and foreign judgments, here we are faced with para-legal alternatives to State law. However, at the same time, regulatory issues are concerned, as in comparable national constellations, with the solution for which the State law lacks resources and expertise.[55] The transition to procedural forms of regulation in national law correlates with the willingness to recognize the results of societal norm-generation, which, first, is bound to substantial preconditions, second, follows some procedural demands or at least corresponds to recognized practices, and, third, whose results do not have to be accepted by State legal systems, with whose *ordre public* they are not compatible.

The notion of the recognition of non-State law in the conflict of laws under preconditions does not represent a radically new turn in thinking about the conflict of laws. Instead, an approach is adopted and generalized which has long since been accepted and practised in private international law, namely, the recognition of the rulings of private courts of arbitration by State law (paragraphs 1059 *et seq*. of the German Code of Civil Procedure);[56] they are also subject to objective preconditions as well as procedural and material requirements, which are more substantial than the recognition of foreign law (Article 6 of the German Code on the Conflict of Laws) or the recognition of foreign judicial decisions (Article 328 of the German Code of Civil Procedure). This analogy also stresses the asymmetry of what has already been outlined: private standardization seeks the recognition of State or European law; the former

[55] E. Schanze, 'International Standards – Functions and Links to Law' in P. Nobel (ed.), *International Standards and the Law* (Bern: Stämpfli, 2005), pp. 84–103, pp. 90–1; H. Schepel, 'Sources and Legal Recognition of Standardisation' in Ch. Joerges and E.-U. Petersmann (eds.), *Constitutionalism, Multilevel Trade Governance and Social Regulation* (Oxford: Hart Publishing, 2006), pp. 397–409.

[56] See, in the context of the debate about a 'private law beyond the State', F. Rödl, 'Private Law beyond the Democratic Order?', *American Journal of Comparative Law* 56 (2008) 743–66, pp. 764 *et seq*.

depends upon the latter and therefore operates in its shadow.[57] This enables us, in 'old European' terms, to stick to the notion that law can only claim validity if those legally or factually subject to it can see themselves as its equivalent authors – this seems only conceivable in procedures that come under public constitution.

3. Outlook

We are of course aware of the need to elaborate further and concretize our approach in all of its three dimensions; we have to be more precise in outlining links with legal theory, integration theory and theories of International Relations. However, it should, nevertheless, have become clear what our reference points are, and where we would like to go.

Most important for us are the challenges to law posed by the post-national constellation. We are concerned with advancing law's two-fold task: to grant and safeguard individual *and* social freedom. This requires the forms of individual freedom to find articulation in public-democratic procedures. The post-national constellation leads, on the one hand, to ('vertical') collisions of societally generated norms with publicly constitutionalized law, and to ('horizontal') collisions among these norms, on the other hand. In such a pluralist context, law can only remain democratically legitimate if societal norm-generation becomes endorsed as an exercise of autonomy granted by public authority. Moreover, there are also conflicts of publicly constituted legal orders in the fragmented global multi-level system. Here, law can preserve its democratic legitimacy only if it protects democratic autonomy and compensates for the democratic deficits of political fragmentation.[58]

[57] This aspect seems also to be central in M. Herberg, *Globalisierung und private Selbstregulierung* (Frankfurt: Campus, 2007). K. Günther defends similar positions and intentions: see his 'Kann das Zivilrecht im Zuge der Globalisierung das öffentliche Recht ersetzen?' in Ch. Joerges and G. Teubner (eds.), *Rechtsverfassungsrecht: Recht-Fertigung zwischen Privatrechtsdogmatik und Gesellschaftstheorie* (Baden-Baden: Nomos, 2003), pp. 295–311, pp. 305 *et seq.*; and Ch. Möllers, 'Transnational Governance without a Public Law?' in Ch. Joerges, I.-J. Sand and G. Teubner (eds.), *Constitutionalism and Transnational Governance* (Oxford: Hart Publishing, 2004), pp. 329–37.

[58] J. Bast, 'Das Demokratiedefizit internationaler Fragmentierung', *Soziale Welt* (2009) 185–94; Ch. Möllers, *Gewaltengliederung* (Tübingen: Mohr Siebeck, 2005), p. 223.

12

Fundamental rights as sources of trust and voices of distrust in the European Internal Market

ANTOINE BAILLEUX

1. Introduction

In the case law of the European Court of Justice, the relationship between the protection of fundamental rights and the establishment of the Internal Market is characterized by a deep ambivalence.[1] To be sure, many lawyers are now familiar with the ever-growing slew of cases in which fundamental rights are invoked by Member States in order to *escape* the requirements of the free movement principles.[2] In such instances, public authorities rely on the need to protect rights such as the freedom of expression, the freedom of assembly or human dignity in an attempt to justify a measure *prima facie* incompatible with the basic principles of the Common Market. The Court had long paved the way for such a development by recognizing fundamental rights as 'general principles of Community law' in its early case law.[3] It is therefore not surprising that the European judicature proved receptive to this line of argument and readily accepted that the protection of fundamental rights may amount to an 'overriding' or 'mandatory' requirement of general

[1] See A. Bailleux, *Les interactions entre libre circulation et droits fondamentaux dans la jurisprudence communautaire. Essai sur la figure du juge traducteur* (Brussels: FUSL-Bruylant, 2009).

[2] On this case law, see, e.g., J. Morijn, 'Balancing Fundamental Rights and Common Market Freedoms in Union Law: Schmidberger and Omega in the Light of the European Constitution', *European Law Journal* 12 (2006) 15–40; A. Alemanno, 'A la recherche d'un juste équilibre entre libertés fondamentales et droits fondamentaux dans le cadre du marché intérieur', *Revue du droit de l'Union européenne* 4 (2004) 709–51.

[3] Case 26/69, *Stauder* [1969] ECR 419; Case 11/70, *Internationale Handelsgesellschaft* [1970] ECR 1125; Case 4/73, *Nold* [1974] ECR 491.

interest capable of justifying a deviation from the free movement principles enshrined in the Treaty.[4]

One should be careful, however, not to regard the protection of fundamental rights as a systematic obstacle to the free exercise of the 'four freedoms' and to the establishment of a European Common Market. In numerous cases, fundamental rights come into play to *bolster* the free movement dynamic, whether by supporting the removal of regulatory barriers to free trade[5] or by advancing the cause of the free movement of non-economically active citizens.[6] In a number of occurrences, combined claims relating to breaches of free movement *and* fundamental rights resulted in the Court exercising a particularly extensive or vigorous scrutiny of the impugned measure.[7]

This ambivalent relationship between fundamental rights and free movement (featuring both 'conflicts' and 'alliances') provides the background to this chapter. The aim of the following pages is to unravel further the chemistry of this interaction by analyzing it through the lens of the promising – yet relatively unexplored – notion of 'trust'. In this respect, it will be argued that trust is indeed the centrepiece of the relationship between fundamental rights and free movement. First, the notion of trust sheds a new light on – and, to a certain extent, provides an explanation for – the ambivalence of this relationship. Second, the issue of trust seems to bear a direct influence on the Court's reasoning and final verdict in many cases where fundamental rights and free movement come to meet.

These observations will emerge from a short – and selective – overview of the case law on fundamental rights and free movement. Section 2 of the chapter focuses on cases in which fundamental rights appear as a trust-enhancing factor, either buttressing the trust between Member States or strengthening the citizen's confidence in foreign Member States. Section 3 of the chapter explores the cases where fundamental rights act as channels for the expression of distrust both among Member States and between citizens and foreign Member States.

[4] See, e.g., Case C-353/89, *Commission* v. *Netherlands* [1991] ECR I-4069; Case C-288/89, *Stichting Collectieve Antennevoorziening Gouda* [1991] ECR I-4007; and Case C-368/95, *Familiapress* [1997] ECR I-3689.

[5] See, e.g., Case 222/86, *Heylens* [1987] ECR 4097; and Case C-260/89, *ERT* [1991] ECR I-2925.

[6] See, e.g., Case C-60/00, *Carpenter* [2002] ECR I-6279; and Case C-109/01, *Akrich* [2003] ECR I-9607.

[7] See, e.g., Case C-370/05, *Festersen* [2007] ECR I-1129, paras. 35 and 37.

2. Fundamental rights as sources of trust

In a number of cases brought before the Court, fundamental rights are presented as the touchstone of a common legal heritage. These shared common values, it is argued, are the backbone of the European integration project and the bedrock of trust relationships between the Member States. Such references to human rights aim to strengthen the mutual recognition principle and – whether directly or indirectly – to further the free movement dynamic. An analysis of the case law reveals that, depending on the circumstances of the case, fundamental rights can be used to bolster the trust of the host State, of the home State, or of the European citizen.

2.1 Building up the host State's trust

In *Dynamic Medien*,[8] the Court was called upon to rule on the compatibility, with the free movement of goods, of a German rule prohibiting the sale of image media that had not been examined and classified by the German authority for the purpose of protecting children and the youth. This legislation precluded Avides, a German company, from selling in Germany video media that had only been approved by the British authority responsible for the protection of children. Germany claimed that this restriction to the free movement of goods was justified by the protection of morality, the rights of the child and human dignity.

We will come back later to this argument which sets the stage for a conflict between fundamental rights and free movement. Of more direct relevance here is the reply of Avides to the defence of the German government, to be found in the Opinion of Advocate General Mengozzi:

> Avides points out in this regard that the examination criteria for the protection of young persons used by the competent British and German authorities are equivalent, since both the United Kingdom and Germany have signed and ratified the Convention on the Rights of the Child adopted in New York on 20 November 1989, in the preamble to which the States Parties recognise 'that the child should be fully prepared to live an individual life in society, and brought up in the spirit of the ideals proclaimed in the Charter of the United Nations, and in particular in the spirit of peace, dignity, tolerance, freedom, equality and solidarity'.[9]

Striking here is the use of fundamental rights as a trust-building factor. The argument goes as follows: from the fact that both Germany and the

[8] Case C-244/06, *Dynamic Medien* [2008] ECR I-505. [9] *Ibid.*, para. 73.

United Kingdom have ratified the Convention on the Rights of the Child, it must be inferred that these two countries share the same standards as regards the protection of the youth. *Ergo*, Germany (the host State) should be confident that the control exercised by the British authorities (the home State) on the contents of image media is sufficient to ensure the protection of German children. By setting a common floor of core values, adherence to fundamental rights is used to support the mutual recognition principle that lies at the heart of the Common Market.

It should be noted that this argument was not taken up by the Court. The Court preferred to follow the line of reasoning developed in the *Omega* judgment that will be discussed below.

2.2 *Building up the home State's trust*

Trust relationships cannot work one way. In some instances, it is for the *home* Member State to place confidence in the *host* State in the name of a shared commitment towards fundamental rights.

An illustration of this situation is provided by the *United Pan-Europe*[10] case, which concerned a Belgian measure requiring cable operators to broadcast in Brussels programmes transmitted by certain broadcasters established in Belgium. Foreign broadcasters, which *de facto* did not benefit from this regime of 'must carry', claimed that the Belgian law was discriminatory and unduly restricted their right to freely provide services. Belgium justified this *prima facie* breach of free movement by the need to maintain pluralism and protect the freedom of expression in Brussels: cable operators had to transmit programmes in Dutch and in French in order to preserve the right of the Dutch- and French-speaking populations of Brussels to receive local information in their own language. Just like the German government in the *Dynamic Medien* case, Belgium used the protection of fundamental rights as a shield against the requirements of the free movement principles.

The call for mutual trust did not come from the claimant this time, but from the Court itself. The Court accepted Belgium's argument and considered that:

> the national legislation at issue in the main proceedings pursues an aim in the general interest, since it seeks to preserve the pluralist nature of the range of television programmes available in the bilingual region of

[10] Case C-250/06, *United Pan-Europe* [2007] ECR I-11135.

> Brussels-Capital and thus forms part of a cultural policy the aim of which is to safeguard, in the audiovisual sector, the *freedom of expression of the different social, cultural, religious, philosophical or linguistic components* which exist in that region.[11]

The Court did not only recognize the legitimacy of the need to safeguard the freedom of expression of the population of Brussels. Following the reasoning adopted in the *Schmidberger*[12] case, the Court went as far as to grant Belgium a wide margin of appreciation in its efforts to protect pluralism and free speech:

> As regards, thirdly, the question whether the legislation at issue in the main proceedings is necessary in order to attain the aim pursued, it must be noted that, while the maintenance of pluralism, through a cultural policy, is connected with the fundamental right of freedom of expression and, accordingly, that the national authorities *have a wide margin of discretion* in that regard, the requirements imposed under measures designed to implement such a policy must in no case be disproportionate in relation to that aim and the manner in which they are applied must not bring about discrimination against nationals of other Member States.[13]

It is submitted that trust played a pivotal role in the Court's decision to grant Belgium significant leeway and convert its classic proportionality test into a 'non-disproportionality' review. Behind this decision lies the notion that the home State (and all the other Member States) should trust the host State's judgment in its efforts to safeguard common fundamental values. Interestingly, fundamental rights are used by the Court to enlarge the scope of the mutual trust and mutual recognition principles, with the effect of creating an obstacle to the '*laissez faire, laissez passer*' dynamic inherent in the Common Market. It could be argued, however, that, even in this case, the role played by trust indirectly fosters economic integration by setting the ground for the establishment of a genuinely *common market*, premised on shared 'constitutional' standards.

[11] *Ibid.*, para. 42 (emphasis added).

[12] Case C-112/00, *Schmidberger* [2003] ECR I-5659. On this case, see, e.g., A. Biondi, 'Free Trade, A Mountain Road and the Right to Protest: European Economic Freedoms and Fundamental Individual Rights', *European Human Rights Law Review* 1 (2004) 51–61; F. Ronkes Agerbeek, 'Freedom of Expression and Free Movement in the Brenner Corridor: The Schmidberger Case', *European Law Review* 29 (2004) 255–66.

[13] Case C-250/06, *United Pan-Europe* [2007] ECR I-11135, para. 44.

2.3 Building up the European citizen's trust

Fundamental rights may also be viewed as a necessary condition for European *citizens* to make confident use of their free movement rights. There are good grounds to believe that respect of European standards of fundamental rights by a foreign Member State is likely to strengthen the migrant citizen's trust in that Member State and act as an incentive to move. This reasoning was set out for the first time by Advocate General Jacobs in the *Konstantinidis*[14] case:

> Suppose that a Member State introduces a draconian penal code under which theft is punishable by amputation of the right hand. A national of another Member State goes to that country in exercise of the rights of free movement . . . steals a loaf of bread and is sentenced to have his right hand cut off. Such a penalty could undoubtedly constitute inhuman and degrading punishment contrary to Article 3 of the European Convention on Human Rights. But would it also be a breach of the individual's right under Community law, even though it were applied in a non-discriminatory manner? I believe it would . . . In my opinion, a Community national who goes to another Member State . . . is in addition entitled to assume that, wherever he goes to earn his living in the European Community, he will be treated in accordance with a common code of fundamental values, in particular those laid down in the European Convention on Human Rights.[15]

This revolutionary stance was never endorsed by the Court, which prompted Advocate General Maduro recently to submit a milder version thereof. In *Centro Europa 7*,[16] Advocate General Maduro suggested that the trust necessary to the European integration project and to the exercise of free movement would be compromised by serious and persistent violations of fundamental rights in a given country. Therefore, such violations had to be regarded as breaches of the free movement principles falling under the Court's jurisdiction:

> My suggestion is not that any violation of fundamental rights within the meaning of Article 6(2) EU constitutes, of itself, an infringement of the rules on free movement. Only serious and persistent violations which highlight a problem of systemic nature in the protection of fundamental rights in the Member State at issue, would, in my view, qualify as violations of the rules on free movement, by virtue of the direct threat they would pose to the transnational dimension of European citizenship and to the integrity of the EU legal order.

[14] Case C-168/91, *Konstantinidis* [1993] ECR I-1191. [15] *Ibid.*, paras. 46–7.
[16] Case C-380/05, *Centro Europa 7 Srl* [2008] ECR I-1349.

To date, the Court does not seem to have endorsed this reasoning. It is submitted, however, that, having recognized – at least implicitly – that the exercise of free movement heavily depends on trust in the host State's regulatory regime, it might not take more than a clear (but low-profile) case for the Court to establish a further link between free movement and the respect of fundamental rights.

3. Fundamental rights as voices of distrust

Fundamental rights are not always used as trust-enhancing tools before the Court of Justice. It emerges from the case law that these same rights may carry a divisive force and may be used to voice distrust towards the neighbour and shield the Member States' constitutional identities and regulatory diversity from the unifying dynamic of the Internal Market.

3.1 Expressing the host State's distrust

A first spate of cases features fundamental rights as channels of expression of the host State's distrust *vis-à-vis* the home State's regulatory standards. The nature and the extent of this mistrust may, however, differ considerably from one case to another, as it appears from the *Omega Spielhallen*[17] and *Laval*[18] cases.

In *Omega*, the Court was called upon to assess the compatibility with the free movement of goods and services of an order from the police in Bonn prohibiting the operation of a game commercialized in the United Kingdom which involved simulated killing actions. In support of this prohibition, Germany invoked the protection of human dignity and of public policy. It argued that, in view of the specific history of Germany, such games were considered by the population as violating the highest value of the German Constitution, i.e., human dignity. Importantly, through such a measure, Germany did not express blunt distrust towards

[17] Case C-36/02, *Omega* [2004] ECR I-9609. On this case, see, e.g., C. Smith and T. Fetzer, 'The Uncertain Limits of the European Court of Justice's Authority: Economic Freedom Versus Human Dignity', *Columbia Journal of European Law* 10 (2004) 445–90; G. Chu, '"Playing at Killing" Freedom of Movement', *Legal Issues of Economic Integration* 33 (2006) 85–94.

[18] Case C-341/05, *Laval* [2007] ECR I-11767. On this case, see, e.g., B. Bercusson, 'The Trade Union Movement and the European Union: Judgment Day', *European Law Journal* 13 (2007) 279–308; N. Reich, 'Free Movement v. Social Rights in an Enlarged Union: The Laval and Viking Cases before the European Court of Justice', *German Law Journal* 9 (2008) 125–61.

the British standards, neither did it blame the British authorities for being too lax in the enforcement of such standards. Indeed, Germany did nothing more than stress the specificity of its own 'constitutional public order' and express its concern that this specificity could not be adequately safeguarded by foreign standards.

Both the Court and its Advocate General approved this line of defence. The Court stated that '[i]t is not indispensable in that respect for the restrictive measure issued by the authorities of a Member State to correspond to a conception shared by all Member States as regards the precise way in which the fundamental right or legitimate interest in question is to be protected'. Accordingly, the Court vested Germany with a significant margin of appreciation to determine (1) the existence of a breach of its constitutional values and (2) the measures needed to remedy that violation.

As a matter of fact, although this case illustrates a situation of conflict between free movement and fundamental rights, it is disputable whether it provides an instance of mistrust between Member States. To be sure, Germany distanced itself from the British standards and made a case for the protection of diversity in the Common Market. Yet, concern for specificity can hardly be equated with distrust. In addition, it should be noted that the Court's reasoning is once more premised on a powerful sense of trust – the trust that Germany will not abuse the latitude that it enjoys by adopting protectionist measures under the umbrella of its Constitution.

This example should be contrasted with the examination of the Swedish 'Lex Britannia' in the *Laval* case. This legislation authorized collective actions only against undertakings which were not bound by collective agreements in Sweden, regardless of whether such undertakings were already bound by collective agreements in any other Member State. In other words, under Swedish labour law, 'collective action is authorised against undertakings bound by a collective agreement subject to the law of another Member State in the same way as such action is authorised against undertakings which are not bound by any collective agreement'.[19]

It is submitted that the Swedish 'Lex Britannia' in *Laval* does not fulfil the same function as the order of the police of Bonn in *Omega*. Whereas the latter genuinely seeks to protect the specificity of the German constitutional order, the former merely encapsulates blunt distrust towards the other Member State's labour regime. This 'Lex Britannia' relies on the (non-rebuttable) assumption that the only trustworthy labour

[19] Case C-341/05, *Laval* [2007] ECR I-11767, para. 113.

protection instruments are those which are signed on its own territory according to its own laws. This blind defiance – applicable not only to Latvia or Estonia but also to Finland or Denmark – brings us back to the early years of European integration, when States did not know each other very well and had trouble trusting each other's standards.

It is therefore not surprising that the Court dealt with the 'Lex Britannia' as it would have forty years ago. The Court considered that the Swedish law was discriminatory and that this discrimination was contrary to EU law as it could not be justified by the public policy, public morality or public health reasons laid down in the Treaty. Admittedly, this statement is lamentable for two reasons. First, it maintains the aged and ill-suited dividing line between the express derogation grounds contained in the Treaty (capable of justifying discriminatory measures) and the mandatory or overriding requirements of general interest developed by the case law (only able to justify non-discriminatory breaches of free movement). Second, it denies any special status to the 'fundamental rights defence' by failing to recognize that the need to protect fundamental rights (such as the right to collective action) carries a particular significance in the European legal order and should therefore be placed on the same footing as the express derogation grounds enshrined in the Treaty.

However, it could be argued that the content of the 'Lex Britannia' can at least partly explain the Court's conservative position. By expressing blind distrust *vis-à-vis* all the Member States' labour legislation, the 'Lex Britannia' strikes at the heart of the European project. It is therefore only natural that the Court treated Sweden like parents would treat a boisterous child, taking the view that behaviours reminiscent of those in the early days of European integration should be sanctioned in accordance with the standards of that time.

3.2 Expressing the European citizen's distrust

European *citizens* can also use fundamental rights to express distrust towards Member States of which they are not a national. In *Viking*,[20] for instance, collective actions were taken to preclude a Finnish ship-owner from registering one of its vessels under the flag of Estonia. Those actions were taken in accordance with the policy of the International Transport Workers' Federation (ITWF). Under this policy, the ITWF was obliged to take collective actions at the request of the Finnish trade unions, even

[20] Case C-438/05, *Viking* [2007] ECR I-10779.

though Viking (the Finnish ship-owner) had eventually promised to maintain the same working conditions, and even if (hypothetically) Viking had decided to register its vessel in a State which guarantees workers a higher level of protection than Finland.[21] However legitimate and praiseworthy the goal of these collective actions may be, it is submitted that in the automatic character of such actions lies the spectre of the 'blind distrust' already found in *Laval*.

This was rightly observed by the Court and by Advocate General Maduro. Both considered that breaches of free movement caused by collective actions could be objectively justified if such actions genuinely aimed to protect the 'social identity' of the country or if they sought to improve the working conditions of all the Union workers. By contrast, such collective actions could not be allowed if they boiled down to a blunt expression of distrust *vis-à-vis* the other Member States' standards and workers.

In this respect, Advocate General Maduro's call for trust in the governments of the Member States should also be highlighted. In his Opinion in the *Viking* case, the Advocate General called upon European citizens to trust the European integration project and willingly suffer a few sacrifices in exchange for greater benefits to come:

> The European economic order is firmly anchored in a social contract: workers throughout Europe must accept the recurring negative consequences that are inherent to the common market's creation of increasing prosperity, in exchange for which society must commit itself to the general improvement of their living and working conditions, and to the provision of economic support to those workers who, as a consequence of market forces, come into difficulties.[22]

The Advocate General states further that this trust must, however, not be blind. Fundamental rights come into play here: 'The right to associate and the right to collective action are essential instruments for workers to express their voice and to make governments and employers live up to their part of the social contract'.[23]

[21] 'As Viking argued during the hearing without being contradicted by [the International Transport Workers' Federation] in that regard, the policy of reserving the right of collective negotiations to trade unions of the State of which the beneficial owner of a vessel is a national is also applicable where the vessel is registered in a State which guarantees workers a higher level of social protection than they would enjoy in the first State.' *Ibid.*, para. 89.

[22] *Ibid.*, Opinion of Advocate General Maduro, para. 59.

[23] *Ibid.*, para. 60.

The *AGM Cos.Met*[24] case provides another illustration of the role that fundamental rights can play in expressing a citizen's distrust. In this case, a Finnish official, Mr Lehtinen, publicly aired his doubts as to the safety of vehicle lifts marketed by AGM, an Italian company. These products benefited from the 'CE' label and were therefore presumed to comply with the safety requirements of secondary legislation. The only way for the Finnish authorities to lawfully restrict the marketing of these products would have been to alert the Commission and follow the procedure laid down in secondary legislation. The warnings expressed by Mr Lehtinen caused the sale in Finland of the vehicle lifts to plummet. Finland accepted that this entailed a restriction on the free movement of goods but claimed that this restriction was dictated, *inter alia*, by the need to secure the freedom of expression of Mr Lehtinen. In a rather clumsy judgment, the Court seemed to consider that Mr Lehtinen had given the impression that he was talking on behalf of the Finnish government and that therefore the restriction on free movement was imputable to Finland itself. The Court considered further that Finland did not enjoy any right to freedom of expression for itself and that, consequently, the disruption of the free flow of trade caused by Mr Lehtinen could not be justified under Union law.

From this case, it appears that the Court is again not very happy with statements or actions that jeopardize the mutual trust underpinning the European integration project. However, it is submitted that the Court went too far here. It is one thing to say that fundamental rights cannot serve as a cloak to disseminate the fear of one's neighbour and to convey mutual defiance. It is yet another to consider that the protection of fundamental rights is less important than compliance with secondary legislation on the free movement of products.

4. Conclusion

Three main trends seem to emerge from the overview of the case law on the relation between trust, free movement and fundamental rights.

First, it appears from several cases that, as a set of common values, fundamental rights can bolster trust between the Member States and

[24] Case C-470/03, *AGM Cos.Met* [2007] ECR I-2749. On this case, see, e.g., A. Bailleux, 'Les droits de l'homme face à la libre circulation – un nouveau conflit porté devant la Cour de justice', *Revue trimestrielle des droits de l'homme 72* (2007) 1171–1184; S. de Vries, 'Case C–470/03, AGM-Cos.Met Srl v. Suomen valtio, Tarmo Lehtinen', *Common Market Law Review* 45 (2008) 569–85.

hence further the dynamic of economic integration. In some instances, reliance on the Member States' adherence to the same fundamental values can make it more difficult for a State to justify obstacles to the free flow of trade. In other situations, while successfully justifying restrictions to the free movement, fundamental rights indirectly foster mutual trust and economic integration by setting the ground for the establishment of a genuinely *common market*, premised on shared 'constitutional' standards.

Second, the Court recognizes that fundamental rights can be invoked in order to secure the protection of a country's identity – whether constitutional, social or otherwise – against the unifying dynamic of the Internal Market. In such situations, the 'burden of trust' weighs on the host Member State, requested not to pursue a protectionist agenda under its constitutional umbrella.

It appears from the above that the Court takes fundamental rights seriously insofar as these rights are aimed at protecting non-market values or at preserving diversity against the imperatives of the Common Market. However – and this is my third observation – the Court has so far never admitted that fundamental rights could serve as a means to express blind defiance towards the other participants in the European integration project. This limit, placed by the Court, sheds new light on the interactions between fundamental rights and free movement. It reveals that there are things more important to the Court than the free flow of trade and the ever-closer integration of Europe – which can be both challenged and countered on fundamental rights grounds. As the touchstone of the European project, the sense of trust between and towards the Member States is carefully preserved by the Court and kept beyond the reach of litigants.

Should it be confirmed in subsequent judgments, this trend in the case law could legitimately raise a few eyebrows. Certainly, one can understand the Court's desire to keep a close eye on the jewel of the Union crown. It is respectfully submitted, however, that the Court can only be regarded as 'taking rights seriously'[25] as long as it takes care not to sacrifice individual liberty on the altar of the mutual trust underpinning the European project.

[25] See J. Coppel and A. O'Neill, 'The European Court of Justice: Taking Rights Seriously?', *Common Market Law Review* 29 (1992) 227–39; J. Weiler and N. Lockhart, '"Taking Rights Seriously" Seriously: The European Court of Justice and Its Fundamental Rights Jurisprudence', *Common Market Law Review* 32 (1995) 51–92 (Part I) and 579–627 (Part II).

PART VI

Extensions: the relevance of the 'trust theory' of integration in the context of the WTO

13

I now recognize you (and only you) as equal: an anatomy of (mutual) recognition agreements in the GATS

JUAN A. MARCHETTI AND PETROS C. MAVROIDIS*

1. Introduction

There is a plethora of writings regarding mutual recognition, which has long been recognized as a useful, and potentially powerful, means to tackle regulatory barriers impeding trade in services. Paradoxically, very little attention has been paid to empirical issues regarding recognition, such as the extent of unilateral or mutual recognition around the world. Observers, from both academic and policy quarters, have therefore been left with the impression that either recognition agreements were kept relatively secret, so that their benefits would not have to be extended to third parties, or they were not really so widespread as their merits would warrant, which could constitute an indication of countries' reluctance to venture into service market integration beyond a purely negative integration approach (i.e., one that focuses solely on the elimination of market access barriers and discriminatory measures).

This was certainly the question that prompted us to study this issue: How much recognition is out there? In which sectors? Among which countries? Are there discernible patterns? In order to address these issues we made use of the only systematic database on recognition available: the WTO. Indeed, through the notification obligations contained in Article VII GATS, the WTO has gathered an interesting amount of information,

* We have benefited from excellent research assistance by Carlo Cantore. Rhian-Mary Wood Richards, as always, was instrumental in helping us put this chapter together. We thank participants in the *Modern Law Review* conference organized in London and Cambridge (July 2009) for their comments, and, in particular, Panagiotis Delimatsis, Rob Howse, Christian Joerges, Ioannis Lianos, Kalypso Nicolaïdis, Federico Ortino and Florian Wagner-von Papp. The views expressed here should not be attributed to the WTO.

virtually a database, waiting to be analyzed. And this is basically what we have attempted in this chapter. Our data are determined then by the extent of information found in notifications to the WTO.

This chapter has another objective as well: theory predicts that recognition agreements would occur across countries that trust each other's regulatory regime. Trust is necessary since through recognition a party accepts another country's regime as equivalent to its own: crucially, it cannot influence the shaping of the regime it accepts as equivalent. Trust, however, is hard to quantify. Recourse to proxies is thus necessary to establish whether trust exists. A number of proxies have been identified in literature, such as language, geographic proximity, similarity across legal regimes, religion, etc. We will be leaning on some of them to show whether empirical evidence (who has signed agreements with who?) supports the theoretical intuitions.

Section 2 of the chapter discusses the economic rationales for recognition. In section 3 we revert to a legal discussion of recognition. Section 4 explores recognition within preferential trade agreements. Section 5 contains the data on recognition and our analysis of it. Section 6 concludes.

2. The basic economics of recognition

Asymmetric information provides the most important rationale for economic regulation: it is pervasive in service activities, and can, under certain circumstances, reduce consumer demand for services, or lead to expenses that would not otherwise have been incurred. For instance, in a situation where consumers know there are good and bad products or firms but, due to insufficient credible information, are unable to distinguish them at the point of purchase because the quality is revealed only after a lapse of time, the demand for some products may decline. Under some circumstances, and with known asymmetric information features, risk-averse consumers may exit the market altogether. In its extreme form (Akerlof's lemons), the market breaks down completely. This is because the perceived costs of purchasing a low-quality product are valued highly, and consumers may forego the possibility of purchasing what might be a high-quality product because of the high risk and high cost of unwittingly purchasing a poor product. In such a situation, consumers do not purchase products they believe might be beneficial because they are unable to distinguish high- and low-quality products.

Based on information theory, and focusing on the moment in which the consumer can assess quality, three types of products have been identified by the literature: 'search' goods, 'experience' goods and 'credence' goods.

In the case of search goods, the quality is known *ex ante*, i.e., either it can be ascertained at low cost prior to purchase, or a warranty is attached.[1] The majority of goods that we purchase (e.g., from basic commodities such as flour or petrol, to clothes, footwear, and furniture) falls into this category. The degree of uncertainty with these transactions is low and causes no problems for the consumer. The consumer knows what he or she is buying and simply searches for the lowest price, hence the name 'search' goods (these are goods where typically competition is quite stiff, and hence it is the rivalry in the market that reduces search to price elements). The consumer has confidence in her purchases, although of course this does not mean that quality is guaranteed. Nevertheless, there is a high degree of certainty about quality precisely because of the rivalry which is typical in these markets.

In the case of 'experience' goods, the quality becomes obvious *ex post*. This type of product features high pre-buying costs of quality detection. Hence, the buyer learns the product's attributes typically only after buying and consuming. The post-buying costs of quality detection are low for such goods: in other words, experience is more effective and cheaper than search. The information can be used for further (additional, future) consumption of the product. Examples of such goods include wine, restaurant meals, hotels, music records, movies and second-hand cars. While the element of uncertainty at the point of purchase is clearly higher than in the case of search goods, the degree of uncertainty is bounded. The key issue with experience goods is whether firms have incentives to supply quality products. Once again, the degree of rivalry in the market will influence the incentives.

In the case of 'credence' goods, the quality can be ascertained only at some cost after purchase and consumption, and eventually might never be fully open to objective evaluation. They basically feature high pre-buying costs and high post-buying costs of quality detection. A frequent characteristic of these goods and services is that the value of the purchase is either spread over a long period of time, or emerges only after a considerable lapse of time. Most non-network services fall into this category: health services, legal advice, and child day care, financial services, car repair and airline services. These are services in which there is a serious imbalance of information, and, ultimately, most consumers must have faith in the professionals that provide the service, and/or the process regulating the profession, hence the name 'credence' goods. Markets in credence goods are made on the basis of trust, which in turn depends on the suppliers' reputations for

[1] P. Nelson, 'Information and Consumer Behavior', *Journal of Political Economy*, 78(2) (1970) 311–29.

quality and probity, which are built over long periods of time. As noted by Darby and Karni,[2] these goods are often subject to public policy intervention for consumer protection purposes.

The informational problems that plague service industries have prompted regulatory reaction, through the use of (minimum) quality standards. Leland[3] points out that, when consumers cannot identify high-quality professionals (in his example, physicians), all professionals must charge the same fee (equal to the average quality). As a result, the most talented individuals choose other professions (where their superior ability can be revealed), assuming of course reasonable switching costs. Only the low-quality providers (the 'lemons') will be left in the market in this scenario. Under these conditions, Leland[4] shows that setting minimum quality standards will raise the average price and quality of the product. The intuition is that barriers (in the form of minimum quality standards) not only exclude the least skilled, but they increase earnings, attracting more able individuals to the market.

In effect, licensing can be considered a cost-raising mechanism, i.e., it raises the costs of entry by requiring investments in education and training. Entrants may be required to attend and complete an accredited university programme that has specific time and content characteristics. The explicit costs of this investment include payments for tuition and books, but the primary cost is usually implicit – the opportunity cost of the applicant's time. Entry fees, State- or profession-administered examinations and other requirements (such as residence and citizenship) also make entry more costly. Only licensed individuals can provide the services. As costs rise,[5] some service providers will be discouraged from entering the market. The price of services rises, as supply declines through retirements, or if demand grows faster than supply. Not until earnings rise to offset the increase in costs of entry will new professionals be attracted to the market. The new market equilibrium will be one with a lower stock of practitioners and higher prices than would have been observed in an unregulated market.

In a nutshell, then, other things being equal, licensing and qualification requirements raise the cost of entry into the market. Licensing and

[2] M. R. Darby and E. Karni. 'Free Competition and the Optimal Amount of Fraud', *Journal of Law and Economics* 16 (1973) 67–88.

[3] H. E. Leland, 'Quacks, Lemons, and Licensing: A Theory of Minimum Quality Standards', *Journal of Political Economy* 87(6) (1979) 1328–1346.

[4] *Ibid.* [5] In relation to expected earnings, of course.

qualification requirements can (and do) differ across markets: a number of independent variables, ranging from the need to regulate asymmetric information to political economy-type of considerations. Viewed against this background, recognition (be it mutual or unilateral) is a way for foreign suppliers to reduce the cost of entry, by avoiding (part of) the investment costs in education and training to accede to the foreign market: absent recognition, foreign suppliers might have been requested to carry the burden of proof that they meet the licensing and qualification requirements in the (foreign) country where they wish to provide their service. Recognition refers to situations where country A accepts the qualification standards or even the licence of another, country B, as a valid basis for licensing in its market: without such recognition, professionals from country B must take licensing exams and meet other conditions of entry imposed by country A when they seek to practice there. Sometimes recognition is only partial, and therefore the professionals from country B will be obliged to compensate for any lacunae in their background (e.g., by sitting for a competence exam or by completing a course of studies) before they are actually licensed in country A.[6] The very objective of mutual recognition, then, is to reduce transaction costs, thereby facilitating market access. Mutual recognition is in fact a way to consolidate commercial relationship.

As explained by Pelkmans,[7] in practice the starting point for mutual recognition is that trading partners have more or less equivalent regulatory objectives in, for example, safety, health, environment and consumer protection, or whatever regulatory objectives the two (or more) countries deem relevant for the regulation of a particular service sector. If and when regulatory objectives are equivalent, and thus the market failure (information asymmetry) is addressed, full harmonization is no longer necessary and cross-border trade in services is facilitated. Mutual recognition implies, in practice, that services and service suppliers originating in other trading partners must be allowed access to the host country, even if the detailed specifications in the relevant domestic regulation differ from those in the country of origin, as long as the regulatory objectives are *equivalent*: it is in this sense that the importing

6 Similar solutions have been proposed by the European Court of Justice in Case 222/86, *Heylens* [1987] ECR 4097.

7 J. Pelkmans, 'Mutual Recognition in Goods and Services: An Economic Perspective' in F. K. P. Schioppa (ed.), *The Principle of Mutual Recognition in the European Integration Process* (Basingstoke: Palgrave Macmillan, 2005).

(host) country 'recognizes' the regulatory regime of the exporting country. Equivalence is, *de facto*, a mix of qualitative and quantitative judgment.

Mutual recognition is not feasible or even necessary in all cases.[8] It is not necessary for example in non-regulated services, such as tourism, or business services, such as consulting. On the other hand, it is not feasible, or only partially feasible, in sectors where asymmetric information is not the dominant economic rationale for regulation. This is the case of the so-called network industries (e.g., broadcasting, postal, telecommunications, rail transport and gas and electricity distribution). Indeed, the economic case for regulating network industries rests basically on consumption externalities, switching costs, and significant economies of scale in production. Consumption externalities arise because the utility derived by the consumption of, for example, telephone services, is affected by the number of consumers using similar or compatible services. Consumers of network services, such as telephony, also face high costs of changing suppliers or technology, which are usually referred to as switching costs. Finally, in network industries, the long-run average cost function declines with the number of services produced, leading to the absence of competitive equilibrium in the market and to monopolistic situations. Within strict limits, selective and/or residual instances of mutual recognition (in the field of licensing or safety) remain possible in some of these services (e.g., air transport). It is in the realm of regulated non-network services (e.g., financial, some forms of transport, professional services) that mutual recognition has regulatory and economic significance.

In the presence of recognition agreements trust works in two different ways:

(1) Consumers must trust their government to have adequately regulated a particular profession so that, when purchasing, say, medical services, they will be dealing with competent professionals.
(2) They must further trust their government's selection of recognition partners. If the government commits a type I error and picks the wrong partner (adverse selection), then consumers might have to pay the price by purchasing services from incompetent professionals. Depending on the nature of the service supplied, the costs stemming from 'wrong' recognition might be quite high.

[8] *Ibid.*

3. The law regarding recognition

3.1 The legal discipline

Article VII GATS regulates recognition. It is placed in Part II of GATS, entitled 'General Obligations and Disciplines', making it clear that WTO Members are bound by it irrespective of whether they have made *specific commitments* in a particular sector. However, Article VII GATS is not really an obligation; rather, Article VII GATS is a sort of 'permission' granted to WTO Members to decide whether to recognize foreign qualifications or licences or not, subject to certain disciplines. It is when a country unilaterally (or bilaterally) recognizes foreign qualifications and licences that the obligations imposed by Article VII GATS become pertinent. It is through Article VI:4 that the GATS makes it mandatory for all WTO Members that make specific commitments regarding professional services 'to provide for adequate procedures to verify the competence of professionals of other Members'.

As explained by Delimatsis,[9] Article VI:4 is not directly related to recognition, but it is contiguous to it, as it refers to the establishment of 'adequate procedures' for verifying the competence of professionals covered by the Member's specific commitments, without defining what those 'adequate procedures' may or should be.

Coming back to Article VII GATS, we remark that:

(1) The GATS does not define 'recognition', like other agreements do.[10]
(2) Recognition can be *unilateral* or *bilateral* (Article VII:1 GATS): the former refers to cases where country A recognizes that, say, architects from country B have qualifications which are similar to those that can be obtained in country A, and that therefore enable country B architects to practice their profession in country A; whereas bilateral recognition refers to cases where the opposite obtains as well (that is, it is country B who also recognizes the qualification of architects from country A).
(3) Recognition, irrespective of whether it is unilateral or bilateral, can be achieved through harmonization, or without it: in the former case, countries A and B harmonize their standards for architects (i.e., both

[9] P. Delimatsis, *International Trade in Services and Domestic Regulations: Necessity, Transparency and Regulatory Diversity* (Oxford University Press, 2008).

[10] For example, the Convention on the Recognition of Qualifications concerning Higher Education in the European Region, concluded in Lisbon on 11 April 1997, defines recognition as 'a formal acknowledgement by a competent authority of the value of a foreign educational qualification with a view to access to educational and/or employment activities'.

apply the same standards), whereas, in the absence of harmonization, both countries continue to unilaterally define qualifications for architects, but accept nonetheless that they are equivalent (Article VII:1 GATS).[11]

(4) Recognition *should*, but does *not have to*, be based on multilaterally agreed criteria: this provision is particularly important whenever recognition is based on harmonization, the language of Article VII:5 GATS leaving no doubt as to its best endeavours nature in this respect. WTO Members, nonetheless, agree to cooperate within international organizations and with non-governmental organizations (NGOs) with a view to establishing common standards (Article VII:5 GATS).

(5) Recognition cannot serve as means of discrimination across WTO Members: Article VII:3 GATS makes this point explicit, although WTO Members must observe this obligation anyway by virtue of Article II GATS, which is legal context to Article VII GATS. Interestingly, Article VII:3 GATS speaks about 'discrimination between countries', instead of using the usual formulation for non-discrimination (in the MFN sense), that is, 'treatment no less favourable' than that accorded to own services and services suppliers.

(6) To this effect, that is, in order to guarantee that recognition does not *de facto* amount to discrimination, Article VII:2 GATS requests from those who have either unilaterally recognized or are members of a bilateral (mutual) recognition agreement (MRA) to afford adequate opportunities to all other WTO Members who wish to benefit from this. Article VII:2 GATS does not impose an *obligation of result* (i.e., petitioners must accede to an MRA), but an *obligation of specific conduct* (i.e., petitioners will be afforded adequate opportunity (whatever this means) to negotiate accession to an existing agreement, to negotiate a comparable agreement, or to demonstrate that their own qualifications should also be recognized). To cement this obligation, Article VII:4 GATS requests from all WTO Members to notify all existing recognition measures, the opening of any negotiation on recognition, as well as recognition outcomes.

(7) Recognition cannot serve as 'a disguised restriction on trade in services' either (Article VII:3 GATS). This term, which remains un-interpreted so far, could cover cases which would not formally qualify as discriminatory:

[11] Pursuant to the Decision on Professional Services adopted by Ministers at the end of the Uruguay Round, in May 1997, the WTO Working Party on Professional Services issued non-binding guidelines for the negotiation of mutual recognition agreements or arrangements (see WTO document S/L/39, 28 May 1997).

it could, for example, be the case that unnecessary non-discriminatory legislation comes under the purview of this term.

3.2 *Non-discrimination?*

All recognition (unilateral or bilateral) has to be on an MFN basis: as we saw above, both the text of Article VII GATS explicitly as well as the context of this provision (Article II GATS) make this point clear. How will recognition occur in practice?

There is no doubt as to the *burden of production* of proof: it is for the *demandeur* (i.e., the countries whose qualifications are not being recognized) to request MFN extension;[12] Article VII GATS explicitly states that the WTO Member that has recognized the regulatory standards of another WTO Member must afford adequate opportunities to the *demandeur* to present its case.

The law, however, does not address the issue of *burden of persuasion*: how much proof is necessary for the burden of production of proof to shift to the other party? There is no indication in Article VII as to what exactly has to be produced or demonstrated as proof. And this contrasts with the wording of recognition provisions regarding financial services (paragraph 3(b) of the GATS Annex on Financial Services), where it is foreseen that the *demandeur* must demonstrate the existence of specific circumstances, namely, '[the existence of] equivalent regulation, oversight, implementation of such regulation, and, if appropriate, procedures concerning the sharing of information between the parties to the agreement or arrangement'. Additionally, there is no case law in this context, and some have feared that the lack of disputes might be due to the fact that the burden of persuasion associated with successful complaints in this respect must be quite high.[13] Nicolaïdis,[14] siding with this view, goes so far as to call the obligation of MFN recognition

[12] WTO Members thus cannot, from a legal perspective, sign recognition agreements with their preferential partners only, although in practice this is often the case. By this, we mean that WTO Members cannot exclude *demandeurs* from their recognition agreement simply because a *demandeur* is not a member of their PTA.

[13] See A. Beviglia-Zampetti, 'Market Access through Mutual Recognition' in P. Sauvé and R. Stern (eds.), *The GATS 2000: New Directions in Services Trade Liberalization* (Washington, DC: Brookings Institution, 2000), pp. 283–306; and A. Mattoo, 'MFN and the GATS' in T. Cottier and P. C. Mavroidis (eds.), *Regulatory Barriers and the Principle of Non Discrimination* (Ann Arbor, MI: University of Michigan Press, 2000), pp. 51–99.

[14] K. Nicolaïdis, 'Non-Discriminatory Mutual Recognition: An Oxymoron in the New WTO Lexicon?' in T. Cottier and P. C. Mavroidis (eds.), *Regulatory Barriers and the Principle of Non Discrimination* (Ann Arbor, MI: University of Michigan Press, 2000), pp. 267–301.

an oxymoron. In the view of this author, it is not thus bizarre that recognition happens contractually and not following litigation to this effect.[15]

The regulation of the burden of persuasion is a matter of case law in WTO practice, and case law has hardly been consistent in this respect: there are cases where the burden has shifted with little evidence and cases where the opposite has happened, all in the name of the so-called *prima facie* standard that the WTO Appellate Body invented; this standard is hardly quantifiable, and leaves ample room for discretion in the hands of the adjudicator.[16] For these reasons (ample discretion, inconsistent practice), it is almost impossible to predict how the Appellate Body will use its discretion in future cases.

There are, nevertheless, good reasons to believe that there is a lot of merit in the views expressed in the doctrine so far: the recognition agreements that have been duly notified to the WTO are all *process-based* agreements, that is, a WTO Member accepts that the process for becoming, say, an architect in another WTO Member is equivalent to the one applied to its own architects. A third country will thus have to demonstrate that its own process is equivalent (or comparable at the very least)[17] to that of the WTO Member that benefited from recognition (or to that of the recognizing WTO Member). It is highly unlikely that there will be no differences across the two processes (such as the quality of education, the years of training, etc.), and, consequently, the question will be what value should the judge attach to observed differences.[18] A risk-averse panel will most likely take a conservative view and attach significant value to observed differences. Assuming the existence of differences such as the number of years of education, or the subject matter of education, to name a few – a rather safe assumption for a large number of transactions – it is to be expected that

[15] See A. Beviglia-Zampetti, 'Mutual Recognition in the Transatlantic Context: Some Reflections on Future Negotiations', in T. Cottier and P. C. Mavroidis (eds.), *Regulatory Barriers and the Principle of Non Discrimination* (Ann Arbor, MI: University of Michigan Press, 2000), pp. 303–28; and K. Nicolaïdis and J. Trachtman, 'From Policed Regulation to Managed Recognition in GATS' in P. Sauvé and R. Stern (eds.), *The GATS 2000: New Directions in Services Trade Liberalization* (Washington, DC: Brookings Institution, 2000), pp. 241–82.

[16] P. C. Mavroidis, 'No Outsourcing of Law? WTO Law as Practised by WTO Courts', *American Journal of International Law* 102 (2008) 421–74.

[17] To be sure, in the absence of practice, we do not know at this stage whether panels will adopt a more stringent equivalence – or a less stringent comparability – standard when confronting challenges regarding the extension of recognition agreements.

[18] Compare A. Mattoo, 'MFN and the GATS' in T. Cottier and P. C. Mavroidis (eds.), *Regulatory Barriers and the Principle of Non Discrimination* (Ann Arbor, MI: University of Michigan Press, 2000), pp. 51–99.

adjudicators will see differences as objective evidence justifying asymmetric treatment: the onus will be on the *demandeur* to demonstrate that, notwithstanding the differences, its own education programme is comparable to the one (from another country) benefiting from recognition.

It is probably the high burden of persuasion that explains why there has so far been no request to extend a recognition agreement. The counter-argument here would be that no request has been tabled because trade flows diverted through recognition agreements are not that significant to start with. There is no reliable empirical evidence on this score. If the European experience is of any value, however, this argument should be dismissed: it is through recognition that market access has been effectively provided for a number of professional services since other classic market integration tools, such as national treatment, proved to be of limited use in this context.[19]

Against this background, it seems reasonable to conclude that the burden of persuasion associated with requests for extension is an insulating factor effectively providing incumbents with an effective legal shield against requests for extension of their recognition agreement. The original choice of partners is, thus cemented.

4. Recognition in PTAs

Before turning to the actual anatomy of unilateral and mutual recognition around the world, we turn our attention to recognition provisions in preferential trade agreements (PTAs). The reason is the following: if PTA partners can avoid requests for extension because their recognition agreement comes under a PTA, then the preceding discussion concerning the high burden of persuasion becomes obsolete. The question we address here is, in other words, the following: do PTAs provide a safe haven under the GATS for recognition agreements?

Article V GATS allows for the conclusion of PTAs assuming the conditions embedded in this provision have been observed. Fifty-nine PTAs have been notified to the WTO at the time of writing. Twenty of these PTAs do not contain provisions on recognition (see Table 13.5 below), which means that two-thirds of the existing PTAs contain provisions on this score. Recognition is not regulated in the same manner across all PTAs: in some,

[19] See J. Pelkmans, 'Mutual Recognition in Goods and Services: An Economic Perspective' in F. K. P. Schioppa (ed.), *The Principle of Mutual Recognition in the European Integration Process* (Basingstoke: Palgrave Macmillan, 2005).

trading partners have opted for legally binding obligations,[20] whereas in others they have agreed to discuss this issue further by establishing a forum to this effect or by simply encouraging the conclusion of recognition agreements between them. In Table 13.5, we denote the former as 'Y' (Yes), and the latter as 'Other'. The overwhelming majority of PTA partners have opted for 'Other' and only four PTAs exhibit legally binding language regarding recognition: these four PTAs concern liberal professions and banking. It is interesting to note that these have been concluded between geographically proximate partners (EC, EFTA, India–Singapore and Korea–Singapore).

An interesting legal question arises: does the conclusion of a PTA provide a shield against all claims for extension of recognition? In other words, assume countries A and B have concluded a PTA in accordance with Article V GATS. Their agreement contains provisions on recognition. Country C requests an extension of these provisions for the benefit of its citizens, arguing that its own regulatory arsenal is equivalent to that of the two PTA partners in the sector concerned. Can country A (or B) reject this request by claiming that the very existence of their PTA is a factor justifying the exclusive treatment they grant to each other?

This question has not been discussed either in the preparatory work, or in WTO practice (at the Committee level or before an adjudicating body). It seems that the best arguments would dictate a negative response to the question. Article V:1(b) GATS calls for elimination of all discrimination in the sense of Article XVII GATS across PTA partners. It does not say a word, however, on the *manner* in which this should be done. Arguably, this could be done in various ways. Country A, for example, could simply subject B's lawyers to its own regulation regarding accession to the legal profession: in case of asymmetric regulation of the legal profession across A and B, A is not recognizing B's regulation as equivalent to its own; it requires B's citizens to follow the same path as its own citizens in order to accede to the legal profession in A's market. Only four of the fifty-nine PTAs contain legally binding language on recognition.

Recognition is, thus, not a *legal requirement* for the conclusion of PTAs. The legal requirements are only two: substantial sectoral coverage and

[20] Our benchmark to decide whether this has indeed been the case is the language used: when the parties use terms such as 'recognizes', we count it as legally binding; conversely, language to the effect 'a party may recognize' or 'the parties shall encourage' is in our view tantamount to a step towards recognition albeit not a legally binding obligation. We thus classify the latter under 'Other' in Table 13.5.

absence of discrimination. In the Appellate Body's words in *Turkey – Textiles*,[21] PTAs can provide legal shelter for measures which are necessary for their establishment, that is, absent which, a PTA cannot be established in the first place:

> Accordingly, on the basis of this analysis of the text and the context of the chapeau of paragraph 5 of Article XXIV, we are of the view that Article XXIV may justify a measure which is inconsistent with certain other GATT provisions. However, in a case involving the formation of a customs union, this 'defence' is available only when two conditions are fulfilled. First, the party claiming the benefit of this defence must demonstrate that the measure at issue is introduced upon the formation of a customs union that fully meets the requirements of sub-paragraphs 8(a) and 5(a) of Article XXIV. And, second, that party must demonstrate that the formation of that customs union would be prevented if it were not allowed to introduce the measure at issue. Again, *both* these conditions must be met to have the benefit of the defence under Article XXIV.[22]

As explained above, recognition is not necessary for the establishment of a PTA: both the wording of Article V GATS and subsequent practice in this area point in this direction. The Appellate Body report on *Turkey – Textiles* concerns a GATT – and not a GATS – case. Still, we believe that it provides guidance for GATS cases as well; it would be odd for the Appellate Body to suggest that the establishment of PTAs can provide legal shelter only for measures necessary to its establishment in the GATT context, and not also in the GATS context. In both legal settings, PTAs are an exception to the overarching principle not to discriminate (MFN), and this construction is consonant with the idea that exceptions should be limited to what is strictly necessary for them to exist.

It follows that country C can request an extension of recognition for the benefit of its own citizens from the PTA partners. However, as we noted in section 2.2 above, the burden of persuasion associated with similar requests should not be underestimated. It is this factor that probably explains the absence to date – to our knowledge – of requests in this vein.

5. Recognition: an anatomy

As explained in the introduction to this chapter, our main interest is empirical, not theoretical. We asked ourselves some basic questions regarding the

[21] WTO Appellate Body Report, *Turkey – Restrictions on Imports of Textile and Clothing Products*, WT/DS34/AB/R, 1999, adopted 19 November 1999.

[22] Appellate Body, *Turkey – Textiles*, § 58 (emphasis in the original).

facts of recognition. How much recognition is out there? In which sectors? Among which countries? Are there discernible patterns? In order to address these issues, we made use of the only systematic database on recognition available: the WTO. Indeed, through the notification obligations contained in Article VII GATS, the WTO has gathered much information, virtually a database.

A caveat is in order in that regard: we are fortunate to have access to the WTO 'dataset' (which is publicly available anyway) and constrained at the same time since our analysis is based on notifications to the WTO, which are not always optimal.[23]

Between December 1995 (the date of the first notification) and May 2007 (the date of the latest notification received), the WTO received forty-seven notifications under Article VII GATS by twenty WTO Members (see Table 13.1). Twelve of those notifications concern diverse forms of unilateral recognition granted by Macau, Singapore and Switzerland. That leaves us with only thirty-five notifications of bilateral and plurilateral recognition agreements.

WTO Members have usually included more than one agreement per notification, and some notifications include both bilateral and plurilateral agreements. Thus, although there are only thirty-five notifications of MRAs by eighteen WTO Members, there are actually 119 MRAs notified (106 bilateral and thirteen plurilateral).[24] The agreements notified are both bilateral and plurilateral, which means that the WTO Members for which we have information about their recognition arrangements are a multiple of the eighteen really notifying. In other words, each notification actually provides information about the recognition granted not only by the notifying WTO Member but also by its trading partners as well. We checked the agreements notified by different WTO Members in order to avoid double counting. In doing so, we have realized that, as a matter of fact, there were only a few instances in which both participants to a bilateral MRA or some of the participants to a plurilateral MRA have made the same notification. As can be seen from Table 13.2, there are eighty-nine parties involved in the notifications, including all the parties that are involved in at least one bilateral or plurilateral MRA notified. Some of the parties are not WTO Members.

[23] It is worth noting that we attempted to obtain copies of the agreements notified by getting in touch with the notifying countries' contact points supposedly established as per Article III GATS. We actually contacted all of them by email twice, the last time on 27 April 2009, but were unable to get any answer.

[24] We counted each agreement notified only once, to avoid double counting.

Table 13.1 *Notifications under Article VII:4 GATS (in alphabetical order, between 22 December 1995 and 15 July 2007)*

WTO Member	Number of notifications	Unilateral recognition	Mutual recognition arrangements
Argentina	1		X
Armenia	2		X
Australia	6		X
Brazil	1		X
Chile	1		X
Colombia	1		X
Costa Rica	1		X
Cuba	1		X
El Salvador	1		X
European Communities	2		X
Guatemala	1		X
Japan	1		X
Latvia	2		X
Liechtenstein	1		X
Macau	1	X	
Norway	1		X
Singapore	1	X	
Switzerland	14	X (10)	X
United States	4		X
Venezuela	4		X
Total	47	12	35

We may well have 119 agreements notified, but, because of the existence of plurilateral agreements, which can be considered as being formed by a multitude of 'bilateral' agreements, we have actually many more 'bilateral' agreements. In fact, a plurilateral agreement between A, B, C and D implies six bilateral agreements: A–B, A–C, A–D, B–C, B–D and C–D. Mathematically, this can be expressed by the following formula:

$$\frac{[n \times (n-1)]}{2}$$

where n is the number of parties to the plurilateral agreement. Counting both the bilateral and the plurilateral agreements in this way,

Table 13.2 *MRAs' purpose and sectoral coverage (in numbers)*

Parties	Total	MRA's purpose						Professional purpose: sectors covered								
		Unknown purpose	Both academic and professional	Insurances	Credit institutions	Academic purposes	Professional purposes	Accountants	Engineers	Architects	Surveyors	University professions	Doctors, dentists, veterinary surgeons	Lawyers	Patents representatives	No sector
Angola	1	0	0	0	0	1	0	0	0	0	0	0	0	0	0	0
Antigua and Barbuda	1	0	0	0	0	1	0	0	0	0	0	0	0	0	0	0
Argentina	14	2	1	0	0	10	1	0	0	0	0	0	0	0	0	1
Armenia	2	0	0	0	0	0	2	0	0	0	0	0	0	0	0	2
Australia	21	0	0	0	0	0	21	17	2	1	1	0	0	0	0	0
Azerbaijan	1	0	0	0	0	0	1	0	0	0	0	0	0	0	0	1
Bahamas	1	0	0	0	0	1	0	0	0	0	0	0	0	0	0	0
Barbados	1	0	0	0	0	1	0	0	0	0	0	0	0	0	0	0
Belarus	1	0	0	0	0	0	1	0	0	0	0	0	0	0	0	1
Belgium	1	0	0	0	0	1	0	0	0	0	0	0	0	0	0	0
Belize	1	0	0	0	0	1	0	0	0	0	0	0	0	0	0	0
Bolivia	9	0	1	0	0	4	4	0	0	0	0	0	0	0	0	4
Brazil	29	0	1	0	0	26	2	0	0	0	0	0	0	0	0	2
Bulgaria	3	0	0	0	0	3	0	0	0	0	0	0	0	0	0	0
Canada	5	0	0	0	0	0	5	2	2	1	0	0	0	0	0	0
Cape Verde	1	0	0	0	0	1	0	0	0	0	0	0	0	0	0	0
Chile	14	0	1	0	0	6	7	0	0	0	0	0	0	0	0	7
China	2	0	0	0	0	1	1	1	0	0	0	0	0	0	0	0
Colombia	33	0	2	0	0	22	9	0	0	0	0	0	0	0	0	9
Congo	1	0	0	0	0	1	0	0	0	0	0	0	0	0	0	0
Costa Rica	16	0	2	0	0	11	3	0	0	0	0	0	0	0	0	3
Cuba	3	0	1	0	0	2	0	0	0	0	0	0	0	0	0	0
Czech Republic	1	0	0	0	0	1	0	0	0	0	0	0	0	0	0	0
Dominica	1	0	0	0	0	1	0	0	0	0	0	0	0	0	0	0
Dominican Republic	4	0	0	0	0	3	1	0	0	0	0	0	0	0	0	1
Ecuador	10	0	1	0	0	6	3	0	0	0	0	1	0	0	0	2
El Salvador	10	0	3	0	0	3	4	0	0	0	0	2	0	0	0	2
Estonia	2	0	0	0	0	2	0	0	0	0	0	0	0	0	0	0

European Commission	2	0	0	1	0	0	1	0	0	0	0	0	1	0	0	0
France	1	0	0	0	0	1	0	0	0	0	0	0	0	0	0	0
Georgia	1	0	0	0	0	0	1	0	0	0	0	0	0	0	0	0
Germany	3	0	0	0	2	1	0	0	0	0	0	0	0	0	0	0
Grenada	1	0	0	0	0	1	0	0	0	0	0	0	0	0	0	0
Guatemala	8	0	1	0	0	6	1	0	0	0	0	0	0	0	0	0
Guyana	1	0	0	0	0	1	0	0	0	0	0	0	0	0	0	0
Haiti	3	0	1	0	0	2	0	0	0	0	0	0	0	0	0	0
Holy See	2	0	0	0	0	2	0	0	0	0	0	0	0	0	0	0
Honduras	6	0	1	0	0	3	2	0	0	0	0	0	0	0	0	2
Hong Kong	3	0	0	0	0	0	3	1	2	0	0	0	0	0	0	0
Iceland	1	0	0	0	0	0	1	0	0	0	0	0	0	1	0	0
Iran	1	0	0	0	0	0	1	0	0	0	0	0	0	0	0	1
Ireland	4	0	0	0	0	0	4	2	2	0	0	0	0	0	0	0
Jamaica	2	0	0	0	0	2	0	0	0	0	0	0	0	0	0	0
Japan	2	0	0	0	1	0	1	0	1	0	0	0	0	0	0	0
Kazakhstan	1	0	0	0	0	0	1	0	0	0	0	0	0	0	0	1
Korea	2	0	1	0	0	0	1	0	0	0	0	0	0	0	0	0
Kyrgyzstan	1	0	0	0	0	0	1	0	0	0	0	0	0	0	0	1
Latvia	2	0	0	0	0	2	0	0	0	0	0	0	0	0	0	0
Liechtenstein	3	0	0	1	0	0	2	0	0	0	0	0	0	0	1	1
Lithuania	2	0	0	0	0	2	0	0	0	0	0	0	0	0	0	0
Luxembourg	1	0	0	0	0	0	1	0	0	0	0	0	0	0	0	0
Malaysia	1	0	0	0	0	0	1	1	0	0	0	0	0	0	0	0
Mexico	3	0	1	0	0	2	0	0	0	0	0	0	0	0	0	0
Moldova	1	0	0	0	0	0	1	0	0	0	0	0	0	0	0	0
Morocco	1	0	0	0	0	1	0	0	0	0	0	0	0	0	0	0
Netherlands	1	0	0	0	0	1	0	0	0	0	0	0	0	0	0	0
Netherlands Antilles	1	0	0	0	0	1	0	0	0	0	0	0	0	0	0	0
New Zealand	4	0	0	0	0	0	4	1	2	1	0	0	0	0	0	0
Nicaragua	4	0	0	0	0	2	2	0	0	0	0	0	0	0	0	0
Norway	1	0	0	0	0	0	1	0	0	0	0	0	0	1	0	0
Panama	5	0	1	0	0	4	0	0	0	0	0	0	0	0	0	0
Paraguay	4	1	1	0	0	1	1	0	0	0	0	0	0	0	0	1
Peru	10	0	1	0	0	5	4	0	0	0	0	0	0	0	0	4
Philippines	1	0	0	0	0	0	1	1	0	0	0	0	0	0	0	0
Portugal	2	0	0	0	0	2	0	0	0	0	0	0	0	0	0	0
Romania	1	0	0	0	0	1	0	0	0	0	0	0	0	0	0	0

Table 13.2 (*cont.*)

Parties	Total	MRA's purpose						Professional purpose: sectors covered								
		Unknown purpose	Both academic and professional	Insurances	Credit institutions	Academic purposes	Professional purposes	Accountants	Engineers	Architects	Surveyors	University professions	Doctors, dentists, veterinary surgeons	Lawyers	Patents representatives	No sector
Russia	1	0	0	0	0	0	1	0	0	0	0	0	0	0	0	1
Saint Kitts and Nevis	1	0	0	0	0	1	0	0	0	0	0	0	0	0	0	0
Saint Lucia	1	0	0	0	0	1	0	0	0	0	0	0	0	0	0	0
Saint Vincent and the Grenadines	1	0	0	0	0	1	0	0	0	0	0	0	0	0	0	0
Singapore	1	0	0	0	0	0	1	1	0	0	0	0	0	0	0	0
Slovak Republic	1	0	0	0	0	1	0	0	0	0	0	0	0	0	0	0
South Africa	3	0	0	0	0	0	3	1	2	0	0	0	0	0	0	0
Soviet Union	2	0	0	0	0	2	0	0	0	0	0	0	0	0	0	0
Spain	6	0	0	0	0	3	3	0	0	0	0	2	0	0	0	1
Suriname	2	0	0	0	0	2	0	0	0	0	0	0	0	0	0	0
Switzerland	4	0	0	2	0	0	2	0	0	0	0	0	1	0	1	0
Tajikistan	1	0	0	0	0	0	1	0	0	0	0	0	0	0	0	1
Trinidad and Tobago	2	0	0	0	0	2	0	0	0	0	0	0	0	0	0	0
Turkey	1	0	0	0	0	1	0	0	0	0	0	0	0	0	0	0
Turkmenistan	1	0	0	0	0	0	1	0	0	0	0	0	0	0	0	1
UK	6	0	0	0	0	1	5	2	2	0	1	0	0	0	0	0
Ukraine	1	0	0	0	0	0	1	0	0	0	0	0	0	0	0	1
Uruguay	5	1	0	0	0	2	2	0	0	0	0	0	0	0	0	2
USA	8	0	0	0	1	0	7	4	2	1	0	0	0	0	0	0
Uzbekistan	1	0	0	0	0	0	1	0	0	0	0	0	0	0	0	1
Venezuela	19	0	2	0	0	**17**	0	0	0	0	0	0	0	0	0	0
Vietnam	1	0	0	0	0	0	1	1	0	0	0	0	0	0	0	0
Yugoslavia	1	0	0	0	0	1	0	0	0	0	0	0	0	0	0	0
TOTAL	352	4	23	4	4	187	130	35	17	4	2	5	2	2	2	54

we have 1,049 'bilateral' agreements notified to the WTO, with only 106 'true' bilateral agreements, and the rest arising from this 'bilateralization' procedure applied to plurilateral agreements.[25]

In order to have a first evaluation of recognition agreements notified to the WTO, we ask six questions:

(1) What is the purpose of these agreements?

Here, we distinguish between academic and professional purposes: an MRA may provide for the recognition of qualifications (diplomas, degrees or certificates of studies) for purely academic purposes such as enrolment in (further) studies or teaching. But such recognition does not *necessarily* entail market access in the relevant profession at the end of studies (academic purpose); other MRAs may provide for the recognition of qualifications with a view to exercising a specific profession (professional purpose).

As can be seen in Table 13.2, 53 per cent of the MRAs notified have academic purposes (187 MRAs out of 352); while only 37 per cent of the MRAs notified have a professional purpose (130 MRAs out of 352). Some MRAs (7 per cent, or 23 out of 352) provide for both academic and professional purposes.

(2) What are the sectors covered?

As can be seen from Table 13.2, most MRAs having a professional purpose provide for recognition of qualifications or licences in professional services. Eight MRAs notified refer to other sectors, in this case insurance and financial services. In any case, the sectoral coverage of MRAs confirms our hypothesis in section 2 of this paper that MRAs are

[25] As a matter of fact, one could even go further by looking not only at pairs of countries involved in plurilateral agreements but also at 'individual recognition cases'. Let us explain: the agreements notified, both bilateral and plurilateral, are about 'mutual' recognition, that is to say, recognition runs in both directions: an MRA between A and B, notified only by A, represents only one bilateral agreement but two 'cases' of recognition, from A to B, and from B to A. In the case of plurilateral MRAs, one notification contains several 'cases' of recognition. For example, an MRA between A, B, C and D can imply the following recognition 'cases': from A to B, C and D; from B to A, C and D; from C to A, B and D; and from D to A, B and C. So, in this example, we get a total of twelve recognition 'cases'. This can be expressed through a simple formula: $[n \times (n - 1)]$, where n is the number of parties to the agreement. Counting notifications this way, i.e., calculating the number of 'individual recognition cases' per agreement notified, we have identified 2,098 'cases' of recognition (1,876 of them in thirteen plurilateral agreements notified).

particularly relevant in non-network regulated services, such as financial and professional services.

In most cases, the MRAs for professional purposes identify specific professions (see the right-hand side of Table 13.2). Fifty-four MRAs notified (41.5 per cent of all MRAs dealing with the recognition for professional purposes) do not mention any specific sector but, rather, make reference only to professional services in general. Five of the MRAs notified simply make reference to 'university professions'. Accountancy (thirty-five MRAs, or 26.9 per cent of all MRAs dealing with professions) and engineering (seventeen MRAs, or 13 per cent of all MRAs dealing with professions) are the professions most commonly referred to. Others include architecture, surveying, and legal, medical and dental services.

(3) Are there 'hubs' and 'spokes'?

The question here is whether there are countries which have embraced mutual recognition, therefore becoming a sort of 'hub'. In that regard, Table 13.2 shows clearly that only a handful of countries (Argentina, Australia, Bolivia, Brazil, Chile, Colombia, Costa Rica, Ecuador, El Salvador, Peru and Venezuela) have signed more than ten MRAs (bilateral and plurilateral). Bolivia, Guatemala and the United States follow next, with eight MRAs each. Most other countries seem to be 'spokes', having signed only one MRA (in most cases, of a plurilateral nature). There are in fact seventy-six 'spokes' (89 minus 13). It is worth noting that the EU has only notified two MRAs (one on behalf of Germany), thus covering extra-EU recognition.

(4) Is it more common in some regions than in others?

Here, again, the answer seems to be yes. As can be seen in Table 13.3, MRAs are much more common among Latin American countries than countries in other regions.[26]

(5) With which partners do countries sign?

We are interested here in knowing whether countries have shown specific preferences in the choice of their trading partners. As can be seen in Table 13.3, this seems to be the case, particularly with regard to two features: language and geographical region. In fact, countries have shown a clear preference for signing MRAs with trading partners in the same region

[26] We do not count intra-EU trade. Indeed, for many services, the EU is an MRA across its constituents.

Table 13.3 *MRAs sharing common language and common region*

Parties	Same region (number)	Same region (% of MRAs signed by the party)	Same language	Same language (% of MRAs signed by the party)	At least same region or same language	At least same region or same language (% of MRAs signed by the party)	Total
Angola	0	0	1	100	1	100	1
Antigua and Barbuda	1	100	1	100	1	100	1
Argentina	12	86	12	86	13	93	14
Armenia	2	100	0	0	2	100	2
Australia	4	19	17	81	17	81	21
Azerbaijan	1	100	0	0	1	100	1
Bahamas	1	100	1	100	1	100	1
Barbados	1	100	1	100	1	100	1
Belarus	1	100	0	0	1	100	1
Belgium	1	100	1	100	1	100	1
Belize	1	100	1	100	1	100	1
Bolivia	9	100	9	100	9	100	9
Brazil	21	72	3	10	22	76	29
Bulgaria	0	0	0	0	0	0	3
Canada	4	80	5	100	5	100	5
Cape Verde	0	0	1	100	1	100	1
Chile	13	93	12	86	14	100	14
China	0	0	0	0	0	0	2
Colombia	23	70	21	64	24	73	33
Congo	0	0	0	0	0	0	1
Costa Rica	14	88	12	75	14	88	16
Cuba	3	100	3	100	3	100	3
Czech Republic	0	0	0	0	0	0	1
Dominica	1	100	1	100	1	100	1

Table 13.3 (*cont.*)

Parties	Same region (number)	Same region (% of MRAs signed by the party)	Same language	Same language (% of MRAs signed by the party)	At least same region or same language	At least same region or same language (% of MRAs signed by the party)	Total
Dominican Republic	4	100	4	100	4	100	4
Ecuador	10	100	9	90	10	100	10
El Salvador	8	80	8	80	10	100	10
Estonia	2	100	0	0	2	100	2
European Commission	2	100	2	100	2	100	2
France	0	0	0	0	0	0	1
Georgia	1	100	0	0	1	100	1
Germany	0	0	0	0	0	0	3
Grenada	1	100	1	100	1	100	1
Guatemala	8	100	8	100	8	100	8
Guyana	1	100	1	100	1	100	1
Haiti	3	100	2	67	3	100	3
Holy See	0	0	0	0	0	0	2
Honduras	6	100	6	100	6	100	6
Hong Kong	0	0	3	100	3	100	3
Iceland	1	100	0	0	1	100	1
Iran	1	100	0	0	1	100	1
Ireland	0	0	4	100	4	100	4
Jamaica	2	100	0	0	2	100	2
Japan	0	0	0	0	0	0	2
Kazakhstan	1	100	0	0	1	100	1

Korea	0	0	0	0	0	0	2
Kyrgyzstan	1	100	0	0	1	100	1
Latvia	2	100	0	0	2	100	2
Liechtenstein	3	100	2	67	3	100	3
Lithuania	2	100	0	0	2	100	2
Luxembourg	1	100	1	100	2	200	1
Malaysia	0	0	0	0	0	0	1
Mexico	3	100	3	100	3	100	3
Moldova	1	100	0	0	1	100	1
Morocco	0	0	0	0	0	0	1
Netherlands	1	100	1	100	1	100	1
Netherlands Antilles	1	100	0	0	1	100	1
New Zealand	4	100	4	100	4	100	4
Nicaragua	4	100	4	100	2	50	4
Norway	1	100	0	0	1	100	1
Panama	5	100	4	80	5	100	5
Paraguay	4	100	4	100	4	100	4
Peru	10	100	9	90	10	100	10
Philippines	0	0	1	100	1	100	1
Portugal	0	0	1	50	1	50	2
Romania	0	0	0	0	0	0	1
Russia	1	100	0	0	1	100	1
Saint Kitts and Nevis	1	100	1	100	1	100	1
Saint Lucia	1	100	1	100	1	100	1
Saint Vincent and the Grenadines	1	100	1	100	1	100	1
Singapore	0	0	1	100	1	100	1

Table 13.3 (*cont.*)

Parties	Same region (number)	Same region (% of MRAs signed by the party)	Same language	Same language (% of MRAs signed by the party)	At least same region or same language	At least same region or same language (% of MRAs signed by the party)	Total
Slovak Republic	0	0	0	0	0	0	1
South Africa	0	0	3	100	3	100	3
Soviet Union	0	0	0	0	0	0	2
Spain	0	0	6	100	6	100	6
Suriname	2	100	0	0	2	100	2
Switzerland	4	100	4	100	4	100	4
Tajikistan	1	100	0	0	1	100	1
Trinidad and Tobago	2	100	0	0	2	100	2
Turkey	0	0	0	0	0	0	1
Turkmenistan	1	100	0	0	1	100	1
UK	0	0	5	83	5	83	6
Ukraine	1	100	0	0	1	100	1
Uruguay	5	100	5	100	5	100	5
USA	7	88	2	25	7	88	8
Uzbekistan	1	100	0	0	1	100	1
Venezuela	18	95	14	74	18	95	19
Vietnam	0	0	0	0	0	0	1
Yugoslavia	0	0	0	0	0	0	1
Total	253	72	227	64	298	85	352

(72 per cent of all MRAs notified) or with trading partners speaking the same language (64 per cent of all MRAs notified).

(6) Does the level of development matter?

The basic idea here is to see whether, in addition to being part of the same region or sharing the same language, level of development matters. In other words, do countries tend to sign MRAs with countries at the same level of development or not?

For that, we divided countries on the basis of their 2007 GNI (gross national income) per capita, calculated using the *World Bank Atlas* method (see Table 13.4). The groups are: low income (US$935 or less); middle income (US$936 to US$11,455); and high income (US$11,456 or more). We add another category, called G-2, which includes only the US and the EC as a whole. Additionally, we grouped countries in pairs, looking only at the bilateral MRAs notified.

Out of all the 'bilateral agreements' identified, the bulk of them (56 per cent) are between middle-income countries. Neither the US nor the EC (G-2) has signed MRAs with low-income or middle-income countries. The US and the EC have only signed MRAs with high-income countries. High-income countries tend to sign either with other high-income countries or with middle-income countries. Low-income countries are not very active participants in MRAs. Hence, although one cannot draw definitive conclusions, the data seem to support the idea that the level of development matters and helps to explain the partnerships that we observe.

Table 13.4 *Bilateral MRAs by level of income (total: 106 agreements)*

	G2–G2	G2–HIC	G2–LIC	G2–MIC	HIC–HIC	HIC–LIC	HIC–MIC	MIC–MIC	LIC–LIC	MIC–LIC
Nunber of agreements	0	8	0	0	14	2	20	59	0	3
Percentage of total number of agreements	0	8	0	0	13	2	19	56	0	3

Note: G-2 includes the US and the EC. HIC = 'High-income countries'; MIC = 'Middle-income countries'; and LIC = 'Low-income countries'. Percentages may not add up to 100 due to rounding.

Table 13.5 *Mutual recognition provisions in PTAs notified to the WTO*

Parties	Recognition	Type of provision	Date of entry into force
ASEAN–China	Other		2007
Australia–Chile	Other	A party 'may recognize'	2009
Australia–New Zealand	N		1989
Brunei Darussalam–Japan	Other	A party 'may recognize'	2008
Canada–Chile	Other	The parties agree to foster	1997
CARICOM	Other	The parties shall establish common standard to recognize	1997
Chile–Costa Rica	Other	A party 'may recognize'	2002
Chile–El Salvador	N		2002
Chile–Japan	Other	A party 'may recognize' (Article 113)	2007
Chile–Mexico	N		1999
China–Hong Kong	N		2004
China–Macao	N		2004
China–Singapore	Other	A party 'may recognize'	2009
Costa Rica–Mexico	Other	The parties shall encourage	1995
Dominican Republic–Central America–United States Free Trade Agreement	Other	A party 'may recognize'	2006
EC	Y		1958
EC–CARIFORUM States EPA	N		2008
EC–Chile	Other	A party 'may recognize'	2003
EC–Mexico	N		2000
EEA	N		1994

EFTA	?		2002
EFTA–Chile	Other	The parties shall encourage (Article 29)	2004
EFTA–Korea	Other	The parties shall encourage	2006
EFTA–Mexico	Other	The parties shall encourage	2001
EFTA–Singapore	N		2003
El Salvador–Mexico	N		2001
Guatemala–Mexico	N		2001
Honduras–Mexico	N		2001
Iceland–Faroe Islands	N		2006
India–Singapore	Y		2005
Japan–Indonesia	N		2008
Japan–Malaysia	Other	A party 'may recognize'	2006
Japan–Mexico	Other	Hortatory (Article 104)	2005
Japan–Philippines	Other	A party 'may recognize'	2008
Japan–Singapore	Other	A party 'may recognize'	2002
Japan–Thailand	Other	A party 'may recognize' (Article 118)	2007
Jordan–Singapore	N		2005
Korea–Chile	N		2004
Korea–Singapore	Y	Korea recognizes two Singaporean universities; Singapore recognizes twenty Korean universities (Annex 9D)	2006
MERCOSUR	Other	Possibility to recognize	2005
Mexico–Nicaragua	N		1998
NAFTA	Y	The parties agree to foster	1994
New Zealand–Singapore	Other	The parties shall encourage	2001
Pakistan–Malaysia	Other	A party 'may recognize'	2008
Panama–Chile	Other	The parties agree to foster	2008

Table 13.5 (*cont.*)

Parties	Recognition	Type of provision	Date of entry into force
Panama–El Salvador	Other	The parties agree to negotiate on mutual recognition of higher education diplomas (Table 51.13)	2003
Panama–Singapore	N		2006
Singapore–Australia	Other	The parties shall encourage	2003
Thailand–Australia	Other	A party may recognize (Article 808)	2005
Thailand–New Zealand	N		2005
Trans-Pacific Strategic Economic Partnership (Brunei Darussalam, Chile, Singapore, New Zealand)	Other	Hortatory (Article 12)	2006
US–Australia	Other	The parties shall encourage (Table 50–A)	2005
US–Bahrain	Other	The parties shall encourage	2006
US–Chile	Other	The parties shall encourage	2004
US–Jordan	N		2001
US–Morocco	Other	A party 'may recognize'	2006
US–Oman	Other	A party 'may recognize'	2009
US–Peru	Other	A party 'may recognize'	2009
US–Singapore	Other	The parties shall encourage	2004

Note: 'Y' applies to PTAs providing for mutual recognition; 'N' applies to PTAs not providing for mutual recognition; and 'Other' applies to PTAs providing for a best-endeavours provision on mutual recognition.

6. Concluding remarks

Theory predicts that recognition agreements should be signed between countries that 'trust' each other. This is reasonable in light of the fact that they will accept each other's regulation as equivalent to theirs, although they have no say in the design of their partner's regulation. On the other hand, they can feel relatively comforted by the fact that, in light of the high burden of persuasion associated with the extension of a recognition agreement to outsiders, they will in all likelihood be in a position to resist similar requests. The quantification of trust is of course not a walk in the park. It is for this reason that theory has had recourse to proxies such as language, education, geographic proximity – in other words, cultural factors – the presence of which would increase trust across States wishing to enter into a recognition agreement. The data that we have discussed provide adequate support for these theoretical conclusions: WTO Members will usually enter into recognition agreements with other WTO Members that are either their PTA-partners, share the same language, are in geographic proximity to them, or share all of the above characteristics.

14

'Importing' regulatory standards and principles into WTO dispute settlement: the challenge of interpreting the GATS arrangements on telecommunications

ROBERT HOWSE

1. Introduction

This chapter examines the importation of regulatory standards and principles from other specialized international regimes into the World Trade Organization (WTO). It reflects on the systemic issues that must be taken note of in such importation and the administrative challenges that these create for the WTO adjudicator, who has to *define*, in context, the appropriate relationship between the specialized regimes and the WTO and *adapt* the external standards and principles to the purposes of the WTO – it cannot simply *apply* external norms in the WTO as if they were treaty norms, to be interpreted in accordance with the Vienna Convention on the Law of Treaties. The case I have chosen to illustrate these challenges is telecommunications, where the market access supposedly guaranteed by WTO free trade disciplines depends crucially on the shape of the domestic regulatory landscape, as well as institutions and norms of international regulatory cooperation.

During the earlier era of the multilateral trading system, based on the General Agreement on Tariffs and Trade (GATT) of 1947, the concern with domestic regulation was largely focused on discrimination problems: against imports in favour of domestic products (National Treatment) and between imports from different Members (Most-Favoured Nation). The multilateral trading system was viewed mostly as a framework for negotiated bindings on the reduction or elimination of discriminatory border measures restricting trade, such as tariffs or quotas. In order to sustain such a bargain, it was necessary to ensure that Members did not 'cheat' on, or circumvent, these commitments through reintroducing measures amounting to import-discrimination in their domestic policies. The official theology of the trading system sanctioned complete regulatory autonomy and wide regulatory diversity: as long as they did not discriminate, Members were free to adopt whatever approach to domestic regulation they saw as appropriate. This outlook was well suited to an international regime like the GATT, which lacked the institutions, expertise or explicit mandate to engage in 'positive integration' through regulatory *rapprochement* or harmonization.

It is notable, however, that not even the non-discrimination norm is an absolute constraint on regulatory autonomy in the GATT regime. In practice, it is largely impossible to determine, in a given case, which regulatory distinctions amount to impermissible 'discrimination', and which do not, without reference to *some* benchmarks or standards for, crudely speaking, 'legitimate' regulation. This has been clearly seen in the debates about the meaning of 'like' products in the National Treatment obligation, such as whether social, environmental, ethical and health considerations may be taken into account in determining whether products are 'like' for purposes of domestic regulatory treatment. Moreover, policies that violate National Treatment or Most-Favoured Nation might be justified, under certain conditions, where necessary or rationally related to particular policy objectives, such as public morals, health and the conservation of exhaustible natural resources. While it is often suggested that in such cases the adjudicative exercise is limited to considering the relationship between means and objectives, and thus involves no substantive judgments about the purposes of regulation or its desirability, in practice judging the necessity or rationality of a particular regulatory device necessarily entails second-guessing a set of domestic regulatory choices informed by diverse concerns (culture, social and community structures, administrability, the constitutional system, etc.) and representing a balance of values. Without some conception, at least implicit, of best or acceptable regulatory practices, it is hard to make fine judgments about whether a given instrument choice is really the necessary or rational means to a particular objective.

In part due to recognition of this difficulty, as well as the related instability of the non-discrimination norm as a means of disciplining domestic policy, two of the specialized agreements that emerged out of the Uruguay Round[1] gave a significant role to international standards as a means of managing the interface between domestic regulation and trade liberalization in the

[1] The Uruguay Round negotiations ran from 1986 to 1994, culminating in the Marrakech Declaration and Final Act of 15 April 1995, announcing the creation of the WTO.

case of trade in goods. These were the Agreement on Technical Barriers to Trade (TBT) and the Agreement on Sanitary and Phytosanitary Measures (SPS). The international standards were imported in various ways from non-WTO standardization regimes, such as the International Standards Organization (ISO) or the Codex Alimentarius, as normative benchmarks for judging the acceptability of WTO Members' domestic regulations from the viewpoint of trade liberalization.

The Uruguay Round negotiations coincided with an era of regulatory reform and privatization where many traditional approaches to regulation and the public sector (such as public monopolies in services like telecommunications) were put in question, and changed or dismantled in a number of important jurisdictions within the multilateral trading system. The traditional approaches were viewed as too restrictive of market forces; legitimate public policy goals, it was thought, could be attainable through more market-friendly regulatory instruments. The durability of the older approaches was often attributed to vested interests in the *status quo*. This mindset migrated to the multilateral trading system, where non-discriminatory domestic regulatory policies began to be questioned as 'barriers' to market access. It was thought that shifting to less restrictive regulatory instruments could, at the same time, make domestic markets more efficient and open up the possibility of international trade.

Nowhere was the linkage between the philosophy of regulatory reform or 'deregulation' and the shift from non-discrimination to market access more evident than in the area of trade in services. There were relatively few explicit border restrictions on such trade, and where discriminatory measures existed they were often plausibly related to non-protectionist policy objectives, such as ensuring the quality of services (such measures included licensing, certification and assuring adequate investment in infrastructure in network industries). Thus, the interests of those most intent on pushing for liberalization of trade in services (such as the United States) lay with inducing trade partners to lock in as binding concessions, pro-competitive or pro-market regulatory changes. Many countries, especially developing countries, tried to resist the insertion of the 'deregulation' agenda into the multilateral trading system.

The resulting set of legal instruments, the General Agreement on Trade in Services (GATS) and related agreements, reflects a messy compromise between these points of view. The basic GATS Agreement contains GATT-like Most-Favoured Nation and National Treatment obligations. But there is also a very broad Market Access clause, Article XVI, which prohibits most quantitative limits on access to service markets even where these limits are non-discriminatory, i.e., domestic service providers are equally subject to them. Significantly, the National Treatment obligation and the Market Access obligation are only binding with respect to sectors and activities listed by individual WTO Members in their Schedules of Specific Commitments. Moreover, WTO Members are permitted in these schedules to qualify or limit the extent to which these obligations apply to particular measures, sub-sectors or activities. At the same time, Article VI, the provision on domestic regulation, provides for the future negotiation of regulatory codes applicable to particular sectors. Finally, there is an excepting provision, Article XIV, very similar in design and content to Article XX GATT. Reflecting the lack of and resistance to the creation of a regulatory culture at the WTO, in only one case has a code been developed under Article VI, that of accounting standards.

This raises the question of where the WTO dispute settlement organs will go to find the regulatory standards and principles to interpret the scope and nature of Members' commitments under the GATS in specific contexts. This question is especially obvious or acute in the case of telecommunications and financial services, because through WTO instruments that have supplemented the basic GATS text, and on the basis of which specific commitments have been negotiated, certain norms concerning competition and regulatory structure, including the appropriate balance of regulatory objectives, have been made explicitly part of the GATS framework.

While open-ended and general, these norms explicitly point to concepts and methodologies in domestic regulatory and administrative practice that (unlike concepts such as non-discrimination or transparency) are largely alien to the culture of the multilateral trading regime. The few competition-related norms already present in the GATT (such as the norms related to the operation of State trading enterprises including public monopolies) were largely ignored or interpreted with great caution by the dispute settlement organs. This is understandable, given the resistance of many WTO Members to the notion that the WTO should be used as a forum to harmonize competition policies. This was reflected most dramatically at the Cancun Ministerial, following the objections of developing countries, to drop competition law from the negotiation agenda of the Doha Round. Thus, particularly acute legitimacy questions would arise were an expectation of *minimum* standards in competition policy to be imported through treaty interpretation into the WTO system, at least without a clear and bounded mandate in the text. Applying the regulatory and competition-related norms with respect to telecommunications therefore represents a delicate hermeneutic challenge for the dispute settlement organs.

2. Systemic issues in the importation of norms through interpretation

Where the WTO adjudicator uses normative material from outside the WTO Agreements to interpret provisions of those treaties, a range of issues arise, which are, broadly speaking, issues of *fragmentation*: the relation between different international regimes. This section will outline these issues in the course of developing a broad conceptual framework for the importation of norms into the GATS. It will begin by asserting that a broad range of sources may be drawn upon as sources of external norms, provided they conform to applicable criteria, such as internal legitimacy, global adherence, etc. It will then explain that the relevant criteria in each case depend upon how the WTO adjudicator conceives the GATS, as well as towards the nature of the standards being imported.

2.1 Conceptions of the GATS and criteria for importation of external norms

In some cases, the nature of the material and its relation to the WTO norm in question is specified, at some level of detail, in the treaty text itself (SPS and TBT); the relationship may even be one of actual incorporation (for instance, many of the standards in TRIPs are taken directly from the WIPO conventions). Even these cases raise important interpretative issues, such as to what extent ought the interpretative practice of the other regime be taken regard of when these norms are imported into the WTO.

Even where not specified in the WTO Agreements themselves, the use of certain kinds of normative material external to the treaty text is mandated by Article 31 of the Vienna Convention on the Law of Treaties (VCLT). Thus, Article 31 of the VCLT provides that the treaty interpreter must take into account, as context, 'any agreement relating to the treaty which was made between all the parties in connection with the conclusion of the treaty' and 'any instrument which was made by one or more of the parties in connection with the conclusion of the treaty and accepted by the other parties as an instrument related to the treaty'. In addition, the treaty interpreter is to take into account '(a) any subsequent agreement between the parties regarding the interpretation of the treaty or the application of its provisions; (b) any subsequent practice in the application of the treaty which establishes the agreement of the parties regarding its interpretation; (c) any relevant rules of international law applicable in the relations between the parties'.

As is discussed at length in the International Law Commission's Report on Fragmentation,[2] these categories ought not to be read as exhausting the kind of normative material from other international regimes that can be taken into account in interpretation. In the context of regulatory norms within the WTO, regulatory standards, principles or benchmarks may well be found in soft law. This would include recommendations, guidelines, statements of best practices made by various networks or bodies concerned with regulatory coordination, including bodies that are of a predominately private nature, as well as ones which engage only a subset of WTO Members.

In a recent WTO panel ruling, *EC – Biotech*,[3] the panel refused to consider the Cartagena Protocol on Biosafety, a treaty containing specific standards, relevant to the management of risk from trade in genetically modified organisms. As I have discussed at length elsewhere,[4] the panel's reasoning was that the exclusive route by which a non-WTO legal instrument can be given legal weight in WTO dispute settlement is Article 31(3)(c) of the VCLT; the panel further interpreted the language 'applicable in relations between the parties' as limiting the scope of Article 31(3)(c) to legal instruments binding as among all the parties to the WTO treaty being interpreted. This is a highly problematic reading of the VCLT, unjustifiably reading into Article 31(3)(c) an *exclusion* of other material (whereas the context of Article 31 clearly shows that it is intended to set out what a treaty interpreter is required to take into account, and not to exclude other sources); a critique along similar lines has been made by the ILC Working Group on Fragmentation.[5] Moreover, in general, the Appellate Body has had resort to a range of

[2] International Law Commission, 'Fragmentation of International Law: Difficulties Arising from Diversification and Expansion of International Law', Report of the Study Group of the International Law Commission, finalized by M. Koskenniemi, UN Doc. A/CN.4/1682 (13 April 2006).

[3] Panel Report, *European Communities – Measures Affecting the Approval and Marketing of Biotech Products (Biotech)*, WT/DS291/R, WT/DS292/R, WT/DS293R (adopted 29 September 2006).

[4] R. Howse, 'The Use and Abuse of Other "Relevant Rules of International Law" in Treaty Interpretation: Insights from WTO Trade/Environment Litigation', Institute for International Law and Justice Working Paper 2007/1, pp. 20–8.

[5] See International Law Commission, 'Fragmentation of International Law: Difficulties Arising from Diversification and Expansion of International Law', Report of the Study

material from non-WTO international regimes, without strict regard for whether it is binding (i.e., the material included soft law) or whether all WTO Members are bound. Had the *EC – Biotech* case been appealed, the Appellate Body might have had to address directly the issue of how and when benchmarks from other regimes can be imported into WTO dispute settlement, in the process of interpreting WTO treaty provisions.

A range of issues needs to be addressed in order to develop an adequate conceptual framework for a broader use of non-WTO legal norms than that suggested by the *EC – Biotech* panel. The telecommunications and financial services examples raise some of the most interesting of these issues, because they relate to the use of non-WTO legal norms to articulate baselines or benchmarks against which to judge WTO Members' regulatory interventions as either acceptable, legitimate or reasonable public policy actions permissible and protected under the GATS compromises in question, or as unjustified barriers to market access of the kind legally prohibited under GATS commitments. This goes to the very understanding of the nature of these compromises.

A first perspective, common in the WTO epistemic community, including many of those involved in the conception and negotiation of GATS arrangements in these sectors, is that the *telos* of the arrangements is *full international competition* facilitated by progressively deeper or more complete deregulation[6] and/or privatization. From this perspective, the accommodations in these agreements to more traditional regulatory approaches represent concessions to political reality, which is likely to change as the trend towards deregulation and free markets continues to spread globally.

The second perspective of the GATS compromise is that it represents a careful *balance of values*, with those public policy values that may be in tension with full liberalization given significant play, and with considerable policy space guaranteed for a diversity of regulatory approaches at the domestic level.

A third perspective, broadly speaking consistent with the second, is that liberalization of global markets may lead to increased spillovers or

Group of the International Law Commission, finalized by M. Koskenniemi, UN Doc. A/CN.4/1682 (13 April 2006), p. 471.

[6] The concept of deregulation here in fact denotes the reform of regulation in the direction of 'lighter', more market-friendly or incentive-oriented regulatory instruments. In some instances, the market-access approach to the WTO implies more or higher regulatory standards, for instance intellectual property and competition-related regulatory standards. Thus, the turn to 'deregulation' really means a tendency to minimize competition or market-access-limiting regulation and to maximize regulation that enhances or guarantees competition and market access.

negative effects of regulatory failure in one jurisdiction on the interests of other jurisdiction; from this point of view, liberalization of trade may well *imply* or *require* the *upward harmonization of regulation*. As was well put by Gkoutzinis with respect to the financial services sector: '[I]international regulatory convergence through a process of re-regulation may ... be a necessary step towards the acceptability of international economic integration and the sustainability of unobstructed financial linkages.'[7] One difference between the second perspective and the third is that the second perspective places more emphasis on the protection of domestic policy space as an element of the GATS compromise.

Depending upon which of the three perspectives, or combination thereof, the WTO adjudicator adopts, the function that he sees the importation of standards as achieving will differ. On the *first perspective*, international regulatory standards would most likely be employed as benchmarks against which domestic measures would be evaluated. Furthermore, trade-restrictive measures would be viewed with suspicion, as unnecessary barriers to trade, and at a *minimum* subjected to greater scrutiny. Indeed, this function of international standards is explicitly incorporated into WTO law in a different context, that of food and agricultural health and safety. Thus, the SPS Agreement provides a special justificatory procedure (entailing scientific risk assessment) that WTO Members must follow if they are to regulate trade in a more restrictive way than what is indicated by international standards. Obviously, where international regulatory standards have the function of *enhancing* competition or market access (for instance, antitrust norms), it will be the domestic measures' failure to live up to these standards that will concern the WTO adjudicator, not their greater strictness.

Where the adjudicator adopts the *second perspective* on the GATS compromise, of a balance of values and interests that does not necessarily privilege trade liberalization or market access over other values and interests, importing baselines or benchmarks from international regulatory regimes may help ensure this balance is properly protected. This is important, given that the institutional culture of the WTO is one where the non-trade liberalization/market access values and interests are less likely to be

[7] A. Gkoutzinis, 'How Far Is Basel from Geneva?: International Regulatory Convergence and the Elimination of Barriers to International Financial Integration' in K. Alexander and M. Andenas (eds.), *The World Trade Organization and Trade in Services* (2008), pp. 635–711.

appreciated or understood.[8] On this perspective, the weight and value afforded to international regulatory standards from outside the WTO may well depend on the extent to which they *legitimately* reflect non-trade values and interests that are an integral part of the GATS compromise itself.

On the *third perspective*, the non-WTO international regulatory standards will have the function of assuring external conditions that are required for or presupposed by the trade liberalization project, if it is to be successful in achieving its own purposes. The legitimacy of the standards for purposes of their use in WTO adjudication will stem from this instrumental effectiveness, and not (as in the second perspective) their expression or legitimate reflection of particular non-trade values and interests.

2.2 Fragmentation and related systemic concerns

As is implicit in the above analysis, the function of international regulatory standards in WTO adjudication is likely to bear a complex and conceivably conflictual relationship to the internal understanding and functionality of those standards within the non-WTO regimes of their origin. What if the determinative meaning given to the standards in WTO adjudication produces normative effects other than, or even opposite to, those intended by the regime from which they originate?

Some commentators (I am one example), attracted to the second perspective articulated above, see the importation of regulatory standards from other regimes as a means of ensuring that WTO law is read in a manner that does not undermine or minimize the non-trade values and interests protected by those other regimes. However, other scholars assume that the first perspective above is the one almost certainly to be adopted by the WTO adjudicator, with the result that international regulatory standards will be given a determinative meaning in adjudication that privileges trade liberalization and indeed the entire related outlook or ethos of the trade 'epistemic community'. This concern may be particularly acute where the international regulatory standards in question are voluntary or of a 'soft law' character, and their original regime lacks the institutional mechanisms or legitimacy to develop its own counter-interpretations, as it were, of the norms in question. In effect, the WTO dispute settlement process becomes the conduit for giving 'hard law' effects to these norms at the international

[8] I have argued along these lines elsewhere. See R. Howse, 'Adjudicative Legitimacy and Treaty Interpretation in International Trade Law' in R. Howse, *The WTO System: Law, Politics and Legitimacy* (London: Cameron May, 2007), pp. 231–2.

level, and these effects will be filtered through a trade liberalization *telos*, again assuming the adjudicator adopts the first perspective described above.[9]

To understand whether this points to an insoluble problem of 'fragmentation', we need to consider the normative functionality of the international regulatory standards within the regimes that generate them, as well as the sources of their legitimacy *within* those regimes. We will then have a better grasp on the points of conflict or convergence with their functionality and legitimacy within the WTO adjudicative process.

2.2.1 Normative functions and legitimacy of international standards

Standards can have a wide range of intended normative effects within regulatory regimes. First of all, standards may be viewed as *minimum requirements*, prescribing a threshold level of regulation that parties to the regime undertake not to go below, though upward regulatory diversity – in regulating more strictly or extensively – may be encouraged. A different normative function of standards could be described as *aspirational*, that is, intended to demarcate the level or kind of regulation that parties are encouraged eventually to attain, with regulatory diversity being tolerated or encouraged to the extent it refers to the speed and/or the means by which the regulatory objective is attained. Third, standards may be *facilitative*, but not directive, of a particular regulatory approach. This role of standards is in principle quite consistent with deep regulatory diversity: for instance, with respect to telecommunications services, a standard might set out technical requirements to allow for interconnection of competing service providers to a network in order to facilitate the smooth functioning of a newly competitive sector, but this standard may not in itself contain any normative imperative that any party shift to pro-competitive regulation.

[9] See J. A. Beckett, 'Fragmentation, Openness, and Hegemony: Pauwelyn and the WTO' (unpublished draft, University of Leicester, December 2007, on file with the author). According to Beckett, the only way in which the hegemonic effect of WTO adjudication could be avoided is if expert representatives of the other regimes 'are invited on to the Panels and the Appellate Body, not as experts or witnesses but as *judges*: their expertise is raised to a level equal to, or greater than, their trade law brethren.' See also H. G. Ruse-Khan, 'Proportionality and Balancing within Objectives for Intellectual Property Protection' in P. Torremans (ed.), *Intellectual Property and Human Rights*, Enhanced Edition of *Copyright and Human Rights* (Kluwer Law International, 2008), p. 161.

Fourth, some standards may serve the function of boilerplate or *default rules*. These standards do not express a normative preference for harmonization, even in principle. They may serve to reduce the costs of regulation, and facilitate regulatory cooperation, where particular States desire it, but entail no negative judgment upon States that formulate domestic regulations without regard to the default rules. Similarly, the standards may be intended as default options that industry players can adopt by choice to coordinate purely private or largely private activity; again this would be the case where use of the standards is seen to reduce transaction and/or coordination costs.

Finally, standards may be expressed as *guidelines* or other material that is intentionally under-determined in its normative effect. The expectation is that the standards will provide some shaping guidance for domestic regulation, but the substantive regulatory outcome will be the product of the domestic political and/or administrative process. This is the case, frequently, with standards that are procedural in nature – suggesting certain inputs in the regulatory process or evoking certain best practices. In such instances, it is arguably the case that accountability for the substantive balance of values and interests reflected in regulatory outcomes is expected to remain at the domestic level.

This brings us to the question of legitimacy. Unlike domestic regulations, international standards are often the product of informal, non-transparent, expert-elite-driven processes that are not subject to direct or effective democratic control. A much debated question is whether in fact this matters, given that in most cases the standards only acquire a determinative, binding, coercive effect through being translated into regulations. There is an increasing appreciation that standard-setting at the international level may nevertheless shape the behaviour and opportunities of various agents, as well as increasing awareness of the difficulty of *ex post* democratic control through the regulatory process, given the agency costs and information asymmetries entailed in relying on expert elites to shape the standards in the first place.

Addressing this problem is central to the agenda of Global Administrative Law.[10] This approach emphasizes the importance of administrative law values of participation, transparency and rule of law in enhancing the legitimacy of global norm-creation; it is particularly apposite in fields such as telecommunications, where these values underpin in many democracies

[10] B. Kingsbury, N. Krisch and R. B. Stewart, 'The Emergence of Global Administrative Law', *Law and Contemporary Problems* 68 (2005) 15–61.

the legitimacy of *domestic* rule-making. Evaluating where, and to what extent, *global* norm-creation requires enhancement of legitimacy by these means involves assessing both the formal and intended effects of the norms as well as their actual real-world effects. Arguably, the more that global norms constrain or determine, whether formally or effectively, democratic policy choices or trade-offs between competing values, create winners and losers, or redistribute resources and opportunities between diverse social actors, the more that legitimation is required through 'public law values'. On the other hand, the more standards reflect technical or scientific choices, or seek to solve purely technical problems (such as of interface, coordination, etc.), the more legitimation can or should depend on the quality of the expertise generating the standards, and the demonstrated experts' capacity to fulfill these 'technical' functions. Of course, the difficulty is that many standardization decisions perceived as technical by the expert elites that make them are, in fact, important value choices, risk/risk, risk/benefit trade-offs etc.; nevertheless, there is a question of degree here.

2.2.2 Specific concerns

Now let us return to the problem of importing regulatory standards into WTO adjudication. Even where the legitimacy of international regulatory standards is well matched to their formal or intended normative effects within the regime of their origin, this legitimacy may not be well suited to the normative effects created by virtue of the use made of these standards by the WTO adjudicator. Depending on the perspective she adopts concerning the function of the international regulatory standards, the WTO adjudicator may or may not care about their legitimacy in the regime of their origin. Their legitimacy for purposes of WTO adjudication may be different from the kind of legitimacy required by the original regime.

This is most easily illustrated by assuming the WTO adjudicator adopts the *first perspective* (that is, full international competition) discussed above. For instance, in assessing whether a measure can be justified under an exception in the GATS for legitimate public policies, she will look to the international standards as a benchmark or baseline against which to determine whether a domestic measure is unnecessarily trade-restrictive, by entailing either a stricter standard in the case of market-access-limiting regulation or a laxer standard in the case of market-access-enhancing regulation. The assumption is that deviation reflects, or is more likely to reflect, motivations inconsistent with the purposes of the GATS, such as the protection of domestic industry. Clearly, it is not the normative aspiration of the standard that is important here, but rather its evidence of common or shared practice or understandings. In other words, what the adjudicator is supposed to be suspicious or sceptical of is trade-restricting regulatory diversity *per se*. The very fact of non-conformity raises the red flag. Reference to international standards is simply a shortcut to finding out what common or community practice is, for the purpose of identifying non-conformists.

Therefore, though the legitimacy of the regime that generates the standards does not matter here, what does matter is that the standards reflect common or community practice. Logically, then, the WTO adjudicator would need to be sensitive to whether the standards are actually followed, by how large and diverse a group of States, and to what extent. Significantly, the international standards may themselves reflect political capture by powerful States or multinational corporations. That is to say, the standards may themselves reflect the impermissible motivations that the adjudicator seeks to ferret out by referring to a benchmark or baseline of common practice.

Then there may be a legitimacy question related to the international system as a whole – of fragmentation. Given that, other than the hierarchy established by the UN Charter and the notion of *ius cogens*, the international legal system is characterized by decentralized and horizontal relations between specialized regimes, does a principle of deference or comity impose itself as a structural principle of international order? Thus, should the WTO adjudicator who operates upon the first perspective nevertheless be concerned about the creation of normative effects in contradiction to, or undermining of, the intended effects of the international regime of origin of the standards? This is not, strictly speaking, a 'conflict of laws' problem as, for instance, Joost Pauwelyn would characterize it, because the competing normative effects come out of the interpretation of WTO law itself (also, a conflict-of-laws framework may not apply if the norms are voluntary or soft law).[11]

The most obvious situation is the one where the regime of origin regards the standards in question as bare *minima* and has an active policy to encourage parties to the regime to adopt, where possible, higher, or more trade-restrictive, standards. Clearly, were the WTO interpreter to regard these standards as prescribing the ceiling beyond which a Member's regulatory activity is illegitimate, it would undermine the policy of the regime of origin. Another example is where an international regime offers standards primarily as boilerplate or default rules,

[11] See generally J. Pauwelyn, *Conflict of Norms in Public International Law: How WTO Law Relates to Other Rules of International Law* (Cambridge University Press, 2003).

subsidiary to regulatory diversity where States have the capacity to tailor regulations to their specific needs. Here, use of such standards as a baseline or benchmark for legitimacy of trade-restricting regulatory measures would pose a barrier to desired regulatory diversity.

In the *second perspective* (balance of values) that the WTO adjudicator might adopt in importing regulatory standards, the internal legitimacy of the original regime and its standards ought to matter. That is, in this case, he must enquire whether the original regime and the norms it legitimates actually legitimately represent the non-trade values essential to the GATS compromise. To this understanding of legitimacy, significant for its virtual representation, as it were, of certain non-trade constituencies, concerns about transparency, the quality and extent of participation and deliberation, the giving of reasons, etc. – the values of Global Administrative Law – would be important. Further, to the extent that the original regime is legitimate in the sense of being representative of those constituencies, the WTO adjudicator would want to be careful that the use of the standards does not undermine the effects or purposes intended by that regime, or stretch its internal legitimacy beyond what it can bear. Thus, the adjudicator will be attentive to elements of subsidiarity in the original regime, the extent to which the standards are designed and implemented within that regime so as to preserve domestic regulatory diversity or 'policy space'.

Such subsidiarity – which can take many forms, one of which is leaving the norms open to being shaped through implementation in domestic democratic processes – may reflect the notion that the balance of interests and values at stake varies considerably: from jurisdiction to jurisdiction, due to appreciation of different needs given different levels of development and geographic and cultural variations. But it may also indicate that the standardization process in that original international regime *is not strongly enough legitimated* to produce norms that appropriately displace or tightly constrain domestic regulatory choices.

Thus, the second perspective requires that the WTO adjudicator pays close attention to the regulatory practice, culture and process of the international regime of origin of standards; this arguably means understanding the other regime in terms of Global Administrative Law, and looking behind the formal norms it produces. This challenge is not to be dictated by some meta- or structural norm of comity between different international regimes. Rather, it is required given the function that standards are seen as serving within the WTO system itself.

In the case of the *third perspective* (upward regulatory harmonization), the concern with importing these standards into WTO dispute settlement will be their effectiveness in making a shift to liberal trade successful, that is, in solving problems relating to spillover effects and distribution of global public goods under conditions of globalization. The legitimacy that concerns the WTO adjudicator will be output-related and technocratic or expertise-based.

Of course, any particular solution to spillovers or public goods problems requires implicit or explicit property or liability rules that have distributive effects and engage controversies concerning the principles for allocation of rights and responsibilities with respect to the commons. Hence, from the internal point of view of the original regime, legitimacy may depend on public law values as they relate to accountability and forms of democratic control. But the WTO adjudicator will not be concerned with the distributive effects of allocating rights and responsibilities over the commons, rather only with whether the solution adopted is effective in underpinning or appropriately complementing trade liberalization.

However, a comity issue would arise if the way in which the WTO adjudicator imports international standards actually *produces* distributive effects that are unintended and not legitimate under original international regime. Again, we would have to ask whether such a meta-norm of comity between regimes with putatively equal status in the international legal universe does exist, or if it is required to make the overall project of international legal order legitimate under the challenge of fragmentation.

3. Telecommunications: the role of ITU standards

3.1 Interconnection and the relationship of the ITU to the WTO

Even where no competition exists in telecommunications markets whatsoever, the ability of a telecommunications monopoly in one jurisdiction to provide its own domestic customers with international long-distance services implies the ability to connect with the network of the telecommunications monopoly in the destination jurisdictions. In other words, connection and cooperation of the destination jurisdiction is required to 'complete' the calls. This raises the issue of how the costs and revenues of these calls should be shared between the originating and destination jurisdictions, in addition to many technical issues of interconnection. A central function of the International Telecommunications Union (ITU), a multilateral, intergovernmental organization, has been the management of these issues through intergovernmental bargaining.[12] Underlying bargaining about the allocation of costs and revenues are controversies about how public policy goals such as the provision of universal service and the maintenance or creation of an adequate domestic telecommunications infrastructure should be funded, both in terms of domestic regulatory values and global distributive justice.[13] In the specific example provided above, what results from bargaining is a series of charges called 'accounting rates' that determine what the originating telecommunications operator must pay the terminating operator for completion of the call.

Where there is a shift to competitive international telecommunications markets – a move often viewed by the WTO trade policy community as the exclusive *telos* of the WTO telecommunications arrangements – interconnection of calls is seen not only as a means by which a foreign telecommunications operator can assure long-distance service for its own domestic customers, but also a means of access to the network in the other WTO Member States so that the foreign operator can compete for customers located there. In theory, the foreign operator could enter the market in that other WTO Member State by creating its own network infrastructure, but its services would be of limited value if customers could only connect with other customers on that same network, and not customers of other providers in the country concerned. So interconnection is an issue even where each provider has its own network. In any event, creating one's own network infrastructure is a very significant barrier to entry for a foreign telecommunications provider.

The shift to competition in many jurisdictions has led the basic telecommunications network or significant elements of it (and this is a shifting story as technology changes) being controlled by a major player, often a former monopolist, who dominates the provision of some telecommunications services in that particular jurisdiction or region. The question is of the terms and conditions on which this major domestic player, sometimes in collusion with other major domestic players, determines the access of competing foreign suppliers to the network so that they connect the calls of their customers *within* this jurisdiction. From a trade-liberalization perspective, the concern can be articulated as either protectionism or market access. The traditional GATT-era point of view was that private decisions of this nature, if they could not be attributable in some way to governmental

[12] The ITU has the status of a specialized agency of the United Nations.

[13] S. O. Siochru, 'The ITU, the WTO and Accounting Rates: Limited Prospects for the South?', *The Public* 4 (1997) 47–57.

direction or control, were not contrary to the norms of the multilateral trading system, even if discriminatory against other WTO Members. This stemmed from the lack of consensus concerning the incorporation of antitrust or competition principles or norms into the multilateral trading system.

The issue was eventually dealt with in the WTO telecommunications arrangements through the drafting of a Reference Paper[14] that states a number of norms concerning interconnection; the Reference Paper applies as a binding instrument to any WTO Member that has incorporated the paper into its Schedule of Commitments on basic telecommunications, and this includes the vast majority of WTO Members who have made such commitments.[15]

The reference paper on basic telecommunications provides:

> Interconnection with a major supplier will be ensured at any technically feasible point in the network. Such interconnection is provided:
>
> (a) under non-discriminatory terms, conditions (including technical standards and specifications) and rates and of a quality no less favourable than that provided for its own like services or for like services of non-affiliated service suppliers or for its subsidiaries or other affiliates;
> (b) in a timely fashion, on terms, conditions (including technical standards and specifications) and cost-oriented rates that are transparent, reasonable, having regard to economic feasibility, and sufficiently unbundled so that the supplier need not to pay for network components or facilities that it does not require for the service to be provided; and
> (c) upon request, at points in addition to the network termination points offered to the majority of users, subject to charges that reflect the cost of construction of necessary additional facilities.

The expressions 'reasonable' and 'cost-oriented' leave open to a large extent the range of economic and non-economic considerations that can be taken into account in determining the actual connection charges that apply. This makes the ITU instruments with respect to accounting rates arguably relevant to establishing the benchmarks or baselines against which the meaning of 'reasonableness' and 'cost-orientation' can be determined.

[14] Reference Paper to the Fourth Protocol to the General Agreement on Trade in Services, 36 ILM 367 (1997).

[15] D. Roseman, 'Domestic Regulation and Trade in Telecommunications Services: Experience and Prospects under the GATS' in A. Mattoo and P. Sauvé (eds.), *Domestic Regulation and Service Trade Liberalization* (World Bank and Oxford University Press, 2005), pp. 83–107, p. 88.

However, although the ITU has come to be generally supportive of the shift to competition, at the same time values other than competition/ free trade/market access have traditionally played a large role in the way the ITU guides the determination of connection rates through the accounting rate concept – including values of domestic and international distributive justice. The application of the Reference Paper then logically raises the question of the role of ITU standards in WTO adjudication.

Another element of the WTO architecture on telecommunications services, the Telecommunications Annex, explicitly addresses the relationship between the WTO and the ITU. Thus Article 7(a) of the Annex provides: 'Members recognize the importance of international standards for global compatibility and inter-operability of telecommunications networks and services and undertake to promote such standards through the work of relevant international bodies, including the [ITU].' Article 7(b) further provides: 'Members recognize the role played by intergovernmental and non-governmental organizations and agreements in ensuring the efficient operation of domestic and global telecommunications services, in particular, the [ITU]. Members shall make appropriate arrangements, where relevant, for consultations with such organizations.' What is clear from these and other references in the Annex is that the ITU is viewed largely, if not exclusively, from what I have described as the *third perspective*, as relevant to the facilitation of global telecommunications markets by providing the regulatory coordination necessary for global telecommunications trade to function smoothly. There seems to be no recognition of the importance of the ITU as a defender of non-trade values that are part of the GATS compromise.

3.2 The Telmex case

In the *Telmex* case,[16] the United States challenged connection rates and practices charged to US telecommunications operators by the dominant Mexican operator, Telmex, arguing that these rates and practices violated several provisions of the WTO Reference Paper. The relevance and meaning of ITU standards to the interpretation of the Reference Paper became a major issue in this WTO dispute. An unusual feature of this dispute is that the rates in question were being charged by Telmex for completion of calls

[16] Panel Report, *Mexico – Measures Affecting Telecommunications Services*, WT/DS204/R, adopted on 1 June 2004.

by US customers of the US telecoms operators in question; the US operators were not seeking access to the Mexican market. A threshold issue never properly addressed by the panel is whether the Reference Paper is even applicable in a situation where no access is being sought to the domestic telecommunications market of a WTO Member. In other words, where the issue is only of facilitating international long-distance services provided by an operator to its domestic customers, is it not exclusively the domain of the ITU, and indeed its function even when international competition in telecommunications markets did not exist?[17]

First of all, the United States claimed that Mexico had violated the Reference Paper by failing to ensure that Telmex's interconnection rates for 'completion' of US-originating calls were 'cost-oriented' and 'reasonable', since the rates exceeded the long-run incremental cost of providing the service. In seeking to defend its rates, Mexico invoked a number of ITU instruments that concerned regulatory standards for interconnection rates.

A threshold argument of Mexico was that an 'Understanding' negotiated at the time at which the WTO telecommunications arrangements were being concluded left intact the accounting rate regime of the ITU, notwithstanding the Reference Paper. In essence, Mexico's argument was that the Understanding in question came from the ITU leadership of the process by which its traditional accounting rate regime would be altered to adjust to a world of global competition in telecommunications services, despite the central interest of the WTO in such a world being realized. The Understanding states:[18]

> In light of the fact that the accounting rate system established under the International Telecommunications Regulations is the usual method of terminating international traffic and by its nature involves differential rates, and in order to avoid the submission of further such exemptions, it is the understanding of the Group that:
>
> - the application of such accounting rates would not give rise to actions by Members under dispute settlement under the WTO; and
> - this understanding will be reviewed not later than the commencement of the further round of negotiations of service Commitments due to begin not later than 1 January 2000.

[17] For a powerful argument to this effect, see D. Neven and P. Mavroidis, 'Mexico – Measures Affecting Telecommunications Services (WT/DS204/R): A Comment on "El Mess in Telmex"', in H. Horn and P. Mavroidis (eds.), *WTO Case Law of 2003: The American Law Institute Reporters' Studies* (2006), p. 188.

[18] Report of the Group on Basic Telecommunications, S/GBT/4 (15 February 1997).

The panel, in rejecting Mexico's argument, read down the Understanding to apply only inasmuch as accounting rates apply to the traditional interconnection between telecommunications monopolies, that is, where there has been no move towards competition. In other words, its purpose is not that of preserving the role of the ITU in introducing distributive concerns into standards concerning interconnection rates in the context of a transition to competition, but of grandfathering accounting rates where obsolescent monopoly practices still apply, presumably due to political realities.[19] The logic of the panel's interpretation is *prima facie* difficult to see: since the Reference Paper is only binding in the first place in a context where the WTO Member in question has committed to competition in telecommunications services in its Schedule, in the case of monopoly-to-monopoly connection, it would be hard to understand the concern to shield accounting rates from challenge in the WTO dispute settlement. The panel's answer is that the intent must have been to provide an exemption from the MFN obligations, one of the few substantive GATS obligations that apply regardless of scheduled commitments. However, even this obligation only applies where there is trade in the service in question, defined under the GATS as the supply of the service by providers of one WTO Member to the consumers of another, by one of four modes of delivery, including transboundary movement of the service and local commercial presence. As observed by Neven and Mavroidis, the main problem with the panel's logic is its failure to ask whether, in fact, telecommunications services were being traded in the relevant sense on the facts.[20]

However flawed, the panel's logic is revealing of its teleological view concerning telecommunications deregulation: accounting rates reflecting distributive values are an anachronism that belongs to the passing world of monopoly. Here the panel's view went even further in *laissez-faire* ideology than the *first perspective* on importation, in that the panel viewed the WTO as guarantor of a hyperliberal approach to deregulation – that rates are not an acceptable tool for distributive purposes – even where such an approach was not required to underpin global market access or free trade. One can only speculate that it may be significant that one of the panellists, Ernst-Ulrich Petersmann, has long been committed to the view that the WTO is a

[19] Panel Report, *Mexico – Measures Affecting Telecommunications Services*, paras. 7.137 *et seq.*

[20] D. Neven and P. Mavroidis, 'Mexico – Measures Affecting Telecommunications Services (WT/DS204/R): A Comment on "El Mess in Telmex"', in H. Horn and P. Mavroidis (eds.), *WTO Case Law of 2003: The American Law Institute Reporters' Studies* (2006), p. 188.

charter or constitution for economic 'liberty' and free competition generally, not just free trade.[21]

A further argument of Mexico was that its connection rates were consistent with the target rates recommended by ITU Study Group 3 for Mexico.[22] The panel hardly addressed at all this argument of Mexico, and, when Mexico objected, the panel dismissively noted that 'ITU "target rates" are just that, and are not, themselves, cost oriented rates'.[23] Now the panel noted in support of its views that cost-orientation is a regulatory principle that prevails at the ITU as well as the WTO. However, this very fact, when put together with the fact that Mexico's rates were consistent with ITU target rates for Mexico, might lead to the opposite conclusion to that of the panel, namely, that ITU standards and practice indicate that the principle of cost-orientation does not exclude the possibility of taking into account other concerns, even distributive concerns, in the determination of rates, even if they must have some relationship to costs. It is the hyperliberal teleological perspective of the panel that apparently blinds it to this possible reading, which is not even considered.

The effects of this perspective are further seen in the way that the panel disposed of a further recourse by Mexico to ITU regulatory standards. Mexico invoked an ITU document, Recommendation D.140, which, in the words of the panel, 'lays down guidelines for establishing accounting rates for international telephone services'.[24] According to the panel, Recommendation D.140 not only establishes the principle of cost-orientation, it also 'enumerates the cost elements to be taken into account when determining accounting rates'.[25]

An examination of these cost elements reveals that they include direct and indirect or common costs, with the proviso that they cannot solely be attributed to the international telephone service, that is, these indirect or common costs cannot be totally subsidized through charges to foreign telecommunications operators. This exactly articulates a concept of cost-orientation that allows some, if not considerable, coverage of indirect or common costs through interconnection charges, and does not exclude in any of its provisions that such charges could reflect distributive concerns. Thus Recommendation D.140, except when interpreted through a hyperliberal teleological perspective, is quite consistent with

[21] See, e.g., E.-U. Petersmann, 'The WTO Constitution and Human Rights', *Journal of International Economics Law* 3 (2000) 19.

[22] Panel Report, *Mexico – Measures Affecting Telecommunications Services*, para. 6.42.

[23] *Ibid.* [24] *Ibid.*, para. 7.170. [25] *Ibid.*

target rates for Mexico that exceed the long-term incremental cost of providing the interconnection service itself. Perhaps itself insecure about the textual foundations of its reading of Recommendation D.140, the panel proceeded to invoke another ITU document, a report merely noting or observing domestic regulatory practices. The panel cited the report as stating that 'incremental cost methodologies are becoming the *de facto* standard for interconnection around the world'.[26] In other words, in the panel's vision, as the trend to this form of deregulation prevails in practice, the permitted scope of regulatory diversity in the ITU's standards shrinks.

It should be apparent how differently a WTO adjudicator with the *second perspective* on importation of standards – the value pluralism perspective – would interpret and import ITU standards. Such an adjudicator might well view the Understanding as an effort to preserve the integrity of the ITU process for negotiating interconnection rates in the face of the shift to international competition, based on particular institutional characteristics of the ITU that allow its standards to reflect values and interests that have weight in the GATS compromise. As Siochru suggests, in the ITU 'the scope for dominance of individual powerful countries (or indeed [telecommunications operators] through their country representatives) is relatively restricted ... [T]he ITU is thus relatively democratic, and it percolates down to bilateral negotiations ... [T]he USA ... cannot simply use its power to impose its preferred solution on a reluctant majority ... Indeed, this is what motivates the broader US strategy of shifting the overall communications global forum from the ITU to the WTO and other trade organizations.'[27]

A WTO adjudicator operating from the second perspective would emphasize, not dismiss, the elements of choice that are offered to regulators in Recommendation D140 to decide what range of costs, direct and indirect, are to be taken into account in creating a 'cost-oriented' rate. Moreover, a focus on costs would accommodate a variety of public policy values and goals, not just market efficiency; reading the requirement of 'cost-orientation' in the WTO Reference Paper in light of the broad conception

[26] International Telecommunications Union, *Trends in Telecommunications Reform: Interconnection Regulation*, 3rd edn (2001), available at www.itu.int/pub/D-REG-TTR.4-2001 (last visited 15 September 2010).

[27] S. O. Siochru, 'The ITU, the WTO and Accounting Rates: Limited Prospects for the South?', *The Public* 4 (1997) 47–57, pp. 51–2. See also E. Mahoney, 'The Utilization of International Communications Organizations 1978–1992' in K. Nordenstreng and H. Schill (eds.), *Beyond National Sovereignty* (Norwood, NJ: Ablex Publishing, 1993), pp. 314–42.

of relevant costs in Recommendation D.140, a WTO adjudicator adopting the second perspective would understand the concept of cost-orientation in the Reference Paper as sustaining a balance of trade and non-trade values in the GATS compromise.[28]

How might the panel have imported ITU standards if it had adopted the *third perspective*, that understands the non-WTO regime as necessary for addressing issues relating to the global commons and transboundary externalities that arise with global markets and must be addressed to make those markets sustainable? Under such a perspective, the sum of interconnected domestic telecommunications networks could be seen as itself a global commons, and the ITU as a repository of specialized knowledge concerning the requirements of maintaining that commons with a view to sustaining and perhaps enhancing global markets. A panel operating from this third perspective would likely be less dismissive of the target rates for Mexico determined by the ITU Study Group 3 for Mexico, assuming that these rates were a function of expertise being applied to understand the kind of rates appropriate to sustain Mexico's network as part of the global telecommunications commons. Moreover, the panel would be attentive to the ITU's role in addressing the global commons dimensions of telecommunications trade liberalization and might view the ITU's approach – to not impose long-run incremental cost as a single permissible approach to cost-orientation – as perhaps a reflection of its concern with commons issues. Neven and Mavroidis, citing a range of economic literature, make the point that pricing of access to networks typically reflects a balance of concerns, including 'the need to finance infrastructure (in particular in the presence of large fixed and common costs)'.[29] As they explain, long-run incremental cost may in some circumstances be an optimal approach to pricing access, but 'only if there is no issue with respect to the financing of the existing

[28] As one telecommunications expert suggests, the meaning of costs with respect to the pricing of interconnection has never been limited to long-run incremental cost of providing the interconnection itself. Rather, '[t]he pricing of interconnection takes into account three basic cost elements: one-time start-up costs, costs of network elements that incumbents make available to new entrants, and contributions to the funding of universal service'. D. Roseman, 'Domestic Regulation and Trade in Telecommunications Services: Experience and Prospects under the GATS' in A. Mattoo and P. Sauvé (eds.), *Domestic Regulation and Service Trade Liberalization* (World Bank and Oxford University Press, 2005), pp. 83–107, p. 95.

[29] D. Neven and P. Mavroidis, 'Mexico – Measures Affecting Telecommunications Services (WT/DS204/R): A Comment on "El Mess in Telmex"', in H. Horn and P. Mavroidis (eds.), *WTO Case Law of 2003: The American Law Institute Reporters' Studies* (2006), p. 212.

infrastructure, or in other words, where there is no risk of important stranded costs'.[30]

4. Conclusion: the WTO's absent administrative function and Global Administrative Law

The nature of WTO law in regulatory domains such as telecommunications is such that the WTO adjudicator, in interpreting WTO treaty norms, must draw on normative material from other specialized international regimes. As I have argued in this chapter, there are several different ways of conceptualizing this exercise, in terms of the interaction of regimes. As a general matter, while sometimes appearing in the guise of international law, the normative material in question is often better understood in light of the specific regulatory goals and practice of the regimes in question, i.e., in terms of Global Administrative Law. A Global Administrative Law perspective should sensitize the WTO adjudicator to the complexity of the regulatory instruments used by the specialized regimes in question, which cannot simply be applied in the WTO as if they were treaty norms, to be interpreted in accordance with the VCLT.

Despite various attempts at cooperation and exchange of information between the secretariats of the WTO and specialized regulatory regimes, what one might call a regulatory culture has not yet emerged within the administrative and diplomatic/political organs of the WTO. The committees within the WTO charged with implementing WTO Agreements that concern specialized regulatory fields have generally avoided profound or sustained dialogue with either domestic or international regulatory agencies. There is no effective administrative or regulatory process in the WTO for adaptation of normative material from other regulatory regimes to the purposes of the WTO. Under these circumstances, the burden is likely to fall largely on the WTO adjudicator to define the appropriate relationship between those regimes and the WTO.

From a Global Administrative Law perspective, it is worth considering some of the practices and procedures that can facilitate the adjudicator playing this role. Participation of officials or experts from specialized regulatory regimes on WTO panels; solicitation of interpretations or opinions from the secretariats of such regimes; the use of international or

30 *Ibid.*

domestic regulators as experts in WTO panel proceedings; *amicus curiae* briefs from domestic and international regulatory agencies to both the panel and the Appellate Body (as well as stakeholders) are all possibilities, consistent with the existing Dispute Settlement Understanding as interpreted in the Appellate Body jurisprudence.

INDEX